"Few books on economic and social observation ever written in any land posses the enduring interest of Olmsted's.... He did more than any other man of the times to make the discussion of slavery realistic by examining in detail its practical workings, and describing all its concomitants in the life of the people."

—**Allan Nevins**, author of *The Ordeal of the Union*

"Olmsted's literary fame rests on his full-bodied travel books, which are judicious without being dull, colorful without being lurid; they restore the reader's faith in the human capacity of precise and reliable observation, when few others seemed capable of it.... There is no better introduction to Southern life on the brink of the [Civil] War [than *The Cotton Kingdom*], and there are few comparable travel books in all American history." —**Daniel Boorstin**, *The Americans*

"The best travel account of 'that peculiar institution,' more authoritative than many secondary works."

—**John Hope Franklin**, *From Slavery to Freedom*

"I have learned more about the South from [Olmsted's] books than from all others put together, and I valued them the more that an American who can be patient and accurate is so rare a phenomenon."

—**James Russell Lowell**, author of *The Bigelow Papers*

"The conversations reported by Olmsted give the impression of all having been reproduced, without any art of selection, precisely as Olmsted remembered them, and he seems to have remembered everything. He tenaciously and patiently and lucidly made his way through the whole South, undiscouraged by churlish natives, almost impassable roads or the cold inns and uncomfortable cabins in which he spent most of his nights. He talked to everybody and he sized up everything, and he wrote it all down.... Olmsted's reporting today can provide an indispensable antidote to the later crop of spoony fancy pictures that had already reached ripeness in the [eighteen-]eighties with the fiction of Thomas Nelson Page, and which has more or less continued into our own day." —**Edmund Wilson**, *Patriotic Gore*

THE
COTTON KINGDOM

A Traveller's Observations on
Cotton and Slavery
IN THE AMERICAN SLAVE STATES

---

*Based upon Three Former Volumes of Journeys and Investigations
by the Same Author*

BY

FREDERICK LAW OLMSTED

EDITED, WITH AN INTRODUCTION, BY
ARTHUR M. SCHLESINGER

DA CAPO PRESS • NEW YORK

Library of Congress Cataloging in Publication Data

Olmsted, Fredrick Law, 1822–1903.
   The cotton kingdom: a traveller's observations on cotton and slavery in the American slave states: based upon three former volumes of journeys and investigations by the same author / by Frederick Law Olmsted: edited with an introduction by Arthur M. Schlesinger.
      p.   cm.
   Includes bibliographical references (p.) and index.
   ISBN 0-306-80723-8 (alk. paper)
   1. Southern States—Description and travel. 2. Southern States—Economic conditions. 3. Slavery—Southern States. 4. Cotton growing—Southern States—History—19th century. 5. Olmsted, Frederick Law, 1822–1903. I. Title.
   F213.O53 1996
   975′.03—dc20   96-24350
                                                                                                                  CIP

First Da Capo Press edition 1996

This Da Capo Press paperback edition of *The Cotton Kingdom* is an unabridged republication of the edition published in New York in 1953. It is reprinted by arrangement with Alfred A. Knopf, Inc.

Published by Da Capo Press, Inc.
A Subsidiary of Plenum Publishing Corporation
233 Spring Street, New York, N.Y. 10013

TO

ELIZABETH F. HOXIE

GENERAL TABLE OF CONTENTS

Editor's Introduction

OLMSTED recorded his memorable impressions of the South and slavery in the fateful decade between the Compromise of 1850, which sought to avert national disunion, and Lincoln's election as President, which precipitated it. His writings do more than reveal a little-known chapter in the life of a world-famous landscape architect. Far more important, they present a uniquely candid and realistic picture of the pre-Civil War South. The *Cotton Kingdom*, which abridges and synthesizes his observations, is the nearest thing posterity has to an exact transcription of a civilization which time has tinted with hues of romantic legend. Olmsted's account, in other words, is an indispensable work in the process of recapturing the American past.

Olmsted's Early Years

Frederick Law Olmsted was born in Hartford, Connecticut, on April 26, 1822, the son of John Olmsted, a prosperous merchant, and Charlotte Law (Hull) Olmsted. His formal education fell largely to a succession of country parsons, with whom he lodged, but he obviously derived more of lasting value from his father, who nourished his love of travel and trained his powers of observation by taking the family on summer trips through the countryside. Before Fred was twelve he had traversed, on foot or by wagon, the Connecticut Valley, the White Mountains and most of the New England coast from Kennebec to Naugatuck. "We were our own servants," he wrote in fond retrospect, "my father seldom trusting strangers in these journeys with the feeding, cleaning or harnessing of his horses." [1] By wagon, stagecoach, canalboat and steamer he had, moreover, gone farther afield—to West Point, Trenton Falls, Lake George and Quebec. Sensitive to natural beauty, he also observed agriculture at every stage of development, from the wasteful practices of

[1] F. L. Olmsted, "Passages in the Life of an Unpractical Man," F. L. Olmsted, Jr., and Theodora Kimball, eds., *Frederick Law Olmsted, Landscape Architect* (New York, 1922–1928), I, 46. My biographical summary is based upon this volume and upon Broadus Mitchell, *Frederick Law Olmsted, A Critic of the Old South* (Baltimore, 1924), chap. i.

the backwoodsman to the tidy management of the long-settled Yankee. These observations were to serve him well when he himself took
up farming.

In 1836, when he was fourteen years old, a bad case of sumac
poisoning affected his eyes, and instead of entering Yale College, as
planned, he led what he afterward called a "decently restrained
vagabond life" for two and a half years, while "nominally" studying
with a topographical engineer in Andover, Massachusetts, and later
in Collinsville, Connecticut.[2] He next tried clerking in a French im-
porting house in New York (which he heartily disliked, but which
afforded considerable time for reading on his own); then in 1842,
and again in 1847, he attended science classes at Yale as a special
student. In the interval, partly for reasons of health, he shipped before the mast to Canton. This experience, which bridged the years
1843–1844, taught him more about the brutal discipline at sea, however, than it did about the strange life in Chinese ports, all too briefly
visited. He was later to be reminded of the voyage when evaluating
the treatment of slaves on Southern plantations.[3] During his second
term of residence at Yale two of his intimates were his younger
brother John, who was headed toward medicine, and Charles Loring
Brace, who was afterward to distinguish himself as a pioneer social
worker in the New York slums. They tramped, fished and boated
together and argued religion and the topics of the day, as college
youths are wont to do. John and Charles were to play an important
part in Fred's travels of the 1850's.

He had already worked summers on several farms, acquiring
practical knowledge and supplementing it with the latest information in agricultural journals. He aimed to be a scientific farmer according to the standards of his time. In 1847 the elder Olmsted established him on a small tract of his own near Guilford, Connecticut,
where he did so well that the next year his father bought him a
much larger place of 130 acres at South Side, Staten Island, New York.
The twenty-six-year-old owner speedily improved the unsightly
grounds of the old Dutch farmhouse by shifting the roadway and
outbuildings, restoring the lawn and setting out fruit and shade trees.

[2] Olmsted, "Life of an Unpractical Man," 61.

[3] Olmsted, A Journey in the Back Country (New York, 1860), 83–84 (The
Cotton Kingdom, 453). For the convenience of the reader, all references in this
Introduction to the Cotton Kingdom are to the present edition rather than to
the original work of 1861.

He then proceeded to put the soil into full production. Soon he was winning prizes for the best crops of wheat and turnips and the finest assortment of fruits. He also imported English machinery for better results, and in partnership with a friend he installed the first cylindrical-drainage-tile system in the United States. Always eager to learn new methods, he visited farms in various parts of the North, defraying his expenses and sharing his observations with others by writing for newspapers and magazines.

His interest in agriculture and his wandering foot now prompted him to accompany his brother John and their friend Charles Brace on a walking trip in Europe. John had impaired his eyes and general health while studying medicine in New York after graduation from Yale and needed a vacation from books. Charles, then a theological student in New York whose thoughts were turning more and more toward philanthropic work, wished to note the "varying developments of human nature under different biases and institutions." All agreed they would pay principal heed to "those classes which form the majority of the people" as the best way of gauging the "wisdom of national institutions." Hurrying the spring work on the farm, Fred embarked with his companions on the sailing vessel *Henry Clay* for Liverpool on May 3, 1850, for an excursion which took them to England, Wales, Ireland, Germany, Belgium, France and Scotland before the brothers returned to New York on October 4, leaving Charles Brace behind for further adventures on the Continent.

Frederick wrote up a portion of the trip—the ocean voyage and the first four weeks in England and Wales—in *Walks and Talks of an American Farmer in England,* published in 1852 by the firm of G. P. Putnam, New York.[4] The trio did not neglect medieval castles

4 The quotations in this and the preceding paragraph are, unless otherwise indicated, from this work, page 2. The book was originally published in two parts in *Putnam's Semi-monthly Library,* with the first part also issued in London by D. Bogue. On January 11, 1851, Olmsted informed Brace that he had begun the writing, and on October 17, 1852, he told another friend of college days, Frederick J. Kingsbury, that the two parts bound in a single volume had appeared two days before. Correspondence in the Olmsted Papers (Library of Congress). There was sufficient demand for Putnam to reprint the book in 1854. A revised and enlarged edition, published in 1859 by J. H. Riley and Company, Columbus, Ohio, compressed the original narrative from 246 to 206 pages and added 158 pages (thirteen chapters and two appendices). The new matter dealt almost wholly with rural life, London being dismissed in half a page. Letters from Charles Brace during the walking trip are in Emma Brace, *The Life of Charles Loring Brace* (London, 1894), 89–97.

and ancient ruins, and though Olmsted passed over the fact in his book, they also visited London. They spent most of their outing, however, observing rural folk and ways of living. At first they tramped at the rate of a hundred miles in six days, knapsacks on back, but later, when their feet had sufficiently hardened, they covered two hundred in the same length of time at a brisk four miles an hour. Bed and board averaged 75 cents a day for each.[5] The Staten Island farmer was greatly impressed by the cleanliness, orderliness and neatness of the English countryside, the sturdiness of the farm buildings and the unvarying hospitality of the innkeepers—all of which he was to miss in his travels in the American slave states. Where British methods of tillage diverged from those at home, he carefully noted the differences, with results not always complimentary to the English, though his balance sheet favored the older country. His purpose in publishing a narrative of the trip was to impart to his "brother farmers and their families" in the United States the "practical agricultural information" and "useful suggestions" he had gleaned abroad.

This was Olmsted's first book. Quite apart from the light it cast on English rural life, it is important as disclosing many of the qualities that were to mark his writings on the South. Like these subsequent accounts, it was a circumstantial day-by-day portrayal of common people and common things and particularly of agricultural practices, with the author expressing his own ideas along with the evidence pro and con. As he said in the Preface, he provided material from which his readers should have no difficulty in "forming their own views from the facts that I give them, and taking my opinions for only just what they shall seem to be worth." As in his later works, too, he used the device of citing concrete incidents to clinch general observations and conclusions. He took particular pains to write clearly and straightforwardly, an ideal he did not always achieve in his books on the South. Commenting on a reviewer who remarked that his style showed "unaffected simplicity," he said that "the most simple parts are those I worked hardest at to make simple." [6] His

[5] *Walks and Talks* (1859 ed.), 354, 359. Olmsted evidently had reservations about the frugal mode of travel, for after his return he wrote on November 12, 1850, to Brace, still abroad, "I wish I had spent more money. I wish that I had borrowed money if necessary. I advise you to." Olmsted Papers (in the Library of Congress).

[6] Mitchell, *Olmsted*, 25 *n.*

ear for peculiarities of speech was revealed in the occasional bits of dialogue. Olmsted also gained greater intellectual maturity from the experience. "I should say," he wrote to Brace after the trip, "that I had more independance [sic], freedom of thought," and am "less influenced by the mere fact of other's opinions." He had at the same time learned "more charity and brotherhood with those who differ totally with me." [7]

In addition, his methods of inquiry and reporting were to stand him in good stead in his journeys through the slave states. He took along letters of introduction to British farmers from such persons as the widely traveled Charles Eliot Norton, afterward to be a distinguished Harvard professor, and Andrew Jackson Downing, the well-known landscape gardener of Newburgh, New York. He scribbled notes on the spot and kept a diary, usually in the form of letters sent to his family and friends at home. To sharpen his impressions he made drawings from time to time, twelve of which appear in the 1852 edition of *Walks and Talks*. (He would later intersperse his book on the seaboard South with nine sketches, and preface his volume on Texas with a charming illustration of himself and John camping beside a river.[8])

The student of Olmsted's life career will, moreover, find unmistakable traces in *Walks and Talks* of his developing preoccupation with landscape design. His fondness for Nature almost burst its bonds in his praise of the English countryside after a May shower— "green, dripping, glistening, gorgeous!" The hawthorn hedges, fragrant with pink and white blossoms, enchanted him, at least until the practical farmer inside him reflected that they often shaded the growing crops and drew valuable nourishment from the soil. No such doubts assailed him, however, as to the spacious public gardens, on some of which he descanted with loving detail. "Probably there is no object of art that Americans of cultivated taste generally more long to see in Europe, than an English park," he remarked.[9]

[7] Olmsted to Brace, January 11, 1851. Olmsted Papers.

[8] Though the artist's name is not given in these works, there can be no doubt as to his identity. See, for example, *A Journey in the Seaboard Slave States* (New York, 1856), 424.

[9] *Walks and Talks* (1852 ed.), 87, 133, 178. In the revised edition (263) he observes, "The sublime or the picturesque in nature is much more rare in England, except on the sea-coast, than in America; but there is every where a great deal of quiet, peaceful, graceful beauty which the works of man have generally added to, and which I remember but little like at home."

Curiously, little evidence of this burgeoning interest appears in his published accounts of the South, though some of the hedges in Louisiana and Mississippi pleased him almost as much as those of Herefordshire, and in Raleigh, North Carolina, he severely criticized the lack of landscaping about the State House.[1] In Dixie he apparently found human conditions too absorbing to devote much space to the inanimate beauties of Nature.[2]

The Journeys in the Slave States

A photograph of Olmsted in 1850, the year he went to England, shows a young man of twenty-eight, slight of build, with a high forehead, long wavy dark hair parted on the right, wide-set eyes, mobile lips, and well-molded nose and chin. His appearance suggested studiousness and artistic perception rather than the tiller of the soil or the adventurous youth who gloried in an "aptitude for *roughing it.*"[3] In after years his wife remembered him at this period as "fond of arguments" and "full of life and fun,"[4] and his book on Britain does reveal occasional glints of humor. To most outsiders, however, the photograph probably came closer to their conception of the man. "His face is generally very placid, with all the expressive delicacy of a woman's," remarked an associate in Civil War relief work of a somewhat older Olmsted, adding that "there is a deep, calm thoughtfulness about him which is always attractive and sometimes—provoking." And Charles Eliot Norton wrote a little later, "All the lines of his face imply refinement and sensibility to such a degree that it is not till one has looked through them to what is beneath, that the force of his will and reserved power of his character become evident."[5]

---

[1] *Seaboard Slave States*, 318–319, and *Back Country*, 13–14, 35 (*Cotton Kingdom*, 134, 406–407, 423).

[2] "Yet," Mrs. Schuyler van Rensselaer wrote forty years later in commenting on this neglect, "one hardly needs to hear Mr. Olmsted talk about his Southern journeys to feel that, like his boyish wanderings, like his saunters among English parks and meadows, they helped his artistic development." "Frederick Law Olmsted," *Century Magazine*, XLVI (1893), 862.

[3] Olmsted's phrase in a letter to his father. Mitchell, *Olmsted*, 43.

[4] Olmsted and Kimball, *Olmsted*, I, 79.

[5] Letter of Katharine P. Wormeley, May 21, 1862, in her *The Other Side of War with the Army of the Potomac* (Boston, 1888), 63; Norton to George W. Curtis, September 21, 1863, in Norton, *Letters* (Sara Norton and M. A. De W. Howe, eds., Boston, 1913), I, 264.

Olmsted's next expedition was to a strange part of his own country. This came about as the result of a combination of things. One was his zest for travel, and another his interest in learning about an unfamiliar type of agriculture. But the precipitating cause was a recurrent debate with Charles Brace, which doubtless began in college days and reached fiery heights at the Staten Island farm, where Charles often went from Manhattan to spend a Sunday. Brace was a "red hot abolitionist," while Olmsted, though disliking slavery, pleaded extenuating circumstances for the slaveholders.[6] Brace may have been referring to one of these verbal bouts when he wrote to a mutual friend of the "torrent of argument, mixed with divers oaths on Fred's part, and abuse on both!" It is evident that with his intimates Olmsted did not always display that "charity and brotherhood with those who differ totally with me," which he had counted as one of the gains of his English trip. On one occasion Charles took Theodore Parker with him as reinforcement, and on another William Lloyd Garrison.[7]

In the end the two cronies agreed that the best way to settle their dispute would be for Olmsted to go south and judge conditions at first hand. This Olmsted was all the readier to do because the Compromise of 1850 had for the most part stilled the "unwholesome excitement" which had long warped popular consideration of the slavery issue in both sections, and in the relaxed state of the public mind he believed he might contribute to a rational and conciliatory understanding of the problem. "Men are never so likely to settle a question rightly as when they discuss it freely," was a favorite quotation of his from Macaulay.[8] He was also weary of "the deluge of spoony fancy pictures" of the South which was pouring from the press.[9]

Brace broached the project to Henry J. Raymond, editor of the recently established *New York Times* (then called the *New-York Daily Times*). Raymond talked five minutes with Olmsted, made no inquiry concerning his views on slavery or on any other subject, and promptly engaged him as a special correspondent. "The only intima-

---

[6] Olmsted to F. J. Kingsbury, October 17, 1852. Olmsted Papers. For Brace's sentiments on slavery, see Brace, *Brace*, 57, 72, 102, 116, 265. Olmsted's views are analyzed at some length later in this Introduction.

[7] Brace, *Brace*, 61; Mitchell, *Olmsted*, 44.

[8] *Seaboard Slave States*, pp. xvi, 178; *Back Country*, p. vi.

[9] Olmsted to F. J. Kingsbury, October 17, 1852. Olmsted Papers.

tion I received of his expectations as to the matter I should write," Olmsted stated later, "was a request that it should be confined to personal observations, and the expression of a wish that I would not feel myself at all restricted or constrained by regard to consistency with the general position of the paper or anything else." [1] The editor's confidence in a young man whom he had never before seen doubtless stemmed from the qualities Olmsted had shown in his recently published book on England.

Olmsted set forth from Washington on December 11, 1852. "I wish to see for myself," he told the readers of the *Times* in his introductory article, "and shall endeavor to report with candor and fidelity, to you, the ordinary condition of the laborers of the South, with respect to material comfort and moral and intellectual happiness." [2] After a month on the way he wrote back that the trip was costing him $2.00 a day above traveling expenses and that he expected to do the whole for about $300.[3] Proceeding by steamboat, train and stagecoach, and occasionally on horseback, he visited the eastern sections of Virginia, the Carolinas and Georgia as far south as Savannah, then struck westward across Georgia and Alabama, taking the steamer from Mobile for New Orleans. Spending most of his time in the hill country, he studied the mode of life assiduously wherever he went and constantly reflected on his experiences. He returned from Louisiana by way of Vicksburg, Memphis and then "along the eastern base of the Appalachian Chain in the upper parts of the States of Mississippi, Alabama, Georgia, the Carolinas and Virginia." [4] The entire journey took three months.

His letters began appearing in the *Times* on February 16, 1853, under the pseudonym of "Yeoman" and the running title of "The South," and they continued at short intervals for forty-nine more installments, the last on February 13, 1854. Raymond in prefacing the series commended the "accurate, complete and dispassionate statement of facts," which he hoped would correct the usual accounts written to "fortify some preconceived opinion" or "to aid the attainment of some political purpose." Olmsted himself was a bit unhappy about his efforts since he felt that in covering so much of the South

[1] *New York Times*, February 13, 1854, p. 2; Mitchell, *Olmsted*, 44.
[2] *New York Times*, February 16, 1853, p. 2.
[3] Mitchell, *Olmsted*, 47.
[4] *New York Times*, November 21, 1853, p. 2.

so fast he could do "no more than to glance at the outside of things." [5]
Moreover, he was disappointed in his expectation that Charles Brace
would polish the style of the letters before they were printed.

Raymond, for his part, seems at first to have expressed privately
some dissatisfaction with the articles, for Olmsted exploded to Brace,
"I can't write a different sort of letters. If Raymond wanted statesmanship and generalizations he is at the wrong shop." He admitted,
however, that his first two pieces were the "poorest of the lot." Whatever Raymond's doubts, he did not communicate them directly to
Olmsted, and soon, according to Brace, he was praising his roving
correspondent's "powers of observation and detailed reporting—giving just the facts that people want and seldom get." [6] With the appearance of the final installment of the letters he wrote editorially,
"We think we run no hazard in saying that they constitute decidedly
the best report that has ever been made, of the industrial condition
and prospects of the Southern section of the Union." [7]

The series aroused considerable interest in the South as well as
the North. Raymond spoke of receiving "warm commendations"
from men in both sections and of widely differing convictions.[8] The
Southern Literary Messenger, which said after the first two letters
that it could find no objections to them, warmly endorsed Olmsted's
undertaking, adding that *"this is exactly what we wish all well-disposed and well-behaved Northern people, who desire to know something of the South, would do."* [9] Correspondence printed in the
Times as Olmsted moved farther into Dixie was similarly approving.
If an Alabamian noted that the traveler was "looking at things
through a pair of sharp Northern eyes," he too considered the general tone of the articles "acceptable to unbiased Southerners." [1]

Yet all was not sweetness and light. The *Savannah Republican*

---

[5] Olmsted to F. J. Kingsbury, February 26, 1853. Olmsted Papers.

[6] Mitchell, *Olmsted*, 47, 48, 49.

[7] *New York Times*, February 13, 1854, p. 4.

[8] *Ibid.*

[9] Copied in the *Times*, March 10, 1853, p. 3. An advertisement for the *Seaboard Slave States* in *ibid.*, January 28, 1856, quotes the *New Orleans Delta*
to like effect.

[1] "A Native Southerner" in the *Times*, June 6, 1853, p. 2. For other expressions of approval, see "R. J. W." (a Virginian) in *ibid.*, March 22, p. 3, and
"H. W. P." (a New Yorker who had resided in the South) in the issue of April
7, p. 2. Olmsted reprinted these two letters in the *Seaboard Slave States*, 717–
720, and the *Cotton Kingdom*, 601–604.

accused the *Times* of seeking to disturb the existing harmony between the sections: "It sends a stranger among us 'to spy out the
nakedness of the land.' What is its object, if it be not an evil one?"
It denied that any Northerner, however honest and intelligent, could
grasp the ramifications of the slavery system; it doubted whether
even a Southerner could do so.[2] At the opposite pole, as Raymond
ruefully pointed out, "violent Anti-Slavery journals" denounced the
pieces as "designed to gloss over the evils of Slavery, and to discuss
the subject upon a false basis." [3] They were irked because Olmsted
concerned himself with the economic rather than the moral aspects
of the institution.

Such criticisms only confirmed Raymond's opinion of the value
of the series. As a result he commissioned Olmsted on his return
to make a trip to a different part of the South. This time Olmsted
had an additional reason for going—his brother John s weak lungs,
which, it was hoped, a long jaunt in the saddle, camping along the
way, would remedy. Heading for Texas, the two left Baltimore on
November 10, 1853, by the Baltimore & Ohio Railroad for Wheel-
ing on the Ohio River, continued by steamboat, stage and rail
through Kentucky and Tennessee to Nashville, observing conditions
as they went, and then proceeded on the Mississippi to New Orleans.
In mid-December at Natchitoches, Louisiana, on the Red River
near the Texas border, they bought horses and supplies for the further journey, together with a pack mule "endowed with the bigotry
of his race." Their equipment ranged from blankets, overcoats, guns
and a tent with an India-rubber mat, to medicines, emergency rations and pocket classics. In a saddle trip of some two thousand
miles they visited the ranching and farming country which lay between the Gulf of Mexico and a roughly parallel line running from
Natchitoches through Nacogdoches and Austin in Texas to the Rio
Grande at Eagle Pass. They took time also to dip south across the
border into Mexico for a week. By May they were back in New
Orleans.[4] They had originally planned on seeing California as well
as Texas, but Indian outbreaks made this impossible.[5]

[2] Copied from the *Savannah Republican*, February 22, 1853, in the *Times*,
March 9, p. 3. Raymond replied editorially on the next page.

[3] *Ibid.*, February 13, 1853, p. 4.

[4] F. L. Olmsted, *A Journey through Texas; or, a Saddle-Trip on the South-
western Frontier* (New York, 1857), *passim*.

[5] Rensselaer, "Olmsted," 862.

Olmsted's letters, signed "Yeoman" as before, commenced in the *New York Times* on March 6, 1854, and, under the usual caption of "A Tour in the Southwest," appeared irregularly till June 7. The series, which told nothing of the month spent in reaching Natchitoches, gave a day-by-day account of the brothers' wanderings thereafter to April 5, shortly before venturing into Mexico, when they were at Fort Inge on the Leona River, a tributary of the Rio Grande. The fifteen articles were less than a third as many as for the first trip, though the entire journey took twice as long. The reason for this is uncertain. There may have been exceptional difficulties of communication or, what is more likely, the *Times* now found its space taxed by the exciting discussions in Congress over the Kansas-Nebraska bill, as well as by other political events at home and abroad. Three weeks before the series began appearing, Raymond had announced that he had on hand several installments which he could not yet publish because of the "pressure of news upon our columns." [6] Nor was there the same immediate evidence of reader response as before. This was probably due to the remoteness of the region, added to the distractions arising from the revival of sectional controversy after the false calm of the Compromise of 1850. Olmsted's total pay from the *Times* for the two series of articles was $720. [7]

Upon reaching New Orleans the brothers parted company. John, having failed to derive the expected good from the tour, now hurried home. "The abominable diet, and the fatigue, sometimes relatively too severe, had served to null the fresh benefits of pure air and stimulating travel." [8] The insatiable Frederick, seizing the occasion to round out his knowledge of the South, took to the saddle alone, wending his way across central Mississippi and through the Appalachian highlands of Alabama, Tennessee, Georgia, North Carolina and Virginia to Richmond, whence he returned to New York by steamer. This third trip, covering what Olmsted called the back country, lasted from May, 1854, to early August.

Though he apparently made this final jaunt on his own initiative, he eventually published ten articles about it under the title "The

---

[6] *New York Times*, February 13, 1854, p. 4.

[7] Olmsted to his father, December 31, 1854, cited in Laura Wood Roper, "Frederick Law Olmsted in the 'Literary Republic,'" *Mississippi Valley Historical Review*, XXXIX (1952–1953), 466.

[8] *Journey through Texas*, pp. v, 380.

Southerners at Home" in the *New York Tribune*, a new medium for him. The only indication of authorship at the time was that the pieces, which appeared between June 3 and August 24, 1857, were announced as "From the Journal of a Northern Traveler on Horseback." They were advance portions of the book he was then writing on his latest travels and described that part of the journey from the river town of St. Francisville, Louisiana, on the lower Mississippi, to northern Alabama near the Tennessee line. The account corresponds roughly with the first five chapters of the *Back Country*, published three years later.

Altogether, Olmsted reckoned that the three expeditions occupied fourteen months. Some places he visited more than once. Of the eleven states which were to join the Southern Confederacy he missed only Arkansas and Florida, and he went to two slave states—Kentucky and Maryland—which did not secede. He tried every known means of conveyance, constantly using his "sharp Northern eyes" and recording at the first opportunity his conversations with people and his impressions of the country. James Russell Lowell, no mean judge, praised his faithful rendition of dialect.[9] Unfortunately his notebooks and manuscript journals have not survived; presumably they perished in a fire on his Staten Island farm in 1863.

After the manner of his English trip, he had armed himself with letters of introduction, some of them "from distinguished men, both of the North and the South," and in his second and third tours he carried a general letter of credence from the governor of New York.[1] Though he evidently found these credentials helpful, most of his contacts came about more casually. He chatted not only with fellow travelers but also with farmers of every kind, merchants, miners, lumbermen, lawyers, white laborers, women, Negroes—anyone who came to hand. At least five hundred white men, he estimated, "told me something of their lives and fortunes, across their own tables."[2] He discovered, however, that "The rank-and-file plantation negroes are not to be made ready acquaintance with by chance or through letters of introduction."[3] But that merely spurred him to extra exertions. As to the freedom with which people ex-

[9] Unsigned review of the *Back Country* in the *Atlantic Monthly*, VI (1860), 636.

[1] *Back Country*, 425, 426.

[2] *Cotton Kingdom*, 12.

[3] *Back Country*, 72 (*Cotton Kingdom*, 445).

pressed themselves, we can rely upon the evidence of his own pages, which goes far to confirm his statement that he was "usually taken for and treated as a Southerner" until he explained otherwise.[4]

Being regardful always of the retail traffic of life, Olmsted's observations shed light on all manner of things: dress, diet, health, drinking habits, travel accommodations, agricultural practices, cattle drives, land values, class distinctions, cultural attainments, religious attitudes, moral standards, social diversions, even the songs of river boatmen. Inescapably, though, his overriding interest was the institution of slavery and its effects on both races. It was for this reason above all others that he had gone south, and as his journeys broadened his knowledge, he constantly noticed new manifestations of its influence. His study of conditions, however, was practical rather than theoretical, realistic rather than emotional. These qualities underline the special character of his accomplishment.

Olmsted's Trilogy on the South

Even before setting out on his first trip to the South, Olmsted planned to give his observations more permanent form than fleeting newspaper pieces.[5] Anticipating this task, he asked his father, after a month on the way, to mark in the *Times* articles infelicities of style and factual inaccuracies "that I may have the advantage of them in revising." [6] He became conscious also of faults of reporting due to insufficient knowledge of the historical background, and by the same token he felt the need of fuller statistics to fortify or modify his findings. Hence on his return from the journey he busied himself in various New York libraries, delving into Virginia history, for example, "to follow down the influence of aristocracy and slavery on the conditions of the state." [7] These inquiries he supplemented by wide reading in agricultural journals as well as in Northern and Southern newspapers. To deal adequately with the moot question of the relative well-being of Northern workingmen and Negro slaves, he collected information at first and second hand concerning "the food, the wages, and the habits" of the laborers in some hundred farm families in every free state (except California) and in Canada.[8]

---

4 *Back Country*, 407 (*Cotton Kingdom*, 549).
5 Letter to F. J. Kingsbury, October 17, 1852. Olmsted Papers.
6 Letter of January 10, 1853, from Raleigh, N.C. Mitchell, *Olmsted*, 47.
7 Olmsted to his father, December 31, 1854. *Ibid.*, 50.
8 *Seaboard Slave States*, 702 (*Cotton Kingdom*, 485).

Moreover, since he did not actually write the book till after his subsequent travels in the South, he took occasion to utilize these later experiences "to correct the erroneous impressions of the earlier." [9] This led in some cases to the expression of stiffer judgments than in his *Times* articles.

He began writing the first volume of what was to be a trilogy in the late summer or early autumn of 1854. Constant interruptions—further researches, the management of the Staten Island farm, a siege of dyspepsia in December—slowed his pace, however, while his change of residence to New York the following spring to join the shaky publishing house of Dix & Edwards proved an added distraction. At one stage he reported that he had been able to sweat out only thirty-six pages in six weeks. [1] But the birth pangs finally came to an end. With the Preface dated January 9, 1856, *A Journey in the Seaboard Slave States, with Remarks on Their Economy*, appeared under the imprint of the author's own house, Dix & Edwards; abroad it was marketed by Sampson Low, Son & Company of London. The 724-page account enlarged considerably upon the *Times* articles, though it did not include the trip back from New Orleans. This he omitted because when he came to write the work he had traveled a second time through that part of the South, and he was planning to combine the later material with the earlier in a subsequent book. The *Seaboard Slave States* bore the over-all title of *Our Slave States*, thus serving notice that other volumes were to follow.

The second of the series, that on the Texas expedition, received far less personal attention from Olmsted. He was now absorbed in the publishing business, going for his firm to Europe in February, 1856. Hence he arranged with John to compile the work in return for two thirds of the royalties. [2] He himself, however, supplied some fresh matter in an introductory "Letter to a Southern Friend." John later described his part in the undertaking as "that of connecting, by a slender thread of reminiscence," his brother's "copious notes" and of drawing freely upon his memory for the purpose. [3] In reality

---

[9] *Seaboard Slave States*, p. ix.
[1] Mitchell, *Olmsted*, 50–52.
[2] Roper, "Olmsted in the 'Literary Republic,' " 475
[3] *Journey through Texas*, p. v.

he understated his role. If one may judge from his revision of the part of the narrative published in the *Times*—where comparison is alone possible—he transposed material, rectified occasional misstatements and sometimes strove for a more polished diction. Obviously, no one would question his correcting the population of Nacogdoches from 2000 to 500,[4] but his literary sense was less sure. Thus, when Frederick quoted a harassed farmer's wife as saying, "Good God! what's the matter with the child?" John altered it to "Jupiter! what's the matter with this child?" [5] On the whole, however, the style of the book seems to be Frederick's rather than John's, and Frederick is not known to have ever complained of the collaboration. In fact, he even allowed the "Jupiter" emendation to stand when he could have restored the original exclamation in the *Cotton Kingdom*.[6]

The raw material which John reworked included, in addition to his brother's field notes, information Frederick had gathered after his return from the Texas trip, doubtless at the same time he was digging up data for the *Seaboard Slave States*. The nature of these further investigations is indicated in the Appendix of the completed volume. This contains a chronology of Texas history, a digest of the state constitution and elaborate statistical tables, together with a list of thirty-three historical and geographical treatises and personal accounts. Obviously other books were drawn upon as well, since this bibliography omits some titles referred to in the main text. The volume issued from the press in mid-January, 1857, under the title *A Journey through Texas; or, a Saddle-Trip on the Southwestern Frontier; with a Statistical Appendix*. Dix, Edwards & Company were again the publishers, with Sampson Low, Son & Company in London and Thomas Constable & Company in Edinburgh managing the foreign sales. The 516 pages—far more extensive than the selections printed in the *Times*—included the interesting journey from Baltimore to Natchitoches as well as the less germane jaunt into Mexico.

After Olmsted got back from Europe he turned to preparing the final volume of the trilogy, the one on the back-country South. He pitched into it with enthusiasm, informing his father on February 7,

---

4 Compare the *New York Times*, March 21, 1854, p. 2, with *Texas*, 80.
5 Compare the *Times*, March 3, p. 2, with *Texas*, 49.
6 *Cotton Kingdom*, 282.

1857, "I busy myself in my book. Write every night till four o'clock and get on grandly." [7] He had a little material in shape to begin with, because in the first *Times* series he had recorded some of his impressions of the region formed while returning from his tour of the seaboard states. [8] As before, he also garnered supplementary data from reference works. By the middle of the year he had made enough progress to publish some portions in the *New York Tribune*, and in another six months he had finished the first draft of the entire volume.

This was no mean achievement, for he had been beset by many cares: the failure of his publishing house, worries over his enforced neglect of the Staten Island farm, grief over John's death from tuberculosis after a lingering illness. On top of these distractions had come the obligations arising from his appointment in September as superintendent of New York's Central Park, a post which was to be the steppingstone to his subsequent career as a landscape architect. He still planned to write a chapter on the "natural history of southern politics," but the multiplying responsibilities of the park (of which he became architect in chief in May, 1858), together with a trip to Europe late in 1859 in connection with these duties, kept him from ever doing so. [9]

The book finally appeared in the summer of 1860 from the press of Mason Brothers in New York, with Sampson Low, Son & Company as the London agents. Entitled *A Journey in the Back Country*, the 492 pages also included an Index for the three volumes. As originally conceived, the work, like its two predecessors, was to have consisted "almost exclusively of simple *observation* with little theorizing or summarizing," but as the manuscript grew under his pen, Olmsted amplified its scope. "Facts of general observation and conclusions of judgment," he explained in the Preface, "form a larger part of this volume than of the others, because they are appropriately deduced from all preceding details." [1] He was at last ready to play

[7] Mitchell, *Olmsted*, 52.

[8] These articles in the *New York Times*, November 21, December 3, 28, 1853 (p. 2 in each issue), were incorporated with minor changes in chaps. ii and iii of the *Back Country*.

[9] Mitchell, *Olmsted*, 52–53; Olmsted and Kimball, *Olmsted*, 7; *Back Country*, p. v; Edward Cary, *George William Curtis* (Boston, 1894), 106–107.

[1] Letter to John Olmsted, June, 1854, Mitchell, *Olmsted*, 49; *Back Country*, p. v.

the statesman, a role he had deemed unsuitable when he embarked on his initial Southern trip. The deepening sectional crisis plus the fact that he believed he was now saying his last say on the South were no doubt the determining factors. He had the Mason Brothers send specially bound copies of the book, with his compliments, to Henry J. Raymond of the *Times* and Charles A. Dana of the *Tribune*.[2]

As for Olmsted's publication arrangements, he (or, rather, his father) underwrote the costs of the *Seaboard Slave States*, including the advertising, and he paid Dix & Edwards a percentage on the sales for bringing it out. His contract for the *Journey through Texas* provided that the firm, after being reimbursed for the publication charges, should pay him 12½ per cent royalty. He received a similar return from the Mason Brothers for the *Back Country*. Sales records are fragmentary, but the first three printings of the *Seaboard Slave States* consisted of 2000, 1000 and 2000 copies respectively, and the first edition of *Texas*, of 2500. Olmsted noted that he obtained profits of only $52 in 1859, when the original interest in the books had temporarily slumped.[3]

More significant is the fact that the continuing demand proved sufficient to induce the Mason Brothers, who had taken over the works after the failure of Dix, Edwards & Company in 1857, to re-issue the *Seaboard Slave States* in 1859, 1861 and 1863 and the *Journey through Texas* in 1859 and 1860. Moreover, the Texas volume was published in German translation in Leipzig in 1857, 1865 and 1874, because of its extensive account of German settlements in the Lone Star state. The *Back Country*, the concluding volume of the series, sold slowly for a time, the Masons reporting on January 28, 1861, that it had been "remunerative neither to author nor publishers,"[4] but it too was reprinted in both New York and London during that year and again in New York in 1863.[5]

The favorable reception of the books is further evidenced by the

[2] Mason Brothers to Olmsted, February 21, 1861. Olmsted Papers.

[3] For a fuller account of these business matters, see Roper, "Olmsted in the 'Literary Republic,'" *passim*, and Mitchell, *Olmsted*, 53–54.

[4] Mason Brothers to Olmsted. Olmsted Papers.

[5] Long afterward, in response to a revived historical interest in the prewar South, Putnam republished the *Seaboard Slave States* (with an introduction by W. P. Trent and a biographical sketch by F. L. Olmsted, Jr.) in 1904, and the *Back Country* in 1907, both in two-volume editions.

praise that greeted them in both America and Britain. James Russell Lowell and Edwin L. Godkin were reminded—as historical scholars would later be—of Arthur Young's classic description of France before the Revolution, though Godkin considered Olmsted's account superior "in vividness of description and in photographic minuteness." [6] Godkin's estimate has particular value, for he was in an unusually good position to judge. Arriving in the United States from England in November, 1856, the journalist had immediately sought out Olmsted because of his writings on the South, and had himself then set forth on a similar mission through the seaboard slave states for the London *Daily News*. He afterward testified, "I saw nothing of the 'peculiar institution' which Olmsted had not already recorded." [7] Charles Dickens, another Briton with personal knowledge of the South, agreed that Olmsted, though offering no solution for slavery, had reported the situation accurately and reflected on it with care, and Harriet Beecher Stowe praised him for "the most thorough exposé of the economical view of this subject which has ever appeared." [8] Charles Eliot Norton also recommended the three volumes as the "most important contributions to an exact acquaintance with the conditions and results of slavery in this country that have ever been published." [9] Nearly all other contemporary comments and reviews were of like tenor.[1] An even greater compliment

[6] Lowell's review of the *Back Country* in *Atlantic Monthly*, VI (1860), 635; Rollo Ogden, *Life and Letters of Edwin Lawrence Godkin* (New York, 1907), I, 113. For similar comparisons by historians, see John Morley, *The Life of William Ewart Gladstone* (London, 1903), II, 71 n.; two letters of J. Franklin Jameson in the 1920's, in "Senator Beveridge, J. Franklin Jameson, and Abraham Lincoln" (Elizabeth Donnan and L. F. Stock, eds.), *Mississippi Valley Historical Review*, XXXV (1948–1949), 651, 659; and Mitchell, *Olmsted*, 92.

[7] Ogden, *Life and Letters*, I, 114. For excerpts from the *Daily News* series, which ran from December 6, 1856, to April 7, 1857, see 118–164.

[8] Comments on the *Seaboard Slave States* in *Household Words*, XIV (August 23, 1856), 138, and the *Independent*, VIII (February 21, 1856), 57.

[9] Letter to A. H. Clough, September 24, 1860. Norton, *Letters*, I, 211.

[1] See Roper, "Olmsted in the 'Literary Republic,'" *passim*, for summaries of the reviews of the three volumes in newspapers and magazines in the United States and Great Britain. The one conspicuous exception to the rule was *De Bow's Review*, XXIII (1857), 113–131, whose editor, J. D. B. De Bow, New Orleans economist and professional Southerner, accused Olmsted in a raging and discursive article of writing books "abounding in bitterness and prejudices of every sort" in order to make them sell well in the North. Olmsted quotes from this review in the *Back Country*, 398 (*Cotton Kingdom*, 543).

perhaps was the Bostonian Henry Lee Higginson's decision to try living in Dixie after the war as a result of reading Olmsted.[2]

The Cotton Kingdom

When the *Back Country* came off the press in mid-1860, the country was in the thick of a presidential campaign, with the tension between North and South reaching a dangerous pitch. The previous autumn John Brown had made his reckless attempt at Harpers Ferry to start a servile insurrection, and a few months later had suffered death by hanging at the hands of Virginia to outraged cries in the North. The atmosphere in both sections reeked with fear and hatred. The Democrats, unable to resolve their differences over the constitutional status of slavery in the territories, were split into two parties with rival candidates, and Abraham Lincoln was running for the Republicans on a platform which, their opponents rightly said, "could not cross the Ohio River."

The secession of the Lower South following Lincoln's victory in November, 1860, dismayed no one more than Olmsted. This triumph of the proslavery extremists meant that his endeavors to cool sectional fevers by fostering mutual understanding had irremediably failed. Unlike many Northerners, however, he had no doubts as to what course the government should pursue in the emergency. As he had avowed years before, ". . . I am tremendously patriotic. . . . it's the strongest principle in my nature." [3] He had warned the South in the final pages of the *Back Country* that secession would bring war; and though the new administration had yet to take office and Northern opinion was wavering and confused, he wrote Charles Brace on December 8 that "my mind is made up for a fight. The sooner we get used to the idea the better, I think." [4] Was there any way now in which he could use his unrivaled knowledge of slavery and its practices to strengthen the national cause?

At this moment Sampson Low, Son & Company of London, who had handled Olmsted's three Southern volumes in England, made an appealing proposition. They invited him to revise and abridge his

[2] Van Wyck Brooks, *New England: Indian Summer* (New York, 1940), 184–185; Bliss Perry, *Life and Letters of Henry Lee Higginson* (Boston, 1921), II, 250.

[3] Olmsted to F. J. Kingsbury, September 23, 1847. Olmsted Papers.

[4] *Back Country*, 457, 459; Mitchell, *Olmsted*, 54.

writings into a single work for British readers.[5] Olmsted had long given thought to the English attitude on the slavery question and keenly realized its importance in the present crisis. He had taken soundings of popular sentiment on his 1850 trip and no doubt also on his later visits.[6] At one juncture he had tried unsuccessfully, as we shall see, to enlist British businessmen in a project to colonize free laborers in Texas. Olmsted realized that influential Britons favored the South, and he knew that the secessionists counted on the Ministry's support in the event of war with the North. This expectation rested largely on the South's proud boast that "Cotton is King," trumpeted on the floor of the United States Senate by James H. Hammond of South Carolina in 1858.[7] "What would happen if no cotton was furnished for three years? " he cried. ". . . England would topple headlong and carry the whole civilized world with her save the South." In the circumstances Olmsted was eager to do anything he could to guide English thought along pro-Northern lines.

Though the Lows' proposal involved no remuneration for Olmsted, they promised to supply the plates free for an American edition. On the advice of his New York publishers, the Mason Brothers, who for their part offered him a royalty of 12½ per cent, he entered into the arrangement. The Masons predicted a good sale both at home and abroad and pointed out that in any case he could lose nothing but his time.[8] If Olmsted hesitated at all, it was only to figure out how he could fit the undertaking in with his heavy duties at Central Park. He surmounted the obstacle by asking the journalist Daniel R. Goodloe to help him with the revision in return for half the profits. Goodloe, an antislavery North Carolinian, had worked since 1844 on various Washington newspapers, a career briefly interrupted by a

[5] Lows to Olmsted, January 11, 1861. Olmsted Papers.

[6] *Walks and Talks of an American Farmer* (1852 ed.), 220–221.

[7] *Congressional Globe*, 35 Cong., 1 Sess., p. 961. David Christy probably coined the phrase in his *Cotton Is King: or the Culture of Cotton, and Its Relation to Agriculture, Manufactures and Commerce; to the Free Colored People; and to Those Who Hold That Slavery Is in Itself Sinful* (Cincinnati, 1855). F. L. Owsley, *King Cotton Diplomacy* (Chicago, 1931), chap. i, discusses the assumptions and beliefs underlying the concept. For the use of this propaganda in England, see E. D. Adams, *Great Britain and the American Civil War* (New York, 1925), II, chap. x.

[8] Mason Brothers to Olmsted, January 28, February 19, 21, 1861. Olmsted Papers.

clerkship under the Taylor administration, which he lost for writing a letter commending *Uncle Tom's Cabin*. He was now editor of the *National Era*, a moderate antislavery paper published in the capital. Though Olmsted had met him only casually, the choice was a natural one because of Goodloe's many articles and pamphlets on the economics of slavery. Olmsted broached the project to him in a letter of February 12, 1861, and Goodloe instantly accepted.[9]

The two worked at high speed, for the rapid march of events—the onset of the war at Fort Sumter in April and England's recognition of the South's belligerency in May—rendered time of the essence. Under the circumstances Olmsted prepared a brand-new introductory chapter on "The Present Crisis" to point up observations originally penned for calmer days. Occasional misunderstandings arose between author and editor because of their residence in different cities, and others because Goodloe wanted to inject more of himself into the book than Olmsted would allow. Olmsted wished him mainly to condense the earlier volumes and to bring the statistics in line with the later census of 1860; but Goodloe, in addition, hankered to include some of his own "thoughts and inferences." On one occasion he suggested appending brief annotations to the text and supplying a "copious introduction, upon the nature and condition of Slavery."[1]

Such an introduction would have given Goodloe an opportunity to expound his own reasons for the South's economic backwardness. The true cause, he instructed Olmsted, was the concentration on cotton culture. This preoccupation absorbed capital and labor and handicapped all other undertakings, though the incompetence of unpaid workers was doubtless a contributing element. "Slavery *is* profitable to the few," he went on, "because it is simply a privilege of robbing the many." The institution not only impoverished the white community as a whole, but it rendered the Negro population a "meagre market for the products of manufacturing and commercial enterprize." "What I maintain is simply this:" he said in widening the base of his argument, "that Slavery is an unnecessary investment

---

[9] Goodloe to Olmsted, February 15, 1861. Olmsted Papers.

[1] Olmsted to his father, March 22, 1861; Goodloe to Olmsted, February 15, 24, 1861. This account of the collaboration is derived from the Olmsted Papers, where, however, only Goodloe's side of the correspondence is preserved.

of Capital, because Slaves, being rational beings can be induced to work without owning them—or if that is not true of negroes, they may be dispensed with and white men will take their places. . . . and do their work 3 or 4 times as well." Hence it followed that emancipation, though destroying three billion dollars of slave property, would not diminish in actuality the South's productive resources.

This was a somewhat different approach to the matter from that of Olmsted, who attributed the slaveholder's plight largely to the inefficiency of forced labor, the inflated price of slaves and the high overhead cost of their maintenance from womb to tomb. Yet Olmsted's account of conditions, as Goodloe contended, afforded "implicit illustration" also of another interpretation.[2] In reality the two positions were not mutually exclusive. The differences were chiefly of emphasis.

Olmsted stuck by his guns, however, as he also did when Goodloe queried certain statistical conclusions in the newly written chapter. The editor thought it misleading to state that a Negro produced only a bale and a third of cotton annually when the figure was arrived at by dividing the total crop by the total number of slaves, including the aged and children: "this is not what you talk of elsewhere, when you say that on large plantations they make ten bales to the hand." Usually the field workers did not comprise more than a third of the slaves, he pointed out. On the same basis he considered that Olmsted had underrated the profits of the small cotton farmers. These men, he added, gave a good deal of attention also to grain growing, hog raising etc., with the help of house servants and children. He argued that if such farms didn't really pay they would be abandoned.[3] Olmsted likewise did nothing with Goodloe's suggestion that the situation in Virginia and North Carolina had substantially improved since 1853–1854, thanks to the building of additional railroads.[4] On the other hand, Goodloe performed a lot of useful leg work for the book, ascertaining the number of large slaveholders, for example, and supplying detailed information about the 1849 cotton crop. But on neither these nor other matters was he able to

---

[2] Goodloe to Olmsted, February 23, 24, March 1, 8, 1861.

[3] Goodloe to Olmsted, March 19, 1861. Compare the *Cotton Kingdom*, 13, 15–16.

[4] Goodloe to Olmsted, March 1, 1861.

consult the 1860 census returns, which were "not yet sufficiently verified and digested to be given to the public." [5]

The work of compression and consolidation, Goodloe's principal task, had to be an act of major surgery to meet the wishes of the English publishers. He had complete liberty from the author to do as he pleased, but since he felt "some delicacy" about acting without advice, he and Olmsted agreed that the main savings should come from the *Back Country* and, particularly, from the *Journey through Texas*, which played up a single state disproportionately. As for the *Seaboard Slave States*, the editor confessed, "I have thus far found scarcely a page which could be dropped without injury to the picture you give of the South." [6] Proceeding along these lines, Goodloe amputated the bulk of the *Journey through Texas*, leaving only 27,-625 words out of the 185,765, and sacrificing among other things the valuable chapter on the first leg of the expedition through western Kentucky and Tennessee to Louisiana. He retained more of the *Back Country*, however, than he probably had originally intended, and, with whatever regrets, he was compelled to dispense with more of the *Seaboard Slave States* than he had planned.

Wherever he could, he economized space not only by pruning individual sentences, but by deleting long passages and, as notably in the instance of the *Journey through Texas*, whole chapters. Generally, he omitted historical digressions and purely descriptive and travelogue matter, and he also shortened considerably the material on the poor whites as well as on agricultural practices and affairs. Focusing on the current scene, he aimed at a representative portrayal of conditions without the needless repetition which formed a natural part of a traveler's day-by-day jottings. And, oddly enough, despite the political purpose of the book and the editor's own antislavery convictions, he eliminated more things adverse to the South than those that were favorable. In merging Olmsted's earlier writings he often brought together observations scattered in different volumes. Though this had certain obvious advantages, it sometimes destroyed the narrative thread, surprising the reader by an abrupt transposition to a new locality. The net result of Goodloe's labors was to cut the 606,000 words of the original works to 276,500 words, a reduction of more than half.

[5] Goodloe to Olmsted, February 23, March 19, 1861; *Cotton Kingdom*, 8 *n.*
[6] Goodloe to Olmsted, February 24, March 1, 1861.

How *The Cotton Kingdom* was Compiled

1861 ED. (VOL. I)	PRESENT ED.	ORIGINAL SOURCE
1–27	3–23	New matter
28–107	24–83	*Seaboard Slave States*, 1–118
108–114	84–88	New matter
114–116	88–90	*Seaboard Slave States*, 212–213
116–117	90–91	New matter
117–137	91–107	*Seaboard Slave States*, 185–200, 145–148, 203–207
137–140	107–109	New matter
140–263	110–204	*Seaboard Slave States*, 133–138, 149–156, 351–8, 158–163, 305–337, 348–351, 366–453
263–265	204–206	*Back Country*, 134–135
265–308	206–240	*Seaboard Slave States*, 454–461, 546–602
308–317	240–247	*Back Country*, 187–196
317–341	247–266	*Seaboard Slave States*, 656–686
342–343	267	New matter
343–356	267–278	*Seaboard Slave States*, 603–620
356–357	278	New matter
357–358	278–279	*Seaboard Slave States*, 631–632
358–376	279–293	*Texas*, 45–70

1861 ED. (VOL. II)	PRESENT ED.	ORIGINAL SOURCE
1–43	294–326	*Texas*, 80–132, 241–258, 362–405
43–54	326–335	*Seaboard Slave States*, 646–656, 643–645
55–235	336–479	*Back Country*, 125–272, 11–65, 72–93, 107–109, 65–71, 105–106, 109–123
236–251	480–493	*Seaboard Slave States*, 686–711
252–257	494–498	*Back Country*, 337–342
257–258	498–499	*Seaboard Slave States*, 586–587
258–292	499–525	*Back Country*, 342–355, 381–396, 304–311
292–293	525–526	*Seaboard Slave States*, 504–505, 510
293–294	526–527	*Back Country*, 310
294	527	*Seaboard Slave States*, 514
294–296	527–529	*Back Country*, 311–320
296–298	529–531	*Seaboard Slave States*, 533–534, 576–577
298–303	531–535	*Back Country*, 320–325

1861 ED.			
(VOL. II)	PRESENT ED.	ORIGINAL SOURCE
303–304	535–536	*Seaboard Slave States*, 289, 278, 280
304–308	536–539	*Back Country*, 325–329
308–309	539–541	New matter
310–327	541–555	*Back Country*, 397, 297, 397–415
327–329	555–557	New matter
329–363	557–584	*Back Country*, 415–424, 431–457
364–384	585–605	*Seaboard Slave States*, 164–173, 32–40, 717–722
385–392	606–613	*Back Country*, 312–319

This feat, moreover, he achieved in spite of some freshly inserted material. Besides the chapter on "The Present Crisis," Olmsted prefixed six and a half pages to the chapter on "The Economy of Virginia," which were directed particularly at English readers,[7] and he interpolated in the next to the last chapter a long letter by an Illinois farmer concerning the South, which he had just noticed in the *New York Tribune*, June 7, 1861.[8] There were also new or expanded footnotes here and there,[9] as well as an occasional added sentence, such as: "That 'slaves are liars,' or, as they say here, 'niggers will lie,' always has been proverbial."[1] Presumably the many purely verbal changes—apart from the English spelling, which, though not consistently observed, came about as the result of transatlantic publication—were Goodloe's. Thus the editor altered "I have the impression that it was customary" to "I understand that it was customary," and he preferred " 'Very well, my dear,' " to " 'Very well, my beauty' " (referring to a horse).[2] Such revisions were matters of taste (*non disputandum*); but he made others for the sake of greater clarity, as when he substituted "rich cotton country" for

[7] Olmsted's authorship, rather than Goodloe's, is indicated in part by his inquiries to Goodloe regarding the use of white and colored labor in Virginia, which falls in these pages. Goodloe to Olmsted, March 19, 1861.

[8] Olmsted to Charles A. Dana, June 7, 1861; *Cotton Kingdom*, 539–541. The other new matter for which Olmsted was probably responsible was widely scattered and does not amount in all to more than eight or nine pages of the 1861 edition. Only the longer passages are noted in the table showing how the *Cotton Kingdom* was compiled.

[9] *Ibid.*, 40, 46, 160, 298, 321, 328, 332, 405, 418–419, 457–458, 494, 514–515.

[1] *Ibid.*, 82. Cf. the *Seaboard Slave States*, 116.

[2] *Cotton Kingdom*, 43, 52. Cf. the *Seaboard Slave States*, 47, 65.

"planting country," [3] while still others arose from the need to square Olmsted's data with the conditions as they existed at this later time. An instance is the selling price of Negroes, which he gave as $1400 instead of $1000 a head.[4]

Olmsted shipped the last of the manuscript to London on June 11, 1861. Only three months had elapsed since he had teamed up with Goodloe. The English publishers acted with equal alacrity, reporting on June 29 that the printers were already hard at work on the book. The author received his first copy on October 25, and the Masons had their edition off the press on November 7.[5] The work, in two volumes and 768 pages (exclusive of the Index), bore the title *The Cotton Kingdom: a Traveller's Observations on Cotton and Slavery in the American Slave States*. It was issued abroad also as *Journeys and Explorations in the Cotton Kingdom*. Olmsted dedicated it to John Stuart Mill, champion of "moral and political freedom" in England and, incidentally, a stout friend of the Northern cause. The book carried no mention of Goodloe's editorial services. The Masons reported a brisk advance sale,[6] and in fact the work had to be reissued in both the United States and Great Britain the next year.

The title was a play upon Senator Hammond's defiant speech in 1858 vaunting King Cotton, from which Olmsted quoted in his opening chapter. Far from being a pillar of strength to the South, Olmsted insisted that the "cotton monopoly" had been a source of weakness, despite the large profits accruing to a few great planters. In a graphic passage on the "so-called cotton States" he told of traveling "at least three thousand miles of roads, from which not a cotton plant was to be seen, and the people living by the side of which certainly had not been made rich by cotton or anything else." [7] Cotton, he concluded, was a cruel and ruinous monarch.

Olmsted is said to have been dissatisfied with the abridgment,[8] perhaps as authors generally are when someone lays profane hands on their brain children. The product nevertheless seems fully to warrant the contemporary estimate of the *North American Review*:

[3] *Cotton Kingdom*, 392. Cf. the *Back Country*, 220.

[4] *Cotton Kingdom*, 411. Cf. the *Back Country*, 20.

[5] Olmsted to C. A. Dana, June 7, 1861; Sampson Low, Son & Company to Olmsted, June 29; Olmsted to his wife, October 25. Olmsted Papers.

[6] Olmsted to his wife, October 25, 1861.

[7] *Cotton Kingdom*, 7, 8, 11.

[8] Conversation with Frederick Law Olmsted, Jr., August 1, 1941.

Whatever praise we have bestowed on the previous volumes belongs more emphatically to these two; for they enable the reader with a much smaller expense of time, not only to acquaint himself with Mr. Olmsted's generalizations, results, and conclusions, but to examine specimens of each class of observations, and of every kind of evidence from which he drew his inferences.[9]

James Russell Lowell, telling Olmsted he was "particularly impressed with the compactness and quiet power" of the introductory chapter, added, "I have learned more about the South from your books than from all others put together, and I valued them the more that an American who can be patient and accurate is so rare a phenomenon." To Senator Charles Sumner the treatise was "a positive contribution to Civilization," while Henry T. Tuckerman, the essayist and biographer, hailed it as "the most powerful and permanent argument in favor of every sacrifice to preserve our nationality intact." [1]

The effect of the *Cotton Kingdom* on England is impossible to measure. It was one of a great many factors in Anglo-American relations, even in the realm of propaganda.[2] The work, however, enraged the ultra-Tory *Saturday Review*, which declared it to be no more trustworthy than "the facts of a first-class Old Bailey barrister retained for the defence of a wealthy client on trial for his life." Obviously the political climate in England had changed since the same journal, only a year before, had said of the *Back Country* that the author "is so candid and unprejudiced, and he is apparently so precise and exact, that we yield him a confidence which can only be displaced by the testimony of a witness equally reliable." [3]

Probably Olmsted exerted his greatest influence indirectly, through the writings of the Irish economist John Elliot Cairnes, notably *The Slave Power*, published in London in May, 1862. This treatise, a potent indictment of the Southern system on economic grounds,

---

[9] *North American Review*, XCIV (1862), 272.

[1] Letters to Olmsted from Lowell, January 25, 1862, Sumner, December 18, 1861, and Tuckerman, November 8, 1861. Olmsted Papers.

[2] For Northern propaganda at the time, see Donaldson Jordan and E. J. Pratt, *Europe and the American Civil War* (Boston, 1931), chaps. i–vii; J. H. Kiger, "Federal Government Propaganda in Great Britain during the American Civil War," *Historical Outlook*, XIX (1928), 204–209; and Jay Monaghan, *Diplomat in Carpet Slippers* (Indianapolis, 1945), chap. xiv.

[3] *Saturday Review*, X (October 20, 1860), 486; XII (November 2, 1861), 460.

inspired John Stuart Mill to say in the *Westminster Review*: "A work more needed, or one better adapted to the need, could scarcely have been produced at the present time. It contains more than enough to give a new turn to English feeling on the subject, if those who guide and sway public opinion were ever likely to reconsider a question on which they have so deeply committed themselves."[4] Cairnes quoted constantly from Olmsted, relying upon the *Seaboard Slave States* and the *Journey through Texas*, however, rather than on the *Cotton Kingdom*, which may not have come to his hand in time.

The Problem of Bias

When Olmsted wrangled over the slavery question with Charles Brace far into the night at the Staten Island farm before his first Southern trip, both disapproved of the institution but in significantly different degrees. To evaluate properly Olmsted's writings on the South, it is necessary to know just what his position was and whether it was such as to impugn his credibility as a witness. Fortunately, the evidence is reasonably complete, for he expressed his views repeatedly in private as well as in public.

In 1846, six years before he first went south, the twenty-four-year-old Olmsted informed his father, "The tyranny of priests and churches is as great a curse to the country and the world as negro Slavery." He had been pondering John C. Calhoun's justification of the system, for he wrote Charles Brace that the South Carolinian's arguments had persuaded him "that Slavery is not the greatest sin in the world—that a Slaveholder may be a conscientious Christian." Olmsted, in fact, could not "believe Slaveholding to be *either* a unforgiveable sin or a 'beneficial Institution sanctioned by God.'" Though he felt that Calhoun had overstated the case, "he *may* be right. God knows, I honestly believe he may be right."[5] Nevertheless he was

[4] Cited in J. E. Cairnes, *The Revolution in America* (5th ed., Dublin, n.d.), opposite the title page. Temporarily it also gave a new turn to Charles Darwin's views on the Civil War, making him "for a time wish honestly for the North; but," he candidly added to his American colleague Asa Gray, "I could never help, though I honestly tried, all the time thinking how we should be bullied and forced into a war by you, when you were triumphant." Francis Darwin, *Life and Letters of Charles Darwin* (New York, 1888), II, 195–196.

[5] Olmsted to his father, August 12, 1846, and to Brace, March 22, 1846. These and later letters in this section are cited from the Olmsted Papers unless otherwise indicated.

troubled that the Southern students he had known at Yale, whom he thought admirable in other respects, "do not seem to have a fundamental sense of right," having "no power of comprehending a hatred of slavery in itself," and ascribing Northern objections merely to a "regard for self-interest." [6] At the same time he deplored the blackguarding of slaveholders in the Northern press, "exasperating them—Acting as if we hated them as much as we did their doctrines." The proper way was to "*reason* with them as though *we might* be the mistaken ones, for truly I think in my heart we *may* be." [7]

Notwithstanding such doubts he wrote his father in 1846, at an early stage of the fight in Congress over the Wilmot Proviso, that he hoped the admitting of Texas into the Union with slavery meant that Oregon and California—other recent or prospective acquisitions—would be given the status of free soil. "If we can but secure that," he said, "before the lines are irretrievably drawn—then at least I hope it will be North and freedom vs. South and slavery," thus opening the way for gradual emancipation and the colonization of the freedmen in Africa.[8] This solution of the problem was one which would increasingly engage Olmsted's attention. A year later, in 1847, he dismissed a recent declaration of principles by the Liberty party as too Garrisonian in spirit and "far from convincing." By contrast, he described himself as a lukewarm Whig, a choice he justified on the score that the Whigs were the more national-minded of the two major parties.[9]

During his trip abroad in 1850 he resented the prevalent British view that the North, except for "a few martyrs, called abolitionists," was as responsible for slavery as the South, but in almost the same breath he declared the English practice of primogeniture "more naturally abhorrent and wrong" than Negro bondage. He counseled the Southerners to send some lecturers to England to counter abolitionist misrepresentations.[1] Returning home amid the "fearful reaction" in the North to the new Fugitive Slave Act (a part of the Compromise of 1850, passed during his absence), he blamed both

---

[6] Olmsted to F. J. Kingsbury, June, 1846. Mitchell, *Olmsted*, 38.

[7] Olmsted to Brace, May 27, 1846.

[8] Olmsted to his father, August 12, 1846.

[9] Olmsted to Brace, September 20, 1847, and to Kingsbury, September 23, 1847.

[1] *Walks and Talks* (1852 ed.), 215, 221.

sections for the uproar, but thought the "free principles" of Northerners would succumb to the danger of losing Southern trade. "Money," he said, "is at the bottom of the sin on both sides." [2] In the 1852 campaign he supported the Whigs, who, like the Democrats, pledged continuance of the Compromise, though he declared privately that he "would take in a fugitive slave and shoot the man that was likely to get him. On the whole I guess I represent pretty fairly the average sentiment of good thinking men on our side." [3]

The *New York Times* correspondent who went south shortly after the election truthfully said that "few men could have been so little inclined to establish previously formed opinions as I was." [4] To an extraordinary degree he had kept his mind free from the passions which had for so long inflamed his countrymen's thinking on the slavery issue. As a believer in democracy he could not approve of human bondage in principle, but he recognized the "clear constitutional right" of the Southern states "to continue their peculiar institution, as it is, and where it is," and he regarded abolition as no more immediately practicable than the abolition of penitentiaries and hospitals.[5] He could even cry, "Who are we to condemn our brother? . . . No slave freezes to death for want of habitation and fuel, as have men in Boston. . . . Remember that, Mrs. Stowe. Remember that, indignant sympathizers." At the most, as we have seen, he desired to keep the institution from spreading farther—he "would rather the Union be dissolved" than have this occur [6]—and he considered it a dirty business for Northerners to return escaped Negroes.

Then and later, he viewed slavery *per se* as "an unfortunate circumstance for which the people of the South were in no wise to blame," and held that "much mischief had resulted from statements and descriptions of occurrences which were exceptional, as if they were the ordinary phenomena attending slavery." On the contrary, he believed the whites to be discharging an "unenviable duty" at much personal inconvenience, and that the gains to the Negroes from enforced association with a superior race "far outweighed the occasional cruelties, and other evils incidental to the system." De-

[2] Olmsted to Brace, November 12, 1850.
[3] Olmsted to Kingsbury, October 17, 1852.
[4] *Back Country*, p. vi.
[5] *Seaboard Slave States*, p. x; *New York Times*, February 13, 1854, p. 2 (not later reprinted); *Back Country*, p. vi.
[6] *New York Times*, February 13, 1854, p. 2; April 8, p. 2.

termined to examine conditions "carefully and fairly," he would also do so "cheerfully and kindly," seeking for "the causes and extenuating circumstances, past and present, of those phenomena which are commonly reported to the prejudice of the slaveholding community; and especially of those features which are manifestly most to be regretted."[7]

Though Olmsted adhered to some of these ideas for more than twelve months of his wanderings, rejecting counterevidence as probably atypical, he felt obliged in the end to abandon most of them.[8] As he confessed at the close of his wayfaring, "I saw much more of what I had not anticipated and less of what I had, in the Slave States, than, with a somewhat extended traveling experience, in any other country I ever visited."[9] His new convictions, though, did not render him dogmatic or denunciatory, or lead him to withhold from his readers facts that did not document his views. And even as late as 1860 he still felt that the dominant race was caught in a historical trap and that, everything considered, the "subjection of the negroes" to the "mastership of the whites" was "justifiable and necessary."[1]

By the same token Olmsted continued to decry the course of the Northern abolitionists, whose high moral tone ignored the practical difficulties of emancipation. He likewise deplored their loathing of Southerners as individuals and their willingness to imperil the very survival of the Union for their cause. In his view they were as wrongheaded as those at the other pole of the argument who stood for "hopeless, dawnless, unredeeming slavery."[2] "The extremists of the South," he said, "esteem their opponents as madmen, or robbers," while "The extremists of the North esteem the slave-holders as

[7] This paragraph rests upon the *Seaboard Slave States*, p. x, and on the *Back Country*, pp. vi and 70–71. The last reference reappears in the *Cotton Kingdom*, 466.

[8] *Back Country*, 71 (*Cotton Kingdom*, 466–467).

[9] *Seaboard Slave States*, 179. Though this was the first volume of the trilogy, it will be recalled that he had completed his second and third journeys before he wrote it.

[1] *Back Country*, p. viii. Despite his avowed belief in democracy he had written in the *New York Times*, February 13, 1854, p. 2, "I do not consider slaveholding—the simple exercise of the authority of a master over the negroes who have so wickedly been enslaved—in itself, necessarily wrong, any more than all forcible constraint of a child or lunatic is wrong," though he added, "*Slavery as it is*, in the vast majority of cases, is shamefully cruel, selfish and wicked."

[2] *Walks and Talks* (1859 ed.), 278.

robbers and tyrants, willfully and malevolently oppressive and cruel." [3] In his "Letter to a Southern Friend," which prefaced the *Journey through Texas,* he denied, however, that any "formidable number" of Northerners wished to interfere with slavery where it was already entrenched, though perhaps half the population (of whom he was, of course, one) held it to be an evil which should not be extended elsewhere.[4] Moreover, he questioned the common Southern contention that the militancy of abolitionism had badgered the people of the slave states into a firmer attachment to the institution. That attitude he attributed, rather, to the South's increasing economic stake in the system.[5]

Olmsted's sojourn in Texas, though shedding no additional light on his antislavery sentiments, put them to the test of action. He and John spent considerable time among the Germans in the New Braunfels district of Western Texas between San Antonio and Austin, where the thrifty management of the settlers and their repugnance to human bondage greatly impressed the brothers. So strong was the feeling against slavery that Olmsted estimated that not more than thirty out of the nearly twenty-five thousand Germans in Western Texas owned Negroes.[6] Since Texas as admitted to the Union in 1845 exceeded in area New England, the Middle Atlantic states, Maryland, Virginia and Kentucky combined, Congress had provided that, as the population increased, it might be divided into as many as five commonwealths with the state's consent. The possibility therefore existed that slavery might be barred from part of the broad expanse.

Dr. Adolf Douai, editor of the *San Antonio Zeitung,* whom the Olmsteds had met and admired, was leader of the movement for making Western Texas into a free state; and when some of the paper's stockholders, unwilling to antagonize their Anglo-American neighbors, tried to muzzle him, he appealed in September, 1854, to the Olmsted brothers, then back in New York, for a loan to enable him to continue publishing on his own. They quickly secured the

[3] *Seaboard Slave States,* 177.
[4] *Journey through Texas,* p. xv.
[5] *Seaboard Slave States,* 283–284.
[6] *Journey through Texas,* 428, 432. The account that follows rests upon *ibid.,* 434–439, and Laura Wood Roper, "Frederick Law Olmsted and the Western Texas Free-Soil Movement," *American Historical Review,* LVI (1950–1951), 58–61.

money from Charles Brace, Henry Ward Beecher and other anti-slavery sympathizers, helped Douai get printing equipment in New York and drummed up subscribers for the publication. Moreover, Olmsted, besides agreeing to write a fortnightly letter for the *Zeitung*, induced the *New York Times* to publish editorials and articles to encourage Northern emigration to Western Texas. These pieces, for political reasons, intentionally side-stepped the free-soil angle for the economic advantages. Douai, however, finding the local opposition too powerful, quit the paper and the hopeless cause in May, 1856, and removed to the more congenial atmosphere of Boston.

Meanwhile Olmsted had become involved in a similar campaign to keep slavery out of Kansas, an issue much more prominent nationally. The dispute over this area, growing out of the passage of the Kansas-Nebraska Act, had reached the stage of bloodshed, and Olmsted, with the assistance of Horace Greeley, David Dudley Field and others, raised funds to provide the free-state party in Kansas with its first cannon. The howitzer arrived in time to help beat off the attack of the proslavery forces on Lawrence in December, 1855.[7] In his "Letter to a Southern Friend" in the *Journey through Texas*, Olmsted bitterly denounced the "fraud and violence" of the slavery elements in both Kansas and Texas, and in the Introduction to a book on the Kansas situation by a London *Times* reporter he flayed the pro-Southern course of the federal administration as well.[8]

Olmsted's deeper concern, however, remained with Western Texas, perhaps because he felt that the North was already sufficiently stirred up over "Bleeding Kansas," which the newly formed Republican party made one of its major issues in the 1856 campaign. His volume on Texas, appearing a few months after the election, did not openly urge Northern emigration to the Lone Star state, but that was its tenor, and he took every occasion to use the book as a pro-

[7] J. B. Abbott, "The Abbott Howitzer—Its History," *Kansas State Historical Society, Transactions*, I–II (1881), 221–226.

[8] *Journey through Texas*, p. xix; T. H. Gladstone, *The Englishman in Kansas; or Squatter Life and Border Warfare* (London, 1857), Introduction and chap. xxvi (both by Olmsted). Gladstone arrived in New York in January, 1856, and after traveling in the Lower South went by way of Missouri to Kansas in the spring. Olmsted quotes part of his Introduction in the *Back Country*, 440–447 (*Cotton Kingdom*, 571–576).

motional tract. Though the prospect of carving a free state out of Texas had now faded, he nevertheless believed that free labor, by demonstrating its superior efficiency in the growing of cotton, would lead to the curtailment or abandonment of slave labor.[9] Hearing that some of the Kansas free-soilers were hoping to "take Western Texas next," he offered Edward Everett Hale of the New England Emigrant Aid Company a hundred copies of his book at cost to distribute among them. He gave others to leading antislavery men like Theodore Parker and John Greenleaf Whittier, and even circulated selected pages of the work to New England newspaper editors.[1]

He also tried to stimulate English migration to the region, on the plea that the greater productivity of free labor would relieve British fears that the Southern output of cotton would not keep abreast of the mounting industrial demand in that country.[2] Besides writing to J. T. Delane of the London *Times* and other English acquaintances, he appealed directly to the Cotton Supply Associations of Manchester and Liverpool, buttressing his arguments with copies of his book and offering to present the case to them in person. Nor did the outbreak of the war exhaust his interest in Western Texas. Joining with the Massachusetts textile manufacturer Edward Atkinson and others, he urged that an "army of colonization" be dispatched to detach the area from the Confederacy and so repair the North's shortage of cotton. The ill-starred attack on Galveston at the close of 1862 was the sole outcome.

These concerns and activities in no sense belied the careful distinction Olmsted invariably drew between slavery as a pre-existing institution and its transplantation to fresh soil. Despite his firsthand acquaintance with the aggressive nature of the slavocracy, he continued to look upon Negro servitude where it was already rooted as "an entailed misfortune which, with the best disposition, it might

[9] *Back Country*, 184 (*Cotton Kingdom*, 373–374).

[1] Roper, "Olmsted and the Western Texas Free-Soil Movement," 61–62.

[2] This account is based on *ibid.*, 62–65; P. W. Bidwell, ed., "The New England Emigrant Aid Company and English Cotton Supply Associations: Letters of Frederick L. Olmsted," *American Historical Review*, XXIII (1917–1918), 114–119; H. F. Williamson, *Edward Atkinson* (Boston, 1934), 5–8; and G. W. Smith, "The Banks Expedition of 1862," *Louisiana Historical Quarterly*, XXVI (1943), 341–360. Olmsted comments on the attitude of the Cotton Supply Associations in the *Back Country*, 353–354 (*Cotton Kingdom*, 508–509).

require centuries to wholly dispose of." [3] In sympathizing with the white man's plight, however, he did not ignore the black man's, for the system in his judgment misdirected and debased the laborer's ambition, withholding "all the natural motives, which lead men to increase their capacity of usefulness to their country and the world." [4] Yet he opposed instant emancipation by federal edict, not only on constitutional grounds but also because he doubted whether it would accomplish what was expected: "An extraction of the bullet does not at once remedy the injury of a gun-shot wound; it sometimes aggravates it." [5]

Olmsted's own solution was gradual manumission by action of the slaveholders themselves. [6] This he regarded as not improbable, once they faced up to the economic drawbacks of the system. As steps toward the goal, an owner should systematically foster habits of self-reliance in his thralls and permit them to buy their liberation by accumulating financial credits as payment for their toil. Even so, Olmsted was not starry-eyed about the outcome. He did not believe the ex-slaves would ever "become Teutons or Celts," rather that they would be "of tenfold more in value to the commonwealth than they are." This answer to the problem was far different from that of the abolitionists, who held that freedom was a God-given right and that the master class, having exploited the Negroes for long generations, deserved no further compensation of any kind. Olmsted, moreover, foresaw a difficult race problem when enough Negroes should be freed, and hence he hoped that "something" would "force, or encourage and facilitate, a voluntary and spontaneous separation" of the two peoples at that time. In all this, Olmsted was indebted to Thomas Jefferson's scheme of gradual emancipation, and he attributed certain features of his plan to the self-liberation law in Cuba and the reformatory system of some of the British penal colonies. [7] He was undoubtedly acquainted also with the program of the American Colonization Society, in existence since 1817.

In the *Back Country*, in the summer of 1860, he presented his

---

[3] Gladstone, *Englishman in Kansas*, p. xxxvii.

[4] *Seaboard Slave States*, 711 (*Cotton Kingdom*, 493).

[5] *Back Country*, p. vii.

[6] *Seaboard Slave States*, 443–445 (*Cotton Kingdom*, 198–200); *Back Country*, pp. viii–ix, 482–483.

[7] Olmsted discusses Jefferson's plan in the *Seaboard Slave States*, 261–265, and refers to the two others in *ibid.*, 445–446 (*Cotton Kingdom*, 199–200).

proposal with a fresh note of urgency, declaring that it was the only means of averting an eventual military clash between the sections. So long as human bondage endured, he wrote, the very existence of the North organized on a basis of voluntary labor would be a standing threat to the servile system, and the South's increasing demand for federal legislation to protect and nurture slavery would sooner or later, perhaps "ten or twenty years hence," impel the free states to call a halt on further concessions. Though he did not deny the South's abstract right to secede when that moment should come, he warned that the Northern people would take up arms to prevent it.[8]

Far more swiftly than he had anticipated, the exodus of slave states began after Lincoln's election in the autumn, and, as we have seen, Olmsted took his stand unqualifiedly with the Union—that Union which he had so long and earnestly striven to hold together by peaceful means. With the North and South at war, his cherished scheme of voluntary gradual emancipation became of the figment of dreams. The "first *shotted*-gun that was fired" at Fort Sumter had outmoded it, he declared in discussing "The Present Crisis" in the *Cotton Kingdom*. The issue was now the stark one of power: "The one system or the other is to thrive and extend, and eventually possess and govern this whole land." Either we must "subjugate slavery, or be subjugated by it." [9]

Nonetheless, the fate of the Southern Negroes under the altered conditions was never far from his mind. He did not share Brace's expectation that they would voluntarily rise against their masters, but he called on the government to seize strategic points to which they could escape and thus help demoralize the South. He also believed they should be enlisted as soldiers.[1] But the increasing certainty that the government would abolish slavery gave him pause, for it was not easy to shed long-held convictions as to the Negroes' unpreparedness. To him they were still "half savage Africans." He voiced the fear, after six months or so of the fighting, that "the slaves will get emancipated long before we are in a condition to deal with them decently in any other way than as slaves." In the

---

[8] *Back Country*, 455–457 (*Cotton Kingdom*, 582–584), 459, 481.

[9] *Cotton Kingdom*, 5.

[1] Olmsted to Brace, October 4, 1862, Olmsted Papers; "Yeoman" in the *New York Times*, December 4, 1861, p. 2.

midst of his exacting duties as chief executive officer of the United States Sanitary Commission (for which he had obtained leave in June, 1861, from Central Park), he urged the federal authorities to provide constructive employment for freedmen in districts occupied by the troops, and he even toyed with the idea of himself taking over the "management of a large negro colony." After the Emancipation Proclamation on January 1, 1863, he participated actively in the discussions that led Congress in March, 1865, to create the Bureau for the Relief of Freedmen and Refugees.[2] Unfortunately, this agency accomplished only a small part of what Olmsted had desired.

In a backward look a quarter of a century later, Olmsted took stock of the social and economic changes which defeat had forced upon the South, and with characteristic frankness confessed wherein his own judgment had been amiss. He noted that after the war thoughtful Northerners, even though they recognized that "the great mass of the freedmen were as yet ludicrously unfitted to be trusted with the ballot," had nevertheless favored enfranchisement on the ground that the vote would protect the Negroes against the danger of "some sort of quasi-slavery" after the withdrawal of the Union troops. In line with such views, Congress had made Negro suffrage central to its Reconstruction program, but he himself had thought this unwise.

"If I could," he wrote, "I would have secured to the freedmen the full rights of intending citizens yet unnaturalized" and so have made "political equality a privilege to be earned." He still hoped that the Southern states would enact a literacy test for voting, applicable, however, to both races. Notwithstanding such reservations he freely admitted:

The negroes have been doing a great deal better as freedmen than I had ever imagined it possible that they would. The whites have accepted the situation about as well as it was in human nature that they should, and we have been advancing toward prosperity and in prosperity under the new state of things at the South amazingly more than I had thought would be possible in so short a time after so great a catastrophe.[3]

    [2] This account is based on Mitchell, *Olmsted*, 57–58, and his quotations from Olmsted's correspondence.
    [3] Letter to Thomas H. Clark, August 5, 1889, in Clark's article, "Frederick Law Olmsted on the South, 1889," *South Atlantic Quarterly*, III (1904), 11–15.

In the light of this inventory of Olmsted's views on the slavery question over the years, he might perhaps be charged with obtuseness to some of the moral implications of the institution; he can hardly be accused of undue prejudice against the South. From first to last he pursued an individual course between extremes of opinion, seeking to perform a mediatorial role. He addressed himself to the human reason in matter-of-fact tones while voices screamed all about him. He stressed the economic aspects of slavery because they particularly interested him, but he may also have felt that that approach afforded the best antidote to passion and intolerance in both sections. If, as someone has said, a first-rate mind is one that can entertain antagonistic ideas and still retain the capacity to function, Olmsted amply met the specifications. While frankly expressing his own judgments—in the *Seaboard Slave States* he called himself an "honest growler"—he carefully presented the evidence from which others might draw their own conclusions. As he stated in the *Back Country*, "my first conscious purpose has been to obtain and report the facts of ordinary life at the South, not to supply arguments." That indeed was the reason he assigned for the bulkiness of his works.[4]

It is difficult to conceive of a more objective critic of Southern life. This in fact was the almost universal opinion of contemporaneous reviewers, who characterized Olmsted's writings as " temperate," "singularly fair," "impartial," "dispassionate," "unbiased," "conciliatory," "authentic." [5] Since these commentators, however, may themselves have been swayed by antislavery predilections, the cooler judgment of historians in after years obviously merits greater weight. That verdict is equally impressive, for with few exceptions such scholars, whether of Northern or Southern birth, have accorded Olmsted like praise.[6] Even those who have questioned some of his

---

[4] *Seaboard Slave States*, p. ix; *Back Country*, pp. ix, 292. Echoing Olmsted's characterization of himself, Thomas H. Clark, an Alabamian, wrote in 1904, "The South may well be grateful that this kindly, growling note-taker came amongst us." "Olmsted on the South," 12.

[5] *Household Words*, XIV (August 23, 1856), 138; *New Englander*, XIV (1856), 265; *North American Review*, LXXXIII (1856), 279, LXXXIV (1857), 566, XCI (1860), 571; *Atlantic Monthly*, VI (1860), 635; H. T. Tuckerman, *America and Her Commentators* (New York, 1864), 417–418. De Bow's angry dissent has earlier been noted.

[6] A. J. Beveridge, *Abraham Lincoln* (Boston, 1928), II, 6 n.; P. W. Bidwell in *American Historical Review*, XXIII (1917–1918), 114; Clement Eaton, *Freedom of Thought in the Old South* (Durham, 1930), 112; A. B. Hart, *Slavery*

inferences have generally trusted his factual data.[7] Olmsted, in the eyes of those best qualified to judge, thus emerges as a disinterested and reliable witness of conditions in the Old South. No other contemporary observer possessed equivalent credentials.

The South through Olmsted's Eyes

Alexis de Tocqueville, traveling in the United States in the 1830's, maintained "that almost all the differences which may be noticed between the Americans in the Southern and in the Northern states have originated in slavery."[8] Olmsted, out of a much fuller knowledge of conditions, came to a like conclusion. The American, how-

---

and Abolition (New York, 1906), 335; H. M. Henry, *The Police Control of the Slave in South Carolina* (Emory, 1914), 204; Richard Hofstadter, "U. B. Phillips and the Plantation Legend," *Journal of Negro History,* XXIX (1944), 121; J. F. Jameson in *Mississippi Valley Historical Review,* XXXV (1948–1949), 659 (letter of May 24, 1926, to A. J. Beveridge); Broadus Mitchell, *Olmsted,* 68–70, 97–98; Allan Nevins, *The Emergence of Lincoln* (New York, 1950), I, 203; J. F. Rhodes, *History of the United States,* I (New York, 1892), 304 n.; F. B. Simkins, *The South Old and New* (New York, 1947), 498; and W. P. Trent, "Introduction," *Seaboard Slave States* (New York, 1904), p. xxxv.

[7] Of these dissidents, W. E. Dodd (*The Cotton Kingdom,* New Haven, 1919, p. 148) and F. L. Owsley (*Plain Folk of the Old South,* Baton Rouge, 1949, pp. 2–3) praise Olmsted's reporting of facts, but caution against the antislavery slant of his conclusions. More extreme are U. B. Phillips, who, though constantly citing data from Olmsted, implies that he went south to make out a case against slavery (*American Negro Slavery,* New York, 1918, pp. 287, 293); S. B. Weeks, who, emulating De Bow, finds him guilty of "bitterness, prejudice, misrepresentation and contradictions" (J. N. Larned, ed., *The Literature of American History,* Boston, 1902, p. 195); and J. C. Bonner, who is in agreement with both Phillips and Weeks ("Profile of a Late Ante-Bellum Community," *American Historical Review,* XLIX, 1943–1944, p. 663). Both Hofstadter and Mitchell take specific issue with Phillips, a Georgian and a well-known authority on slavery, Hofstadter holding that "a fuller and more accurate knowledge of the late antebellum South can be obtained from the volumes of Olmsted than from Professor Phillips' own writings" ("Phillips and the Plantation Legend," 121; Mitchell, *Olmsted,* 70 n., 90). "The real question is," as Thomas H. Clark suggests in the *South Atlantic Quarterly,* III (1904), 12, "did the writer tell the truth?" and the answer of this Southerner was: "There is a transparent candor in every line Olmsted wrote."

[8] *Democracy in America* (Phillips Bradley, ed., New York, 1945), I, 365. Mitchell, *Olmsted,* chaps. ii–iii, compares Olmsted's observations with those of other contemporaries, foreign and domestic. For additional British commentators, consult Max Berger, "American Slavery as Seen by British Visitors, 1836–1860," *Journal of Negro History,* XXX (1945), 181–202, and Laura A. White, "The South in the 1850's as Seen by British Consuls," *Journal of Southern History,* I (1935), 29–48.

ever, did not make the mistake of regarding the South as a uniform economic and social section. He was impressed not only by the contrasts between the "grand divisions of old settlement and of recent settlement," but also by the divergences between seaboard and interior, between lowlands and hill country, as well as the differences between the Gulf zone and the border states. But, though he perceived Souths rather than *the* South, he found the common denominator—the ligature binding the various parts—in the practice of human bondage. In this fundamental sense there was one South, distinct from the rest of the United States and from most of the Western world.

Slavery, as Olmsted viewed Southern life and society, everywhere determined mental attitudes, ways of living, human relations, politics, customs, manners and laws. It enslaved the white man almost as much as the black, yielding advantages to each incommensurate with the disadvantages. Olmsted rejected the idea that it was the hot weather, rather than the labor system, that accounted for the South's economic and social backwardness. Discussing this point in connection with Virginia, he noted that the most "successful and prosperous States of antiquity were of a climate warmer than that of Virginia." In fact, the protracted heat should have favored the slave states over the free states, since it lengthened the season during which the soil could be worked and reduced the cost of wintering cattle, while it also ensured the operations of manufacturing, trade and mining against interruptions by ice and snow.[9]

Holding such views, he naturally denied the favorite Southern contention that only the African could withstand the blazing sun. On the contrary, he said, "The recent German settlers in Texas and in South Carolina, the whites on steamboats and railroads and in trade, the white workmen in New Orleans, as well as thousands of exceptional, hardworking and successful laboring Southerners, testify that the climate is no preventive of persevering toil by the white race in any part of the slave States." He further pointed out that Caucasians displayed "no lack of strength or endurance when engaged in athletic exercise which is immediately gratifying to their ambition,

---

[9] *Seaboard Slave States*, 181. It was perhaps with some malice that he quoted Dr. E. H. Barton of New Orleans to the effect that the Southern climate was much more bearable summer and winter than the Northern. *Back Country*, 344 (*Cotton Kingdom*, 500).

passions, or their tastes." [1] The aversion to manual toil arose, rather, from the fact that "to work industriously and steadily, especially under directions from another man," was regarded by the master race as the lot of slaves—whence came the Southern expression: "to work like a nigger." [2]

Olmsted was equally certain that the primitive manner of living— the lack of conveniences, the slovenly ways, the addiction to violence, the intellectual destitution—did not stem from frontier conditions. In the free states pioneer life was a transitional stage, a spur to improvement, something to surmount and leave behind. "The child born to-day on the northern frontier," he observed, "in most cases, before it is ten years old, will be living in a well organized and tolerably well provided community," with access to schools, churches and printing presses, or at least be within a day's journey of them and always within reach of their influence. In the slave states, on the other hand, the rude order of existence tended to be permanent. "There are improvements, and communities loosely and gradually cohering in various parts of the South," he conceded, "but so slowly, so feebly, so irregularly, that men's minds and habits are knit firm quite independently of this class of social influences." [3]

He could not avoid the conclusion that slavery prolonged "the evils which properly belong only to a frontier." In his "Letter to a Southern Friend" he amplified the point by contrasting the rate of advance in Texas with that in Iowa, both newly settled areas.[4] His crowning example, however, was Virginia, oldest of the slave states, where "an essentially frontier condition of society" still persisted after more than two centuries. In fact, he asserted, "Beasts and birds of prey, forests and marshes are increasing; bridges, schools, churches and shops are diminishing in number, where slavery has existed longest. The habits of the people correspond." [5]

[1] *Back Country*, 298–299. For observations of similar import, see *ibid.*, 342–344, 349–350 (*Cotton Kingdom*, 497–500, 505). On the predominance of white labor in New Orleans, see the *Seaboard Slave States*, 590–591 (*Cotton Kingdom*, 233).

[2] *Cotton Kingdom*, 19.

[3] Texas, p. xix n.; *Back Country*, 321–325, 414 (*Cotton Kingdom*, 532–535, 554–555). See also the *Cotton Kingdom*, 17–18, 21–22.

[4] *Texas*, pp. viii–xii. Though admitting that he spoke at second hand of conditions in Iowa, he went on to extend the comparison to New York, where he had personal knowledge (pp. xii–xiii).

[5] *Back Country*, 292.

Olmsted further insisted that the slavery system had enhanced the economic liabilities which the presence of several million Negroes undeniably created for the South. Servile labor, though sometimes profitable, had in general a blighting effect. It not only stunted the intelligence and initiative of the bondsmen, but encouraged "sogering" on the job, accounted for the shiftless poor-white class and arrested the inflow of enterprising individuals from the North and Europe. It also depleted the soil, increased greatly the overhead costs of farming and locked up capital that might have nourished a more diversified economic development. With handicaps like these, how could the whites hope to thrive?

Put the best race of men under heaven into a land where all industry is obliged to bear the weight of such a system, and inevitably their ingenuity, enterprise, and skill will be paralyzed, the land will be impoverished, its resources of wealth will remain undeveloped, or will be wasted; and only by the favor of some extraordinary advantage can it compare, in prosperity, with countries adjoining, in which a more simple, natural, and healthy system of labor prevails.[6]

As we have seen, Olmsted did not think that the magic wand of immediate emancipation was the answer. The Negroes must be helped to unlearn the bad habits which slavery had drilled into them before striking out for themselves.

Olmsted's preoccupation with the common life of Dixie opens him to the criticism that he neglected the more gracious features of Southern civilization and hence painted an unduly dark picture. He may have been anticipating this reproach when he wrote:

Men of literary taste or clerical habits are always apt to overlook the working-classes, and to confine the records they make of their own times, in a great degree, to the habits and fortunes of their own associates, or to those of people of superior rank to themselves, of whose sayings and doings their vanity, as well as their curiosity, leads them to most carefully inform themselves. The dumb masses have often been so lost in this shadow of egotism, that, in later days, it has been impossible to discern the very real influence their character and condition has had on the fortune and fate of nations.[7]

He might have justified his attitude further by noting that, in any event, the great planters were few. Indeed, slaveholders, whether

[6] *Seaboard Slave States,* 479.   [7] *Ibid.,* 214–215.

large or small, constituted but a minority of the white population—
something like a quarter of the families, according to J. B. D. De
Bow, Superintendent of the 1850 Census.[8] Of this favored group, 26.6
per cent in 1850 owned only one to ten Negroes apiece, and 51.8 per
cent owned more than ten but fewer than fifty apiece. That left a
mere 21.6 per cent to comprise the planting aristocracy; in other
words, a little more than one in five masters and perhaps a twentieth
of the whole white population.[9] But, of course, as a Southern historical scholar has recently said, "This small privileged class of
planters tended to think of themselves as 'the South'; they confused
their narrow class interests as identical with the welfare of the whole
South." [1]

Olmsted, if little concerned with this exclusive element, did not
ignore it. He had known and admired some of these Southern pa-
tricians at Yale, and en route to Texas late in 1853 he and John had
visited one of them in Nashville. Interestingly enough, the brothers
fell into a discussion with their host over whether "gentlemen in the
Southern sense" were known in the free states. Olmsted, though con-
ceding their absence, "tried to show him that there were compensations in the *general* elevation of all classes at the North, but he did
not seem to care for it." [2] Again and again Olmsted made it clear
in his published writings that the greatest good of the greatest number was for him the touchstone of a well-ordered society.

Nonetheless, he visited as many large estates as their proportionate
number probably merited. In the *Cotton Kingdom*, for example, he
describes a 2000-acre farm in Maryland, nationally known for its
"excellent management"; some "show plantations" in Georgia, two
of which, under a single owner, employed 200 slaves; several sugar
estates in Louisiana with a comparable labor force; an extensive
cotton property in Texas; two others in Mississippi, with 135 and 500
blacks respectively, as well as an "opulent" plantation in Tennessee.
The "most profitable estate" he saw—identified merely as on a "tributary of the Mississippi"—comprised four contiguous plantations

---

[8] *The Industrial Resources, etc., of the Southern and Western States* (New
Orleans, 1852–1853), II, 108, cited in the *Back Country*, 297 (*Cotton Kingdom*,
541).

[9] L. C. Gray, *History of Agriculture in the Southern United States to 1860*
(Washington, 1933), I, 530.

[1] Clement Eaton, *A History of the Old South* (New York, 1949), 445.

[2] Letter of December, 1853. Mitchell, *Olmsted*, 48.

under separate overseers bossing more than a hundred Negroes apiece.[3] He found the general manager well educated and a delightful companion and the slaves excellently cared for, many of them living in commodious cabins—though it was also on this occasion that he first saw a woman flogged.

On the basis of this sampling and of other knowledge gained at first or second hand, he arrived at certain generalizations concerning the Southern upper class. He noted a marked difference between the seaboard aristocrats and those of the newer Gulf states. Though there were fewer wealthy families in the older region, they were superior in "refinement and education." In fact, he discovered "less vulgar display, and more intrinsic elegance, and habitual refinement in the best society of South Carolina, than in any distinct class" of the North. In Mississippi, on the other hand, as in New York and Manchester, the "farce of the vulgar-rich" evidenced "the rapidity with which certain values have advanced, especially that of cotton, and, simultaneously, that of cotton lands and negroes." Even here he encountered occasional men of breeding. With all his praise of the South Carolina gentry, however, they had failed to perform the function which in his judgment society had a right to expect of them. They had done little "for the advancement of learning and science, and there have been fewer valuable inventions and discoveries, or designs in art, or literary compositions of a high rank," than in "any community of equal numbers and wealth, probably in the world."[4]

In general, he felt that Southerners reputed to be worth $400,000 enjoyed fewer advantages than men with $100,000 in the older Northern states.[5] He also thought the conventional picture of "a master's occupying the position of a father toward his slaves and of the slaves accepting this relation, affectionately, faithfully and confidingly," was grossly exaggerated, being particularly improbable for practical reasons where the owner had a numerous labor force.[6]

[3] For this last instance, see the *Cotton Kingdom*, 445–460 (*Back Country*, 72–93). The estate was actually on the Red River, and the total slave population was nearly a thousand. See the *New York Times*, November 21, 1853, p. 2.

[4] *Back Country*, 27–28 (*Cotton Kingdom*, 416–417); *Seaboard Slave States*, 501–502.

[5] *Cotton Kingdom*, 107. For comparable statements, see the *Seaboard Slave States*, 652, and the *Back Country*, 326 (*Cotton Kingdom*, 330, 536–537).

[6] *Back Country*, 288. He saw more of this "patriarchal character" in North Carolina than in any other state, because "of the less concentration of wealth in families or individuals." *Seaboard Slave States*, 367 (*Cotton Kingdom*, 149).

Mulling over the discussion with his Nashville friend early in his wanderings, Olmsted concluded upon further observation and reflection that "The Southern gentleman, as we ordinarily conceive him to be, is as rare a phenomenon in the South at the present day as is the old squire of Geoffrey Crayon in modern England." [7] Indeed, "there is unquestionably at this time a very much larger number of thoroughly well bred and even high bred people in the free than in the slave States. It is equally certain that the proportion of such people to the whole population of whites is larger at the North than the South." [8]

There are few aspects of the pre-Civil War South which Olmsted does not illumine, whether you accept his judgments at face value or not. Perhaps no vanished civilization has suffered more misrepresentation at the hands of both friend and foe. But after visiting the slave states in Olmsted's company the reader is in a position to form his own opinion. It is true that Olmsted found little to interest him in the cities, but, apart from Baltimore and St. Louis, his itinerary included all the largest ones (New Orleans, Louisville, Charleston, Richmond, Mobile, Savannah, Norfolk, Lexington and Nashville, ranging in population according to the 1850 census from 116,000 to 10,000, in the order named), as well as many of the smaller ones. Except for a few of the major centers, he reported that half the streets were usually "tolerably good pastures, the other half intolerable cart-roads," with the "majority of shops selling raisins, nailrods [iron strips to be cut into nails] and nigger cloth, from the same counter with silks, and school books and 'bitters.'" [9] He tried every possible mode of transportation and describes graphically the mean accommodations commonly afforded by the hotels and inns.

Since the South was primarily an agricultural section and he an agriculturist, he familiarized himself with a variety of rural industries—tobacco, rice, cotton and sugar culture, lumbering, the extraction of turpentine—and he probed into the practical aspects of

[7] *Back Country*, 117–118 (*Cotton Kingdom*, 476).

[8] *Back Country*, 424 (slightly rephrased in *Cotton Kingdom*, 563). See also, to like effect, the *Back Country*, 391–400 (*Cotton Kingdom*, 517–520, 542–545). Olmsted, after a good deal of backing and filling, expresses substantially the same view in the essay reprinted as Editor's Appendix (E) in the present work, 614–622.

[9] *Back Country*, 279–280.

plantation management as only an experienced farmer could. This led him to investigate such features as absentee ownership, the overseer system, the slave traffic, the efficiency and adaptability of the labor force, the utilization of the soil, the hiring out of slaves, the use of white workers, the range of plantation occupations other than tillage and, in general, the question of whether the institution of servile labor paid off in dollars and cents.

He also inquired into the wider social consequences of human bondage: the effect on the masters, on the slaveless farmers, on the poor whites, on the free Negroes and, most of all, on the chattels themselves. Were the slaves better off than black or white wageworkers in the free states? Were they better off than they would have been in Africa? What opportunities did they have for self-improvement? Was cruelty an incidental or inseparable part of the system? Did their treatment vary according to the master, the region, the size of the plantation, the nature of their work? Olmsted's scrupulousness as a witness is indicated by his avowal that in fourteen months in the South he did not himself once see a slave auction.[1] He also touches upon a side of the "peculiar institution" that posterity has generally forgotten: the fact that Negroes themselves sometimes owned slaves—a phenomenon which suggests that the system of involuntary servitude was something more than simply a convenient method of policing race relations.

On other phases of Southern life Olmsted is equally informative. He contrasts the South's stifling of the public discussion of slavery with the Northern practice of freely ventilating social abuses as a way of remedying them. If slavery was as perfect a social arrangement as Southerners commonly alleged, he saw all the more reason why they should allow its merits to be debated. On the other hand, he occasionally heard private condemnations of the institution and even came across instances of familiarity with *Uncle Tom's Cabin*. Interestingly enough, he discovered one of the strongest champions of slavery in a Northern woman in Texas, herself the owner of several house servants.[2]

The meager standard of living—the shabby dwellings, the coarse

---

[1] *Seaboard Slave States*, 31 (*Cotton Kingdom*, 40–41). At another point in the *Cotton Kingdom* (14), however, Olmsted might give the unwary reader the impression that he had attended one.

[2] *Journey through Texas*, 119–121 (*Cotton Kingdom*, 302–304).

and monotonous fare, the absence of cleanliness and ordinary comforts, the dearth of newspapers and other reading matter—appalled this Yankee who had never encountered anything like it in even the humblest Northern homes. From the banks of the James to the banks of the Mississippi he saw scarcely a volume of Shakespeare, a sheet of music, a good art engraving or a reading lamp. Random conversations along the way suggested, moreover, that the level of general information was not much better. One person supposed New York was in New Orleans, another that Iowa lay somewhere west of Texas, another that New York was a slave state, while still another hadn't heard that the war with Mexico was over. Olmsted's strictures on the vaunted Southern hospitality provoked a furious rebuttal from De Bow, the New Orleans editor, only to bring from Olmsted an additional bill of particulars.[3] All these and other insights into Southern life, favorable and unfavorable, await the reader of the *Cotton Kingdom*.

The present edition closely follows the original work of 1861. Certain deviations should be noted, however. The chapters are numbered consecutively throughout; the chapter titles of Volume I of the 1862 imprint have been used as more accurately descriptive of that portion of the contents; and the text of chapter i of Volume I of the 1862 imprint has been preferred because, as a marked copy in the family library in Brookline, Massachusetts, shows, it had the benefit of Olmsted's corrections. In other respects editorial emendations have been kept to a minimum so as not unduly to distract the reader. In general, the names of authors and books and Olmsted's page references to publications have been amended when faulty, misprints have been eliminated, and punctuation and capitalization have occasionally been changed for the sake of clarity. Such alterations, being routine, have not been indicated. When feasible, individuals have been more fully identified (in brackets), though in many cases this proved impossible, since the traveler, for reasons of

---

[3] *De Bow's Review*, XXIII (1857), 118–121. In support of his own observations Olmsted cites Godkin's similar experiences in the South in 1856–1857. *Back Country*, 61–62, 408–409 (*Cotton Kingdom*, 441–443, 551–552). He could easily have multiplied quotations from this source. See Ogden, *Life and Letters of Edwin Lawrence Godkin*, I, 133, 135, 137–140, 148, 155–156. In the *Times* article reprinted in Editor's Appendix (E) of the present work (614–622), Olmsted, however, at one point praises Southern hospitality. Further reflection and fuller knowledge evidently caused him to alter this opinion.

delicacy, usually avoided naming the persons with whom he talked and visited. He even referred to their places of abode in such a way as intentionally to mislead the reader.[4] Though Olmsted does not observe the modern practice of verbatim transcription of quotations, he never warps the sense, and the slight modifications he introduces were evidently designed to improve the literary quality. His version has in every instance been allowed to stand. Bracketed matter within quotations originated with the author of the *Cotton Kingdom*.

To Olmsted's appendices I have added two others. The one, Appendix (E), is his perceptive discussion of the differences between the Southern and Northern characters. This extra dividend to the reader appeared in the *New York Times*, January 12, 1854, but, for some reason difficult to understand, Olmsted did not see fit to give it more permanent form. The other, Appendix (F), lists the principal books cited in the *Cotton Kingdom*, as well as the works and articles referred to in the Editor's Introduction.

In preparing this edition I am indebted to Mr. Frederick Law Olmsted, Jr., and Mrs. Laura Wood Roper for restricted access to the Frederick Law Olmsted Papers in the Library of Congress. Mrs. Roper, who is engaged in writing a full-length life of the elder Olmsted, kindly aided me in other ways as well. I wish further to thank Dr. Samuel R. Spencer, Jr., of Davidson College, Professor Jeter A. Isely of Princeton University, Mr. Walter S. Oswald, Jr., of Anderson, Indiana, and Miss Stella D. Obst of Brookline, Massachusetts, for helpful suggestions; Professor Donald Born of Boston University for indispensable assistance in proofreading; and my wife Elizabeth Bancroft Schlesinger and my son and colleague Arthur M. Schlesinger, Jr., for a critical reading of the Introduction. In particular, my appreciation goes to my research secretary Elizabeth F. Hoxie, to whom I have dedicated this work in gratitude for her invaluable services over the years.

ARTHUR M. SCHLESINGER

---

[4] *Back Country*, 400 (*Cotton Kingdom*, 544).

THE

COTTON KINGDOM:

A TRAVELLER'S OBSERVATIONS ON COTTON AND SLAVERY
IN THE AMERICAN SLAVE STATES.

BASED UPON THREE FORMER VOLUMES OF JOURNEYS AND INVESTIGATIONS
BY THE SAME AUTHOR.

BY

FREDERICK LAW OLMSTED.

IN TWO VOLUMES.

VOL. I.

NEW YORK:
PUBLISHED BY MASON BROTHERS,
5 and 7 MERCER STREET.
LONDON : SAMPSON LOW, SON & CO., 47 LUDGATE HILL
1861.

Facsimile setup of title page of original edition

DEDICATION

CONTENTS

Contents

CHAPTER I

Introductory. The Present Crisis

THE MOUNTAIN ranges, the valleys, and the great waters of America, all trend north and south, not east and west. An arbitrary political line may divide the north part from the south part, but there is no such line in nature: there can be none, socially. While water runs downhill, the currents and counter currents of trade, of love, of consanguinity, and fellowship, will flow north and south. The unavoidable comminglings of the people in a land like this, upon the conditions which the slavery of a portion of the population impose, make it necessary to peace that we should all live under the same laws and respect the same flag. No government could long control its own people, no government could long exist, that would allow its citizens to be subject to such indignities under a foreign government as those to which the citizens of the United States heretofore have been required to submit under their own, for the sake of the tranquillity of the South. Nor could the South, with its present purposes, live on terms of peace with any foreign nation, between whose people and its own there was no division, except such an one as might be maintained by means of forts, frontier-guards and custom-houses, edicts, passports and spies. Scotland, Wales, and Ireland are each much better adapted for an independent government, and under an independent government would be far more likely to live at peace with England, than the South to remain peaceably separated from the North of this country.

It is said that the South can never be subjugated. It must be, or we must. It must be, or not only our American republic is a failure, but our English justice and our English law and our English freedom are failures. This Southern repudiation of obligations upon the result of an election is but a clearer warning than we have had before, that these cannot be maintained in this land any longer in such intimate association with slavery as we have hitherto tried to hope that they might. We now know that we must give them up, or give up trying to accommodate ourselves to what the South has declared, and demonstrated, to be the necessities of its state of society. Those necessities would not be less, but, on the contrary, far more impera-

tive, were the South an independent people. If the South has reason to declare itself independent of our long-honoured constitution,
and of our common court or our common laws, on account of a past
want of invariable tenderness on the part of each one of our people
towards its necessities, how long could we calculate to be able to
preserve ourselves from occurrences which would be deemed to ab-
rogate the obligations of a mere treaty of peace? A treaty of peace
with the South as a foreign power, would be a cowardly armistice,
a cruel aggravation and prolongation of war.

Subjugation! I do not choose the word, but take it, and use it in
the only sense in which it can be applicable. This is a Republic, and
the South must come under the yoke of freedom, not to work for us,
but to work with us, on equal terms, as a free people. To work with
us, for the security of a state of society, the ruling purpose and
tendency of which, spite of all its bendings heretofore, to the necessities of slavery; spite of the incongruous foreign elements which it
has had constantly to absorb and incorporate; spite of a strong element of excessive backwoods individualism, has, beyond all question, been favourable to sound and safe progress in knowledge, civilization, and Christianity. To this yoke the head of the South must
now be lifted, or we must bend our necks to that of slavery, con-
senting and submitting, even more than we have been willing to do
heretofore, to labour and fight, and pay for the dire needs of a small
portion of our people living in an exceptional state of society, in
which Cowper's poems must not be read aloud without due precautions against the listening of family servants; in which it may be
treated as a crime against the public safety to teach one of the labouring classes to write; in which the names of Wilberforce and
Buxton are execrated; within which the slave trade is perpetuated,
and at the capital of whose rebellion, black seamen born free, taken
prisoners, in merchant ships, not in arms, are even already sold into
slavery with as little hesitation as ever in Barbary. One system or
the other is to thrive and extend, and eventually possess and govern
this whole land.

This has been long felt and acted upon at the South; and the purpose of the more prudent and conservative men, now engaged in the
attempt to establish a new government in the South, was for a long
time simply to obtain an advantage for what was talked of as "reconstruction"; namely, a process of change in the form and rules of

our government that would disqualify us of the Free States from offering any resistance to whatever was demanded of our government, for the end in view of the extension and eternal maintenance of slavery. That men to whom the terms prudent and conservative can in any way be applied, should not have foreseen that such a scheme must be unsuccessful, only presents one more illustration of that, of which the people of England have had many in their own history, the moral myopism, to which the habit of almost constantly looking down and never up at mankind, always predisposes. That the true people of the United States could have allowed the mutiny to proceed so far, before rising in their strength to resist it, is due chiefly to the instinctive reliance which every grumbler really gets to have under our forms of society, in the ultimate common-sense of the great body of the people, and to the incredulity with which the report has been regarded, that slavery had made such a vast difference between the character of the South and that of the country at large. Few were fully convinced that the whole proceedings of the insurgents meant anything else than a more than usually bold and scandalous way of playing the game of brag, to which we had been so long used in our politics, and of which the people of England had a little experience shortly before the passage of a certain Reform Bill. The instant effect of the first *shotted*-gun that was fired proves this. We knew then that we had to subjugate slavery, or be subjugated by it.

Peace is now not possible until the people of the South are well convinced that the form of society, to fortify which is the ostensible purpose of the war into which they have been plunged, is not worthy fighting for, or until we think the sovereignty of our convictions of Justice, Freedom, Law and the conditions of Civilization in this land to be of less worth than the lives and property of our generation.

From the St. Lawrence to the Mexican Gulf, freedom must everywhere give way to the necessities of slavery, or slavery must be accommodated to the necessary incidents of freedom.

Where the hopes and sympathies of Englishmen will be, we well know.

"The necessity to labour is incompatible with a high civilization, and with heroic spirit in those subject to it."

"The institution of African slavery is a means more effective than any other yet devised, for relieving a large body of men from the necessity of labour; consequently, states which possess it must be stronger in statesmanship and in war, than those which do not; especially must they be stronger than states in which there is absolutely no privileged class, but all men are held to be equal before the law."

"The civilized world is dependent upon the Slave States of America for a supply of cotton. The demand for this commodity has, during many years, increased faster than the supply. Sales are made of it, now, to the amount of two hundred millions of dollars in a year, yet they have a vast area of soil suitable for its production which has never been broken. With an enormous income, then, upon a steadily rising market, they hold a vast idle capital yet to be employed. Such a monopoly under such circumstances must constitute those who possess it the richest and most powerful people on the earth. The world must have cotton, and the world depends on them for it. Whatever they demand, that must be conceded them; whatever they want, they have but to stretch forth their hands and take it."

These fallacies, lodged in certain minds, generated, long ago, grand ambitions, and bold schemes of conquest and wealth. The people of the North stood in the way of these schemes. In the minds of the schemers, labour had been associated with servility, meekness, cowardice; and they were persuaded that all men not degraded by labour at the North "kept aloof from politics," or held their judgment in entire subjection to the daily wants of a working population, of no more spirit and no more patriotism than their own working men—slaves. They believed this whole people to be really in a state of dependence, and that they controlled that upon which they depended. So, to a hitherto vague and inert local partisanship, they brought a purpose of determination to overcome the North, and, as this could not be safely avowed, there was the necessity for a conspiracy, and for the cloak of a conspiracy. By means the most mendacious, the ignorant, proud, jealous, and violent free population of the cotton States and their dependencies, were persuaded that less consideration was paid to their political demands than the importance of their contentment entitled them to expect from their government, and were at length decoyed into a state of angry passion, in which they only needed leaders of sufficient audacity to bring them into open rebellion. Assured that their own power if used would be supreme, and that they had but to offer sufficient evidence of a violent and dangerous determination to overawe the sordid North, and make it submit to a "reconstruction" of the nation in a form more advantageous to themselves, they were artfully led along in a constant advance, and constant failure of attempts at intimidation, until at length they must needs take part in a desperate rebellion, or accept a position which, after the declarations they had made for the purpose of intimidation, they could not do without humiliation.

The conspirators themselves have, until recently, been able, either directly or by impositions upon patriotic, but too confiding and generous instruments, to control the treasury of the United States, its post-office, its army and navy, its arsenals, workshops, dockyards and fortresses, and, by the simple means of perjury, to either turn these agencies against the government, or at least render them ineffectual to aid it, and this at a time, when its very existence, if it were anything but a democratic republican government, and, as we think for all good purposes, by far the strongest that ever existed, would have depended on a perfect instant and unquestionable command of them. Yet I doubt not that the conspirators themselves, trust at this moment, as they ever have trusted, even less to the supposed helpless condition of the government than to the supposed advantages of the cotton monopoly to the Slave States, and to the supposed superiority of a community of privileged classes over an actual democracy.

"No! you dare not make war upon cotton; no power on earth dares to make war upon it. Cotton is king; until lately the Bank of England was king; but she tried to put her screws, as usual, the fall before the last, on the cotton crop, and was utterly vanquished. The last power has been conquered: who can doubt, that has looked at recent events, that cotton is supreme?"

These are the defiant and triumphant words of Governor [James H.] Hammond, of South Carolina, addressed to the Senate of the United States, March 4th, 1858. Almost every important man of the South, has at one time or other, within a few years, been betrayed into the utterance of similar exultant anticipations; and the South would never have been led into the great and terrible mistake it has made, had it not been for this confident conviction in the minds of the men who have been passing for its statesmen. Whatever moral strength the rebellion has, abroad or at home, lies chiefly in the fact that this conviction is also held, more or less distinctly, by multitudes who know perfectly well that the commonly assigned reasons for it are based on falsehoods.

Recently, a banker, who is and always has been a loyal union man, said, commenting upon certain experiences of mine narrated in this book: "The South cannot be poor. Why, their last crop alone was worth two hundred million. They must be rich": ergo, say the conspirators, adopting the same careless conclusion, they must be powerful, and the world must feel their power, and respect them and their institutions.

My own observation of the real condition of the people of our Slave States, gave me, on the contrary, an impression that the cotton monopoly in some way did them more harm than good; and, although the written narration of what I saw was not intended to set this forth, upon reviewing it for the present publication, I find the impression has become a conviction. I propose here, therefore, to show how the main body of the observations of the book arrange themselves in my mind with reference to this question, and also to inquire how far the conclusion to which I think they tend is substantiated by the Census returns of those States.[1]

Coming directly from my farm in New York to Eastern Virginia, I was satisfied, after a few weeks' observation, that the most of the people lived very poorly; that the proportion of men improving their condition was much less than in any Northern community; and that the natural resources of the land were strangely unused, or were used with poor economy. It was "the hiring season," and I had daily opportunities of talking with farmers, manufacturers, miners, and labourers, with whom the value of labour and of wages was then the handiest subject of conversation. I soon perceived that labour was much more readily classified and measured with refer-

[1] I greatly regret, after visiting Washington for this purpose, to find that the returns of the Census of 1860, are not yet sufficiently verified and digested to be given to the public. I have therefore had to fall back upon those of 1850. The rate of increase of the slave population in the meantime is stated at 25 per cent.

ence to its quality than at the North. The limit of measure I found to be the ordinary day's work of a "prime field-hand," and a prime field-hand, I found universally understood to mean, not a man who would split two cords of wood, or cradle two acres of grain in a day, but a man for whom a "trader" would give a thousand dollars, or more, to take on South, for sale to a cotton planter. I do not mean that the alternative of a sale to a trader was always had in view in determining how a man should be employed. To be just, this seldom appeared to be the case—but that, in estimating the market value of his labour, he was viewed, for the time, from the trader's point of view, or, as if the question were—What is he worth for cotton?

I soon ascertained that a much larger number of hands, at much larger aggregate wages, was commonly reckoned to be required to accomplish certain results, than would have been the case at the North. Not all results, but certain results, of a kind in which it happened that I could most readily make a confident comparison. I have been in the habit of watching men at work, and of judging of their industry, their skill, their spirit; in short, of whatever goes to make up their value to their employers, or to the community, as instruments of production; and from day to day I saw that, as a landowner, or as a citizen, in a community largely composed, or dependent upon the productive industry, of working people of such habits and disposition as I constantly saw evinced in those of Virginia, I should feel disheartened, and myself lose courage, spirit, and industry. The close proximity of the better and cheaper labour—labour seeking a field of labour—which I had left behind me, added greatly to my interest in the subject, and stimulated close inquiry. It seemed, indeed, quite incredible that there really could be such a want of better labour in this region as at first sight there appeared to be, when a supply was so near at hand. I compared notes with every Northern man I met who had been living for some time in Virginia, and some I found able to give me quite exact statements of personal experience, with which, in the cases they mentioned, it could not be doubted that labourers costing, all things considered, the same wages, had taken four times as long to accomplish certain tasks of rude work in Virginia as at the North, and that in house service, four servants accomplished less, while they required vastly more looking after, than one at the North.

I left Virginia, having remained much longer than I at first intended, in trying to satisfy myself about this matter—quite satisfied as to the general fact, not at all satisfied with any theories of demand and supply which had been offered me, or which had occurred to me, in the way of explanation of it.

My perplexity was increased by certain apparent exceptions to the general rule; but they were, all things considered, unimportant, and rather served as affording contrasts, on the ground, to satisfy me of the correctness of my general conclusion.

I subsequently returned, and spent another month in Virginia, after visiting the cotton States, and I also spent three months in Kentucky and other parts of the Slave States where the climate is unsuitable for the production of cotton, and with the information which I had in the meantime obtained, I continued to study both the question of fact, and the question of cause. The following conclusions to which my mind tended strongly in the first month, though I did not then adopt them altogether with confidence, were established at length in my convictions.

1. The cash value of a slave's labour in Virginia is, practically, the cash value of the same labour minus the cost of its transportation, acclimatizing, and breaking in to cotton-culture in Mississippi.
2. The cost of production, or the development of natural wealth in Virginia, is regulated by the cost of slave-labour: (that is to say) the competition of white labour does not materially reduce it; though it doubtless has some effect, at least in certain districts, and with reference to certain productions or branches of industry.
3. Taking infants, aged, invalid, and vicious and knavish slaves into account, the ordinary and average cost of a certain task of labour is more than double in Virginia what it is in the Free States adjoining.
4. The use of land and nearly all other resources of wealth in Virginia is much less valuable than the use of similar property in the adjoining Free States, these resources having no real value until labour is applied to them. (The Census returns of 1850 show that the sale value of farm lands by the acre in Virginia is less than one-third the value of farm lands in the adjoining Free State of Pennsylvania, and less than one-fifth than that of the farm lands of the neighbouring Free State of New Jersey.) [2]
5. Beyond the bare necessities of existence, poor shelter, poor cloth-

[2] See Appendix, A 2.

ing, and the crudest diet, the mass of the citizen class of Virginia earn very little and are very poor—immeasurably poorer than the mass of the people of the adjoining Free States.

6. So far as this poverty is to be attributed to personal constitution, character, and choice, it is not the result of climate.

7. What is true of Virginia is measurably true of all the border Slave States, though in special cases the resistance of slavery to a competition of free labour is more easily overcome. In proportion as this is the case, the cost of production is less, the value of production greater, the comfort of the people is greater; they are advancing in wealth as they are in intelligence, which is the best form or result of wealth.

I went on my way into the so-called cotton States, within which I travelled over, first and last, at least three thousand miles of roads, from which not a cotton plant was to be seen, and the people living by the side of which certainly had not been made rich by cotton or anything else. And for every mile of road-side upon which I saw any evidence of cotton production, I am sure that I saw a hundred of forest or waste land, with only now and then an acre or two of poor corn half smothered in weeds; for every rich man's house, I am sure that I passed a dozen shabby and half-furnished cottages, and at least a hundred cabins—mere hovels, such as none but a poor farmer would house his cattle in at the North. And I think that, for every man of refinement and education with whom I came in contact, there were a score or two superior only in the virtue of silence, and in the manner of self-complacency, to the sort of people we should expect to find paying a large price for a place from which a sight could be got at a gallows on an execution day at the North, and a much larger number of what poor men at the North would themselves describe as poor men: not that they were destitute of certain things which are cheap at the South,—fuel for instance,—but that they were almost wholly destitute of things the possession of which, at the North, would indicate that a man had begun to accumulate capital—more destitute of these, on an average, than our day-labourers. In short, except in certain limited districts, mere streaks by the side of rivers, and in a few isolated spots of especially favoured soil away from these, I found the same state of things which I had seen in Virginia, but in a more aggravated form.

At least five hundred white men told me something of their own lives and fortunes, across their own tables, and with the means of measuring the weight of their words before my eyes; and I know that while men seldom want an abundance of coarse food in the cotton States, the proportion of the free white men who live as well in any respect as our working classes at the North, on an average, is small, and the citizens of the cotton States, as a whole, are poor. They work little, and that little, badly; they earn little, they sell little; they buy little, and they have little—very little—of the common comforts and consolations of civilized life. Their destitution is not material only; it is intellectual and it is moral. I know not what virtues they have that rude men everywhere have not; but those which are commonly attributed to them, I am sure that they lack: they are not generous or hospitable; and, to be plain, I must say that their talk is not the talk of even courageous men elsewhere. They boast and lack self-restraint, yet, when not excited, are habitually reserved and guarded in expressions of opinion very much like cowardly men elsewhere.

But, much cotton is produced in the cotton States, and by the labour of somebody; much cotton is sold and somebody must be paid for it; there are rich people; there are good markets; there is hospitality, refinement, virtue, courage, and urbanity at the South. All this is proverbially true. Who produces the cotton? who is paid for it? where are, and who are, the rich and gentle people?

I can answer in part at least.

I have been on plantations on the Mississippi, the Red River, and the Brazos bottoms, whereon I was assured that ten bales of cotton to each average prime field-hand had been raised. The soil was a perfect garden mould, well drained and guarded by levees against the floods; it was admirably tilled; I have seen but few Northern farms so well tilled: the labourers were, to a large degree, tall, slender, sinewy, young men, who worked from dawn to dusk, not with spirit, but with steadiness and constancy. They had good tools; their rations of bacon and corn were brought to them in the field, and eaten with efficient despatch between the cotton plants. They had the best sort of gins and presses, so situated that from them cotton bales could be rolled in five minutes to steamboats, bound direct to the ports on the Gulf. They were superintended by skilful and vigilant overseers. These plantations were all large, so large as to yet contain much fresh land, ready to be worked as soon as the culti-vated fields gave out in fertility. If it was true that ten bales of cotton to the hand had been raised on them, then their net profit for the year had been not less than two hundred and fifty dollars for each hand employed. Even at seven bales to the hand the profits of cotton planting are enormous. Men who have plantations producing at this rate, can well afford to buy fresh hands at fourteen hundred dollars a head. They can even afford to employ such hands for a year or two in clearing land, ditching, leveeing, fencing, and other preparatory work, buying, meantime, all the corn and bacon they need, and getting the best kind of tools and cattle, and paying fifteen per cent. per annum interest on all the capital required for this, as many of them do. All this can be well afforded to establish new plantations favourably situated, on fresh soil, if there is a reasonable probability that they can after all be made to produce half a dozen seven-bale crops. And a great many large plantations do produce seven bales to the hand for years in succession. A great many more produce seven bales occasionally. A few produce even ten bales occasionally, though by no means as often as is reported.

Now, it is not at a Roman lottery alone that one may see it, but all over the world, where a few very large prizes are promised and many very small ones, and the number of tickets is limited; these are always speculated on, and men will buy them at third and fourth hand at prices which, it is useless to demonstrate to them, must be extravagant. They go to the Jews and pledge the clothes on their back to get another biacchi to invest; they beggar themselves; they ruin their families; they risk damnation in their passionate eagerness to have a chance, when they know perfectly well that the average of chances is not worth a tithe of what they must pay for it.

The area of land on which cotton may be raised with profit is practically limitless; it is cheap; even the best land is cheap; but to the large planter it is much more valuable when held in large parcels, for obvious reasons, than when in small; consequently the best land can hardly be obtained in small tracts or without the use of a considerable capital. But there are millions of acres of land yet untouched, which if leveed and drained and fenced, and well cultivated, might be made to produce with good luck seven or more bales to the hand. It would cost comparatively little to accomplish it—one lucky crop would repay all the outlay for land and improvements—if it were not for "the hands." The supply of hands is limited. It does not increase in the ratio of the increase of the cotton demand. If cotton should double in price next year, or become worth its weight in gold, the number of negroes in the United States would not increase four per cent. unless the African slave-trade were re-established. Now step into a dealer's "jail" in Memphis, Montgomery, Vicksburg, or New Orleans, and you will hear the mezzano [muezzin] of the cotton lottery crying his tickets in this way: "There's a cotton nigger for you! Genuine! Look at his toes! Look at his fingers! There's a pair of legs for you! If you have got the right sile and the right sort of overseer, buy him, and put your trust in Providence! He's just as good for ten bales as I am for a julep at eleven o'clock." And this is just as true as that any named horse is sure to win the Derby. And so the price of good labourers is constantly gambled up to a point, where, if they produce ten bales to the hand, the purchaser will be as fortunate as he who draws the high prize of the lottery; where, if they produce seven bales to the hand, he will still be in luck; where, if rot, or worm, or floods, or untimely rains or frosts occur, reducing the crop to one or two bales to the hand, as is often the case, the purchaser will have drawn a blank.

That, all things considered, the value of the labour of slaves does not, on an average, by any means justify the price paid for it, is constantly asserted by the planters, and it is true. At least beyond question it is true, and I think that I have shown why, that there is no difficulty in finding purchasers for all the good slaves that can be got by traders, at prices considerably more than they are worth for the production of cotton *under ordinary circumstances*. The supply being limited, those who grow cotton on the most productive soils, and with the greatest advantages in all other respects, not only can afford to pay more than others, for all the slaves which can be brought into market, but they are driven to a ruinous competition among themselves, and slaves thus get a fictitious value like stocks "in a corner." The buyers indeed are often "cornered," and it is only the rise which almost annually has occurred in the value of cotton that has hitherto saved them from general bankruptcy. Nearly all the large planters carry a heavy load of debt from year to year, till a lucky crop coincident with a rise in the price of cotton relieves them.

The whole number of slaves engaged in cotton culture at the Census of 1850 was reckoned by De Bow to be 1,800,000,[3] the crops at 2,400,000 bales, which is a bale and a third to each head of slaves. This was the largest crop between 1846 and 1852. Other things being equal, for reasons already indicated, the smaller the estate of slaves, the less is their rate of production per head; and, as a rule, the larger the slave estate the larger is the production per head. The number of slaves in cotton plantations held by owners of fifty and upwards is, as nearly as it can be fixed by the Census returns, 420,000.

If these produce on an average only two and a half bales per head (man, woman, and child), and double this is not extraordinary on the large plantations of the South-west,[4] it leaves an average for the smaller plantations of seven-eighths of a bale per head. These plantations are mostly in the interior, with long haulage and boatage to market. To the small planter in the interior, his cotton crop does not realize, as an average plantation price, more than seven cents a pound, or thirty dollars the bale.[5] Those who plant cotton in this small way usually raise a crop of corn, and some little else, not enough, take the country through, one year with another, to supply themselves and their slaves with food; certainly not more than enough to do so, on an average. To this the Southern agricultural periodicals frequently testify. They generally raise nothing *for sale,* but cotton. And of cotton their sale, as has been shown, amounted in 1849—a favourable year—to less than the value of twenty-five dollars for each slave, young and old, which they had kept through the year.[6] Deducting those who hold slaves only as domestic servants from the whole number of slaveholders returned by the Census, more than half of all the slaveholders, and fully half of all the cot-

---

[3] Official Census—Compend., p. 94.

[4] Messrs. Neill Brothers, cotton merchants of New Orleans, the most painstaking collectors of information about the cotton crop in the country, state, in a recent circular, that many of the Mississippi cotton plantations last year, after an extraordinary fertilizing flood, produced sixteen bales to the hand. The slaves on these plantations being to a large extent picked hands, as I elsewhere show, the production per head was fully eight bales.

[5] In a careful article in the *Austin State Gazette,* six and a quarter cents is given as the average net price of cotton in Texas. The small planters, having no gins or presses of their own, usually have their cotton prepared for market by large planters, for which service they of course have to pay.

[6] There have been much larger aggregate crops since, and the price may be a cent more to the planter, but the number of slaves drawn to the larger plantations in the meantime has increased in quite equal proportion.

ton-sellers, own each, not more than one family, on an average, of five slaves of all ages.[7] The ordinary total cash income, then, in time of peace, of fully half our cotton-planters, cannot be reckoned at more than one hundred and twenty-five dollars, or, in extraordinary years, like the last, at, say, one hundred and fifty dollars. From this they must purchase whatever clothing and other necessaries they require for the yearly supply of an average of more than ten persons (five whites and five slaves), as well as obtain tools, mechanics' work and materials, and whatever is necessary for carrying on the work of a plantation, usually of some hundred acres,[8] and must yet save enough to pay the fees of doctors, clergy, and lawyers, if they have had occasion to employ them, and their county and state taxes (we will say nothing of the education of their children, or of accumulations for the war expenses of the Confederation). My personal experience of the style of living of the greater number of cotton-planters leads me to think this not an unfair estimate. It is mainly based upon the official returns and calculations of the United States Census of 1850, as prepared by Mr. [J. D. B.] De Bow, a leading secessionist, and it assumes nothing which is not conceded in the article on cotton in his Resources of the South [*The Industrial Resources, etc., of the Southern and Western States*]. A majority of those who sell the cotton crop of the United States must be miserably poor—poorer than the majority of our day-labourers at the North.

A similar calculation will indicate that the planters who own on an average two slave families each, can sell scarcely more than three hundred dollars' worth of cotton a year, on an average; which also entirely agrees with my observations. I have seen many a workman's lodging at the North, and in England too, where there was double the amount of luxury that I ever saw in a regular cotton-planter's house on plantations of three cabins.

The next class of which the Census furnishes us means of considering separately, are planters whose slaves occupy, on an average, seven cabins, lodging five each on an average, including the house servants, aged, invalids, and children. The average income of plant-

---

[7] "Census Compend.," p. 95.

[8] The average size of plantations in the South-west, including the farms and "patches" of the non-slaveholders, is 273 acres (p. 170, "C. Compend."). Cotton plantations are not generally of less than 400 acres.

ers of this class, I reckon from similar data, to be hardly more than that of a private of the New York Metropolitan Police Force. It is doubtless true that cotton is cultivated profitably, that is to say, so as to produce a fair rate of interest on the capital of the planter, on many plantations of this class; but this can hardly be the case on an average, all things considered.

It is not so with many plantations of the next larger class even, but it would appear to be so with these on an average. That is to say, where the quarters of a cotton plantation number half a score of cabins or more (which method of classification I use that travellers may the more readily recall their observations of the appearance of such plantations, when I think that their recollections will confirm these calculations), there are usually other advantages for the cultivation, cleaning, pressing, shipping, and disposing of cotton, by the aid of which the owner obtains a fair return for the capital invested, and may be supposed to live, if he knows how, in a moderately comfortable way. The whole number of slaveholders of this large class in all the Slave States is, according to De Bow's Compendium of the Census, 7,929, among which are all the great sugar, rice, and tobacco-planters. Less than seven thousand, certainly, are cotton-planters.

A large majority of these live, when they live on their plantations at all, in districts, almost the only white population of which consists of owners and overseers of the same class of plantations with their own. The nearest other whites will be some sand-hill vagabonds, generally miles away, between whom and these planters, intercourse is neither intimate nor friendly.

It is hardly worth while to build much of a bridge for the occasional use of two families, even if they are rich. It is less worth while to go to much pains in making six miles of good road for the use of these families. A school-house will hardly be built for the children of six rich men who will all live on an average six miles away from it, while private tutors or governesses can be paid by the earnings of a single field-hand. If zeal and fluency can be obtained in a preacher coming occasionally within reach, the interest on the cost of a tolerable education is not likely to be often paid by all who would live within half a day's journey of a house of worship, which can be built anywhere in the midst of a district of large plantations. It is not necessary to multiply illustrations like these. In short, then, if all the wealth produced in a certain district is concentrated in the hands of a few men living remote from each other, it may possibly bring to the district comfortable houses, good servants, fine wines, food and furniture, tutors and governesses, horses and carriages, for these few men, but it will not bring thither good roads and bridges, it will not bring thither such means of education and of civilized comfort as are to be drawn from libraries, churches, museums, gardens, theatres, and assembly rooms; it will not bring thither local newspapers, telegraphs, and so on. It will not bring thither that subtle force and discipline which comes of the myriad relations with and duties to a well-constituted community which every member of it is daily exercising, and which is the natural unseen compensation and complement of its more obvious constraints and inconveniences. There is, in fact, a vast range of advantages which our civilization has made so common to us that they are hardly thought of, of which the people of the South are destitute. They chiefly come from or connect with acts of co-operation, or exchanges of service; they are therefore possessed only in communities, and in communities where a large proportion of the people have profitable employment. They grow, in fact, out of employments in which the people of the community are associated, or which they constantly give to and receive from one another, with profit. The slaves of the South, though often living in communities upon plantations, fail to give or receive these advantages because the profits of their labour are not distributed to them; the whites, from not engaging in profitable employment. The whites are not engaged in profitable employment, because the want of the advantages of capital in the application of their labour, independently of the already rich, renders the prospective result of their labour so small that it is inoperative in most, as a motive for exerting themselves further than is necessary to procure the bare means of a rude subsistence; also because common labour is so poorly rewarded in the case of the slaves as to assume in their minds, as it must in the minds of the slaves themselves, a hateful aspect.

In the late act of treason of the usurpers of government in Louisiana, the commercial demand which induces a man to go to work is considered to be equivalent to slavery; and the fear that the election of Lincoln, by its tendency to open a way for the emancipation of the negroes, may lead on to a necessity for the whites to go to work, is gravely set forth as a justification for the surrender of the State to the conspiracy. Thus:—

"Fully convinced as we are that slavery . . . leaves to the *black labourer* a more considerable sum of comfort, happiness, and liberty than the inexorable labour required from the free servants of the whole universe, and that each emancipation of an African, without being of any benefit to him, would necessarily *condemn to slavery* one of our own race, etc."

To work industriously and steadily, especially under directions from another man, is, in the Southern tongue, to "work like a nigger"; and, from childhood, the one thing in their condition which has made life valuable to the mass of whites has been that the niggers are yet their inferiors. It is this habit of considering themselves of a privileged class, and of disdaining something which they think beneath them, that is deemed to be the chief blessing of slavery. It is termed "high tone," "high spirit," and is supposed to give great military advantages to those who possess it. It should give advantages of some sort, for its disadvantages are inexpressibly great.

But if the poor whites were ever so industriously disposed, the rich planter has a natural distaste to exchange absolute for partial authority over the instruments by which he achieves his purpose; and the employment of free and slave labour together, is almost as difficult as working, under the same yoke, an unbroken horse and a docile ox. Again, however repugnant it may be to the self-esteem, and contrary to the habits of the rich man to treat his labourers with respect, he has to do it when employing white men, from motives of self-interest which lie below the surface, and he consequently habitually avoids arranging his affairs in such a way as will make it necessary for him to offer them employment.

It may be said that on the more profitable cotton plantations, where little is raised except cotton, supplies for the maintenance of the slaves, and for carrying on the work of the plantation, are largely bought, which are raised elsewhere at the South; and that those who supply the commodities, thus required by the cotton-planter, draw from his profits which are thus distributed throughout the South, even to the non-cotton-producing States, the people of which are thus enriched. As far as all articles are concerned, in the production of which labour is a comparatively unimportant item of cost,—mules for instance, and in certain circumstances, within certain limits, swine,—this is true. But these are of small consequence. It is constantly assumed by nearly all writers on this subject, that the labour directed to the cultivation of Indian corn for the necessary sustenance of slaves engaged in cotton culture, must be just as profitably directed as if it were devoted to the cultivation of cotton itself. This is not true, although the Southern agricultural journals, and to a large extent our national agriculture reports, have for years been assuming it to be so. It is frequently spoken of, indeed, as a mystery, that the cotton-planters cannot be induced to raise the food required by their force. The reason of it is a very simple one; namely, that in the cultivation of corn their labour must come into competition with the free labour of the Northern States, as it does not in the production of cotton: and the corn-raisers of the Northern Slave States, without enjoying any monopoly of production, like that of the cotton-raisers, have to share with these, all the manifold inconveniences which result from the scarcity of good workmen, and the necessary concentration of all the effective working force of the country, limited as it is, upon the one purpose of getting cotton.

The interests of the owners of all soil in the Slave States which is not adapted to cotton culture, and of all capital not engaged in cotton culture, or in supplying slaves for it, are thus injured by the demand for cotton, they being, in fact, forced to be co-partners in an association in which they do not share the profits.

And as to what are commonly called the Cotton States, if we assume that cotton cultivation is profitable only where the production is equal to two bales for each slave employed, it will be seen that wherever the land will not yield as much as this, the owner of it suffers all the disadvantages of the difficulty of getting good labourers as much as the owner of the land which produces seven or ten bales to the hand, although none of the profits of supplying the cotton demand, which gives this extraordinary price to labour, come to him.

According to the Census,[9] the whole crop of cotton is produced on 5,000,000 acres. It could be produced, at the rate common on good South-western plantations, on less than half that area. The rest of the land of the Slave States, which amounts to over 500,000,000 acres, is condemned, so far as the tendencies I have indicated are

[9] Compendium, p. 176.

not overweighed here and there by some special advantages, to non-cultivation, except for the hand-to-mouth supply of its people. And this is true not only of its agricultural but of all other of its resources.

That for all practical purposes this is not an exaggerated statement is clearly enough shown by the difference in the market value of land, which, as officially given by De Bow, is, notwithstanding the extraordinary demand of the world upon the cotton land, between four and five hundred per cent. higher in the Free than in the Slave States, the frontier and unsettled districts, Texas, California, and the territories not being considered.

One of the grand errors, out of which this rebellion has grown, came from supposing that whatever nourishes wealth and gives power to an ordinary civilized community must command as much for a slave-holding community. The truth has been overlooked that the accumulation of wealth and the power of a nation are contingent not merely upon the primary value of the surplus of productions of which it has to dispose, but very largely also upon the way in which the income from its surplus is distributed and reinvested. Let a man be absent from almost any part of the North twenty years, and he is struck, on his return, by what we call the "improvements" which have been made. Better buildings, churches, school-houses, mills, railroads, etc. In New York city alone, for instance, at least two hundred millions of dollars have been reinvested merely in an improved housing of the people; in labour-saving machinery, waterworks, gasworks, etc., as much more. It is not difficult to see where the profits of our manufacturers and merchants are. Again, go into the country, and there is no end of substantial proof of twenty years of agricultural prosperity, not alone in roads, canals, bridges, dwellings, barns and fences, but in books and furniture, and gardens, and pictures, and in the better dress and evidently higher education of the people. But where will the returning traveller see the accumulated cotton profits of twenty years in Mississippi? Ask the cotton-planter for them, and he will point in reply, not to dwellings, libraries, churches, school-houses, mills, railroads, or anything of the kind; he will point to his negroes—to almost nothing else. Negroes such as stood for five hundred dollars once, now represent a thousand dollars. We must look then in Virginia and those Northern Slave States which have the monopoly of supplying negroes, for the real wealth which the sale of cotton has brought to the South. But where is the evidence of it? where anything to compare with the evidence of accumulated profits to be seen in any Free State? If certain portions of Virginia have been a little improving, others unquestionably have been deteriorating, growing shabbier, more comfortless, less convenient. The total increase in wealth of the population during the last twenty years shows for almost nothing. One year's improvements of a Free State exceed it all.

It is obvious that to the community at large, even in Virginia, the profits of supplying negroes to meet the wants occasioned by the cotton demand, have not compensated for the bar which the high cost of all sorts of human service, which the cotton demand has also occasioned, has placed upon all other means of accumulating wealth; and this disadvantage of the cotton monopoly is fully experienced by the negro-breeders themselves, in respect to everything else they have to produce or obtain.[1]

I say all sorts of human service. What the South will have to pay for the service of true statesmanship, the world has now to see.

Whither the profits of cotton go, it is not my purpose, here, to undertake to show. I will barely notice the hypocritical statement made for the English market as an apology for this mad crime of the slaveholders, that they are greatly absorbed in contributions made by the planting States to our national treasury in payment of duties on importations. The cotton-planters pay duties only on what they consume of foreign goods. A very large part of all our duties are collected on a class of goods for which there is almost no demand at all from the South, either directly or indirectly—woollen and fur goods, for instance: of the goods required for the South not a few have been practically free. The whole slave population of the South consumes almost nothing imported (nor would it, while slave, under any circumstances). The majority of the white population habitually makes use of no foreign production except chickory, which, ground with peas, they call coffee. I have never seen reason to believe that with absolute free trade the cotton States would take a tenth part of the value of our present importations. And as far as I can judge from observation of the comparative use of foreign goods at the South and at the North, not a tenth part of our duties have been defrayed by the South in the last twenty years. The most in-

---

[1] Evidence from Virginian witnesses is given in the Appendix, A.

defensible protective duty we have is one called for by the South, and which has been maintained solely to benefit the South. Our protective system had a Southern origin; its most powerful advocates have been Southerners; and there has not been a year in the last twenty, in which it could have been maintained but for Southern votes.

Chapter II

Washington

Washington, Dec. 10th [1852].—To accomplish the purposes which brought me to Washington, it was necessary, on arriving here, to make arrangements to secure food and shelter while I remained. There are two thousand visitors now in Washington under a similar necessity. There are a dozen or more persons who, for a consideration, undertake to provide what they want. Mr. Dexter is reported to be the best of them, and really seems a very obliging and honestly disposed person. To Mr. Dexter, therefore, I commit myself.

I commit myself by inscribing my name in a Register. Five minutes after I have done so, Clerk No. 4, whose attention I have hitherto been unable to obtain, suddenly catches the Register by the corner, swings it round with a jerk, and throws a hieroglyph at it, which strikes near my name. Henceforth, I figure as Boarder No. 201 (or whatever it may be). Clerk No. 4 pipes "Boarder away!" and throws key No. 201 upon the table. Turnkey No. 3 takes it, and me, and my travelling bag, up several flights of stairs, along corridors and galleries, and finally consigns me to this little square cell.

I have faith that there is a tight roof above the much-cracked ceiling; that the bed is clean; and that I shall, by-and-by, be summoned, along with hundreds of other boarders, to partake, in silent sobriety, of a "splendid" dinner.

Food and shelter. Therewith should a man be content. But my perverse nature will not be content: will be wishing things were otherwise. They say this uneasiness—this passion for change—is a peculiarity of our diseased Northern nature. The Southern man finds Providence in all that is: Satan in all that might be. That is good; and, as I am going South, when I have accomplished my purposes at Washington, I will not here restrain the escape of my present discontent.

In my perversity I wish the dinner were not going to be so grand. My idea is that, if it were not, Mr. Dexter would save moneys, which I would like to have him expend in other ways. I wish he had more clerks, so that they would have time to be as polite to an unknown man as I see they are to John P. Hale [Senator from New Hampshire]; and, at least, answer civil questions, when his boarders ask them. I don't like such a fearful rush of business as there is down stairs. I wish there were men enough to do the work quietly.

I don't like these cracked and variegated walls; and, though the roof may be tight, I don't like this threatening aspect of the ceiling. It should be kept for boarders of Damoclesian ambition: I am humble.

I am humble, and I am short, and soon curried; but I am not satisfied with a quarter of a yard of towelling, having an irregular vacancy in its centre, where I am liable to insert my head. I am not proud; but I had rather have something else, or nothing, than these three yards of ragged and faded quarter-ply carpeting. I also would like a curtain to the window, and I wish the glass were not so dusty, and that the sashes did not rattle so in their casements; though, as there is no other ventilation, I suppose I ought not to complain. Of course not; but it is confoundedly cold, as well as noisy.

I don't like that broken latch; I don't like this broken chair; I would prefer that this table were not so greasy; I would rather the ashes and cinders, and the tobacco juice around the grate, had been removed before I was consigned to the cell.

I wish that less of my two dollars and a half a day went to pay for game at dinner, and interest on the cost of the mirrors and mahogany for the public parlours, and of marble for the halls, and more of it for providing me with a private room, which should be more than a barely habitable cell, which should also be a little bit tasteful, home-like, and comfortable.

I wish more of it could be expended in servants' wages.

Six times I rang the bell; three several times came three different Irish lads; entered, received my demand for a fire, and retired. I was writing, shiveringly, a full hour before the fire-man came. Now he has entered, bearing on his head a hod of coal and kindling wood, without knocking. An aged negro, more familiar and more indifferent to forms of subserviency than the Irish lads, very much bent, seemingly with infirmity; an expression of impotent anger in his face, and a look of weakness, like a drunkard's. He does not look at me, but mutters unintelligibly.

"What's that you say?"

"Tink I can make a hundred fires at once?"

"I don't want to sit an hour waiting for a fire, after I have ordered one, and you must not let me again."

"Nebber let de old nigger have no ress—hundred gemmen tink I kin mak dair fires all de same minit; all get mad at an ole nigger; I ain't a goin to stan it—nebber get no ress—up all night—haint got nautin to eat nor drink dis blessed mornin—hundred gemmen—"

"That's not my business; Mr. Dexter should have more servants."

"So he ort ter, master, dat he had; one ole man ain't enough for all dis house, is it, master? hundred gemmen—"

"Stop—here's a quarter for you: now I want you to look out that I have a good fire, and keep the hearth clean in my room as long as I stay here. And when I send for you I want you to come immediately. Do you understand?"

"I'le try, master—you jus look roun and fine me when you want yer fire; I'll be roun somewhere. You got a newspaper, sir, I ken take for a minit? I won't hurt it."

I gave him one; and wondered what use he could put it to, that would not hurt it. He opened it to a folio, and spread it before the grate, so the draft held it in place, and it acted as a blower. I asked if there were no blowers? "No." "But haven't you got any brush or shovel?" I inquired, seeing him get down upon his knees again and sweep the cinders and ashes he had thrown upon the floor with the sleeve of his coat, and then take them up with his hands;—No, he said, his master did not give him such things.

"Are you a slave?"

"Yes, sir."

"Do you belong to Mr. Dexter?"

"No, sir—he hires me of de man dat owns me. Don't you tink I'se too ole a man for to be knock roun at dis kind of work, massa?—hundred gemmen all want dair fires made de same minute, and caus de old nigger can't do it all de same minute, ebbery one tinks dey's boun to scold him all de time; nebber no rest for him, no time."

Washington, Dec. 14th.—I called to-day on Mr. C., whose fine farm, from its vicinity to Washington, and its excellent management, as well as from the hospitable habits of its owner, has a national reputation. It is some two thousand acres in extent, and situated just without the District, in Maryland.

The residence is in the midst of the farm, a quarter of a mile from the high road—the private approach being judiciously carried through large pastures which are divided only by slight, but close and well-secured wire fences. The kept grounds are limited, and in simple but quiet taste; being surrounded only by wires, they merge, in effect, into the pastures. There is a fountain, an ornamental dove-cote, and ice-house, and the approach road, nicely gravelled and rolled, comes up to the door with a fine sweep.

I had dismounted and was standing before the door, when I heard myself loudly hailed from a distance.

"Ef yer wants to see master, sah, he's down thar—to the new stable."

I could see no one; and when tired of holding my horse, I mounted, and rode on in search of the new stable. I found it without difficulty; and in it Mr. and Mrs. C. With them were a number of servants, one of whom now took my horse with alacrity. I was taken at once to look at a very fine herd of cows, and afterwards led upon a tramp over the farm, and did not get back to the house till dinner-time.

Mr. C. is a large hereditary owner of slaves, which, for ordinary field and stable work, constitute his labouring force. He has employed several Irishmen for ditching; and for this work, and this alone, he thought he could use them to better advantage than negroes. He would not think of using Irishmen for common farm-labour, and made light of their coming in competition with slaves. Negroes at hoeing and any steady field-work, he assured me, would "do two to their one"; but his main objection to employing Irishmen was derived from his experience of their unfaithfulness—they were dishonest, would not obey explicit directions about their work, and required more personal supervision than negroes. From what he had heard and seen of Germans, he supposed they did better than Irish. He mentioned that there were several Germans who had come here as labouring men, and worked for wages several years, who had now got possession of small farms, and were reputed to be getting rich.[1] He was disinclined to converse on the topic of slavery; and I there-

---

[1] "There is a small settlement of Germans, about three miles from me, who, a few years since (with little or nothing beyond their physical abilities to aid them), seated themselves down in a poor, miserable, old field, and have, by their industry, and means obtained by working round among the neighbours, effected a change which is really surprising and pleasing to behold, and who will, I have no doubt, become wealthy, provided they remain prudent, as they have hitherto been industrious."—F. A. CLOPPER (Montgomery Co.), Maryland, in Patent Of. Rept., 1851.

fore made no inquiries about the condition and habits of his negroes, or his management of them. They seemed to live in small and
rude log-cabins, scattered in different parts of the farm. Those I
saw at work appeared to me to move very slowly and awkwardly,
as did also those engaged in the stable. These also were very stupid
and dilatory in executing any orders given to them, so that Mr. C.
would frequently take the duty off their hands into his own, rather
than wait for them, or make them correct their blunders: they were
much, in these respects, like what our farmers call dumb Paddies,
that is, Irishmen who do not readily understand the English language, and who are still weak and stiff from the effects of the emigrating voyage. At the entrance-gate was a porter's lodge, and as I
approached, I saw a black face peeping at me from it, but, both
when I entered and left, I was obliged to dismount and open the
gate myself.

Altogether it struck me—slaves coming here as they naturally did
in direct comparison with free labourers, as commonly employed on
my own and my neighbours' farms, in exactly similar duties—that
they must be difficult to direct efficiently, and that it must be irksome and trying to one's patience to have to superintend their
labour.

Washington, Dec. 16th.—Visiting the market-place, early on Tuesday morning, I found myself in the midst of a throng of a very different character from any I have ever seen at the North. The majority of the people were negroes; and, taken as a whole, they appeared
inferior in the expression of their face and less well-clothed than
any collection of negroes I had ever seen before. All the negro characteristics were more clearly marked in each than they often are in
any at the North. In their dress, language, manner, motions—all
were distinguishable almost as much by their colour, from the white
people who were distributed among them, and engaged in the same
occupations—chiefly selling poultry, vegetables, and small country
produce. The white men were, generally, a mean-looking people,
and but meanly dressed, but differently so from the negroes.

Most of the produce was in small, rickety carts, drawn by the
smallest, ugliest, leanest lot of oxen and horses that I ever saw.
There was but one pair of horses in over a hundred that were tolerably good—a remarkable proportion of them were maimed in some

way. As for the oxen, I do not believe New England and New York together could produce a single yoke as poor as the best of them.

The very trifling quantity of articles brought in and exposed for sale by most of the market-people was noticeable; a peck of ,potatoes, three bunches of carrots, two cabbages, six eggs and a chicken, would be about the average stock in trade of all the dealers. Mr. F. said that an old negro woman once came to his door with a single large turkey, which she pressed him to buy. Struck with her fatigued appearance, he made some inquiries of her, and ascertained that she had been several days coming from home, had travelled mainly on foot, and had brought the turkey and nothing else with her. "Ole massa had to raise some money somehow, and he could not sell anyting else, so he tole me to catch the big gobbler, and tote um down to Washington and see wot um would fotch."

Land may be purchased, within twenty miles of Washington, at from ten to twenty dollars an acre. Most of it has been once in cultivation, and, having been exhausted in raising tobacco, has been, for many years, abandoned, and is now covered by a forest growth. Several New Yorkers have lately speculated in the purchase of this sort of land, and, as there is a good market for wood, and the soil, by the decay of leaves upon it, and other natural causes, has been restored to moderate fertility, have made money by clearing and improving it. By deep ploughing and liming, and the judicious use of manures, it is made quite productive; and, as equally cheap farms can hardly be found in any Free State, in such proximity to as good markets for agricultural produce, there are inducements for a considerable Northern immigration hither. It may not be long before a majority of the inhabitants will be opposed to slavery, and desire its abolition within the District. Indeed, when Mr. [William H.] Seward proposed in the Senate to allow them to decide that matter, the advocates of "popular sovereignty" made haste to vote down the motion.

There are, already, more Irish and German labourers and servants than *slaves;* and, as many of the objections which free labourers have to going further south, do not operate in Washington, the proportion of white labourers is every year increasing. The majority of servants, however, are now *free* negroes, which class constitutes one-fifth of the entire population. The slaves are one-fifteenth, but are mostly owned out of the District, and hired annually to those who require their services. In the assessment of taxable property, for 1853, the slaves, owned or hired in the District, were valued at three hundred thousand dollars.

The coloured population voluntarily sustain several churches, schools, and mutual assistance and improvement societies, and there are evidently persons among them of no inconsiderable cultivation of mind. Among the police reports of the City newspapers, there was lately (April, 1855), an account of the apprehension of twenty-four "genteel coloured men" (so they were described), who had been found by a watchman assembling privately in the evening, and been lodged in the watch-house. The object of their meeting appears to have been purely benevolent, and, when they were examined before a magistrate in the morning, no evidence was offered, nor does there seem to have been any suspicion that they had any criminal purpose. On searching their persons, there were found a Bible; a volume of *Seneca's Morals*; *Life in Earnest* [a publication of the American Sunday School Union written by James Hamilton]; the printed constitution of a society, the object of which was said to be *"to relieve the sick and bury the dead"*; and a subscription paper *to purchase the freedom of Eliza Howard*, a young woman, whom her owner was willing to sell at $650.

I can think of nothing that would speak higher for the character of a body of poor men, servants and labourers, than to find, by chance, in their pockets, just such things as these. And I cannot value that man as a countryman, who does not feel intense humiliation and indignation, when he learns that such men may not be allowed to meet privately together, with such laudable motives, in the capital city of the United States, without being subject to disgraceful punishment. One of the prisoners, a slave named Joseph Jones, was ordered to be flogged; four others, called in the papers free men, and named John E. Bennett, Chester Taylor, George Lee, and Aquila Barton, were sent to the workhouse; and the remainder, on paying costs of court, and fines, amounting, in the aggregate, to one hundred and eleven dollars, were permitted to range loose again.

CHAPTER III

Virginia

Richmond, Dec. 16th [1852].—From Washington to Richmond, Virginia, by the regular great southern route—steamboat on the Potomac to Acquia Creek, and thence direct by rail. The boat makes 55 miles in 3½ hours, including two stoppages (12½ miles an hour); fare $2 (3.6 cents a mile). Flat rail; distance, 75 miles; time 5½ hours (13 miles an hour); fare, $3.50 (4⅔ cents a mile).

Not more than a third of the country, visible on this route, I should say, is cleared; the rest mainly a pine forest. Of the cleared land, not more than one quarter seems to have been lately in cultivation; the rest is grown over with briars and bushes, and a long, coarse grass of no value. But two crops seem to be grown upon the cultivated land—maize and wheat. The last is frequently sown in narrow beds and carefully surface-drained, and is looking remarkably well.

A good many old plantation mansions are to be seen; generally standing in a grove of white oaks, upon some hill-top. Most of them are constructed of wood, of two stories, painted white, and have, perhaps, a dozen rude-looking little log-cabins scattered around them, for the slaves. Now and then, there is one of more pretension, with a large porch or gallery in front, like that of Mount Vernon. These are generally in a heavy, compact style; less often, perhaps, than similar establishments at the North, in markedly bad, or vulgar taste, but seem in sad need of repairs.

The more common sort of habitations of the white people are either of logs or loosely boarded frames, a brick chimney running up outside, at one end: everything very slovenly and dirty about them. Swine, hounds, and black and white children, are commonly lying very promiscuously together on the ground about the doors.

I am struck with the close cohabitation and association of black and white—negro women are carrying black and white babies together in their arms; black and white children are playing together (not going to school together); black and white faces are constantly thrust together out of the doors, to see the train go by.

A fine-looking, well-dressed, and well-behaved coloured young man sat, together with a white man, on a seat in the cars. I suppose the man was his master; but he was much the less like a gentleman of the two. The railroad company advertise to take coloured people only in second-class trains; but servants seem to go with their masters everywhere. Once, to-day, seeing a lady entering the car at a way-station, with a family behind her, and that she was looking about to find a place where they could be seated together, I rose, and offered her my seat, which had several vacancies round it. She accepted it, without thanking me, and immediately installed in it a stout negro woman; took the adjoining seat herself, and seated the rest of her party before her. It consisted of a white girl, probably her daughter, and a bright and very pretty mulatto girl. They all talked and laughed together; and the girls munched confectionary out of the same paper, with a familiarity and closeness of intimacy that would have been noticed with astonishment, if not with manifest displeasure, in almost any chance company at the North. When the negro is definitely a slave, it would seem that the alleged natural antipathy of the white race to associate with him is lost.

I am surprised at the number of fine-looking mulattoes, or nearly white-coloured persons, that I see. The majority of those with whom I have come personally in contact are such. I fancy I see a peculiar expression among these—a contraction of the eyebrows and tightening of the lips—a spying, secretive, and counsel-keeping expression.

But the great mass, as they are seen at work, under overseers, in the fields, appear very dull, idiotic, and brute-like; and it requires an effort to appreciate that they are, very much more than the beasts they drive, our brethren—a part of ourselves. They are very ragged, and the women especially, who work in the field with the men, with no apparent distinction in their labour, disgustingly dirty. They seem to move very awkwardly, slowly, and undecidedly, and almost invariably stop their work while the train is passing.

One tannery and two or three saw-mills afforded the only indications I saw, in seventy-five miles of this old country—settled before any part of Massachusetts—of any industrial occupation other than corn and wheat culture, and fire-wood chopping. At Fredericksburg we passed through the streets of a rather busy, poorly-built town; but altogether, the country seen from the railroad, bore less signs of an active and prospering people than any I ever travelled through before, for an equal distance.

Richmond, at a glance from adjacent high ground, through a dull cloud of bituminous smoke, upon a lowering winter's day, has a very picturesque appearance, and I was reminded of the sensation produced by a similar *coup d'œil* of Edinburgh. It is somewhat similarly situated upon and among some considerable hills; but the moment it is examined at all in detail, there is but one spot, in the whole picture, upon which the eye is at all attracted to rest. This is the Capitol, a Grecian edifice, standing alone, and finely placed on open and elevated ground, in the centre of the town. It was built soon after the Revolution, and the model was obtained by Mr. Jefferson, then Minister to France, from the Maison Carrée.

A considerable part of the town, which contains a population of 28,000, is compactly and somewhat substantially built, but is without any pretensions to architectural merit, except in a few modern private mansions. The streets are not paved, and but few of them are provided with side walks other than of earth or gravel. The town is lighted with gas, and furnished with excellent water by an aqueduct.

On a closer view of the Capitol, a bold deviation from the Grecian model is very noticeable. The southern portico is sustained upon a very high blank wall, and is as inaccessible from the exterior as if it had been intended to fortify the edifice from all ingress other than by scaling-ladders. On coming round to the west side, however, which is without a colonnade, a grand entrance, reached by a heavy buttress of stone steps, is found. This incongruity diminishes, in some degree, the usual inconvenience of the Greek temple for modern public purposes, for it gives speedy access to a small central rotunda, out of which doors open into the legislative halls and offices.

If the walling up of the legitimate entrance has caused the impression, in a stranger, that he is being led to a prison or fortress, instead of the place for transacting the public business of a Free State by its chosen paid agents, it is not removed when on approaching this side door, he sees before it an armed sentinel—a meek-looking man in a livery of many colours, embarrassed with a bright-bayoneted firelock, which he hugs gently, as though the cold iron, this frosty day, chilled his arm.

He belongs to the Public Guard of Virginia, I am told; a company of a hundred men (more or less), enlisted under an Act of the State, passed in 1801, after a rebellion of the coloured people, who, under one "General Gabriel," attempted to take the town, in hopes to gain the means of securing their freedom. Having been betrayed by a traitor, as insurgent slaves almost always are, they were met, on their approach, by a large body of well-armed militia, hastily called out by the Governor. For this, being armed only with scythe-blades, they were unprepared, and immediately dispersed. "General Gabriel" and the other leaders, one after another, were captured, tried, and hanged, the militia in strong force guarding them to execution. Since then, a disciplined guard, bearing the warning motto, "*Sic semper tyrannis!*" has been kept constantly under arms in the Capitol, and no man can enter the legislative temple of Virginia without being reminded that "Eternal vigilance is the price of—."

It was not till I had passed the guard, unchallenged, and stood at the door-way, that I perceived that the imposing edifice, as I had thought it at a distance, was nothing but a cheap stuccoed building; nor would anything short of test by touch have convinced me that the great State of Virginia would have been so long content with such a parsimonious pretence of dignity as is found in imitation granite and imitation marble.

There is an instance of parsimony, without pretence, in Richmond, which Ruskin himself, if he were a traveller, could not be expected to applaud. The railroad company which brings the traveller from Washington, so far from being open to the criticism of having provided edifices of a style of architecture only fitted for palaces, instead of a hall suited to conflicts with hackney-coachmen, actually has no sort of stationary accommodations for them at all, but sets them down, rain or shine, in the middle of one of the main streets. The adjoining hucksteries, barbers' shops, and bar-rooms, are evidently all the better patronized for this fine simplicity; but I should doubt if the railroad stock advanced in value by it.

Richmond.—On a Sunday afternoon I met a negro funeral procession, and followed after it to the place of burial. There was a decent hearse, of the usual style, drawn by two horses; six hackneyed coaches followed it, and six well-dressed men, mounted on handsome saddle-horses, and riding them well, rode in the rear of these. Twenty or thirty men and women were also walking together with the procession, on the side walk. Among all there was not a white person.

Passing out into the country, a little beyond the principal cemetery of the city (a neat, rural ground, well filled with monuments and evergreens), the hearse halted at a desolate place, where a dozen coloured people were already engaged heaping the earth over the grave of a child, and singing a wild kind of chant. Another grave was already dug immediately adjoining that of the child, both being near the foot of a hill, in a crumbling bank—the ground below being already occupied, and the graves advancing in irregular terraces up the hill-side—an arrangement which facilitated labour.

The new comers, setting the coffin—which was neatly made of stained pine—upon the ground, joined in the labour and the singing, with the preceding party, until a small mound of earth was made over the grave of the child. When this was completed, one of those who had been handling a spade, sighed deeply and said—

"Lord Jesus, have marcy on us—now! you Jim—you! see yar! you jes lay dat yar shovel cross dat grave—so fash—dah—yes, dat's right."

A shovel and a hoe-handle having been laid across the unfilled grave, the coffin was brought and laid upon them, as on a trestle; after which, lines were passed under it, by which it was lowered to the bottom.

Most of the company were of a very poor appearance, rude and unintelligent, but there were several neatly-dressed and very good-looking men. One of these now stepped to the head of the grave, and, after a few sentences of prayer, held a handkerchief before him as if it were a book, and pronounced a short exhortation, as if he were reading from it. His manner was earnest, and the tone of his voice solemn and impressive, except that, occasionally, it would break into a shout or kind of howl at the close of a long sentence. I noticed several women near him, weeping, and one sobbing intensely. I was deeply influenced myself by the unaffected feeling, in connection with the simplicity, natural, rude truthfulness, and absence of all attempt at formal decorum in the crowd.

I never in my life, however, heard such ludicrous language as was sometimes uttered by the speaker. Frequently I could not guess the idea he was intending to express. Sometimes it was evident that he was trying to repeat phrases that he had heard used before, on similar occasions, but which he made absurd by some interpolation or distortion of a word, thus: "We do not see the end here! oh no, my friends! there will be a *putrification* of this body!" the context failing to indicate whether he meant purification or putrefaction, and leaving it doubtful if he attached any definite meaning to the word himself. He quoted from the Bible several times, several times from hymns, always introducing the latter with "In the words of the poet, my brethren"; he once used the same form, before a verse from the New Testament, and once qualified his citation by saying, "I *believe* the Bible says that."

He concluded by throwing a handful of earth on the coffin, repeating the usual words, slightly disarranged, and then took a shovel, and, with the aid of six or seven others, proceeded very rapidly to fill the grave. Another man had in the mean time, stepped into the place he had first occupied at the head of the grave; an old negro, with a very singularly distorted face, who raised a hymn, which soon became a confused chant—the leader singing a few words alone, and the company then either repeating them after him or making a response to them, in the manner of sailors heaving at the windlass. I could understand but very few of the words. The music was wild and barbarous, but not without a plaintive melody. A new leader took the place of the old man, when his breath gave out (he had sung very hard, with much bending of the body and gesticulation), and continued until the grave was filled, and a mound raised over it.

A man had, in the mean time, gone into a ravine near by, and now returned with two small branches, hung with withered leaves, that he had broken off a beech tree: these were placed upright, one at the head, the other at the foot of the grave. A few sentences of prayer were then repeated in a low voice by one of the company, and all dispersed. No one seemed to notice my presence at all. There were about fifty coloured people in the assembly, and but one other white man besides myself. This man lounged against the fence, outside the crowd, an apparently indifferent spectator, and I judged he was a police officer, or some one procured to witness the funeral, in compliance with the law which requires that a white man shall always be present at any meeting, for religious exercises, of the negroes.

The greater part of the coloured people, on Sunday, seemed to be dressed in the cast-off fine clothes of the white people, received, I suppose, as presents, or purchased of the Jews, whose shops show that there must be considerable importation of such articles, probably from the North, as there is from England into Ireland. Indeed, the lowest class, especially among the younger, remind me much, by their dress, of the "lads" of Donnybrook; and when the funeral procession came to its destination, there was a scene precisely like that you may see every day in Sackville Street, Dublin,—a dozen boys in ragged clothes, originally made for tall men, and rather folded round their bodies than worn, striving who should hold the horses of the gentlemen when they dismounted to attend the interment of the body. Many, who had probably come in from the farms near the town, wore clothing of coarse gray "negro-cloth," that appeared as if made by contract, without regard to the size of the particular individual to whom it had been allotted, like penitentiary uniforms. A few had a better suit of coarse blue cloth, expressly made for them evidently, for "Sunday clothes."

Some were dressed with foppish extravagance, and many in the latest style of fashion. In what I suppose to be the fashionable streets, there were many more well-dressed and highly-dressed coloured people than white; and among this dark gentry the finest French cloths, embroidered waistcoats, patent-leather shoes, resplendent brooches, silk hats, kid gloves, and *eau de mille fleurs*, were quite common. Nor was the fairer, or rather the softer sex, at all left in the shade of this splendour. Many of the coloured ladies were dressed not only expensively, but with good taste and effect, after the latest Parisian mode. Some of them were very attractive in appearance, and would have produced a decided sensation in any European drawing-room. Their walk and carriage were more often stylish and graceful. Nearly a fourth part seemed to me to have lost all African peculiarity of feature, and to have acquired, in place of it, a good deal of that voluptuousness of expression which characterizes many of the women of the South of Europe.

There was no indication of their belonging to a subject race, except that they invariably gave the way to the white people they

met. Once, when two of them, engaged in conversation and looking at each other, had not noticed his approach, I saw a Virginian
gentleman lift his walking-stick and push a woman aside with it. In
the evening I saw three rowdies, arm-in-arm, taking the whole of
the sidewalk, hustle a black man off it, giving him a blow, as they
passed, that sent him staggering into the middle of the street. As he
recovered himself he began to call out to, and threaten them. Perhaps he saw me stop, and thought I should support him, as I was
certainly inclined to: "Can't you find anything else to do than to be
knockin' quiet people round! You jus' come back here, will you?
Here, you! *don't care if you is white.* You jus' come back here, and
I'll teach you how to behave—knockin' people round!—don't care if
I does hab to go to der watch-house." They passed on without noticing him further, only laughing jeeringly—and he continued: "You
come back here, and I'll make you laugh; you is jus' three white
nigger cowards, dat's what *you* be."

I observe, in the newspapers, complaints of growing insolence
and insubordination among the negroes, arising, it is thought, from
too many privileges being permitted them by their masters, and
from too merciful administration of the police laws with regard to
them. Except in this instance, however, I have seen not the slightest
evidence of any independent manliness on the part of the negroes
towards the whites. As far as I have yet observed, they are treated
very kindly and even generously as servants, but their manner to
white people is invariably either sullen, jocose, or fawning.

The pronunciation and dialect of the negroes, here, is generally
much more idiomatic and peculiar than with us. As I write, I hear
a man shouting, slowly and deliberately, meaning to say *there:*
" *Dah! dah!* DAH!"

Among the people you see in the streets, full half, I should think,
are more or less of negro blood, and a very decent, civil people
these seem, in general, to be; more so than the labouring class of
whites, among which there are many very ruffianly-looking fellows.
There is a considerable population of foreign origin, generally of
the least valuable class; very dirty German Jews, especially, abound,
and their characteristic shops (with their characteristic smells, quite
as bad as in Cologne) are thickly set in the narrowest and meanest
streets, which seem to be otherwise inhabited mainly by negroes.

Immense waggons, drawn by six mules each, the teamster always riding on the back of the near-wheeler, are a characteristic feature of the streets. On the canal, a long, narrow, canoe-like boat, perhaps fifty feet long and six wide, and drawing but a foot or two of water, is nearly as common as the ordinary large boats, such as are used on our canals. They come out of some of the small, narrow, crooked streams, connected with the canals, in which a difficult navigation is effected by poling. They are loaded with tobacco, flour, and a great variety of raw country produce. The canal boatmen seem rude, insolent, and riotous, and every facility is evidently afforded them, at Richmond, for indulging their peculiar appetites and tastes. A great many low eating, and, I should think, drinking, shops are frequented chiefly by the negroes. Dancing and other amusements are carried on in these at night.

From reading the comments of Southern statesmen and newspapers on the crime and misery which sometimes result from the accumulation of poor and ignorant people, with no intelligent masters to take care of them, in our Northern towns, one might get the impression that Southern towns—especially those not demoralized by foreign commerce—were comparatively free from a low and licentious population. From what I have seen, however, I am led to think that there is at least as much vice, and of what we call rowdyism, in Richmond, as in any Northern town of its size.

Richmond.—Yesterday morning, during a cold, sleety storm, against which I was struggling, with my umbrella, to the post-office, I met a comfortably-dressed negro leading three others by a rope; the first was a middle-aged man; the second a girl of, perhaps, twenty; and the last a boy, considerably younger. The arms of all three were secured before them with hand-cuffs, and the rope by which they were led passed from one to another; being made fast at each pair of hand-cuffs. They were thinly clad, the girl especially so, having only an old ragged handkerchief around her neck, over a common calico dress, and another handkerchief twisted around her head. They were dripping wet, and icicles were forming, at the time, on the awning bars.

The boy looked most dolefully, and the girl was turning around, with a very angry face, and shouting, "O pshaw! Shut up!"

"What are they?" said I, to a white man, who had also stopped, for a moment, to look at them. "What's he going to do with them?"

"Come in a canal boat, I reckon: sent down here to be sold.—That ar's a likely gal."

Our ways lay together, and I asked further explanation. He informed me that the negro-dealers had confidential servants always in attendance, on the arrival of the railroad trains and canal packets, to take any negroes that might have come consigned to them, and bring them to their marts.

Nearly opposite the post-office was another singular group of negroes. They consisted of men and boys, and each carried a coarse, white blanket, drawn together at the corners so as to hold some articles; probably, extra clothes. They stood in a row, in lounging attitudes, and some of them, again, were quarrelling, or reproving one another. A villainous-looking white man stood in front of them. Presently, a stout, respectable man, dressed in black according to the custom, and without any overcoat or umbrella, but with a large, golden-headed walking-stick, came out of the door of an office, and, without saying a word, walked briskly up the street; the negroes immediately followed, in file; the other white man bringing up the rear. They were slaves that had been sent into the town to be hired out as servants or factory hands. The gentleman in black was, probably, the broker in the business.

Near the post-office, opposite a large livery and sale stable, I turned into a short, broad street, in which were a number of establishments, the signs on which indicated that they were occupied by "Slave Dealers," and that "Slaves, for Sale or to Hire," were to be found within them. They were much like Intelligence Offices, being large rooms partly occupied by ranges of forms, on which sat a few comfortably and neatly clad negroes, who appeared perfectly cheerful, each grinning obsequiously, but with a manifest interest or anxiety, when I fixed my eye on them for a moment.

In Chambers' Journal for October, 1853,[1] there is an account of the Richmond slave marts, and the manner of conducting business in them, to which I shall refer the reader, in lieu of any further narration of my own observations on this subject. (See Appendix B.) I did not myself happen to witness, during fourteen months that I spent in the Slave States, any sale of negroes by auction. This must

---

[1] William Chambers has published the article in a separate form, with some others, under the title of American Slavery and Colours. Mr. [Robert] Russell, of the [London] Times, has given a later case at Montgomery.

not be taken as an indication that negro auctions are not of frequent occurrence (I did not, so far as I now recollect, witness the sale of anything else, at auction, at the South). I saw negroes advertised to be sold at auction, very frequently.

The hotel at which I am staying, "The American," Milberger Smith, from New York, proprietor, is an excellent one. I have never, this side the Atlantic, had my comforts provided for better, in my private room, with so little annoyance from the servants. The chamber-servants are negroes, and are accomplished in their business; (the dining-room servants are Irish). A man and a woman attend together upon a few assigned rooms, in the hall adjoining which they are constantly in waiting; your bell is answered immediately, your orders are quickly and quietly followed, and your particular personal wants anticipated as much as possible, and provided for, as well as the usual offices performed, when you are out. The man becomes your servant while you are in your room; he asks, at night, when he comes to request your boots, at what time he shall come in the morning, and then, without being very exactly punctual, he comes quietly in, makes your fire, sets the boots before it, brushes and arranges your clothes, lays out your linen, arranges your dressing gear, asks if you want anything else of him before breakfast, opens the shutters, and goes off to the next room. I took occasion to speak well of him to my neighbour one day, that I might judge whether I was particularly favoured.

"Oh, yes," he said, "Henry was a very good boy, very—valuable servant—quite so—would be worth two thousand dollars, if he was a little younger—easy."

At dinner, a venerable looking man asked another—

"Niggers are going high now, aint they?"

"Yes, sir."

"What would you consider a fair price for a woman thirty years old, with a young-one two years old?"

"Depends altogether on her physical condition, you know.—Has she any other children?"

"*Yes; four.*"

"—Well—I reckon about seven to eight hundred."

"I bought one yesterday—gave six hundred and fifty."

"Well, sir, if she's tolerable likely, you did well."

This morning I visited a farm, situated on the bank of James River, near Richmond.

The labour upon it was entirely performed by slaves. I did not inquire their number, but I judged there were from twenty to forty. Their "quarters" lined the approach-road to the mansion, and were well-made and comfortable log cabins, about thirty feet long by twenty wide, and eight feet tall, with a high loft and shingle roof. Each divided in the middle, and having a brick chimney outside the wall at either end, was intended to be occupied by two families. There were square windows, closed by wooden ports, having a single pane of glass in the centre. The house-servants were neatly dressed, but the field-hands wore very coarse and ragged garments.

During the three hours, or more, in which I was in company with the proprietor, I do not think ten consecutive minutes passed uninterrupted by some of the slaves requiring his personal direction or assistance. He was even obliged, three times, to leave the dinner-table.

"You see," said he, smiling, as he came in the last time, "a farmer's life, in this country, is no sinecure." Then turning the conversation to slavery, he observed, in answer to a remark of mine, "I only wish your philanthropists would contrive some satisfactory plan to relieve us of it; the trouble and the responsibility of properly taking care of our negroes, you may judge, from what you see yourself here, is anything but enviable. But what can we do that is better? Our free negroes—and I believe it is the same at the North as it is here—are a miserable set of vagabonds, drunken, vicious, worse off, it is my honest opinion, than those who are retained in slavery. I am satisfied, too, that our slaves are better off, as they are, than the majority of your free labouring classes at the North."

I expressed my doubts.

"Well, they certainly are better off than the English agricultural labourers, or, I believe, those of any other Christian country. Free labour might be more profitable to us: I am inclined to think it would be. The slaves are excessively careless and wasteful, and, in various ways—which, without you lived among them, you could hardly be made to understand—subject us to very annoying losses.

"To make anything by farming, here, a man has got to live a hard life. You see how constantly I am called upon—and, often, it is about as bad at night as by day. Last night I did not sleep a wink till near morning; I am quite worn out with it, and my wife's health is failing. But I cannot rid myself of it."

I asked why he did not employ an overseer.

"Because I do not think it right to trust to such men as we have to use, if we use any, for overseers."

"Is the general character of overseers bad?"

"They are the curse of this country, sir; the worst men in the community. . . . But lately, I had another sort of fellow offer—a fellow like a dancing-master, with kid gloves, and wrist-bands turned up over his coat-sleeves, and all so nice, that I was almost ashamed to talk to him in my old coat and slouched hat. Half a bushel of recommendations he had with him, too. Well, he was not the man for me—not half the gentleman, with all his airs, that Ned here is"—(a black servant, who was bursting with suppressed laughter, behind his chair).

"Oh, they are interesting creatures, sir," he continued, "and, with all their faults, have many beautiful traits. I can't help being attached to them, and I am sure they love us." In his own case, at least, I did not doubt it; his manner towards them was paternal— familiar and kind; and they came to him like children who have been given some task, and constantly are wanting to be encouraged and guided, simply and confidently. At dinner, he frequently addressed the servant familiarly, and drew him into our conversation as if he were a family friend, better informed, on some local and domestic points, than himself.

I have been visiting a coal-pit: the majority of the mining labourers are slaves, and uncommonly athletic and fine-looking negroes; but a considerable number of white hands are also employed, and they occupy all the responsible posts. The slaves are, some of them, owned by the mining company; but the most are hired of their owners, at from $120 to $200 a year, the company boarding and clothing them. (I understood that it was customary to give them a certain allowance of money and let them find their own board.)

The white hands are mostly English or Welsh. One of them, with whom I conversed, told me that he had been here several years; he had previously lived some years at the North. He got better wages here than he earned at the North, but he was not contented, and did not intend to remain. On pressing him for the reason of his discontent, he said, after some hesitation, he would rather live where he could be more free; a man had to be too "discreet" here: if one happened to say anything that gave offence, they thought no more of drawing a pistol or a knife upon him, than they would of kicking a dog that was in their way. Not long since, a young English fellow came to the pit, and was put to work along with a gang of negroes. One morning, about a week afterwards, twenty or thirty men called on him, and told him that they would allow him fifteen minutes to get out of sight, and if they ever saw him in those parts again they would "give him hell." They were all armed, and there was nothing for the young fellow to do but to move "right off."

"What reason did they give him for it?"

"They did not give him any reason."

"But what had he done?"

"Why, I believe they thought he had been too free with the niggers; he wasn't used to them, you see, sir, and he talked to 'em free like, and they thought he'd make 'em think too much of themselves."

He said the slaves were very well fed, and well treated—not worked over hard. They were employed night and day, in relays.

The coal from these beds is of special value for gas manufacture, and is shipped, for that purpose, to all the large towns on the Atlantic sea-board, even to beyond Boston. It is delivered to shipping at Richmond, at fifteen cents a bushel: about thirty bushels go to a ton.

Petersburg.—The train was advertised to leave at 3.30 p.m. At that hour the cars were crowded with passengers, and the engineer, punctually at the minute, gave notice that he was at his post, by a long, loud whistle of the locomotive. Five minutes afterwards he gave us an impatient jerk; ten minutes afterwards we advanced three rods; twelve minutes afterwards, returned to first position: continued, "backing and filling," upon the bridge over the rapids of the James River, for half an hour. At precisely four o'clock, crossed the bridge and fairly started for Petersburg.

Ran twenty miles in exactly an hour and thirty minutes, (thirteen miles an hour; mail train, especially recommended by advertise-ment as "fast"). Brakes on three times, for cattle on the track; twenty minutes spent at way-stations. Flat rail. Locomotive built at Philadelphia. I am informed that most of those used on the road—perhaps all those of the *slow* trains—are made at Petersburg.

At one of the stoppages, smoke was to be seen issuing from the truck of a car. The conductor, on having his attention called to it, nodded his head sagely, took a morsel of tobacco, put his hands in his pocket, looked at the truck as if he would mesmerize it, spat upon it, and then stept upon the platform and shouted, "All right! Go ahead!" At the next stoppage, the smoking was furious; conductor bent himself over it with an evidently strong exercise of his will, but not succeeding to tranquillize the subject at all, he suddenly relinquished the attempt, and, deserting Mesmer for Preisnitz, shouted, "Ho! boy! bring me some water here." A negro soon brought a quart of water in a tin vessel.

"Hain't got no oil, Columbus?"

"No, sir."

"Hum—go ask Mr. Smith for some: this yer's a screaking so, I durstn't go on. You Scott! get some salt. And look here, some of you boys, get me some more water. D'ye hear?"

Salt, oil, and water, were crowded into the box, and, after five minutes' longer delay, we went on, the truck still smoking, and the water and oil boiling in the box, until we reached Petersburg. The heat was the result, I suppose, of a neglect of sufficient or timely oiling. While waiting, in a carriage, for the driver to get my baggage, I saw a negro oiling all the trucks of the train; as he proceeded from one to the other, he did not give himself the trouble to elevate the outlet of his oiler, so that a stream of oil, costing probably a dollar and a half a gallon, was poured out upon the ground the whole length of the train.

There were, in the train, two first-class passenger cars, and two freight cars. The latter were occupied by about forty negroes, most of them belonging to traders, who were sending them to the cotton States to be sold. Such kind of evidence of activity in the slave trade of Virginia is to be seen every day; but particulars and statistics of it are not to be obtained by a stranger here. Most gentlemen of character seem to have a special disinclination to converse on the subject; and it is denied, with feeling, that slaves are often reared, as is supposed by the Abolitionists, with the intention of selling them to the traders. It appears to me evident, however, from the manner in which I hear the traffic spoken of incidentally, that the cash value of a slave for sale, above the cost of raising it from infancy to the age at which it commands the highest price, is generally considered among the surest elements of a planter's wealth. Such a nigger is worth such a price, and such another is too old to learn to pick cotton, and such another will bring so much, when it has grown a little more, I have frequently heard people say, in the street, or the public-houses. That a slave woman is commonly esteemed least for her working qualities, most for those qualities which give value to a brood-mare is, also, constantly made apparent.[2]

By comparing the average decennial ratio of slave increase in all the States with the difference in the number of the actual slave-population of the slave-breeding States, as ascertained by the Census, it is apparent that the number of slaves exported to the cotton States is considerably more than twenty thousand a year.[3]

While calling on a gentleman occupying an honourable official position at Richmond, I noticed upon his table a copy of Professor Johnson's Agricultural Tour in the United States. Referring to a paragraph in it, where some statistics of the value of the slaves raised and annually exported from Virginia were given, I asked if he knew how these had been obtained, and whether they were authentic. "No," he replied, "I don't know anything about it; but if they are anything unfavourable to the institution of slavery, you may be sure they are false." This is but an illustration, in extreme, of the manner in which I find a desire to obtain more correct but *definite* information, on the subject of slavery, is usually met, by gentlemen otherwise of enlarged mind and generous qualities.

A gentleman, who was a member of the "Union Safety Committee" of New York, during the excitement which attended the discussion of the Fugitive Slave Act of 1850, told me that, as he was passing through Virginia this winter, a man entered the car in which he was seated, leading in a negro girl, whose manner and expression

[2] A slaveholder writing to me with regard to my cautious statements on this subject, made in the *Daily Times*, says:—"In the States of Maryland, Virginia, North Carolina, Kentucky, Tennessee, and Missouri, as much attention is paid to the breeding and growth of negroes as to that of horses and mules. Further South, we raise them both for use and for market. Planters command their girls and women (married or unmarried) to have children; and I have known a great many negro girls to be sold off, because they did not have children. A breeding woman is worth from one-sixth to one-fourth more than one that does not breed."

[3] Mr. Ellison, in his work, Slavery and Secession, gives the annual importation of negroes, for the ten years ending 1860, into seven of the Southern Slave States, from the Slave-breeding States, as 26.301.

of face indicated dread and grief. Thinking she was a criminal, he asked the man what she had done.

"Done? Nothing."

"What are you going to do with her?"

"I'm taking her down to Richmond, to be sold."

"Does she belong to you?"

"No; she belongs to ——; he raised her."

"Why does he sell her—has she done anything wrong?"

"Done anything? No: she's no fault, I reckon."

"Then, what does he want to sell her for?"

"Sell her for! Why shouldn't he sell her? He sells one or two every year; wants the money for 'em, I reckon."

The irritated tone and severe stare with which this was said, my friend took as a caution not to pursue his investigation.

A gentleman with whom I was conversing on the subject of the cost of slave labour, in answer to an inquiry—What proportion of all the stock of slaves of an old plantation might be reckoned upon to do full work?—answered, that he owned ninety-six negroes; of these, only thirty-five were field-hands, the rest being either too young or too old for hard work. He reckoned his whole force as only equal to twenty-one strong men, or "*prime* field-hands." But this proportion was somewhat smaller than usual, he added, "because his women were uncommonly good breeders; he did not suppose there was a lot of women anywhere that bred faster than his; he never heard of babies coming so fast as they did on his plantation; it was perfectly surprising; and every one of them, in his estimation, was worth two hundred dollars, as negroes were selling now, the moment it drew breath."

I asked what he thought might be the usual proportion of workers to slaves, supported on plantations, throughout the South. On the large cotton and sugar plantations of the more Southern States, it was very high, he replied; because their hands were nearly all bought and *picked for work;* he supposed, on these, it would be about one-half; but, on any old plantation, where the stock of slaves had been an inheritance, and none had been bought or sold, he thought the working force would rarely be more than one-third, at most, of the whole number.

This gentleman was out of health, and told me, with frankness, that such was the trouble and annoyance his negroes occasioned him—although he had an overseer—and so wearisome did he find the lonely life he led on his plantation, that he could not remain upon it; and as he knew everything would go to the dogs if he did not, he was seriously contemplating to sell out, retaining only his foster-mother and a body servant. He thought of taking them to Louisiana and Texas, for sale; but, if he should learn that there was much probability that Lower California would be made a Slave State, he supposed it would pay him to wait, as probably, if that should occur, he could take them there and sell them for twice as much as they would now bring in New Orleans. He knew very well, he said, that, as they were, raising corn and tobacco, they were paying nothing at all like a fair interest on their value.[4]

Some of his best hands he now rented out, to work at a furnace, and for the best of these he had been offered, for next year, two hundred dollars. He did not know whether he ought to let them go, though. They were worked hard, and had too much liberty, and were acquiring bad habits. They earned money by overwork, and spent it for whisky, and got a habit of roaming about and *taking care of themselves;* because when they were not at work in the furnace, nobody looked out for them.

I begin to suspect that the great trouble and anxiety of Southern gentlemen is:—How, without quite destroying the capabilities of the negro for any work at all, to prevent him from learning to take care of himself.

Petersburg, Dec. 28th.—It was early on a fine, mild, bright morning, like the pleasantest we ever have in March, that I alighted from a train of cars, at a country station. Besides the shanty that stood for a station-house, there was a small, comfortable farm-house on the right, and a country store on the left, and around them, perhaps, fifty acres of clear land, now much flooded with muddy water;—all framed in by thick pine wood.

A few negro children, staring as fixedly and posed as lifelessly as if they were really figures "carved in ebony," stood, lay, and lounged on the sunny side of the ranks of locomotive-firewood; a white man, smoking a cigar, looked out of the door of the store, and another,

---

[4] Mr. [Henry A.] Wise is reported to have stated, in his electioneering tour, when candidate for Governor, in 1855, that, if slavery were permitted in California, negroes would sell for $5,000 apiece.

chewing tobacco, leaned against a gate-post in front of the farm-house; I advanced to the latter, and asked him if I could hire a horse in the neighbourhood.

"How d'ye do, sir?" he replied, spitting and bowing with cere-mony; "I have some horses—none on 'em very good ones, though—rather hard riders; reckon, perhaps, they wouldn't suit you."

"Thank you; do you think I could find anything better about here?"

"Colonel Gillin, over here to the store, 's got a right nice saddle-horse, if he'll let you take her. I'll go over there with you, and see if he will. . . . Mornin', Colonel;—here's a gentleman that wants to go to Thomas W.'s: couldn't you let him have your saddle-horse?"

"How do you do, sir; I suppose you'd come back to-night?"

"That's my intention; but I might be detained till to-morrow, un-less it would be inconvenient to you to spare your horse."

"Well, yes, sir, I reckon you can have her;—Tom!—Tom!—*Tom!* Now, has that devilish nigger gone again? Tom! *Oh,* Tom! saddle the filly for this gentleman.—Have you ever been to Mr. W.'s, sir?"

"No, I have not."

"It isn't a very easy place for strangers to go to from here; but I reckon I can direct you, so you'll have no difficulty."

He accordingly began to direct me; but the way appeared so diffi-cult to find, I asked him to let me make a written memorandum, and, from this memorandum, I now repeat the directions he gave me.

"You take this road here—you'll see where it's most travelled, and it's easy enough to keep on it for about a mile; then there's a fork, and you take the right; pretty soon, you'll cross a creek and turn to the right—the creek's been up a good deal lately, and there's some big trees fallen along there, and if they ha'n't got them out of the way, you may have some difficulty in finding where the road is; but you keep bearing off to the right, where it's the most open [*i.e.,* the wood], and you'll see it again pretty soon. Then you go on, keeping along in the road—you'll see where folks have travelled before—for may be a quarter of a mile, and you'll find a cross road; you must take that to the left; pretty soon you'll pass two cabins; one of 'em's old and all fallen in, the other one's new, and there's a white man lives into it: you can't mistake it. About a hundred yards beyond it, there's a fork, and you take the left—it turns square off, and it's fenced for a good bit; keep along by the fence, and you can't miss it. It's right straight beyond that till you come to a school-house, there's a gate opposite to it, and off there there's a big house—but I don't reckon you'll see it neither, for the woods. But somewhere, about three hundred yards beyond the school-house, you'll find a little road running off to the left through an old field; you take that, and in less than half a mile you'll find a path going square off to the right; you take that, and keep on it till you pass a little cabin in the woods; ain't nobody lives there now: then it turns to the left, and when you come to a fence and a gate, you'll see a house there, that's Mr. George Rivers' plantation—it breaks in two, and you take the right, and when you come to the end of the fence, turn the corner—don't keep on, but turn there. Then it's straight, till you come to the creek again—there's a bridge there; don't go over the bridge, but turn to the left, and keep along nigh the creek, and pretty soon you'll see a meeting-house in the woods; you go to that, and you'll see a path bearing off to the right—it looks as if it was going right away from the creek, but you take it, and pretty soon it'll bring you to a saw-mill on the creek, up higher a piece; you just cross the creek there, and you'll find some people at the mill, and they'll put you right straight on the road to Mr. W.'s."

"How far is it all, sir?"

"I reckon it's about two hours' ride, when the roads are good, to the saw-mill. Mr. W.'s gate is only a mile or so beyond that, and then you've got another mile, or better, after you get to the gate, but you'll see some nigger-quarters—the niggers belong to Mr. W., and I reckon ther'll be some of 'em round, and they'll show you just where to go."

After reading over my memorandum, and finding it correct, and agreeing with him that I should pay two dollars a day for the mare, we walked out, and found her saddled and waiting for me.

I remarked that she was very good looking.

"Yes, sir; she ain't a bad filly; out of a mare that came of Lady Rackett by old Lord-knows-who, the best horse we ever had in this part of the country: I expect you have heard of him. Oh! she's maybe a little playful, but you'll find her a pleasant riding-horse."

The filly was just so pleasantly playful, and full of well-bred life, as to create a joyful, healthy, sympathetic, frolicsome heedlessness in her rider, and, in two hours, we had lost our way, and I was trying to work up a dead reckoning.

First, we had picked our way from the store down to the brook, through a deeply corrugated clay-road; then there was the swamp, with the fallen trees and thick underwood, beaten down and barked in the miry parts by waggons making a road for themselves, no traces of which road could we find in the harder, pebbly ground. At length, when we came to drier land, and among pine trees, we discovered a clear way cut through them, and a distinct road before us again; and this brought us soon to an old clearing, just beginning to be grown over with pines, in which was the old cabin of rotten logs, one or two of them falling out of rank on the door side, and the whole concern having a dangerous lurch to one corner, as if too much whisky had been drunk in it: then a more recent clearing, with a fenced field and another cabin, the residence of the white man we were told of, probably. No white people, however, were to be seen, but two negroes sat in the mouth of a wigwam, husking maize, and a couple of hungry hounds came bounding over the zigzag, gateless fence, as if they had agreed with each other that they would wait no longer for the return of their master, but would straightway pull down the first traveller that passed, and have something to eat before they were quite famished. They stopped short, however, when they had got within a good cart-whip's length of us, and contented themselves with dolefully youping as long as we continued in sight. We turned the corner, following some slight traces of a road, and shortly afterwards met a curious vehicular establishment, probably belonging to the master of the hounds. It consisted of an axle-tree and wheels, and a pair of shafts made of unbarked saplings, in which was harnessed, by attachments of raw hide and rope, a single small black ox. There was a bit, made of telegraph wire, in his mouth, by which he was guided, through the mediation of a pair of much-knotted rope reins, by a white man—a dignified sovereign, wearing a brimless crown—who sat upon a two-bushel sack (of meal, I trust, for the hounds' sake), balanced upon the axle-tree, and who saluted me with a frank "How are you?" as we came opposite each other.

Soon after this, we reached a small grove of much older and larger pines than we had seen before, with long and horizontally stretching branches, and duller and thinner foliage. In the middle of it was another log cabin, with a door in one of the gable ends, a stove pipe, half rusted away, protruding from the other, and, in the middle of one of the sides, a small square port-hole, closed by a wooden shutter. This must have been the school-house; but there were no children then about it, and no appearance of there having been any lately. Near it was a long string of fence, and a gate and lane, which gave entrance, probably, to a large plantation, though there was no cultivated land within sight of the road.

I could remember hardly anything after this, except a continuation of pine trees, big, little, and medium in size, and hogs, and a black, crooked, burnt sapling, that we had made believe was a snake springing at us and had jumped away from, and then we had gone on at a trot—it must have been some time ago, that—and then I was paying attentions to Jane (the filly's name was Jane Gillan), and finally my thoughts had gone wool-gathering, and we must have travelled some miles out of our way and—"Never mind," said Jane, lifting her head, and turning in the direction we had been going, "I don't think it's any great matter if we are lost; such a fine day—so long since I've been out; if you don't care, I'd just as lief be lost as not; let's go on and see what we shall come to."

"Very well, my beauty; you know the country better than I do. If you'll risk your dinner, I'm quite ready to go anywhere you choose to take me. It's quite certain we have not passed any meeting-house, or creek, or saw-mill, or negro-quarters, and, as we have been two hours on the road, it's evident we are not going straight to Mr. W.'s; I must see what we do pass after this," and I stood up in the stirrups as we walked on, to see what the country around us was like.

"Old fields"—a coarse, yellow, sandy soil, bearing scarcely anything but pine trees and broom-sedge. In some places, for acres, the pines would not be above five feet high—that was land that had been in cultivation, used up and "turned out," not more than six or eight years before; then there were patches of every age; sometimes the trees were a hundred feet high. At long intervals, there were fields in which the pine was just beginning to spring in beautiful green plumes from the ground, and was yet hardly noticeable among the dead brown grass and sassafras bushes and blackberry vines, which nature first sends to hide the nakedness of the impoverished earth.

Of living creatures, for miles, not one was to be seen (not even a crow or a snow-bird), except hogs. These—long, lank, bony, snake-headed, hairy, wild beasts—would come dashing across our path, in packs of from three to a dozen, with short, hasty grunts, almost always at a gallop, and looking neither to right nor left, as if they were in pursuit of a fox, and were quite certain to catch him in the next hundred yards; or droves of little pigs would rise up suddenly in the sedge, and scamper off squealing into cover, while their heroic mothers would turn round and make a stand, looking fiercely at us, as if they were quite ready to fight if we advanced any further, but always breaking, as we came near, with a loud *booschl*

Once I saw a house, across a large, new old field, but it was far off, and there was no distinct path leading towards it out of the waggon-track we were following; so we did not go to it, but continued walking steadily on through the old fields and pine woods for more than an hour longer.

We then arrived at a grove of tall oak-trees, in the midst of which ran a brook, giving motion to a small grist-mill. Back of the mill were two log cabins, and near these a number of negroes, in holiday clothes, were standing in groups among the trees. When we stopped one of them came towards us. He wore a battered old hat, stiffly starched shirt collar, cutting his ears; a red cravat, and an old black dress coat, threadbare and a little ragged, but adorned with new brass buttons. He knew Mr. Thomas W., certainly he did, and he reckoned I had come about four miles (he did not know but it might be eight, if I thought so) off the road I had been directed to follow. But that was of no consequence, because he could show me where to go by a straight road—a cross cut—from here, that would make it just as quick for me as if I had gone the way I had intended.

"How far is it from here?" I asked.

"Oh, 'taint far, sar."

"How far do you think?"

"Well, massa, I spec—I spec"—(looking at my horse) "I spec, massa, ef you goes de way, sar, dat I show you, sar, I reckon it'll take you—"

"How far is it—how many miles?"

"How many miles, sar? ha! masser, I don 'zactly reckon I ken tell ou—not 'cisely, sar—how many miles it is, not 'zactly, 'cisely, sar."

"How is that?—you don't what?"

"I don't 'zactly reckon I can give you de drection excise about de miles, sar."

"Oh! but how many miles do you think it is; is it two miles?"

"Yes, sar; as de roads is now, I tink it is just about two miles. Dey's long ones, dough, I reckon."

"Long ones? you think it's more than two miles, don't you, then?"

"Yes, sar, I reckon it's four or five miles."

"Four or five! four or five long ones or short ones, do you mean?"

"I don 'zactly know, sar, wedder dey is short ones or long ones, sar, but I reckon you find em middlin' long; I spec you'll be about two hours 'fore you be done gone all the way to Mass W.'s."

He walked on with us a few rods upon a narrow path, until we came to a crossing of the stream; pointing to where it continued on the other side, he assured me that it went right straight to Mr. W.'s plantation. "You juss keep de straight road, massar," he repeated several times, "and it'll take you right dar, sar."

He had been grinning and bowing, and constantly touching his hat, or holding it in his hand during our conversation, which I understood to mean, that he would thank me for a dime. I gave it to him, upon which he repeated his contortions and his form of direction— "Keep de straight road." I rode through the brook, and he called out again—"You keep dat road right straight, and it'll take you right straight dar." I rode up the bank and entered the oak wood, and still again heard him enjoining me to "keep dat road right straight."

Within less than a quarter of a mile there was a fork in the road to the left, which seemed a good deal more travelled than the straight one; nevertheless I kept the latter, and was soon well satisfied that I had done so. It presently led me up a slope out of the oak woods into a dark evergreen forest; and though it was a mere bridle-path, it must have existed, I thought, before the trees began to grow, for it was free of stumps, and smooth and clean as a garden walk, and the pines grew thickly up, about four feet apart, on each side of it, their branches meeting, just clear of my head, and making a dense shade. There was an agreeable, slightly balsamic odour in the air; the path was covered with a deep, elastic mat of pine leaves, so that our footsteps could hardly be heard; and for a time we greatly enjoyed going along at a lazy, pacing walk of Jane's. It was noonday, and had been rather warmer than was quite agreeable on the open road, and I took my hat off, and let the living pine leaves brush my hair. But, after a while, I felt slightly chilly; and when Jane, at the same time, gave a little sympathizing caper, I bent my head down, that the limbs might not hit me, until it nearly rested on her neck, dropped my hands and pressed my knees tightly against her. Away we bounded!

A glorious gallop Jane had inherited from her noble grandfather!

Out of the cool dark-green alley, at last, and soon, with a more cautious step, down a steep, stony declivity, set with deciduous trees—beech, ash, oak, gum—"gum," beloved of the "minstrels." A brawling shallow brook at the bottom, into which our path descended, though on the opposite shore was a steep high bank, faced by an impenetrable brake of bush and brier.

Have we been following a path only leading to a watering-place, then? I see no continuance of it. Jane does not hesitate at all; but, as if it was the commonest thing here to take advantage of nature's engineering in this way, walking into the water, turns her head up stream.

For more than a mile we continued following up the brook, which was all the time walled in by insurmountable banks, overhung by large trees. Sometimes it swept strongly through a deep channel, contracted by boulders; sometimes purled and tinkled over a pebbly slope; and sometimes stood in broad, silent pools, around the edges of which remained a skirt of ice, held there by bushes and long broken water-grasses.

At length came pine woods again. Jane was now for leaving the brook. I let her have her own way, and she soon found a beaten track in the woods. It certainly was not the "straight road" we had been directed to follow; but its course was less crooked than that of the brook, and after some time it led us out into a more open country, with young pines and enclosed fields. Eventually we came to a gate and lane, which we followed till we came to another cross-lane leading straight to a farm-house.

As soon as we turned into the cross-lane, half a dozen little negro boys and girls were seen running toward the house, to give alarm. We passed a stable, with a cattle-pen by its side, opposite which was a vegetable garden, enclosed with split palings; then across a running stream of water; then by a small cabin on the right; and a corn-crib and large pen, with a number of fatting hogs in it, on the left; then into a large, irregular yard, in the midst of which was the farm-house, before which were now collected three white children, six black ones, two negro women, and an old lady wearing spectacles.

"How dy do, sir?" said the old lady, as we reined up, lifted our hat, and put our black foot foremost.

"Thank you, madam, quite well; but I have lost my way to Mr. Thomas W.'s, and will trouble you to tell me how to go from here to get to his house."

By this time a black man came cautiously walking in from the field back of the house, bringing an axe; a woman, who had been washing clothes in the brook, left her work and came up on the other side, and two more girls climbed upon a great heap of logs that had been thrown upon the ground, near the porch, for fuel. The swine were making a great noise in their pen, as if feeding-time had come; and a flock of turkeys were gobbling so incessantly and loudly that I was not heard. The old lady ordered the turkeys to be driven away, but nobody stirred to do it, and I rode nearer and repeated my request. No better success. "Can't you shew away them turkeys?" she asked again; but nobody "shewed." A third time I endeavoured to make myself understood. "Will you please direct me how to go to Mr. W.'s?"

"No, sir—not here."

"Excuse me—I asked if you would direct me to Mr. W.'s."

"If some of you niggers don't shew them turkeys, I'll have you all whipped as soon as your mass John comes home," exclaimed the old lady, now quite excited. The man with the axe, without moving towards them at all, picked up a billet of wood, and threw it at the biggest cock-turkey, who immediately collapsed; and the whole flock scattered, chased by the two girls who had been on the log-heap.

"An't dat Colonel Gillin's mare, master?" asked the black man, coming up on my left.

"You want to go to Thomas W.'s?" asked the old lady.

"Yes, madam."

"It's a good many years since I have been to Thomas W.'s, and I reckon I can't tell you how to go there now."

"If master'll go over to Missy Abler's, I reckon dey ken tell 'em dah, sar."

"And how shall I go to Mrs. Abler's?"

"You want to go to Missy Abler's; you take dat path right over 'yond dem bars, dar, by de hog-pen, dat runs along by dat fence into de woods, and dat'll take you right straight dar."

"Is you come from Colonel Gillin's, massa?" asked the wash-woman.

"Yes."

"Did you see a black man dar, dey calls Tom, sar?"

"Yes."

"Tom's my husband, massa; if you's gwine back dah, wish you'd tell um, ef you please, sar, dat I wants to see him partiklar; will ou, massa?"

"Yes."

"Tank you, massa."

I bowed to the old lady, and, in turning to ride off, saw two other negro boys who had come out of the woods, and were now leaning over the fence, and staring at us, as if I were a giant and Jane was a dragoness.

We trotted away, found the path, and in course of a mile had our choice of at least twenty forks to go "straight to Mrs. Abler's." At length, cleared land again, fences, stubble-fields and a lane, that took us to a little cabin, which fronted, much to my surprise, upon a broad and well-travelled road. Over the door of the cabin was a sign, done in black, upon a hogshead stave, showing that it was a "GROSERY," which, in Virginia, means the same thing as in Ireland— a dram-shop.

I hung the bridle over a rack before the door, and walked in. At one end of the interior was a range of shelves, on which were two decanters, some dirty tumblers, a box of crackers, a canister, and several packages in paper; under the shelves a table and a barrel. At the other end of the room was a fire-place; near this, a chest, and another range of shelves, on which stood plates and cooking uten-sils: between these and the grocery end were a bed and a spinning-wheel. Near the spinning-wheel sat a tall, bony, sickly, sullen young woman, nursing a languishing infant. The faculty would not have discouraged either of them from trying hydropathic practice. In a corner of the fire-place sat a man, smoking a pipe. He rose, as I entered, walked across to the grocery-shelves, turned a chair round at the table, and asked me to take a seat. I excused myself, and re-quested him to direct me to Mr. W.'s. He had heard of such a man living somewhere about there, but he did not know where. He repeated this, with an oath, when I declined to "take" anything, and added, that he had not lived here long, and he was sorry he had ever come here. It was the worst job, for himself, ever he did, when he came here, though all he wanted was to just get a living.

I rode on till I came to another house, a very pleasant little house, with a steep, gabled roof, curving at the bottom, and extending over a little gallery, which was entered, by steps, from the road; back of it were stables and negro-cabins, and by its side was a small garden, and beyond that a peach-orchard. As I approached it, a well-dressed young man, with an intelligent and pleasant face, came out into the gallery. I asked him if he could direct me to Mr. W.'s. "Thomas W.'s?" he inquired.

"Yes, sir."

"You are not going in the right direction to go to Mr. W.'s. The shortest way you can take to go there is, to go right back to the Court House."

I told him I had just come out of the lane by the grocery on to the road. "Ah! well, I'll tell you; you had better turn round, and keep right straight upon this road till you get to the Court House, and anybody can tell you, there, how to go."

"How far is it, sir?"

"To the Court House?—not above a mile."

"And to Mr. W.'s?"

"To Mr. W.'s, I should think it was as much as ten miles, and long ones, too."

I rode to the Court House, which was a plain brick building in the centre of a small square, around which there were twenty or thirty houses, two of them being occupied as stores, one as a saddler's shop, one had the sign of "Law Office" upon it; one was a jail; two were occupied by physicians, one other looked as if it might be a meeting-house or school-house, or the shop of any mechanic needing much light for his work, and two were "Hotels." At one of these we stopped to dine; Jane had "corn and fodder" (they had no oats or hay in the stable), and I had ham and eggs (they had no fresh meat in the house). I had several other things, however, that were very good, besides the company of the landlady, who sat alone with me, at the table, in a long, dining hall, and was very pretty, amiable, and talkative.

In a course of apologies, which came in the place of soup, she gave me the clue to the assemblage of negroes I had seen at the mill. It was Christmas week; all the servants thought they must go, for at least one day, to have a frolic, and to-day (as luck would have it, when I was coming,) her cook was off with some others; she did not suppose they'd be back till to-morrow, and then, likely as not, they'd be drunk. She did not think this custom, of letting servants go so, at Christmas, was a good one; niggers were not fit to be let to take care of themselves, anyhow. It was very bad for them, and she didn't think it was *right*. Providence had put the servants into our hands to be looked out for, and she didn't believe it was intended they should be let to do all sorts of wickedness, even if Christmas did come but once a year. She wished, for her part, it did not come but once in ten years.

(The negroes, who were husking maize near the cabin where the white man lived, were, no doubt, slaves, who had hired themselves out by the day, during the holiday-week, to earn a little money on their own account.)

In regard to the size of the dining-hall, and the extent of sheds in the stable-yard, the landlady told me that though at other times they very often did not have a single guest in a day, at "Court time" they always had more than they could comfortably accommodate. I judged, also, from her manners and the general appearance of the house, as well as from the charges, that, at such times, the company might be of a rather respectable character. The appearance of the other public-house indicated that it expected a less select patronage.

When I left, my direction was to keep on the main road until I came to a fork, about four miles distant, then take the left, and keep *the best-travelled road,* until I came to a certain house, which was so described that I should know it, where I was advised to ask further directions.

The sky was now clouding over; it was growing cold; and we went on, as fast as we conveniently could, until we reached the fork in the road. The direction to keep the best-travelled road, was unpleasantly prominent in my mind; it was near sunset, I reflected, and however jolly it might be at twelve o'clock at noon, it would be quite another thing to be knocking about among those fierce hogs in the pine-forest, if I should be lost, at twelve o'clock at night. Besides, as the landlady said about her negroes, I did not think it was right to expose Jane to this danger, unnecessarily. A little beyond the fork, there was a large, gray, old house, with a grove of tall poplars before it; a respectable, country-gentleman-of-the-old-school look it had.—These old Virginians are proverbially hospitable.—It's rather impudent; but I hate to go back to the Court House, and I am—I will ride on, and look it in the face, at any rate.

Zigzag fences up to a large, square yard, growing full of Lombardy poplar sprouts, from the roots of eight or ten old trees, which were planted some fifty years ago, I suppose, in a double row, on two sides of the house. At the further end of this yard, beyond the house, a gate opened on the road, and out of this was just then coming a black man.

I inquired of him if there was a house, near by, at which I could get accommodation for the night. Reckoned his master'd take me in, if I'd ask him. Where was his master? In the house: I could go right in here (at a place where a panel of the paling had fallen over) and see him if I wanted to. I asked him to hold my horse, and went in.

It was a simple two-story house, very much like those built by the wealthier class of people in New England villages, from fifty to a hundred years ago, except that the chimneys were carried up outside the walls. There was a porch at the front door, and a small wing at one end, in the rear: from this wing to the other end extended a broad gallery.

A dog had been barking at me after I had dismounted; and just as I reached the steps of the gallery, a vigorous, middle-aged man, with a rather sullen and suspicious expression of face, came out without any coat on, to see what had excited him.

Doubting if he were the master of the house, I told him that I had come in to inquire if it would be convenient to allow me to spend the night with them. He asked where I came from, whither I was going, and various other questions, until I had given him an epitome of my day's wanderings and adventures; at the conclusion of which he walked to the end of the gallery to look at my horse; then, without giving me any answer, but muttering indistinctly something about servants, walked into the house, shutting the door behind him!

Well, thought I, this is not overwhelmingly hospitable. What can it mean?

While I was considering whether he expected me to go without any further talk—his curiosity being, I judged, satisfied—he came out again, and said, "Reckon you can stay, sir, if you'll take what we'll give you." (The good man had been in to consult his wife.) I replied that I would do so thankfully, and hoped they would not give themselves any unnecessary trouble, or alter their usual family arrangements. I was then invited to come in, but I preferred to see my horse taken care of first. My host called for "Sam," two or three times, and then said he reckoned all his "people" had gone off, and he would attend to my horse himself. I offered to assist him, and we walked out to the gate, where the negro, not being inclined to wait for my return, had left Jane fastened to a post. Our host conducted us to an old square log-cabin which had formerly been used for curing tobacco, there being no room for Jane, he said, in the stables proper.

The floor of the tobacco-house was covered with lumber, old ploughs, scythes and cradles, a part of which had to be removed to make room for the filly to stand. She was then induced, with some difficulty, to enter it through a low, square doorway; saddle and bridle were removed, and she was fastened in a corner by a piece of old plough-line. We then went to a fodder-stack, and pulled out from it several small bundles of maize leaves. Additional feed and water were promised when "some of the niggers" came in; and, after righting up an old door that had fallen from one hinge, and setting a rail against it to keep it in its place, we returned to the house.

My host (whom I will call Mr. Newman) observed that his buildings and fences were a good deal out of order. He had owned the place but a few years, and had not had time to make much improvement about the house yet.

Entering the mansion, he took me to a large room on the first floor, gave me a chair, went out and soon returned (now wearing a coat) with two negro girls, one bringing wood and the other some flaming brands. A fire was made with a great deal of trouble, scolding of the girls, bringing in more brands, and blowing with the mouth. When the room had been suffocatingly filled with smoke, and at length a strong bright blaze swept steadily up the chimney, Mr. Newman again went out with the girls, and I was left alone for nearly an hour, with one interruption, when he came in and threw some more wood upon the fire, and said he hoped I would make myself comfortable.

It was a square room, with a door from the hall on one side, and two windows on each of the other sides. The lower part of the walls was wainscoted, and the upper part, with the ceiling, plastered and whitewashed. The fire-place and mantel-piece were somewhat carved, and were painted black; all the wood-work lead colour. Blue paper curtains covered the windows; the floor was uncarpeted, and the only furniture in the room was some strong plain chairs, painted yellow, and a Connecticut clock, which did not run. The house had evidently been built for a family of some wealth, and, after having been deserted by them, had been bought at a bargain by the present resident, who either had not the capital or the inclination to furnish and occupy it appropriately.

When my entertainer called again, he merely opened the door and said, "Come! get something to eat!" I followed him out into the gallery, and thence through a door at its end into a room in the wing—a family room, and a very comfortable homely room. A bountifully spread supper-table stood in the centre, at which was sitting a very neat, pretty little woman, of as silent habits as her husband, but neither bashful nor morose. A very nice little girl sat at her right side, and a peevish, ill-behaved, whining glutton of a boy at her left. I was requested to be seated adjoining the little girl, and the master of the house sat opposite me. The fourth side of the table was unoccupied, though a plate and chair were placed there, as if some one else had been expected.

The two negro girls waited at table, and a negro boy was in the room, who, when I asked for a glass of water, was sent to get it. An old negro woman also frequently came in from the kitchen, with hot biscuit and corn-cake. There was fried fowl, and fried bacon and eggs, and cold ham; there were preserved peaches, and preserved quinces and grapes; there was hot wheaten biscuit, and hot short-cake, and hot corn-cake, and hot griddle cakes, soaked in butter; there was coffee, and there was milk, sour or sweet, whichever I preferred to drink. I really ate more than I wanted, and extolled the corn-cake and the peach preserve, and asked how they were made; but I evidently disappointed my pretty hostess, who said she was afraid there wasn't anything that suited me,—she feared there wasn't anything on the table I could eat; and she was sorry I couldn't make out a supper. And this was about all she would say. I tried to get a conversation started, but could obtain little more than very laconic answers to my questions.

Except from the little girl at my side, whose confidence I gained by taking an opportunity, when her mother was engaged with young Hopeful t'other side the coffee-pot, to give her a great deal of quince and grape, and by several times pouring molasses very freely on her cakes and bacon; and finally by feeding Pink out of my hand. (Hopeful had done this first, and then kicked him away, when he came round to Martha and me.) She told me her name, and that she had got a kitten, and that she hated Pink; and that she went to a Sunday-school at the Court House, and that she was going to go to an every-day school next winter—she wasn't big enough to walk so far now, but she would be then. But Billy said he didn't mean to go, because he didn't like to, though Billy was bigger nor she was, a heap. She reckoned when Billy saw Wash. Baker going past every day, and heard how much fun he had every day with the other boys at the school, he would want to go too, wouldn't he? etc. etc. When supper was ended, I set back my chair to the wall, and took her on my knee; but after she had been told twice not to trouble the gentleman, and I had testified that she didn't do it, and after several mild hints that I would perhaps find it pleasanter in the sitting-room—(the chairs in the supper-room were the easiest, being country-made, low, and seated with undressed calf-skin), she was called to, out of the kitchen, and Mr. Newman said—going to the door and opening it for me—"Reckon you'd better walk into the sittin'-room, sir."

I walked out at this, and said I would go and look at the filly. Mr. Newman called "Sam" again, and Sam, having at that moment arrived at the kitchen door, was ordered to go and take care of this gentleman's horse. I followed Sam to the tobacco-house, and gave him to know that he would be properly remembered for any attentions he could give to Jane. He watered her, and brought her a large supply of oats in straw, and some maize on the cob; but he could get no litter, and declared there was no straw on the plantation, though the next morning I saw a large quantity in a heap (not a stack), at a little greater distance than he was willing to go for it, I suppose, at a barn on the opposite side of the road. Having seen her rubbed clean and apparently well contented with her quarters and her supper, I bade her good-night, and returned to the house.

I did not venture again into the supper-room, but went to the sitting-room, where I found Miss Martha Ann and her kitten; I was having a good time with her, when her father came in and told her she was "troubling the gentleman." I denied it, and he took a seat by the fire with us, and I soon succeeded in drawing him into a conversation on farming, and the differences in our methods of work at the North and those he was accustomed to.

I learned that there were no white labouring men here who hired themselves out by the month. The poor white people that had to labour for their living, never would work steadily at any employment. "They generally followed boating"—hiring as hands on the bateaus that navigate the small streams and canals, but never for a longer term at once than a single trip of a boat, whether that might be long or short. At the end of the trip they were paid by the day. Their wages were from fifty cents to a dollar, varying with the demand and individual capacities. They hardly ever worked on farms except in harvest, when they usually received a dollar a day, sometimes more. In harvest-time, most of the rural mechanics closed their shops and hired out to the farmers at a dollar a day, which would indicate that their ordinary earnings are considerably less than this. At other than harvest-time, the poor white people, who had no trade, would sometimes work for the farmers by the job; not often any regular agricultural labour, but at getting rails or shingles, or clearing land.

He did not know that they were particular about working with negroes, but no white man would ever do certain kinds of work (such as taking care of cattle, or getting water or wood to be used in the house); and if you should ask a white man you had hired, to do such things, he would get mad and tell you he wasn't a nigger. Poor white girls never hired out to do servants' work, but they would come and help another white woman about her sewing and quilting, and take wages for it. But these girls were not very respectable generally, and it was not agreeable to have them in your house, though there were some very respectable ladies that would go out to sew. Farmers depended almost entirely upon their negroes; it was only when they were hard pushed by their crops, that they ever got white hands to help them.

Negroes had commanded such high wages lately, to work on railroads and in tobacco-factories, that farmers were tempted to hire out too many of their people, and to undertake to do too much work with those they retained; and thus they were often driven to employ white men, and to give them very high wages by the day, when they found themselves getting much behind-hand with their crops. He had been driven very hard in this way this last season; he had been so unfortunate as to lose one of his best women, who died in child-bed just before harvest. The loss of the woman and her child, for the child had died also, just at that time, came very hard upon him. He would not have taken a thousand dollars of any man's money for them. He had had to hire white men to help him, but they were poor sticks, and would be half the time drunk, and you never know what to depend upon with them. One fellow that he had hired, who had agreed to work for him all through harvest, got him to pay him some wages in advance (he said it was to buy him some clothes with, so that he could go to meeting on Sunday, at the Court House), and went off the next day, right in the middle of harvest, and he had never seen him since. He had heard of him—he was on a boat— but he didn't reckon he should ever get his money again.

Of course, he did not see how white labourers were ever going to come into competition with negroes here, at all. You never could depend on white men, and you couldn't *drive* them any; they wouldn't stand it. Slaves were the only reliable labourers—you could command them and make them do what was right.

From the manner in which he talked of the white labouring people, it was evident that, although he placed them in some sort on an equality with himself, and that in his intercourse with them he wouldn't think of asserting for himself any superior dignity, or even feel himself to be patronizing them in not doing so, yet he, all the time, recognized them as a distinct and a rather despicable class, and wanted to have as little to do with them as he conveniently could.

I have been once or twice told that the poor white people, meaning those, I suppose, who bring nothing to market to exchange for money but their labour, although they may own a cabin and a little furniture, and cultivate land enough to supply themselves with (maize) bread, are worse off in almost all respects than the slaves. They are said to be extremely ignorant and immoral, as well as indolent and unambitious. That their condition is not so unfortunate by any means as that of negroes, however, is most obvious, since from among them, men sometimes elevate themselves to positions and habits of usefulness, and respectability. They are said to "corrupt" the negroes, and to encourage them to steal, or to work for them at night and on Sundays, and to pay them with liquor, and also to constantly associate licentiously with them. They seem, nevertheless, more than any other portion of the community, to hate and despise the negroes.

In the midst of our conversation, one of the black girls had come into the room and stood still with her head dropped forward, staring at me from under her brows, without saying a word. When she had waited, in this way, perhaps two minutes, her master turned to her and asked what she wanted.

"Miss Matty says Marta Ann go to bed now."

But Martha Ann refused to budge; after being told once or twice by her father to go with Rose, she came to me and lifted up her hands, I supposed to kiss me and go, but when I reached down, she took hold of my shoulders and climbed up on to my knees. Her father seemed to take no notice of this proceeding, but continued talking about guano; Rose went to a corner of the fire-place, dropped down upon the floor, and presently was asleep, leaning her head against the wall. In about half an hour the other negro girl came to the door, when Mr. Newman abruptly called out, "Girl! take that child to bed!" and immediately got up himself and walked out. Rose roused herself, and lifted Martha Ann out of my arms, and carried her off fast asleep. Mr. Newman returned holding a small candle, and, without entering the room, stood at the door and said, "I'll show you your bed if you are ready, sir." As he evidently meant, "I am ready to show you to bed if you will not refuse to go," I followed him up stairs.

Into a large room, again, with six windows, with a fire-place, in which a few brands were smoking, with some wool spread thinly upon the floor in a corner; with a dozen small bundles of tobacco leaves; with a lady's saddle; with a deep feather-bed, covered with a bright patch-work quilt, on a maple bedstead, and without a single item of any other furniture whatever. Mr. Newman asked if I wanted the candle to undress by; I said yes, if he pleased, and waited a moment for him to set it down: as he did not do so, I walked towards him, lifting my hand to take it. "No—I'll hold it," said he, and I then perceived that he had no candlestick, but held the lean little dip in his hand: I remembered also that no candle had been brought into the "sitting-room," and that while we were at supper only one candle had stood upon the table, which had been immediately extinguished when we rose, the room being lighted only from the fire.

I very quickly undressed and hung my clothes upon a bedpost: Mr. Newman looked on in silence until I had got into bed, when, with an abrupt "Good-night, sir," he went out and shut the door.

It was not until after I had consulted Sam the next morning that I ventured to consider that my entertainment might be taken as a mere business transaction, and not as "genuine planter's hospitality," though this had become rather a ridiculous view of it, after a repetition of the supper, in all respects, had been eaten for breakfast, with equal moroseness on the part of my host and equal quietness on the part of his kind-looking little wife. I was, nevertheless, amused at the promptness with which he replied to my rather hesitating inquiry—what I might pay him for the trouble I had given him—"I reckon a dollar and a quarter will be right, sir."

I have described, perhaps with tedious prolixity, what adventures befell me, and what scenes I passed through in my first day's random riding, for the purpose of giving an idea of the uncultivated and unimproved—rather, sadly worn and misused—condition of some parts, and I judge, of a very large part, of all Eastern Virginia, and of the isolated, lonely, and dissociable aspect of the dwelling-places of a large part of the people. I subsequently rode for three weeks in Eastern and Central Virginia, the country differing not very greatly in its characteristics from that here described.

Much the same general characteristics pervade the Slave States, everywhere, except in certain rich regions, or on the banks of some rivers, or in the vicinity of some great routes of travel and transportation, which have occasioned closer settlement or stimulated public spirit. For hours and hours one has to ride through the unlimited, continual, all-shadowing, all-embracing forest, following roads, in the making of which no more labour has been given than was necessary to remove the timber which would obstruct the passage of waggons; and even for days and days he may sometimes travel, and see never two dwellings of mankind within sight of each other; only, at long distances, often several miles asunder, these isolated plantation patriarchates. If a traveller leaves the main road to go any distance, it is not to be imagined how difficult it is for him to find his way from one house to any other in particular; his only safety is in the fact that, unless there are mountains or swamps in the way, he is not likely to go many miles upon any waggon or horse track without coming to some white man's habitation.

The country passed through, in the early part of my second day's ride, was very similar in general characteristics to that I have already described; only that a rather larger portion of it was cleared, and plantations were more frequent. About eleven o'clock I crossed a bridge and came to the meeting-house I had been expecting to reach by that hour the previous day. It was in the midst of the woods, and the small clearing around it was still dotted with the stumps of the trees out of whose trunks it had been built; for it was a log structure. In one end there was a single square port, closed by a sliding shutter; in the other end were two doors, both standing open. In front of the doors, a rude scaffolding had been made of poles and saplings, extending out twenty feet from the wall of the house, and this had been covered with boughs of trees, the leaves now withered; a few benches, made of split trunks of trees slightly hewn with the axe, were arranged under this arbour, as if the religious service was sometimes conducted on the outside in preference to the interior of the edifice. Looking in, I saw that a gallery or loft extended from over the doors, across about one-third the length of the house, access to which was had by a ladder. At the opposite end was a square unpainted pulpit, and on the floor were rows of rude benches. The house was sufficiently lighted by crevices between the upper logs.

Half an hour after this I arrived at the negro-quarters—a little hamlet of ten or twelve small and dilapidated cabins. Just beyond them was a plain farm-gate, at which several negroes were standing: one of them, a well-made man, with an intelligent countenance and prompt manner, directed me how to find my way to his owner's house. It was still nearly a mile distant; and yet, until I arrived in its immediate vicinity, I saw no cultivated field, and but one clearing. In the edge of this clearing, a number of negroes, male and female, lay stretched out upon the ground near a small smoking charcoal pit. Their master afterwards informed me that they were burning charcoal for the plantation blacksmith, using the time allowed them for holidays—from Christmas to New Year's Day—to earn a little money for themselves in this way. He paid them by the bushel for it. When I said that I supposed he allowed them to take what wood they chose for this purpose, he replied that he had five hundred acres covered with wood, which he would be very glad to have any one burn, or clear off in any way.

Mr. W.'s house was an old family mansion, which he had himself remodelled "in the Grecian style," and furnished with a large wooden portico. An oak forest had originally occupied the ground where it stood; but this having been cleared and the soil worn out in cultivation by the previous proprietors, pine woods now surrounded it in every direction, a square of a few acres only being kept clear immediately about it. A number of the old oaks still stood in the rear of the house, and, until Mr. W. commenced "his improvements," there had been some in its front. But as he deemed these to have an aspect of negligence and rudeness, not quite proper to be associated with a fine house, he had cut them away, and substituted formal rows of miserable little ailanthus trees. I could not believe my ears till this explanation had been twice repeated to me.

On three sides of the outer part of the cleared square, which was called "the lawn," but which was no more like a lawn than it was like a sea-beach, there was a row of negro-cabins, stables, tobacco-houses, and other offices, all built of rough logs.

Mr. W. was one of the few large planters of his vicinity who still made the culture of tobacco their principal business. He said there was a general prejudice against tobacco, in all the tide-water region of the State, because it was through the culture of tobacco that the once fertile soils had been impoverished; but he did not believe that, at the present value of negroes, their labour could be applied to the culture of grain, with any profit, except under peculiarly favourable circumstances. Possibly, the use of guano might make wheat a paying crop, but he still doubted. He had not used it, himself. Tobacco required fresh land, and was rapidly exhausting, but it returned more money, for the labour used upon it, than anything else; enough more, in his opinion, to pay for the wearing out of the land. If he was well paid for it, he did not know why he should not wear out his land.

His tobacco-fields were nearly all in a distant and lower part of his plantation; land which had been neglected before his time, in a great measure, because it had been sometimes flooded, and was, much of the year, too wet for cultivation. He was draining and clearing it, and it now brought good crops.

He had had an Irish gang draining for him, by contract. He thought a negro could do twice as much work, in a day, as an Irishman. He had not stood over them and seen them at work, but judged entirely from the amount they accomplished: he thought a good gang of negroes would have got on twice as fast. He was sure they must have "trifled" a great deal, or they would have accomplished more than they had. He complained much, also, of their sprees and quarrels. I asked why he should employ Irishmen, in preference to doing the work with his own hands. "It's dangerous work [unhealthy?], and a negro's life is too valuable to be risked at it. If a negro dies, it's a considerable loss, you know."

He afterwards said that his negroes never worked so hard as to tire themselves—always were lively, and ready to go off on a frolic at night. He did not think they ever did half a fair day's work. They could not be made to work hard: they never would lay out their strength freely, and it was impossible to make them do it.

This is just what I have thought when I have seen slaves at work —they seem to go through the motions of labour without putting strength into them. They keep their powers in reserve for their own use at night, perhaps.

Mr. W. also said that he cultivated only the coarser and lower-priced sorts of tobacco, because the finer sorts required more painstaking and discretion than it was possible to make a large gang of negroes use. "You can make a nigger work," he said, "but you cannot make him think."

Although Mr. W. was so wealthy (or, at least, would be considered anywhere at the North), and had been at college, his style of living was very farmer-like, and thoroughly Southern. On their plantations, generally, the Virginia gentlemen seem to drop their full dress and constrained town habits, and to live a free, rustic, shooting-jacket life. We dined in a room that extended out, rearwardly, from the house, and which, in a Northern establishment, would have been the kitchen. The cooking was done in a detached log-cabin, and the dishes brought some distance, through the open air, by the servants. The outer door was left constantly open, though there was a fire in an enormous old fire-place, large enough, if it could have been distributed sufficiently, to have lasted a New York seamstress the best part of the winter. By the door there was indiscriminate admittance to negro children and fox-hounds, and, on an average, there were four of these, grinning or licking their chops, on either side of my chair, all the time I was at the table. A stout woman acted as head waitress, employing two handsome little mulatto boys as her aids in communicating with the kitchen, from which relays of hot corn-bread, of an excellence quite new to me, were brought at frequent intervals. There was no other bread, and but one vegetable served—sweet potato, roasted in ashes, and this, I thought, was the best sweet potato, also, that I ever had eaten; but there were four preparations of swine's flesh, besides fried fowls, fried eggs, cold roast turkey, and opossum, cooked, I know not how, but it somewhat resembled baked sucking-pig. The only beverages on the table were milk and whisky.

I was pressed to stay several days with Mr. W., and should have been glad to do so, had not another engagement prevented. When I was about to leave, an old servant was directed to get a horse, and go with me, as guide, to the railroad station at Col. Gillin's. He followed behind me, and I had great difficulty in inducing him to ride near enough to converse with me. I wished to ascertain from him how old the different stages of the old-field forest-growth, by the side of our road, might be; but for a long time, he was, or pretended to be, unable to comprehend my questions. When he did so, the most accurate information he could give me was, that he reckoned such a field (in which the pines were now some sixty feet high) had been planted with tobacco the year his old master bought him. He thought he was about twenty years old then, and that now he was forty. He had every appearance of being seventy.

He frequently told me there was no need for him to go any further, and that it was a dead straight road to the station, without any forks. As he appeared very eager to return, I was at length foolish enough to allow myself to be prevailed upon to dispense with his guidance; gave him a quarter of a dollar for his time that I had employed, and went on alone. The road, which for a short distance further was plain enough, soon began to ramify, and, in half an hour, we were stumbling along a dark wood-path, looking eagerly for a house. At length, seeing one across a large clearing, we went through a long lane, opening gates and letting down bars, until we met two negroes, riding a mule, who were going to the plantation near the school-house which we had seen the day before. Following them thither, we knew the rest of the way (Jane gave a bound and neighed, when we struck the old road, showing that she had been lost, as well as I, up to the moment).

It was twenty minutes after the hour given in the time-table for the passage of the train, when I reached the station, but it had not arrived; nor did it make its appearance for a quarter of an hour longer; so I had plenty of time to deliver Tom's wife's message and take leave of Jane. I am sorry to say she appeared very indifferent, and seemed to think a good deal more of Tom than of me. Mr. W. had told me that the train would, probably, be half an hour behind its advertised time, and that I had no need to ride with haste, to reach it. I asked Col. Gillin if it would be safe to always calculate on the train being half an hour late: he said it would not; for, although usually that much behind the time-table, it was sometimes half an hour ahead of it. So those, who would be safe, had commonly to wait an hour. People, therefore, who wished to go not more than twenty miles from home, would find it more convenient, and equally expeditious, taking all things into account, to go in their own conveyances—there being but few who lived so near the station that they would not have to employ a horse and servant to get to it.

————. ——. I have been visiting a farm, cultivated entirely by free labour. The proprietor told me that he was first led to disuse slave-labour, not from any economical considerations, but because he had become convinced that there was an essential wrong in holding men in forced servitude with any other purpose than to benefit them alone, and because he was not willing to allow his own children to be educated as slave-masters. His father had been a large slaveholder, and he felt very strongly the bad influence it had had on his own character. He wished me to be satisfied that Jefferson uttered a great truth when he asserted that slavery was more pernicious to the white race than the black. Although, therefore, a chief part of his inheritance had been in slaves, he had liberated them all.

Most of them had, by his advice, gone to Africa. These he had frequently heard from. Except a child that had been drowned, they were, at his last account, all alive, in general good health, and satisfactorily prospering. He had lately received a letter from one of them, who told him that he was "*trying* to preach the Gospel," and who had evidently greatly improved, both intellectually and morally, since he left here. With regard to those going North, and the common opinion that they encountered much misery, and would be much better off here, he said that it entirely depended on the general character and habits of the individual: it was true of those who were badly brought up, and who had acquired indolent and vicious habits, especially if they were drunkards, but, if of some intelligence and well trained, they generally represented themselves to be successful and contented.

He mentioned two remarkable cases, that had come under his own observation, of this kind. One was that of a man who had been free, but, by some fraud and informality of his papers, was re-enslaved. He ran away, and afterwards negotiated, by correspondence, with his master, and purchased his freedom. This man he had accidentally met, fifteen years afterwards, in a Northern city; he was engaged in profitable and increasing business, and showed him, by his books, that he was possessed of property to the amount of ten thousand dollars. He was living a great deal more comfortably and wisely than ever his old master had done. The other case was that of a coloured woman, who had obtained her freedom, and who became apprehensive that she also was about to be fraudulently made a slave again. She fled to Philadelphia, where she was nearly starved, at first. A little girl, who heard her begging in the streets to be allowed to work for bread, told her that her mother was wanting some washing done, and she followed her home. The mother, not knowing her, was afraid to trust her with the articles to be washed. She prayed so earnestly for the job, however—suggesting that she might be locked into a room until she had completed it—that it was given her.

So she commenced life in Philadelphia. Ten years afterwards he had accidentally met her there; she recognized him immediately, recalled herself to his recollection, manifested the greatest joy at seeing him, and asked him to come to her house, which he found a handsome three-story building, furnished really with elegance; and she pointed out to him, from the window, three houses in the vicinity that she owned and rented. She showed great anxiety to have her children well educated, and was employing the best instructors for them which she could procure in Philadelphia.

He considered the condition of slaves to have much improved since the Revolution, and very perceptibly during the last twenty years. The original stock of slaves, the imported Africans, he observed, probably required to be governed with much greater severity, and very little humanity was exercised or thought of with regard to them. The slaves of the present day are of a higher character; in fact, he did not think more than half of them were full-blooded Africans. Public sentiment condemned the man who treated his slaves with cruelty. The owners were mainly men of some cultivation, and felt a family attachment to their slaves, many of whom had been the playmates of their boyhood. Nevertheless, they were frequently punished severely, under the impulse of temporary passion, often without deliberation, and on unfounded suspicion. This was especially the case where they were left to overseers, who, though sometimes men of intelligence and piety, were more often coarse, brutal, and licentious; drinking men, wholly unfitted for the responsibility imposed on them.

With regard to the value of slave-labour, this gentleman is confident that, at present, he has the advantage in employing free men instead of it. It has not been so until of late, the price of slaves having much advanced within ten years, while immigration has made free white labourers more easy to be procured.

He has heretofore had some difficulty in obtaining hands when he needed them, and has suffered a good deal from the demoralizing influence of adjacent slave-labour, the men, after a few months' residence, inclining to follow the customs of the slaves with regard to the amount of work they should do in a day, or their careless mode of operation. He has had white and black Virginians, sometimes Germans, and latterly Irish. Of all these, he has found the Irish on the whole the best. The poorest have been the native white Virginians; next, the free blacks: and though there have been exceptions, he has not generally paid these as high as one hundred dollars a year, and has thought them less worth their wages than any he has had. At present, he has two white natives and two free coloured men, but both the latter were brought up in his family, and are worth twenty dollars a year more than the average. The free black, he thinks, is generally worse than the slave, and so is the poor white man. He also employs, at present, four Irish hands, and is expecting two more to arrive, who have been recommended to him, and sent for by those he has. He pays the Irishmen $120 a year, and boards them. He has had them for $100; but these are all excellent men, and well worth their price. They are less given to drinking than any men he has ever had; and one of them first suggested improvements to him in his farm, that he is now carrying out with prospects of considerable advantage. Housemaids, Irish girls, he pays $3 and $6 a month.

He does not apprehend that in future he shall have any difficulty in obtaining steady men, who will accomplish much more work than any slaves. There are some operations, such as carting and spreading dung, and all work with the fork, spade, or shovel, at which his Irishmen will do, he thinks, over fifty per cent. more in a day than any negroes he has ever known. On the whole, he is satisfied that at present free-labour is more profitable than slave-labour, though his success is not so evident that he would be willing to have attention particularly called to it. His farm, moreover, is now in a transition state from one system of husbandry to another, and appearances are temporarily more unfavourable on that account.

The wages paid for slaves, when they are hired for agricultural labour, do not differ at present, he says, from those which he pays for his free labourers. In both cases the hiring party boards the labourer, but, in addition to money and board, the slave-employer has to furnish clothing, and is subject, without redress, to any losses which may result from the carelessness or malevolence of the slave. He also has to lose his time if he is unwell, or when from any cause he is absent or unable to work.

The slave, if he is indisposed to work, and especially if he is not treated well, or does not like the master who has hired him, will sham sickness—even make himself sick or lame—that he need not work. But a more serious loss frequently arises, when the slave, thinking he is worked too hard, or being angered by punishment or unkind treatment, "getting the sulks," takes to "the swamp," and comes back when he has a mind to. Often this will not be till the year is up for which he is engaged, when he will return to his owner, who glad to find his property safe, and that it has not died in the swamp, or gone to Canada, forgets to punish him, and immediately sends him for another year to a new master.

"But, meanwhile, how does the negro support life in the swamp?" I asked.

"Oh, he gets sheep and pigs and calves, and fowls and turkeys; sometimes they will kill a small cow. We have often seen the fires, where they were cooking them, through the woods, in the swamp yonder. If it is cold, he will crawl under a fodder-stack, or go into the cabins with some of the other negroes, and in the same way, you see, he can get all the corn, or almost anything else he wants."

"He steals them from his master?"

"From any one; frequently from me. I have had many a sheep taken by them."

"It is a common thing, then?"

"Certainly, it is, very common, and the loss is sometimes exceedingly provoking. One of my neighbours here was going to build, and hired two mechanics for a year. Just as he was ready to put his house up, the two men, taking offence at something, both ran away, and did not come back at all till their year was out, and then their owner immediately hired them out again to another man."

These negroes "in the swamp," he said, were often hunted after, but it was very difficult to find them, and, if caught, they would run again, and the other negroes would hide and assist them. Dogs to track them he had never known to be used in Virginia.

Saturday, Dec. 25th.—From Christmas to New-Year's Day, most of the slaves, except house servants, enjoy a freedom from labour; and Christmas is especially holiday, or Saturnalia, with them. The young ones began last night firing crackers, and I do not observe that they are engaged in any other amusement to-day; the older ones are generally getting drunk, and making business for the police. I have seen large gangs coming in from the country, and these contrast much in their general appearance with the town negroes. The latter are dressed expensively, and frequently more elegantly than the whites. They seem to be spending money freely, and I observe that they, and even the slaves that wait upon me at the hotel, often have watches, and other articles of value.

The slaves have a good many ways of obtaining "spending money," which though in law belonging to their owner, as the property of a son under age does to his father, they are never dispossessed of, and use for their own gratification, with even less restraint than a wholesome regard for their health and moral condition may be thought to require. A Richmond paper, complaining of the liberty allowed to slaves in this respect, as calculated to foster an insubordinate spirit, speaks of their "champagne suppers." The police broke into a gambling cellar a few nights since, and found about twenty negroes at "high play," with all the usual accessories of a first-class "Hell." It is mentioned that, among the number taken to the watch-house, and treated with lashes the next morning, there were some who had previously enjoyed a high reputation for piety, and others of a very elegant or foppish appearance.

Passing two negroes in the street, I heard the following:

"—Workin' in a tobacco factory all de year roun', an' come Christmas only twenty dollars! Workin' mighty hard, too—up to twelve o'clock o' night very often—an' then to hab a nigger oberseah!"

"A nigger!"

"Yes—dat's it, yer see. Wouldn't care if 'twarn't for dat. Nothin' but a dirty nigger! orderin' 'round, jes' as if he was a wite man!"

It is the custom of tobacco manufacturers to hire slaves and free negroes at a certain rate of wages per year. A task of 45 lbs. per day is given them to work up, and all that they choose to do more than this they are paid for—payment being made once a fortnight; and invariably this over-wages is used by the slave for himself, and is usually spent in drinking, licentiousness, and gambling. The man was grumbling that he had saved but $20 to spend at the holidays.

Sitting with a company of smokers last night, one of them, to show me the manner in which a slave of any ingenuity or cunning would manage to avoid working for his master's profit, narrated the following anecdote. He was executor of an estate in which, among other negroes, there was one very smart man, who, he knew perfectly well, ought to be earning for the estate $150 a year, and who could do it if he chose, yet whose wages for a year, being let out by the day or job, had amounted to but $18, while he had paid for medical attendance upon him $45. Having failed in every other way to make him earn anything, he proposed to him that he should purchase his freedom and go to Philadelphia, where he had a brother. He told him that if he would earn a certain sum ($400 I believe), and pay it over to the estate for himself, he would give him his free papers. The man agreed to the arrangement, and by his overwork in a tobacco factory, and some assistance from his free brother, soon paid the sum agreed upon, and was sent to Philadelphia. A few weeks afterwards he met him in the street, and asked him why he had returned. "Oh, I don't like dat Philadelphy, massa; an't no chance for coloured folks dere; spec' if I'd been a runaway, de wite folks dere take care o' me; but I couldn't git anythin' to do, so I jis borrow ten dollar of my broder, and cum back to old Virginny."

"But you know the law forbids your return. I wonder that you are not afraid to be seen here; I should think Mr. —— [an officer of police] would take you up."

"Oh! I look out for dat, massa; I juss hire myself out to Mr. —— himself, ha! ha! He tink I your boy."

And so it proved; the officer, thinking that he was permitted to hire himself out, and tempted by the low wages at which he offered himself, had neglected to ask for his written permission, and had engaged him for a year. He still lived with the officer, and was an active, healthy, good servant to him.

A well-informed capitalist and slave-holder remarked, that negroes could not be employed in cotton factories. I said that I understood they were so in Charleston, and some other places at the South.

"It may be so, yet," he answered, "but they will have to give it up."

The reason was, he said, that the negro could never be trained to exercise judgment; he cannot be made to use his mind; he always depends on machinery doing its own work, and cannot be made to watch it. He neglects it until something is broken or there is great waste. "We have tried rewards and punishments, but it makes no difference. It's his nature and you cannot change it. All men are indolent and have a disinclination to labour, but this is a great deal stronger in the African race than in any other. In working niggers, we must always calculate that they will not labour at all except to avoid punishment, and they will never do more than just enough to save themselves from being punished, and no amount of punishment will prevent their working carelessly and indifferently. It always seems on the plantation as if they took pains to break all the tools and spoil all the cattle that they possibly can, even when they know they'll be directly punished for it."

As to rewards, he said, "They only want to support life: they will not work for anything more; and in this country it would be hard to prevent their getting that." I thought this opinion of the power of rewards was not exactly confirmed by the narrative we had just heard, but I said nothing. "If you could move," he continued, "all the white people from the whole seaboard district of Virginia and give it up to the negroes that are on it now, just leave them to themselves, in ten years' time there would not be an acre of land cultivated, and nothing would be produced, except what grew spontaneously."

(The Hon. Willoughby Newton, by the way, seems to think that if it had not been for the introduction of guano, a similar desolation would have soon occurred without the Africanization of the country. He is reported to have said:—

("I look upon the introduction of guano, and the success attending its application to our barren lands, in the light of a special interposition of Divine Providence, to save the northern neck of Virginia from reverting entirely into its former state of wilderness and utter desolation. Until the discovery of guano—more valuable to us than the mines of California—I looked upon the possibility of renovating our soil, of ever bringing it to a point capable of producing remunerating crops, as utterly hopeless. Our up-lands were all worn out, and our bottom-lands fast failing, and if it had not been for guano, to revive our last hope, a few years more and the whole country must have been deserted by all who desired to increase their own wealth, or advance the cause of civilization by a proper cultivation of the earth.")

I said I supposed that they were much better off, more improved intellectually, and more kindly treated in Virginia than further South. He said I was mistaken in both respects—that in Louisiana, especially, they were more intelligent, because the amalgamation of the races was much greater, and they were treated with more familiarity by the whites; besides which, the laws of Louisiana were much more favourable to them. For instance, they required the planter to give slaves 200 pounds of pork a year: and he gave a very apt anecdote, showing the effect of this law, but which, at the same time, made it evident that a Virginian may be accustomed to neglect providing sufficient food for his force, and that they sometimes suffer greatly for want of it. I was assured, however, that this was very rare—that, generally, the slaves were well provided for—always allowed a sufficient quantity of meal, and, generally, of pork—were permitted to raise pigs and poultry, and in summer could always grow as many vegetables as they wanted. It was observed, however, that they frequently neglect to provide for themselves in this way, and live mainly on meal and bacon. If a man does not provide well for his slaves, it soon becomes known; he gets the name of a "nigger killer," and loses the respect of the community.

The general allowance of food was thought to be a peck and a half of meal, and three pounds of bacon a week. This, it was observed, is as much meal as they can eat, but they would be glad to have more bacon; sometimes they receive four pounds, but it is oftener that they get less than three. It is distributed to them on Saturday nights; or, on the better managed plantations, sometimes on Wednesday, to prevent their using it extravagantly, or selling it for whisky on Sunday. This distribution is called the "drawing," and is made by the overseer to all the heads of families or single negroes. Except on the smallest plantations, where the cooking is done in the house of the proprietor, there is a cook-house, furnished with a large copper for boiling, and an oven. Every night the negroes take their "mess," for the next day's breakfast and dinner, to the cook, to be prepared for the next day. Custom varies as to the time it is served out to them; sometimes at morning and noon, at other times at noon and night. Each negro marks his meat by cuts, so that he shall know it from the rest, and they observe each other's rights with regard to this, punctiliously.

After breakfast has been eaten early in the cabins, at sunrise, or a little before in winter, and perhaps a little later in summer, they go to the field. At noon dinner is brought to them, and, unless the work presses, they are allowed two hours' rest. Very punctually at sunset they stop work and are at liberty, except that a squad is detached once a week for shelling corn, to go to the mill for the next week's drawing of meal. Thus they work in the field about eleven hours a day, on an average. Returning to the cabins, wood "ought to have been" carted for them; but if it has not been, they then go to the woods and "tote" it home for themselves. They then make a fire—a big, blazing fire at this season, for the supply of fuel is unlimited—and cook their own supper, which will be a bit of bacon fried, often with eggs, corn-bread baked in the spider after the bacon, to absorb the fat, and perhaps some sweet potatoes roasted in the ashes. Immediately after supper they go to sleep, often lying on the floor or a bench in preference to a bed. About two o'clock they very generally rouse up and cook and eat, or eat cold, what they call their "mornin' bit"; then sleep again till breakfast. They generally save from their ration of meal: commonly as much as five bushels of meal was sent to town by my informant's hands every week, to be sold for them. Upon inquiry, he almost always found that it belonged to only two or three individuals, who had traded for it with the rest; he added, that too often the exchange was for whisky, which, against his rules, they obtained of some rascally white people in the neighbourhood, and kept concealed. They were very fond of whisky, and sometimes much injured themselves with it.

To show me how well they were supplied with eggs, he said that once a vessel came to anchor, becalmed, off his place, and the captain came to him and asked leave to purchase some eggs of his people. He gave him permission, and called the cook to collect them for him. The cook asked how many she should bring. "Oh, all you can get," he answered—and she returned after a time, with several boys assisting her, bringing nearly two bushels, all the property of the slaves, and which they were willing to sell at four cents a dozen.

One of the smokers explained to me that it is bad economy, not to allow an abundant supply of food to "a man's force." If not well provided for, the negroes will find a way to provide for themselves. It is, also, but simple policy to have them well lodged and clothed. If they do not have comfortable cabins and sufficient clothing, they will take cold, and be laid up. He lost a valuable negro, once, from having neglected to provide him with shoes.

The houses of the slaves are usually log-cabins, of various degrees of comfort and commodiousness. At one end there is a great open fire-place, which is exterior to the wall of the house, being made of clay in an inclosure, about eight feet square and high, of logs. The chimney is sometimes of brick, but more commonly of lath or split sticks, laid up like log work and plastered with mud. They enjoy great roaring fires, and, as the common fuel is pine, the cabin, at night when the door is open, seen from a distance, appears like a fierce furnace. The chimneys often catch fire, and the cabin is destroyed. Very little precaution can be taken against this danger.[5] Several cabins are placed near together, and they are called

[5] "AN INGENIOUS NEGRO.—In Lafayette, Miss., a few days ago, a negro, who, with his wife and three children, occupied a hut upon the plantation of Col. Peques, was very much annoyed by fleas. Believing that they congregated in great numbers beneath the house, he resolved to destroy them by fire; and accordingly, one night when his family were asleep, he raised a plank in the floor

"the quarters." On a plantation of moderate size there will be but one "quarters." The situation chosen for it has reference to convenience of obtaining water from springs and fuel from the woods.

As to the clothing of the slaves on the plantations, they are said to be usually furnished by their owners or masters, every year, each with a coat and trousers, of a coarse woollen or woollen and cotton stuff (mostly made, especially for this purpose, in Providence, R.I.) for winter, trousers of cotton osnaburghs for summer, sometimes with a jacket also of the same; two pairs of strong shoes, or one pair of strong boots and one of lighter shoes for harvest; three shirts, one blanket, and one felt hat.

The women have two dresses of striped cotton, three shifts, two pairs of shoes, etc. The women lying-in are kept at knitting short sacks, from cotton, which, in Southern Virginia, is usually raised for this purpose on the farm, and these are also given to the negroes. They also purchase clothing for themselves, and, I notice especially, are well supplied with handkerchiefs, which the men frequently, and the women nearly always, wear on their heads. On Sundays and holidays they usually look very smart, but when at work, very ragged and slovenly.

At the conclusion of our bar-room session, some time after midnight, as we were retiring to our rooms, our progress upstairs and along the corridors was several times impeded, by negroes lying fast asleep, in their usual clothes only, upon the floor. I asked why they were not abed, and was answered by a gentleman, that negroes never wanted to go to bed; they always preferred to sleep on the floor.

That "slaves are liars," or, as they say here, "niggers will lie," always has been proverbial. "They will lie in their very prayers to God," said one, and I find illustrations of the trouble that the vice occasions on every hand here. I just heard this, from a lady. A housemaid, who had the reputation of being especially devout, was suspected by her mistress of having stolen from her bureau several trinkets. She was charged with the theft, and vociferously denied it. She was watched, and the articles discovered openly displayed on

---

of the cabin, and, procuring an armful of shucks, scattered them on the ground beneath, and lighted them. The consequence was, that the cabin was consumed, and the whole family, with the exception of the man who lighted the fire, was burned to death."—*Journal of Commerce.*

her person as she went to church. She still, on her return, denied having them—was searched, and they were found in her pockets. When reproached by her mistress, and lectured on the wickedness of lying and stealing, she replied with the confident air of knowing the ground she stood upon, "Law, mam, don't say I's wicked; ole Aunt Ann says it allers right for us poor coloured people to 'popiate whatever of de wite folk's blessins de Lord puts in our way"; old Aunt Ann being a sort of mother in the coloured Israel of the town.

It is told me as a singular fact, that everywhere on the plantations, the agrarian notion has become a fixed point of the negro system of ethics: that the result of labour belongs of right to the labourer, and on this ground, even the religious feel justified in using "massa's" property for their own temporal benefit. This they term "taking," and it is never admitted to be a reproach to a man among them that he is charged with it, though "stealing," or taking from another than their master, and particularly from one another, is so. They almost universally pilfer from the household stores when they have a safe opportunity.

Jefferson says of the slaves [*Notes on Virginia* (1784), Query 14]:

Whether further observation will or will not verify the conjecture, that nature has been less bountiful to them in the endowments of the head, I believe that in those of the heart she will have done them justice. That disposition to theft, with which they have been branded, must be ascribed to their situation, and not to any depravity of the moral sense. The man in whose favour no laws of property exist, probably feels himself less bound to respect those made in favour of others. When arguing for ourselves, we lay it down as fundamental, that laws, to be just, must give a reciprocation of right; that without this, they are mere arbitrary rules, founded in force, and not in conscience; and it is a problem which I give to the master to solve, whether the religious precepts against the violation of property were not framed for him as well as his slave? and whether the slave may not as justifiably take a little from one who has taken all from him, as he may slay one who would slay him? That a change of the relations in which a man is placed should change his ideas of moral right and wrong, is neither new, nor peculiar to the colour of the blacks. Homer tells us it was so, 2,600 years ago:

> Jove fixed it certain, that whatever day
> Makes man a slave, takes half his worth away.

Chapter IV

The Economy of Virginia

An Englishman will cross three thousand miles of sea, and, landing in our Free States, find, under a different sky and climate, a people speaking the same language, influenced by the same literature, giving allegiance to the same common law, and with not very dissimilar tastes, manners, or opinions, on the whole, to those of his own people. What most strikes him is an apparent indifference to conditions of living which he would at home call shabby. He will find men, however, at whose homes he will hardly see anything, either of substance, custom, or manner, by which he would know that he was out of England, and if he asks how these manage to get waiters who do not smell of the stable; and grooms who keep stirrups bright; roofs which do not leak; lawns which are better than stubble fields; walks which are not grassy; fences which do not need shoring up; staunch dogs; clean guns; strong boots and clothes that will go whole through a thicket; the true answer will be, by taking double the pains and paying double as much as would be necessary to secure the same results in England, and that few men are willing or able to do this.

I make half a day's journey southward here, and I find, with an equal resemblance between the people and those I left, an indifference to conditions of living, which Mrs. Stowe's Ophelia describes as "shiftless," and which makes the same sort of impression on my mind, as the state of things at the North does upon an Englishman's. But, in this case, there has been no change in the skies; I wear the same clothing, or if I come from the low sea-board and, going inland, gain elevation, I need some better protection against cold. I also find exceptions; how are they to be accounted for? The first step does not seem difficult. In this well-provided, hospitable, and most agreeable household, for instance, there are four times as many servants as in one which would otherwise be as similar as possible to it at the North; to say nothing of the governess, or of the New York plumber, who has been at work here for a month; or of the doctor, who, having come fifteen miles to lance the baby's gums, stays of course to dine with us; or of the German, who I am told—such is the value of railroads even at a distance—left Richmond only at nine o'clock last night, and having tuned the piano, will return in time for his classes there to-morrow; or of the patent chain-pump peddler, whose horses have been knocked up in crossing the swamp; or of the weekly mail-carrier, who cannot go on till the logs which have floated off the bridge are restored. Mr. T. means soon, he tells me, to build a substantial bridge there, because his nearest respectable neighbours are in that direction. His nearest neighbours on this side of the creek, by the way, he seems to regard with suspicion. They live in solitary cabins, and he don't think they do a day's work in a year; but they somehow manage to always have corn enough to keep themselves from starving, and as they certainly don't raise half enough for this, the supposition is that his negroes steal it and supply it in exchange for whisky. Clearly the negroes do get whisky, somewhere; for even their preacher, who has been a capital blacksmith, and but for this vice would be worth $2,500, was taken with delirium tremens last Sunday night, and set one of the outhouses on fire, so that the energetic Mr. T., who will have things right about his "place," has determined to get rid of him, and will have him sold for what he will fetch at the sheriff's sale at the County House to-morrow; and Prior, the overseer, must go to Richmond immediately, to see about a new blacksmith, for the plumber says that until one is got he must stand idle, and the ploughs are all needing repair. A less energetic man would keep old Joe, in spite of his vice, on account of his old wife and many children, and out of regard to the spiritual interests of his flock, for when not very drunk, old Joe is reckoned the best preacher in five counties. But Mr. T. is determined to live like a gentleman; he is not going to have the hoofs of his thorough-breds spoiled; and he will have hot and cold water laid on; and he tells Prior that if he can find a first-rate shoer, young, healthy, active, and strong, and handy at anything in the way of his trade, not to lose him, if he has to go as high as $250, for the year; or, if necessary, he will buy such an one outright, at any fair price, if he can have him on trial for a month. If there is none in market, he must try to induce that Scotchman who hung the bells to come up again for a few days. "Treat him like a gentleman," he says, "and tell him he will be paid whatever he asks, and make as if it were a frolic."

$250 a year, and a man's board and clothing, with iron, coal, and, possibly, doctor's bills to be added, is certainly a high price to pay for the blacksmith's work of a single farm. This exceptional condition, then, it is obvious on the face of things, is maintained at an enormous expense, not only of money, but of nerve, time, temper, if not of humanity, or the world's judgment of humanity. There is much inherited wealth, a cotton plantation or two in Mississippi and a few slips of paper in a broker's office in Wall Street, that account for the comfort of this Virginia farmer, as, with something of the pride which apes humility, he likes to style himself. And after all he has no road on which he can drive his fine horses; his physician supposes the use of chloric ether, as an anaesthetic agent, to be a novel and interesting subject of after-dinner eloquence; he has no church within twenty miles, but one of logs, attendance on which is sure to bring on an attack of neuralgia with his wife, and where only an ignorant ranter of a different faith from his own preaches at irregular intervals; there is no school which he is willing that his children should attend; his daily papers come weekly, and he sees no books except such as he has especially ordered from Norton or Stevens.

This being the exception, how is it with the community as a whole?

As a whole, the community makes shift to live, some part tolerably, the most part wretchedly enough, with arrangements such as one might expect to find in a country in stress of war. Nothing which can be postponed or overlooked, without immediate serious inconvenience, gets attended to. One soon neglects to inquire why this is not done or that; the answer is so certain to be that there is no proper person to be got to do it without more trouble (or expense) than it is thought to be worth. Evidently habit reconciles the people to do without much, the permanent want of which would seem likely to be intolerable to those who had it in possession. Nevertheless, they complain a good deal, showing that the evil is an increasing one. Verbal statements to the same effect as the following, written by a Virginian to the Journal of Commerce, are often heard.

Hundreds of farmers and planters, mill owners, tobacconists, cotton factories, iron works, steam-boat owners, master builders, contractors, carpenters, stage proprietors, canal boat owners, railroad companies, and others, are, and have been short of hands these five years past, in Maryland, Virginia, and the Carolinas. They pay $150 or $200 a year each hand, and his board, and stealing, and if that hand be present or absent, sick or well, it is all the same. His clothes cost say $30 more, and in many cases the hirer has to pay his policy of life insurance.

For all that, labourers are being constantly sent away. I have not been on or seen a railroad train, departing southward, that it did not convey a considerable number of the best class of negro labourers, in charge of a trader who was intending to sell them to cotton-planters. Thus it is evident that, great as is the need for more labourers here, there is a still greater demand for them to raise cotton; and in order to supply this demand, the Virginians suffer the most extreme inconvenience. The wonder is, that their own demand for labour is not supplied by free labourers. But it appears that where negro slavery has long existed, certain occupations are, by custom, assigned to the slaves, and a white man is not only reluctant to engage himself in those occupations, but is greatly disinclined to employ other whites in them. I have often asked: "Why do you not employ white men?" (for this or that purpose for which slaves could not be procured); and, almost always, the reply has been given in a tone which indicated a little feeling, which, if I do not misapprehend it, means that the employment of whites in duties upon which slaves are ordinarily employed is felt to be not only humiliating to the whites employed, but also to the employer.

Nor is this difficulty merely a matter of sentiment. I have been answered: "Our poor white men will not do such work if they can very well help it, and they will do no more of it than they are obliged to. They will do a few days' work when it is necessary to provide themselves with the necessaries of life, but they are not used to steady labour; they work reluctantly, and will not bear driving; they cannot be worked to advantage with slaves, and it is inconvenient to look after them, if you work them separately." And then, when I push the inquiries by asking, why not send North and get some of our labourers? "Well—the truth is, I have been used to driving niggers, and I don't think I could drive white men. I should not know how to manage them." So far as I understand the matter, then, Virginia is in this position: there are slaves enough in most of the country to mainly exclude white labourers from labouring men's occupations and to make the white people dependent on slave-labour for certain things; but the slaves being drawn off almost as fast as they grow up to grow cotton in the more Southern States, and those which remain being managed with almost as much regard for this demand as for the local demand for labour, this local demand is not systematically provided for; and even if there were the intention to provide for it, there are no sufficient means to do so, as the white population increases in number much more rapidly than the slave.[1] I do not mean that no whites are employed in the ordinary occupations of slaves in Virginia. In some parts there are few or no slaves, and the white people who live in these parts, of course do not live without having work done; but even in these districts it is hardly possible to find men or women, who are willing and able to serve others well and faithfully, on wages. In some parts white working men also drift in slowly from the Free States, but they are too few and scattered to perceptibly affect the habits of the people and customs of the country, while they rapidly adapt themselves to these habits and customs. Thus it is questionable if as yet they do not add more to the general demand for labour than they supply to reduce it.

Still, it is where slaves remain in the greatest numbers, proportionately to the whites, that the scarcity of labourers, or what is practically the same thing, the cost of getting desirable work done, is most obvious. Schools, churches, roads, bridges, fences, houses, stables, are all more frequent, and in better repair, where the proportion of whites to slaves is large, than in the "negro counties," as some are popularly designated, from the preponderance of the slave population in them. I find this observation confirmed by an examination in the Census returns and other documents.

In the North-western counties, Cabell, Mason, Brooke, and Tyler, in or adjoining which there are no large towns, but a free labouring population, with slaves in ratio to the freemen as one to fifteen only, the value of land is over seven dollars and three quarters an acre.

In Southampton, Surrey, James Town and New Kent, in which

---

[1] From 1850 to 1860, the rate of increase of the free population has been 16.44 per cent.; of the slave, 3.88. (From a recent official statement of the Census Office.) A somewhat parallel case to that of the Virginia slaveholder is that of a breeder of blooded stock. A Flying Dutchman is used upon occasion as a charger, but under no pressure of the harvest will you find him put before the cart. I have more than once heard the phrase used, "Niggers are worth too much" to be used in such and such work. Instances of this are given hereafter.

the slave population is as 1 to 2.2, the value of land is but little more than half as much—$4.50 an acre.

The value of land of course rises with its availability to contribute to the wants of men, and it can only be made available as labour can be applied to it.

In Surrey, Prince George, Charles City, and James, adjoining counties on James River, and originally having some of the most productive soil in the State, and now supplied with the public conveniences which have accrued in two hundred years of occupation by a civilized and Christian community, the number of slaves being at present, to that of whites as 1 to 1.9, the value of land is but $6 an acre.

In Fairfax, another of the first settled counties, and in which, twenty years ago, land was even less in value than in the James River counties, it is now become worth twice as much.

The slave population, once greater than that of whites, has been reduced by emigration and sale, till there are now less than half as many slaves as whites. In the place of slaves has come another sort of people. The change which has taken place, and the cause of it, is thus simply described in the Agricultural Report of the County to the Commissioner of Patents.[2]

In appearance, the county is so changed in many parts, that a traveller who passed over it ten years ago would not now recognize it. Thousands and thousands of acres had been cultivated in tobacco by the former proprietors, would not pay the cost, and were abandoned as worthless, and became covered with a wilderness of pines. These lands have been purchased by Northern emigrants; the large tracts divided and subdivided and cleared of pines; and neat farm-houses and barns, with smiling fields of grain and grass in the season, salute the delighted gaze of the beholder. Ten years ago it was a mooted question whether Fairfax lands could be made productive; and if so, would they pay the cost? This problem has been satisfactorily solved by many, and in consequence of the above altered state of things school-houses and churches have doubled in number.

The following substantiates what I have said of the inavailability of the native whites for supplying the place of the negroes exported to the cotton plantations.

[2] See Patent Office Report, 1852.

From the Patent Office Report for 1847

As to the price of labour, our mechanics charge from one to two dollars a day. As to agricultural labour, we have none. Our poor are poor because *they will not work,* therefore are seldom employed.

CHAS. YANCEY,
Buckingham Co., Virginia.

The sentence, "As to agricultural labour, we have none," must mean no free labour, the number of slaves in this county being according to the Census 8,161, or nearly 3,000 more than the whole white population. There are also 250 free negroes in the county.

From a Correspondent of the 'American Agriculturist,' Feb. 14, 1855.

As to labourers, we work chiefly slaves, not because they are cheaper, but rather because they are the only *reliable* labour we can get. The whites here engage to work for *less price than the blacks* can be got for; yet they will not work well, and *rarely work out the time specified.* If any of your friends come here and wish to work whites, I would advise them by all means to bring them with them; for our white labourers are far inferior to our blacks, and our black labour is far inferior to what we read and hear of your labourers.   C. G. G.

Albemarle Co., Virginia.

In Albemarle there are over thirteen thousand slaves to less than twelve thousand whites.

Among the native Virginians I find most intelligent men, very ready to assert that slavery is no disadvantage to Virginia, and, as necessary to the maintenance of this assertion, that slave-labour is no dearer than free-labour, that is, than free-labour would be, if slavery did not exist. It is even said—and, as I have shown, it is practically true, at least wherever slavery has not in a great measure withdrawn from the field—that white labour cannot live in competition with slave-labour. In other words, the holder of slave-labour controls the local market for labour, and the cost of slave-labour fixes the cost of everything which is produced by slave-labour. But it is a mistake which the Virginians generally make, when they jump from this to the conclusion that slave-labour is therefore cheaper under all circumstances than free-labour. It is evident that slaves are valuable for another purpose than to supply the local demand for their labour, namely, to supply the demand of the cotton planter; consequently those slaves which are employed to supply the local demand, must be employed either at a loss, or at what they are worth to the cotton planter. Whether this is more or less than free-labour would cost if the field were open, can only be ascertained by comparing the cost of slave-labour in Virginia with the cost of free-labour in the Free States.

An exact comparison on a large scale I cannot find the means of making, but I have taken a great many notes which lead me with confidence to a few important general conclusions.

Wages.—Many thousand slaves have been hired in Eastern Virginia during the time of my visit. The wages paid for able working men—sound, healthy, in good condition, and with no especial vices, from twenty to thirty years old—are from $110 to $140; the average, as nearly as I can ascertain, from very extended inquiry, being $120 per year, with board and lodging, and certain other expenses. These wages must represent exactly the cost of slave-labour, because any considerations which would prevent the owner of a slave disposing of his labour for those wages, when the labour for his own purposes would not be worth as much, are so many hindrances upon the free disposal of his property, and thereby deduct from its actual value, as measured with money.

As the large majority of slaves are employed in agricultural labour, and many of those, hired at the prices I have mentioned, are taken directly from the labour of the farm, and are skilled in no other, these wages represent the cost of agricultural labour in Eastern Virginia.

In New York, the usual wages for similar men, if Americans, white or black, are exactly the same in the money part; for Irish or German labourers the most common wages are $10 per month, for summer, and $8 per month, for winter, or from $96 to $120 a year, the average being about $108.

The hirer has, in addition to paying wages for the slave, to feed and to clothe him; the free labourer requires also to be boarded, but not to be clothed by his employer. The opinion is universal in Virginia, that the slaves are better fed than the Northern labourers. This is, however, a mistake, and we must consider that the board of the Northern labourer would cost at least as much more as the additional cost of clothing to the slave. Comparing man with man, with reference simply to equality of muscular power and endurance, my final judgment is, that the wages for common labourers are twenty-five per cent. higher in Virginia than in New York.

Loss from disability of the labourer.—This to the employer of free labourers need be nothing. To the slave-master it is of varying consequence: sometimes small, often excessively embarrassing, and always a subject of anxiety and suspicion. I have not yet made the inquiry on any plantation where as many as twenty negroes are employed together, that I have not found one or more of the field-hands not at work, on account of some illness, strain, bruise, or wound, of which he or she was complaining; and in such cases the proprietor or overseer has, I think, never failed to express his suspicion that the invalid was really as well able to work as anyone else on the plantation. It is said to be nearly as difficult to form a satisfactory diagnosis of negroes' disorders as it is of infants', because their imagination of symptoms is so vivid, and because not the smallest reliance is to be placed on their accounts of what they have felt or done. If a man is really ill, he fears lest he should be thought to be simulating, and therefore exaggerates all his pains, and locates them in whatever he supposes to be the most vital parts of his system.

Frequently the invalid slaves neglect or refuse to use the remedies prescribed for their recovery. They conceal pills, for instance, under their tongue, and declare that they have swallowed them, when, from their producing no effect, it will be afterwards evident that they have not. This general custom I heard ascribed to habit, acquired when they were not very ill, and were loth to be made quite well enough to have to go to work again.

Amusing incidents, illustrating this difficulty, I have heard narrated, showing that the slave rather enjoys getting a severe wound that lays him up:—he has his hand crushed by the fall of a piece of timber, and after the pain is alleviated, is heard to exclaim, "Bress der Lord—der haan b'long to masser—don't reckon dis chile got no more corn to hoe dis yaar, no how."

Mr. H., of North Carolina, observed to me, in relation to this difficulty, that a man who had had much experience with negroes could generally tell, with a good deal of certainty, by their tongue, and their pulse, and their general aspect, whether they were really ill or not.

"Last year," said he, "I hired out one of my negroes to a railroad contractor. I suppose that he found he had to work harder than he would on the plantation, and became discontented, and one night he left the camp without asking leave. The next day he stopped at a public-house, and told the people he had fallen sick working on the railroad, and was going home to his master. They suspected he had run away, and, as he had no pass, they arrested him and sent him to the jail. In the night the sheriff sent me word that there was a boy, who said he belonged to me, in the jail, and he was very sick indeed, and I had better come and take care of him. I suspected how it was, and, as I was particularly engaged, I did not go near him till towards night, the next day. When I came to look at him, and heard his story, I felt quite sure that he was not sick; but, as he pretended to be suffering very much, I told the sheriff to give him plenty of salts and senna, and to be careful that he did not get much of anything to eat. The next day I got a letter from the contractor, telling me that my nigger had run away, without any cause. So I rode over to the jail again, and told them to continue the same treatment until the boy got a good deal worse or a good deal better. Well, the rascal kept it up for a week, all the time groaning so, you'd think he couldn't live many hours longer; but, after he had been in seven days, he all of a sudden said he'd got well, and wanted something to eat. As soon as I heard of it, I sent them word to give him a good paddling,[3] and handcuff him, and send him back to the railroad. I had to pay them for taking up a runaway, besides the sheriff's fees, and a week's board of the boy to the county."

But the same gentleman admitted that he had sometimes been mistaken, and had made men go to work when they afterwards proved to be really ill; therefore, when one of his people told him he was not able to work, he usually thought, "Very likely he'll be all the better for a day's rest, whether he's really ill or not," and would let him off without being particular in his examination. Lately he had been getting a new overseer, and when he was engaging him, he told him that this was his way. The overseer replied, "It's my way, too, now; it didn't use to be, but I had a lesson. There was a nigger one day at Mr. ——'s who was sulky and complaining; he said he couldn't work. I looked at his tongue, and it was right

---

[3] Not something to eat, but punishment with an instrument like a ferule.

clean, and I thought it was nothing but damned sulkiness, so I pad-
dled him, and made him go to work; but, two days after, he was
under ground. He was a good eight hundred dollar nigger, and it
was a lesson to me about taming possums, that I ain't agoing to forget in a hurry."

The liability of women, especially, to disorders and irregularities
which cannot be detected by exterior symptoms, but which may
be easily aggravated into serious complaints, renders many of them
nearly valueless for work, because of the ease with which they can
impose upon their owners. "The women on a plantation," said one
extensive Virginian slaveowner to me, "will hardly earn their salt,
after they come to the breeding age: they don't come to the field,
and you go to the quarters, and ask the old nurse what's the matter,
and she says, 'Oh, she's not well, master; she not fit to work, sir';
and what can you do? You have to take her word for it that something or other is the matter with her, and you dare not set her to
work; and so she lays up till she feels like taking the air again, and
plays the lady at your expense."

I was on a plantation where a woman had been excused from
any sort of labour for more than two years, on the supposition that
she was dying of phthisis. At last the overseer discovered that she
was employed as a milliner and dress-maker by all the other coloured ladies of the vicinity; and upon taking her to the house, it was
found that she had acquired a remarkable skill in these vocations.
She was hired out the next year to a fashionable dress-maker in
town, at handsome wages; and as, after that, she did not again
"raise blood," it was supposed that when she had done so before,
it had been by artificial means. Such tricks every army and navy
surgeon is familiar with.

The interruption and disarrangement of operations of labour, occasioned by slaves "running away," frequently causes great inconvenience and loss to those who employ them. It is said to often
occur when no immediate motive can be guessed at for it—when
the slave has been well treated, well fed, and not over-worked; and
when he will be sure to suffer hardship from it, and be subject to
severe punishment on his return, or if he is caught.

This is often mentioned to illustrate the ingratitude and especial
depravity of the African race. I should suspect it to be, if it cannot
be otherwise accounted for, the natural instinct of freedom in a

man, working out capriciously, as the wild instincts of domesticated beasts and birds sometimes do.

But the learned Dr. [Samuel A.] Cartwright, of the University of Louisiana, believes that slaves are subject to a peculiar form of mental disease, termed by him *Drapetomania*, which, like a malady that cats are liable to, manifests itself by an irrestrainable propensity to *run away*; and in a work on the diseases of negroes [*Report on the Diseases and Physical Peculiarities of the Negro Race*, prepared for the Louisiana State Medical Society], highly esteemed at the South for its patriotism and erudition, he advises planters of the proper preventive and curative measures to be taken for it.

He asserts that, "with the advantage of proper medical advice, strictly followed, this troublesome practice of running away, that many negroes have, can be almost entirely prevented." Its symptoms and the usual empirical practice on the plantations are described: "Before negroes run away, unless they are frightened or panic-struck, they become sulky and dissatisfied. The cause of this sulkiness and dissatisfaction should be inquired into and removed, or they are apt to run away or fall into the negro consumption." When sulky or dissatisfied without cause, the experience of those having most practice with *drapetomania*, the Doctor thinks, has been in favour of "whipping them *out of it*." It is vulgarly called, "whipping the devil *out of them*," he afterwards informs us.

Another droll sort of "indisposition," thought to be peculiar to the slaves, and which must greatly affect their value, as compared with free labourers, is described by Dr. Cartwright, as follows:—

DYSÆSTHESIA ÆTHIOPICA, or Hebetude of Mind and Obtuse Sensibility of Body. . . . From the careless movements of the individuals affected with this complaint, they are apt to do much mischief, which appears as if intentional, but is mostly owing to the stupidness of mind and insensibility of the nerves induced by the disease. Thus they break, waste, and destroy everything they handle—abuse horses and cattle—tear, burn, or rend their own clothing, and, paying no attention to the rights of property, steal others to replace what they have destroyed. They wander about at night, and keep in a half-nodding state by day. They slight their work —cut up corn, cane, cotton, and tobacco, when hoeing it, as if for pure mischief. They raise disturbances with their overseers, and among their fellow-servants, without cause or motive, and seem to be insensible to pain when subjected to punishment. . . .

When left to himself, the negro indulges in his natural disposition to idleness and sloth, and does not take exercise enough to expand his lungs and vitalize his blood, but dozes out a miserable existence in the midst of filth and uncleanliness, being too indolent, and having too little energy of mind, to provide for himself proper food and comfortable clothing and lodging. The consequence is, that the blood becomes so highly carbonized and deprived of oxygen that it not only becomes unfit to stimulate the brain to energy, but unfit to stimulate the nerves of sensation distributed to the body. . . .

This is the disease called *Dysæsthesia* (a Greek term expressing the dull or obtuse sensation that always attends the complaint). When roused from sloth by the stimulus of hunger, he takes anything he can lay his hands on, and tramples on the rights as well as on the property of others, with perfect indifference. When driven to labour by the compulsive power of the white man, he performs the task assigned to him in a headlong, careless manner, treading down with his feet or cutting with his hoe the plants he is put to cultivate—breaking the tools he works with, and spoiling everything he touches that can be injured by careless handling. Hence the overseers call it "rascality," supposing that the mischief is intentionally done. . . .

The term, "rascality," given to this disease by overseers, is founded on an erroneous hypothesis, and leads to an incorrect empirical treatment, which seldom or never cures it.

There are many complaints described in Dr. Cartwright's treatise, to which the negroes, in slavery, seem to be peculiarly subject.

More fatal than any other is congestion of the lungs, *peripneumonia notha,* often called cold plague, etc. . . .

The *Frambæsia,* Piam, or Yaws, is a *contagious* disease, communicable by contact among those who greatly neglect cleanliness. It is supposed to be communicable, in a modified form, to the white race, among whom it resembles pseudo syphilis, or some disease of the nose, throat, or larynx. . . .

Negro-consumption, a disease almost unknown to medical men of the Northern States and of Europe, is also sometimes fearfully prevalent among the slaves. "It is of importance," says the Doctor, "to know the pathognomic signs in its early stages, not only in regard to its treatment, but to detect impositions, as negroes afflicted with this complaint are often for sale; the acceleration of the pulse, on exercise, incapacitates them for labour, as they quickly give out, and have to leave their work. This induces their owners to sell them, although they may not know the cause of their inability to labour. Many of the negroes brought South, for sale, are in the incipient stages of this disease; they are found to be inefficient labourers, and are sold in consequence thereof. The effect of superstition—a firm belief that he is poisoned or conjured—upon the patient's mind, already in a morbid state (dysæsthesia), and his health affected from hard usage, over-tasking or exposure, want of wholesome food, good clothing, warm, comfortable lodging, with the distressing idea (sometimes) that he is an object of hatred or dislike, both to his master or fellow-servants, and has no one to befriend him, tends directly to generate that erythism of mind which is the essential cause of negro-consumption." . . . "Remedies should be assisted by removing the *original cause* of the dissatisfaction or trouble of mind, and by using every means to make the patient comfortable, satisfied, and happy."

Longing for home generates a distinct malady, known to physicians as *Nostalgia*, and there is a suggestive analogy between the treatment commonly employed to cure it and that recommended in this last advice of Dr. Cartwright.

Discipline.—Under the slave system of labor, discipline must always be maintained by physical power. A lady of New York, spending a winter in a Southern city, had a hired slave-servant, who, one day, refused outright to perform some ordinary light domestic duty required of her. On the lady's gently remonstrating with her, she immediately replied: "You can't make me do it, and I won't do it: I aint afeared of you whippin' me." The servant was right; the lady could not whip her, and was too tender-hearted to call in a man, or to send her to the guard-house to be whipped, as is the custom with Southern ladies, when their patience is exhausted, under such circumstances. She endeavoured, by kindness and by appeals to the girl's good sense, to obtain a moral control over her; but, after suffering continual annoyance and inconvenience, and after an intense trial of her feelings, for some time, she was at length obliged to go to her owner, and beg him to come and take her away from the house, on any terms. It was no better than having a lunatic or a mischievous and pilfering monomaniac quartered on her.[4]

But often when courage and physical power, with the strength

[4] The *Richmond American* has a letter from Raleigh, N.C., dated Sept. 18, which says: "On yesterday morning, a beautiful young lady, Miss Virginia Frost, daughter of Austin Frost, an engineer on the Petersburg and Weldon Railroad, and residing in this city, was shot by a negro girl, and killed instantly. Cause—reproving her for insolent language."

of the militia force and the army of the United States, if required, at the back of the master, are not wanting, there are a great variety of circumstances that make a resort to punishment inconvenient, if not impossible.

Really well-trained, accomplished, and docile house-servants are seldom to be purchased or hired at the South, though they are found in old wealthy families rather oftener than first-rate English or French servants are at the North. It is, doubtless, a convenience to have even moderately good servants who cannot, at any time of their improved value or your necessity, demand to have their pay increased, or who cannot be drawn away from you by prospect of smaller demands and kinder treatment at your neighbour's; but I believe few of those who are incessantly murmuring against this healthy operation of God's good law of supply and demand would be willing to purchase exemption from it, at the price with which the masters and mistresses of the South do. They would pay, to get a certain amount of work done, three or four times as much, to the owner of the best sort of hired slaves, as they do to the commonest, stupidest Irish domestic drudges at the North, though the nominal wages by the week or year, in Virginia, are but little more than in New York.

The number of servants usually found in a Southern family, of any pretension, always amazes a Northern lady. In one that I have visited, there are exactly three negroes to each white, the negroes being employed solely in the house.

(A Southern lady, of an old and wealthy family, who had been for some time visiting a friend of mine in New York, said to her, as she was preparing to return home: "I cannot tell you how much, after being in your house so long, I dread to go home, and to have to take care of our servants again. We have a much smaller family of whites than you, but we have twelve servants, and your two accomplish a great deal more, and do their work a great deal better than our twelve. You think your girls are very stupid, and that they give you much trouble: but it is as nothing. There is hardly one of our servants that can be trusted to do the simplest work without being stood over. If I order a room to be cleaned, or a fire to be made in a distant chamber, I never can be sure I am obeyed un- less I go there and see for myself. If I send a girl out to get anything I want for preparing the dinner, she is as likely as not to forget what is wanted, and not to come back till after the time at which dinner should be ready. A hand-organ in the street will draw all my girls out of the house; and while it remains near us I have no more command over them than over so many monkeys. The parade of a military company has sometimes entirely prevented me from having any dinner cooked; and when the servants, standing in the square looking at the soldiers, see my husband coming after them, they only laugh, and run away to the other side, like playful children.[5] And, when I reprimand them, they only say they don't mean to do anything wrong, or they won't do it again, all the time laughing as though it was all a joke. They don't mind it at all. They are just as playful and careless as any wilful child; and they never will do any work if you don't compel them.")

The slave employer, if he finds he has been so unfortunate as to hire a sulky servant, who cannot be made to work to his advantage, has no remedy but to solicit from his owner a deduction from the price he has agreed to pay for his labour, on the same ground that one would from a livery-stable keeper, if he had engaged a horse to go a journey, but found that he was not strong or skilful enough to keep him upon the road. But, if the slave is the property of his employer, and becomes "rascally," the usual remedy is that which the veterinary surgeon recommended when he was called upon for advice how to cure a jibing horse: "*Sell* him, my lord." "Rascals" are "sent South" from Virginia, for the cure or alleviation of their complaint, in much greater numbers than consumptives are from the more Northern States.

"How do you manage, then, when a man misbehaves, or is sick?" I have been often asked by Southerners, in discussing this question.

If he is sick, I simply charge against him every half day of the time he is off work, and deduct it from his wages. If he is careless, or refuses to do what in reason I demand of him, I discharge him, paying him wages to the time he leaves. With new men in whom I have not confidence, I make a written agreement, before witnesses, on engaging them, that will permit me to do this. As for "rascality," I never had but one case of anything approaching to what you call

[5] In the city of Columbia, S.C., the police are required to prevent the negroes from running in this way after the military. Any negro neglecting to leave the vicinity of a parade, when ordered by a policeman or any military officer, is required, by the ordinance, to be whipped at the guard-house.

so. A man insolently contradicted me in the field: I told him to leave his job and go to the house, took hold and finished it myself, then went to the house, made out a written statement of account, counted out the balance in money due to him, gave him the statement and the money, and told him he must go. He knew that he had failed of his duty, and that the law would sustain me, and we parted in a friendly manner, he expressing regret that his temper had driven him from a situation which had been agreeable and satisfactory to him. The probability is, that this single experience educated him so far that his next employer would have no occasion to complain of his "rascality"; and I very much doubt if any amount of corporeal punishment would have improved his temper in the least.

"*Sogering.*"—That slaves have to be "humoured" a great deal, and that they very frequently cannot be made to do their master's will, I have seen much evidence. Not that they often directly refuse to obey an order, but when they are directed to do anything for which they have a disinclination, they undertake it in such a way that the desired result is sure not to be accomplished. They cannot be driven by fear of punishment to do that which the labourers in free communities do cheerfully from their sense of duty, self-respect, or regard for their reputation and standing with their employer. A gentleman who had some free men in his employment in Virginia, that he had procured in New York, told me that he had been astonished, when a dam that he had been building began to give way in a freshet, to see how much more readily than negroes they would obey his orders, and do their best without orders, running into the water waist-deep, in mid-winter, without any hesitation or grumbling.

The manager of a large candle-factory in London, in which the labourers are treated with an unusual degree of confidence and generosity, writes thus in a report to his directors:—

The present year promises to be a very good one as regards profit, in consequence of the enormous increase in the demand for candles. No mere driving of the men and boys, by ourselves and those in authority under us, would have produced the sudden and very great increase of manufacture, necessary for keeping pace with this demand. It has been effected only by the hearty good-will with which the factory has worked, the men and boys making the great extra exertion, which they saw to be necessary to prevent our getting hopelessly in arrears with the orders, as heartily as if the question had been, how to avert some difficulty threatening themselves personally. One of the foremen remarked with truth, a few days back: "To look on them, one would think each was engaged in a little business of his own, so as to have only himself affected by the results of his work."

A farmer in Lincolnshire, England, told me that once, during an extraordinary harvest season, he had a number of labourers at work without leaving the field or taking any repose for sixty hours—he himself working with them, and eating and drinking only with them during all the time. Such services men may give voluntarily, from their own regard to the value of property to be saved by it, or for the purpose of establishing their credit as worth good wages; but to require it of slaves would be intensely cruel, if not actually impossible. A man can work excessively on his own impulse as much easier than he can be driven to by another, as a horse travels easier in going towards his accustomed stable than in going from it. I mean—and every man who has ever served as a sailor or a soldier will know that it is no imaginary effect—that the actual fatigue, the waste of bodily energy, the expenditure of the physical capacity, is greater in one case than the other.

Sailors and soldiers both, are led by certain inducements to place themselves within certain limits, and for a certain time, both defined by contract, in a condition resembling, in many particulars, that of slaves; and, although they are bound by their voluntary contract and by legal and moral considerations to obey orders, the fact that force is also used to secure their obedience to their officers, scarcely ever fails to produce in them the identical vices which are complained of in slaves. They obey the letter, but defeat the intention of orders that do not please them; they are improvident, wasteful, reckless: they sham illness, and as Dr. Cartwright gives specific medical appellations to discontent, laziness, and rascality, so among sailors and soldiers, when men suddenly find themselves ill and unable to do their duty in times of peculiar danger, or when unusual labor is required, they are humorously said to be suffering under an attack of the powder-fever, the cape-fever, the ice-fever, the coast-fever, or the reefing-fever. The counteracting influences to these vices, which it is the first effort of every good officer to foster, are, first, regard to duty; second, patriotism; third, *esprit du corps,* or professional pride; fourth, self-respect, or personal pride; fifth, self-interest, hope of promotion, or of bounty, or of privileges in mitigation of their hard service, as reward for excellence. Things are never quickly done at sea, unless they are done with a will, or "cheerly," as the sailor's word is—that is, cheerfully. An army is never effective in the field when depressed in its *morale.*

None of these promptings to excellence can be operative, except in a very low degree, to counteract the indolent and vicious tendencies of the Slavery, much more pure than the slavery of the army or the ship, by which the exertions of the Virginia labourer are obtained for his employer.

Incidents, trifling in themselves, constantly betray to a stranger what must be the necessary consequences. The catastrophe of one such occurred since I began to write this letter. I requested a fire to be made in my room, as I was going out this morning. On my return, I found a grand fire—the room door having been closed upon it, and, by the way, I had to obtain assistance to open it, the lock being "out of order." Just now, while I was writing, down tumbled upon the floor, and rolled away close to the valance of the bed, half a hodful of ignited coal, which had been so piled up on the grate, and left without a fender or any guard, that this result was almost inevitable. And such carelessness of servants you have momentarily to notice.

But the constantly-occurring delays, and the waste of time and labour that you encounter everywhere, are most annoying and provoking to a stranger. At an hotel, for instance, you go to your room and find no conveniences for washing; ring and ring again, and hear the office-keeper ring again and again. At length two servants appear together at your door, get orders, and go away. A quarter of an hour afterwards, perhaps, one returns with a pitcher of water, but no towels; and so on. Yet as the servants seem anxious to please, it can only result from want of system and order.

Until the negro is big enough for his labor to be plainly profitable to his master, he has no training to application or method, but only to idleness and carelessness. Before the children arrive at a working age, they hardly come under the notice of their owner. An inventory of them is taken on the plantation at Christmas; and a planter told me that sometimes they escaped the attention of the overseer and were not returned at all, till twelve or thirteen years old. The only whipping of slaves I have seen in Virginia, has been of these wild, lazy children, as they are being broke in to work. They cannot be depended upon a minute, out of sight.

You will see how difficult it would be, if it were attempted, to eradicate the indolent, careless, incogitant habits so formed in youth. But it is not systematically attempted, and the influences that continue to act upon a slave in the same direction, cultivating every quality at variance with industry, precision, forethought, and providence, are innumerable.

It is not wonderful that the habits of the whole community should be influenced by, and be made to accommodate to these habits of its labourers. It irresistibly affects the whole industrial character of the people. You may see it in the habits and manners of the free white mechanics and trades-people. All of these must have dealings or be in competition with slaves, and so have their standard of excellence made low, and become accustomed to, until they are content with slight, false, unsound workmanship. You notice in all classes, vagueness in ideas of cost and value, and injudicious and unnecessary expenditure of labour by a thoughtless manner of setting about work.[6] For instance, I noticed a rivet loose in my umbrella, as I was going out from my hotel during a shower, and stepped into an adjoining shop to have it repaired.

"I can't do it in less than half an hour, sir, and it will be worth a quarter," said the locksmith, replying to inquiries.

"I shouldn't think it need take you so long—it is merely a rivet to be tightened."

"I shall have to take it all to pieces, and it will take me all of half an hour."

"I don't think you need take it to pieces."

"Yes, I shall—there's no other way to do it."

"Then, as I can't well wait so long, I will not trouble you with it"; and I went back to the hotel, and with the fire-poker did the work myself, in less than a minute, as well as he could have done it in a week, and went on my way, saving half an hour and quarter of a dollar, like a "Yankee."

Virginians laugh at us for such things: but it is because they are

[6] A ship's officer told me that he had noticed that it took just about three times as long to have the same repairs made in Norfolk that it did in New York.

indifferent to these fractions, or, as they say, above regarding them, that they cannot do their own business with the rest of the world; and all their commerce, as they are absurdly complaining, only goes to enrich Northern men. A man forced to labour under their system is morally driven to indolence, carelessness, indifference to the results of skill, heedlessness, inconstancy of purpose, improvidence, and extravagance. Precisely the opposite qualities are those which are encouraged, and inevitably developed in a man who has to make his living, and earn all his comfort by his voluntarily-directed labour.

"It is with dogs," says an authority [W. W. Hutchinson] on the subject, "as it is with horses; no work is so well done as that which is done cheerfully." And it is with men, both black and white, as it is with horses and with dogs; it is even more so, because the strength and cunning of a man is less adapted to being "broken" to the will of another than that of either dogs or horses.

Work accomplished in a given time.—Mr. T. R. Griscom, of Petersburg, Virginia, stated to me, that he once took accurate account of the labour expended in harvesting a large field of wheat; and the result was that one quarter of an acre a day was secured for each able hand engaged in cradling, raking, and binding. The crop was light, yielding not over six bushels to the acre. In New York a gang of fair cradlers and binders would be expected, under ordinary circumstances, to secure a crop of wheat, yielding from twenty to thirty bushels to the acre, at the rate of about two acres a day for each man.

Mr. Griscom formerly resided in New Jersey; and since living in Virginia has had the superintendence of very large agricultural operations, conducted with slave-labour. After I had, in a letter, intended for publication, made use of this testimony, I called upon him to ask if he would object to my giving his name with it. He was so good as to permit me to do so, and said that I might add that the ordinary waste in harvesting wheat in Virginia, through the carelessness of the negroes, beyond that which occurs in the hands of ordinary Northern labourers, is equal in value to what a Northern farmer would often consider a satisfactory profit on his crop. He also wished me to say that it was his deliberate opinion, formed not without much and accurate observation, that four Virginia slaves do not, when engaged in ordinary agricultural operations, accomplish as much, on an average, as one ordinary free farm labourer in New Jersey.

Mr. Griscom is well known at Petersburg as a man remarkable for accuracy and preciseness; and no man's judgment on this subject could be entitled to more respect.

Another man, who had superintended labour of the same character at the North and in Virginia, whom I questioned closely, agreed entirely with Mr. Griscom, believing that four negroes had to be supported on every farm in the State to accomplish the same work which was ordinarily done by one free labourer in New York.

A clergyman from Connecticut, who had resided for many years in Virginia, told me that what a slave expected to spend a day upon, a Northern labourer would, he was confident, usually accomplish by eleven o'clock in the morning.

In a letter on this subject, most of the facts given in which have been already narrated in this volume, written from Virginia to the *New York Times,* I expressed the conviction that, at the most, not more than one-half as much labour was ordinarily accomplished in Virginia by a certain number of slaves, in a given time, as by an equal number of free labourers in New York. The publication of this letter induced a number of persons to make public the conclusions of their own experience or observations on this subject. So far as I know, these, in every case, sustained my conclusions, or, if any doubt was expressed, it was that I had under-estimated the superior economy of free-labour. As affording evidence more valuable than my own on this important point, from the better opportunities of forming sound judgment, which a residence at different times, in both Virginia and a Free State had given the writers, I have reprinted, in an Appendix, two of these letters, together with a quantity of other testimony from Southern witnesses on this subject, which I beg the reader, who has any doubt of the correctness of my information, not to neglect.

"*Driving.*"—On mentioning to a gentleman in Virginia (who believed that slave-labour was better and cheaper than free-labour) Mr. Griscom's observation, he replied: that without doubting the correctness of the statement of that particular instance, he was sure that if four men did not harvest more than an acre of wheat a day, they could not have been well "driven." He knew that, if properly driven, threatened with punishment, and punished if necessary, negroes would do as much work as it was possible for any white man to do. The same gentleman, however, at another time, told me that negroes were seldom punished; not oftener, he presumed, than apprentices were, at the North; that the driving of them was generally left to overseers, who were the laziest and most worthless dogs in the world, frequently not demanding higher wages for their services than one of the negroes whom they were given to manage might be hired for. Another gentleman told me that he would rather, if the law would permit it, have some of his negroes for overseers, than any white man he had ever been able to obtain in that capacity.

Another planter, whom I requested to examine a letter on the subject, that I had prepared for the *Times*, that he might, if he could, refute my calculations, or give me any facts of an opposite character, after reading it said: "The truth is, that, in general, a slave does not do half the work he easily might; and which, by being harsh enough with him, he can be made to do. When I came into possession of my plantation, I soon found the overseer then upon it was good for nothing, and told him I had no further occasion for his services: I then went to driving the negroes myself. In the morning, when I went out, one of them came up to me and asked what work he should go about. I told him to go into the swamp and cut some wood. 'Well, massa,' said he, 's'pose you wants me to do kordins we's been use to doin'; ebery nigger cut a cord a day.' 'A cord! that's what you have been used to doing, is it?' said I. 'Yes, massa, dat's wot dey always makes a nigger do roun' heah—a cord a day, dat's allers de task.' 'Well, now, old man,' [7] said I, 'you go and cut me two cords to-day.' 'Oh, massa! two cords! Nobody couldn' do dat. Oh! massa, dat's too hard! Nebber heard o' nobody's cuttin' more'n a cord o' wood in a day, roun' heah. No nigger couldn' do it.' 'Well, old man, you have two cords of wood cut to-night, or to-morrow morning you will have two hundred lashes—that's all there is about it. So, look sharp!' Of course, he did it, and

---

[7] "Old Man" is a common title of address to any middle-aged negro in Virginia whose name is not known. "Boy" and "Old Man" may be applied to the same person. Of course, in this case, the slave is not to be supposed to be beyond his prime of strength.

no negro has ever cut less than two cords a day for me since, though my neighbors still get but one cord. It was just so with a great many other things—mauling rails: I always have two hundred rails mauled in a day; just twice what it is the custom, in our country, to expect of a negro, and just twice as many as my negroes had been made to do before I managed them myself."

This only makes it more probable that the amount of labour ordinarily and generally performed by slaves in Virginia is very small, compared with that done by the labourers of the Free States.

Of course, it does not follow that all articles produced by such labour cost four times as much as in New York. There are other elements of cost besides labour, as land and fuel. I could not have a bushel of lime or salt or coal dug for me on my farm at Staten Island at any price. There are farms in Virginia where either could be obtained by an hour's labour.

Yet now, as I think of all the homes of which I have had a glimpse, it does not seem to me that men who are reputed to be worth $400,000 have equal advantages of wealth here with those whose property is valued at a quarter that, in the Eastern Free States; men with $40,000 live not as well here, all things considered, as men worth $10,000 at the North; and the farmer who owns half a dozen negroes, and who I suppose must be called worth $4000, does not approach in his possession of civilized comfort, the well-to-do working man with us, who rents a small house, and whose property consists in its furniture, his tools, skill, and strength, and who has a few hundred dollars laid up in the Savings-Bank, against a rainy day. I do not need to ask a farmer, then, any longer why he lifts his stable door into its place, and fastens it by leaning a log against it, as he evidently has been doing for years. He cannot afford to buy or hire a blacksmith for his little farm, and what with going and coming, and paying in corn which must be carried a number of miles over scarcely passable roads, our thriftiest farmers would wait for better times, perhaps, before they would take half the trouble or give a third as much corn as the blacksmith will want for the job, to save a minute's time whenever they needed to enter and leave their stable. And so with everything. Any substantial work costs so much, not alone in money or corn directly, but in the time and trouble of effecting the exchange, that the people make shift and do without it. And this is evidently the case not only with the people as individuals and families, but in their community. It is more obvious, if possible, in the condition of the houses of worship, the schools, the roads, the public conveyances; finally, it accounts for what at first sight appears the marvellous neglect or waste of the natural resources of the country, and it no longer surprises me that a farmer points out a coal bed, which has never been worked, in the bank of a stream which has never been dammed, in the midst of a forest of fine timber trees, with clay and lime and sand convenient, and who yet lives in a miserable smoky cabin of logs on a diet almost exclusively formed of pounded maize and bacon. Nor, when I ask, if a little painstaking here and there would not save much waste of fertility, that he should reply, that inasmuch as land enough, equally good, can be bought for six dollars an acre, the whole fertile matter can be better lost than a week's labour be spent to save all that will not go into this year's crop.

To this general rule of make shift, there is but rare exception; to the general rule of the difficulty or expense of accomplishing any ordinary aim of civilized, in distinction from savage society, I am inclined to think that there is none in Virginia. There are, however, individuals and localities and communities and enterprises, upon which the forces of wealth—including both capital and talent, or energy—seem to have concentrated, just as we sometimes observe to be the case at the North. It is true also, as Virginians are fond of asserting, that absolute destitution of the means of preserving life is more rare than at the North, but then life is barely preserved with little labour by a naked savage in the wilderness; and it must be said that a great number, I almost think a majority, of the Eastern Virginians live but one step removed from what we should deem great destitution at the North. I am sure, upon consideration, that this phrase would convey no unjust idea of the life of the majority of the Virginians, whom I have seen, to the people of a New England manufacturing town.

I have said that there are points where the forces of wealth seem to have concentrated. As a rule the farm-labour of a slave accomplishes not half as much in a day, as at the North; that of a white man, probably, not a third; that of most mechanics, because of their carelessness and unfaithfulness, much less than of most at the North, although they are paid more than there. But it is true, there are apparent exceptions, and I have been at times a good deal puzzled by them. Generally a patient study discovers a concealed force. Most commonly, I think, the explanation is given in the converse of the maxim that "high wages are the cheapest." The workman who commands much more than the ruling rate of wages is hard to be got, and proverbially accomplishes much more for his employer than the excess of his wages indicates. The man who cannot command the current rates is the first to be dropped off on a reduction, the last to be taken on at an increase of force. As prime field-hand slaves furnish the standard of labour in Virginia, and the vast majority of labourers are far below that standard in quality, their labour is paid much less, and it is of less value relative to its cost. Most of the labouring class of Virginia are of a quality which our farmers would call "dear at any price." If, then, by unusually skilful and energetic management, under favourable circumstances, the labour of slaves, in certain instances, seems to accomplish as much for its course as that of free labourers at the North, it does not follow that results of labour of all kinds in Virginia do not cost ordinarily, and on average, twice or thrice as much as in the adjoining Free States.

Whenever I have found unusual efficiency apparent in any enterprise in Virginia—as sometimes in railroad *construction,* milling, and mining—I have thus far invariably found the negroes employed to be picked men, and, when my inquiries have been frankly answered, that they were working under some unusual stimulus. For instance, a tobacco manufacturer pays the owner of a valuable negro $140 a year for his services, undertaking also to feed and clothe him and otherwise care for his permanent value. He then offers to pay the negro a certain rate per pound for all the tobacco he works up beyond a certain quantity. One of the largest manufacturers informed me that he paid seldom less than $60 a year, and sometimes over $300, to each slave he used, in addition to the rent paid their masters, which was from $100 to $150 a year. I did not learn the averages, but suppose that, while the nominal wages for the labour of these slaves was but little more than the ruling market-rate of $120 a year, their labour really cost the manufacturer at least double that. Hardly any of the white labour employed in enterprises which are pursued with energy and efficiency is native, nor does it ever, so far as I have seen, seem to be established and at home.

Chapter V

The Carolinas

Norfolk.—In order to be in time for the train of cars in which I was to leave Petersburg for Norfolk, I was called up at an unusual hour in the morning and provided with an apology for breakfast, on the ground that there had not been time to prepare anything better (though I was charged full time on the bill), advised by the landlord to hurry when I seated myself at the table, and two minutes afterwards informed that, if I remained longer, I should be too late.

Thanks to these kind precautions, I reached the station twenty minutes before the train left, and was afterwards carried, with about fifty other people, at the rate of ten miles an hour, to Citypoint, where all were discharged under a dirty shed, from which a wharf projected into James River.

The train was advertised to connect here with a steamboat for Norfolk. Finding no steamboat at the wharf, I feared, at first, that the delay in leaving Petersburg and the slow speed upon the road had detained us so long that the boat had departed without us. But observing no disappointment or concern expressed by the other passengers, I concluded the boat was to call for us, and had yet to arrive. An hour passed, during which I tried to keep warm by walking up and down the wharf; rain then commenced falling, and I returned to the crowded shed and asked a young man, who was engaged in cutting the letters G. W. B., with a dirk-knife, upon the head of a tobacco-cask, what was supposed to have detained the steamboat.

"Detained her? there aint no detention to her, as I know on; 'taint hardly time for her to be along yet."

Another half-hour, in fact, passed, before the steamboat arrived, nor was any impatience manifested by the passengers. All seemed to take this hurrying and waiting process as the regular thing. The women sat sullenly upon trunks and packing-cases, and watched their baggage and restrained their children; the men chewed tobacco and read newspapers; lounged first on one side and then on the other; some smoked, some walked away to a distant tavern; some reclined on the heaps of freight and went to sleep, and a few conversed quietly and intermittently with one another.

The shores of the James River are low and level—the scenery uninteresting; but frequent planters' mansions, often of considerable size and of some elegance, stand upon the bank, and sometimes these have very pretty and well-kept grounds about them, and the plantations surrounding them are cultivated with neatness and skill. Many men distinguished in law and politics here have their homes.

I was pleased to see the appearance of enthusiasm with which some passengers, who were landed from our boat at one of these places, were received by two or three well-dressed negro servants, who had come from the house to the wharf to meet them. Black and white met with kisses; and the effort of a long-haired sophomore to maintain his dignity, was quite ineffectual to kill the kindness of a fat mulatto woman, who joyfully and pathetically shouted, as she caught him off the gang-plank, "Oh Massa George, is you come back!" Field negroes, standing by, looked on with their usual besotted expression, and neither offered nor received greetings.

Jan. 10th [1853].—Norfolk is a dirty, low, ill-arranged town, nearly divided by a morass. It has a single creditable public building, a number of fine private residences, and the polite society is reputed to be agreeable, refined, and cultivated, receiving a character from the families of the resident naval officers. It has all the immoral and disagreeable characteristics of a large seaport, with very few of the advantages that we should expect to find as relief to them. No lyceum or public libraries, no public gardens, no galleries of art, and though there are two "Bethels," no "home" for its seamen; no public resorts of healthful amusement; no place better than a filthy, tobacco-impregnated bar-room or a licentious dance-cellar, so far as I have been able to learn, for the stranger of high or low degree to pass the hours unoccupied by business.

Lieut. [Matthew F.] Maury has lately very well shown what advantages were originally possessed for profitable commerce at this point, in a report, the intention of which is to advocate the establishment of a line of steamers hence to Para, the port of the mouth of the Amazon. He says—

Norfolk is in a position to have commanded the business of the Atlantic sea-board: it is midway the coast. It has a back country of great facility and resources; and, as to approaches to the ocean, there is no harbour from the St. John's to the Rio Grande that has the same facilities of ingress and egress at all times and in all weathers. . . . The back country of Norfolk is all that which is drained by the Chesapeake Bay—embracing a line drawn along the ridge between the Delaware and the Chesapeake, thence northerly, including all of Pennsylvania that is in the valley of the Susquehanna, all of Maryland this side of the mountains, the valleys of the Potomac, Rappahannock, York, and James Rivers, with the Valley of the Roanoke, and a great part of the State of North Carolina, whose only outlet to the sea is by the way of Norfolk.

In a letter to the *National Intelligencer,* Oct. 31, 1854, after describing similar advantages which the town possesses, to those enumerated above, Lieut. Maury, who is a Virginian, again says—

Its climate is delightful. It is of exactly that happy temperature where the frosts of the North bite not, and the pestilence of the South walks not. Its harbour is commodious and safe as safe can be. It is never blocked up by ice. It has the double advantage of an inner and an outer harbour. The inner harbour is as smooth as any mill-pond. In it vessels lie with perfect security, where every imaginable facility is offered for loading and unloading. . . . The back country, which without portage is *naturally* tributary to Norfolk, not only surpasses that which is tributary to New York in mildness of climate, in fertility of soil, and variety of production, but in geographical extent by many square miles. The proportion being as *three to one* in favour of the Virginia port. . . . The *natural* advantages, then, in relation to the sea or the back country, are superior, *beyond comparison,* to those of New York.

There is little, if any exaggeration in this estimate; yet, if a deadly, enervating pestilence had always raged here, this Norfolk could not be a more miserable, sorry little seaport town than it is. It was not possible to prevent the existence of some agency here for the transhipment of goods, and for supplying the needs of vessels, compelled by exterior circumstances to take refuge in the harbour. Beyond this bare supply of a necessitous demand, and what results from the adjoining naval rendezvous of the nation, there is nothing.

Jan. 18th.—The "Great Dismal Swamp," together with the smaller "Dismals" (for so the term is used here), of the same character, along the North Carolina coast, have hitherto been of considerable commercial importance as furnishing a large amount of lumber, and especially of shingles for our Northern use, as well as for exportation. The district from which this commerce proceeds is all a

vast quagmire, the soil being entirely composed of decayed vegetable fibre, saturated and surcharged with water; yielding or *quak-
ing* on the surface to the tread of a man, and a large part of it,
during most of the year, half inundated with standing pools. It is
divided by creeks and water-veins, and in the centre is a pond six
miles long and three broad, the shores of which, strange to say, are
at a higher elevation above the sea, than any other part of the
swamp, and yet are of the same miry consistency. The Great Dismal
is about thirty miles long and ten miles wide, on an average; its
area about 200,000 acres. And the little Dismal, Aligator, Catfish,
Green, and other smaller swamps, on the shores of Albemarle and
Pamlico, contain over 2,000,000 acres.

The swamp belongs to a great many proprietors. Most of them
own only a few acres, but some possess large tracts and use a heavy
capital in the business. One, whose acquaintance I made, employed more than a hundred hands in getting out shingles alone.
The value of the swamp land varies with the wood upon it, and the
facility with which it can be got off, from 12½ cents to $10 an acre.
It is made passable in any desired direction in which trees grow,
by laying logs, cut in lengths of eight or ten feet, parallel and
against each other on the surface of the soil, or "sponge," as it is
called. Mules and oxen are used to some extent upon these roads,
but transportation is mainly by hand to the creeks, or to ditches
communicating with them or the canal.

Except by those log-roads, the swamp is scarcely passable in
many parts, owing not only to the softness of the sponge, but to the
obstruction caused by innumerable shrubs, vines, creepers, and
briars, which often take entire possession of the surface, forming a
dense brake or jungle. This, however, is sometimes removed by
fires, which of late years have been frequent and very destructive
to the standing timber. The most common shrubs are various
smooth-leafed evergreens, and their dense, bright, glossy foliage
was exceedingly beautiful in the wintry season of my visit. There
is a good deal of game in the swamp—bears and wildcats are sometimes shot, raccoons and opossums are plentiful, and deer are found
in the drier parts and on the outskirts. The fishing, in the interior
waters, is also said to be excellent.

Nearly all the valuable trees have now been cut off from the
swamp. The whole ground has been frequently gone over, the best

timber selected and removed at each time, leaving the remainder standing thinly, so that the wind has more effect upon it; and much of it, from the yielding of the soft soil, is uprooted or broken off. The fires have also greatly injured it. The principal stock, now worked into shingles, is obtained *from beneath the surface*—old trunks that have been preserved by the wetness of the soil, and that are found by "sounding" with poles, and raised with hooks or pikes by the negroes.

The quarry is giving out, however; and except that lumber, and especially shingles, have been in great demand at high prices of late, the business would be almost at an end. As it is, the principal men engaged in it are turning their attention to other and more distant supplies. A very large purchase had been made by one company in the Florida everglades, and a schooner, with a gang of hands trained in the "Dismals," was about to sail from Deep Creek, for this new field of operations.

The labour in the swamp is almost entirely done by slaves; and the way in which they are managed is interesting and instructive. They are mostly hired by their employers at a rent, perhaps of one hundred dollars a year for each, paid to their owners. They spend one or two months of the winter—when it is too wet to work in the swamp—at the residence of their master. At this period little or no work is required of them; their time is their own, and if they can get any employment, they will generally keep for themselves what they are paid for it. When it is sufficiently dry—usually early in February—they go into the swamp in gangs, each gang under a white overseer. Before leaving, they are all examined and registered at the Court House; and "passes," good for a year, are given them, in which their features and the marks upon their persons are minutely described. Each man is furnished with a quantity of provisions and clothing, of which, as well as of all that he afterwards draws from the stock in the hands of the overseer, an exact account is kept.

Arrived at their destination, a rude camp is made; huts of logs, poles, shingles, and boughs being built, usually, upon some places where shingles have been worked before, and in which the shavings have accumulated in small hillocks upon the soft surface of the ground.

The slave lumberman then lives measurably as a free man; hunts, fishes, eats, drinks, smokes and sleeps, plays and works, each when and as much as he pleases. It is only required of him that he shall have made, after half a year has passed, such a quantity of shingles as shall be worth to his master so much money as is paid to his owner for his services, and shall refund the value of the clothing and provisions he has required.

No "driving" at his work is attempted or needed. No force is used to overcome the indolence peculiar to the negro. The overseer merely takes a daily account of the number of shingles each man adds to the general stock, and employs another set of hands, with mules, to draw them to a point from which they can be shipped, and where they are, from time to time, called for by a schooner.

At the end of five months the gang returns to dry land, and a statement of account from the overseer's book is drawn up, something like the following:—

Sam Bo to John Doe, Dr.

Feb. 1. To clothing (outfit)	$ 5 00
Mar. 10. To clothing, as per overseer's account	2 25
Feb. 1. To bacon and meal (outfit) . . .	19 00
July 1. To stores drawn in swamp, as per over-	
seer's account	4 75
July 1. To half-yearly hire, paid his owner . .	50 00
	$ 81 00

Per Contra, Cr.

July 1. By 10,000 shingles, as per overseer's		
account, 10c.	100 00	
Balance due Sambo	———	$19 00

which is immediately paid him, and of which, together with the proceeds of sale of peltry which he has got while in the swamp, he is always allowed to make use as his own. No liquor is sold or served to the negroes in the swamp, and, as their first want when they come out of it is an excitement, most of their money goes to the grog-shops.

After a short vacation, the whole gang is taken in the schooner to spend another five months in the swamp as before. If they are good hands and work steadily, they will commonly be hired again, and so continuing, will spend most of their lives at it. They almost invariably have excellent health, as have also the white men engaged in the business. They all consider the water of the "Dismals" to have a medicinal virtue, and quite probably it is a mild tonic. It is greenish in colour, and I thought I detected a slightly resinous taste upon first drinking it. Upon entering the swamp also, an agreeable resinous odour, resembling that of a hemlock forest, was perceptible.

The negroes working in the swamp were more sprightly and straightforward in their manner and conversation than any field-hand plantation negroes that I saw at the South; two or three of their employers with whom I conversed spoke well of them, as compared with other slaves, and made no complaints of "rascality" or laziness.

One of those gentlemen told me of a remarkable case of providence and good sense in a negro that he had employed in the swamp for many years. He was so trustworthy, that he had once let him go to New York as cook of a lumber schooner, when he could, if he had chosen to remain there, have easily escaped from slavery.

Knowing that he must have accumulated considerable money, his employer suggested to him that he might *buy* his freedom, and he immediately determined to do so. But when, on applying to his owner, he was asked $500 for himself, a price which, considering he was an elderly man, he thought too much, he declined the bargain; shortly afterwards, however, he came to his employer again, and said that although he thought his owner was mean to set so high a price upon him, he had been thinking that if he was to be an old man he would rather be his own master, and if he did not live long, his money would not be of any use to him at any rate, and so he had concluded he would make the purchase.

He did so, and upon collecting the various sums that he had loaned to white people in the vicinity, he was found to have several hundred dollars more than was necessary. With the surplus, he paid for his passage to Liberia, and bought a handsome outfit. When he was about to leave, my informant had made him a present, and, in thanking him for it, the free man had said that the first thing he should do, on reaching Liberia, would be to learn to write, and, as soon as he could, he would write to him how he liked the country: he had been gone yet scarce a year, and had not been heard from.

Deep River, Jan. 18th.—The shad and herring fisheries upon the
sounds and inlets of the North Carolina coast are an important
branch of industry, and a source of considerable wealth. The men
employed in them are mainly negroes, slave and free; and the manner in which they are conducted is interesting, and in some respects
novel.

The largest sweep seines in the world are used. The gentleman to
whom I am indebted for the most of my information, was the proprietor of a seine over two miles in length. It was manned by a force
of forty negroes, most of whom were hired at a dollar a day, for the
fishing season, which usually commences between the tenth and fif-
teenth of March, and lasts fifty days. In favourable years the profits
are very great. In extremely unfavourable years many of the proprietors are made bankrupt.

Cleaning, curing, and packing houses are erected on the shore, as
near as they conveniently may be to a point on the beach, suitable
for drawing the seine. Six or eight windlasses, worked by horses, are
fixed along the shore, on each side of this point. There are two large
seine-boats, in each of which there is one captain, two seine-tenders,
and eight or ten oarsmen. In making a cast of the net, one-half of it
is arranged on the stern of each of the boats, which, having previously been placed in a suitable position—perhaps a mile off shore,
in front of the buildings—are rowed from each other, the captains
steering, and the seine-tenders throwing off, until the seine is all cast
between them. This is usually done in such a way that it describes
the arc of a circle, the chord of which is diagonal with the shore. The
hawsers attached to the ends of the seine are brought first to the
outer windlasses, and are wound in by the horses. As the operation
of gathering in the seine occupies several hours, the boat hands, as
soon as they have brought the hawsers to the shore, draw their boats
up, and go to sleep.

As the wings approach the shore, the hawsers are from time to
time carried to the other windlasses, to contract the sweep of the
seine. After the gaff of the net reaches the shore, lines attached toward the bunt are carried to the windlasses, and the boats' crews are
awakened, and arrange the wing of the seine, as fast as it comes in,
upon the boat again. Of course, as the cast was made diagonally
with the shore, one wing is beached before the other. By the time the
fish in the bunt have been secured, both boats are ready for another

cast, and the boatmen proceed to make it, while the shore gang is engaged in sorting and gutting the "take."

My informant, who had $50,000 invested in his fishing establishment, among other items of expenditure, mentioned that he had used seventy kegs of gunpowder the previous year, and amused himself for a few moments with letting me try to conjecture in what way villainous saltpetre could be put to use in taking fish.

There is evidence of a subsidence of this coast, in many places, at a comparatively recent period; many stumps of trees, evidently standing where they grew, being found some way below the present surface, in the swamps and salt marshes. Where the formation of the shore and the surface, or the strength of the currents of water, which have flowed over the sunken land, has been such as to prevent a later deposit, the stumps of great cypress trees, not in the least decayed, protrude from the bottom of the sounds. These would obstruct the passage of a net, and must be removed from a fishing-ground.

The operation of removing them is carried on during the summer, after the close of the fishing season. The position of a stump having been ascertained by divers, two large seine-boats are moored over it, alongside each other, and a log is laid across them, to which is attached perpendicularly, between the boats, a spar, fifteen feet long. The end of a chain is hooked to the log, between the boats, the other end of which is fastened by divers to the stump which it is wished to raise. A double-purchase tackle leads from the end of the spar to a ring-bolt in the bows of one of the boats, with the fall leading aft, to be bowsed upon by the crews. The mechanical advantages of the windlass, the lever, and the pulley being thus combined, the chain is wound on to the log, until either the stump yields, and is brought to the surface, or the boats' gunwales are brought to the water's edge.

When the latter is the case, and the stump still remains firm, a new power must be applied. A spile, pointed with iron, six inches in diameter, and twenty feet long, is set upon the stump by a diver, who goes down with it, and gives it that direction which, in his judgment, is best, and driven into it by mauls and sledges, a scaffold being erected between the boats for men to stand on while driving it. In very large stumps, the spile is often driven till its top reaches the water; so that when it is drawn out, a cavity is left in the stump, ten feet in depth. A tube is now used, which is made by welding together three musket-barrels, with a breech at one end, in which is the tube of a percussion breech, with the ordinary position of the nipple reversed, so that when it is screwed on with a detonating cap, the latter will protrude within the barrel. This breech is then inserted within a cylindrical tin box, six inches in diameter, and varying in length, according to the supposed strength of the stump; and soap or tallow is smeared about the place of insertion to make it water tight. The box contains several pounds of gunpowder.

The long iron tube is elevated, and the diver goes down again, and guides it into the hole in the stump, with the canister in his arms. It has reached the bottom—the diver has come up, and is drawn into one of the boats—an iron rod is inserted in the mouth of the tube— all hands crouch low, and hold hard—the rod is let go—crack!—whoo —oosch! The sea swells, boils, and breaks upward. If the boats do not rise with it, they must sink; if they rise, and the chain does not break, the stump must rise with them. At the same moment the heart of cypress is riven; its furthest rootlets quiver; the very earth trembles, and loses courage to hold it; "up comes the stump, or down go the niggers!"

The success of the operation evidently depends mainly on the discretion and skill of the diver. My informant, who thought that he removed last summer over a thousand stumps, using for the purpose seventy kegs of gunpowder, employed several divers, all of them negroes. Some of them could remain under water, and work there to better advantage than others; but all were admirably skilful, and this, much in proportion to the practice and experience they had had. They wear, when diving, three or four pairs of flannel drawers and shirts. Nothing is required of them when they are not wanted to go to the bottom, and, while the other hands are at work, they may lounge, or go to sleep in the boat, which they do, in their wet garments. Whenever a diver displays unusual hardihood, skill, or perseverance, he is rewarded with whisky; or, as they are commonly allowed, while diving, as much whisky as they want, with money. Each of them would generally get every day from a quarter to half a dollar in this way, above the wages paid for them, according to the skill and industry with which they had worked. On this account, said my informant, "the harder the work you give them to do, the better they like it." His divers very frequently had intermittent fevers, but would very rarely let this keep them out of their boats. Even in the midst of a severe "shake," they would generally insist that they were "well enough to dive."

What! slaves eager to work, and working cheerfully, earnestly, and skilfully? Even so. Being for the time managed as freemen, their ambition stimulated by wages, suddenly they, too, reveal sterling manhood, and honour their Creator.

Norfolk, Jan. 19*th.*—The market gardens at Norfolk—which have been profitably supplying New York markets with poor early vege-tables, and half-hardy luxuries for several years past—do not differ at all from market gardens elsewhere. They are situated in every direction for many miles from the city, offering a striking contrast, in all respects, to the large, old-fashioned Virginian farms, among which they are scattered.

On one of the latter, of over a thousand acres, a friend told me he had seen the negroes moving long, strawy manure with shovels, and upon inquiry found there was not a dung-fork on the place.

The soil is a poor sandy loam, and manure is brought by shipping from Baltimore, as well as from the nearer towns, to enrich it. The proprietors of the market gardens are nearly all from New Jersey, and brought many of their old white labourers with them. Except at picking-time, when everything possessing fingers is in demand, they do not often employ slaves.

The *Norfolk Argus* says that, from about the 20th June to the 20th July, from 2,000 to 2,500 barrels of potatoes will be shipped daily from that city to Philadelphia and New York, together with 300 to 500 barrels of cucumbers, muskmelons, etc.

Norfolk, Jan. 20*th.*—While driving a chaise from Portsmouth to Deep River, I picked up on the road a jaded-looking negro, who proved to be a very intelligent and good-natured fellow. His ac-count of the lumber business, and of the life of the lumbermen in the swamps, in answer to my questions, was clear and precise, and was afterwards verified by information obtained from his master.

He told me that his name was Joseph, that he belonged (as prop-erty) to a church in one of the inland counties, and that he was hired from the trustees of the church by his present master. He ex-pressed contentment with his lot, but great unwillingness to be sold to go on to a plantation. He liked to "mind himself," as he did in the swamps. Whether he would still more prefer to be entirely his own master, I did not ask.

The Dismal Swamps are noted places of refuge for runaway negroes. They were formerly peopled in this way much more than at present; a systematic hunting of them with dogs and guns having been made by individuals who took it up as a business about ten years ago. Children were born, bred, lived, and died here. Joseph Church told me he had seen skeletons, and had helped to bury bodies recently dead. There were people in the swamps still, he thought, that were the children of runaways, and who had been runaways themselves "all their lives." What a life it must be! born outlaws; educated self-stealers; trained from infancy to be constantly in dread of the approach of a white man as a thing more fearful than wildcats or serpents, or even starvation.

There can be but few, however, if any, of these "natives" left. They cannot obtain the means of supporting life without coming often either to the outskirts to steal from the plantations, or to the neighbourhood of the camps of the lumbermen. They depend much upon the charity or the wages given them by the latter. The poorer white men, owning small tracts of the swamps, will sometimes employ them, and the negroes frequently. In the hands of either they are liable to be betrayed to the negro-hunters. Joseph said that they had huts in "back places" hidden by bushes, and difficult of access; he had, apparently, been himself quite intimate with them. When the shingle negroes employed them, he told me, they made them get up logs for them, and would give them enough to eat, and some clothes, and perhaps two dollars a month in money. But some, when they owed them money, would betray them, instead of paying them.

I asked if they were ever shot. "Oh, yes," he said; when the hunters saw a runaway, if he tried to get from them, they would call out to him, that if he did not stop they would shoot, and if he did not, they would shoot, and sometimes kill him.

"*But some on 'em would rather be shot than be took, sir,*" he added, simply.

A farmer living near the swamp confirmed this account, and said he knew of three or four being shot in one day.

No particular breed of dogs is needed for hunting negroes: blood-hounds, fox-hounds, bull-dogs, and curs were used,[1] and one white man told me how they were trained for it, as if it were a common or notorious practice. They are shut up when puppies, and never allowed to see a negro except while training to catch him. A negro is made to run from them, and they are encouraged to follow him until he gets into a tree, when meat is given them. Afterwards they learn to follow any particular negro by scent, and then a shoe or a piece of clothing is taken off a negro, and they learn to find by scent who it belongs to, and to tree him, etc. All this the farmer told me. I don't think dogs are employed in the ordinary "driving" in the swamp, but only to overtake some particular slave, as soon as possible, after it is discovered that he has fled from a plantation. Joseph said that it was easy for the drivers to tell a fugitive from a regularly employed slave in the swamps.

"How do they know them?"

"Oh, dey looks *strange.*"

"How do you mean?"

"*Skeared* like, you know, sir, and kind o' strange, cause dey hasn't much to eat, and ain't decent [not decently clothed], like we is."

When the hunters take a negro who has not a pass, or "free papers," and they don't know whose slave he is, they confine him in jail, and advertise him. If no one claims him within a year he is sold to the highest bidder, at a public sale, and this sale gives title in law against any subsequent claimant.

The form of the advertisements used in such cases is shown by the following, which are cut from North Carolina newspapers, published in counties adjoining the Dismals. Such advertisements are quite as common in the papers of many parts of the Slave States as those of horses or cattle "Taken up" in those of the North:—

WAS TAKEN UP and committed to the Jail of Halifax County, on the 26th day of May, a dark coloured boy, who says his name is JORDAN ARTIS. Said boy says he was born free, and was bound out to William Beale, near Murfreesboro', Hertford County, N.C., and is now 21 years of age. The owner is requested to come forward, prove property, pay

---

[1] I have since seen a pack of negro-dogs, chained in couples, and probably going to the field. They were all of a breed, and in appearance between a Scotch stag-hound and a fox-hound.

charges, and take the said boy away, within the time prescribed by law; otherwise he will be dealt with as the law directs.

O. P. SHELL, *Jailer.*

Halifax County, N.C., June 8, 1855.

TAKEN UP,

AND COMMITTED to the Jail of New Hanover County, on the 5th of March, 1855, a Negro Man, who says his name is EDWARD LLOYD. Said negro is about 35 or 40 years old, light complected, 5 feet 9½ inches high, slim built, upper fore teeth out; says he is a Mason by trade, that he is free, and belongs in Alexandria, Va., that he served his time at the Mason business under Mr. Wm. Stuart, of Alexandria. He was taken up and committed as a runaway. His owner is notified to come forward, prove property, pay charges, and take him away, or he will be dealt with as the law directs.   E. D. HALL, *Sheriff.*

In the same paper with the last are four advertisements of Runaways: two of them, as specimens, I transcribe.

$200 REWARD

RAN AWAY from the employ of Messrs. Holmes & Brown, on Sunday night, 20th inst., a negro man named YATNEY or MEDICINE, belonging to the undersigned. Said boy is stout built, about 5 feet 4 inches high, 22 years old, and dark complected, and has the appearance, when walking slow, of one leg being a little shorter than the other. He was brought from Chapel Hill, and is probably lurking either in the neighbourhood of that place, or Beatty's Bridge, in Bladen County.

The above reward will be paid for evidence sufficient to convict any white person of harbouring him, or a reward of $25 for his apprehension and confinement in any Jail in the State, so that I can get him, or for his delivery to me in Wilmington.

J. T. SCHONWALD.

RUNAWAY

FROM THE SUBSCRIBER, on the 27th of May, his negro boy ISOME. Said boy is about 21 years of age; rather light complexion; very coarse hair; weight about 150 lbs.; height about 5 feet 6 or 7 inches; rather pleasing countenance; quick and easy spoken; rather a downcast look. It is thought that he is trying to make his way to Franklin county, N.C., where he was hired in Jan. last, of Thomas J. Blackwell. A liberal Reward will be given for his confinement in any Jail in North or South Carolina, or to any one who will give information where he can be found.

W. H. PRIVETT,

Canwayboro', S.C.

Handbills, written or printed, offering rewards for the return of runaway slaves, are to be constantly seen at nearly every court-house, tavern, and post-office. The frequency with which these losses must occur, however, on large plantations, is most strongly evidenced by the following paragraph from the domestic-news columns of the *Fayetteville Observer*. A man who would pay these prices must anticipate frequent occasion to use his purchase.

Mr. J. L. Bryan, of Moore county, sold at public auction, on the 20th instant, a pack of ten hounds, trained for hunting runaways, for the sum of $1,540. The highest price paid for any one dog was $301; lowest price, $75; average for the ten, $154. The terms of sale were six months' credit, with approved security, and interest from date.

The newspapers of the South-western States frequently contain advertisements similar to the following, which is taken from the *West Tennessee Democrat:—*

BLOOD-HOUNDS.—I have TWO of the FINEST DOGS for CATCHING NEGROES in the Southwest. They can take the trail TWELVE HOURS after the NEGRO HAS PASSED, and catch him with ease. I live just four miles southwest of Boliver, on the road leading from Boliver to Whitesville. I am ready at all times to catch runaway negroes.—March 2, 1853.

DAVID TURNER.

The largest and best "hotel" in Norfolk had been closed, shortly before I was there, from want of sufficient patronage to sustain it, and I was obliged to go to another house, which, though quite pretending, was shamefully kept. The landlord paid scarcely the smallest attention to the wants of his guests, turned his back when inquiries were made of him, and replied insolently to complaints and requests. His slaves were far his superiors in manners and morals; but, not being one quarter in number what were needed, and consequently not being able to obey one quarter of the orders that were given them, their only study was to disregard, as far as they would be allowed to, all requisitions upon their time and labour. The smallest service could only be obtained by bullying or bribing. Every clean towel that I got during my stay was a matter of special negotiation.

I was first put in a very small room, in a corner of the house, next under the roof. The weather being stormy, and the roof leaky, water was frequently dripping from the ceiling upon the bed and driving in at the window, so as to stand in pools upon the floor. There was no fire-place in the room; the ladies' parlour was usually crowded by ladies and their friends, among whom I had no acquaintance, and, as it was freezing cold, I was obliged to spend most of my time in the stinking bar-room, where the landlord, all the time, sat with his boon companions, smoking and chewing and talking obscenely.

This crew of old reprobates frequently exercised their indignation upon Mrs. Stowe, and other "Infidel abolitionists"; and, on Sunday, having all attended church, afterwards mingled with their ordinary ribaldry laudations of the "evangelical" character of the sermons they had heard.

On the night I arrived, I was told that I would be provided, the next morning, with a room in which I could have a fire, and a similar promise was given me every twelve hours, for five days, before I obtained it; then, at last, I had to share it with two strangers.

When I left, the same petty sponging operation was practised upon me as at Petersburg. The breakfast, for which half a dollar had been paid, was not ready until an hour after I had been called; and, when ready, consisted of cold salt fish; dried slices of bread and tainted butter; coffee, evidently made the day before and half re-warmed; no milk, the milkman not arriving so early in the morning, the servant said; and no sooner was I seated than the choice was presented to me, by the agitated book-keeper, of going without such as this, or of losing the train, and so being obliged to stay in the house twenty-four hours longer.

Of course I dispensed with the breakfast, and hurried off with the porter, who was to take my baggage on a wheelbarrow to the station. The station was across the harbour, in Portsmouth. Notwithstanding all the haste I could communicate to him, we reached the ferry-landing just as the boat left, too late by three seconds. I looked at my watch; it lacked but twenty minutes of the time at which the landlord and the book-keeper and the breakfast-table waiter and the railroad company's advertisements had informed me that the train left. "Nebber mine, massa," said the porter, "dey won't go widout 'ou

—Baltimore boat haant ariv yet; dey doan go till dat come in, sueh."

Somewhat relieved by this assurance, and by the arrival of others at the landing, who evidently expected to reach the train, I went into the market and got a breakfast from the cake and fruit stalls of the negro-women.

In twenty minutes the ferry-boat returned, and after waiting some time at the landing, put out again; but when midway across the harbour, the wheels ceased to revolve, and for fifteen minutes we drifted with the tide. The fireman had been asleep, the fires had got low, and the steam given out. I observed that the crew, including the master or pilot, and the engineer, were all negroes.

We reached the railroad station about half an hour after the time at which the train should have left. There were several persons, prepared for travelling, waiting about it, but there was no sign of a departing train, and the ticket-office was not open. I paid the porter, sent him back, and was added to the number of the waiters.

The delay was for the Baltimore boat, which arrived in an hour after the time the train was advertised, unconditionally, to start, and the first forward movement was more than an hour and a half behind time. A brakeman told me this delay was not very unusual, and that an hour's waiting might be commonly calculated upon with safety.

The distance from Portsmouth to Welden, N.C., eighty miles, was run in three hours and twenty minutes—twenty-five miles an hour. The road, which was formerly a very poor and unprofitable one, was bought up a few years ago, mainly, I believe, by Boston capital, and reconstructed in a substantial manner. The grades are light, and there are few curves. Fare, 2¾ cents a mile.

At a way-station a trader had ready a company of negroes, intended to be shipped South; but the "servants' car" being quite full already, they were obliged to be left for another train. As we departed from the station, I stood upon the platform of the rear car with two other men. One said to the other:—

"That's a good lot of niggers."

"Damn'd good; I only wish they belonged to me."

I entered the car, and took a seat, and presently they followed, and sat near me. Continuing their conversation thus commenced, they spoke of their bad luck in life. One appeared to have been a bar-keeper; the other an overseer. One said the highest wages he had ever been paid were two hundred dollars a year, and that year he hadn't laid up a cent. Soon after, the other, speaking with much energy and bitterness, said:—

"I wish to God, old Virginny was free of all the niggers."

"It would be a good thing if she was."

"Yes, sir; and, I tell you, it would be a damn'd good thing for us poor fellows."

"I reckon it would, myself."

When we stopped at Weldon, a man was shouting from a stage-coach, "Passengers for Gaston! Hurry up! Stage is waiting!" As he repeated this the third time, I threw up to him my two valises, and proceeded to climb to the box, to take my seat.

"You are in a mighty hurry, aint ye?"

"Didn't you say the stage was waiting?"

"If ye'r goin' ter get any dinner to-day, better get it here; won't have much other chance. Be right smart about it, too."

"Then you are not going yet?"

"You can get yer dinner, if ye want to."

"You'll call me, will you, when you are ready to go?"

"I shan't go without ye, ye needn't be afeard—go 'long in, and get yer dinner; this is the place, if anywar;—don't want to go without yer dinner, do ye?"

Before arriving at Weldon, a handbill, distributed by the proprietors of this inn, had been placed in my hands, from which I make the following extracts:—

We pledge our word of honour, as gentlemen, that if the fare at our table be inferior to that on the table of our enterprising competitor, we will not receive a cent from the traveller, but relinquish our claims to pay, as a merited forfeit, for what we would regard as a wanton imposition upon the rights and claims of the unsuspecting traveller.

We have too much respect for the Ladies of our House, to make even a remote allusion to their domestic duties in a public circular. It will not however, be regarded indelicate in us to say, that the duties performed by them have been, and are satisfactory to us, and, as far as we know, to the public. And we will only add, in this connection, that we take much pleasure in superintending both our "Cook-House" and Table in person, and in administering in person to the wants of our guests.

We have made considerable improvements in our House of late, and those who wish to remain over at Weldon, will find, with us, airy rooms clean beds, brisk fires, and attentive and orderly servants, with abundance of FRESH OYSTERS during the season, and every necessary and luxury that money can procure.

It is not our wish to deceive strangers nor others; and if, on visiting our House, they do not find things as here represented, they can publish us to the world as impostors, and the ignominy will be ours.

Going into the house, I found most of the passengers by the train at dinner, and the few negro boys and girls in too much of a hurry to pay attention to any one in particular. The only palatable viand within my reach was some cold sweet potatoes; of these I made a slight repast, paid the landlord, who stood like a sentry in the doorway, half a dollar, and in fifteen minutes, by my watch, from the time I had entered, went out, anxious to make sure of my seat on the box, for the coach was so small that but one passenger could be conveniently carried outside. The coach was gone.

"O, yes, sir," said the landlord, hardly disguising his satisfaction; "gone—yes, sir, some time ago; you was in to dinner, was you, sir—pity! you'll have to stay over till to-morrow now, won't you?"

"I suppose so," said I, hardly willing to give up my intention to sleep in Raleigh that night, even to secure a clean bed and fresh oysters. "Which road does the stage go upon?"

"Along the county road."

"Which is that—this way through the woods?"

"Yes, sir.—Carried off your baggage, did he?—Pity! Suppose he forgot you. Pity!"

"Thank you—yes, I suppose he did. Is it a pretty good road?"

"No, sir, 'taint first-rate—good many pretty bad slews. You might go round by the Petersburg Railroad, to-morrow. You'd overtake your baggage at Gaston."

"Thank you. It was not a very fast team, I know. I'm going to take a little run; and, if I shouldn't come back before night, you needn't keep a bed for me. Good day, sir."

In about half an hour I overhauled the coach: as I came up, the driver hailed me—

"Hallo! that you?"

"Why did not you wait for me, or call me when you wanted to go, as you promised?"

"Reckoned yer was inside—didn't look in, coz I asked if 'twas all right, and somebody, this 'ere gentleman here"—[who had got my seat]—"'Yes,' says he, 'all right'; so I reckoned 'twas, and driv along. Mustn't blame me. Ortn't to be so long swallerin' yer dinner—mind, next time!"

The road was as bad as anything under the name of a road can be conceived to be. Wherever the adjoining swamps, fallen trees, stumps, and plantation fences would admit of it, the coach was driven, with a great deal of dexterity, out of the road. When the wheels sunk in the mud, below the hubs, we were sometimes requested to get out and walk. An upset seemed every moment inevitable. At length, it came; and the driver, climbing on to the upper side, opened the door, and asked—

"Got mixed up some in here then, didn't ye? Ladies, hurt any? Well, come, get out here; don't want to stay here all night I reckon, do ye?—Aint nothing broke, as I see. We'll right her right up. Nary durn'd rail within a thousan' mile, I don't s'pose; better be lookin' roun'; got to get somethin' for a pry."

In four hours after I left the hotel at Weldon, the coach reached the bank of the Roanoke, a distance of fourteen miles, and stopped. "Here we are," said the driver, opening the door.

"Where are we—not in Gaston?"

"Durned nigh it. That ere's Gaston, over thar; and you jast holler, and they'll come over arter you in the boat."

Gaston was a mile above us, and on the other side of the river. Nearly opposite was a house, and a scow drawn up on the beach; the distance across the river was, perhaps, a quarter of a mile. When the driver had got the luggage off, he gathered his reins, and said—

"Seems to me them ther gol-durned lazy niggers aint a goin' to come over arter you now; if they won't you'd better go up to the railroad bridge, some of ye, and get a boat, or else go down here to Free Town; some of them cussed free niggers 'll be glad of the job, I no doubt."

"But, confound it, driver! you are not going to leave us here, are you? we paid to be carried to Gaston."

"Can't help it; you are clus to Gaston, any how, and if any man thinks he's goin' to hev me drive him up to the bridge to-night, he's damnably mistaken, he is, and I ain't a goin' to do it not for no man, I ain't."

And away he drove, leaving us, all strangers, in a strange country, just at the edge of night, far from any house, to "holler."

The only way to stop him was to shoot him; and, as we were all good citizens, and travelled with faith in the protection of the law, and not like knights-errant, armed for adventure, we could not do that.

Good citizens? No, we were not, for we have all, to this day, neglected to prosecute the fellow, or his employers. It would, to be sure, have cost us ten times any damages we should have been awarded; but, if we had been really good citizens, we should have been as willing to sacrifice the necessary loss, as knights-errant of old were to risk life to fight bloody giants. And, until many of us can have the nobleness to give ourselves the trouble and expense of killing off these impudent highwaymen of our time, at law, we have all got to suffer in their traps and stratagems.

We soon saw the "gol-durned lazy niggers" come to their scow, and after a scrutiny of our numbers, and a consultation among themselves, which evidently resulted in the conclusion that the job wouldn't pay, go back.

When it began to grow dark, leaving me as a baggage-guard, the rest of the coach's company walked up the bank of the river, and crossed by a railroad bridge to Gaston. One of them afterwards returned with a gang of negroes, whom he had hired, and a large freight-boat, into which, across the snags which lined the shore, we passed all the baggage. Among the rest, there were some very large and heavy chests, belonging to two pretty women, who were moving, with their effects; and, although they remained in our company all the next day, they not only neglected to pay their share of the boat and negro-hire, but forgot to thank us, or even gratefully to smile upon us, for our long toil in the darkness for them.

Working up the swollen stream of the Roanoke, with setting-poles and oars, we at length reached Gaston. When I bought my tickets at the station in Portsmouth, I said, "I will take tickets to any place this side of Raleigh at which I can arrive before night. I wish to avoid travelling after dark." "You can go straight through to Raleigh, before dark," said the clerk. "You are sure of that?" "Yes, sir." On reaching Gaston, I inquired at what time the train for Raleigh had passed: "At three o'clock."

According to the advertisement, it should have passed at two o'clock; and, under the most favourable circumstances, it could not have been possible for us, leaving Portsmouth at the time we did, to reach Gaston before four o'clock, or Raleigh in less than twenty-eight hours after the time promised. The next day, I asked one of the railroad men how often the connection occurred, which is advertised in the Northern papers, as if it were a certain thing to take place at Gaston. "Not very often, sir; it hain't been once, in the last two weeks." Whenever the connection is not made, all passengers whom these railroad freebooters have drawn into their ambush, are obliged to remain over a day, at Gaston; for, as is to be supposed, with such management, the business of the road will support but one train a day.

The route by sea, from Baltimore to Portsmouth, and thence by these lines, is advertised as the surest, cheapest, and most expeditious route to Raleigh. Among my stage companions, were some who lived beyond Raleigh. This was Friday. They would now not reach Raleigh till Saturday night, and such as could not conscientiously travel on Sunday, would be detained from home two days longer than if they had come the land route. One of them lived some eighty miles beyond Raleigh, and intended to proceed by a coach, which was to leave Saturday morning. He would probably be now detained till the following Wednesday, as the coach left Raleigh but twice a week.

The country from Portsmouth to Gaston, eighty miles, partly in Virginia, and partly in North Carolina, is almost all pine forest, or cypress swamp; and on the little land that is cultivated, I saw no indication of any other crop than maize. The soil is light and poor. Between Weldon and Gaston there are heavier soils, and we passed several cotton fields, and planters' mansions. On the low, flat lands bordering the banks of the Roanoke, the soil is of the character of that of James River, fine, fertile, mellow loam; and the maize crop seemed to have been heavy.

Gaston is a village of some twenty houses, shops, and cabins, besides the railroad storehouses, the hotel, and a nondescript building, which may be either a fancy barn, or a little church, getting high. From the manner in which passengers are forced, by the management of the trains arriving here, to patronize it, the hotel, I presume, belongs to the railroad companies. It is ill-kept, but affords some entertainment from its travesty of certain metropolitan vulgarities. I was chummed with a Southern gentleman, in a very small room. Finding the sheets on both our beds had been soiled by previous occupants, he made a row about it with the servants, and, after a long delay, had them changed; then observing that it was probably the mistress's fault, and not the servants', he paid the negro, whom he had been berating, for his trouble.

Among our inside passengers, in the stage-coach, was a free coloured woman; she was treated in no way differently from the white ladies. My room-mate said this was entirely customary at the South, and no Southerner would ever think of objecting to it. Notwithstanding which, I have known young Southerners to get very angry because negroes were not excluded from the public conveyances in which they had taken passage themselves, at the North; and I have always supposed that when they were so excluded, it was from fear of offending Southern travellers, more than anything else.[2]

---

[2] *A South Carolina View of the Subject.* (*Correspondence of Willis's Musical World, New York.*)—"Charlestown, Dec. 31.—I take advantage of the season of compliments (being a subscriber to your invaluable sheet), to tender you this scrap, as a reply to a piece in your paper of the 17th ult., with the caption: 'Intolerance of coloured persons in New York.' The piece stated that uptown families (in New York) objected to hiring coloured persons as servants, in consequence of 'conductors and drivers refusing to let them ride in city cars and omnibuses,' and coloured boys, at most, may ride on the top. And after dwelling on this, you say, 'Shame on such intolerant and outrageous prejudice and persecution of the coloured race at the North!' You then say, 'Even the slaveholder would cry shame upon us.' You never made a truer assertion in your life. For you first stated that they were even rejected when they had white children in their arms. My dear friend, if this was the only persecution that your coloured people were compelled to yield submission to, then I might say nothing. Are they allowed (if they pay) to sit at the tables of your fashionable hotels? Are they allowed a seat in the 'dress circle' at your operas? Are they not subject to all kinds of ill-treatment from the whites? Are they not pointed at, and hooted at, by the whites (natives of the city), when dressed up a little extra, and if they offer a reply, are immediately overpowered by gangs of whites? You appear to be a reasonable writer, which is the reason I put these queries, knowing they can only be answered in the affirmative.

"We at the South feel proud to allow them to occupy seats in our omnibuses (public conveyances), while they, with the affection of mothers, embrace our white children, and take them to ride. And in our most fashionable carriages, you will see the slave sitting alongside of *their owner.* You will see the slave clothed in the most comfortable of wearing apparel. And more. Touch that slave, if you dare, and you will see the owner's attachment. And thus, in a very few words, you have the contrast between the situation of the coloured people at the North and South. Do teach the *detestable* Abolitionist of the North his duty, and open his eyes to the misery and starvation that surround his own

Sitting near some men lounging on the river-bank, I took notes of the following interesting information, delivered in a high-keyed, blatant drawl:—

"The best medicine there is, is this here Idee of Potasun. It's made out of two minerals; one on 'em they gets in the mountains of Scotland—that's the Idee; the other's steel-filings, and they mixes them eschemically until they works altogether into a solid stuff like saltpetre. Now, I tell you that's the stuff for medicine. It's the best thing a man can ever put into his self. It searches out every narve in his body."

The train by which we were finally able to leave Gaston arrived the next day an hour and a half after its advertised time. The road was excellent and the speed good, a heavy U rail having lately been substituted for a flat one. A new equipment of the road, throughout, is nearly complete. The cars of this train were very old, dirty, and with dilapidated and moth-eaten furniture. They furnished me with a comfort, however, which I have never been able to try before—a full-length lounge, on which, with my overcoat for a pillow, the car being warmed, and unintentionally well ventilated, I slept soundly after dark. Why night-trains are not furnished with sleeping apartments, has long been a wonder to me. We have now smoking-rooms and water-closets on our trains; why not sleeping, dressing, and refreshment rooms? With these additions, and good ventilation, we could go from New York to New Orleans, by rail, without stopping: as it is, a man of ordinary constitution cannot go a quarter that distance without suffering serious indisposition. Surely such improvements could not fail to be remunerative, particularly on lines competing with water communication.

The country passed through, so far as I observed, was almost entirely covered with wood; and such of it as was cultivated, very unproductive.

The city of Raleigh (old Sir Walter), the capital of North Carolina, is a pleasing town—the streets wide, and lined with trees, and many white wooden mansions, all having little court-yards of flowers and shrubbery around them. The State-house is, in every way,

---

home. *Teach him* to love his brethren of the South, and teach him to let Slavery alone in the South, while starvation and destitution surround him at the North; and oblige,

"BARON."

a noble building, constructed of brownish-gray granite, in Grecian style. It stands on an elevated position, near the centre of the city, in a square field, which is shaded by some tall old oaks, and could easily be made into an appropriate and beautiful little park; but which, with singular negligence, or more singular economy (while $500,000 has been spent upon the simple edifice), remains in a rude state of undressed nature, and is used as a hog-pasture. A trifle of the expense, employed with doubtful advantage, to give a smooth exterior face to the blocks of stone, if laid out in grading, smoothing, and dressing its ground base, would have added indescribably to the beauty of the edifice. An architect should always begin his work upon the ground.

It is hard to admire what is common; and it is, perhaps, asking too much of the citizens of Raleigh, that they should plant for ornament, or even cause to be retained about such institutions as their Lunatic Asylum, the beautiful evergreens that crowd about the town; but can any man walk from the Capitol oaks to the pine grove, a little beyond the Deaf and Dumb Institution, and say that he would not far rather have the latter than the former to curtain in his habitation? If he can in summer, let him try it again, as I did, in a soft winter's day, when the evergreens fill the air with a balsamic odour, and the green light comes quivering through them, and the foot falls silently upon the elastic carpet they have spread, deluding one with all the feelings of spring.

The country, for miles about Raleigh, is nearly all pine forest, unfertile, and so little cultivated, that it is a mystery how a town of 2,500 inhabitants can obtain sufficient supplies from it to exist.

The public-house at which I stayed was, however, not only well supplied, but was excellently well kept, for a house of its class, in all other respects. The landlord superintended his business personally, and was always attentive and obliging to his guests; and the servants were sufficiently numerous, intelligent, and well instructed. Though I had no acquaintances in Raleigh, I remained, finding myself in such good quarters, several days. I think the house was called "The Burlinghame."

After this stay, rendered also partly necessary for the repair of damages to my clothing and baggage on the Weldon stage, I engaged a seat one day on the coach, advertised to leave at nine o'clock for Fayetteville. At half-past nine, tired of waiting for its departure,

I told the agent, as it was not ready to start, I would walk on a bit, and let them pick me up. I found a rough road—for several miles a clayey surface and much water—and was obliged to pick my way a good deal through the woods on either side. Stopping frequently, when I came to cultivated land, to examine the soil and the appearance of the stubble of the maize—the only crop—in three different fields I made five measurements at random, of fifty feet each, and found the stalks had stood, on an average, five feet by two feet one inch apart, and that, generally, they were not over an inch in diameter at the butt. In one old-field, in process of clearing for new cultivation, I examined a most absurd little plough, with a share not more than six inches in depth, and eight in length on the sole, fastened by a socket to a stake, to which was fitted a short beam and stilts. It was drawn by one mule, and its work among the stumps could only be called scratching. A farmer told me that he considered twenty-five bushels of corn a large crop, and that he generally got only as much as fifteen. He said that no money was to be got by raising corn, and very few farmers here "made" any more than they needed for their own force. It cost too much to get it to market, and yet sometimes they had to buy corn at a dollar a bushel, and waggon it home from Raleigh, or further, enough not having been raised in the country for home consumption. Cotton was the only crop they got any money for. I, nevertheless, did not see a single cotton-field during the day. He said that the largest crop of corn that he knew of, reckoned to be fifty bushels to the acre, had been raised on some reclaimed swamp, while it was still so wet that horses would mire on it all the summer, and most of it had been tended entirely with hoes.

After walking a few miles, the country became more flat, and was covered with old forests of yellow pine, and, at nine miles south of Raleigh, there were occasionally young long-leaved pines: exceedingly beautiful they are while young, the colour being more agreeable than that of any other pine, and the leaves, or "straw," as its foliage is called here, long, graceful, and lustrous. As the tree gets older, it becomes of a stiffer character and darker colour.

I do not think I passed, in ten miles, more than half a dozen homesteads, and of these but one was at all above the character of a hut or cabin. The same remarkable appearance of listlessness, which I had noticed so often in Virginia, characterized the men who stood leaning against the logs of the hovels. They blinked at me as I passed, as if unable to withdraw their hands from their pockets to shade their eyes. Every dwelling sent its pack of curs to meet me, and as often as they opened cry, a woman, with a pipe in her mouth, would come to the door and call them off; the men and boys blinking on in rest and silence.

A little after one o'clock I reached "Banks's," a plantation where the stage horses are changed, eleven miles from Raleigh. Here I waited nearly an hour, till the coach arrived, when, fresh horses having been put on, I took an outside seat.

"There ain't a man in North Car'lina could drive them horses up the hills without a whip," said the driver. "You ought to get yesef a whip, massa," said one of the negroes. "Durnation! think I'm going to buy whips! the best whip in North Car'lina wouldn't last a week on this road." "Dat's a fac—dat ar is a fac; but look yeah, massa, ye let me hab yer stick, and I'll make a whip for ye; ye nebber can make Bawley go widout it, no how." The stick was a sapling rod, of which two or three lay on the coach top; the negro fastened a long leather thong to it. "Dah! ye can fetch old Bawley wi' dat." "Bawley" had been tackled in as the leader of the "spike team"; but, upon attempting to start, it was found that he couldn't be driven in that way at all, and the driver took him out and put him to the pole, within reach of the butt of his stick, and another horse was put on the lead.

One negro now took the leader by the head, and applied a stick lustily to his flanks; another, at the near wheeler, did the same; and the driver belaboured Bawley from the box. But as soon as they began to move forward, and the negro let go the leader's head, he would face about. After this had been repeated many times, a new plan of operations was arranged that proved successful. Leaving the two wheelers to the care of the negroes, the driver was enabled to give all his attention to the leader. When the wheelers started, of course he was struck by the pole, upon which he would turn tail and start for the stable. The negroes kept the wheelers from following him, and the driver with his stick, and another negro with the bough of a tree, thrashed his face; he would then turn again, and, being hit by the pole, start ahead. So, after ten minutes of fearful outcry, we got off.

"How far is it to Mrs. Barclay's?" a passenger had asked. "Thirteen miles," answered a negro; "but I tell 'ou, massa, dais a heap to be said and talk 'bout 'fore 'ou see Missy Barclay's wid dem hosses." There was, indeed.

"Bawley—*you*! Bawley—Bawley! wha' 'bout?—ah!"

"*Rock!* wha' you doin'?—(durned sick horse—an't fit to be in a stage, nohow)."

"Bawley! you! g'up!"

"Oh! you dod-rotted Bob—*Bob!*—(he don't draw a pound, and he an't a gwine to)—*you*, Bob!—(well, he can't stop, can he, as long as the wheelers keep movin'?) Bob! I'll break yer legs, you don't git out the way."

"Oh, Bawley!—(no business to put such a lame hoss into the stage.) Blamnation, Bawley! Now, if you stop, I'll kill you."

"Wha' 'bout, Rock? Dod burn that Rock! You stop if you dare! (I'll be durned to Hux if that 'ere hoss arn't all used up.)"

"You, *Bob!* get out de way, or I'll be ——."

"Oh! d'rot yer soul, Bawley—y're gwine to stop! G'up! G'up! *Rock!* You all-fired ole villain! Wha' 'bout? (If they jus' git to stoppin', all hell couldn't git the mails through to-night.)"

After about three miles of this, they did stop. The driver threw the reins down in despair. After looking at the wheels, and seeing that we were on a good piece of road, nothing unusual to hinder progress, he put his hands in his pockets, and sat quietly a minute, and then began, in a business-like manner, to swear, no longer confining himself to the peculiar idiomatic profanity of the country, but using real, outright, old-fashioned, uncompromising English oaths, as loud as he could yell. Then he stopped, and after another pause, began to talk quietly to the horses:

"You, Bob, you won't draw? Didn't you git enough last night? (I jabbed my knife into his face twice when we got into that fix last night"; and the wounds on the horse's head showed that he spoke the truth.) "I swar, Bob, if I have to come down thar, I'll cut your throat."

He stopped again, and then sat down on the foot-board, and began to beat the wheelers as hard and as rapidly as possible with the butt of his stick. They started, and, striking Bob with the pole, he jumped and turned round; but a happy stroke on "the raw" in his face brought him to his place; and the stick being applied just in time to the wheelers, he caught the pole and jumped ahead. We were off again.

"Turned over in that 'ere mire hole last night," said the driver. "Couldn't do anythin' with 'em—passengers camped out—thar's were they had their fire, under that tree; didn't get to Raleigh till nine o'clock this mornin'. That's the reason I weren't along after you any sooner—hadn't got my breakfast; that's the reason the hosses don't draw no better to-day, too, I s'pose. *You,* Rock!—*Bawley!*—Bob!"

After two miles more, the horses stopped once more. The driver now quietly took the leader off (he had never drawn at all), and tied him behind the coach. He then began beating the near wheeler, a passenger did the same to Bawley—both standing on the ground—while I threw off my overcoat and walked on. For a time I could occasionally hear the cry, "Bawl—Rock!" and knew that the coach was moving again; gradually I outwalked the sound.

The road was a mere opening through a forest of the long-leafed pine; the trees from eight to eighteen inches in diameter, with straight trunks bare for nearly thirty feet, and their evergreen foliage forming a dense dark canopy at that height, the surface of the ground undulating with long swells, occasionally low and wet. In the latter case, there was generally a mingling of deciduous trees and a watercourse crossing the road, with a thicket of shrubs. The soil sandy, with occasionally veins of clay; the latter more commonly in the low ground, or in the descent to it. Very little grass, herbage, or underwood; and the ground covered, except in the road, with the fallen pine-leaves. Every tree, on one, two, or three sides, was scarified for turpentine. In ten miles, I passed half a dozen cabins, one or two small clearings, in which corn had been planted, and one turpentine distillery, with a dozen sheds and cabins clustered about it.

In about an hour after I left the coach, the driver, mounted on Bob, overtook me: he was going on to get fresh horses.

After dark, I had some difficulty in keeping the road, there being frequent forks, and my only guide the telegraph wire. I had to cross three or four brooks, which were now high, and had sometimes floated off the logs which, in this country, are commonly placed, for the teamsters, along the side of the road, where it runs through water. I could generally jump from stump to stump; and, by wading a little at the edges in my staunch Scotch shooting-boots, get across dry-shod. Where, however, the water was too deep, I always found, by going up or down stream, a short way, a fallen trunk across it, by which I got over.

I met the driver returning with two fresh horses; and at length, before eight o'clock, reached a long one-story cabin, which I found to be Mrs. Barclay's. It was right cheerful and comforting to open the door, from the dark, damp, chilly night, into a large room, filled with blazing light from a great fire of turpentine pine, by which two stalwart men were reading newspapers, a door opening into a background of supper-table and kitchen, and a nice, stout, kindly-looking, Quaker-like old lady coming forward to welcome me.

As soon as I was warm, I was taken out to supper: seven preparations of swine's flesh, two of maize, wheat cakes, broiled quails, cold roast turkey, coffee, and tea.

My bed-room was a house by itself, the only connection between it and the main building being a platform, or gallery, in front. A great fire burned here also in a broad fire-place; a stuffed easy-chair had been placed before it, and a tub of hot water, which I had not thought to ask for, to bathe my weary feet.

And this was a piny-woods stage-house! But genius will find its development, no matter where its lot is cast; and there is as much genius for inn-keeping as for poetry. Mrs. Barclay is a Burns in her way, and with even more modesty; for, after twenty-four hours of the best entertainment that could be asked for, I was only charged one dollar. I paid two dollars for my stage-coach privileges—to wit, riding five miles and walking twenty-one.

At three o'clock in the morning, the three gentlemen that I had left ten miles back at four o'clock the previous day, were dragged, shivering in the stage-coach, to the door. They had had no meal since breakfasting at Raleigh; and one of them was now so tired that he could not eat, but dropt prone on the floor before the fire and slept the half-hour they were changing horses, or rather resting horses, for no relay was left.

I afterwards met one of the company in Fayetteville. Their night's adventure after I left them, and the continued cruelty to the horses, were most distressing. The driver once got off the box, and struck the poor, miserable, sick "Rock" with a rail, and actually knocked him down in the road. At another time, after having got fresh horses, when they, too, were "stalled," he took them out of the harness and turned them loose, and, refusing to give any answer to the inquiries of the passengers, looked about for a dry place, and lay down and went to sleep on the ground. One of the passengers had then walked on to Mrs. Barclay's and obtained a pair of mules, with which the coach was finally brought to the house. The remainder kindled a fire, and tried to rest themselves by it. They were sixteen hours in coming thirty miles, suffering much from cold, and without food.

The next day I spent in visiting turpentine and rosin works, piny-wood farms, etc., under the obliging guidance of Mrs. Barclay's son-in-law, and in the evening again took the coach. The horses were better than on the previous stage: upon my remarking this to the driver, he said that the reason was, that they took care of this team themselves (the drivers); on the last stage the horses were left to negroes, who would not feed them regularly, nor take any decent care of them. "Why, what do you think?" said he; "when I got to Banks's, this morning, I found my team hadn't been fed all day; they hadn't been rubbed nor cleaned, nary durned thing done to 'em, and thar the cussed darkey was, fast asleep. Reckon I didn't gin him a wakin' up!"

"You don't mean the horses that you drove up?"

"Yes, I do, and they hadn't a cussed thing to eat till they got back to Barclay's!"

"How was it possible for you to drive them back?"

"Why, I don't suppose I could ha' done it if I'd had any passengers: (you Suze!) shall lose a mail again to-night, if this mare don't travel better, (durn ye, yer ugly, I believe). She's a good mare—a heap of go in her, but it takes right smart of work to get it out. Suze!"

So we toiled on, with incessant shouting, and many strange piny-wood oaths, and horrid belabouring of the poor horses' backs, with the butt-end of a hickory whip-stalk, till I really thought their spinal-columns must break. The country, the same undulating pine forest, the track tortuous among the trees, which frequently stood so close that it required some care to work between them. Often we made detours from the original road, to avoid a fallen tree, or a mire-hole, and all the time we were bouncing over protruding roots and small stumps. There was but little mud, the soil being sand, but now and then a deep slough. In one of these we found a waggon, heavily laden, stuck fast, and six mules and five negroes tugging at it. With our help it was got out of the way, and we passed on. Soon after-wards we met the return coach, apparently in a similar predicament; but one of the passengers, whom I questioned, replied: "No, not stalled, exactly, but somehow *the horses won't draw*. We have been more than three hours coming about four miles."

"How is it you have so many balky horses?" I asked the driver.

"The old man buys 'em up cheap, 'cause nobody else can do anything with 'em."

"I should not think you could do much with them, either—except to kill them."

"Well, that's what the old man says he buys 'em for. He was blowing me up for losing the mail t'other night; I told him, says I, 'You have to a'most kill them horses, 'fore you can make 'em draw a bit,' says I. 'Kill 'em, damn 'em, kill 'em, then; that's what I buy 'em for,' says he. 'I buy 'em a purpose to kill; that's all they are good for, ain't it?' says he. 'Don't s'pose they're going to last for ever, do ye?' says he."

We stopped once, nearly half an hour, for some unexplained reason, before a house on the road. The door of the house was open, an enormous fire was burning in it, and, at the suggestion of the driver, I went in to warm myself. It was a large log-cabin, of two rooms, with beds in each room, and with an apartment overhead, to which access was had by a ladder. Among the inmates were two women; one of them sat in the chimney-corner smoking a pipe, and rocking a cradle; the other sat directly before the fire, and full ten feet distant. She was apparently young, but her face was as dry and impassive as a dead man's. She was doing nothing, and said but little; but, once in about a minute, would suddenly throw up her chin, and spit with perfect precision into the hottest embers of the fire. The furniture of the house was more scanty and rude than I ever saw before in any house, with women living in it, in the United States. Yet these people were not so poor but that they had a negro woman cutting and bringing wood for their fire.

It must be remembered that this is a long-settled country, having been occupied by Anglo-Saxons as early as any part of the Free States, and that it is the main road between the capital of North Carolina and its chief sea-port.

There is nothing that is more closely connected, both as cause and effect, with the prosperity and wealth of a country, than its means and modes of travelling, and of transportation of the necessities and luxuries of life. I saw this day, as I shall hereafter describe, three thousand barrels of resin, worth a dollar and a half a barrel in New York, thrown away, a mere heap of useless offal, because it would cost more to transport it than it would be worth. There was a single waggon, with a ton or two of sugar, and flour, and tea, and axes, and cotton cloths, unable to move, with six mules, and five negroes at work upon it. Raleigh is a large distributing post-office, getting a very heavy mail from the North; here was all that is sent by one of its main radii, travelling one day two miles an hour, the next four miles, and on each occasion failing to connect with the conveyances which we pay to scatter further the intelligence and wealth transmitted by it. Barbarous is too mild a term to apply to the manner in which even this was done. The improvidence, if not the cruelty, no sensible barbarian could have been guilty of.

Afterwards, merely to satisfy my mind (for there is a satisfaction in seeing even scoundrelism consistently carried out, if attempted at all in a business), I called on the agent of the line at Fayetteville, stated the case, and asked if any part of what I had paid for my passage would be returned me, on account of the disappointment and delay which I had suffered from the inability of the proprietor to carry out his contract with me. The impudence of the suggestion, of course, only created amusement; and I was smilingly informed that the business was not so "lucky" that the proprietor could afford to pay back money that he had once got into his hands. What I had seen was regarded by no one, apparently, as at all unusual.

At one of the stations for changing horses, an old coloured man was taken into the coach. I ascertained from him that he was a blacksmith, and had been up the line to shoe the horses at the different stables. Probably he belonged (poor fellow!) to the man who bought horses to be killed in doing his work. After answering my inquiries, he lay down in the bottom of the coach, and slept until we reached Fayetteville. The next time we changed, the new driver inquired of the old one what passengers he had. "Only one gentleman, and old man Ned."

"Oh! is old man along—that's good—if we should turn over, or break down, or anything, reckon he could nigh about pray us up— he's right smart at prayin'."

"Well, I tell you, now, ole man can trot out as smart a prayer, when he's a mind to go in for't, as any man I ever heerd, durned if he can't."

The last ten miles we came over rapidly, smoothly, and quietly, by a plank-road, reaching Fayetteville about twelve, of a fine, clear, frosty night.

Entering the office or bar-room of the stage-house, at which I had been advised to stay while in Fayetteville, I found it occupied by a group of old soakers, among whom was one of perhaps sixteen years of age. This lad, without removing the cigar which he had in his mouth, went to the bar, whither I followed him, and, without saying a word, placed an empty tumbler before me.

"I don't wish anything to drink," said I; "I am cold and tired, and I would like to go to a room. I intend to stay here some days, and I should be glad if you could give me a private room with a fire in it."

"Room with a fire in it?" he inquired, as he handed me the registry-book.

"Yes; and I will thank you to have it made immediately, and let my baggage be taken up."

He closed the book, after I had written my name, and returned to his seat at the stove, leaving me standing, and immediately engaged in conversation, without paying any attention to my request. I waited some time, during which a negro came into the room, and went out again. I then repeated my request, necessarily aloud, and in such a way as to be understood, not only by the boy, but by all the company. Immediately all conversation ceased, and every head was turned to look at me. The lad paused a moment, spit upon the stove, and then—

"Want a room to yourself?"

"Yes, if convenient."

No answer and no movement, all the company staring at me as if at a detected burglar.

"Perhaps you can't accommodate me?"

"Want a fire made in your room?"

"Why, yes, if convenient; but I should like to go to my room, at any rate; I am very tired."

After puffing and spitting for a moment, he rose and pulled a bell; then took his seat again. In about five minutes a negro came in, and during all this time there was silence.

"What'll you drink, Baker?" said the lad, rising and going to the bar, and taking no notice of the negro's entrance. A boozy man followed him, and made some reply; the lad turned out two glasses of spirits, added water to one, and drank it in a gulp.[3]

"Can this boy show me to my room?" I asked.

"Anybody in number eleven, Peter?"

"Not as I knows on, sar."

"Take this man's baggage up there."

I followed the negro up to number eleven, which was a large back room in the upper story, with four beds in it.

"Peter," said I, "I want a fire made here."

"Want a fire, sar?"

"Yes, I want you to make a fire."

"Want a fire, master, this time o' night?"

"Why, yes; I want a fire. Where are you going with the lamp?"

"Want a lamp, massa?"

"Want a lamp? Certainly, I do."

After about ten minutes, I heard a man splitting wood in the yard, and, in ten more, Peter brought in three sticks of green wood, and some chips; then, the little bed-lamp having burned out, he went into an adjoining room, where I heard him talking to some one, evidently awakened by his entrance to get a match; that failing, he went for another. By one o'clock, my fire was made.

"Peter," said I, "are you going to wait on me, while I stay here?"

"Yes, sar; I 'tends to dis room."

"Very well; take this, and, when I leave, I'll give you another, if you take good care of me. Now, I want you to get me some water."

"I'll get you some water in de morning, sar."

"I want some to-night—some water and some towels; don't you think you can get them for me?"

"I reckon so, massa, if you wants 'em. Want 'em 'fore you go to bed?"

"Yes; and get another lamp."

"Want a lamp?"

"Yes, of course."

"Won't the fire do you?"

[3] The mother of this young man remonstrated with a friend of mine, for permitting his son to join a company of civil engineers, engaged, at the time, in surveying a route for a road—he would be subject to such fatiguing labour, and so much exposure to the elements; and congratulated herself that her own child was engaged in such an easy and gentleman-like employment as that of hotel-clerk and bar keeper.

"No; bring a lamp. That one won't burn without filling; you need not try it."

The water and the lamp came, after a long time.

In the morning, early, I was awakened by a knock at the door.

"Who's there?"

"Me, massa; I wants your boots to black."

I got up, opened the door, and returned to bed. Falling asleep, I was soon again awakened by Peter throwing down an armful of wood upon the floor. Slept again, and was again awakened, by Peter's throwing up the window, to empty out the contents of the wash bowl, etc. The room was filled with smoke of the fat light wood: Peter had already made a fire for me to dress by; but I again fell asleep, and, when I next awoke, the breakfast bell was ringing. Peter had gone off, and left the window and door open, and the fire had burned out. My boots had been taken away, and the bell-wire was broken. I dressed, and walking to the bar-room, asked the bar-keeper—a complaisant, full-grown man—for my boots. He did not know where they were, and rang the bell for Peter. Peter came, was reprimanded for his forgetfulness, and departed. Ten minutes elapsed, and he did not return. I again requested that he should be called; and this time he brought my boots. He had had to stop to black them; having, he said, been too busy to do it before breakfast.

The following evening, as it grew too cold to write in my room, I went down, and found Peter, and told him I wanted a fire again, and that he might get me a couple of candles. When he came up, he brought one of the little bed-lamps, with a capacity of oil for fifteen minutes' use. I sent him down again to the office, with a request to the proprietor that I might be furnished with candles. He returned, and reported that there were no candles in the house.

"Then, get me a larger lamp."

"Aint no larger lamps, nuther, sar;—none to spare."

"Then go out, and see if you can't buy me some candles, some-where."

"Aint no stores open, Sunday, massa, and I don't know where I can buy 'em."

"Then go down, and tell the bar-keeper, with my compliments, that I wish to write in my room, and I would be obliged to him if he would send me a light, of some sort; something that will last longer, and give more light, than these little lamps."

"He won't give you none, massa—not if you hab a fire. Can't you see by da light of da fire? When a gentlemen hab a fire in his room, dey don't count he wants no more light 'n dat."

"Well, make the fire, and I'll go down and see about it."

As I reached the foot of the stairs, the bell rang, and I went in to tea. The tea table was moderately well lighted with candles. I waited till the company had generally left it, and then said to one of the waiters—

"Here are two dimes: I want you to bring me, as soon as you can, two of these candles to number eleven; do you understand?"

"Yes, sar; I'll fotch 'em, sar."

And he did.

About eight o'clock, there was an alarm of fire. Going into the street, I was surprised to observe how leisurely the people were walking toward the house in flames, standing very prominently, as it did, upon a hill, at one end of the town. As I passed a church, the congregation was coming out; but very few quickened their step above a strolling pace. Arrived near the house, I was still more astonished to see how few, of the crowd assembled, were occupied in restraining the progress of the fire, or in saving the furniture, and at the prevailing stupidity, confusion, and want of system and concert of action, in the labour for this purpose. A large majority of those engaged were negroes. As I returned toward the hotel, a gentleman, walking, with a lady, before me, on the side walk, accosted a negro whom he met:

"What! Moses! That you? Why were you not here sooner?"

"Why, Mass Richard, I was singing, an' I didn' her de bells and—I see twant in our ward, sar, and so I didn' see as dar was zactly 'casion for me to hurry myself to def. Ef eed a been in our ward, Mass Richard, I'd a rallied, you knows I would. Mose would ha rallied, ef eed a been in our ward—ha! ha! ha!—you knows it, Mass Richard!"

And he passed on, laughing comically, without further reproof.

Fayetteville.—The negroes employed in the turpentine business, to which during the last week I have been giving some examination, seem to me to be unusually intelligent and cheerful, decidedly more so than most of the white people inhabiting the turpentine forest. Among the latter there is a large number, I should think a majority,

of entirely uneducated, poverty-stricken vagabonds. I mean by vagabonds, simply, people without habitual, definite occupation or reliable means of livelihood. They are poor, having almost no property but their own bodies; and the use of these, that is, their labour,
they are not accustomed to hire out statedly and regularly, so as to
obtain capital by wages, but only occasionally by the day or job,
when driven to it by necessity. A family of these people will commonly hire, or "squat" and build, a little log cabin, so made that it
is only a shelter from rain, the sides not being chinked, and having
no more furniture or pretension to comfort than is commonly provided a criminal in the cell of a prison. They will cultivate a little
corn, and possibly a few roods of potatoes, cow-peas, and coleworts.
They will own a few swine, that find their living in the forest; and
pretty certainly, also, a rifle and dogs; and the men, ostensibly, occupy most of their time in hunting. I am, mainly, repeating the statements of one of the turpentine distillers, but it was confirmed by
others, and by my own observation, so far as it went.

A gentleman of Fayetteville told me that he had, several times,
appraised, under oath, the whole household property of families of
this class at less than $20. If they have need of money to purchase
clothing, etc., they obtain it by selling their game or meal. If they
have none of this to spare, or an insufficiency, they will work for a
neighbouring farmer for a few days, and they usually get for their
labour fifty cents a day, *finding themselves*. The farmers and distillers say, that that they do not like to employ them, because they
cannot be relied upon to finish what they undertake, or to work
according to directions; and because, being white men, they cannot
"drive" them. That is to say, their labour is even more inefficient
and unmanageable than that of slaves.

That I have not formed an exaggerated estimate of the proportion
of such a class, will appear to the reader more probable from the
testimony of a pious colporteur, given before a public meeting in
Charleston, in February, 1855. I quote from a Charleston paper's
report. The colporteur had been stationed at —— county, N.C.:—
"*The larger portion* of the inhabitants seemed to be totally given up
to a species of mental hallucination, which carried them captive at its
will. They nearly all believed implicitly in witchcraft, and attributed everything that happened, good or bad, to the agency of persons whom they supposed possessed of evil spirits."

The majority of what I have termed turpentine-farmers—meaning the small proprietors of the long-leafed pine forest land—are people but a grade superior, in character or condition, to these vagabonds. They have habitations more like houses—log-cabins, commonly, sometimes chinked, oftener not—without windows of glass, but with a few pieces of substantial old-fashioned heir-loom furniture; a vegetable garden, in which, however, you will find no vegetable but what they call "collards" (colewort) for "greens"; fewer dogs, more swine, and larger clearings for maize, but no better crops than the poorer class. Their property is, nevertheless, often of considerable money value, consisting mainly of negroes, who, associating intimately with their masters, are of superior intelligence to the slaves of the wealthier classes.

Some of the larger proprietors, who are also often cotton planters, cultivating the richer low lands, are said to be gentlemen of good estate—intelligent, cultivated, and hospitable.

North Carolina has a proverbial reputation for the ignorance and torpidity of her people; being, in this respect, at the head of the Slave States. I do not find the reason of this in any innate quality of the popular mind; but, rather, in the circumstances under which it finds its development. Owing to the general poverty of the soil in the eastern part of the State, and to the almost exclusive employment of slave labour on the soils productive of cotton; owing, also, to the difficulty and expense of reaching market with bulky produce from the interior and western districts, population and wealth are more divided than in the other Atlantic States; industry is almost entirely rural, and there is but little communication or concert of action among the small and scattered proprietors of capital. For the same reason, the advantages of education are more difficult to be enjoyed, the distance at which families reside apart preventing children from coming together in such numbers as to give remunerative employment to a teacher. The teachers are, generally, totally unfitted for their business; young men, as a clergyman informed me, themselves not only unadvanced beyond the lowest knowledge of the elements of primary school learning, but often coarse, vulgar, and profane in their language and behaviour, who take up teaching as a temporary business, to supply the demand of a neighbourhood of people as ignorant and uncultivated as themselves.

The native white population of North Carolina is . . 550,267
The whole white population under 20 years is . . . 301,106
Leaving white adults over 20 249,161
Of these there are natives who cannot read and write . 73,226 [4]

Being more than one-fourth of the native white adults.

But the aspect of North Carolina with regard to slavery, is, in some respects, less lamentable than that of Virginia. There is not only less bigotry upon the subject, and more freedom of conversation, but I saw here, in the institution, more of patriarchal character than in any other State. The slave more frequently appears as a family servant—a member of his master's family, interested with him in his fortune, good or bad. This is a result of the less concentration of wealth in families or individuals, occasioned by the circumstances I have described. Slavery thus loses much of its inhumanity. It is still questionable, however, if, as the subject race approaches civilization, the dominant race is not proportionately detained in its onward progress. One is forced often to question, too, in viewing slavery in this aspect, whether humanity and the accumulation of wealth, the prosperity of the master, and the happiness and improvement of the subject, are not in some degree incompatible.

These later observations are made after having twice again passed through the State, once in a leisurely way on horseback. In some of the western and northern central parts of the State, there is much more enterprise, thrift, and comfort than in the eastern part, where I had my first impressions.

I left Fayetteville in a steamboat (advertised for 8 o'clock, left at 8.45) bound down Cape Fear River to Wilmington. A description of the river, with incidents of the passage, will serve to show the character of most of the navigable streams of the cotton States, flowing into the Atlantic and the Gulf, and of the manner of their navigation.

The water was eighteen feet above its lowest summer stages; the banks steep, thirty feet high from the present water surface—from fifty to one hundred feet apart—and covered with large trees and luxuriant vegetation; the course crooked; the current very rapid; the trees overhanging the banks, and frequently falling into the chan-

[4] Official Census Report, pp. 309, 299, 317.

nel—making the navigation hazardous. The river is subject to very rapid rising. The master told me that he had sometimes left his boat aground at night, and, on returning in the morning, found it floating in twenty-five feet of water, over the same spot. The difference between the extremes of low stages and floods is as much as seventy feet. In summer, there are sometimes but eighteen inches of water on the bars: the boat I was in drew but fourteen inches, light. She was a stern-wheel craft—the boiler and engine (high pressure) being placed at opposite ends, to balance weights. Her burden was three hundred barrels, or sixty tons measurement. This is the character of most of the boats navigating the river—of which there are now twelve. Larger boats are almost useless in summer, from their liability to ground; and even the smaller ones, at low stages of water, carry no freight, but are employed to tow up "flats" or shallow barges. At this season of the year, however, the steamboats are loaded close to the water's edge.

The bulk of our freight was turpentine; and the close proximity of this to the furnaces suggested a danger fully equal to that from snags or grounding. On calling the attention of a fellow-passenger to it, he told me that a friend of his was once awakened from sleep, while lying in a berth on one of these boats, by a sudden, confused sound. Thinking the boiler had burst, he drew the bed-clothing over his head, and lay quiet, to avoid breathing the steam; until, feeling the boat ground, he ran out, and discovered that she was on fire near the furnace. Having some valuable freight near by, which he was desirous to save, and seeing no immediate danger, though left alone on the boat, he snatched a bucket, and, drawing water from alongside, applied it with such skill and rapidity as soon to quench the flames, and eventually to entirely extinguish the fire. Upon the return of the crew, a few repairs were made, steam was got up again, and the boat proceeded to her destination in safety. He afterwards ascertained that three hundred kegs of gunpowder were stowed beneath the deck that had been on fire—a circumstance which sufficiently accounted for the panic-flight of the crew.

Soon after leaving, we passed the Zephyr, wooding up: an hour later, our own boat was run to the bank, men jumped from her fore and aft, and fastened head and stern lines to the trees, and we also commenced wooding.

The trees had been cut away so as to leave a clear space to the top of the bank, which was some fifty feet from the boat, and moderately steep. Wood, cut, split, and piled in ranks, stood at the top of it, and a chute of plank, two feet wide and thirty long, conveyed it nearly to the water. The crew rushed to the wood-piles—master, passengers, and all, but the engineer and chambermaid, deserting the boat—and the wood was first passed down, as many as could, throwing into the chute, and others forming a line, and tossing it, from one to another, down the bank. From the water's edge it was passed, in the same way, to its place on board, with great rapidity—the crew exciting themselves with yells. They were all blacks, but one.

On a tree, near the top of the bank, a little box was nailed, on which a piece of paper was tacked, with this inscription:

" " *Notic*
" " *to all persons takin wood from this landin pleas to leav a*
" " *ticket payable to the subscriber, at $1,75 a cord as heretofore.*
" " *Amos Sikes.* " "

and the master—just before the wood was all on board—hastily filled a blank order (torn from a book, like a checkbook, leaving a memorandum of the amount, etc.) on the owner of the boat for payment, to Mr. Sikes, for two cords of pine-wood, at $1.75, and two cords of light-wood, at $2—and left it in the box. The wood used had been measured in the ranks with a rod, carried for the purpose, by the master, at the moment he reached the bank.

Before, with all possible haste, we had finished wooding, the Zephyr passed us; and, during the rest of the day, she kept out of our sight. As often as we met a steamboat, or passed any flats or rafts, our men were calling out to know how far ahead of us she was; and when the answer came back each time, in an increasing number of miles, they told us that our boat was more than usually sluggish, owing to an uncommonly heavy freight; but still, for some time, they were ready to make bets that we should get first to Wilmington.

Several times we were hailed from the shore, to take on a passenger, or some light freight; and these requests, as long as it was possible, were promptly complied with—the boat being run up, so as to rest her bow upon the bank, and then shouldered off by the men, as if she had been a skiff.

There were but three through-passengers, besides myself. Among them, was a glue-manufacturer, of Baltimore—getting orders from the turpentine-distillers,—and a turpentine-farmer and distiller. The glue-manufacturer said that, in his factory, they had formerly employed slaves; had since used Irishmen, and now employed Germans. Their operations were carried on night and day, and one gang of the men had to relieve another. The slaves they had employed never would be *on hand,* when the hour for relieving came. It was also necessary to be careful that certain operations should be performed at a certain time, and some judgment and watchfulness was necessary, to fix this time: the slaves never could be made to care enough for the matter, to be depended upon for discretion, in this respect; and great injury was frequently done in consequence. Some of the operations were disagreeable, and they would put one another up to thinking and saying that they ought not to be required to do such dirty work—and try to have their owners get them away from it.

Irishmen, he said, worked very well, and to a certain extent faithfully, and, for a time, they liked them very much; but they found that, in about a fortnight, an Irishman always thought he knew more than his master, and would exercise his discretion a little too much, as well as often directly disregard his orders. Irishmen were, he said, "*too* faithful"—that is, self-confident and officious.

At length, at a hurried time, they had employed one or two Germans. The Irishmen, of course, soon quarrelled with them, and threatened to leave, if they were kept. Whereupon, they were, themselves, all discharged, and a full crew of Germans, at much less wages, taken; and they proved excellent hands—steady, plodding, reliable, though they never pretended to know anything, and said nothing about what they could do. They were easily instructed, obeyed orders faithfully, and worked fairly for their wages, without boasting or grumbling.

The turpentine-distiller gave a good account of some of his men; but said he was sure they never performed half as much work as he himself could; and they sometimes would, of their own accord, do twice as much in a day, as could usually be got out of them. He employed a Scotchman at the "still"; but he never would have white people at ordinary work, because he couldn't drive them. He added, with the utmost simplicity—and I do not think any one present saw, at the time, how much the remark expressed more than it was intended to—"I never can drive a white man, for I know I could never bear to be driven, myself, by anybody."

The other passenger was "a North of England man," as I suspected from the first words I heard from him—though he had been in this country for about twenty years. He was a mechanic, and employed several slaves; but testified strongly of the expensive character of their labour; and declared, without any reserve, that the system was ruinous in its effects upon the character and value of all classes of working men.

The country on the river-bank was nearly all wooded, with, occasionally, a field of corn, which, even in the low alluvial meadows, sometimes overflowed by the river, and enriched by its deposit, had evidently yielded but a very meagre crop—the stalks standing singly, at great distances, and very small. The greater part, even of these once rich low lands, that had been in cultivation, were now "turned out," and covered either with pines or broom-sedge and brushwood.

At some seventy or eighty miles, I should think, below Fayette-ville, the banks became lower, and there was much swamp land, in which the ground was often covered with a confusion of logs and sawn lumber, mingled with other rubbish, left by floods of the river. The standing timber was very large, and many of the trees were hung with the long, waving drapery of the tylandria, or Spanish moss, which, as well as the mistletoe, I here first saw in profusion. There was also a thick network among the trees, of beautiful climbing plants. I observed some very large grape-vines, and many trees of greater size than I ever saw of their species before. I infer that this soil, properly reclaimed, and protected from floods of the river, might be most profitably used in the culture of the various half-tropical trees and shrubs, of whose fruits we now import so large and costly an amount. The fig, I have been informed, grows and bears luxuriantly at Wilmington, seldom or never suffering in its wood, though a crop of fruit may be occasionally injured by a severe late spring frost. The almond, doubtless, would succeed equally well, so also the olive; but of none of these is there the slightest commercial value produced in North Carolina, or in all our country.

In the evening we passed many boats and rafts, blazing with great fires, made upon a thick bed of clay, and their crews singing at their sweeps. Twenty miles above Wilmington, the shores became marshy, the river wide, and the woody screen that had hitherto, in a great

degree, hid the nakedness of the land, was withdrawn, leaving open
to view only broad, reedy savannahs, on either side.

We reached Wilmington, the port at the mouth of the river, at
half-past nine. Taking a carriage, I was driven first to one hotel and
afterwards to another. They were both so crowded with guests, and
excessive business duties so prevented the clerks from being tolerably civil to me, that I feared if I remained in either of them I should
have another Norfolk experience. While I was endeavouring to ascertain if there was a third public-house, in which I might, perhaps,
obtain a private room, my eye fell upon an advertisement of a new
railroad line of passage to Charleston. A boat, to take passengers to
the railroad, was to start every night, from Wilmington, at ten
o'clock. It was already something past ten; but being pretty sure
that she would not get off punctually, and having a strong resisting
impulse to being packed away in a close room, with any chance
stranger the clerk of the house might choose to couple me with, I
shouldered my baggage and ran for the wharves. At half-past ten I
was looking at Wilmington over the stern of another little wheel-
barrow-steamboat, pushing back up the river. When or how I was
to be taken to Charleston, I had not yet been able to ascertain. The
captain assured me it was all right, and demanded twenty dollars.
Being in his power I gave it to him, and received in return a pocket-
ful of tickets, guaranteeing the bearer passage from place to place;
of not one of which places had I ever heard before, except Charleston.

The cabin was small, dirty, crowded, close, and smoky. Finding a
warm spot in the deck, over the furnace, and to leeward of the
chimney, I pillowed myself on my luggage and went to sleep.

The ringing of the boat's bell awoke me, after no great lapse of
time, and I found we were in a small creek, heading southward.
Presently we reached a wharf, near which stood a locomotive and
train. A long, narrow plank having been run out, half a dozen white
men, including myself, went on shore. Then followed as many negroes, who appeared to be a recent purchase of their owner. Owing,
probably, to an unusually low tide, there was a steep ascent from
the boat to the wharf, and I was amused to see the anxiety of this
gentleman for the safe landing of his property, and especially to hear
him curse them for their carelessness, as if their lives were of much
greater value to him than to themselves. One was a woman. All car-

ried over their shoulders some little baggage, probably all their personal effects, slung in a blanket; and one had a dog, whose safe landing caused him nearly as much anxiety as his own did *his* owner.

"Gib me da dog, now," said the dog's owner, standing half way up the plank.

"Damn the dog," said the negro's owner; "give me your hand up here. Let go of the dog; d'ye hear! Let him take care of himself."

But the negro hugged the dog, and brought him safely on shore.

After a short delay the train started: the single passenger car was a fine one (made at Wilmington, Delaware), and just sufficiently warmed. I should have slept again if it had not been that two of the six inmates were drunk—one of them uproariously.

Passing through long stretches of cypress swamps, with occasional intervals of either pine-barrens, or clear water ponds, in about two hours we came, in the midst of the woods, to the end of the rails. In the vicinity could be seen a small tent, a shanty of loose boards, and a large, subdued fire, around which, upon the ground, a considerable number of men were stretched out asleep. This was the camp of the hands engaged in laying the rails, and who were thus daily extending the distance which the locomotive could run.

The conductor told me that there was here a break of about eighty miles in the rail, over which I should be transferred by a stage-coach, which would come as soon as possible after the driver knew that the train had arrived. To inform him of this, the locomotive trumpeted loud and long.

The negro property, which had been brought up in a freight car, was immediately let out on the stoppage of the train. As it stepped on to the platform, the owner asked, "Are you all here?"

"Yes, massa, we is all heah," answered one. "Do dysef no harm, for we's all heah," added another, in an undertone.

The negroes immediately gathered some wood, and taking a brand from the railroad hands, made a fire for themselves; then, all but the woman, opening their bundles, wrapped themselves in their blankets and went to sleep. The woman, bare-headed, and very inadequately clothed as she was, stood for a long time alone, erect and statue-like, her head bowed, gazing in the fire. She had taken no part in the light chat of the others, and had given them no assistance in making the fire. Her dress too was not the usual plantation apparel. It was all sadly suggestive.

The principal other freight of the train was one hundred and twenty bales of Northern hay. It belonged, as the conductor told me, to a planter who lived some twenty miles beyond here, and who had bought it in Wilmington at a dollar and a half a hundred weight, to feed his mules. Including the steamboat and railroad freight, and all the labour of getting it to his stables, its entire cost to him would not be much less than two dollars a hundred, or at least four times as much as it would have cost to raise and make it in the interior of New York or New England. There are not only several forage crops which can be raised in South Carolina, that cannot be grown on account of the severity of the winter in the Free States, but, on a farm near Fayetteville, a few days before, I had seen a crop of natural grass growing in half-cultivated land, dead upon the ground; which, I think, would have made, if it had been cut and well treated in the summer, three tons of hay to the acre. The owner of the land said that there was no better hay than it would have made, but he hadn't had time to attend to it. He had as much as his hands could do of other work at the period of the year when it should have been made.

Probably the case was similar with the planter who had bought this Northern hay at a price four times that which it would have cost a Northern farmer to make it. He had preferred to employ his slaves at other business.

The inference must be, either that there was most improbably-foolish, bad management, or that the slaves were more profitably employed in cultivating cotton, than they could have been in cultivating maize, or other forage crops.

I put the case, some days afterwards, to an English merchant, who had had good opportunities, and made it a part of his business to study such matters.

"I have no doubt," said he, "that if hay cannot be obtained here, other valuable forage can, with less labour than anywhere at the North; and all the Southern agricultural journals sustain this opinion, and declare it to be purely bad management that neglects these crops, and devotes labour to cotton, so exclusively. Probably, it is so—at the present cost of forage. Nevertheless, the fact is also true, as the planters assert, that they cannot afford to apply their labour to anything else but cotton. And yet, they complain that the price of cotton is so low that there is no profit in growing it, which is evidently false. You see that they prefer buying hay to raising it at, to say the least, three times what it costs your Northern farmers to raise it. Of course, if cotton could be grown in New York and Ohio, it could be afforded at one-third the cost it is here—say at three cents per pound. And that is my solution of the slavery question. Bring cotton down to three cents a pound, and there would be more abolitionists in South Carolina than in Massachusetts. If that can be brought about, in any way—and it is not impossible that we may live to see it, as our railways are extended in India, and the French enlarge their free-labour plantations in Algiers—there will be an end of slavery."

It was just one o'clock when the stage-coach came for us. There was but one passenger beside myself—a Philadelphia gentleman, going to Columbia. We proceeded very slowly for about three miles, across a swamp, upon a "corduroy road"; then more rapidly, over rough ground, being tossed about in the coach most severely, for six or eight miles further. Besides the driver, there was on the box the agent or superintendent of the coach line, who now opened the doors, and we found ourselves before a log stable, in the midst of a forest of large pines. The driver took out a horse, and, mounting him, rode off, and we collected wood, splitting it with a hatchet that was carried on the coach, and, lighting it from the coach lamp, made a fire. It was very cold, ice half an inch thick, and a heavy hoar frost. We complained to the agent that there was no straw in the coach bottom, while there were large holes bored in it, that kept our feet excessively cold. He said there was no straw to be had in the country. They were obliged to bed their horses with pine leaves, which were damp, and would be of no service to us. The necessity for the holes he did not immediately explain, and we, in the exercise of our Yankee privilege, resolved that they were made with reference to the habit of expectoration, which we had observed in the car to be very general and excessive.

In about half an hour the driver of the new stage came to us on the horse that the first had ridden away. A new set of horses was brought out and attached to the coach, and we were driven on again. An hour later, the sun rose; we were still in pine-barrens, once in several miles passing through a clearing, with a log farm-house, and a few negro huts about it; often through cypress swamps, and long pools of water. At the end of ten miles we breakfasted, and changed horses and drivers at a steam saw-mill. A few miles further on, we were asked to get on the top of the coach, while it was driven through a swamp, in which the water was over the road, for a quarter of a mile, to such a depth that it covered the foot-board. The horses really groaned, as they pushed the thin ice away with their necks, and were very near swimming. The holes in the coach bottom, the agent now told us, were to allow the water that would here enter the body to flow out. At the end of these ten miles we changed again, at a cotton planter's house—a very neat, well-built house, having pine trees about it, but very poor, old, negro quarters.

Since the long ford we had kept the top, the inside of the coach being wet, and I had been greatly pleased with the driving—the coachman, a steady-going sort of a fellow, saying but little to his horses, and doing what swearing he thought necessary in English; driving, too, with great judgment and skill. The coach was a fine, roomy, old-fashioned, fragrant, leathery affair, and the horses the best I had seen this side of Virginia. I could not resist expressing my pleasure with the whole establishment. The new team was admirable; four sleek, well-governed, eager, sorrel cobs, and the driver, a staid, bronzed-faced man, keeping them tight in hand, drove quietly and neatly, his whip in the socket. After about fifteen minutes, during which he had been engaged in hushing down their too great impetuosity, he took out a large silver hunting-watch, and asked what time it was.

"Quarter past eleven," said the agent.

"Twelve minutes past," said the Philadelphian.

"Well, fourteen, only, I am," said the agent.

"Thirteen," said I.

"Just thirteen, I am," said the driver, slipping back his watch to its place, and then, to the agent, "ha'an't touched a hand of her since I left old Lancaster."

Suddenly guessing the meaning of what had been for some time astonishing me—"You are from the North?" I asked.

"Yes, sir."

"And you, too, Mr. Agent?"

"Yes, sir."

"And the coach, and the cattle, and all?"

"All from Pennsylvania."

"How long have you been here?"

"We have been here about a fortnight, stocking the road. We commenced regular trips yesterday. You are the first passenger through, sir."

It was, in fact, merely a transfer from one of the old National Road lines, complete. After a little further conversation, I asked, "How do you like the country, here?"

"Very nice country," said the agent.

"It's the cussedest poor country God ever created," snapped out the driver.

"You have to keep your horses on—"

"*Shucks!* [5] damn it."

The character of the scenery was novel to me, the surface very flat, the soil a fine-grained, silvery white sand, shaded by a continuous forest of large pines, which had shed their lower branches, so that we could see from the coach-top, to the distance of a quarter of a mile, everything upon the ground. In the swamps, which were frequent and extensive, and on their borders, the pines gave place to cypresses, with great pedestal trunks, and protuberant roots, throwing up an awkward dwarf progeny of shrub, cypress, and curious bulbous-like stumps, called "cypress-knees." Mingled with these were a few of our common deciduous trees, the white-shafted sycamore, the gray beech, and the shrubby blackjack oak, with broad leaves, brown and dead, yet glossy, and reflecting the sunbeams. Somewhat rarely, the red cedar, and more frequently than any other except the cypress, the beautiful American holly. Added to these, there was often a thick undergrowth of evergreen shrubs. Vines and creepers of various kinds grew to the tops of the tallest trees and dangled beneath and between their branches, in intricate net-work. The tylandria hung in festoons, sometimes several feet in length, and often completely clothed the trunks, and every branch of the trees in the low ground. It is like a fringe of tangled hair, of a light gray pearly colour, and sometimes produces exquisite effects when slightly veiling the dark green, purple, and scarlet of the cedar, and the holly with their berries. The mistletoe also grew in large, vivid, green tufts, on the ends of the branches of the oldest and largest trees. A small fine and wiry dead grass, hardly perceptible, even in the most open ground, from the coach-tops, was the only sign of herbage. Large black buzzards were constantly in sight, sailing slowly, high above the treetops. Flocks of larks, quails,

[5] Husks of maize.

and robins were common, as were also doves, swiftly flying in small companies. The redheaded woodpecker could at any time be heard hammering the old tree-trunks, and would sometimes show himself, after his rat-tat, cocking his head archly, and listening to hear if the worm moved under the bark. The drivers told me that they had on previous days, as they went over the road, seen deer, turkeys, and wild hogs.

At every tenth mile, or thereabout, we changed horses; and, generally, were allowed half an hour to stroll in the neighbourhood of the stable—the agent observing that we could reach the end of the staging some hours before the cars should leave to take us further; and, as there were no good accommodations for sleeping there, we would pass the time quite as pleasantly on the road. We dined at "Marion County House," a pleasant little village (and the only village we saw during the day), with a fine pine-grove, a broad street, a court-house, a church or two, a school-house, and a dozen or twenty dwellings. Towards night, we crossed the Great Pedee [Pee Dee] of the maps, the *Big* Pedee of the natives, in a flat boat. A large quantity of cotton, in bales, was upon the bank, ready for loading into a steamboat—when one should arrive—for Charleston.

The country was very thinly peopled; lone houses often being several miles apart. The large majority of the dwellings were of logs, and even those of the white people were often without glass windows. In the better class of cabins, the roof is usually built with a curve, so as to project eight or ten feet beyond the log-wall; and a part of this space, exterior to the logs, is enclosed with boards, making an additional small room—the remainder forms an open porch. The whole cabin is often elevated on four corner-posts, two or three feet from the ground, so that the air may circulate under it. The fire-place is built at the end of the house, of sticks and clay, and the chimney is carried up outside, and often detached from the log-walls; but the roof is extended at the gable, until in a line with its outer side. The porch has a railing in front, and a wide shelf at the end, on which a bucket of water, a gourd, and hand-basin, are usually placed. There are chairs, or benches, in the porch, and you often see women sitting at work in it, as in Germany.

The logs are usually hewn but little; and, of course, as they are laid up, there will be wide interstices between them—which are increased by subsequent shrinking. These, very commonly, are not "chinked," or filled up in any way; nor is the wall lined on the inside. Through the chinks, as you pass along the road, you may often see all that is going on in the house; and, at night, the light of the fire shines brightly out on all sides.

Cabins, of this class, would almost always be flanked by two or three negro huts. The cabins of the poor whites, much the largest in number, were of a meaner sort—being mere square pens of logs, roofed over, provided with a chimney, and usually with a shed of boards, supported by rough posts, before the door.

Occasionally, where, near the banks of a water-course, the silvery sand was darkened by a considerable intermixture of mould, there would be a large plantation, with negro-quarters, and a cotton-press and gin-house. We passed half a dozen of these, perhaps, during the day. Where the owners resided in them, they would have comfortable-looking residences, not unlike the better class of New England farm-houses. On the largest, however, there was no residence for the owner, at all, only a small cottage, or whitewashed cabin, for the overseer. The negro-cabins, here, were the smallest I had seen—I thought not more than twelve feet square, inside. They stood in two rows, with a wide street between them. They were built of logs, with no windows—no opening at all, except the doorway, with a chimney of sticks and mud; with no trees about them, no porches, or shades, of any kind. Except for the chimney—the purpose of which I should not readily have guessed if I had seen one of them in New England—I should have conjectured that it had been built for a powder-house, or perhaps an ice-house—never for an animal to sleep in.

We stopped, for some time, on this plantation, near where some thirty men and women were at work, repairing the road. The women were in majority, and were engaged at exactly the same labour as the men; driving the carts, loading them with dirt, and dumping them upon the road; cutting down trees, and drawing wood by hand, to lay across the miry places; hoeing, and shovelling. They were dressed in coarse gray gowns, generally very much burned, and very dirty; which, for greater convenience of working in the mud, were reefed up with a cord drawn tightly around the body, a little above the hips—the spare amount of skirt bagging out between this and the waist-proper. On their legs were loose leggings, or pieces of blanket or bagging wrapped about, and lashed with thongs; and they wore very heavy shoes. Most of them had handkerchiefs, only, tied around their heads; some wore men's caps, or old slouched hats, and several were bareheaded.

The overseer rode about among them, on a horse, carrying in his hand a raw-hide whip, constantly directing and encouraging them; but, as my companion and I, both, several times noticed, as often as he visited one end of the line of operations, the hands at the other end would discontinue their labour, until he turned to ride towards them again. Clumsy, awkward, gross, elephantine in all their movements; pouting, grinning, and leering at us; sly, sensual, and shameless, in all their expressions and demeanour; I never before had witnessed, I thought, anything more revolting than the whole scene.

At length, the overseer dismounted from his horse, and, giving him to a boy to take to the stables, got upon the coach, and rode with us several miles. From the conversation I had with him, as well as from what I saw of his conduct in the field, I judged that he was an uncommonly fit man for his duties; at least ordinarily amiable in disposition, and not passionate; but deliberate, watchful, and efficient. I thought he would be not only a good economist, but a firm and considerate officer or master.

If these women, and their children after them, were always naturally and necessarily to remain of the character and capacity stamped on their faces—as is probably the opinion of their owner, in common with most wealthy South Carolina planters—I don't know that they could be much less miserably situated, or guided more for their own good and that of the world, than they were. They were fat enough, and didn't look as if they were at all overworked, or harassed by cares, or oppressed by a consciousness of their degradation. If that is all—as some think.

Afterwards, while we were changing at a house near a crossing of roads, strolling off in the woods for a short distance, I came upon two small white-topped waggons, each with a pair of horses feeding at its pole; near them was a dull camp fire, with a bake-kettle and coffee-pot, some blankets and a chest upon the ground, and an old negro sitting with his head bowed down over a meal sack, while a negro boy was combing his wool with a common horse-card. "Good evening, uncle," said I, approaching them. "Good evening, sar," he answered, without looking up.

"Where are you going?"

"Well, we ain't gwine nower, master; we's peddlin' tobacco roun."

"Where did you come from?"

"From Rockingham County, Norf Car'lina, master."

"How long have you been coming from there?"

"'Twill be seven weeks, to-morrow, sar, sin we leff home."

"Have you most sold out?"

"We had a hundred and seventy-five boxes in both waggons, and we's sold all but sixty. Want to buy some tobacco, master?" (Looking up.)

"No, thank you; I am only waiting here, while the coach changes. How much tobacco is there in a box?"

"Seventy-five pound."

"Are these the boxes?"

"No, them is our provision boxes, master. Show de genman some of der tobacco, dah." (To the boy.)

A couple of negroes here passed along near us; the old man hailed them:

"Ho dah, boys! Doan you want to buy some backey?"

"No." (Decidedly.)

"Well, I'm sorry for it." (Reproachfully.)

"Are you bound homeward, now?" I asked.

"No, master; wish me was; got to sell all our backey fuss; you don't want none, master, does you? Doan you tink it pretty fair tobacco, sar? Juss try it: it's right sweet, reckon you'll find."

"I don't wish any, thank you; I never use it. Is your master with you?"

"No, sar; he's gone across to Marion, to-day."

"Do you like to be travelling about, in this way?"

"Yes, master; I likes it very well."

"Better than staying at home, eh?"

"Well, I likes my country better dan dis; must say dat, master; likes my country better dan dis. I'se a free niggar in my country, master."

"Oh, you are a free man, are you! North Carolina is a better country than this, for free men, I suppose."

"Yes, master, I likes my country de best; I gets five dollar a month for dat boy." (Hastily, to change the subject.)

"He is your son, is he?"

"Yes, sar; he drives dat waggon, I drives dis; and I haant seen him fore, master, for six weeks, till dis mornin'."

"How were you separated?"

"We separated six weeks ago, sar, and we agreed to meet here, last night. We didn', dough, till dis mornin'."

The old man's tone softened, and he regarded his son with earnestness.

"'Pears, dough, we was bofe heah, last night; but I couldn't find um till dis mornin'. Dis mornin' some niggars tole me dar war a niggar camped off yander in de wood; and I knew 'twas him, and I went an' found him right off."

"And what wages do you get for yourself?"

"Ten dollars a month, master."

"That's pretty good wages."

"Yes, master, any niggar can get good wages if he's a mind to be industrious, no matter wedder he's slave or free."

"So you don't like this country as well as North Carolina?"

"No, master. Fac is, master, 'pears like wite folks doan' ginerally like niggars in dis country; day doan' ginerally talk so to niggars like as do in my country; de niggars ain't so happy heah; 'pears like de wite folks was kind o' different, somehow. I doan' like dis country so well; my country suits me very well."

"Well, I've been thinking, myself, the niggers did not look so well here as they did in North Carolina and Virginia; they are not so well clothed, and they don't appear so bright as they do there."

"Well, master, Sundays dey is mighty well clothed, dis country; 'pears like dere an't nobody looks better Sundays dan dey do. But Lord! workin' days, seems like dey haden no close dey could keep on 'um at all, master. Dey is a'mos' naked, wen deys at work, some on 'em. Why, master, up in our country, de wite folks—why, some on 'em has ten or twelve niggars; dey doan' hev no real big plantation, like day has heah, but some on 'em has ten or twelve niggars, may be, and dey juss lives and talks along wid 'em; and dey treats 'um most as if dem was dar own chile. Dey doan' keep no niggars dey can't treat so; dey won't keep 'em, won't be bodered wid 'em. If dey gets a niggar and he doan behave himself, dey won't keep him; dey juss tell him, sar, he must look up anudder master, and if he doan' find hisself one, I tell 'ou, when de trader cum along, dey sells him, and he totes him away. Dey allers sell off all de bad niggars out of our country; dat's de way all de bad niggar and all dem no-account niggar keep a cumin' down heah; dat's de way on't, master."

"Yes, that's the way of it, I suppose; these big plantations are not just the best thing for niggers, I see that plainly."

"Master, you wan't raise in dis country, was 'ou?"

"No; I came from the North."

"I tort so, sar; I knew 'ou wan't one of dis country people; 'peared like 'ou was one o' my country people, way 'ou talks; and I loves dem kine of people. Won't you take some whisky, sar? Heah, you boy! bring dat jug of whisky dah, out o' my waggon; in dah,—in dat box under dem foddar."

"No, don't trouble yourself, I am very much obliged to you; but I don't like to drink whisky."

"Like to have you drink some, master, if you'd like it. You's right welcome to it. 'Pears like I knew you was one of my country people. Ever been in Greensboro', master? dat's in Guilford."

"No, I never was there. I came from New York, further North than your country."

"New York, did 'ou, master? I heerd New York was what dey calls a Free State; all de niggars free dah."

"Yes, that is so."

"Not no slaves at all; well, I expec dat's a good ting, for all de niggars to be free. Greensboro' is a right comely town; tain't like dese heah Souf Car'lina towns."

"I have heard it spoken of as a beautiful town, and there are some fine people there."

"Yes, dere's Mr. —— ——, I knows him—he's a mighty good man."

"Do you know Mr. ——?"

"O, yes, sar, he's a mighty fine man, he is, master; ain't no better kind of man dan him."

"Well, I must go, or the coach will be kept waiting for me. Good-bye to you."

"Far'well, master, far'well; 'pears like it's done me good to see a man dat's cum out of my country again. Far'well, master."

We took supper at a neat log-cabin, standing a short distance off the road, with a beautiful evergreen oak, the first I had observed, in front of it. There was no glass in the windows, but drapery of white muslin restrained the currents of air, and during the day would let in sufficient light, while a blazing wood-fire both warmed and lighted the room by night. A rifle and powder-horn hung near the fire-place, and the master of the house, a fine, hearty, companionable fellow, said that he had lately shot three deer, and that there were plenty of cats, and foxes, as well as turkeys, hares, squirrels, and other small game in the vicinity. It was a perfectly charming little backwoods farm-house—good wife, supper, and all; but one disagreeable blot darkened the otherwise most agreeable picture of rustic civilization—we were waited upon at table by two excessively dirty, slovenly-dressed, negro girls. In the rear of the cabin were two hovels, each lighted by large fires, and apparently crowded with other slaves belonging to the family.

Between nine and ten at night, we reached the end of the completed railroad, coming up in search for that we had left the previous night. There was another camp and fire of the workmen, and in a little white frame-house we found a company of engineers. There were two trains and locomotives on the track, and a gang of negroes was loading cotton into one of them.

I strolled off until I reached an opening in the woods, in which was a cotton-field and some negro-cabins, and beyond it large girdled trees, among which were two negroes with dogs, barking, yelping, hacking, shouting, and whistling, after 'coons and 'possums. Returning to the railroad, I found a comfortable, warm passenger-car, and, wrapped in my blanket, went to sleep. At midnight I was awakened by loud laughter, and, looking out, saw that the gang of negroes had made a fire, and were enjoying a right merry repast. Suddenly, one raised such a sound as I never heard before; a long, loud, musical shout, rising and falling, and breaking into falsetto, his voice ringing through the woods in the clear, frosty night air, like a bugle-call. As he finished, the melody was caught up by another, and' then another, and then by several in chorus. When there was silence again, one of them cried out, as if bursting with amusement: "Did yer see de dog?—when I began eeohing, he turn roun' an' look me straight into der face; ha! ha! ha!" and the whole party broke into the loudest peals of laughter, as if it was the very best joke they had ever heard.

After a few minutes I could hear one urging the rest to come to work again, and soon he stepped towards the cotton bales, saying,

"Come, brederen, come; let's go at it; come now, eoho! roll away! eeoho-eeoho-weeioho-i!"—and the rest taking it up as before, in a few moments they all had their shoulders to a bale of cotton, and were rolling it up the embankment.

About half-past three, I was awakened again by the whistle of the locomotive, answering, I suppose, the horn of a stage-coach, which in a few minutes drove up, bringing a mail. A negro man and woman who had been sleeping near me, replenished the fire; two other passengers came in, and we started.

In the woods I saw a negro by a fire, while it was still night, shaving shingles very industriously. He did not even stop to look at the train. No doubt he was a slave, working by task, and of his own accord at night, that he might have the more daylight for his own purposes.

The negroes enjoy fine blazing fires in the open air, and make them at every opportunity. The train on this road was provided with a man and maid-servant to attend to the fire and wait on the passengers—a very good arrangement, by the way, yet to be adopted on our own long passenger trains. When we arrived at a junction where we were to change cars, as soon as all the passengers had left the train, they also left; but instead of going into the station-house with us, they immediately collected some pine branches and chips, and getting a brand from the locomotive, made a fire upon the ground, and seated themselves by it. Other negroes soon began to join them, and as they approached were called to: "Doan' yer cum widout som' wood! Doan' yer cum widout som' wood!" and every one had to make his contribution. At another place, near a cotton plantation, I found a woman collecting pine leaves into heaps, to be carted to the cattle-pens. She, too, had a fire near her. "What are you doing with a fire, aunty?" "Oh, jus' to warm my hans wen dey gits cold, massa." The weather was then almost uncomfortably warm.

We were running during the forenoon, for a hundred miles, or more, in a southerly direction, on nearly a straight course, through about the middle of the State of South Carolina. The greater part of this distance, the flat, sandy pine barrens continued, scarcely a foot of grading, for many miles at a time, having been required in the construction of the railroad. As the swamps, which were still frequent, were crossed on piles and tressel-work, the roads must have been built very cheaply—the land damages being nothing. We passed from the track of one company to that of another, several times during the day—the speed was from fifteen to twenty miles an hour, with long stoppages at the stations. A conductor said they could easily run forty miles, and had done it, including stoppages; but they were forbidden now to make fast time, from the injury it did the road—the superstructure being much more shaken and liable to displacement in these light sands than on our Northern roads. The locomotives that I saw were all made in Philadelphia; the cars were all from the Hartford, Conn., and Worcester, Mass., manufactories, and invariably, elegant and comfortable. The roads seemed to be doing a heavy freighting business with cotton. We passed at the turn-outs half a dozen trains, with nearly a thousand bales on each, but the number of passengers was always small. A slave country can never, it is evident, furnish a passenger traffic of much value. A majority of the passenger trains, which I saw used in the South, were not paying for the fuel and wages expended in running them.

For an hour or two we got above the sandy zone, and into the second, middle, or "wave" region of the State. The surface here was extremely undulating, gracefully swelling and dipping in bluffs and dells—the soil a mellow brown loam, with some indications of fertility, especially in the valleys. Yet most of the ground was occupied by pine woods (probably old-field pines, on exhausted cotton-fields). For a few miles, on a gently sloping surface of the same sort of soil, there were some enormously large cotton-fields.

I saw women working again, in large gangs with men. In one case they were distributing manure—ditch scrapings it appeared to be—and the mode of operation was this: the manure had been already carted into heaps upon the ground; a number of the women were carrying it in from the heap in baskets, on their heads, and one in her apron, and spreading it with their hands between the ridges on which the cotton grew last year; the rest followed with great, long-handled, heavy, clumsy hoes, and pulled down the ridges over the manure, and so made new ridges for the next planting. I asked a young planter who continued with me a good part of the day, why they did not use ploughs. He said this was rather rough land, and a plough wouldn't work in it very well. It was light soil, and smooth enough for a parade ground. The fact is, in certain parts of South Carolina, a plough is yet an almost unknown instrument of tillage.

About noon we turned east, on a track running direct to Charleston. Pine barrens continued alternating with swamp, with some cotton and corn fields on the edges of the latter. A few of the pines were "boxed" for turpentine; and I understood that one or two companies from North Carolina had been operating here for several years. Plantations were not very often seen along the road through the sand; but stations, at which cotton was stored and loading, were comparatively frequent.

At one of the stations an empty car had been attached to the train; I had gone into it, and was standing at one end of it, when an elderly countryman with a young woman and three little children entered and took seats at the other. The old man took out a roll of deerskin, in which were bank-bills, and some small change.

"How much did he say 'twould be?" he inquired.

"Seventy cents."

"For both on us?"

"For each on us."

"Both on us, I reckon."

"Reckon it's each."

"I've got jess seventy-five cents in hard money."

"Give it to him, and tell him it's all yer got; reckon he'll let us go."

At this I moved, to attract their attention; the old man started, and looked towards me for a moment, and said no more. I soon afterwards walked out on the platform, passing him, and the conductor came in, and collected their fare; I then returned, and stood near them, looking out of the window of the door. The old man had a good-humoured, thin, withered, very brown face, and there was a speaking twinkle in his eye. He was dressed in clothes much of the Quaker cut—a broad-brimmed, low hat; white cotton shirt, open in front, and without cravat, showing his hairy breast; a long-skirted, snuff-coloured coat, of very coarse homespun; short trousers, of brown drilling; red woollen stockings, and heavy cow-hide shoes. He presently asked the time of day; I gave it to him, and we continued in conversation, as follows:—

"Right cold weather."

"Yes."

"G'wine to Branchville?"

"I am going beyond there—to Charleston."

"Ah—come from Hamburg this mornin'?"

"No—from beyond there."

"Did ye?—where 'd you come from?"

"From Wilmington."

"How long yer ben comin'?"

"I left Wilmington night before last, about ten o'clock. I have been ever since on the road."

"Reckon yer a night-bird."

"What?"

"Reckon you are a night-bird—what we calls a night-hawk; keeps a goin' at night, you know."

"Yes—I've been going most of two nights."

"Reckon so; kinder red your eyes is. Live in Charleston, do ye?"

"No, I live in New York."

"New York—that's a good ways, yet, ain't it?"

"Yes."

"Reckon yer arter a chicken, up here."

"No."

"Ah, ha—reckon ye are."

The young woman laughed, lifted her shoulder, and looked out of the window.

"Reckon ye'll get somebody's chicken."

"I'm afraid not."

The young woman laughed again, and tossed her head.

"Oh, reckon ye will—ah, ha! But yer mustn't mind my fun."

"Not at all, not at all. Where did *you* come from?"

"Up here to ——; g'wine hum; g'wine to stop down here, next deeper. How do you go, w'en you get to Charleston?"

"I am going on to New Orleans."

"Is New York beyond New Orleans?"

"Beyond New Orleans? Oh, no."

"In New Orleans, is't?"

"What?"

"New York is somewhere in New Orleans, ain't it?"

"No; it's the other way—beyond Wilmington."

"Oh! Been pretty cold thar?"

"Yes; there was a foot and a half of snow there, last week, I hear."

"Lord o'massy! why! have to feed all the cattle!—whew!—ha!—whew! don't wonner ye com' away."

"You are a farmer."

"Yes."

"Well, I am a farmer, too."

"Be ye—to New York?"

"Yes; how much land have you got?"

"A hundred and twenty-five acres; how much have you?"

"Just about the same. What's your land worth, here?"

"Some on't—what we call swamp-land—kinder low and wet like, you know—that's worth five dollars an acre; and mainly it's worth a dollar and a half or two dollars—that's takin' a common trac' of up-land. What's yours worth?"

"A hundred and fifty to two hundred dollars."

"What!"

"A hundred and fifty to two hundred."

"Dollars?"

"Yes."

"Not an acre?"

"Yes."

"Good Lord! yer might as well buy niggers to onst. Do you work any niggers?"

"No."

"May be they don't have niggers—that is, slaves—to New York."

"No, we do not. It's against the law."

"Yes, I heerd 'twas, some place. How do yer get yer work done?"

"I hire white men—Irishmen generally."

"Do they work good?"

"Yes, better than negroes, I think, and don't cost nearly as much."

"What do yer have to give 'em?"

"Eight or nine dollars a month, and board, for common hands, by the year."

"Hi, Lordy! and they work up right smart, do they? Why, yer can't get any kind of a good nigger less'n twelve dollars a month."

"And board?"

"And board 'em? yes; and clothe, and blank, and shoe 'em, too."

He owned no negroes himself and did not hire any. "They," his family, "made their own crap." They raised maize, and sweet potatoes, and cow-peas. He reckoned, in general, they made about three barrels of maize to the acre; sometimes, as much as five. He described to me, as a novelty, a plough, with "a sort of a wing, like, on one side," that pushed off, and turned over a slice of the ground; from which it appeared that he had, until recently, never seen a mould-board; the common ploughs of this country being constructed on the same principles as those of the Chinese, and only rooting the ground, like a hog or a mole—not cleaving and turning. He had never heard of working a plough with more than one horse. He was frank and good-natured; embarrassed his daughter by coarse jokes about herself and her babies, and asked me if I would not go home with him, and, when I declined, pressed me to come and see them when I returned. That I might do so, he gave me directions how to get to his farm; observing that I must start pretty early in the day—because it would not be safe for a stranger to try to cross the swamp after dark. The moment the train began to check its speed, before stopping at the place at which he was to leave, he said to his daughter, "Come, gal! quick now; gather up yer young ones!" and stepped out, pulling her after him, on to the platform. As they walked off, I noticed that he strode ahead, like an Indian or a gipsy man, and she carried in her arms two of the children and a bundle, while the third child held to her skirts.

A party of fashionably-dressed people took the train for Charleston—two families, apparently, returning from a visit to their plantations. They came to the station in handsome coaches. Some minutes before the rest, there entered the car, in which I was then again alone, and reclining on a bench in the corner, an old nurse, with a baby, and two young negro women, having care of half a dozen children, mostly girls, from three to fifteen years of age. As they closed the door, the negro girls seemed to resume a conversation, or quarrel. Their language was loud and obscene, such as I never heard before from any but the most depraved and beastly women of the streets. Upon observing me, they dropped their voices, but not with any appearance of shame, and continued their altercation, until their mistresses entered. The white children, in the mean time, had listened, without any appearance of wonder or annoyance. The moment the ladies opened the door, they became silent.[6]

<hr>

[6] *From the Southern Cultivator, June,* 1855.—"Children are fond of the company of negroes, not only because the deference shown them makes them feel perfectly at ease, but the subjects of conversation are on a level with their capacity; while the simple tales, and the witch and ghost stories, so common among negroes, excite the young imagination and enlist the feelings. If, in this association, the child becomes familiar with indelicate, vulgar, and lascivious manners and conversation, an impression is made upon the mind and heart, which lasts for years—perhaps for life. Could we, in all cases, trace effects to

their real causes, I doubt not but many young men and women, of respectable parentage and bright prospects, who have made shipwreck of all their earthly hopes, have been led to the fatal step by the seeds of corruption which, in the days of childhood and youth, were sown in their hearts by the indelicate and lascivious manners and conversation of their father's negroes."

From an Address of Chancellor [William] Harper, prepared for and read before the Society for the Advancement of Learning, of South Carolina.—"I have said the tendency of our institution is to elevate the female character, as well as that of the other sex, for similar reasons.

"And, permit me to say, that this elevation of the female character is no less important and essential to us, than the moral and intellectual cultivation of the other sex. It would, indeed, be intolerable, if, when one class of society is necessarily degraded in this respect, no compensation were made by the superior elevation and purity of the other. Not only essential purity of conduct, but the utmost purity of manners. And, I will add, though it may incur the formidable charge of affectation or prudery, *a greater severity of decorum than is required elsewhere, is necessary among us.* Always should be strenuously resisted the attempts, which have sometimes been made, to introduce among us the freedom of foreign European, and, especially, of continental manners. Let us say: we will not have *the manners* of South Carolina changed."

Chapter VI

The Rice District

Savannah.—While riding, aimlessly, in the suburbs, I came upon a square field, in the midst of an open pine-wood, partially inclosed with a dilapidated wooden paling. It proved to be a grave-yard for negroes. Dismounting, and fastening my horse to a gate-post, I walked in, and found much in the monuments to interest me. Some of these were mere billets of wood, others were of brick and marble, and some were pieces of plank, cut in the ordinary form of tomb-stones. Many family-lots were inclosed with railings, and a few flowers or evergreen shrubs had sometimes been planted on the graves; but these were generally broken down and withered, and the ground was overgrown with weeds and briars. I spent some time in examining the inscriptions, the greater number of which were evidently painted by self-taught negroes, and were curiously illustrative both of their condition and character. I transcribed a few of them, as literally as possible, as follow:

SACRED
TO THE MEMORY
OF HENRY. Gleve, ho
Dide January 19 1849
Age 44.

BALDWING
In men of Charles
who died NOV
20. The 1846
aged 62 years Blessed are the
dead who dieth
in the Lord
Even so said
the SPerit. For
the Rest From
Thair

[The remainder rotted off.]

DEAR
WIFE OF
JAMES DELBUG
BORN 1814 DIED 1852.

In Memr
y, of,
M a
gare
-t. Born
August
29 and
died oc
tober 29 1852

[The following on marble.]

To record the worth fidelity and virtue of Reynolda Watts, (who died on the 2d day of May 1829 at the age of 24 years, in giving birth to her 3d child).

Reared from infancy by an affectionate mistress and trained by her in the paths of virtue, She was strictly moral in her deportment, faithful and devoted in her duty and heart and soul a

[Sand drifted over the remainder.]

There were a few others, of similar character to the above, erected by whites to the memory of favourite servants. The following was on a large brick tomb:—

This tablet is erected to record the demise of Rev. HENRY CUN-NINGHAM, Founder and subsequent pastor of the 2d African Church for 39 years, who yielded his spirit to its master the 29 of March 1842, aged 83 years.

[Followed by an inscription to the memory of Mrs. Cunningham.]

This vault is erected by the 2d African Church, as a token of respect.

The following is upon a large stone table. The reader will observe its date; but I must add that, while in North Carolina, I heard of two recent occasions, in which public religious services had been interrupted, and the preachers—very estimable coloured men—publicly whipped.

Sacred to the memory of Andrew Brian pastor of 1st colored Baptist church in Savannah. God was Pleased to lay his honour near his heart and impress the worth and weight of souls upon his mind that he was constrained to Preach the Gospel to dieng world, particularly to the sable sons of africa. though he labored under many disadvantage yet thought in the school of Christ, he was able to bring out new and old out of the treasury And he has done more good among the poor slaves than all the learned Doctors in America, He was im prisoned for the Gospel without any ceremony was severely whipped. But while under the lash he told his prosecutor he rejoiced not only to be whipped but he was willing for to suffer death for the cause of CHRIST.

He continued preaching the Gospel until Oct 6 1812. He was supposed to be 96 years of age, his remains were interd with peculiar respect an address was delivered by the Rev. Mr Johnston Dr. Kolluck Thomas Williams and Henry Cunningham He was an honour to human nature an ornament to religion and a friend to mankind. His memory is still precious in the (hearts) of the living.

> *Afflicted long he bore the rod*
> *With calm submission to his maker God.*
> *His mind was tranquil and serene*
> *No terrors in his looks was seen*
> *A* SAVIOURS *smile dispelled the gloom*
> *And smoothed the passage to the tomb.*

I heard a voice from Heaven saying unto me, Write, Blessed are the dead which die in the Lord from henceforth! Yea saith the Spirit that they may rest from the labours.

This stone is erected by the First Colored Church as a token of love for their most faithful pastor. A.D. 1821.

Plantation, February [1853].—I left town yesterday morning, on horseback, with a letter in my pocket to Mr. X., under whose roof I am now writing. The weather was fine, and, indeed, since I left Virginia, the weather for out-of-door purposes has been as fine as can be imagined. The exercise of walking or of riding warms one, at any time between sunrise and sunset, sufficiently to allow an overcoat to be dispensed with, while the air is yet brisk and stimulating. The public-houses are overcrowded with Northerners, who congratulate themselves on having escaped from the severe cold, of which they hear from home.

All, however, who know the country, out of the large towns, say that they have suffered more from cold here than ever at the North; because, except at a few first-class hotels, and in the better sort of mansions and plantation residences, any provision for keeping houses warm is so entirely neglected. It is, indeed, too cool to sit quietly, even at midday, out of sunshine, and at night it is often frosty. As a general rule, with such exceptions as I have indicated, it will be full two hours after one has asked for a fire in his room before the servants can be got to make it. The expedient of closing a door or window to exclude a draught of cold air seems really to be unknown to the negroes. From the time I left Richmond, until I arrived at Charleston, I never but once knew a servant to close the door on leaving a room, unless he was requested at the moment to do so.

The public-houses of the smaller towns, and the country houses generally, are so loosely built, and so rarely have unbroken glass windows, that to sit by a fire, and to avoid remaining in a draught at the same time, is not to be expected.

As the number of Northerners, and especially of invalids, who come hither in winter, is every year increasing, more comfortable accommodations along the line of travel must soon be provided; if not by native, then by Northern enterprise. Some of the hotels in Florida, indeed, are already, I understand, under the management of Northerners; and this winter, cooks and waiters have been procured for them from the North. I observe, also, that one of them advertises that meats and vegetables are received by every steamer from New York.

Whenever comfortable quarters, and means of conveyance are extensively provided, at not immoderately great expense, there must be a great migration here every winter. The climate and the scenery, as well as the society of the more wealthy planters' families, are attractive, not to invalids alone, but even more to men and women who are able to enjoy invigorating recreations. Nowhere in the world could a man, with a sound body and a quiet conscience, live more pleasantly, at least as a guest, it seems to me, than here where I am. I was awakened this morning by a servant making a fire in my chamber. Opening the window, I found a clear, brisk air, but without frost—the mercury standing at 35° F. There was not a sign of winter, except that a few cypress trees, hung with seed attached to pretty pendulous tassels, were leafless. A grove which surrounded the house was all in dark verdure; there were green oranges on trees nearer the window; the buds were swelling on a jessamine-vine, and a number of camelia-japonicas were in full bloom; one of them, at least seven feet high, and a large compact shrub, must have had several hundred blossoms on it. Sparrows were chirping, doves cooing, and a mocking-bird whistling loudly. I walked to the stable, and saw clean and neatly-dressed negroes grooming thorough-bred horses, which pawed the ground, and tossed their heads, and drew deep inspirations, and danced as they were led out, in exuberance of animal spirits; and I felt as they did. We drove ten miles to church, in the forenoon, with the carriage-top thrown back, and with our overcoats laid aside; nevertheless, when we returned, and came into the house, we found a crackling wood fire, as comfortable as it was cheerful. Two lads, the sons of my host, had returned the night before from a "marooning party," with a boat-load of venison, wild fowl, and fish; and at dinner this evening there were delicacies which are to be had in perfection, it is said, nowhere else than on this coast. The woods and waters around us abound, not only with game, but with most interesting subjects of observation to the naturalist and the artist. Everything encourages cheerfulness, and invites to healthful life.

Now to think how people are baking in their oven-houses at home, or waddling out in the deep snow or mud, or across the frozen ruts, wrapped up to a Falstaffian rotundity in flannels and furs, one can but wonder that those, who have means, stay there, any more than these stay here in summer; and that my host would no more think of doing than the wild-goose.

But I must tell how I got here, and what I saw by the way.

A narrow belt of cleared land—"vacant lots"—only separated the town from the pine forest—that great broad forest which extends uninterruptedly, and merely dotted with a few small corn and cotton fields, from Delaware to Louisiana.

Having some doubt about the road, I asked a direction of a man on horseback, who overtook and was passing me. In reply, he said it was a straight road, and we should go in company for a mile or two. He inquired if I was a stranger; and, when he heard that I was from the North, and now first visiting the South, he remarked that there was "no better place for me to go to than that for which I had inquired. Mr. X. was a very fine man—rich, got a splendid plantation, lived well, had plenty of company always, and there were a number of other show plantations near his. He reckoned I would visit some of them."

I asked what he meant by "show plantations." "Plantations belonging to rich people," he said, "where they had everything fixed up nice. There were several places that had that name; their owners always went out and lived on them part of the year, and kept a kind of open house, and were always ready to receive company. He reckoned I might go and stay a month round on them kind of places on —— River, and it would not cost me a cent. They always had a great many Northerners going to see them, those gentlemen had. Almost every Northerner that came here was invited right out to visit some of them; and, in summer, a good many of them went to the North themselves."

(It was not till long afterwards, long after the above paragraph was first printed, that I fully comprehended the significance of the statement, that on the show plantations it would not cost me a cent.)

During the forenoon my road continued broad and straight, and I was told that it was the chief outlet and thoroughfare of a very extensive agricultural district. There was very little land in cultivation within sight of the road, however; not a mile of it fenced, in twenty, and the only houses were log-cabins. The soil varied from a coarse, clean, yellow sand, to a dark, brown, sandy loam. There were indications that much of the land had, at some time, been under cultivation—had been worn out, and deserted.

Long teams of mules, driven by negroes, toiled slowly towards the town, with loads of rice or cotton. A stage-coach, with six horses to drag it through the heavy road, covered me, as it passed, with dust; and once or twice, I met a stylish carriage with fashionably-clad gentlemen and ladies, and primly-liveried negro-servants; but much the greatest traffic of the road was done by small one-horse carts, driven by white men, or women.

These carts, all but their wheels, which come from the North, look as if they were made by their owners, in the woods, with no better tools than axes and jack-knives. Very little iron is used in their construction; the different parts being held together by wooden pins, and lashings of hide. The harness is made chiefly of ropes and undressed hide; but there is always a high-peaked riding-saddle, in which the driver prefers to sit, rather than on his cart. Once, I met

a woman riding in this way, with a load of children in the cart behind her. From the axle-tree often hung a gourd, or an iron kettle.
One man carried a rifle on his pommel. Sometimes, these carts would
contain a single bale of cotton, more commonly, an assorted cargo
of maize, sweet potatoes, poultry, game, hides, and peltry, with, always, some bundles of corn-leaves, to be fed to the horse. Women
and children were often passengers, or travelled on foot, in company with the carts, which were usually furnished with a low tilt.
Many of them, I found, had been two or three days on the road,
bringing down a little crop to market; whole families coming with it,
to get reclothed with the proceeds.

The men with the carts were generally slight, with high cheek-
bones and sunken eyes, and were of less than the usual stature of
the Anglo-Saxon race. They were dressed in long-skirted homespun coats, wore slouched hats, and heavy boots, outside their
trousers. As they met me, they usually bowed, and often offered a
remark upon the weather, or the roads, in a bold, but not uncourteous manner—showing themselves to be, at least, in one respect, better
off than the majority of European peasants, whose educated servility
of character rarely fails to manifest itself, when they meet a well-
dressed stranger.

The household markets of most of the Southern towns seem to
be mainly supplied by the poor country people, who, driving in this
style, bring all sorts of produce to exchange for such small stores
and articles of apparel as they must needs obtain from the shops.
Sometimes, owing to the great extent of the back country from which
the supplies are gathered, they are offered in great abundance and
variety: at other times, from the want of regular market-men, there
will be a scarcity, and prices will be very high.

A stranger cannot but express surprise and amusement at the appearance and manners of these country traffickers in the market-
place. The "wild Irish" hardly differ more from the English gentry
than these rustics from the better class of planters and towns-people,
with whom the traveller more commonly comes in contact. Their
language even is almost incomprehensible, and seems exceedingly
droll, to a Northern man. I have found it quite impossible to report
it. I shall not soon forget the figure of a little old white woman, wearing a man's hat, smoking a pipe, driving a little black bull with
reins; sitting herself bolt upright, upon the axle-tree of a little truck,

on which she was returning from market. I was riding with a gentleman of the town at the time, and, as she bowed to him with an expression of ineffable self-satisfaction, I asked if he knew her. He had known her for twenty years, he said, and until lately she had always come into town about once a week, on foot, bringing fowls, eggs, potatoes, or herbs, for sale in a basket. The bull she had probably picked up astray, when a calf, and reared and broken it herself; and the cart and harness she had made herself; but he did not think any lady in the land felt richer than she did now, or prouder of her establishment.

In the afternoon, I left the main road, and, towards night, reached a much more cultivated district. The forest of pines still extended uninterruptedly on one side of the way, but on the other was a continued succession of very large fields, of rich dark soil—evidently reclaimed swamp-land—which had been cultivated the previous year, in Sea Island cotton. Beyond them, a flat surface of still lower land, with a silver thread of water curling through it, extended, Holland-like, to the horizon. Usually at as great a distance as a quarter of a mile from the road, and from half a mile to a mile apart, were the residences of the planters—white houses, with groves of evergreen trees about them; and between these and the road were little villages of slave-cabins.

My directions not having been sufficiently explicit, I rode in, by a private lane, to one of these. It consisted of some thirty neatly-whitewashed cottages, with a broad avenue, planted with Pride-of-China trees between them.

The cottages were framed buildings, boarded on the outside, with shingle roofs and brick chimneys; they stood fifty feet apart, with gardens and pig-yards, enclosed by palings, between them. At one, which was evidently the "sick house," or hospital, there were several negroes of both sexes, wrapped in blankets, and reclining on the door steps or on the ground, basking in the sunshine. Some of them looked ill, but all were chatting and laughing as I rode up to make an inquiry. I learned that it was not the plantation I was intending to visit, and received a direction, as usual, so indistinct and incorrect that it led me wrong.

At another plantation which I soon afterwards reached, I found the "settlement" arranged in the same way, the cabins only being of a slightly different form. In the middle of one row was a well-house, and opposite it, on the other row, was a mill-house, with stones, at which the negroes grind their corn. It is a kind of pestle and mortar; and I was informed afterwards that the negroes prefer to take their allowance of corn and crack it for themselves, rather than to receive meal, because they think the mill-ground meal does not make as sweet bread.

At the head of the settlement, in a garden looking down the street, was an overseer's house, and here the road divided, running each way at right angles; on one side to barns and a landing on the river, on the other toward the mansion of the proprietor. A negro boy opened the gate of the latter, and I entered.

On the either side, at fifty feet distant, were rows of old live-oak trees, their branches and twigs slightly hung with a delicate fringe of gray moss, and their dark, shining, green foliage, meeting and intermingling naturally but densely overhead. The sunlight streamed through, and played aslant the lustrous leaves, and fluttering pendulous moss; the arch was low and broad; the trunks were huge and gnarled, and there was a heavy groining of strong, rough, knotty, branches. I stopped my horse and held my breath; I thought of old Kit North's rhapsody on trees; and it was no rhapsody—it was all here, and real: "Light, shade, shelter, coolness, freshness, music, dew, and dreams dropping through their umbrageous twilight— dropping direct, soft, sweet, soothing, and restorative from heaven."

Alas! no angels; only little black babies, toddling about with an older child or two to watch them, occupied the aisle. At the upper end was the owner's mansion, with a circular court-yard around it, and an irregular plantation of great trees; one of the oaks, as I afterwards learned, seven feet in diameter of trunk, and covering with its branches a circle of one hundred and twenty feet in diameter. As I approached it, a smart servant came out to take my horse. I obtained from him a direction to the residence of the gentleman I was searching for, and rode away, glad that I had stumbled into so charming a place.

After riding a few miles further I reached my destination.

Mr. X. has two plantations on the river, besides a large tract of poor pine forest land, extending some miles back upon the upland, and reaching above the malarious region. In the upper part of this pine land is a house, occupied by his overseer during the malarious season, when it is dangerous for any but negroes to remain during the night in the vicinity of the swamps or rice-fields. Even those few who have been born in the region, and have grown up subject to the malaria, are said to be generally weakly and short-lived. The negroes do not enjoy as good health on rice plantations as elsewhere; and the greater difficulty with which their lives are preserved, through infancy especially, shows that the subtle poison of the miasma is not innocuous to them; but Mr. X. boasts a steady increase of his negro stock, of five per cent. per annum, which is better than is averaged on the plantations of the interior.

The plantation which contains Mr. X.'s winter residence has but a small extent of rice-land, the greater part of it being reclaimed upland swamp soil, suitable for the culture of Sea Island cotton. The other plantation contains over five hundred acres of rice-land, fitted for irrigation; the remainder is unusually fertile reclaimed upland swamp, and some hundred acres of it are cultivated for maize and Sea Island cotton.

There is a "negro settlement" on each; but both plantations, although a mile or two apart, are worked together as one, under one overseer—the hands being drafted from one to another as their labour is required. Somewhat over seven hundred acres are at the present time under the plough in the two plantations: the whole number of negroes is two hundred, and they are reckoned to be equal to about one hundred prime hands—an unusual strength for that number of all classes. The overseer lives, in winter, near the settlement of the larger plantation, Mr. X. near that of the smaller.

It is an old family estate, inherited by Mr. X.'s wife, who, with her children, was born and brought up upon it in close intimacy with the negroes, a large proportion of whom were also included in her inheritance, or have been since born upon the estate. Mr. X. himself is a New England farmer's son, and has been a successful merchant and manufacturer.

The patriarchal institution should be seen here under its most favourable aspects; not only from the ties of long family association, common traditions, common memories, and, if ever, common interests, between the slaves and their rulers, but, also, from the practical talent for organization and administration, gained among the rugged fields, the complicated looms, and the exact and comprehensive counting-houses of New England, which directs the labour.

The house-servants are more intelligent, understand and perform their duties better, and are more appropriately dressed, than any I have seen before. The labour required of them is light, and they are treated with much more consideration for their health and comfort than is usually given to that of free domestics. They live in brick cabins, adjoining the house and stables, and one of these, into which I have looked, is neatly and comfortably furnished. Several of the house-servants, as is usual, are mulattoes, and good-looking. The mulattoes are generally preferred for in-door occupations. Slaves brought up to house-work dread to be employed at field-labour; and those accustomed to the comparatively unconstrained life of the negro-settlement, detest the close control and careful movements required of the house-servants. It is a punishment for a lazy field-hand, to employ him in menial duties at the house, as it is to set a sneaking sailor to do the work of a cabin-servant; and it is equally a punishment to a neglectful house-servant, to banish him to the field-gangs. All the household economy is, of course, carried on in a style appropriate to a wealthy gentleman's residence—not more so, nor less so, that I observe, than in an establishment of similar grade at the North.

It is a custom with Mr. X., when on the estate, to look each day at all the work going on, inspect the buildings, boats, embankments, and sluice-ways, and examine the sick. Yesterday I accompanied him in one of these daily rounds.

After a ride of several miles through the woods, in the rear of the plantations we came to his largest negro-settlement. There was a street, or common, two hundred feet wide, on which the cabins of the negroes fronted. Each cabin was a framed building, the walls boarded and whitewashed on the outside, lathed and plastered within, the roof shingled; forty-two feet long, twenty-one feet wide, divided into two family tenements, each twenty-one by twenty-one; each tenement divided into three rooms—one, the common household apartment, twenty-one by ten; each of the others (bedrooms), ten by ten. There was a brick fire-place in the middle of the long side of each living room, the chimneys rising in one, in the middle of the roof. Besides these rooms, each tenement had a cock-loft, entered by steps from the household room. Each tenement is occupied, on an average, by five persons. There were in them closets, with locks and keys, and a varying quantity of rude furniture. Each cabin stood two hundred feet from the next, and the street in front of them being two hundred feet wide, they were just that distance apart each way. The people were nearly all absent at work, and had locked their outer doors, taking the keys with them. Each cabin has a front and back door, and each room a window, closed by a wooden shutter, swinging outward, on hinges. Between each tenement and the next house, is a small piece of ground, inclosed with palings, in which are coops of fowl with chickens, hovels for nests, and for sows with pig. There were a great many fowls in the street. The negroes' swine are allowed to run in the woods, each owner having his own distinguished by a peculiar mark. In the rear of the yards were gardens—a half-acre to each family. Internally the cabins appeared dirty and disordered, which was rather a pleasant indication that their home-life was not much interfered with, though I found certain police regulations were enforced.

The cabin nearest the overseer's house was used as a nursery. Having driven up to this, Mr. X. inquired first of an old nurse how the children were; whether there had been any births since his last visit; spoke to two convalescent young mothers, who were lounging on the floor of the portico, with the children, and then asked if there were any sick people.

"Nobody, oney dat boy, Sam, sar."

"What Sam is that?"

"Dat little Sam, sar; Tom's Sue's Sam, sar."

"What's the matter with him?"

"Don' 'spec dere's noting much de matter wid him now, sar. He came in Sa'dy, complainin' he had de stomach-ache, an' I gin him some ile, sar; 'spec he mus' be well, dis time, but he din go out dis mornin'."

"Well, I'll see to him."

Mr. X. went to Tom's Sue's cabin, looked at the boy, and, concluding that he was well, though he lay abed, and pretended to cry with pain, ordered him to go out to work. Then, meeting the overseer, who was just riding away, on some business of the plantation, he remained some time in conversation with him, while I occupied myself in making a sketch of the nursery and street of the settlement in my note-book. On the verandah and the steps of the nursery, there were twenty-seven children, most of them infants, that had been left there by their mothers, while they were working their tasks in the fields. They probably make a visit to them once or twice during the day, to nurse them, and receive them to take to their cabins, or where they like, when they have finished their tasks—generally in the middle of the afternoon. The older children were fed with porridge, by the general nurse. A number of girls, eight or ten years old, were occupied in holding and tending the youngest infants. Those a little older—the crawlers—were in the pen, and those big enough to toddle were playing on the steps, or before the house. Some of these, with two or three bigger ones, were singing and dancing about a fire that they had made on the ground. They were not at all dis· turbed or interrupted in their amusement by the presence of their owner and myself. At twelve years of age, the children are first put to regular field-work; until then no labour is required of them, except, perhaps, occasionally they are charged with some light kind of duty, such as frightening birds from corn. When first sent to the field, one quarter of an able-bodied hand's day's work is ordinarily allotted to them, as their task.

From the settlement, we drove to the "mill"—not a flouring mill, though I believe there is a run of stones in it—but a monster barn, with more extensive and better machinery for threshing and storing rice, driven by a steam-engine, than I have ever seen used for grain before. Adjoining the mill-house were shops and sheds, in which blacksmiths, carpenters, and other mechanics—all slaves, belonging to Mr. X.—were at work. He called my attention to the excellence of their workmanship, and said that they exercised as much ingenuity and skill as the ordinary mechanics that he was used to employ in New England. He pointed out to me some carpenter's work, a part of which had been executed by a New England mechanic, and a part by one of his own hands, which indicated that the latter was much the better workman.

I was gratified by this, for I had been so often told, in Virginia, by gentlemen anxious to convince me that the negro was incapable of being educated or improved to a condition in which it would be safe to trust him with himself—that no negro-mechanic could ever be taught, or induced to work carefully or nicely—that I had begun to believe it might be so.

We were attended through the mill-house by a respectable-looking, orderly, and quiet-mannered mulatto, who was called, by his master, "the watchman." His duties, however, as they were described to me, were those of a steward, or intendant. He carried, by a strap at his waist, a very large number of keys, and had charge of all the stores of provisions, tools, and materials of the plantations, as well as of all their produce, before it was shipped to market. He weighed and measured out all the rations of the slaves and the cattle; superintended the mechanics, and made and repaired, as was necessary, all the machinery, including the steam-engine.

In all these departments, his authority was superior to that of the overseer. The overseer received his private allowance of family provisions from him, as did also the head-servant at the mansion, who was his brother. His responsibility was much greater than that of the overseer; and Mr. X. said he would trust him with much more than he would any overseer he had ever known.

Anxious to learn how this trustworthiness and intelligence, so unusual in a slave, had been developed or ascertained, I inquired of his history, which was briefly as follows.

Being the son of a favourite house-servant, he had been, as a child, associated with the white family, and received by chance something of the early education of the white children. When old enough, he had been employed, for some years, as a waiter; but, at his own request, was eventually allowed to learn the blacksmith's trade, in the plantation shop. Showing ingenuity and talent, he was afterwards employed to make and repair the plantation cotton-gins. Finally, his owner took him to a steam-engine builder, and paid $500 to have him instructed as a machinist. After he had become a skilful workman, he obtained employment as an engineer; and for some years continued in this occupation, and was allowed to spend his wages for himself. Finding, however, that he was acquiring dissipated habits, and wasting his earnings, Mr. X. eventually brought him, much against his inclinations, back to the plantations. Being allowed peculiar privileges, and given duties wholly flattering to his self-respect, he soon became contented; and, of course was able to be extremely valuable to his owner.

I have seen another slave-engineer. The gentleman who employed him told me that he was a man of talent, and of great worth of character. He had desired to make him free, but his owner, who was a member of the Board of Brokers, and of Dr. ——'s Church, in New York, believed that Providence designed the negro race for slavery, and refused to sell him for that purpose. He thought it better that he (his owner) should continue to receive two hundred dollars a year for his services, while he continued able to work, because then, as he said, he should feel responsible that he did not starve, or come upon the public for a support, in his old age. The man himself, having light and agreeable duties, well provided for, furnished with plenty of spending money by his employer, patronized and flattered by the white people, honoured and looked up to by those of his own colour, was rather indifferent in the matter; or even, perhaps, preferred to remain a slave, to being transported for life to Africa.

The watchman was a fine-looking fellow: as we were returning from church, on Sunday, he had passed us, well dressed and well mounted, and as he raised his hat, to salute us, there was nothing in his manner or appearance, except his colour, to distinguish him from a gentleman of good breeding and fortune.

When we were leaving the house, to go to church, on Sunday, after all the white family had entered their carriages, or mounted their horses, the head house-servant also mounted a horse—as he did so, slipping a coin into the hands of the boy who had been holding him. Afterwards, we passed a family of negroes, in a light waggon, the oldest among them driving the horse. On my inquiring if the slaves were allowed to take horses to drive to church, I was informed that in each of these three cases, the horses belonged to the negroes who were driving or riding them. The old man was infirm, and Mr. X. had given him a horse, to enable him to move about. He was probably employed to look after the cattle at pasture, or at something in which it was necessary, for his usefulness, that he should have a horse: I say this, because I afterwards found, in similar cases on other plantations, that it was so. But the watchman and the house-servant had bought their horses with money. The watchman was believed to own three horses; and, to account for his wealth, Mr. X.'s son told me that his father considered him a very valuable servant, and frequently encouraged his good behaviour with handsome gratuities. He receives, probably, considerably higher wages, in fact (in the form of presents), than the white overseer. He knew his father gave him two hundred dollars at once, a short time ago. The watchman has a private house, and, no doubt, lives in considerable luxury.

Will it be said, "therefore, Slavery is neither necessarily degrading nor inhumane"? On the other hand, so far as it is not, there is no apology for it. It is possible, though not probable, that this fine fellow, if he had been born a free man, would be no better employed than he is here; but, in that case, where is the advantage? Certainly not in the economy of the arrangement. And if he were self-dependent, if, especially, he had to provide for the present and future of those he loved, and was able to do so, would he not necessarily live a happier, stronger, better, and more respectable man?

After passing through tool-rooms, corn-rooms, mule-stables, store-rooms, and a large garden, in which vegetables to be distributed among the negroes, as well as for the family, are grown, we walked to the rice-land. It is divided by embankments into fields of about twenty acres each, but varying somewhat in size, according to the course of the river. The arrangements are such that each field may be flooded independently of the rest, and they are subdivided by open ditches into rectangular plats of a quarter acre each. We first proceeded to where twenty or thirty women and girls were engaged in raking together, in heaps and winrows, the stubble and rubbish left on the field after the last crop, and burning it. The main object of this operation is to kill all the seeds of weeds, or of rice, on the ground. Ordinarily it is done by tasks—a certain number of the small divisions of the field being given to each hand to burn in a day; but owing to a more than usual amount of rain having fallen lately, and some other causes, making the work harder in some places than others, the women were now working by the day, under the direction of a "driver," a negro man, who walked about among them, taking care that they left nothing unburned. Mr. X. inspected the ground they had gone over, to see whether the driver had done his duty. It had been sufficiently well burned, but not more than a quarter as much ground had been gone over, he said, as was usually burned in task-work,—and he thought they had been very lazy, and reprimanded them. The driver made some little apology, but the women offered no reply, keeping steadily and, it seemed, sullenly, on at their work.

In the next field, twenty men, or boys, for none of them looked as if they were full-grown, were ploughing, each with a single mule, and a light, New-York-made plough. The soil was friable, the ploughing easy, and the mules proceeded at a smart pace; the furrows were straight, regular, and well turned. Their task was nominally an acre and a quarter a day; somewhat less actually, as the measure includes the space occupied by the ditches, which are two to three feet wide, running around each quarter of an acre. The ploughing gang was superintended by a driver, who was provided with a watch; and while we were looking at them he called out that it was twelve o'clock. The mules were immediately taken from the ploughs, and the plough-boys mounting them, leapt the ditches, and cantered off to the stables, to feed them. One or two were ordered to take their ploughs to the blacksmith, for repairs.

The ploughmen got their dinner at this time: those not using horses do not usually dine till they have finished their tasks; but this, I believe, is optional with them. They commence work, I was told, at sunrise, and at about eight o'clock have breakfast brought to them in the field, each hand having left a bucket with the cook for that purpose. All who are working in connection, leave their work together, and gather about a fire, where they generally spend about half an hour. The provisions furnished, consist mainly of meal, rice, and vegetables, with salt and molasses, and occasionally bacon, fish, and coffee. The allowance is a peck of meal, or an equivalent quantity of rice per week, to each working hand, old or young, besides small stores. Mr. X. says that he has lately given a less amount of meat than is now usual on plantations, having observed that the general health of the negroes is not as good as formerly, when no meat at all was customarily given them. (The general impression among planters is, that the negroes work much better for being supplied with three or four pounds of bacon a week.)

Leaving the rice-land, we went next to some of the upland fields, where we found several other gangs of negroes at work; one entirely of men engaged in ditching; another of women, and another of boys and girls, "listing" an old corn-field with hoes. All of them were working by tasks, and were overlooked by negro drivers. They all laboured with greater rapidity and cheerfulness than any slaves I have before seen; and the women struck their hoes as if they were strong, and well able to engage in muscular labour. The expression of their faces was generally repulsive, and their *ensemble* anything but agreeable. The dress of most was uncouth and cumbrous, dirty and ragged; reefed up, as I have once before described, at the hips, so as to show their heavy legs, wrapped round with a piece of old blanket, in lieu of leggings or stockings. Most of them worked with bare arms, but wore strong shoes on their feet, and handkerchiefs on

their heads; some of them were smoking, and each gang had a fire
burning on the ground, near where they were at work, by which to
light their pipes and warm their breakfast. Mr. X. said this was always their custom, even in summer. To each gang a boy or girl was
also attached, whose business it was to bring water for them to drink,
and to go for anything required by the driver. The drivers would
frequently call back a hand to go over again some piece of his or her
task that had not been worked to his satisfaction, and were constantly calling to one or another, with a harsh and peremptory voice,
to strike harder, or hoe deeper, and otherwise taking care that the
work was well done. Mr. X. asked if Little Sam ("Tom's Sue's Sam")
worked yet with the "three-quarter" hands, and learning that he
did, ordered him to be put with the full hands, observing that though
rather short, he was strong and stout, and, being twenty years old,
well able to do a man's work.

The field-hands are all divided into four classes, according to their
physical capacities. The children beginning as "quarter-hands," advancing to "half-hands," and then to "three-quarter hands"; and,
finally, when mature, and able-bodied, healthy, and strong, to "full
hands." As they decline in strength, from age, sickness, or other
cause, they retrograde in the scale, and proportionately less labour
is required of them. Many, of naturally weak frame, never are put
among the full hands. Finally, the aged are left out at the annual
classification, and no more regular field-work is required of them,
although they are generally provided with some light, sedentary
occupation. I saw one old woman picking "tailings" of rice out of a
heap of chaff, an occupation at which she was probably not earning
her salt. Mr. X. told me she was a native African, having been
brought when a girl from the Guinea coast. She spoke almost unintelligibly; but after some other conversation, in which I had not
been able to understand a word she said, he jokingly proposed to
send her back to Africa. She expressed her preference to remain
where she was, very emphatically. "Why?" She did not answer
readily, but being pressed, threw up her palsied hands, and said furiously, "I lubs 'ou, mas'r, oh, I lubs 'ou. I don't want go 'way
from 'ou."

The field-hands are nearly always worked in gangs, the strength
of a gang varying according to the work that engages it; usually it
numbers twenty or more, and is directed by a driver. As on most

large plantations, whether of rice or cotton, in Eastern Georgia and South Carolina, nearly all ordinary and regular work is performed *by tasks:* that is to say, each hand has his labour for the day marked out before him, and can take his own time to do it in. For instance, in making drains in light, clean meadow land, each man or woman of the full hands is required to dig one thousand cubic feet; in swamp-land that is being prepared for rice culture, where there are not many stumps, the task for a ditcher is five hundred feet: while in a very strong cypress swamp, only two hundred feet is required; in hoeing rice, a certain number of rows, equal to one-half or two-thirds of an acre, according to the condition of the land; in sowing rice (strewing in drills), two acres; in reaping rice (if it stands well), three-quarters of an acre; or, sometimes a gang will be required to reap, tie in sheaves, and carry to the stack-yard the produce of a certain area, commonly equal to one fourth the number of acres that there are hands working together. Hoeing cotton, corn, or potatoes; one half to one acre. Threshing; five to six hundred sheaves. In ploughing rice land (light, clean, mellow soil) with a yoke of oxen, one acre a day, including the ground lost in and near the drains—the oxen being changed at noon. A cooper, also, for instance, is required to make barrels at the rate of eighteen a week. Drawing staves, 500 a day. Hoop poles, 120. Squaring timber, 100 ft. Laying worm-fence, 50 panels per hand. Post and rail do., posts set 2½ to 3 ft. deep, 9 ft. apart, nine or ten panels per hand. In getting fuel from the woods, (pine, to be cut and split,) one cord is the task for a day. In "mauling rails," the taskman selecting the trees (pine) that he judges will split easiest, one hundred a day, ends not sharpened.

These are the tasks for first-class able-bodied men; they are lessened by one quarter for three-quarter hands, and proportionately for the lighter classes. In allotting the tasks, the drivers are expected to put the weaker hands where (if there is any choice in the appearance of the ground, as where certain rows in hoeing corn would be less weedy than others,) they will be favoured.

These tasks certainly would not be considered excessively hard, by a Northern labourer; and, in point of fact, the more industrious and active hands finish them often by two o'clock. I saw one or two leaving the field soon after one o'clock, several about two; and between three and four, I met a dozen women and several men coming home to their cabins, having finished their day's work.

Under this "Organization of Labour," most of the slaves work rapidly and well. In nearly all ordinary work, custom has settled the extent of the task, and it is difficult to increase it. The driver who marks it out, has to remain on the ground until it is finished, and has no interest in overmeasuring it; and if it should be systematically increased very much, there is danger of a general stampede to the "swamp"—a danger the slave can always hold before his master's cupidity. In fact, it is looked upon *in this region* as a proscriptive right of the negroes to have this incitement to diligence offered them; and the man who denied it, or who attempted to lessen it, would, it is said, suffer in his reputation, as well as experience much annoyance from the obstinate "rascality" of his negroes. Notwithstanding this, I have heard a man assert, boastingly, that he made his negroes habitually perform double the customary tasks. Thus we get a glimpse again of the black side. If he is allowed the power to do this, what may not a man do?

It is the driver's duty to make the tasked hands do their work well. If, in their haste to finish it, they neglect to do it properly, he "sets them back," so that carelessness will hinder more than it will hasten the completion of their tasks.

In the selection of drivers, regard seems to be had to size and strength—at least, nearly all the drivers I have seen are tall and strong men—but a great deal of judgment, requiring greater capacity of mind than the ordinary slave is often supposed to be possessed of, is certainly needed in them. A good driver is very valuable and usually holds office for life. His authority is not limited to the direction of labour in the field, but extends to the general deportment of the negroes. He is made to do the duties of policeman, and even of police magistrate. It is his duty, for instance, on Mr. X.'s estate, to keep order in the settlement; and, if two persons, men or women, are fighting, it is his duty to immediately separate them, and then to "whip them both."

Before any field of work is entered upon by a gang, the driver who is to superintend them has to measure and stake off the tasks. To do this at all accurately, in irregular-shaped fields, must require considerable powers of calculation. A driver, with a boy to set the stakes, I was told, would accurately lay out forty acres a day, in half-acre tasks. The only instrument used is a five-foot measuring rod. When the gang comes to the field, he points out to each person his or her duty for the day, and then walks about among them, looking out that each proceeds properly. If, after a hard day's labour, he sees that the gang has been overtasked, owing to a miscalculation of the difficulty of the work, he may excuse the completion of the tasks; but he is not allowed to extend them. In the case of uncompleted tasks, the body of the gang begin new tasks the next day, and only a sufficient number are detailed from it to complete, during the day, the unfinished tasks of the day before. The relation of the driver to the working hands seems to be similar to that of the boatswain to the seamen in the navy, or of the sergeant to the privates in the army.

Having generally had long experience on the plantation, the advice of the drivers is commonly taken in nearly all the administration, and frequently they are, *de facto*, the managers. Orders on important points of the plantation economy, I have heard given by the proprietor directly to them, without the overseer's being consulted or informed of them; and it is often left with them to decide when and how long to flow the rice-grounds—the proprietor and overseer deferring to their more experienced judgment. Where the drivers are discreet, experienced, and trusty, the overseer is frequently employed merely as a matter of form, to comply with the laws requiring the superintendence or presence of a white man among every body of slaves; and his duty is rather to inspect and report than to govern. Mr. X. considers his overseer an uncommonly efficient and faithful one, but he would not employ him, even during the summer, when he is absent for several months, if the law did not require it. He has sometimes left his plantation in care of one of the drivers for a considerable length of time, after having discharged an overseer; and he thinks it has then been quite as well conducted as ever. His overseer consults the drivers on all important points, and is governed by their advice.

Mr. X. said, that though overseers sometimes punished the negroes severely, and otherwise ill-treated them, it is their more common fault to indulge them foolishly in their disposition to idleness, or in other ways to curry favour with them, so they may not inform the proprietor of their own misconduct or neglect. He has his overseer bound to certain rules, by written contract; and it is stipulated that he can discharge him at any moment, without remuneration for his loss of time and inconvenience, if he should at any time be dissatisfied with him. One of the rules is, that he shall never punish a negro with his own hands, and that corporeal punishment, when necessary, shall be inflicted by the drivers. The advantage of this is, that it secures time for deliberation, and prevents punishment being made in sudden passion. His drivers are not allowed to carry their whips with them in the field; so that if the overseer wishes a hand punished, it is necessary to call a driver; and the driver has then to go to his cabin, which is, perhaps, a mile or two distant, to get his whip, before it can be applied.

I asked how often the necessity of punishment occurred.

"Sometimes, perhaps, not once for two or three weeks; then it will seem as if the devil had got into them all, and there is a good deal of it."

As the negroes finish the labour required of them by Mr. X., at three or four o'clock in the afternoon, they can employ the remainder of the day in labouring for themselves, if they choose. Each family has a half-acre of land allotted to it, for a garden; besides which, there is a large vegetable garden, cultivated by a gardener for the plantation, from which they are supplied, to a greater or less extent. They are at liberty to sell whatever they choose from the products of their own garden, and to make what they can by keeping swine and fowls. Mr. X.'s family have no other supply of poultry and eggs than what is obtained by purchase from his own negroes; they frequently, also, purchase game from them. The only restriction upon their traffic is a "liquor law." They are not allowed to buy or sell ardent spirits. This prohibition, like liquor laws elsewhere, unfortunately, cannot be enforced; and, of late years, grog-shops, at which stolen goods are bought from the slaves, and poisonous liquors —chiefly the worst whisky, much watered and made stupefying by an infusion of tobacco—are clandestinely sold to them, have become an established evil, and the planters find themselves almost powerless to cope with it. They have, here, lately organized an association for this purpose, and have brought several offenders to trial; but, as it is a penitentiary offence, the culprit spares no pains or expense to avoid conviction—and it is almost impossible, in a community of which so large a proportion is poor and degraded, to have a jury sufficiently honest and intelligent to permit the law to be executed.

A remarkable illustration of this evil has lately occurred. A planter, discovering that a considerable quantity of cotton had been stolen from him, informed the patrol of the neighbouring planters of it. A stratagem was made use of, to detect the thief, and, what was of much more importance—there being no question but that this was a slave—to discover for whom the thief worked. A lot of cotton was prepared, by mixing hair with it, and put in a tempting place. A negro was seen to take it, and was followed by scouts to a grog-shop, several miles distant, where he sold it—its real value being nearly ten dollars—for ten cents, taking his pay in liquor. The man was arrested, and, the theft being made to appear, by the hair, before a justice, obtained bail in $2,000, to answer at the higher court. Some of the best legal counsel of the State has been engaged, to obtain, if possible, his conviction.

This difficulty in the management of slaves is a great and very rapidly increasing one. Everywhere that I have been, I have found the planters provoked and angry about it. A swarm of Jews, within the last ten years, has settled in nearly every Southern town, many of them men of no character, opening cheap clothing and trinket shops; ruining, or driving out of business, many of the old retailers, and engaging in an unlawful trade with the simple negroes, which is found very profitable.[1]

The law which prevents the reception of the evidence of a negro in courts, here strikes back, with a most annoying force, upon the dominant power itself. In the mischief thus arising, we see a striking illustration of the danger which stands before the South, whenever its prosperity shall invite extensive immigration, and lead what

[1] *From the Charleston Standard, Nov. 23rd, 1854.*—"This abominable practice of trading with slaves is not only taking our produce from us, but injuring our slave property. It is true the owner of slaves may lock, watch, and whip, as much as he pleases—the negroes will steal and trade as long as white persons hold out to them temptations to steal and bring to them. Three-fourths of the persons who are guilty, you can get no fine from; and, if they have some property, all they have to do is to confess a judgment to a friend, go to jail, and swear out. It is no uncommon thing for a man to be convicted of offences against the State, and against the persons and property of individuals, and pay the fines, costs, and damages, by swearing out of jail, and then go and commit similar offences. The State, or the party injured, has the cost of all these prosecutions and suits to pay, besides the trouble of attending Court: the guilty is convicted, the injured prosecutor punished."

would otherwise be a healthy competition to flow through its channels of industry.

This injury to slave property, from grog-shops, furnishes the grand argument for the Maine Law at the South.[2]

Mr. X. remarks that his arrangements allow his servants no excuse for dealing with these fellows. He has a rule to purchase everything they desire to sell, and to give them a high price for it himself. Eggs constitute a circulating medium on the plantation. Their par value is considered to be twelve for a dime, at which they may always

[2] *From an Address to the people of Georgia, by a Committee of the State Temperance Society, prior to the election of* 1855.—"We propose to turn the 2,200 *foreign* grog-shop keepers, in Georgia, out of office, and ask them to help us. They (the Know-Nothings) reply, 'We have no time for that now—we are trying to turn *foreigners* out of office'; and when we call upon the Democratic party for aid, they excuse themselves, upon the ground that they have work enough to do in keeping these foreigners in office."

From the Penfield (Ga.) Temperance Banner, Sept. 29th, 1855

"OUR SLAVE POPULATION

"We take the following from the *Savannah Journal and Courier*, and would ask every candid reader if the evils referred to ought not to be corrected. How shall it be done?

" 'By reference to the recent homicide of a negro, in another column, some facts will be seen suggestive of a state of things, in this part of our population, which should not exist, and which cannot endure without danger, both to them and to us. The collision, which terminated thus fatally, occurred at an hour past midnight—at a time when none but the evil-disposed are stirring, unless driven by necessity; and yet, at that hour, those negroes and others, as many as chose, were passing about the country, with ample opportunity to commit any act which might happen to enter their heads. In fact, they did engage, in the public highway, in a broil terminating in homicide. It is not difficult to imagine that their evil passions might have taken a very different direction, with as little danger of meeting control or obstacle.

" 'But it is shown, too, that to the impunity thus given them by the darkness of midnight, was added the incitement to crime drawn from the abuse of liquor. They had just left one of those resorts where the negro is supplied with the most villainously-poisonous compounds, fit only to excite him to deeds of blood and violence. The part that this had in the slaughter of Saturday night, we are enabled only to imagine; but experience would teach us that its share was by no means small. Indeed, we have the declaration of the slayer, that the blow, by which he was exasperated so as to return it by the fatal stab, was inflicted by a bottle of brandy! In this fact, we fear, is a clue to the whole history of the transaction.'

"Here, evidently, are considerations deserving the grave notice of, not only those who own negroes, but of all others who live in a society where they are held."

be exchanged for cash, or left on deposit, without interest, at his kitchen.

Whatever he takes of them that he cannot use in his own family, or has not occasion to give to others of his servants, is sent to town to be resold. The negroes do not commonly take money for the articles he has of them, but the value of them is put to their credit, and a regular account kept with them. He has a store, usually well supplied with articles that they most want, which are purchased in large quantities, and sold to them at wholesale prices; thus giving them a great advantage in dealing with him rather than with the grogshops. His slaves are sometimes his creditors to large amounts; at the present time he says he owes them about five hundred dollars. A woman has charge of the store, and when there is anything called for that she cannot supply, it is usually ordered, by the next conveyance, of his factors in town.

The ascertained practicability of thus dealing with slaves, together with the obvious advantages of the method of working them by tasks, which I have described, seem to me to indicate that it is not so impracticable as is generally supposed, if only it was desired by those having the power, to rapidly extinguish Slavery, and while doing so, to educate the negro for taking care of himself, in freedom. Let, for instance, any slave be provided with all things he will demand, as far as practicable, and charge him for them at certain prices—honest, market prices for his necessities, higher prices for harmless luxuries, and excessive, but not absolutely prohibitory, prices for everything likely to do him harm. Credit him, at a fixed price, for every day's work he does, and for all above a certain easily accomplished task in a day, at an increased price, so that his reward will be in an increasing ratio to his perseverance. Let the prices of provisions be so proportioned to the price of task-work, that it will be about as easy as it is now for him to obtain a bare subsistence. When he has no food and shelter due to him, let him be confined in solitude, or otherwise punished, until he asks for opportunity to earn exemption from punishment by labour.

When he desires to marry, and can persuade any woman to marry him, let the two be dealt with as in partnership. Thus, a young man or young woman will be attractive somewhat in proportion to his or her reputation for industry and providence. Thus industry and providence will become fashionable. Oblige them to purchase food for their children, and let them have the benefit of their children's labour, and they will be careful to teach their children to avoid waste, and to honour labour. Let those who have not gained credit while hale and young, sufficient to support themselves in comfort when prevented by age or infirmity from further labour, be supported by a tax upon all the negroes of the plantation, or of a community. Improvidence, and pretence of inability to labour, will then be disgraceful.

When any man has a balance to his credit equal to his value as a slave, let that constitute him a free man. It will be optional with him and his employer whether he shall continue longer in the relation of servant. If desirable for both that he should, it is probable that he will; for unless he is honest, prudent, industrious, and discreet, he will not have acquired the means of purchasing his freedom.

If he is so, he will remain where he is, unless he is more wanted elsewhere; a fact that will be established by his being called away by higher wages, or the prospect of greater ease and comfort elsewhere. If he is so drawn off, it is better for all parties concerned that he should go. Better for his old master; for he would not refuse him sufficient wages to induce him to stay, unless he could get the work he wanted him to do done cheaper than he would justly do it. Poor wages would certainly, in the long run, buy but poor work; fair wages, fair work.

Of course there will be exceptional cases, but they will always operate as cautions for the future, not only to the parties suffering, but to all who observe them. And be sure they will not be suffered, among ignorant people, to be lost. This is the beneficent function of gossip, with which wise and broad-working minds have nothing to do, such not being benefited by the iteration of the lessons of life.

Married persons, of course, can only become free together. In the appraisement of their value, let that of their young children be included, so that they cannot be parted from them; but with regard to children old enough to earn something more than their living, let it be optional what they do for them.

Such a system would simply combine the commendable elements of the emancipation law of Cuba,[3] and those of the reformatory

---

[3] In Cuba every slave has the privilege of emancipating himself, by paying a price which does not depend upon the selfish exactions of the masters; but it is either a fixed price, or else is fixed, in each case, by disinterested appraisers. The

punishment system, now in successful operation in some of the British penal colonies, with a few practical modifications. Further modifications would, doubtless, be needed, which any man who has had much practical experience in dealing with slaves might readily suggest. Much might be learned from the experience of the system pursued in the penal colonies, some account of which may be seen in the report of the Prisoners' Aid Society of New York, for 1854, or in a previous little work of my own. I have here only desired to suggest, apropos to my friend's experience, the practicability of providing the negroes an education in essential social morality, while they are drawing towards personal freedom; a desideratum with those who do not consider Slavery a purely and eternally desirable thing for both slave and slave-master, which the present system is calculated, as far as possible, in every direction to oppose.

Education in theology and letters could be easily combined with such a plan as I have hinted at; or, if a State should wish to encourage the improvement of its negro constituent—as, in the progress of enlightenment and Christianity, may be hoped to eventually occur—a simple provision of the law, making a certain standard of proficiency the condition of political freedom, would probably create a natural demand for education, which commerce, under its inexorable higher laws, would be obliged to satisfy.

I do not think, after all I have heard to favour it, that there is any good reason to consider the negro, naturally and essentially, the moral inferior of the white; or, that if he is so, it is in those elements of character which should for ever prevent us from trusting him with equal social munities with ourselves.

So far as I have observed, slaves show themselves worthy of trust most, where their masters are most considerate and liberal towards them. Far more so, for instance, on the small farms of North Carolina than on the plantations of Virginia and South Carolina. Mr. X.'s slaves are permitted to purchase fire-arms and ammunition, and to keep them in their cabins; and his wife and daughters reside with him, among them, the doors of the house never locked, or windows closed, perfectly defenceless, and miles distant from any other white family.

---

consequence is, that emancipations are constantly going on, and the free people of colour are becoming enlightened, cultivated, and wealthy. In no part of the United States do they occupy the high social position which they enjoy in Cuba.

Another evidence that negroes, even in slavery, when trusted, may prove wonderfully reliable, I will subjoin, in a letter written by Mr. Alexander Smets, of Savannah, to a friend in New York, in 1853. It is hardly necessary to say, that the "servants" spoken of were negroes, and the "suspicious characters," providentially removed, were whites. The letter was not written for publication:—

The epidemic which spread destruction and desolation through our city, and many other places in most of the Southern States, was, with the exception of that of 1820, the most deadly that was ever known here. Its appearance being sudden, the inhabitants were seized with a panic, which caused an immediate *sauve qui peut* seldom witnessed before. I left, or rather fled, for the sake of my daughters, to Sparta, Hancock county. They were dreadfully frightened.

Of a population of fifteen thousand, six thousand, who could not get away, remained, nearly all of whom were more or less seized with the prevailing disease. The negroes, with very few exceptions, escaped.

Amidst the desolation and gloom pervading the deserted streets, there was a feature that showed our slaves in a favourable light. There were entire blocks of houses, which were either entirely deserted—the owners in many instances having, in their flight, forgotten to lock them up—or left in charge of the servants. A finer opportunity for plunder could not be desired by thieves; and yet the city was remarkable, during the time, for order and quietness. There were scarcely any robberies committed, and as regards fires, so common in the winter, none! Every householder, whose premises had escaped the fury of the late terrific storm, found them in the same condition he had left them. Had not the yellow fever scared away or killed those suspicious characters, whose existence is a problem, and who prowl about every city, I fear that our city might have been laid waste. Of the whole board of directors of five banks, three or four remained, and these at one time were sick. Several of the clerks were left, each in the possession of a single one. For several weeks it was difficult to get anything to eat; the bakers were either sick or dead. The markets closed, no countryman dared venture himself into the city with the usual supplies for the table, and the packets had discontinued their trips. I shall stop, otherwise I could fill a volume with the occurrences and incidents of the dismal period of the epidemic.

On most of the large rice plantations which I have seen in this vicinity, there is a small chapel, which the negroes call their prayer-house. The owner of one of these told me that, having furnished the prayer-house with seats having a back-rail, his negroes petitioned him to remove it, because it did not leave them *room enough to pray.* It was explained to me that it is their custom, in social worship, to work themselves up to a great pitch of excitement, in which they yell and cry aloud, and finally, shriek and leap up, clapping their hands and dancing, as it is done at heathen festivals. The back-rail they found to seriously impede this exercise.

Mr. X. told me that he had endeavoured, with but little success, to prevent this shouting and jumping of the negroes at their meetings on his plantation, from a conviction that there was not the slightest element of religious sentiment in it. He considered it to be engaged in more as an exciting amusement than from any really religious impulse. In the town churches, except, perhaps, those managed and conducted almost exclusively by negroes, the slaves are said to commonly engage in religious exercises in a sober and decorous manner; yet, a member of a Presbyterian church in a Southern city told me, that he had seen the negroes in his own house of worship, during "a season of revival," leap from their seats, throw their arms wildly in the air, shout vehemently and unintelligibly, cry, groan, rend their clothes, and fall into cataleptic trances.

On almost every large plantation, and in every neighbourhood of small ones, there is one man who has come to be considered the head or pastor of the local church. The office among the negroes, as among all other people, confers a certain importance and power. A part of the reverence attaching to the duties is given to the person; vanity and self-confidence are cultivated, and a higher ambition aroused than can usually enter the mind of a slave. The self-respect of the preacher is also often increased by the consideration in which he is held by his master, as well as by his fellows; thus, the preachers generally have an air of superiority to other negroes; they acquire a remarkable memory of words, phrases, and forms; a curious sort of poetic talent is developed, and a habit is obtained of rhapsodizing and exciting furious emotions, to a great degree spurious and temporary, in themselves and others, through the imagination. I was introduced, the other day, to a preacher, who was represented to be quite distinguished among them. I took his hand, respectfully, and said I was happy to meet him. He seemed to take this for a joke, and laughed heartily. He was a "driver," and my friend said—

"He drives the negroes at the cotton all the week, and Sundays he drives them at the Gospel—don't you, Ned?"

He commenced to reply in some scriptural phrase, soberly; but before he could say three words, began to laugh again, and reeled off like a drunken man—entirely overcome with merriment. He recovered himself in a moment, and returned to us.

"They say he preaches very powerfully, too."

"Yes, massa! 'kordin' to der grace—*yah! yah!*"

And he staggered off again, with the peculiar hearty negro guffaw. My friend's tone was, I suppose, slightly humorous, but I was grave, and really meant to treat him respectfully, wishing to draw him into conversation; but he had got the impression that it was intended to make fun of him, and generously assuming a merry humour, I found it impossible to get a serious reply.

A majority of the public houses of worship at the South are small, rude structures of logs, or rough boards, built by the united labour or contributions of the people of a large neighbourhood or district of country, and are used as places of assembly for all public purposes. Few of them have any regular clergymen, but preachers of different denominations go from one to another, sometimes in a defined rotation, or "circuit," so that they may be expected at each of their stations at regular intervals. A late report of the Southern Aid Society states that hardly one-fifth of the preachers are regularly educated for their business, and that "you would starve a host of them if you debarred them from seeking additional support for their families by worldly occupation." In one presbytery of the Presbyterian Church, which is, perhaps, the richest, and includes the most educated body of people of all the Southern Churches, there are twenty-one ministers whose wages are not over two hundred and fifty dollars each. The proportion of ministers, of all sorts, to people, is estimated at one to thirteen hundred. (In the Free States it is estimated at one to nine hundred.) The report of this Society also states, that "within the limits of the United States religious destitution lies comparatively at the South and South-west; and that from the first settlement of the country the North has preserved a decided religious superiority over the South, especially in three important particulars: in ample supply of Christian institutions; extensive supply of Christian truth; and thorough Christian regimen, both in the Church and in the community." It is added that, "while the South-western States have always needed a stronger arm of the Christian ministry to raise them up toward a Christian equality with their Northern brethren, their supply in this respect has always been decidedly inferior." The reason of this is the same with that which explains the general ignorance of the people of the South: The effect of Slavery in preventing social association of the whites, and in encouraging vagabond and improvident habits of life among the poor.

The two largest denominations of Christians at the South are the Methodists and Baptists—the last having a numerical superiority. There are some subdivisions of each, and of the Baptists especially, the nature of which I do not understand. Two grand divisions of the Baptists are known as the Hard Shells and the Soft Shells. There is an intense rivalry and jealousy among these various sects and sub-sects, and the controversy between them is carried on with a bitterness and persistence exceeding anything which I have known at the North, and in a manner which curiously indicates how the terms Christianity, piety, etc., are misapplied to partisanship and conditions of the imagination.

A general want of essential reverence of character seems to be evidenced in the frequent familiar and public use of expressions of rare reverence, and in high-coloured descriptions of personal feelings and sentiments, which, if actual, can only be among a man's dearest, most interior and secret, stillest, and most uncommunicable experiences. Men talk in public places, in the churches, and in barrooms, in the stage-coach, and at the fireside, of their personal communions with the Deity, and of the mutations of their harmony with His Spirit, just as they do about their family and business matters. The familiar use of Scripture expressions by the negroes, I have already indicated. This is not confined to them. A dram-seller advertises thus:—

" FAITH WITHOUT WORKS IS DEAD."

IN order to engage in a more "honorable" business, I offer for sale, cheap for cash, my stock of

LIQUORS, BAR-FIXTURES, BILLIARD TABLE, &c., &c.

If not sold privately, by the 20th day of May, I will sell the same at public auction. "Shew me thy faith without thy works, and I will shew thee my faith by my works."

E. KEYSER

At a Sunday dinner-table, at a village inn in Virginia, two or three men had taken seats with me, who had, as they said, "been to the preachin'." A child had been baptized, and the discourse had been a defence of infant baptism.

"I'm damned," said one, "ef he teched on the primary significance of baptism, at all—buryin' with Jesus."

"They wus the weakest arguments for sprinklin' that ever I heerd," said another—a hot, red-faced, corpulent man—"and his sermon was two hours long, for when he stopped I looked at my watch. I thought it should be a lesson to me, for I couldn't help going to sleep. Says I to Uncle John, says I—he sot next to me, and I whispered to him—says I, 'When he gits to Bunker Hill, you wake me up,' for I see he was bound to go clean back to the beginnin' of things."

"Uncle John is an Episcopalian, aint he?"

"Yes."

"Well, there aint no religion in that, no how."

"No, there aint."

"Well now, you wouldn't think it, but I've studied into religion a heap in my life."

"Don't seem to have done you much good."

"No it aint, not yet, but I've studied into it, and I know what it is."

"There aint but one way, Benny."

"I know it."

"Repent of your sins, and believe in Christ, and be immersed—that's all."

"I know it."

"Well, I hope the Lord'll bring you to it, 'fore you die."

"Reckon he will—hope so, sure."

"You wouldn't hardly think that fat man was a preacher himself, would you?" said the landlady to me, after they left.

"Certainly not."

"He is, though, but I don't think much of that sort"; and the landlady immediately began to describe to me the religious history of the neighbourhood. It was some different here, she said she reckoned, in reply to a remark of mine, from what it was at the North. Most respectable people became pious here before they got to be very old, especially ladies. Young ladies were always gay and went to balls till they were near twenty years old, but from eighteen to twenty-five they generally got religion, and then they stopped right short, and never danced or carried on any after that. Sometimes it wasn't till after they were married, but there weren't many ladies who had children that warn't pious. She herself was an exception, for she had three children and had not got religion yet; sometimes she was frightened to think how old she was—her children growing up about her; but she did so like dancing—she hoped her turn would come—she knew it would—she had a pious and praying mother, and she reckoned her prayers must be heard, and so on.

The religious service which I am about to describe, was held in a less than usually rude meeting-house, the boards by which it was enclosed being planed, the windows glazed, and the seats for the white people provided with backs. It stood in a small clearing of the woods, and there was no habitation within two miles of it. When I reached it with my friends, the services had already commenced. Fastened to trees, in a circle about the house, there were many saddled horses and mules, and a few attached to carts or waggons. There were two smouldering camp-fires, around which sat circles of negroes and white boys, roasting potatoes in the ashes.

In the house were some fifty white people, generally dressed in homespun, and of the class called "crackers," though I was told that some of them owned a good many negroes, and were by no means so poor as their appearance indicated. About one-third of the house, at the end opposite the desk, was covered by a gallery or cock-loft, under and in which, distinctly separated from the whites, was a dense body of negroes; the men on one side, the women on another. The whites were seated promiscuously in the body of the house. The negroes present outnumbered the whites, but the exercises at this time seemed to have no reference to them; there were many more waiting about the doors outside, and they were expecting to enjoy a meeting to themselves, after the whites had left the house. They were generally neatly dressed, more so than the majority of the whites present, but in a distinctly plantation or slave style. A few of them wore somewhat expensive articles, evidently of their own selection and purchase; but I observed with some surprise, that not one of the women had a bonnet upon her head, all wearing handkerchiefs, generally of gay patterns, and becomingly arranged. I inquired if this was entirely a matter of taste, and was told that it, no doubt, was generally so, though the masters would not probably allow them to wear bonnets, if they should be disposed to, and

should purchase them themselves, as it would be thought presuming.
In the towns, the coloured women often, but not generally, wear
bonnets.

During all the exercises, people of both classes were frequently
going out and coming in; the women had brought their babies with
them, and these made much disturbance. A negro girl would sometimes come forward to take a child out; perhaps the child would
prefer not to be taken out, and would make loud and angry objections; it would then be fed. Several were allowed to crawl about
the floor, carrying handfuls of corn-bread and roasted potatoes
about with them; one had a fancy to enter the pulpit; which it succeeded in climbing into three times, and was as often taken away, in
spite of loud and tearful expostulations, by its father. Dogs were not
excluded; and outside, the doors and windows all being open, there
was much neighing and braying, unused as were the mules and
horses to see so many of their kind assembled.

The preliminary devotional exercises—a Scripture reading, singing, and painfully irreverential and meaningless harangues nominally addressed to the Deity, but really to the audience—being concluded, the sermon was commenced by reading a text, with which,
however, it had, so far as I could discover, no further association.
Without often being violent in his manner, the speaker nearly all
the time cried aloud at the utmost stretch of his voice, as if calling
to some one a long distance off; as his discourse was extemporaneous,
however, he sometimes returned with curious effect to his natural
conversational tone; and as he was gifted with a strong imagination,
and possessed of a good deal of dramatic power, he kept the attention of the people very well. There was no argument upon any point
that the congregation were likely to have much difference of opinion upon, nor any special connection between one sentence and
another; yet there was a constant, sly, sectarian skirmishing, and a
frequently recurring cannonade upon French infidelity and social-
ism, and several crushing charges upon Fourier, the Pope of Rome,
Tom Paine, Voltaire, "Roosu," and Joe Smith. The audience were
frequently reminded that the preacher did not want their attention
for any purpose of his own; but that he demanded a respectful
hearing as "the ambassador of Christ." He had the habit of frequently repeating a phrase, or of bringing forward the same idea in
a slightly different form, a great many times. The following passage,

of which I took notes, presents an example of this, followed by one of the best instances of his dramatic talent that occurred. He was leaning far over the desk, with his arm stretched forward, gesticulating violently, yelling at the highest key, and catching breath with an effort:—

"A—ah! why don't you come to Christ? ah! what's the reason? ah! Is it because he was of *lowly birth*? ah! Is that it? *Is it* because he was born in a manger? ah! Is it because he was of a humble origin? ah! Is it because he was lowly born? a-ha! Is it because, ah!—is it because, ah!—because he was called a Nazarene? Is it because he was born in a stable?—or is it because—because he was of humble origin? Or is it—is it because"—He drew back, and after a moment's silence put his hand to his chin, and began walking up and down the platform of the pulpit, soliloquizing. "It can't be—it can't be—?" Then lifting his eyes and gradually turning towards the audience, while he continued to speak in a low, thoughtful tone: "Perhaps you don't like the messenger—is that the reason? I'm the ambassador of the great and glorious King; it's his invitation, 'taint mine. You musn't mind me. I ain't no account. Suppose a ragged, insignificant little boy should come running in here and tell you, 'Mister, your house's a-fire!' would you mind the ragged, insignificant little boy, and refuse to listen to him, because he didn't look respectable?"

At the end of the sermon he stepped down from the pulpit, and, crossing the house towards the negroes, said, quietly, as he walked, "I take great interest in the poor blacks; and this evening I am going to hold a meeting specially for you." With this he turned back, and without re-entering the pulpit, but strolling up and down before it, read a hymn, at the conclusion of which, he laid his book down, and speaking for a moment with natural emphasis, said—

"I don't want to creat a tumultuous scene, now;—that isn't my intention. I don't want to make an excitement,—that aint what I want,—but I feel that there's some here that I may never see again, ah! and, as I may never have another opportunity, I feel it my duty as an ambassador of Jesus Christ, ah! before I go—" By this time he had returned to the high key and whining yell. Exactly what he felt it his duty to do, I did not understand; but evidently to employ some more powerful agency of awakening than arguments and appeals to the understanding; and, before I could conjecture, in the least, of what sort this was to be, while he was yet speaking calmly, deprecating excitement, my attention was attracted to several men, who had previously appeared sleepy and indifferent, but who now suddenly began to sigh, raise their heads, and *shed tears*—some standing up, so that they might be observed in doing this by the whole congregation—the tears running down their noses without any interruption. The speaker, presently, was crying aloud, with a mournful, distressed, beseeching shriek, as if he were himself suffering torture: "Oh, any of you fond parents, who know that any of your dear, sweet, little ones may be, oh! at any moment snatched right away from your bosom, and cast into hell fire, oh! there to suffer torment for ever and ever, and ever and ever—Oh! come out here and help us pray for them! Oh, any of you wives that has got an unconverted husband, that won't go along with you to eternal glory, but is set upon being separated from you, oh! and taking up his bed in hell—Oh! I call upon you, if you love him, now to come out here and jine us in praying for him. Oh, if there's a husband here, whose wife is still in the bond of iniquity," etc., through a long category.

It was immediately evident that a large part of the audience understood his wish to be the reverse of what he had declared, and considered themselves called upon to assist him; and it was astonishing to see with what readiness the faces of those who, up to the moment he gave the signal, had appeared drowsy and stupid, were made to express distressing excitement, sighing, groaning, and weeping. Rising in their seats, and walking up to the pulpit, they grasped each other's hands agonizingly, and remained, some kneeling, others standing, with their faces towards the remainder of the assembly. There was great confusion and tumult, and the poor children, evidently impressed by the terrified tone of the howling preacher, with the expectation of some immediately impending calamity, shrieked, and ran hither and thither, till negro girls came forward, laughing at the imposition, and carried them out.

At length, when some twenty had gathered around the preacher, and it became evident that no more could be drawn out, he stopped a moment for breath, and then repeated a verse of a hymn, which being sung, he again commenced to cry aloud, calling now upon all the unconverted, who were *willing* to be saved, to kneel. A few did so, and another verse was sung, followed by another more fervent exhortation. So it went on; at each verse his entreaties, warnings, and threats, and the responsive groans, sobs, and ejaculations of his coterie grew louder and stronger. Those who refused to kneel were addressed as standing on the brink of the infernal pit, into which a diabolical divinity was momentarily on the point of satisfying the necessities of his character by hurling them off.

All this time about a dozen of the audience remained standing, many were kneeling, and the larger part had taken their seats—all having risen at the commencement of the singing. Those who continued standing were mainly wild-looking young fellows, who glanced with smiles at one another, as if they needed encouragement to brazen it out. A few young women were evidently fearfully excited, and perceptibly trembled, but for some reason dared not kneel, or compromise, by sitting. One of these, a good-looking and gaily-dressed girl, stood near, and directly before the preacher, her lips compressed, and her eyes fixed fiercely and defiantly upon him. He for some time concentrated his force upon her; but she was too strong for him, he could not bring her down. At length, shaking his finger toward her, with a terrible expression, as if he had the power, and did not lack the inclination, to damn her for her resistance to his will, he said: "I tell you this is *the last call!*" She bit her lips, and turned paler, but still stood erect, and defiant of the immense magnetism concentrated upon her; and he gave it up himself, quite exhausted with the effort.

The last verse of the hymn was sung. A comparatively quiet and sober repetition of Scripture phrases, strung together heterogeneously and without meaning, in the form of prayer, followed, a benediction was pronounced, and in five minutes all the people were out of the door, with no trace of the previous excitement left, but most of the men talking eagerly of the price of cotton, and negroes, and other news.

The negroes kept their place during all of the tumult; there may have been a sympathetic groan or exclamation uttered by one or two of them, but generally they expressed only the interest of curiosity in the proceedings, such as Europeans might at a performance of the dancing dervishes, an Indian pow-wow, or an exhibition of "psychological" or "spiritual" phenomena, making it very evident that the emotion of the performers was optionally engaged in, as an appropriate part of divine service. There was generally a self-satisfied smile upon their faces; and I have no doubt they felt that they could do it with a good deal more energy and abandon, if they were called upon. I did not wish to detain my companion to witness how they succeeded, when their turn came; and I can only judge from the fact, that those I saw the next morning were so hoarse that they could scarcely speak, that the religious exercises they most enjoy are rather hard upon the lungs, whatever their effect may be upon the soul.

Chapter VII

Alabama

Mobile.—I left Savannah for the West, by the Macon road; the train started punctually to a second, at its advertised time; the speed was not great, but regular, and less time was lost unnecessarily, at way-stations, than usually on our Northern roads.

I have travelled more than five hundred miles on the Georgia roads, and I am glad to say that all of them seem to be exceedingly well managed. The speed upon them is not generally more than from fifteen to twenty miles an hour; but it is made, as advertised, with considerable punctuality. The roads are admirably engineered and constructed, and their equipment will compare favourably with that of any other roads on the continent. There are now upwards of twelve hundred miles of railroad in the State, and more building. The Savannah and Macon line—the first built—was commenced in 1834. The increased commerce of the city of Savannah, which followed its completion, stimulated many other railroad enterprises, not only within the State, but elsewhere at the South, particularly in South Carolina. Many of these were rashly pushed forward by men of no experience, and but little commercial judgment; the roads were injudiciously laid out, and have been badly managed, and, of course, have occasioned disastrous losses. The Savannah and Macon road has, however, been very successful. The receipts are now over $1,000,000 annually; the road is well stocked, is out of debt, and its business is constantly increasing; the stock is above par, and the stockholders are receiving eight per cent. dividends, with a handsome surplus on hand. It has been always, in a great degree, under the management of Northern men—was engineered, and is still worked chiefly by Northern men, and a large amount of its stock is owned at the North. I am told that most of the mechanics, and of the successful merchants and tradesmen of Savannah came originally from the North, or are the sons of Northern men.

Partly by rail and partly by rapid stage-coaching (the coaches, horses, and drivers again from the North), I crossed the State in about twenty-four hours. The railroad is since entirely completed from Savannah to Montgomery, in Alabama, and is being extended slowly towards the Mississippi; of course with the expectation that it will eventually reach the Pacific, and thus make Savannah "the gate to the commerce of the world." Ship-masters will hope that, when either it or its rival in South Carolina has secured that honour, they will succeed, better than they yet have done, in removing the bars, physical and legal, by which commerce is now annoyed in its endeavours to serve them.

At Columbus, I spent several days. It is the largest manufacturing town, south of Richmond, in the Slave States. It is situated at the Falls, and the head of steamboat navigation of the Chattahoochee, the western boundary of Georgia. The water-power is sufficient to drive two hundred thousand spindles, with a proportionate number of looms. There are, probably, at present from fifteen to twenty thousand spindles running. The operatives in the cotton-mills are said to be mainly "Cracker girls" (poor whites from the country), who earn, in good times, by piece-work, from $8 to $12 a month. There are, besides the cotton-mills, one woollen-mill, one paper-mill, a foundry, a cotton-gin factory, a machine-shop, etc. The labourers in all these are mainly whites, and they are in such a condition that, if temporarily thrown out of employment, great numbers of them are at once reduced to a state of destitution, and are dependent upon credit or charity for their daily food. Public entertainments were being held at the time of my visit, the profits to be applied to the relief of operatives in mills which had been stopped by the effects of a late flood of the river. Yet Slavery is constantly boasted to be a perfect safeguard against such distress.

I had seen in no place, since I left Washington, so much gambling, intoxication, and cruel treatment of servants in public, as in Columbus. This, possibly, was accidental; but I must caution persons, travelling for health or pleasure, to avoid stopping in the town. The hotel in which I lodged was disgustingly dirty; the table revolting; the waiters stupid, inattentive, and annoying. It was the stage-house; but I was informed that the other public-house was no better. There are very good inns at Macon, and at Montgomery, Alabama; and it will be best for an invalid proceeding from Savannah westward, if possible, not to spend a night between these towns.

A day's journey took me from Columbus, through a hilly wilderness, with a few dreary villages, and many isolated cotton farms, with comfortless habitations for black and white upon them, to Montgomery, the capital of Alabama.

Montgomery is a prosperous town, with pleasant suburbs, and a remarkably enterprising population, among which there is a considerable proportion of Northern and foreign-born business-men and mechanics.

I spent a week here, and then left for Mobile, on the steamboat Fashion, a clean and well-ordered boat, with polite and obliging officers. We were two days and a half making the passage, the boat stopping at almost every bluff and landing to take on cotton, until she had a freight of nineteen hundred bales, which was built up on the guards, seven or eight tiers in height, and until it reached the hurricane deck. The boat was thus brought so deep that her guards were in the water, and the ripple of the river constantly washed over them. There are two hundred landings on the Alabama River, and three hundred on the Bigby (Tombeckbee [Tombigbee] of the geographers), at which the boats advertise to call, if required, for passengers or freight. This, of course, makes the passage exceedingly tedious. The so-called landings, however, have not in many cases the slightest artificial accommodations for the purpose of a landing. The boat's hawser, if used, is made fast to a living tree; there is not a sign of a wharf, often no house in sight, and sometimes no distinct road.

The principal town at which we landed was Selma, a pleasant village, in one corner of which I came upon a tall, ill-proportioned, broken-windowed brick barrack; it had no grounds about it, was close upon the highway, was in every way dirty, neglected, and forlorn in expression. I inquired what it was, and was answered, the "Young Ladies' College." There were a number of pretty private gardens in the town, in which I noticed several evergreen oaks, the first I had seen since leaving Savannah.

At Claiborne, another village upon the river, we landed at nine o'clock on a Sunday night. It is situated upon a bluff, a hundred and fifty feet high, with a nearly perpendicular bank, upon the river. The boat came to the shore at the foot of a plank slide-way, down which cotton was sent to it, from a warehouse at the top.

There was something truly Western in the direct, reckless way in which the boat was loaded. A strong gang-plank being placed at right angles to the slide-way, a bale of cotton was let slide from the top, and, coming down with fearful velocity, on striking the gang-plank, it would rebound up and out on to the boat, against a barricade of bales previously arranged to receive it. The moment it struck this barricade, it would be dashed at by two or three men, and jerked out of the way, and others would roll it to its place for the voyage, on the tiers aft. The mate, standing near the bottom of the slide, as soon as the men had removed one bale to what he thought a safe distance, would shout to those aloft, and down would come another. Not unfrequently, a bale would not strike fairly on its end, and would rebound off, diagonally, overboard; or would be thrown up with such force as to go over the barricade, breaking stanchions and railings, and scattering the passengers on the berth deck. Negro hands were sent to the top of the bank, to roll the bales to the side, and Irishmen were kept below to remove them, and stow them. On asking the mate (with some surmisings) the reason of this arrangement, he said—

"The niggers are worth too much to be risked here; if the Paddies are knocked overboard, or get their backs broke, nobody loses anything!"

There were about one hundred passengers on the Fashion, besides a number of poor people and negroes on the lower deck. They were, generally, cotton-planters, going to Mobile on business, or emigrants bound to Texas or Arkansas. They were usually well dressed, but were a rough, coarse style of people, drinking a great deal, and most of the time under a little alcoholic excitement. Not sociable, except when the topics of cotton, land, and negroes, were started; interested, however, in talk about theatres and the turf; very profane; often showing the handles of concealed weapons about their persons, but not quarrelsome, avoiding disputes and altercations, and respectful to one another in forms of words; very ill-informed, except on plantation business; their language ungrammatical, idiomatic, and extravagant. Their grand characteristics—simplicity of motives, vague, shallow, and purely objective habits of thought; and bold, self-reliant movement.

With all their individual independence, I soon could perceive a very great homogeneousness of character, by which they were distinguishable from any other people with whom I had before been thrown in contact; and I began to study it with interest, as the Anglo-Saxon development of the South-west.

I found that, more than any people I had ever seen, they were unrateable by dress, taste, forms, and expenditures. I was perplexed by finding, apparently united in the same individual, the self-possession, confidence, and the use of expressions of deference, of the well-equipped gentleman, and the coarseness and low tastes of the uncivilized boor—frankness and reserve, recklessness and self-restraint, extravagance, and penuriousness.

There was one man, who "lived, when he was to home," as he told me, "in the Red River Country," in the north-eastern part of Texas, having emigrated thither from Alabama, some years before. He was a tall, thin, awkward person, and wore a suit of clothes (probably bought "ready-made") which would have better suited a short, fat figure. Under his waistcoat he carried a large knife, with the hilt generally protruding at the breast. He had been with his family to his former home, for a business purpose, and was now returning to his plantation. His wife was a pale and harassed-looking woman; and he scarce ever paid her the smallest attention, not even sitting near her at the public table. Of his children, however, he seemed very fond; and they had a negro servant in attendance upon them, whom he was constantly scolding and threatening. Having been from home for six weeks, his impatience to return was very great, and was constantly aggravated by the frequent and long-continued stoppages of the boat. "Time's money, time's money!" he would be constantly saying, while we were taking on cotton—"time's worth more'n money to me now; a hundred per cent. more, 'cause I left my niggers all alone; not a dam white man within four mile on 'em."

I asked how many negroes he had.

"I've got twenty on 'em to home, and thar they ar! and thar they ar! and thar aint a dam soul of a white fellow within four mile on 'em."

"They are picking cotton, I suppose?"

"No, I got through pickin' 'fore I left."

"What work have they to do, then, now?"

"I set 'em to clairin', but they aint doin' a dam thing—not a dam thing, they aint; that's wat they are doin', that is—not a dam thing. I know that, as well as you do. That's the reason time's an object. I told the capting so, wen I came aboard: says I, 'capting,' says I, 'time is in the objective case with me.' No, sir, they aint doin' a dam

solitary thing; that's what they are up to. I know that as well as anybody; I do. But I'll make it up, I'll make it up, when I get thar, now
you'd better believe."

Once, when a lot of cotton, baled with unusual neatness, was
coming on board, and some doubt had been expressed as to the
economy of the method of baling, he said very loudly:

"Well, now, I'd be willin' to bet my salvation, that them thar's the
heaviest bales that's come on to this boat."

"I'll bet you a hundred dollars of it," answered one.

"Well, if I was in the habit of bettin', I'd do it. I aint a bettin'
man. But I am a cotton man, I am, and I don't car who knows it.
I know cotton, I do. I'm dam if I know anythin' but cotton. I ought
to know cotton, I had. I've been at it ever sin' I was a chile."

"Stranger," he asked me once, "did you ever come up on the
Leweezay? She's a right smart pretty boat, she is, the Leweezay;
the best I ever see on the Alabamy River. They wanted me to wait
and come down on her, but I told 'em time was in the objective case
to me. She is a right pretty boat and her capting's a high-tone
gentleman; haint no objections to find with him—he's a high-tone
gentleman, that's what he is. But the pilot—well, damn him! He run
her right out of the river, up into the woods—didn't run her in the
river, at all. When I go aboard a steamboat, I like to keep in the
river, somewar; but that pilot, he took her right up into the woods.
It was just clairin' land. Clairin' land, and playin' hell ginerally, all
night; not follering the river at all. I believe he was drunk. He must
have been drunk, for I could keep a boat in the river itself. I'll never
go in a boat where the pilot's drunk all the time. I take a glass too
much myself, sometimes; but I don't hold two hundred lives in the
holler of my hand. I was in my berth, and he run her straight out of
the river, slap up into the furest. It threw me clean out of my berth,
out onter the floor; I didn't sleep any more while I was aboard. The
Leweezay's a right smart pretty little boat, and her capting's a high-
tone gentleman. They hev good livin' aboard of her, too. Haan't no
objections on that score; weddin' fixins all the time; but I won't go in
a boat war the pilot's drunk. I set some vally on the life of two
hundred souls. They wanted to hev me come down on her, but I
told 'em time was in the objective case."

There were three young negroes, carried by another Texan, on
the deck, outside the cabin. I don't know why they were not allowed

to be with the other emigrant slaves, carried on the lower deck, unless the owner was afraid of their trying to get away, and had no handcuffs small enough for them. They were boys; the oldest twelve or fourteen years old, the youngest not more than seven. They had evidently been bought lately by their present owner, and probably had just been taken from their parents. They lay on the deck and slept, with no bed but the passengers' luggage, and no cover but a single blanket for each. Early one morning, after a very stormy night, when they must have suffered much from the driving rain and cold, I saw their owner with a glass of spirits, giving each a few swallows from it. The older ones smacked their lips, and said, "Tank 'ou massa"; but the little one couldn't drink it, and cried aloud, when he was forced to. The older ones were very playful and quarrelsome, and continually teasing the younger, who seemed very sad, or homesick and sulky. He would get very angry at their mischievous fun, and sometimes strike them. He would then be driven into a corner, where he would lie on his back, and kick at them in a perfect frenzy of anger and grief. The two boys would continue to laugh at him, and frequently the passengers would stand about, and be amused by it. Once, when they had plagued him in this way for some time, he jumped up on to the cotton-bales, and made as if he would have plunged overboard. One of the older boys caught him by the ankle, and held him till his master came and hauled him in, and gave him a severe flogging with a rope's end. A number of passengers collected about them, and I heard several say, "That's what he wants." Red River said to me, "I've been a watchin' that ar boy, and I see what's the matter with him; he's got the devil in him right bad, and he'll hev to take a right many of them warmins before it'll be got out."

The crew of the boat, as I have intimated, was composed partly of Irishmen, and partly of negroes; the latter were slaves, and were hired of their owners at $40 a month—the same wages paid to the Irishmen. A dollar of their wages was given to the negroes themselves, for each Sunday they were on the passage. So far as convenient, they were kept at work separately from the white hands; they were also messed separately. On Sunday I observed them dining in a group, on the cotton-bales. The food which was given to them in tubs, from the kitchen, was various and abundant, consisting of bean-porridge, bacon, corn-bread, ship's biscuit, potatoes, duff (pudding), and gravy. There was one knife used only, among ten of them; the bacon was cut and torn into shares; splinters of the bone and of fire-wood were used for forks; the porridge was passed from one to another, and drank out of the tub; but though excessively dirty and beast-like in their appearance and manners, they were good-natured and jocose as usual.

"Heah! you Bill," said one to another, who was on a higher tier of cotton, "pass down de dessart. You! up dar on de hill; de dessart! Augh! don't you know what de dessart be? De duff, you fool."

"Does any of de gemmen want some o' dese potatum?" asked another; and no answer being given, he turned the tub full of potatoes overboard, without any hesitation. It was evident he had never had to think on one day how he should be able to live the next.

Whenever we landed at night or on Sunday, for wood or cotton, there would be many negroes come on board from the neighbouring plantations, to sell eggs to the steward.

Sunday was observed by the discontinuance of public gambling in the cabin, and in no other way. At midnight gambling was resumed, and during the whole passage was never at any other time discontinued, night or day, so far as I saw. There were three men that seemed to be professional sharpers, and who probably played into each other's hands. One young man lost all the money he had with him—several hundred dollars.

Mobile, in its central, business part, is very compactly built, dirty, and noisy, with little elegance, or evidence of taste or public spirit, in its people. A small, central, open square—the only public ground that I saw—was used as a horse and hog pasture, and clothes-drying yard. Out of the busier quarter, there is a good deal of the appearance of a thriving New England village—almost all the dwelling-houses having plots of ground enclosed around them, planted with trees and shrubs. The finest trees are the magnolia and live oak; and the most valuable shrub is the Cherokee rose, which is much used for hedges and screens. It is evergreen, and its leaves are glossy and beautiful at all seasons, and in March it blooms profusely. There is an abundance, also, of the Cape jessamine. It is as beautiful as a camellia; and, when in blossom, scents the whole air with a most delicate and delicious fragrance. At a market-garden, near the town which I visited, I found most of the best Northern and Belgian pears fruiting well, and apparently healthy, and well suited in climate, on quince-stocks. Figs are abundant, and bananas and oranges are said to be grown with some care, and slight winter protection.

The Battle House, kept by Boston men, with Irish servants, I found an excellent hotel; but with higher charge than I had ever paid before. Prices, generally, in Mobile, range very high. There are large numbers of foreign merchants in the population; but a great deficiency of tradesmen and mechanics.

While I was at Montgomery, my hat was one day taken from the dining-room, at dinner-time, by some one who left in its place for me a very battered and greasy substitute, which I could not wear, if I had chosen to. I asked the landlord what I should do. "Be before him, to-morrow." Following this cool advice, and, in the mean time, wearing a cap, I obtained my hat the next day; but so ill used, that I should not have known it, but for the maker's name, stamped within it. Not succeeding in fitting myself with a new hat, I desired to have my old one pressed, when in Mobile; but I could not find a working hatter in the place, though it has a population of thirty thousand souls. Finally, a hat-dealer, a German Jew, I think he was, with whom I had left it while looking further, returned it to me, with a charge of one dollar, for brushing it—the benefit of which brushing I was unable, in the least, to perceive. A friend informed me that he found it cheaper to have all his furniture and clothing made for him, in New York, to order, when he needed any, and sent on by express, than to get it in Mobile.

The great abundance of the best timber for the purpose, in the United States, growing in the vicinity of the town, has lately induced some persons to attempt ship-building at Mobile. The mechanics employed are all from the North.

The great business of the town is the transfer of cotton, from the producer to the manufacturer, from the waggon and the steamboat to the sea-going ship. Like all the other cotton-ports, Mobile labours under the disadvantage of a shallow harbour. At the wharves, there were only a few small craft and steamboats. All large sea-going vessels lie some thirty miles below, and their freights are transhipped in lighters.

There appears to be a good deal of wealth and luxury, as well as senseless extravagance in the town. English merchants affect the character of the society, considerably; some very favourably—some, very much otherwise. Many of them own slaves, and, probably, all employ them; but Slavery seems to be of more value to them from the amusement it affords, than in any other way. "So-and-so advertises 'a valuable drayman, and a good blacksmith and horse-shoer, for sale, on reasonable terms'; an acclimated double-entry book-keeper, kind in harness, is what I want," said one; "those Virginia patriarchs haven't any enterprise, or they'd send on a stock of such goods every spring, to be kept over through the fever, so they could warrant them."

"I don't know where you'll find one," replied another; "but if you are wanting a private chaplain, there's one I have heard, in —— street, several times, that could probably be bought for a fair price; and I will warrant him sound enough in wind, if not in doctrine."

"I wouldn't care for his doctrine, if I bought him; I don't care how black he is; feed him right, and in a month he will be as orthodox as an archbishop."

Chapter VIII

The Lower Mississippi

New Orleans.—The steamboat by which I made the passage along the north shore of the Mexican Gulf to New Orleans, was New York built, and owned by a New-Yorker; and the Northern usage of selling passage tickets, to be returned on leaving the boat, was retained upon it. I was sitting near a group of Texans and emigrating planters, when a waiter passed along, crying the usual request, that passengers who had not obtained tickets would call at the captain's office for that purpose. "What's that? What's that?" they shouted; "What did he mean? What is it?" "Why, it's a dun," said one. "He is dunnin' on us, sure," continued one and another; and some started from the seats, as if they thought it insulting. "Well, it's the first time I ever was dunned by a nigger, I'll swar," said one. This seemed to place it in a humorous aspect; and, after a hearty laugh, they resumed their discussion of the advantages offered to emigrants in different parts of Texas, and elsewhere.

There was a young man on the boat who had been a passenger with me on the boat from Montgomery. He was bound for Texas; and while on board the Fashion I had heard him saying that he had met with "a right smart bad streak of luck" on his way, having lost a valuable negro.

"I thought you were going on with those men to Texas, the other day," said I.

"No," he replied; "I left my sister in Mobile, when I went back after my nigger, and when I came down again, I found that she had found an old acquaintance there, and they had concluded to get married; so I stayed to see the wedding."

"Rather quick work."

"Well, I reckon they'd both thought about it when they knew each other before; but I didn't know it, and it kind o' took me by surprise. So my other sister, she concluded Ann had done so well stopping in Mobile, she'd stop and keep company with her a spell; and so I've got to go 'long alone. Makes me feel kind o' lonesome—losing that nigger too."

"Did you say that you went back after the nigger? I thought he died?"

"Well, you see I had brought him along as far as Mobile, and he got away from me there, and slipped aboard a steamboat going back, and hid himself. I found out that he was aboard of her pretty soon after she got off, and I sent telegraphic despatches to several places along up the river, to the captain, to put him in a jail, ashore, for me. I know he got one of them at Cahawba, but he didn't mind it till he got to Montgomery. Well, the nigger didn't have any attention paid to him. They just put him in irons; likely enough he didn't get much to eat, or have anything to cover himself, and he took cold, and got sick—got pneumonia—and when they got to Montgomery, they made him walk up to the jail, and there wan't no fire, and nothin' to lie on, nor nothin' for him in the jail, and it made quick work with him. Before I could get up there he was dead. I see an attorney here to Mobile, and he offered to take the case, and prosecute the captain; and he says if he don't recover every red cent the man was worth, he won't ask me for a fee. It comes kinder hard on me. I bought the nigger up, counting I should make a speculation on him; reckoned I'd take him to Texas if I couldn't turn him to good advantage at Mobile. As niggers is goin' here now, I expect 'twas a dead loss of eight hundred dollars, right out of pocket."

There were a large number of steerage passengers occupying the main deck, forward of the shaft. Many of them were Irish, late immigrants, but the large majority were slaves, going on to New Orleans to be sold, or moving with their masters to Texas. There was a fiddle or two among them, and they were very merry, dancing and singing. A few, however, refused to join in the amusement, and looked very disconsolate. A large proportion of them were boys and girls, under twenty years of age.

On the forecastle-deck there was a party of emigrants, moving with waggons. There were three men, a father and his two sons, or sons-in-law, with their families, including a dozen or more women and children. They had two waggons, covered with calico and bed-ticks, supported by hoops, in which they carried their furniture and stores, and in which they also slept at night, the women in one, and the men in the other. They had six horses, two mules, and two pair of cattle with them. I asked the old man why he had taken his cattle along with him, when he was going so far by sea, and found that he had informed himself accurately of what it would cost him to hire or buy cattle at Galveston; and that taking into account the probable delay he would experience in looking for them there, he had calculated that he could afford to pay the freight on them, to have them with him, to go on at once into the country on his arrival, rather than to sell them at Mobile.

"But," said he, "there was one thing I didn't cakulate on, and I don't understand it; the capting cherged me two dollars and a half for 'wherfage.' I don't know what that means, do you? I want to know, because I don't car' to be imposed upon by nobody. I payed it without sayin' a word, 'cause I never travelled on the water before; next time I do, I shall be more sassy." I asked where he was going. Didn't know much about it, he said, but reckoned he could find a place where there was a good range, and plenty of game. If 'twas as good a range (pasture) as 'twas to Alabama when he first came there, he'd be satisfied. After he'd got his family safe through acclimating this time, he reckoned he shouldn't move again. He had moved about a good deal in his life. There was his littlest boy, he said, looking kindly at a poor, thin, blue-faced little child—he reckoned they'd be apt to *leave* him; he had got *tropsical,* and was of mighty weak constitution, nat'rally; 'twouldn't take much to carry him off, and, of course, a family must be exposed a good deal, moving so this time of year. They should try to find some heavy timbered land—good land, and go to clearing; didn't calculate to make any crops the first year—didn't calculate on it, though perhaps they might if they had good luck. They had come from an eastern county of Alabama. Had sold out his farm for two dollars an acre; best land in the district was worth four; land was naturally kind of thin, and now 'twas pretty much all worn out there. He had moved first from North Carolina, with his father. They never made anything to sell but cotton; made corn for their own use. Never had any negroes; reckoned he'd done about as well as if he had had them; reckoned a little better on the whole. No, he should not work negroes in Texas. "Niggers is so kerless, and want so much lookin' arter; they is so monstrous lazy; they won't do no work, you know, less you are clus to 'em all the time, and I don't feel like it. I couldn't, at my time of life, begin a-using the lash; and you know they do have to take that, all on 'em—and a heap on't, sometimes."

"I don't know much about it; they don't have slaves where I live."

"Then you come from a Free State; well, they've talked some of makin' Alabama a Free State."

"I didn't know that."

"O, yes, there was a good deal of talk one time, as if they was goin' to do it right off. O, yes; there was two or three of the States this way, one time, come pretty nigh freein' the niggers—lettin' 'em all go free."

"And what do you think of it?"

"Well, I'll tell you what I think on it; I'd like it if we could get rid on 'em to yonst. I wouldn't like to hev 'em freed, if they was gwine to hang round. They ought to get some country, and put 'em war they could be by themselves. It wouldn't do no good to free 'em, and let 'em hang round, because they is so monstrous lazy; if they hadn't got nobody to take keer on 'em, you see they wouldn't do nothin' but juss nat'rally laze round, and steal, and pilfer, and no man couldn't live, you see, war they was—if they was free, no man couldn't live. And then, I've two objections; that's one on 'em—no man couldn't live—and this ere's the other; Now suppose they was free, you see they'd all think themselves just as good as we; of course they would, if they was free. Now, just suppose you had a family of children: how would you like to hev a nigger feelin' just as good as a white man? how'd you like to hev a nigger steppin' up to your darter? Of course you wouldn't; and that's the reason I wouldn't like to hev 'em free; but I tell you, I don't think it's right to hev 'em slaves so; that's the fac—taant right to keep 'em as they is."

I was awakened, in the morning, by the loud ringing of a hand-bell; and, turning out of my berth, dressed by dim lamp-light. The waiters were serving coffee and collecting baggage; and, upon stepping out of the cabin, I found that the boat was made fast to a long wooden jetty, and the passengers were going ashore. A passage-ticket for New Orleans was handed me, as I crossed the gang-plank. There was a rail-track and a train of cars upon the wharf, but no locomotive; and I got my baggage checked, and walked on toward the shore.

It was early daylight—a fog rested on the water, and only the nearest point could be discerned. There were many small buildings near the jetty, erected on piles over the water—bathing-houses, bowling-alleys, and billiard-rooms, with other indications of a place of holiday resort—and, on reaching the shore, I found a slumbering village. The first house from the wharf had a garden about it, with complex alleys, and tables, and arbours, and rustic seats, and cut shrubs, and shells, and statues, and vases, and a lamp was feebly burning in a large lantern over the entrance gate. I was thinking how like it was to a rural restaurant in France or Germany, when a locomotive backed, screaming hoarsely, down the jetty; and I returned to get my seat.

Off we puffed, past the restaurant, into the village—the name of which I did not inquire, everybody near me seemed so cold and cross,—through the little village of white houses—whatever it was—and away into a dense, gray cypress forest. For three or four rods, each side of the track, the trees had all been felled and removed, leaving a dreary strip of swamp, covered with stumps. This was bounded and intersected by broad ditches, or narrow and shallow canals, with a great number of very small punts in them. So it continued, for two or three miles; then the ground became dryer, there was an abrupt termination of the gray wood; the fog was lifting and drifting off, in ragged, rosy clouds, disclosing a flat country, skirted still, and finally bounded, in the background, with the swamp-forest. A few low houses, one story high, all having verandahs before them, were scattered thinly over it.

At length, a broad road struck in by the side of the track; the houses became more frequent; soon forming a village street, with smoke ascending from breakfast fires; windows and doors opening, maids sweeping steps, bakers' waggons passing, and broad streets, little built upon, breaking off at right angles.

At the corners of these streets, were high poles, connected at the top by a rope, and furnished with blocks and halyards, by which great square lanterns were slung over the middle of the carriageway. I thought again of France ("*à la lanterne!*"), and turning to one of my cold and cross companions—a man wrapped in a loose coat, with a cowl over his head—I asked the name of the village, for my geography was at fault. I had expected to be landed at New Orleans by the boat, and had not been informed of the railroad arrangement, and had no idea in what part of Louisiana we might be. "Note Anglische, sare," was the gruff reply.

There was a sign, "*Café du Faubourg*," and, putting my head out of the window, I saw that we must have arrived at New Orleans. We reached the terminus, which was surrounded with *fiacres,* in the style of Paris. "To the Hotel St. Charles," I said to a driver, confused with the loud French and quiet English of the crowd about me. "*Oui,* yer 'onor," was the reply of my Irish-born fellow-citizen: another passenger was got, and away we rattled through narrow dirty streets, among grimy old stuccoed walls; high arched windows and doors, balconies and entresols, and French noises and French smells, French signs, ten to one of English, but with funny polyglotic arrangements, sometimes, from which less influential families were not excluded.

The other fare, to whom I had not ventured to speak, was set down at a *salle pour la vente des* somethings, and soon after the *fiacre* turned out upon a broad place, covered with bales of cotton, and casks of sugar, and weighing scales, and disclosing an astonishing number of steamboats, lying all close together in a line, the ends of which were lost in the mist, which still hung upon the river.

Now the signs became English, and the new brick buildings American. We turned into a broad street, in which shutters were being taken from great glass store-fronts, and clerks were exercising their ingenuity in the display of muslin, and silks, and shawls. In the middle of the broad street there was an open space of waste ground, looking as if the corporation had not been able to pave the whole of it at once, and had left this interval to be attended to when the treasury was better filled. Crossing through a gap in this waste, we entered a narrow street of high buildings, French, Spanish, and English signs, the latter predominating; and at the second block, I was landed before the great Grecian portico of the stupendous, tasteless, ill-contrived, and inconvenient St. Charles Hotel.

After a bath and breakfast, I returned, with great interest, to wander in the old French town, the characteristics of which I have sufficiently indicated. Among the houses, one occasionally sees a relic of ancient Spanish builders, while all the newer edifices have the characteristics of the dollar-pursuing Yankees.

I was delighted when I reached the old Place d'Armes, now a public garden, bright with the orange and lemon trees, and roses, and myrtles, and laurels, and jessamines of the south of France. Fronting upon it is the ancient Hotel de Ville, still the city courthouse, a quaint old French structure, with scaly and vermiculated surface, and deep-worn door-sills, and smooth-rubbed corners; the most picturesque and historic-looking public building, except the highly preserved, little old court-house at Newport, that I can now think of in the United States.

Adjoining it is an old Spanish cathedral, damaged by paint, and late alterations and repairs, but still a fine thing in our desert of the reverend in architecture. Enough, that while it is not new, it is not shabby, and is not tricked out with much frippery,[1] gingerbread and confectionery work. The door is open; coaches and crippled beggars are near it. A priest, with a face the expression of which first makes one think of an ape and then of an owl, is coming out. If he were not otherwise to be heartily welcomed to fresh air and sunlight, he should be so, for the sake of the Sister of Charity who is following him, probably to some death-bed, with a corpse-like face herself, haggard but composed, pensive and absorbed, and with the eyes of a broken heart. I think that I may yet meet them looking down compassionately and soothingly, in some far distant pestilent or war-hospital. In lieu of holy-water, then, here is money for the poor-box, though the devil share it with good angels.

Dark shadows, and dusky light, and deep, subdued, low organ strains pervade the interior; and, on the bare floor, here are the kneeling women—"good" and "bad" women—and, ah! yes, white and black women, bowed in equality before their common Father. "Ridiculously absurd idea," say democratic Governors McDuffie [of South Carolina] and Hammond; "Self-evident," say our ancestors, and so must say the voice of conscience, in all free, humble hearts.

In the crowded market-place, there were not only the pure old Indian Americans, and the Spanish, French, English, Celtic, and African, but nearly all possible mixed varieties of these, and no doubt of some other breeds of mankind.

The various grades of the coloured people are designated by the French as follows, according to the greater or less predominance of negro blood:—

Sacatra	griffe and negress.
Griffe	negro and mulatto.
Marabon	mulatto and griffe.
Mulatto	white and negro.

[1] Contemptible; from the root Fripper, to wear out.—WEBSTER.

Quarteron	. . . .	white and mulatto.
Metif.	. . . .	white and quarteron.
Meamelouc	. . . .	white and metif.
Quarteron	. . . .	white and meamelouc.
Sang-mele	. . . .	white and quarteron.

And all these, with the sub-varieties of them, French, Spanish, English, and Indian, and the sub-sub-varieties, such as Anglo-Indian-mulatto, I believe experts pretend to be able to distinguish. Whether distinguishable or not, it is certain they all exist in New Orleans.

They say that the cross of the French and Spanish with the African produces a finer and a healthier result than that of the more Northern European races. Certainly, the French quadroons are very handsome and healthy in appearance; and I should not be surprised if really thorough and sufficient scientific observation should show them to be—contrary to the common assertion—more vigorous than either of the parent races.

Some of the coloured women spoke French, Spanish, and English, as their customers demanded.[2]

Three taverns, bearing the sign of "The Pig and Whistle," indicated the recent English, a cabaret to the Universal Republic, with a red flag, the French, and the Gasthaus zum Rheinplatz, the Teutonic contributions to the strength of our nation. A policeman, with the richest Irish brogue, directed me back to the St. Charles.

In front of a large New York clothing store, twenty-two negroes were standing in a row. Each wore a blue suit, and a black hat, and each held a bundle of additional clothing, and a pair of shoes, in his hands. They were all, but one, who was probably a driver having charge of them, young men, not over twenty-five, and the majority, I should think, between eighteen and twenty-two years of age. Their owner was probably in the clothing store, settling for the outfit he had purchased for them, and they were waiting to be led to the

---

[2] [*From the New Orleans Picayune*]

FIFTY DOLLARS REWARD.—Ran away from the subscriber, about two months ago, a bright mulatto girl, named Mary, about twenty-five years of age, almost white, and reddish hair, front teeth out, a cut on her upper lip; about five feet five inches high; has a scar on her forehead; she passes for free; talks *French, Italian, Dutch, English, and Spanish.*

ANDRE GRASSO

Upper side of St. Mary's Market

steamboat, which should convey them to his plantation. They were silent and sober, like a file of soldiers standing at ease; and, perhaps, were gratified by the admiration their fine manly figures and uniform dress obtained from the passers by.

"Well, now, that ar's the likeliest lot of niggers I ever see," said one, to me. "Some feller's bin roun', and just made his pick out o' all the jails [3] in Orleens. Must ha' cost him a heap o' rocks. I don't reckon thar's a nigger in that crowd that wouldn't fetch twelve hundred dollars, at a vandue. Twenty thousand dollars wouldn' be no banter for 'em. Dam'd if they aint just the best gang o' cotton-hands ever I see. Give me half on 'em, and I'd sign off—wouldn' ask nothing more."

Louisiana or Texas, thought I, pays Virginia twenty odd thousand dollars for that lot of bone and muscle. Virginia's interest in continuing the business may be imagined, especially if, in their place, could come free labourers, to help her people at the work she needs to have done; but where is the advantage of it to Louisiana, and especially to Texas? Yonder is a steamboat load of the same material—bone and muscle—which, at the same sort of valuation, is worth two hundred and odd thousand dollars; and off it goes, past Texas, through Louisiana—far away yet, up the river, and Wisconsin or Iowa will get it, two hundred thousand dollars' worth, to say nothing of the thalers and silver groschen, in those strong chests—all for nothing.

In ten years' time, how many mills, and bridges, and school-houses, and miles of railroad, will the Germans have built? And how much cloth and fish will they want from Massachusetts, iron from Pennsylvania, and tin from Banka, hemp from Russia, tea from China, and coffee from Brazil, fruit from Spain, wine from Ohio, and oil and gold from the Pacific, silk from France, sugar from Louisiana, cotton from Texas, and rags from Italy, lead from Illinois, notions from Connecticut, and machines from New Jersey, and intelligence from everywhere?

And how much of all these things will the best two hundred Virginians that Louisiana can buy, at any price, demand of commerce, in ten years?

A mechanic, English by birth, who had lived in New Orleans for

[3] The private establishments, in which stocks of slaves are kept for sale in New Orleans, are called jails.

several years, always going up the river in the summer, to escape the danger of fever in the city, told me that he could lay up money much more rapidly than in New York. The expenses of living were not necessarily greater than in New York. If a man kept house, and provided for himself, he could live much cheaper than at boarding-houses. Many unmarried mechanics, therefore, lived with coloured mistresses, who were commonly vile and dishonest. He was at a boarding-house, where he paid four dollars a week. In New York he had paid three dollars, but the board was not as good as in New Orleans. "The reason," said he, "that people say it costs so much more to live here than in New York is, that what they think treats in New York, they consider necessaries here. Everybody lives freer, and spends their money more willingly here." When he first came to New Orleans, a New England mechanic came with him. He supposed him to have been previously a man of sober habits; but almost immediately after he got to New Orleans, he got into bad ways, and in a few months he was so often drunk, and brought so much scandal on their boarding-house, that he was turned out of it. Soon after this, he called on him, and borrowed two dollars. He said he could not live in New Orleans, it was too expensive, and he was going to Texas. This was several years before, and he had not heard from him since. And this he said was a very common course with New England boys, who had been "too carefully brought up at home," when they came to New Orleans. The master mechanics, who bought up slaves, and took contracts for work, he said, made more money than any others. They did so because they did very poor work—poorer than white mechanics could generally be got to do. But nearly all work was done in New Orleans more hastily and carelessly than in New York, though he thought it was bad enough there. The slave-holding bosses could get no white men to work with their slaves, except Irishmen or Germans—no man who had any regard for his position among his fellow-craftsmen would ever let himself be seen working with a negro. He said I could see any day in Canal Street, "a most revolting sight"—Irishmen waiting on negro masons. He had seen, one morning as he was going to his work, a negro carrying some mortar, when another negro hailed him with a loud laugh: "Hallo! you is turned Irishman, is 'ou?" White working men were rapidly displacing the slaves in all sorts of work, and he hoped and believed it would not be many years before every negro would be driven out of the town. He thought acclimated white men could do more hard work than negroes, even in the hottest weather, if they were temperate, and avoided too stimulating food. That, he said, was the general opinion among those of them who stayed over summer. Those who drank much whisky and cordials, and kept up old habits of eating, just as if they were in England, were the ones who complained most of the climate, and who thought white men were not made to work in it. He had stayed as late as July, and returned in September, and he never saw the day in which he could not do as much work as he did in London.

A New-Yorker, whom I questioned about this, said: "I have worked through the very hottest weather, steadily, day after day, and done more work than any three niggers in the State, and been no worse for it. A man has only to take some care of himself."

Going to Lafayette, on the top of an omnibus, I heard an Irishman, somewhat over-stimulated, as Irishmen are apt to be, loudly declare himself an abolitionist: a companion endeavoured in vain to stop him, or make him recant, and finally declared he would not ride any further with him if he could not be more discreet.

The *Morehouse* (Louisiana) *Advocate*, in an article abusive of foreigners, thus describes what, if foreign born working men were not generally so ignorant and easily imposed upon as they are, would undoubtedly be (although they certainly have not yet generally been) their sentiments with regard to Slavery:

The great mass of foreigners who come to our shores are labourers, and consequently come in competition with slave labour. It is to their interest to abolish Slavery; and we know full well the disposition of man to promote all things which advance his own interests. These men come from nations where Slavery is not allowed, and they drink in abolition sentiments from their mothers' breasts; they (all the white race) entertain an utter abhorrence of being put on a level with blacks, whether in the field or in the workshop. Could Slavery be abolished, there would be a greater demand for labourers, and the prices of labour must be greatly enhanced. These may be termed the internal evidences of the abolitionism of foreigners.

But we may find near home facts to corroborate these "internal" evidences: It is well known that there exists a great antipathy among the draymen and rivermen of New Orleans (who are almost to a man foreigners) to the participation of slaves in these branches of industry.

It is obvious that free men have very much gained the field of labour in New Orleans to themselves. The majority of the cartmen, hackney-coach men, porters, railroad hands, public waiters, and common labourers, as well as of skilled mechanics, appear to be white men; and of the negroes employed in those avocations a considerable proportion are free.

This is the case here more than in any other town in the South, although the climate is torrid, and inconvenient or dangerous to strangers; because New Orleans is more extensively engaged in commerce than they are, and because there is, by the passing and sojourning immigration from Europe, constantly in the city a sufficient number of free labourers to sustain, by competition and association with each other, the habits of free-labour communities. It is plainly perceptible that the white working men in New Orleans have more business-like manners, and more assured self-respect, than those of smaller towns. They are even not without some *esprit du corps*.

As Commerce, or any high form of industry requires intelligence in its labourers, slaves can never be brought together in dense communities, but their intelligence will increase to a degree dangerous to those who enjoy the benefit of their labour. The slave must be kept dependent, day by day, upon his master for his daily bread, or he will find, and will declare his independence in all respects, of him. This condition disqualifies the slave for any but the simplest and rudest forms of labour; and every attempt to bring his labour into competition with free labour can only be successful at the hazard of insurrection. Hundreds of slaves in New Orleans must be constantly reflecting and saying to one another, "I am as capable of taking care of myself as this Irish hod-carrier, or this German market-gardener; why can't I have the enjoyment of my labour as well as they? I am as capable of taking care of my own family as much as they of theirs; why should I be subject to have them taken from me by those other men who call themselves our owners? Our children have as much brains as the children of these white neighbours of ours, who not long ago were cooks and waiters at the hotels; why should they be spurned from the school-rooms? I helped to build the school-house, and have not been paid for it. One thing I know, if I can't have my rights, I can have my pleasures; and if they won't give me wages I can take them."

That this influence of association in labour with free-men cannot fail to be appreciated by intelligent observers, will be evident from the following paragraph from the *New Orleans Crescent*, although it was probably written to show only the amusing and picturesque aspect of the slave community:—

GUINEA-LIKE.—Passing along Baronne street, between Perdido and Poydras streets, any Sunday afternoon, the white passer-by might easily suppose himself in Guinea, Caffraria, or any other thickly-peopled region in the land of Ham. Where the darkies all come from, what they do there, or where they go to, constitute a problem somewhat beyond our algebra. It seems to be a sort of nigger exchange. We know there are in that vicinity a coloured church, coloured ice-cream saloon, coloured restaurant, coloured coffee-houses, and a coloured barber-shop, which, we have heard say, has a back communication with one of the groggeries, for the benefit of slaves; but as the police haven't found it out yet, we suppose it ain't so. However, if the ebony dandies who attend Sunday evening 'change, would keep within their various retreats, or leave a path about three feet wide on the side-walk, for the free passage of people who are so unlucky as to be white, we wouldn't complain; but to have to elbow one's way through a crowd of woolly-heads on such a day as yesterday, their natural muskiness made more villainous by the fumes of whisky, is too much for delicate olfactories like ours. A fight, last evening, between two white men at one of the groggeries, afforded much edification to the darkies standing around, and seemed to confirm them in their opinion, that white folks, after all, ain't much.

Similar complaints to the following, which I take from the *New Orleans Crescent*, I have heard, or seen in the journals, at Richmond, Savannah, Louisville, and most other large manufacturing, or commercial towns of the South.

PASSES TO NEGROES.—Something must be done to regulate and prescribe the manner in which passes shall be given to slaves. This is a matter that should no longer be shirked or avoided. The Common Council should act promptly. The slave population of this city is already demoralized to a deplorable extent, all owing to the indiscriminate licence and indulgence extended them by masters, mistresses, and guardians, and to the practice of *forging passes*, which has now become a regular business in New Orleans. The greater portion of the evil flows from forged passes. As things now stand, any negro can obtain a pass for four bits or a dollar, from miserable wretches who obtain a living by such infamous practices. The consequence is that hundreds spend their nights drinking, carousing, gambling, and contracting the worst of habits, which not only make them *useless to their owners*, but dangerous pests to society. We know of many negroes, completely ruined, morally and physically, by such causes. The inherent vice in the negro character always comes out when unrestrained, and there is no degradation too low for him to descend.

Well, for the remedy to cure this crying evil. Prosecuting the forgers is out of the question; for where one conviction could be obtained, thousands of fraudulent passes would be written. *Slave evidence weighs nothing against white forgers and scoundrels.* Hence the necessity of adopting some other mode of prevention. It has been suggested to us, that if the Council would adopt a form for passes, different each month, to be obtained by masters from the Chief of Police, exclusively, that a great deal of good would be at once accomplished. We have no doubt of it. Further, we believe that all owners and guardians would cheerfully submit to the inconvenience in order to obtain so desirable an end. We trust the Common Council will pay some little attention to these suggestions.

How many men, accustomed to the close calculations necessary to successful enterprises, can listen to these suggestions, without asking themselves whether a system, that requires to be sustained by such inconvenient defences, had not better be thrown up altogether?

First and last, I spent some weeks in New Orleans and its vicinity. I doubt if there is a city in the world, where the resident population has been so divided in its origin, or where there is such a variety in the tastes, habits, manners, and moral codes of the citizens. Although this injures civic enterprise—which the peculiar situation of the city greatly demands to be directed to means of cleanliness, convenience, comfort, and health—it also gives a greater scope to the working of individual enterprise, taste, genius, and conscience; so that nowhere are the higher qualities of man—as displayed in generosity, hospitality, benevolence, and courage—better developed, or the lower qualities, likening him to a beast, less interfered with, by law or the action of public opinion.

There is one, among the multitudinous classifications of society in New Orleans, which is a very peculiar and characteristic result of the prejudices, vices, and customs of the various elements of colour, class, and nation, which have been there brought together.

I refer to a class composed of the illegitimate offspring of white men and coloured women (mulattoes or quadroons), who, from habits of early life, the advantages of education, and the use of

wealth, are too much superior to the negroes, in general, to associate with them, and are not allowed by law, or the popular prejudice,
to marry white people. The girls are frequently sent to Paris to be
educated, and are very accomplished. They are generally pretty,
often handsome. I have rarely, if ever, met more beautiful women
than one or two whom I saw by chance, in the streets. They are
better formed, and have a more graceful and elegant carriage than
Americans in general, while they seem to have commonly inherited
or acquired much of the taste and skill, in the selection and arrangement, and the way of wearing dresses and ornaments, that is
the especial distinction of the women of Paris. Their beauty
and attractiveness being their fortune, they cultivate and cherish with diligence every charm or accomplishment they are possessed of.

Of course, men are attracted by them, associate with them, are
captivated, and become attached to them, and, not being able to
marry them legally, and with the usual forms and securities for constancy, make such arrangements "as can be agreed upon." When a
man makes a declaration of love to a girl of this class, she will admit
or deny, as the case may be, her happiness in receiving it; but, supposing she is favourably disposed, she will usually refer the appli-
cant to her mother. The mother inquires, like the "Countess of
Kew," into the circumstances of the suitor; ascertains whether he is
able to maintain a family, and, if satisfied with him, in these and
other respects, requires from him security that he will support her
daughter in a style suitable to the habits in which she has been
bred, and that, if he should ever leave her, he will give her a certain
sum for her future support, and a certain additional sum for each
of the children she shall then have.

The wealth, thus secured, will, of course, vary—as in society with
higher assumptions of morality—with the value of the lady in the
market; that is, with her attractiveness, and the number and value
of other suitors she may have, or may reasonably expect. Of course,
I do not mean that love has nothing at all to do with it; but love is
sedulously restrained, and held firmly in hand, until the road of
competency is seen to be clear, with less humbug than our English
custom requires about it. Everything being satisfactorily arranged,
a tenement in a certain quarter of the town is usually taken, and the
couple move into it and go to housekeeping—living as if they were

married. The woman is not, of course, to be wholly deprived of the society of others—her former acquaintances are continued, and she sustains her relations as daughter, sister, and friend. Of course, too, her husband (she calls him so) will be likely to continue, also, more or less in, and form a part of, this kind of society. There are parties and balls—*bals masqués*—and all the movements and customs of other fashionable society, which they can enjoy in it, if they wish.[4] The women of this sort are represented to be exceedingly affectionate in disposition, and constant beyond reproach.

During all the time a man sustains this relation, he will commonly be moving, also, in reputable society on the other side of the town; not improbably, eventually he marries, and has a family establishment elsewhere. Before doing this, he may separate from his *placée* (so she is termed). If so, he pays her according to agreement, and as much more, perhaps, as his affection for her, or his sense of the cruelty of the proceeding, may lead him to; and she has the world before her again, in the position of a widow. Many men continue for a long time, to support both establishments—particularly if their legal marriage is one *de convenance*. But many others form so strong attachments, that the relation is never discontinued, but becomes, indeed, that of marriage, except that it is not legalized or solemnized. These men leave their estate, at death, to their children, to whom they may have previously given every advantage of education they could command. What becomes of the boys, I am not informed; the girls, sometimes, are removed to other countries, where their colour does not prevent their living reputable lives; but, of

---

[4] **THE GLOBE BALL ROOM,**
Corner of St. Claude and St. Peter Streets, abreast of the Old Basin,
WILL OPEN THIS EVENING, October 16, when a Society Ball will be given.
No ladies admitted without masks.
Gentlemen, fifty cents—Ladies, gratis.
Doors open at 9½ o'clock. Ball to commence at 10 o'clock.
No person admitted with weapons, by order of the Council.
A superior orchestra has been engaged for the season.
The public may be assured of the most strict order, as there will be at all times an efficient police in attendance.
Attached to the establishment is a superior Bar, well stocked with wines and liquors; also, a Restaurant, where may be had all such delicacies as the market affords.
All ladies are requested to procure free tickets in the Mask Room, as no lady will be admitted into the ball-room without one.

A. WHITLOCK, Manager

course, mainly continue in the same society, and are fated to a life similar to that of their mothers.

I have described this custom as it was described to me; I need hardly say, in only its best aspects. The crime and heart-breaking sorrow that must frequently result from it, must be evident to every reflective reader.

A gentleman, of New England education, gave me the following account of his acquaintance with the quadroon society. On first coming to New Orleans, he was drawn into the social circles usually frequented by New England people, and some time afterwards was introduced by a friend to a quadroon family, in which there were three pretty and accomplished young women. They were intelligent and well informed; their musical taste was especially well cultivated; they were well read in the literature of the day, and their conversation upon it was characterized by good sense and refined discrimination. He never saw any indication of a want of purity of character or delicacy of feeling. He was much attracted by them, and for some time visited them very frequently. Having then discontinued his intimacy, at length one of the girls asked him why he did not come to see them as often as he had formerly done. He frankly replied, that he had found their society so fascinating, that he had thought it best to restrict himself in the enjoyment of it, lest it should become necessary to his happiness; and out of regard to his general plans of life, and the feelings of his friends, he could not permit himself to indulge the purpose to be united to one of them, according to the usual custom with their class. The young woman was evidently much pained, but not at all offended, and immediately acknowledged and commended the propriety and good sense of his resolution.

One reason which leads this way of living to be frequently adopted by unmarried men, who come to New Orleans to carry on business, is, that it is much cheaper than living at hotels and boarding-houses. As no young man ordinarily dare think of marrying, until he has made a fortune to support the extravagant style of housekeeping, and gratify the expensive tastes of young women, as fashion is now educating them, many are obliged to make up their minds never to marry. Such a one undertook to show me that it was cheaper for him to *placer* than to live in any other way which could be expected of him in New Orleans. He hired, at a low rent, two apartments in the older part of the town; his *placée* did not, except occasionally, require a servant; she did the marketing, and performed all the ordinary duties of housekeeping herself; she took care of his clothes, and in every way was economical and saving in her habits; it being her interest, if her affection for him were not sufficient, to make him as much comfort and as little expense as possible that he might be the more strongly attached to her, and have the less occasion to leave her. He concluded by assuring me that whatever might be said against it, it certainly was better than the way in which most young men lived who depended on salaries in New York.

It is asserted by Southerners who have lived at the North, and Northerners who lived at the South, that although the facilities for licentiousness are much greater at the South, the evil of licentiousness is much greater at the North. Not because the average standard of "respectable position" requires a less expenditure at the South, for the contrary is the case.[5] But it is said licentiousness at the North is far more captivating, irresistible, and ruinous than at the South. Its very intrigues, cloaks, hazards, and expenses, instead of repressing the passions of young men, exasperate them, and increase its degrading effect upon their character, producing hypocrisy, interfering with high ambitions, destroying self-respect, causing the worst possible results to their health, and giving them habits which are inimical to future domestic contentment and virtue.

Possibly there is some ground for this assertion with regard to young men in towns, though in rural life the advantage of the North, I believe, is incomparable.

Mrs. Douglass, a Virginia woman, who was tried, convicted, and punished, a year or two since, for teaching a number of slaves to read, contrary to law, says in a letter from her jail—

This subject demands the attention, not only of the religious population, but of statesmen and law-makers. It is one great evil hanging over the Southern Slave States, destroying domestic happiness and the peace of thousands. It is summed up in the single word—*amalgamation*. This, and this only, causes the vast extent of ignorance, degradation, and crime

---

[5] A gentleman in an inland Southern town said to me, "I have now but one servant; if I should marry, I should be obliged to buy three more, and that alone would withdraw from my capital at least three thousand dollars."

that lies like a black cloud over the whole South. And the practice is more general than even the Southerners are willing to allow.

Neither is it to be found only in the lower order of the white population. It pervades the entire society. Its followers are to be found among all ranks, occupations, and professions. The white mothers and daughters of the South have suffered under it for years—have seen their dearest affections trampled upon—their hopes of domestic happiness destroyed, and their future lives embittered, even to agony, by those who should be all in all to them, as husbands, sons, and brothers. I cannot use too strong language in reference to this subject, for I know that it will meet with a heartfelt response from every Southern woman.

A negress was hung this year in Alabama, for the murder of her child. At her trial she confessed her guilt. She said her owner was the father of the child, and that her mistress knew it, and treated it so cruelly in consequence, that she had killed it to save it from further suffering, and also to remove a provocation to her own ill-treatment.

A large planter told, as a reason for sending his boys to the North to be educated, that there was no possibility of their being brought up in decency at home. Another planter told me that he was intending to move to a free country on this account. He said that the practice was not occasional or general, it was universal. "There is not," he said, "a likely-looking black girl in this State that is not the concubine of a white man. There is not an old plantation in which the grandchildren of the owner are not whipped in the field by his overseer. I cannot bear that the blood of the —— should run in the veins of slaves." He was of an old Scotch family.

New Orleans, Sunday.—Walking this morning through a rather mean neighbourhood I was attracted, by a loud chorus singing, to the open door of a chapel or small church. I found a large congregation of negroes assembled within, and the singing being just then concluded, and a negro preacher commencing a sermon, I entered an empty pew near the entrance. I had no sooner taken a seat than a negro usher came to me, and, in the most polite manner, whispered—

"Won't you please to let me give you a seat higher up, master, 'long o' tudder white folks?"

I followed him to the uppermost seat, facing the pulpit, where there were three other white persons. One of them was a woman—

old, very plain, and not as well dressed as many of the negroes; another looked like a ship's officer, and was probably a member of the police force in undress—what we call a spy, when we detect it in Europe; both of these remained diligently and gravely attentive during the service; the third was a foreign-looking person, very flashily dressed and sporting a yellow-headed walking-stick, and much cheap jewelry.

The remainder of the congregation consisted entirely of coloured persons, many of them, however, with light hair and hardly any perceptible indications of having African blood. On the step of the chancel were a number of children, and among these one of the loveliest young girls that I ever saw. She was a light mulatto, and had an expression of unusual intelligence and vivacity. During the service she frequently smiled, I thought derisively, at the emotions and excitement betrayed by the older people about her. She was elegantly dressed, and was accompanied by a younger sister, who was also dressed expensively and in good taste, but who was a shade darker, though much removed from the blackness of the true negro, and of very good features and pleasant expression.

The preacher was nearly black, with close woolly hair. His figure was slight, he seemed to be about thirty years of age, and the expression of his face indicated a refined and delicately sensitive nature. His eye was very fine, bright, deep, and clear; his voice and manner generally quiet and impressive.

The text was, "I have fought the good fight, I have kept the faith; henceforth there is laid up for me a crown of glory"; and the sermon was an appropriate and generally correct explanation of the customs of the Olympian games, and a proper and often eloquent application of the figure to the Christian course of life. Much of the language was highly metaphorical; the figures long, strange, and complicated, yet sometimes, however, beautiful. Words were frequently misplaced, and their meaning evidently misapprehended, while the grammar and pronunciation were sometimes such as to make the idea intended to be conveyed by the speaker incomprehensible to me. Vulgarisms and slang phrases occasionally occurred, but evidently without any consciousness of impropriety on the part of the speaker or his congregation.

As soon as I had taken my seat, my attention was attracted by an old negro near me, whom I supposed for some time to be suffering under some nervous complaint; he trembled, his teeth chattered, and his face, at intervals, was convulsed. He soon began to respond aloud to the sentiments of the preacher, in such words as these: "Oh, yes!" "That's it, that's it!" "Yes, yes—glory—yes!" and similar expressions could be heard from all parts of the house whenever the speaker's voice was unusually solemn, or his language and manner eloquent or excited.

Sometimes the outcries and responses were not confined to ejaculations of this kind, but shouts, and groans, terrific shrieks, and indescribable expressions of ecstasy—of pleasure or agony—and even stamping, jumping, and clapping of hands were added. The tumult often resembled that of an excited political meeting; and I was once surprised to find my own muscles all stretched, as if ready for a struggle—my face glowing, and my feet stamping—having been infected unconsciously, as men often are, with instinctive bodily sympathy with the excitement of the crowd. So wholly unintellectual was the basis of this excitement, however, that I could not, when my mind retroverted to itself, find any connection or meaning in the phrases of the speaker that remained in my memory; and I have no doubt it was his "action" rather than his sentiments, that had given rise to the excitement of the congregation.

I took notes as well as I could of a single passage of the sermon. The preacher, having said that among the games of the arena were "raaslin" (wrestling) and boxing, and described how a combatant, determined to win the prize, would come boldly up to his adversary and stand square before him, looking him straight in the eyes, and while he guarded himself with one hand, would give him a "lick" with the other, continued in these words: "Then would he stop, and turn away his face, and let the adversary hit back? No, my brethren, no, no! he'd follow up his advantage, and give him another lick; and if he fell back, he'd keep close after him, and not stop!—and not faint!—not be content with merely driving him back!—but he'd *persevere!* (yes, glory!) and hit him again! (that's it, hit him again! hit him again! oh, glory! hi! hi! glory!) drive him into the corner! and never, never stop till he had him *down!* (glory, glory, glory!) and he had got his foot on his neck, and the crown of wild olive leaves was placed upon his head by the lord of the games. (Ha! ha! glory to the Lord! etc.) It was the custom of the Olympian games, my brethren, for the victor to be crowned with a crown of wild olive leaves; but sometimes, after all, it wouldn't be awarded right, because the lord of the games was a poor, frail, erroneous man, and maybe he couldn't see right, or maybe he wasn't an honest man, and would have his favourites among the combatants, and if his favourite was beaten, he would not *allow* it, but would declare that he was the victor, and the crown would descend on *his* head (*glory!*). But there ain't no danger of that with our fight with the world, for our Lord is throned in justice. (Glory!—oh, yes! yes!—sweet Lord! sweet Lord!) He seeth in secret, and he knoweth all things, and there's no chance for a mistake, and if we only will just persevere and conquer, and conquer and persevere (yes, sir! oh, Lord, yes!) and persevere—not for a year, or for two year, or ten year; nor for seventy year, perhaps; but if we persevere—(yes! yes!) —if we persevere—(oh! Lord! help us!)—if we persevere unto the end—(oh! oh! glory! glory! glory!)—until he calls us home! (Frantic shouting.) Henceforth there is laid up for us a crown of immortal glory—(Ha! ha! HA!)—not a crown of wild olive leaves that begin to droop as soon as they touch our brow, (oh! oh! oh!) but a crown of immortal glory! That fadeth not away! Never begins to droop! But is immortal in the heavens!" (Tremendous uproar, many of the congregation on their feet, and uttering cries and shrieks impossible to be expressed in letters.) The shabby gentleman by my side, who had been asleep, suddenly awakened, dropped his stick, and shouted with all his might, "Glory to the Lord!"

The body of the house was filled by the audience; there were galleries, but few persons were in them; on one side, two or three boys, and on the other, on the seat nearest the pulpit, about a dozen women.

The preacher was drawing his sermon to a close, and offering some sensible and pertinent advice, soberly and calmly, and the congregation was attentive and comparatively quiet, when a small old woman, perfectly black, among those in the gallery, suddenly rose, and began dancing and clapping her hands; at first with a slow and measured movement, and then with increasing rapidity, at the same time beginning to shout "*ha! ha!*" The women about her arose also, and tried to hold her, as there appeared great danger that she would fall out of the gallery, and those below left their pews that she might not fall upon them.

The preacher continued his remarks—much the best part of his

sermon—but it was plain that they were wasted; every one was looking at the dancing woman in the gallery, and many were shouting
and laughing aloud (in joyful sympathy, I suppose). His eye flashed
as he glanced anxiously from the woman to the people, and then
stopping in the middle of a sentence, a sad smile came over his face;
he closed the book and bowed his head upon his hands to the desk.
A voice in the congregation struck into a tune, and the whole congregation rose and joined in a roaring song. The woman was still
shouting and dancing, her head thrown back and rolling from one
side to the other. Gradually her shout became indistinct, she threw
her arms wildly about instead of clapping her hands, fell back into
the arms of her companions, then threw herself forward and embraced those before her, then tossed herself from side to side, gasp-
ing, and finally sunk to the floor, where she remained at the end of
the song, kicking, as if acting a death struggle.

Another man now rose in the pulpit, and gave out a hymn, naming
number and page, and holding a book before him, though I thought
he did not read from it, and I did not see another book in the house.
Having recited seven verses, and repeated the number and page of
the hymn, he closed the book and commenced to address the congregation. He was a tall, full-blooded negro, very black, and with a
disgusting expression of sensuality, cunning, and vanity in his countenance, and a pompous, patronizing manner—a striking contrast,
in all respects, to the prepossessing, quiet, and modest young
preacher who had preceded him. He was dressed in the loosest form
of the fashionable sack overcoat, which he threw off presently,
showing a white vest, gaudy cravat, and a tight cut-away coat, linked
together at the breast with jet buttons. He commenced by propos-
ing to further elucidate the meaning of the apostle's words; they
had an important bearing, he said, which his brother had not had
time to bring out adequately before the congregation. At first he
leaned carelessly on the pulpit cushion, laughing cunningly, and
spoke in a low, deep, hoarse, indistinct, and confidential tone; but
soon he struck a higher key, drawling his sentences like a street
salesman, occasionally breaking out into a yell with all the strength
of extraordinarily powerful lungs, at the same time taking a striking
attitude and gesturing in an extraordinary manner. This would
create a frightful excitement in the people, and be responded to
with the loudest and most terrific shouts. I can compare them to

nothing else human I ever heard. Sometimes he would turn from the audience and assume a personal opponent to be standing by his side in the pulpit. Then, after battling for a few minutes in an awful and majestic manner with this man of Belial, whom he addressed constantly as "sir!" he would turn again to the admiring congregation, and in a familiar, gratulatory, and conversational tone explain the difficulty into which he had got him, and then again suddenly turn back upon him, and in a boxing attitude give another knock-down reply to his heretical propositions.

His language was in a great part unintelligible to me, but the congregation seemed to enjoy it highly, and encouraged and assisted him in his combat with "Sir" Knight of his imagination most tumultuously; and I soon found that this poor gentleman, over whom he rode his high horse so fiercely, was one of those "who take unto themselves the name of Baptist," and that the name of his own charger was *"Perseverance-of-the-Saints."*

The only intelligible argument that I could discover, was presented under the following circumstances. Having made his supposed adversary assert that "if a man would only just believe, and let him bury him under de water, he would be saved,"—he caught up the big pulpit Bible, and using it as a catapult, pretended to hurl from it the reply—"Except ye persevere and fight de good fight unto de end, ye shall be damned!" "That's it, that's it!" shouted the delighted audience. "Yes! you shall be damned! Ah! you've got it now, have ye! Pooh!—Wha's de use o' his tellin' us dat ar?" he continued, turning to the congregation with a laugh; "wha's de use on't, when we know dat a month arter he's buried 'em under de water—whar do we find 'em? Ha? ah ha! Whar? In de grog-shop! (ha! ha! ha! ha!) Yes we do, don't we? (Yes! yes!) In de rum-hole! (Ha! ha! ha! Yes! yes! oh Lord!) and we know de spirit of rum and de Spirit of God hasn't got no 'finities. (Yah! ha! ha! yes! yes! dat's it! dat's it! oh, my Jesus! Oh! oh! glory! glory!) Sut'nly, sah! You may launch out upon de ocean a drop of oil way up to Virginny, and we'll launch anudder one heah to Lusiana, and when dey meets—no matter how far dey been gone—dey'll unite! Why, sah? Because dey's got de 'finities, sah! But de spirit of rum haint got nary sort o' 'finity with de Spirit," etc.

Three of the congregation threw themselves into hysterics during this harangue, though none were so violent as that of the woman in the gallery. The man I had noticed first from his strange convulsive motions, was shaking as if in a violent ague, and frequently snatched the sleeve of his coat in his teeth as if he would rend it. The speaker at length returned to the hymn, repeated the number and page and the first two lines. These were sung, and he repeated the next, and so on, as in the Scotch Presbyterian service. The congregation sang; I think every one joined, even the children, and the collective sound was wonderful. The voices of one or two women rose above the rest, and one of these soon began to introduce variations, which consisted mainly of shouts of Oh! oh! at a piercing height. Many of the singers kept time with their feet, balancing themselves on each alternately, and swinging their bodies accordingly. The reading of the lines would be accompanied also by shouts, as during the previous discourse.

When the preacher had concluded reading the last two lines, as the singing again proceeded, he raised his own voice above all, turned around, clapped his hands, and commenced to dance, and laughed aloud—first with his back, and then with his face to the audience.

The singing ceased, but he continued his movements, leaping, with increasing agility, from one side of the pulpit to the other. The people below laughed and shouted, and the two other preachers who were shut in the pulpit with the dancer, tried hard to keep out of his way, and threw forward their arms or shoulders, to fend off his powerful buffets as he surged about between them. Swinging out his arms at random, with a blow of his fist he knocked the great Bible spinning off the desk, to the great danger of the children below; then threw himself back, jamming the old man, who was trying to restrain him, against the wall.

At the next heave, he pitched headforemost into the young preacher, driving him through the door and falling with him half down the stairs, and after bouncing about a few moments, jerking his arms and legs violently, like a supple jack, in every direction, and all the time driving his breath with all the noise possible between his set teeth, and trying to foam at the mouth and act an epileptic fit, there he lay as if dead, the young preacher, with the same sad smile, and something of shame on his face, sitting on the stair holding his head on his shoulder, and grasping one of his hands, while his feet were extended up into the pulpit.

The third man in the pulpit, a short, aged negro, with a smiling face, and a pleasing manner, took the Bible, which was handed up to him by one of the congregation, laid it upon the desk, and, leaning over it, told the people, in a gentle, conversational tone, that the "love feast" would be held at four o'clock; gave some instructions about the tickets of admission, and severely reproved those, who were in the habit of coming late, and insisted upon being let in after the doors were locked. He then announced that the doxology would be sung, which accordingly followed, another woman going into hysterics at the close. The prostrate man rose, and released the young preacher, who pronounced the Apostles' blessing, and the congregation slowly passed out, chatting and saluting one another politely as they went, and bearing not the slightest mark of the previous excitement.

I came to Mr. R.'s plantation by a steamboat, late at night. As the boat approached the shore, near his house, her big bell having been rung some ten minutes previously, a negro came out with a lantern to meet her. The boat's bow was run boldly against the bank; I leaped ashore, the clerk threw out a newspaper and a package, saying to the negro, "That's for your master, and that's for so-and-so, tell your master, and ask him to give it to him." The boat bounded off at once, by her own elasticity, the starboard wheel was backed for a turn or two, and the next minute the great edifice was driving up the stream again—not a rope having been lifted, nor any other movement having been made on board, except by the pilot and engineer.

"Do you belong to Mr. R.?" I asked the negro. "Yes, sir; is you going to our house, master?" "Yes." "I'll show you the way, then, sir"; and he conducted me in, leaving the parcels the clerk had thrown out, where they had fallen, on the bank.

A negro woman prepared a bed for me, waited at the door till I had put out my light, and then returned to tuck in the musquito-bar tightly about the bed. This was merely from custom, as there were no musquitoes at that season. In the morning the same woman awakened me, opened the curtains, and asked me to take the money which she had found in the pockets of my clothing, while she took it out to be brushed.

Mr. R. is a Southerner by birth, but was educated at the North, where, also, and in foreign countries, he has spent a large part of his life. He is a man of more than usual precision of mind, energetic and humane; and while his negroes seemed to be better disciplined than any others I had seen, they evidently regarded him with affection, respect, and pride.

He had been ill for some weeks previous to my visit, and when he walked out with me, on the second day, it was the first time since the commencement of his illness that his field-hands had seen him.

The first negroes we met were half a dozen women, who were going up to the nursery to suckle their children—the overseer's bell having been just rung (at eleven o'clock), to call them in from work for that purpose. Mr. R. said that he allowed them two hours to be with their children while nursing at noon, and to leave work an hour earlier at night than the other field-hands. The women all stopped as we met them, and asked, with much animation:

"Oh, master! how is 'ou?"

"Well, I'm getting up. How are you, girls?"

"Oh, we's well, sir."

"The children all well?"

"Yes, master, all but Sukey's, sir."

"Sukey's? What, isn't that well yet?"

"No, master."

"But it's getting well, is it not?"

"Yes, master."

Soon after we met a boy, driving a cart. He pulled up as he came against us, and, taking off his hat, asked, "How is 'ou, master?"

"I'm getting well, you see. If I don't get about, and look after you, I'm afraid we shan't have much of a crop. I don't know what you niggers will do for Christmas money."

"Ha!—look heah, massa!—you jus' go right straight on de ways you's goin'; see suthin' make you laugh, ha! ha!" (meaning the work that had been done while he was ill, and the good promise of a crop).

The plantation contained about nine hundred acres of tillage land, and a large tract of "swamp," or woodland, was attached to it. The tillage land was inclosed all in one field by a strong cypress post and rail fence, and was drained by two canals, five feet deep, running about twenty feet apart, and parallel—the earth from both being thrown together, so as to make a high, dry road between them, straight through the middle of the plantation.

Fronting upon the river, and but six or eight rods from the public road, which everywhere runs close along the shore inside the levee, was the mansion of the proprietor: an old Creole house, the lower story of brick and the second of wood, with a broad gallery, shaded by the extended roof, running all around it; the roof steep, and shedding water on four sides, with ornaments of turned wood where lines met, and broken by several small dormer windows. The gallery was supported by round brick columns, and arches. The parlours, library, and sleeping rooms of the white family were all on the second floor. Between the house and the street was a yard, planted formally with orange-trees and other evergreens. A little on one side of the house stood a large two-story, square dove-cot, which is a universal appendage of a sugar-planter's house. In the rear of the house was another large yard, in which, irregularly placed, were houses for the family servants, a kitchen, stable, carriage-house, smoke-house, etc. Behind this rear-yard there was a vegetable garden, of an acre or more, in the charge of a negro gardener; a line of fig-trees were planted along the fence, but all the ground inclosed was intended to be cropped with vegetables for the family, and for the supply of "the people." I was pleased to notice, however, that the negro-gardener had, of his own accord, planted some violets and other flowering plants. From a corner of the court a road ran to the sugar-works and the negro settlement, which were five or six hundred yards from the house.

The negro houses were exactly like those I have described on the Georgia Rice Plantation, except that they were provided with broad galleries in front. They were as neat and well-made externally as the cottages usually provided by large manufacturing companies in New England, to be rented to their workmen. The clothing furnished the negroes, and the rations of bacon and meal, were the same as on other good plantations. During the grinding season extra rations of flour were served, and hot coffee was kept constantly in the sugar-house, and the hands on duty were allowed to drink it almost *ad libitum*. They were also allowed to drink freely of the hot *sirop*, of which they were extremely fond. A generous allowance of *sirop*, or molasses, was also given out to them, with their other rations, every week during the winter and early summer. In extremely hot weather it was thought to be unfavourable to health, and was discontinued. Rations of tobacco were also served. At

Christmas, a sum of money, equal to one dollar for each hogshead of sugar made on the plantation, was divided among the negroes. The last year this had amounted to over two dollars a head. It was usually given to the heads of families. If any had been particularly careless or lazy, it was remembered at this Christmas dole. Of course, the effect of this arrangement, small as was the amount received by each person, was to give the labourers a direct interest in the economical direction of their labour: the advantage of it was said to be evident.

Mr. R. had purchased the plantation but three years before, and had afterwards somewhat increased its area by buying out several poor people, who had owned small farms adjoining. He had greatly extended and improved the drainage, and had nearly doubled the force of negroes employed upon it, adding to the number that he purchased with the land, nearly as many more whom he had inherited, and whom he transferred to it from an old cotton plantation that he had formerly lived upon.

He had considerably more than doubled the stock of mules and oxen; had built entirely new cabins for all the negroes, and new sugar-works and stables. His whole capital, he said, when he first bought the plantation, would not have paid half the price of it and of the cost of stocking it as he had done. Most men when they buy a plantation, he informed me, go very heavily in debt; frequently the purchase is made three quarters on credit.

"Buying a plantation," were his words, "whether a sugar or cotton plantation, in this country, is usually essentially a gambling operation. The capital invested in a sugar plantation of the size of mine ought not to be less than $150,000. The purchaser pays down what he can, and usually gives security for the payment of the balance in six annual installments, with interest (10 per cent. per annum) from the date of the purchase. Success in sugar, as well as cotton planting, is dependent on so many circumstances, that it is as much trusting to luck as betting on a throw of dice. If his first crop proves a bad one, he must borrow money of the Jews in New Orleans to pay his first note; they will sell him this on the best terms they can—often at not less than 25 per cent. per annum. If three or four bad crops follow one another, he is ruined. But this is seldom the case, and he lives on, one year gaining a little on his debts, but almost as often enlarging them. Three or four years ago there was hardly a planter in Louisiana or Mississippi who was not in very embarrassed circumstances, nearly every one having his crops pledged to his creditors long before they were secured. The good prices and good crops of the last few years have set them all on their legs again; and this year all the jewellers' shops, and stores of rich furniture and dry goods, in New Orleans, were cleared out by the middle of the season, and everybody feels strong and cheerful. I have myself been particularly fortunate; I have made three good crops in succession. Last year I made six hundred and fifty hogsheads of sugar, and twelve hundred barrels of molasses. The molasses alone brought me a sum sufficient to pay all my plantation expenses; and the sugar yields me a clear profit of twenty-five per cent. on my whole investment. If I make another crop this year as good as that, I shall be able to discount my outstanding notes, and shall be clear of debt at the end of four years, instead of six, which was all I had hoped for."

On another plantation, which I have since visited, which had a slave population of over two hundred—counted as one hundred field-hands—the sugar works cost $40,000, and seven hundred barrels of sugar were made last year. On this plantation there is a steam-pump, which drains the rear of the plantation over a levee, when the back-water from the swamp would otherwise prevent perfect drainage.

Mr. R. modestly credited his extraordinary success to "luck"; but I was satisfied, upon examining his improvements, and considering the reasons, which he readily gave for every operation which he showed, or described to me, that intelligence, study, and enterprise had seldom better claims to reward. Adjoining his plantation there was another of nearly twice the size, on which an equal number of negroes and only half the number of cattle were employed; and the proprietor, I was told, had had rather *bad luck:* he had, in fact, made but little more than half as much sugar as Mr. R. I inquired of the latter if there was any advantage in his soil over that of his neighbour's. "I think not," he replied; "my best cane was made on a piece of land adjoining his, which, before I bought it, was thought unfit for cultivation. The great advantage I had over him last year, mainly arose from my having secured a more complete drainage of all my land."

The soil of the greater part of the plantation was a fine, dark, sandy loam; some of it, at the greatest distance from the river, was lighter in colour, and more clayey; and in one part, where there was a very slight depression of the surface over about fifty acres, there was a dark, stiffish soil. It was this to which Mr. R. alluded as having produced his best cane. It had been considered too low, wet, tenacious, and unfertile to be worthy of cultivation by the former owner, and was covered with bushes and weeds when he took it. The improvement had been effected entirely by draining and fall-ploughing. In fall-ploughing, as a remedy for tenacity of soil, this gentleman's experience had given him great faith. At various points, on my tour, I found most conflicting opinions upon this point, many (among them the President of a State Agricultural Society) having invariably observed pernicious effects result from it.

The sugar-cane is a perennial-rooted plant, and the stalk does not attain its full size, under favourable circumstances, in less growing time than twelve months; and seed does not usually form upon it until the thirteenth or fourteenth month. This function (termed *arrowing*) it only performs in a very hot and steadily hot climate, somewhat rarely even in the West Indies. The plant is, at all stages, extremely susceptible to cold, a moderate frost not only suspending its growth, but disorganizing it so that the chemical qualities of its sap are changed, and it is rendered valueless for sugar making.

As frosts of considerable severity are common in all parts of Louisiana, during three months of the year, of course the sugar-cane is there never permitted to attain its full growth. To so much greater perfection does it arrive in the West Indies, that the cane produced on one acre will yield from 3,000 to 6,000 lbs. of sugar, while in Louisiana 1,000 is considered the average obtained. "I could make sugar in the climate of Cuba," said a Louisiana planter to me, "for half the price that, under the most favourable circumstances, it must cost here." In addition to the natural uncongeniality of the climate, the ground on which it grows in Louisiana, being lower than the surface of the river, is much of the time made cold by the infiltration of moisture. It is, therefore, only by reason of the extreme fertility of this alluvial deposit, assisted by a careful method of cultivation, that the cane is forced to a state of maturity which enables it to yield an amount of sugar which, with the assistance of a governmental protection against foreign competition, will be remunerative to the planter.

I must confess that there seems to me room for grave doubt if the capital, labour, and especially the human life, which have been and which continue to be spent in converting the swamps of Louisiana into sugar plantations, and in defending them against the annual assaults of the river, and the fever and the cholera, could not have been better employed somewhere else. It is claimed as a great advantage of Slavery, as well as of Protection, that what has been done for this purpose never would have been done without it. If it would not, the obvious reason is, that the wages, or prospect of profit would not have been sufficient to induce free men to undergo the inconveniences and the danger incident to the enterprise. There is now great wealth in Louisiana; but I question if greater wealth would not have been obtained by the same expenditure of human labour, and happiness, and life, in very many other directions.

Planting commences immediately after the sugar-manufacturing season is concluded—usually in January. New or fallow land is prepared by ploughing the whole surface: on this plantation the plough used was made in Kentucky, and was of a very good model, ploughing seven to nine inches deep, with a single pair of mules. The ground being then harrowed, drills are opened with a double mould-board plough, seven feet apart. Cuttings of cane for seed are to be planted in them. These are reserved from the crop in the autumn, when some of the best cane on the plantation is selected for this purpose, while still standing.[6] This is cut off at the roots, and laid up in heaps or stacks, in such a manner that the leaves and tops protect the stalks from frost. The heaps are called mattresses; they are two or three feet high, and as many yards across. At the planting season they are opened, and the cane comes out moist and green, and sweet, with the buds or eyes, which protrude at the joints, swelling. The immature top parts of the stalk are cut off, and they are loaded into carts, and carried to the ground prepared for planting. The carts used are large, with high side-boards, and are drawn by three mules—one large one being in the shafts, and two lighter ones abreast, before her. The drivers are boys, who use the whip a great deal, and drive rapidly.

[6] It is only on the best plantations that the seed-cane is selected with this care. On another plantation that I visited during the planting season I noticed that the best part of the stalk had been cut off for grinding, and only the less valuable part saved for seed; and this, I apprehend, is the general practice. The best cuttings probably produce the most vigorous plants.

In the field I found the labourers working in three divisions—the first, consisting of light hands, brought the cane by arms-full from the cart, and laid it by the side of the furrows; the second planted it, and the third covered it. Planting is done by laying the cuttings at the bottom of the furrow, in such a way that there shall be three always together, with the eyes of each a little removed from those of the others—that is, all "breaking joints." They are thinly covered with earth, drawn over them with hoes. The other tools were so well selected on this plantation, that I expressed surprise at the clumsiness of the hoes, particularly as the soil was light, and entirely free from stones. "Such hoes as you use at the North would not last a negro a day," said the planter.

Cane will grow for several years from the roots of the old plants, and, when it is allowed to do so, a very considerable part of the expense is avoided; but the vigour of the plant is less when growing from this source than when starting from cuttings, and the crop, when thus obtained, is annually less and less productive, until, after a number of years, depending upon the rigour of the seasons, fresh shoots cease to spring from the stubble. This sprouting of cane from the stools of the last crop is termed "ratooning." In the West India plantations the cane is frequently allowed to ratoon for eight successive crops. In Louisiana it is usual to plant once in three years, trusting to the ratooning for two crops only, and this was the practice on Mr. R.'s plantation. The cost of sugar growing would be very greatly increased if the crop needed planting every year; for all the cane grown upon an acre will not furnish seed for more than four acres—consequently one-twelfth of the whole of each crop has to be reserved for the planting of the following crop, even when two-thirds of this is to be of ratoon cane.

Planting is finished in a favourable season—early in March. Tillage is commenced immediately afterwards, by ploughing *from* the rows of young cane, and subsequently continued very much after the usual plans of tillage for potatoes, when planted in drills, with us. By or before the first of July, the crop is all well earthed up, the rows of cane growing from the crest of a rounded bed, seven feet wide, with deep water-furrows between each. The cane is at this time five or six feet high; and that growing from each bed forms arches with that of the next, so as to completely shade the ground. The furrows between the beds are carefully cleaned out; so that in the most drenching torrents of rain, the water is rapidly carried off into the drains, and thence to the swamp; and the crop then requires no further labour upon it until frost is apprehended, or the season for grinding arrives.

The nearly three months' interval, commencing at the intensest heat of summer, corresponds in the allotment of labour to the period of winter in Northern agriculture, because the winter itself, on the sugar-plantations, is the planting-season. The negroes are employed in cutting and carting wood for boiling the cane-juice, in making necessary repairs or additions to the sugar-house, and otherwise preparing for the grinding-season.

The grinding-season is the harvest of the sugar-planter; it commences in October, and continues for two or three months, during which time, the greatest possible activity and the utmost labour of which the hands are capable, are required to secure the product of the previous labour of the year. Mr. R. assured me that during the last grinding-season nearly every man, woman, and child on his plantation, including the overseer and himself, were on duty fully eighteen hours a day. From the moment grinding first commences, until the end of the season, it is never discontinued: the fires under the boiler never go out, and the negroes only rest for six hours in the twenty-four, by relays—three-quarters of them being constantly at work.

Notwithstanding the severity of the labour required of them at this time, Mr. R. said that his negroes were as glad as he was himself to have the time for grinding arrive, and they worked with greater cheerfulness than at any other season. How can those persons who are always so ready to maintain that the slaves work less than free labourers in free countries, and that for that reason they are to be envied by them, account for this? That at Mr. R.'s plantation it was the case that the slaves enjoyed most that season of the year when the hardest labour was required of them, I have, in addition to Mr. R.'s own evidence, good reason to believe, which I shall presently report. And the reason of it evidently is, that they are then better paid; they have better and more varied food and stimulants than usual, but especially they have a degree of freedom, and of social pleasure, and a variety of occupation which brings a recreation of the mind, and to a certain degree gives them strength for, and pleasure in, their labour. Men of sense have discovered that when they desire to get extraordinary exertions from their slaves, it is better to offer them rewards than to whip them; to encourage them, rather than to drive them.

If the season has been favourable, so that the cane is strong, and well matured, it will endure a smart early frost without injury, particularly if the ground is well drained; but as rapidly as possible, after the season has arrived at which frosts are to be expected, the whole crop is cut, and put in mattresses, from which it is taken to the grinding-mill as fast as it can be made to use it.

The business of manufacturing sugar is everywhere carried on in connection with the planting of the cane. The shortness of the season during which the cane can be used is the reason assigned for this: the proprietors would not be willing to trust to custom-mills to manufacture their produce with the necessary rapidity. If cane should be cultivated in connection with other crops—that is, on small farms, instead of great "sugar only" plantations—neighbourhood custom-mills would probably be employed. The profit of a sugar-plantation is now large, much in proportion to its size (if it be proportionately stocked); because only a very large supply of cane will warrant the proprietor in providing the most economical manufacturing apparatus. In 1849 there were 1,474 sugar estates in Louisiana, producing 236,547 hhds. of sugar; but it is thought that half of this quantity was produced on less than 200 estates—that is, that one-eighth of the plantations produced one-half the sugar. The sugar-works on some of the large estates cost over $100,000, and many of them manufacture over 1,000,000 lbs. per annum. The profits of these, under our present tariff, in a favourable season, are immense.

The apparatus used upon the better class of plantations is very admirable, and improvements are yearly being made, which indicate high scientific acquirements, and much mechanical ingenuity on the part of the inventors. The whole process of sugar manufacturing, although chemical analysis proves that a large amount of saccharine is still wasted, has been within a few years greatly improved, principally by reason of the experiments and discoveries of the French chemists, whose labours have been directed by the purpose to lessen the cost of beet-sugar. Apparatus for various processes in the manufacture, which they have invented or recommended, has been improved, and brought into practical operation on a large scale on some of the Louisiana plantations, the owners of which are among the most intelligent, enterprising, and wealthy men of business in the United States. Forty-three plantations in the State are now furnished with apparatus constructed in accordance with the best scientific knowledge on the subject; and 914 are driven by steam-engines—leaving but 560 to be worked by horse-power. Mr. R.'s sugar-house, for making brown sugar, was furnished with the best kind of apparatus, at a cost of $20,000. Preparations were making for the addition of works for the manufacture of white loaf sugar, which would cost $20,000 more. I have visited one plantation on which the sugar-works are said to have cost over $100,000.

At one corner of Mr. R.'s plantation, there was a hamlet consisting of about a dozen small houses or huts, built of wood or clay, in the old French peasant style. The residents owned small farms, on which they raised a little corn and rice; but Mr. R. described them as lazy vagabonds, doing but little work, and spending much time in shooting, fishing, and play. He wanted much to buy all their land, and get them to move away. He had already bought out some of them, and had made arrangements by which he hoped soon to get hold of the land of some of the rest. He was willing to pay two or three times as much as the property was actually worth, to get them to move off. As fast as he got possession, he destroyed their houses and gardens, removed their fences and trees, and brought all their land into his cane-plantation.

Some of them were mechanics. One was a very good mason, and he employed him in building his sugar-works and refinery; but he would be glad to get rid of them all, and depend entirely on slave mechanics—of these he had several already, and he could buy more when he needed them.

Why did he so dislike to have these poor people living near him, I asked? Because, he straightway answered, they demoralized his negroes. Seeing them living in apparent comfort, without much property and without steady labour, the slaves could not help thinking that it was unnecessary for men to work so hard as they themselves were obliged to, and that if they were free they would not work. Besides, the intercourse of these people with the negroes was not favourable to good discipline. They would get the negroes to do them little services, and would pay with luxuries which he did not wish his slaves to have. It was better that they never saw anybody off their own plantation; they should, if possible, have no intercourse with any other white men than their owner or overseer; especially, it was desirable that they should not see white men who did not command their respect, and whom they did not always feel to be superior to themselves, and able to command them.

The nuisance of petty traders dealing with the negroes, and encouraging them to pilfer, which I found everywhere a great annoyance to planters, seems to be greater on the banks of the Mississippi than elsewhere. The traders generally come on boats, which they moor at night on the shore, adjoining the negro-quarters, and float away whenever they have obtained any booty, with very small chance of detection. One day, during my visit at Mr. R.'s, a neighbour called to apprise him that one of these trading-boats was in the vicinity, that he might take precautions to prevent his negroes dealing with it. "The law," he observed, with much feeling, "is entirely inadequate to protect us against these rascals; it rather protects them than us. They easily evade detection in breaking it; and we can never get them punished, except we go beyond or against the law ourselves." To show me how vexatious the evil was, he mentioned that a large brass cock and some pipe had been lately stolen from his sugar-works, and that he had ascertained that one of his negroes had taken it and sold it on board one of these boats for seventy-five cents, and had immediately spent the money, chiefly for whisky, on the same boat. It had cost him thirty dollars to replace it. Mr. R. said that he had lately caught one of his own negroes going towards one of the "chicken-thieves" (so the traders' boats are locally called) with a piece of machinery, unscrewed from his sugar-works, which had cost him eighty dollars, but which would, very likely, have been sold for a drink. If the negro had succeeded in reaching the boat, as he would, if a watch had not been kept, he could never have recovered it. There would have been no witnesses to the sale; the stolen goods would have been hid on board until the boat reached New Orleans; or, if, an officer came to search the boat, they would have been dropped into the river, before he got on board.

This neighbour of Mr. R.'s had been educated in France. Conversing on the inconveniences of Slavery, he acknowledged that it was not only an uneconomical system, but a morally wrong one; "but," he said, "it was not instituted by us—we are not responsible for it. It is unfortunately fixed upon us; we could not do away with it if we wished; our duty is only to make the best of a bad thing; to lessen its evils as much as we can, so far as we have to do with it individually."

Mr. R. himself also acknowledged Slavery to be a very great evil, morally and economically. It was a curse upon the South; he had no doubt at all about it: nothing would be more desirable than its removal, if it were possible to be accomplished. But he did not think it could be abolished without instituting greater evils than those sought to be remedied. Its influence on the character of the whites was what was most deplorable. He was sorry to think that his children would have to be subject to it. He thought that eventually, if he were able to afford it, he should free his slaves and send them to Africa.

When I left Mr. R.'s, I was driven about twenty miles in a buggy, by one of his house servants. He was inclined to be talkative and communicative; and as he expressed great affection and respect for his owner, I felt at liberty to question him on some points upon which I had always previously avoided conversing with slaves. He spoke rapidly, garrulously; and it was only necessary for me to give a direction to his thoughts, by my inquiries. I was careful to avoid leading questions, and not to show such an interest as would lead him to reply guardedly. I charged my memory as much as possible with his very words, when this was of consequence, and made the following record of the conversation within half an hour after I left him.

He first said that he supposed that I would see that he was not a "Creole nigger"; he came from Virginia. He reckoned the Virginia negroes were better looking than those who were raised here; there were no black people anywhere in the world who were so "well made" as those who were born in Virginia. He asked if I lived in New Orleans; and where? I told him that I lived at the North. He asked:

"Da's a great many brack folks dah, massa?"

"No; very few."

"Da's a great many in Virginny; more'n da is heah?"

"But I came from beyond Virginia—from New York."

He had heard there were a great many black folk in New York. I said there were a good many in the city; but few in the country. Did I live in the country? What people did I have for servants? Thought, if I hired all my labour, it must be very dear. He inquired further about negroes there. I told him they were all free, and described their general condition; told him what led them to congregate in cities, and what the effect was. He said the negroes, both slave and free, who lived in New Orleans, were better off than those who lived in the country. Why? Because they make more money, and it is "gayer" there, and there is more "society." He then drew a contrast between Virginia, as he recollected it, and Louisiana. There is but one road in this country. In Virginia, there are roads running in every direction, and often crossing each other. You could see so much more "society," and there was so much more "variety" than here. He would not like now to go back to Virginia to live, because he had got used to this country, and had all his acquaintances here, and knew the ways of the people. He could speak French. He would like to go to New Orleans, though; would rather live in New Orleans than any other place in the world.

After a silence of some minutes, he said, abruptly—

"If I was free, I would go to Virginia, and see my old mudder." He had left her when he was thirteen years old. He reckoned he was now thirty-three. "I don't well know, dough, exactly, how old I is; but, I rec'lect, de day I was taken away, my ole mudder she tell me I was tirteen year old." He did not like to come away at all; he "felt dreadful bad"; but, now he was used to it, he liked living here. He came across the Blue Ridge, and he recollected that, when he first saw it, he thought it was a dark piece of sky, and he wondered what it would be like when they came close to it. He was brought, with a great many other negroes, in waggons, to Louisville; and then they were put on board a steamboat, and brought down here. He was sold, and put on this plantation, and had been on it ever since. He had been twice sold, along with it. Folks didn't very often sell their servants away here, as they did in Virginia. They were selling their servants, in Virginia, all the time; but, here, they did not very often sell them, except they run away. When a man would run away, and they could not do anything with him, they always sold him off. The people were almost all French. "Were there any French in New York?" he asked. I told him there were;

but not as many as in Louisiana. "I s'pose dah is more of French people in Lusiana, dan dah is anywhar else in all de world—a'nt dah, massa?"

"Except in France."

"Wa's dat, sar?"

"France is the country where all the Frenchmen came from, in the first place."

"Wa's dat France, massa?"

"France is a country across the ocean, the big water, beyond Virginia, where all the Frenchmen first came from; just as the black people all came first from Africa, you know."

"I've heered, massa, dat dey sell one anoder dah, in de fus place. Does you know, sar, was dat so?" This was said very gravely.

I explained the savage custom of making slaves of prisoners of war, and described the constant wars of the native Africans. I told him that they were better off here than they would be to be the slaves of cruel savages, in Africa. He turned, and looking me anxiously in the face, like a child, asked:

"*Is* de brack folks better off to be here, massa?"

I answered that I thought so; and described the heathenish barbarism of the people of Africa. I made exception of Liberia, knowing that his master thought of some time sending him there, and described it as a place that was settled by negroes who went back there from this country. He said he had heard of it, and that they had sent a good many free negroes from New Orleans there.

After a moment's pause, he inquired—very gravely, again:

"*Why is it,* massa, when de brack people is free, dey wants to send 'em away out of dis country?"

The question took me aback. After bungling a little—for I did not like to tell him the white people were afraid to have them stay here—I said that it was thought to be a better place for them there. He replied, he should think, that, when they had got used to this country, it was much better that they should be allowed to stay here. He would not like to go out of this country. He wouldn't like even to go to Virginia now, though Virginia was such a pleasant country; he had been here so long, seemed like this was the best place for him to live. To avoid discussion of the point, I asked what he would do, if he were free?

"If I was free, massa; *if I was free*" (with great animation), "I would—well, sar, de fus thing I would do, if I was free, I would go to work for a year, and get some money for myself,—den—den—den, massa, dis is what I do—I buy me, fus place, a little house, and little lot land, and den—no; den—den—I would go to old Virginny, and see my old mudder. Yes, sar, I would like to do dat fus thing; den, when I com back, de fus thing I'd do, I'd get me a wife; den, I'd take her to my house, and I would live with her dar; and I would raise things in my garden, and take 'em to New Orleans, and sell 'em dar, in de market. Dat's de way I would live, if I was free."

He said, in answer to further inquiries, that there were many free negroes all about this region. Some were very rich. He pointed out to me three plantations, within twenty miles, owned by coloured men. These bought black folks, he said, and had servants of their own. They were very bad masters, very hard and cruel—hadn't any feeling. "You might think, master, dat dey would be good to dar own nation; but dey is not. I will tell you de truth, massa; I know I'se got to answer; and it's a fact, dey is very bad masters, sar. I'd rather be a servant to any man in de world, dan to a brack man. If I was sold to a brack man, I'd drown myself. I would dat—I'd drown myself! dough I shouldn't like to do dat nudder; but I wouldn't be sold to a coloured master for anyting."

If he had got to be sold, he would like best to have an American master buy him. The French people did not clothe their servants well; though now they did much better than when he first came to Louisiana. The French masters were very severe, and "dey whip dar niggers most to deff—dey whip de flesh off of 'em."

Nor did they feed them as well as the Americans. "Why, sometimes, massa, dey only gives 'em dry corn—don't give out no meat at all." I told him this could not be so, for the law required that every master would serve out meat to his negroes. "Oh, but some on 'em don't mind Law, if he does say so, massa. Law never here; don't know anything about him. *Very often*, dey only gives 'em dry corn—I knows dat; I sees de niggers. Didn't you see de niggers on our plantation, sar? Well, you nebber see such a good-looking lot of niggers as ours on any of de French plantations, did you, massa? Why, dey all looks fat, and dey's all got good clothes, and dey look as if dey all had plenty to eat, and hadn't got no work to do, ha! ha! ha! Don't dey? But dey does work, dough. Dey does a heap o' work.

But dey don't work so hard as dey does on some ob de French plantations. Oh, dey does work *too* hard on dem, sometimes."

"You work hard in the grinding season, don't you?"

"O, yes; den we works hard; we has to work hard den: harder dan any oder time of year. But, I tell 'ou, massa, I likes to hab de grinding season come; yes, I does—rader dan any oder time of year, dough we work so hard den. I wish it was grinding season all de year roun'—only Sundays."

"Why?"

"Because—oh, because it's merry and lively. All de brack people like it when we begin to grind."

"You have to keep grinding Sundays?"

"Yes, can't stop, when we begin to grind, till we get tru."

"You don't often work Sundays, except then?"

"No, massa! nebber works Sundays, except when der crap's weedy, and we want to get tru 'fore rain comes; den, wen we work a Sunday, massa gives us some oder day for holiday—Monday, if we get tru."

He said that, on the French plantations, they oftener work Sundays than on the American. They used to work almost always on Sundays, on the French plantations, when he was first brought to Louisiana; but they did not so much now.

We were passing a hamlet of cottages, occupied by Acadians, or what the planters call *habitans*, poor white French Creoles. The negroes had always been represented to me to despise the habitans, and to look upon them as their own inferiors; but William spoke of them respectfully; and, when I tempted him to sneer at their indolence and vagabond habits, refused to do so, but insisted very strenuously that they were "very good people," orderly and industrious. He assured me that I was mistaken in supposing that the Creoles, who did not own slaves, did not live comfortably, or that they did not work as hard as they ought for their living. There were no better sort of people than they were, he thought.

He again recurred to the fortunate condition of the negroes on his master's plantation. He thought it was the best plantation in the State, and he did not believe there was a better lot of negroes in the State; some few of them, whom his master had brought from his former plantation, were old; but altogether, they were "as right good a lot of niggers" as could be found anywhere. They could do all the work that was necessary to be done on the plantation. On some old plantations they had not nearly as many negroes as they needed to make the crop, and they "drove 'em awful hard"; but it wasn't so on his master's: they could do all the work, and do it well, and it was the best worked plantation, and made the most sugar to the hand of any plantation he knew of. All the niggers had enough to eat, and were well clothed; their quarters were good, and they got a good many presents. He was going on enthusiastically, when I asked:

"Well, now, wouldn't you rather live on such a plantation than to be free, William?"

"Oh! no, sir, I'd rather be free! Oh, yes, sir, I'd like it better to be free; I would dat, master."

"Why would you?"

"Why, you see, master, if I was free—if I was *free*, I'd have all my time to myself. I'd rather work for myself. Yes. I'd like dat better."

"But then, you know, you'd have to take care of yourself, and you'd get poor."

"No, sir, I would not get poor, I would get rich; for you see, master, then I'd work all the time for myself."

"Suppose all the black people on your plantation, or all the black people in the country were made free at once, what do you think would become of them?—what would they do, do you think? You don't suppose there would be much sugar raised, do you?"

"Why, yes, master, I do. Why not, sir? What would de brack people do? Wouldn't dey hab to work for dar libben? and de wite people own all de land—war dey goin' to work? Dey hire demself right out again, and work all de same as before. And den, wen dey work for demself, dey work harder dan dey do now to get more wages—a heap harder. I tink so, sir. I would do so, sir. I would work for hire. I don't own any land; I hab to work right away again for massa, to get some money."

Perceiving from the readiness of these answers that the subject had been a familiar one with him, I immediately asked: "The black people talk among themselves about this, do they; and they think so generally?"

"Oh! yes, sir; dey talk so; dat's wat dey tink."

"Then they talk about being free a good deal, do they?"

"Yes, sir. Dey—dat is, dey say dey wish it was so; dat's all dey talk, master—dat's all, sir."

His caution was evidently excited, and I inquired no further. We were passing a large old plantation, the cabins of the negroes upon which were wretched hovels—small, without windows, and dilapidated. A large gang of negroes were at work by the road-side, planting cane. Two white men were sitting on horseback, looking at them, and a negro-driver was walking among them, with a whip in his hand.

William said that this was an old Creole plantation, and the negroes on it were worked very hard. There was three times as much land in it as in his master's, and only about the same number of negroes to work it. I observed, however, that a good deal of land had been left uncultivated the previous year. The slaves appeared to be working hard; they were shabbily clothed, and had a cowed expression, looking on the ground, not even glancing at us, as we passed, and were perfectly silent.

"Dem's all Creole niggers," said William: "ain't no Virginny niggers dah. I reckon you didn't see no such looking niggers as dem on our plantation, did you, master?"

After answering some inquiries about the levee, close inside of which the road continually ran, he asked me about the levee at New York; and when informed that we had not any levee, asked me with a good deal of surprise, how we kept the water out? I explained to him that the land was higher than the water, and was not liable, as it was in Louisiana, to be overflowed. I could not make him understand this. He seemed never to have considered that it was not the natural order of things that land should be lower than water, or that men should be able to live on land, except by excluding water artificially. At length, he said:—

"I s'pose dis heah State is de lowest State dar is in de world. Dar ain't no odder State dat is low so as dis is. I s'pose it is five thousand five hundred feet lower dan any odder State."

"What?"

"I s'pose, master, dat dis heah State is five thousand five hundred feet lower down dan any odder, ain't it, sir?"

"I don't understand you."

"I say dis heah is de lowest ob de States, master. I s'pose it's *five thousand five hundred feet* lower dan any odder; lower *down*, ain't it, master?"

"Yes, it's very low."

This is a good illustration of the child-like quality common in the negroes, and which in him was particularly noticeable, notwithstanding the shrewdness of some of his observations. Such an apparent mingling of simplicity and cunning, ingenuousness and slyness, detracted much from the weight of his opinions and purposes in regard to freedom. I could not but have a strong doubt if he would keep to his word, if the opportunity were allowed him to try his ability to take care of himself.

CHAPTER IX

Cotton-planters. Red River

THE LARGEST part of the cotton crop of the United States is now produced in the Mississippi valley, including the lands contiguous to its great Southern tributary streams, the Red River and others. The proportion of the whole crop which is produced in this region is constantly and very rapidly increasing. This increase is chiefly gained by the forming of new plantations and the transfer of slave-labour westward. The common planter of this region lives very differently to those whose plantations I have hitherto described. What a very different person he is, and what a very different thing his plantation is from the class usually visited by travellers in the South, I learned by an extended experience. I presume myself to have been ordinarily well-informed when I started from home, but up to this point in my first journey had no correct idea of the condition and character of the common cotton-planters. I use the word common in reference to the whole region: there are some small districts in which the common planter is a rich man—really rich. But over the whole district there are comparatively few of these, and in this and the next chapter, I shall show what the many are—as I found them. I shall draw for this purpose upon a record of experience extending through nearly twelve months, but obtained in different journeys and in two different years.

My first observation of the common cotton-planters was had on the steamboat, between Montgomery and Mobile, and has already been described. My second experience among them was on a steamboat bound up Red River.

On a certain Saturday morning, when I had determined upon the trip, I found that two boats, the Swamp Fox and the St. Charles, were advertised to leave the same evening, for the Red River. I went to the levee, and, finding the St. Charles to be the better of the two, I asked her clerk if I could engage a state-room. There was just one state-room berth left unengaged; I was requested to place my name against its number on the passenger-book; and did so, understanding that it was thus secured for me.

Having taken leave of my friends, I had my luggage brought

down, and went on board at half-past three—the boat being advertised to sail at four. Four o'clock passed, and freight was still being taken on—a fire had been made in the furnace, and the boat's big bell was rung. I noticed that the Swamp Fox was also firing up, and that her bell rang whenever ours did—though she was not advertised to sail till five. At length, when five o'clock came, the clerk told me he thought, perhaps, they would not be able to get off at all that night—there was so much freight still to come on board. Six o'clock arrived, and he felt certain that, if they did get off that night, it would not be till very late. At half-past six, he said the captain had not come on board yet, and he was quite sure they would not be able to get off that night. I prepared to return to the hotel, and asked if they would leave in the morning. He thought not. He was confident they would not. He was positive they could not leave now, before Monday—Monday noon. Monday at twelve o'clock—I might rely upon it.

Monday morning, *The Picayune* stated, editorially, that the floating palace, the St. Charles, would leave for Shreveport, at five o'clock, and if anybody wanted to make a quick and luxurious trip up Red River, with a jolly good soul, Captain Lickup was in command. It also stated, in another paragraph, that, if any of its friends had any business up Red River, Captain Pitchup was a whole-souled veteran in that trade, and was going up with that remarkably low-draft favourite, the Swamp Fox, to leave at four o'clock that evening. Both boats were also announced, in the advertising columns, to leave at four o'clock.

As the clerk had said noon, however, I thought there might have been a misprint in the newspaper announcements, and so went on board the St. Charles again before twelve. The clerk informed me that the newspaper was right—they had finally concluded not to sail till four o'clock. Before four, I returned again, and the boat again fired up, and rang her bell. So did the Swamp Fox. Neither, however, was quite ready to leave at four o'clock. Not quite ready at five. Even at six—not yet quite ready. At seven, the fires having burned out in the furnace, and the stevedores having gone away, leaving a quantity of freight yet on the dock, without advising this time with the clerk, I had my baggage re-transferred to the hotel.

A similar performance was repeated on Tuesday.

On Wednesday, I found the berth I had engaged occupied by a

very strong man, who was not very polite, when I informed him
that I believed there was some mistake—that the berth he was using
had been engaged to me. I went to the clerk, who said that he was
sorry, but that, as I had not stayed on board at night, and had not
paid for the berth, he had not been sure that I should go, and he
had, therefore, given it to the gentleman who now had it in possession, and whom, he thought, it would not be best to try to reason
out of it. He was very busy, he observed, because the boat was going to start at four o'clock; if I would now pay him the price of passage, he would do the best he could for me. When he had time to examine, he could probably put me in some other state-room, perhaps
quite as good a one as that I had lost. Meanwhile he kindly offered
me the temporary use of his private state-room. I inquired if it was
quite certain that the boat would get off at four; for I had been
asked to dine with a friend, at three o'clock. There was not the
smallest doubt of it—at four they would leave. They were all ready,
at that moment, and only waited till four, because the agent had
advertised that they would—merely a technical point of honour.

But, by some error of calculation, I suppose, she didn't go at four.
Nor at five. Nor at six.

At seven o'clock, the Swamp Fox and the St. Charles were both
discharging dense smoke from their chimneys, blowing steam, and
ringing bells. It was obvious that each was making every exertion
to get off before the other. The captains of both boats stood at the
break of the hurricane deck, apparently waiting in great impatience
for the mails to come on board.

The St. Charles was crowded with passengers, and her decks
were piled high with freight. Bumboatmen, about the bows, were
offering shells, and oranges, and bananas; and newsboys, and peddlers, and tract distributors, were squeezing about with their wares
among the passengers. I had confidence in their instinct; there had
been no such numbers of them the previous evenings, and I made
up my mind, although past seven o'clock, that the St. Charles would
not let her fires go down again.

Among the peddlers there were two of "cheap literature," and
among their yellow covers, each had two or three copies of the
cheap edition (pamphlet) of "Uncle Tom's Cabin." They did not
cry it out as they did the other books they had, but held it forth
among others, so its title could be seen. One of them told me he

carried it because gentlemen often inquired for it, and he sold a good many; at least three copies were sold to passengers on the boat. Another young man, who looked like a beneficiary of the Education Society, endeavouring to pass a college vacation in a useful and profitable manner, was peddling a Bible Defence of Slavery, which he made eloquent appeals, in the manner of a pastoral visit, to us, each personally, to purchase. He said it was prepared by a clergyman of Kentucky, and every slaveholder ought to possess it. When he came to me, I told him that I owned no slaves, and therefore had no occasion for it. He answered that the world was before me, and I perhaps yet might own many of them. I replied so decidedly that I should not, that he appeared to be satisfied that my conscience would not need the book, and turned back again to a man sitting beside me, who had before refused to look at it. He now urged again that he should do so, and forced it into his hands, open at the title-page, on which was a vignette, representing a circle of coloured gentleman and ladies, sitting around a fire-place with a white person standing behind them, like a servant, reading from a book. "Here we see the African race as it is in America, under the blessed—"

"Now you go to hell! I've told you three times I didn't want your book. If you bring it here again I'll throw it overboard. I own niggers; and I calculate to own more of 'em, if I can get 'em, but I don't want any damn'd preachin' about it."

That was the last I saw of the book-peddler.

It was twenty minutes after seven when the captain observed—scanning the levee in every direction, to see if there was another cart or carriage coming towards us—"No use waiting any longer, I reckon: throw off, Mr. Heady." (The Swamp Fox did not leave, I afterwards heard, till the following Saturday.)

We backed out, winded round head up, and as we began to breast the current a dozen of the negro boat-hands, standing on the freight, piled up on the low forecastle, began to sing, waving hats and handkerchiefs, and shirts lashed to poles, towards the people who stood on the sterns of the steamboats at the levee. After losing a few lines, I copied literally into my note-book:

Ye see dem boat way dah ahead.
CHORUS.—*Oahoiohieu.*

De San Charles is arter 'em, dey mus go behine.
    CHO.—*Oahoiohieu.*
So stir up dah, my livelies, stir her up; (pointing to the furnaces).
    CHO.—*Oahoiohieu.*
Dey's burnin' not'n but fat and rosum.
    CHO.—*Oahoiohieu.*
Oh, we is gwine up de Red River, oh!
    CHO.—*Oahoiohieu.*
Oh, we mus part from you dah asho'.
    CHO.—*Oahoiohieu.*
Give my lub to Dinah, oh!
    CHO.—*Oahoiohieu.*
For we is gwine up de Red River.
    CHO.—*Oahoiohieu.*
Yes, we is gwine up de Red River.
    CHO.—*Oahoiohieu.*
Oh, we must part from you dah, oh.
    CHO.—*Oahoiohieu.*

The wit introduced into these songs has, I suspect, been rather over estimated.

As soon as the song was ended, I went into the cabin to remind the clerk to obtain a berth for me. I found two brilliant supper-tables reaching the whole length of the long cabin, and a file of men standing on each side of both of them, ready to take seats as soon as the signal was given.

The clerk was in his room, with two other men, and appeared to be more occupied than ever. His manner was, I thought, now rather cool, not to say rude; and he very distinctly informed me that every berth was occupied, and he didn't know where I was to sleep. He judged I was able to take care of myself; and if I was not, he was quite sure that he had too much to do to give all his time to my surveillance. I then went to the commander, and told him that I thought myself entitled to a berth. I had paid for one, and should not have taken passage in the boat, if it had not been promised me. I was not disposed to fight for it, particularly as the gentleman occupying the berth engaged to me was a deal bigger fellow than I, and also carried a bigger knife; but I thought the clerk was accountable to me for a berth, and I begged that he would inform him so. He replied that the clerk probably knew his business; he had nothing to do with it; and walked away from me. I then addressed myself to a second clerk, or sub-officer of some denomination, who more good-naturedly informed me that half the company were in the same condition as myself, and I needn't be alarmed, cots would be provided for us.

As I saw that the supper-table was likely to be crowded, I asked if there would be a second table. "Yes, they'll keep on eatin' till they all get through." I walked the deck till I saw those who had been first seated at the table coming out; then going in, I found the table still crowded, while many stood waiting to take seats as fast as any were vacated. I obtained one for myself at length, and had no sooner occupied it than two half-intoxicated and garrulous men took the adjoining stools.

It was near nine o'clock before the tables were cleared away, and immediately afterwards the waiters began to rig a framework for sleeping-cots in their place. These cots were simply canvas shelves, five feet and a half long, two wide, and less than two feet apart, perpendicularly. A waiter, whose good will I had purchased at the supper-table, gave me a hint to secure one of them for myself, as soon as they were erected, by putting my hat in it. I did so, and saw that others did the same. I chose a cot as near as possible to the midship doors of the cabin, perceiving that there was not likely to be the best possible air, after all the passengers were laid up for the night, in this compact manner.

Nearly as fast as the cots were ready they were occupied. To make sure that mine was not stolen from me, I also, without much undressing, laid myself away. A single blanket was the only bed-clothing provided. I had not lain long, before I was driven, by an exceedingly offensive smell, to search for a cleaner neighbourhood; but I found all the cots, fore and aft, were either occupied or engaged. I immediately returned, and that I might have a *dernier ressort*, left my shawl in that I had first obtained.

In the forward part of the cabin there was a bar, a stove, a table, and a placard of rules, forbidding smoking, gambling, and swearing in the cabin, and a close company of drinkers, smokers, card-players, and constant swearers. I went out, and stepped down to the boiler-deck. The boat had been provided with very poor wood, and the firemen were crowding it into the furnaces whenever they could find room for it, driving smaller sticks between the larger ones at the top, by a battering-ram method.

Most of the firemen were Irish born; one with whom I conversed was English. He said they were divided into three watches, each working four hours at a time, and all hands liable to be called, when wooding, or landing, or taking on freight, to assist the deck hands. They were paid now but thirty dollars a month—ordinarily forty, and sometimes sixty—and board. He was a sailor bred. This boat-life was harder than seafaring, but the pay was better, and the trips were short. The regular thing was to make two trips, and then lay up for a spree. It would be too hard upon a man, he thought, to pursue it regularly; two trips "on end" was as much as a man could stand. He must then take a "refreshment." Working this way for three weeks, and then refreshing for about one, he did not think it was unhealthy, no more so than ordinary seafaring. He concluded, by informing me that the most striking peculiarity of the business was, that it kept a man, notwithstanding wholesale periodical refreshment, very dry. He was of opinion that after the information I had obtained, if I gave him at least the price of a single drink, and some tobacco, it would be characteristic of a gentleman.

Going round behind the furnace, I found a large quantity of freight: hogsheads, barrels, cases, bales, boxes, nail-rods, rolls of leather, ploughs, cotton, bale-rope, and fire-wood, all thrown together in the most confused manner, with hot steam-pipes, and parts of the engine crossing through it. As I explored further aft, I found negroes lying asleep, in all postures, upon the freight. A single group only, of five or six, appeared to be awake, and as I drew near they commenced to sing a Methodist hymn, not loudly, as negroes generally do, but, as it seemed to me, with a good deal of tenderness and feeling; a few white people—men, women, and children—were lying here and there, among the negroes. Altogether, I learned we had two hundred of these deck passengers, black and white. A stove, by which they could fry bacon, was the only furniture provided for them by the boat. They carried with them their provisions for the voyage, and had their choice of the freight for beds.

As I came to the bows again, and was about to ascend to the cabin, two men came down, one of whom I recognized to have been my cot neighbour. "Where's a bucket?" said he. "By thunder! this fellow was so strong I could not sleep by him, so I stumped him to come down and wash his feet." "I am much obliged to you," said I;

and I was, very much; the man had been lying in the cot beneath mine, to which I now returned and soon fell asleep.

I awoke about midnight. There was an unusual jar in the boat, and an evident excitement among people whom I could hear talking on deck. I rolled out of my cot, and stepped out on the gallery. The steamboat Kimball was running head-and-head with us, and so close that one might have jumped easily from our paddle-box on to her guards. A few other passengers had turned out beside myself, and most of the waiters were leaning on the rail of the gallery. Occasionally a few words of banter passed between them and the waiters of the Kimball; below, the firemen were shouting as they crowded the furnaces, and some one could be heard cheering them: "Shove her up, boys! Shove her up! Give her hell!" "She's got to hold a conversation with us before she gets by, anyhow," said one of the negroes. "Ye har that ar' whistlin'?" said a white man; "tell ye thar an't any too much water in her bilers when ye har that." I laughed silently, but was not without a slight expectant sensation, which Burke would perhaps have called sublime. At length the Kimball slowly drew ahead, crossed our bow, and the contest was given up. "De ole lady too heavy," said a waiter; "if I could pitch a few ton of dat ar freight off her bow, I'd bet de Kimball would be askin' her to show de way mighty quick."

At half-past four o'clock a hand-bell was rung in the cabin, and soon afterwards I was informed that I must get up, that the servants might remove the cot arrangement, and clear the cabin for the breakfast-table.

Breakfast was not ready till half-past seven. The passengers, one set after another, and then the pilots, clerks, mates, and engineers, and then the free coloured people, and then the waiters, chambermaids, and passengers' body servants, having breakfasted, the tables were cleared, and the cabin swept. The tables were then again laid for dinner. Thus the greater part of the cabin was constantly occupied, and the passengers who had no state-rooms were driven to herd in the vicinity of the card-tables and the bar, the lobby (Social Hall, I believe it is called), in which most of the passengers' baggage was deposited, or to go outside. Every part of the boat, except the bleak hurricane deck, was crowded; and so large a number of equally uncomfortable and disagreeable people I think I never saw elsewhere together. We made very slow progress, landing, it seems to me, after we entered Red River, at every "bend," "bottom," "bayou," "point," and "plantation" that came in sight; often for no other object than to roll out a barrel of flour, or a keg of nails; sometimes merely to furnish newspapers to a wealthy planter, who had much cotton to send to market, and whom it was therefore desirable to please.

I was sitting one day on the forward gallery, watching a pair of ducks, that were alternately floating on the river, and flying further ahead as the steamer approached them. A man standing near me drew a long barrelled and very finely-finished pistol from his coat pocket, and, resting it against a stanchion, took aim at them. They were, I judged, full the boat's own length—not less than two hundred feet—from us, and were just raising their wings to fly, when he fired. One of them only rose; the other flapped round and round, and when within ten yards of the boat, dived. The bullet had broken its wing. So remarkable a shot excited, of course, not a little admiration and conversation. Half a dozen other men standing near at once drew pistols or revolvers from under their clothing, and several were fired at floating chips, or objects on the shore. I saw no more remarkable shooting, however; and that the duck should have been hit at such a distance, was generally considered a piece of luck. A man who had been "in the Rangers" said that all his company could put a ball into a tree, the size of a man's body, at sixty paces, at every shot, with Colt's army revolver, not taking steady aim, but firing at the jerk of the arm.

This pistol episode was almost the only entertainment in which the passengers engaged themselves, except eating, drinking, smoking, conversation, and card-playing. Gambling was constantly going on, day and night. I don't think there was an interruption to it of fifteen minutes in three days. The conversation was almost exclusively confined to the topics of steamboats, liquors, cards, blackland, red-land, bottom-land, timber-land, warrants, and locations, sugar, cotton, corn, and negroes.

After the first night, I preferred to sleep on the trunks in the social hall, rather than among the cots in the crowded cabin, and several others did the same. There were, in fact, not cots enough for all the passengers excluded from the state-rooms. I found that some, and I presume most of the passengers, by making the clerk believe that they would otherwise take the Swamp Fox, had obtained their passage at considerably less price than I had paid.

On the third day, just after the dinner-bell had rung, and most of the passengers had gone into the cabin, I was sitting alone on the gallery, reading a pamphlet, when a well-dressed middle-aged man accosted me.

"Is that the book they call Uncle Tom's Cabin, you are reading, sir?"

"No, sir."

"I did not know but it was; I see that there are two or three gentlemen on board that have got it. I suppose I might have got it in New Orleans: I wish I had. Have you ever seen it, sir?"

"Yes, sir."

"I'm told it shows up Slavery in very high colours."

"Yes, sir, it shows the evils of Slavery very strongly."

He took a chair near me, and said that, if it represented extreme cases as if they were general, it was not fair.

Perceiving that he was disposed to discuss the matter, I said that I was a Northern man, and perhaps not well able to judge; but that I thought that a certain degree of cruelty was necessary to make slave-labour generally profitable, and that not many were disposed to be more severe than they thought necessary. I believed there was little wanton cruelty. He answered, that Northern men were much mistaken in supposing that slaves were generally ill-treated. He was a merchant, but he owned a plantation, and he just wished I could see his negroes. "Why, sir," he continued, "my niggers' children all go regularly to a Sunday-school, just the same as my own, and learn verses, and catechism, and hymns. Every one of my grown-up niggers are pious, every one of them, and members of the church. I've got an old man that can pray—well, sir, I only wish I had as good a gift at praying! I wish you could just hear him pray. There are cases in which niggers are badly used; but they are not common. There are brutes everywhere. You have men, at the North, who whip their wives—and they kill them sometimes."

"Certainly, we have, sir; there are plenty of brutes at the North; but our law, you must remember, does not compel women to submit themselves to their power. A wife, cruelly treated, can escape from her husband, and can compel him to give her subsistence, and to cease from doing her harm. A woman could defend herself against her husband's cruelty, and the law would sustain her."

"It would not be safe to receive negroes' testimony against white people; they would be always plotting against their masters, if you did."

"Wives are not always plotting against their husbands."

"Husband and wife is a very different thing from master and slave."

"Your remark, that a bad man might whip his wife, suggested an analogy, sir."

"If the law was to forbid whipping altogether, the authority of the master would be at an end."

"And if you allow bad men to own slaves, and allow them to whip them, and deny the slave the privilege of resisting cruelty, do you not show that you think it is necessary to permit cruelty, in order to sustain the authority of masters, in general, over their slaves? That is, you establish cruelty as a necessity of Slavery—do you not?"

"No more than of marriage, because men may whip their wives cruelly."

"Excuse me, sir; the law does all it can, to prevent such cruelty between husband and wife; between master and slave it does not, because it cannot, without weakening the necessary authority of the master—that is, without destroying Slavery. It is, therefore, a fair argument against Slavery, to show how cruelly this necessity, of sustaining the authority of cruel and passionate men over their slaves, sometimes operates."

He asked what it was Uncle Tom "tried to make out."

I narrated the Red River episode, and asked if such things could not possibly occur.

"Yes," replied he, "but very rarely. I don't know a man, in my parish, that could do such a thing. There are two men, though, in ——, bad enough to do it, I believe; but it isn't a likely story, at all. In the first place, no coloured woman would be likely to offer any resistance, if a white man should want to seduce her."

After further conversation, he said, that a planter had been tried for injuring one of his negroes, at the court in his parish, the preceding summer. He had had a favourite, among his girls, and suspecting that she was unduly kind to one of his men, in an anger of jealousy he mutilated him. There was not sufficient testimony to convict him; "but," he said, "everybody believes he was guilty, and ought to have been punished. Nobody thinks there was any good reason for his being jealous of the boy."

I remarked that this story corroborated "Uncle Tom's Cabin"; it showed that it was all possible.

"Ah!" he answered, "but then nobody would have any respect for a man that treated his niggers cruelly."

I wondered, as I went in to dinner, and glanced at the long rows of surly faces, how many men there were there whose passions would be much restrained by the fear of losing the respect of their neighbours.[1]

My original purpose had been to go high up Red River at this time, but the long delay in the boat's leaving New Orleans, and her slow passage, obliged me to change my plans. The following year, I returned, in company with my brother, as narrated in "The Texas Journey." Some portion of what follows is taken from that volume.

At a place called Alexandria, our progress was arrested by falls in the river which cannot be passed by boats at low stages of the water. The village is every bit a Southern one—all the houses being one story in height, and having an open verandah before them, like the English towns in the West Indies. It contains, usually, about 1,000 inhabitants, but this summer had been entirely depopulated by the yellow fever. Of 300 who remained, 120, we were told, died. Most of the runaway citizens had returned, when we passed, though the last case of fever was still in uncertain progress.

It has apparently not the best reputation for morality. At Natchitoches, the next village above on the river, a couple of men were waiting for their breakfast at the inn, when one, who looked and spoke more like a New Englander than a Southerner, said to the other, whom I presumed to be an Alexandrian—possibly Elder Slocum himself:—

"I had a high old dream, last night."

"What was it?"

"Dreamt I was in hell."

[1] John Randolph, of Roanoke, himself a slaveholder, once said, on the floor of Congress (touching the internal slave-trade): "What are the trophies of this infernal traffic? The handcuff, the manacles, the blood-stained cowhide. *What man is worse received in society for being a hard master? Who denies the hand of sister or daughter to such monsters?*"

"Rough country?"

"Boggy—sulphur bogs. By and by I cum to a great pair of doors. Something kinder drew me right to 'em, and I had to open 'em, and go in. As soon as I got in, the doors slammed to, behind me, and there I see old boss devil lying asleep, on a red-hot sofy. He woke up, and rubbed his eyes, and when he see me, he says, 'Halloo! that you?' 'Yes, sir,' says I. 'Where'd you come from?' says he. 'From Alexandria, sir,' says I. 'Thought so,' says he, and he took down a big book, and wrote something in to't with a red-hot spike. 'Well, sir, what's going on now in Alexandria?' says he. 'Having a "protracted meeting" there, sir,' says I. 'Look here, my friend,' says he, 'you may stop lyin', now you've got here.' 'I aint lyin', sir,' says I. 'Oh!' says he, 'I beg your pardon; I thought it was Alexandria on Red River, you meant.' 'So it was,' says I, 'and they are having a protracted meeting there, sure as you're alive.' 'Hell they are!' says he, jumpin' right up; 'boy, bring my boots!' A little black devil fetched him a pair of hot brass boots, and he began to draw 'em on. 'Whose doin' is that?' says he. 'Elder Slocum's, sir,' says I. 'Elder Slocum's! Why in hell couldn't you have said so, before?' says he. 'Here, boy, take away these boots'; and he kicked 'em off, and laid down again."

French blood rather predominates in the population in the vicinity of Natchitoches, but there is also a considerable amount of the Spanish and Indian mongrel breed. These are often handsome people, but vagabonds, almost to a man. Scarcely any of them have any regular occupation, unless it be that of herding cattle; but they raise a little maize, and fish a little, and hunt a little, and smoke and lounge a great deal, and are very regular in their attendance on divine worship, at the cathedral.

In the public bar-room I heard a person, who I suppose would claim the appellation of a gentleman, narrating how he had overreached a political opponent, in securing the "Spanish vote" at an election, and it appeared from the conversation that it was considered entirely, and as a matter of course, purchasable by the highest bidder. A man who would purchase votes at the North, would, at least, be careful not to mention it so publicly.

We spent several days in Natchitoches, purchasing horses and completing the preparations for our vagrant life in Texas.

One mild day of our stay we made a trip of some ten or fifteen miles out and back, at the invitation of a planter, whose acquaintance we had made at the hotel. We started in good season, but were not long in losing our way and getting upon obscure roads through the woods. The planter's residence we did not find, but one day's experience is worth a note.

We rode on from ten o'clock till three, without seeing a house, except a deserted cabin, or meeting a human being. We then came upon a ferry across a small stream or "bayou," near which was a collection of cabins. We asked the old negro who tended the ferry if we could get something to eat anywhere in the neighbourhood. He replied that his master sometimes took in travellers, and we had better call and try if the mistress wouldn't let us have some dinner.

The house was a small square log cabin, with a broad open shed or piazza in front, and a chimney, made of sticks and mud, leaning against one end. A smaller detached cabin, twenty feet in the rear, was used for a kitchen. A cistern under a roof, and collecting water from three roofs, stood between. The water from the bayou was not fit to drink, nor is the water of the Red River, or of any springs in this region. The people depend entirely on cisterns for drinking water. It is very little white folks need, however—milk, whisky, and, with the better class, Bordeaux wine, being the more common beverages.

About the house was a large yard, in which were two or three China trees, and two fine Cherokee roses; half a dozen hounds; several negro babies; turkeys and chickens, and a pet sow, teaching a fine litter of pigs how to root and wallow. Three hundred yards from the house was a gin-house and stable, and in the interval between were two rows of comfortable negro cabins. Between the house and the cabins was a large post, on which was a bell to call the negroes. A rack for fastening horses stood near it. On the bell-post and on each of the rack-posts were nailed the antlers of a buck, as well as on a large oak-tree near by. On the logs of the kitchen a fresh deer-skin was drying. On the railing of the piazza lay a saddle. The house had but one door and no window, nor was there a pane of glass on the plantation.

Entering the house, we found it to contain but a single room, about twenty feet by sixteen. Of this space one quarter was occupied by a bed—a great four-poster, with the curtains open, made up in the French style, with a strong furniture-calico day-coverlid.

A smaller camp bed stood beside it. These two articles of furniture nearly filled the house on one side the door. At the other end was a great log fire-place, with a fine fire. The outer door was left constantly open to admit the light. On one side the fire, next the door, was a table; a kind of dresser, with crockery, and a bureau stood on the other side, and there were two deer-skin seated chairs and one (Connecticut made) rocking chair.

A bold-faced, but otherwise good-enough-looking woman of a youngish middle age, was ironing a shirt on the table. We stated our circumstances, and asked if we could get some dinner from her. She reckoned we could, she said, if we'd wait till she was done ironing. So we waited, taking seats by the fire, and examining the literature and knick-knacks on the mantel-piece. These consisted of three Natchitoches *Chronicles*, a Patent Office Agricultural Report, "Christie's Galvanic Almanac," a Bible, "The Pirate of the Gulf," a powder-horn, the sheath of a bowie-knife, a whip-lash, and a tobacco-pipe.

Three of the hounds, a negro child, and a white child, had followed us to the door of the cabin, three chickens had entered before us, a cat and kittens were asleep in the corner of the fire-place. By the time we had finished reading the queer advertisements in French of runaway negroes in the *Chronicle* two of the hounds and the black child had retired, and a tan-coloured hound, very lean, and badly crippled in one leg, had entered and stood asking permission with his tail to come to the fire-place. The white child, a frowzy girl of ten, came toward us. I turned and asked her name. She knitted her brows, but made no verbal reply. I turned my chair towards her, and asked her to come to me. She hung her head for an instant, then turned, ran to the hound and struck him a hard blow in the chops. The hound quailed. She struck him again, and he turned half around; then she began with her feet, and kicked him out, taking herself after him.

At length the woman finished her ironing, and went to the kitchen, whence quickly returning, she placed upon the table a plate of cold, salt, fat pork; a cup of what to both eye and tongue seemed lard, but which she termed butter; a plate of very stale, dry, flaky, micaceous corn-bread; a jug of molasses, and a pitcher of milk.

"Well, now it's ready, if you'll eat it," she said, turning to us.

"Best we've got. Sit up. Take some pone"; and she sat down in the rocker at one end of the table. We took seats at the other end.

"Jupiter! what's the matter with this child?" A little white child that had crawled up into the gallery, and now to my side—flushed face, and wheezing like a high-pressure steamboat.

"Got the croup, I reckon," answered the woman. "Take some 'lasses."

The child crawled into the room. With the aid of a hand it stood up and walked round to its mother.

"How long has it been going on that way?" asked we.

"Well, it's been going on some days, now, and keeps getting worse. 'Twas right bad last night, in the night. Reckoned I should lose it, one spell. Take some butter."

We were quite faint with hunger when we rode up, but didn't eat much of the corn-cake and pork. The woman and the high-pressure child sat still and watched us, and we sat still and did our best, making much of the milk.

"Have you had a physician to see that child?" asked my brother, drawing back his chair.

She had not.

"Will you come to me, my dear?"

The child came to him, he felt its pulse and patted its hot forehead, looked down its throat, and leaned his ear on its chest.

"Are you a doctor, sir?"

"Yes, madam."

"Got some fever, hasn't it?"

"Yes."

"Not nigh so much as't had last night."

"Have you done anything for it?"

"Well, thar was a gentleman here; he told me sweet ile and sugar would be good for't, and I gave it a good deal of that: made it sick, it did. I thought, perhaps, that would do it good."

"Yes. You have had something like this in your family before, haven't you? You don't seem much alarmed."

"Oh yes, sir; that ar one" (pointing to the frowzy girl, whose name was Angelina) "had it two or three times—onst most as bad as this. All my children have had it. Is she bad, doctor?"

"Yes. I should say this was a very serious thing."

"Have you any medicine in the house?" he asked, after the woman had returned from a journey to the kitchen. She opened a drawer of the bureau, half full of patent medicines and some common drugs. "There's a whole heap o' truck in thar. I don't know what it all is. Whatever you want just help yourself. I can't read writin'; you must pick it out."

Such as were available were taken out and given to the mother, with directions about administering them, which she promised to obey. "But the first and most important thing for you to do is to shut the door, and make up the fire, and put the child to bed, and try to keep this wind off her."

"Lord! sir, you can't keep *her* in bed—she's too wild."

"Well, you must put some more clothes on her. Wrap her up, and try to keep her warm. The very best thing you can do for her is to give her a warm bath. Have you not got a washing tub?"

"Oh! yes, sir, I can do that. She'll go to bed pretty early; she's used to going 'tween sundown and dark."

"Well, give her the warm bath, then, and if she gets worse send for a physician immediately. You must be very careful of her, madam."

We walked to the stable, and as the horses had not finished eating their corn, I lounged about the quarters, and talked with the negro.

There was not a single soul in the quarters or in sight of the house except ourselves, the woman and her children, and the old negro. The negro women must have taken their sucklings with them, if they had any, to the field where they were at work.

The old man said they had "ten or eleven field-hands, such as they was," and his master would sell sixty to seventy bags of cotton: besides which they made all the corn and pork they wanted, and something over, and raised some cattle.

We found our way back to the town only late in the evening. We had ridden most of the day over heavily-timbered, nearly flat, rich bottom land. It is of very great fertility; but, being subject to overflow, is not very attractive, in spite of its proximity to a market.

But it must be remembered that they were having the first use of a very fine alluvial soil, and were subject to floods and fevers. The yellow fever or cholera another year might kill half their negroes, or a flood of the Red River (such as occurred August, 1849, and October, 1851) destroy their whole crop, and so use up several years' profits.

A slate hung in the piazza, with the names of all the cotton-pickers, and the quantity picked the last picking day by each, thus: Gorge, 152; David, 130; Polly, 98; Hanna, 96; Little Gorge, 52, etc. The whole number of hands noted was fourteen. Probably there were over twenty slaves, big and little, on the plantation.

When our horses were ready, we paid the negro for taking care of them, and I went in and asked the woman what I might pay her.

"What!" she asked, looking in my face as if angry.

I feared she was offended by my offering money for her hospitality, and put the question again as delicately as I could. She continued her sullen gaze at me for a moment, and then answered as if the words had been bullied out of her by a Tombs lawyer—

"Dollar, I reckon."

"What!" thought I, but handed her the silver.

Riding out at the bars let down for us by the old negro, we wondered if the child would be living twenty-four hours later, and if it survived, what its moral chances were. Poor, we thought. Five miles from a neighbour; ten, probably, from a Louisiana [2] school; hound-pups and negroes for playmates.

On the Emigrant Road into Texas.—Five minutes' ride took us deep into the pines. Natchitoches, and with it all the tumult and bother of social civilization, had disappeared. Under the pines and beyond them was a new, calm, free life, upon which we entered with a glow of enthusiasm, which, however, hardly sufficed to light up a whole day of pine shadows, and many times afterwards glimmered very dull over days on days of cold corn-bread and cheerless winter prairies.

For two days, we rode through these pines over a sandy surface, having little rise and fall, watered here and there by small creeks and ponds, within reach of whose overflow, present or past, stand deciduous trees, such as, principally, oaks and cotton-woods, in a firmer and richer soil. Wherever the road crosses or approaches these spots, there is or has been, usually, a plantation.

The road could hardly be called a road. It was only a way where people had passed along before. Each man had taken such a path

[2] The State Superintendent lately recommended that two out of three of the Directors of Common Schools in Louisiana should be required to know how to read and write; and mentioned that in one parish, instead of the signature the mark of twelve different directors was affixed to a teacher's certificate.

as suited him, turning aside to avoid, on high ground, the sand; on low ground, the mud. We chose, generally, the untrodden elastic pavement of pine leaves, at a little distance from the main track.

We overtook, several times in the course of each day, the slow emigrant trains, for which this road, though less frequented than years ago, is still a chief thoroughfare. Inexorable destiny it seems that drags or drives on, always Westward, these toilworn people. Several families were frequently moving together, coming from the same district, or chance met and joined, for company, on the long road from Alabama, Georgia, or the Carolinas. Before you come upon them you hear, ringing through the woods, the fierce cries and blows with which they urge on their jaded cattle. Then the stragglers appear, lean dogs or fainting negroes, ragged and spirit-less. An old granny, hauling on, by the hand, a weak boy—too old to ride and too young to keep up. An old man, heavily loaded, with a rifle. Then the white covers of the waggons, jerking up and down as they mount over a root or plunge into a rut, disappearing, one after another, where the road descends. Then the active and cheery prime negroes, not yet exhausted, with a joke and a suggestion about tobacco. Then the black pickaninnies, staring, in a confused heap, out at the back of the waggon, more and more of their eyes to be made out among the table legs and bedding, as you get near; behind them, further in, the old people and young mothers, whose turn it is to ride. As you get by, the white mother and babies, and the tall, frequently ill-humoured master, on horseback, or walking with his gun, urging up the black driver and his oxen. As a scout ahead, is a brother, or an intelligent slave, with the best gun, on the look-out for a deer or a turkey. We passed in the day perhaps one hundred persons attached to these trains, probably an unusual number; but the immigration this year had been retarded and con-densed by the fear of yellow fever, the last case of which, at Natchitoches, had indeed begun only the night before our arrival. Our chances of danger were considered small, however, as the hard frosts had already come. One of these trains was made up of three large waggons, loaded with furniture, babies, and invalids, two or three light waggons, and a gang of twenty able field-hands. They travel ten or fifteen miles a day, stopping wherever night over-takes them. The masters are plainly dressed, often in home-spun, keeping their eyes about them, noticing the soil, sometimes making a remark on the crops by the roadside; but generally dogged, surly, and silent. The women are silent too, frequently walking, to relieve the teams; and weary, haggard, mud be-draggled, forlorn, and disconsolate, yet hopeful and careful. The negroes, mud-incrusted, wrapped in old blankets or gunny-bags, suffering from cold, plod on, aimless, hopeless, thoughtless, more indifferent, apparently, than the oxen, to all about them.

We met, in course of the day, numerous cotton waggons, two or three sometimes together, drawn by three or four pairs of mules or oxen, going slowly on toward Natchitoches or Grand Ecore, each managed by its negro-driver. The load is commonly five bales (of 400 lbs. each), and the cotton comes in this tedious way, over execrable roads, distances of 100 and even 150 miles. It is usually hauled from the eastern tier of Texan counties to the Sabine; but this year there had been no rise of water in the rivers, and from all this region it must be carried to Red River. The distance from the Sabine is here about fifty miles, and the cost of this transportation about one cent a pound; the freight from Grand Ecore to New Orleans from one to one and a quarter cents. If hauled 150 miles in this way, as we were told, the profit remaining, after paying the charges of transportation and commission, all amounting to about five cents, must be exceedingly small in ordinary years.

At night we met three or four of these teams half-mired in a swamp, distant some quarter of a mile one from another, and cheering themselves in the dark with prolonged and musical "Yohoi's," sent ringing through the woods. We got through this with considerable perplexity ourselves, and were very glad to see the light of the cabin where we had been recommended to stop.

This was "Mrs. Stokers'," about half way to the Sabine. We were received cordially, every house here expecting to do inn-duty, but were allowed to strip and take care of our own horses, the people by no means expecting to do landlord's duty, but taking guests on sufferance. The house was a double log cabin—two log erections, that is, joined by one long roof, leaving an open space between. A gallery, extending across the whole front, serves for a pleasant sitting-room in summer, and for a toilet-room at all seasons. A bright fire was very welcome. Supper, consisting of pork, fresh and salt, cold corn-bread, and boiled sweet potatoes, was served in a little lean-to behind the house. After disposing of this we were shown to our room, the other cabin, where we whiled away our evening, studying, by the light of the great fire, a book of bear stories, and conversing with the young man of the family, and a third guest. The room was open to the rafters, and had been built up only as high as the top of the door upon the gallery side, leaving a huge open triangle to the roof, through which the wind rushed at us with a fierce swoop, both while we were sitting at the fire and after we retreated to bed. Owing to this we slept little, and having had a salt supper, lay very thirsty upon the deep feather bed. About four o'clock an old negro came in to light the fire. Asking him for water, we heard him breaking the ice for it outside. When we washed in the piazza the water was thick with frost, crusty, and half inclined not to be used as a fluid at all.

After a breakfast, similar in all respects to the supper, we saddled and rode on again. The horses had had a dozen ears of corn, night and morning, with an allowance of fodder (maize leaves). For this the charge was $1.25 each person. This is a fair sample of roadside stopping-places in Western Louisiana and Texas. The meals are absolutely invariable, save that fresh pork and sweet potatoes are frequently wanting. There is always, too, the black decoction of the South called coffee, than which it is often difficult to imagine any beverage more revolting. The bread is made of corn-meal, stirred with water and salt, and baked in a kettle covered with coals. The corn for breakfast is frequently unhusked at sunrise. A negro, whose business it is, shells and grinds it in a hand-mill for the cook. Should there be any of the loaf left after breakfast, it is given to the traveller, if he wish it, with a bit of pork, for a noon-"snack," with no further charge. He is conscious, though, in that case, that he is robbing the hounds, always eagerly waiting, and should none remain, none can be had without a new resort to the crib. Wheat bread, if I am not mistaken, we met with but twice, out of Austin, in our whole journey across the State.

The country was very similar to that passed over the day before, with perhaps rather more of the cultivable loam. A good part of the land had, at some time, been cleared, but much was already turned over to the "old-field pines," some of them even fifteen years or more. In fact, a larger area had been abandoned, we thought, than remained under cultivation. With the land, many cabins have, of course, also been deserted, giving the road a desolate air. If you ask, where are the people that once occupied these, the universal reply is, "Gone to Texas."

The plantations occur, perhaps, at an average distance of three or four miles. Most of the remaining inhabitants live chiefly, to appearances, by fleecing emigrants. Every shanty sells spirits, and takes in travellers. We passed through but one village, which consisted of six dwellings. The families obtained their livelihood by the following occupations: one by shoeing the horses of emigrants; one by repairing the wheels of their waggons; one by selling them groceries. The smallest cabin contained a physician. It was not larger than a good-sized medicine chest, but had the biggest sign. The others advertised "corn and fodder." The prices charged for any article sold, or service performed, were enormous; full one hundred per cent. over those of New Orleans.

We met Spaniards once or twice on the road, and the population of this district is thought to be one half of Spanish origin. They have no houses on the road, however, but live in little hamlets in the forest, or in cabins contiguous to each other, about a pond. They make no progress in acquiring capital of their own, but engage in hunting and fishing, or in herding cattle for larger proprietors of the land. For this business they seem to have an hereditary adaptation, far excelling negroes of equal experience.

The number of cattle raised here is now comparatively small, most of the old herd proprietors having moved on to pastures new in Western Texas. The cane, which is a natural growth of most good soils at the South, is killed if closely fed upon. The blue-joint grass (not the blue-grass of Kentucky) takes its place, and is also indigenous upon a poorer class of soils in this region. This is also good food for cattle, but is killed in turn if closely pastured. The ground then becomes bare or covered with shrubs, and the "range" is destroyed. The better class of soils here bear tolerable crops of cotton, but are by no means of value equal to the Red River bottoms or the new soils of any part of Texas. The country is, therefore, here in similar condition to that of the Eastern Slave States. The improvements which the inhabitants have succeeded in making in the way of clearing the forest, fencing and tilling the land, building dwellings, barns, and machinery, making roads and bridges, and introducing the institutions of civilization, not compensating in value the deterioration in the productiveness of the soil, the exhausted land reverts to wilderness.

Eastern Texas.—Shortly after noon rain began to fall from the chilly clouds that had been threatening us, and sleet and snow were soon driving in our faces. Our animals were disposed to flinch, but we were disposed to sleep in Texas, and pushed on across the Sabine. We found use for all our wraps, and when we reached the ferry-house our Mackintoshes were like a coat of mail with the stiff ice, and trees and fields were covered. In the broad river bottom we noticed many aquatic birds, and the browsing line under the dense mass of trees was almost as clean cut as that of Bushy Park. The river, at its low stage, was only three or four rods across. The old negro who ferried us over, told us he had taken many a man to the other side, before annexation, who had ridden his horse hard to get beyond the jurisdiction of the States.

If we were unfortunate in this stormy entrance into Texas, we were very fortunate in the good quarters we lighted upon. The ferry has long been known as Gaines's Ferry, but is now the property of Mr. Strather, an adjacent planter, originally from Mississippi, but a settler of long standing. His log-house had two stories, and being the first we had met having glass windows, and the second, I think, with any windows at all, takes high rank for comfort on the road. At supper we had capital mallard-ducks from the river, as well as the usual Texan diet.

We were detained by the severity of the weather during the following day, and were well entertained with huntsman's stories of snakes, game, and crack shots. Mr. S. himself is the best shot in the county. A rival, who had once a match against him for two thousand dollars, called the day before the trial, and paid five hundred dollars to withdraw. He brought out his rifle for us, and placed a bullet, at one hundred and twenty yards, plump in the spot agreed upon. His piece is an old Kentucky rifle, weighing fourteen pounds, barrel forty-four inches in length, and throwing a ball weighing forty-four to the pound.

A guest, who came in, helped us to pass the day by exciting our anticipations of the West, and by his free and good advice. He confirmed stories we had heard of the danger to slavery in the West

by the fraternizing of the blacks with the Mexicans. They helped
them in all their bad habits, married them, stole a living from them,
and ran them off every day to Mexico. This man had driven stages or
herded cattle in every state of the Union, and had a notion that he
liked the people and the state of Alabama better than any other.
A man would get on faster, he thought, in Iowa, than anywhere else.
He had been stage-driver in Illinois during the cold winter of
1851-2, and had driven a whole day when the mercury was at its
furthest below zero, but had never suffered so much from cold as
on his present trip, during a norther on a Western prairie. He was
now returning from Alexandria, where he had taken a small drove
of horses. He cautioned us, in travelling, always to see our horses
fed with our own eyes, and to "hang around" them till they had
made sure of a tolerable allowance, and never to leave anything
portable within sight of a negro. A stray blanket was a sure loss.

Mr. S. has two plantations, both on upland, but one under the
care of an overseer, some miles from the river. The soil he considers excellent. He averaged, last year, seven and a half bales to
the hand; this year, four and a half bales. The usual crop of corn
here is thirty bushels (shelled) to the acre.

Hearing him curse the neighbouring poor people for stealing
hogs, we inquired if thieves were as troublesome here as in the
older countries. "If there ever were any hog-thieves anywhere," said
he, "it's here." In fact, no slave country, new or old, is free from
this exasperating pest of poor whites. In his neighbourhood were
several who ostensibly had a little patch of land to attend to, but
who really, he said, derived their whole lazy subsistence from their
richer neighbours' hog droves.

The negro-quarters here, scattered irregularly about the house,
were of the worst description, though as good as local custom requires. They are but a rough inclosure of logs, ten feet square,
without windows, covered by slabs of hewn wood four feet long.
The great chinks are stopped with whatever has come to hand—a
wad of cotton here, and a corn-shuck there. The suffering from cold
within them in such weather as we experienced, must be great. The
day before, we had seen a young black girl, of twelve or fourteen
years, sitting on a pile of logs before a house we passed, in a driving sleet, having for her only garment a short chemise. It is im-

possible to say whether such *shiftlessness* was the fault of the master or of the girl. Probably of both, and a part of the peculiar Southern and South-western system of "get along," till it comes better weather.

The storm continuing a third day, we rode through it twenty-five miles further to San Augustine. For some distance the country remains as in Louisiana. Then the pines gradually disappear, and a heavy clay soil, stained by an oxide of iron to a uniform brick red, begins. It makes most disagreeable roads, sticking close, and giving an indelible stain to every article that touches it. This tract is known as the Red Lands of Eastern Texas.

On a plantation not far from the river, we learned they had made eight bales to the hand. Mentioning it, afterwards, to a man who knew the place, he said they had planted earlier than their neighbours, and worked night and day, and, he believed, had lied, besides. They had sent cotton both by Galveston and by Grand Ecore, and had found the cost the same, about $8 per bale of 500 lbs.

We called at a plantation offered for sale. It was described in the hand-bills as having a fine house. We found it a cabin without windows. The proprietor said he had made ten bales to the hand, and would sell with all the improvements, a new gin-house, press, etc., for $6 per acre.

The roadside, though free from the gloom of pines, did not cheer up, the number of deserted wrecks of plantations not at all diminishing. The occupied cabins were no better than before. We had entered our promised land; but the oil and honey of gladness and peace were nowhere visible. The people we met were the most sturdily inquisitive I ever saw. Nothing staggered them, and we found our account in making a clean breast of it as soon as they approached.

We rode through the shire-town, Milam, without noticing it. Its buildings, all told, are six in number.

We passed several immigrant trains in motion, in spite of the weather. Their aspect was truly pitiful. Splashed with a new coating of red mud, dripping, and staggering, beating still the bones of their long worn-out cattle, they floundered helplessly on.

San Augustine made no very charming impression as we entered, nor did we find any striking improvement on longer acquaintance.

It is a town of perhaps fifty or sixty houses, and half a dozen shops. Most of the last front upon a central square acre of neglected mud. The dwellings are clap-boarded, and of a much higher class than the plantation dwellings. As to the people, a resident told us there was but one man in the town that was not in the constant habit of getting drunk, and that this gentleman relaxed his Puritanic severity during our stay in view of the fact that Christmas came but once that year.

Late on Christmas eve [1853], we were invited to the window by our landlady, to see the pleasant local custom of The Christmas Serenade. A band of pleasant spirits started from the square, blowing tin horns, and beating tin pans, and visited in succession every house in the village, kicking in doors, and pulling down fences, until every male member of the family had appeared, with appropriate instruments, and joined the merry party. They then marched to the square, and ended the ceremony with a centupled tin row. In this touching commemoration, as strangers, we were not urged to participate.

A gentleman of the neighbourhood, addicted, as we knew, to a partiality towards a Rip Van Winkle, tavern-lounging style of living, told us he was himself regarded by many of his neighbours with an evil eye, on account of his "stuck-up" deportment, and his habit of minding too strictly his own business. He had been candidate for representative, and had, he thought, probably been defeated on this ground, as he was sure his politics were right.

Not far from the village stands an edifice, which, having three stories and sashed windows, at once attracted our attention. On inquiry, we learned a story, curiously illustrative of Texan and human life. It appeared that two universities were chartered for San Augustine, the one under the protection of the Methodists, the other of the Presbyterians. The country being feebly settled, the supply of students was short, and great was the consequent rivalry between the institutions. The neighbouring people took sides upon the subject so earnestly, that, one fine day, the president of the Presbyterian University was shot down in the street. After this, both dwindled, and seeing death by starvation staring them in the face, they made an arrangement by which both were taken under charge of the fraternity of Masons. The buildings are now used under the style of "The Masonic Institute," the one for boys, the other for girls.

The boys occupy only the third story, and the two lower stories are falling to ludicrous decay—the boarding dropping off, and the windows on all sides dashed in.

The Mexican habitations of which San Augustine was once composed, have all disappeared. We could not find even a trace of them.

Chapter X

South-western Louisiana and Eastern Texas

Nacogdoches.—In this town of 500 inhabitants, we found there was no flour. At San Augustine we had inquired in vain at all the stores for refined sugar. Not satisfied with some blankets that were shown us, we were politely recommended by the shopkeeper to try other stores. At each of the other stores we were told they had none: the only blankets in town we should find at ——'s, naming the one we had just quitted. The same thing occurred with several other articles.

Houston County.—This day's ride and the next were through a very poor country, clay or sand soil, bearing short oaks and black-jack. We passed one small meadow, or prairie, covered with coarse grass. Deserted plantations appeared again in greater numbers than the occupied. One farm, near which we stopped, was worked by eight field hands. The crop had been fifty bales; small, owing to a dry season. The corn had been exceedingly poor. The hands, we noticed, came in from the fields after eight o'clock.

The deserted houses, B. said, were built before the date of Texan Independence. After Annexation the owners had moved on to better lands in the West. One house he pointed out as having been the residence of one of a band of pirates who occupied the country thirty or forty years ago. They had all been gradually killed.

During the day we met two men on horseback, one upon wheels, and passed one emigrant family. This was all the motion upon the principal road of the district.

The second day's camp was a few miles beyond the town of Crockett, the shire-town of Houston County. Not being able to find corn for our horses, we returned to the village for it.

We obtained what we wanted for a day's rest, which we proposed for Sunday, the following day, and loaded it into our emptied hampers. We then looked about the town for current provisions for ourselves. We were rejoiced to find a German baker, but damped by finding he had only molasses-cakes and candies for sale. There was no flour in the town, except the little of which he made his cakes. He was from Hamburg, and though he found a tolerable sale, to emigrants principally, he was very tired of Crockett, and intended to move to San Antonio among his countrymen. He offered us coffee, and said he had had beer, but on Christmas-day a mass of people called on him; he had "treated" them all, and they had finished his supply.

We inquired at seven stores, and at the two inns for butter, flour, or wheat-bread, and fresh meat. There was none in town. One inn-keeper offered us salt beef, the only meat, except pork, in town. At the stores we found crackers, worth in New York 6 cents a pound, sold here at 20 cents; poor raisins, 30 cents; Manilla rope, half-inch, 30 cents a pound. When butter was to be had it came in firkins from New York, although an excellent grazing country is near the town.

Trinity Bottom.—On landing on the west side of the Trinity, we entered a rich bottom, even in winter, of an almost tropical aspect. The road had been cut through a cane-brake, itself a sort of Brob-dingnag grass. Immense trees, of a great variety of kinds, interlaced their branches and reeled with their own rank growth. Many vines, especially huge grape-vines, ran hanging from tree to tree, adding to the luxuriant confusion. Spanish moss clung thick everywhere, supplying the shadows of a winter foliage.

These bottom lands bordering the Trinity are among the richest of rich Texas. They are not considered equal, in degree of fatness, to some parts of the Brazos, Colorado, and Guadalupe bottoms, but are thought to have compensation in reliability for steady cropping.

We made our camp on the edge of the bottom, and for safety against our dirty persecutors, the hogs, pitched our tent *within* a large hog-yard, putting up the bars to exclude them. The trees within had been sparingly cut, and we easily found tent-poles and fuel at hand.

The plantation on which we were thus intruding had just been sold, we learned, at two dollars per acre. There were seven hun-dred acres, and the buildings, with a new gin-house, worth nearly one thousand dollars, were included in the price. With the land were sold eight prime field-hands. A quarter of the land was prob-ably subject to overflow, and the limits extended over some unpro-ductive upland.

When field-hands are sold in this way with the land, the family servants, who have usually been selected from the field-hands, must be detached to follow the fortunes of the seller. When, on the other hand, the land is sold simply, the whole body of slaves move away, leaving frequently wives and children on neighbouring plantations. Such a cause of separation must be exceedingly common among the restless, almost nomadic, small proprietors of the South.

But the very word "sale," applied to a slave, implies this cruelty, leaving, of course, the creature's whole happiness to his owner's discretion and humanity.

As if to give the lie to our reflections, however, the rascals here appeared to be particularly jolly, perhaps adopting Mark Tapley's good principles. They were astir half the night, talking, joking, and singing loud and merrily.

This plantation had made this year seven bales to the hand. The water for the house, we noticed, was brought upon heads a quarter of a mile, from a rain-pool, in which an old negress was washing.

At an old Settler's.—The room was fourteen feet square, with battens of split boards tacked on between the broader openings of the logs. Above, it was open to the rafters, and in many places the sky could be seen between the shingles of the roof. A rough board box, three feet square, with a shelf in it, contained the crockery-ware of the establishment; another similar box held the store of meal, coffee, sugar, and salt; a log crib at the horse-pen held the corn, from which the meal was daily ground, and a log smoke or store-house contained the store of pork. A canopy-bed filled one quarter of the room; a cradle, four chairs seated with untanned deer-hide, a table, a skillet or bake-kettle, a coffee-kettle, a frying-pan, and a rifle laid across two wooden pegs on the chimney, with a string of patches, powder-horn, pouch, and hunting-knife, completed the furniture of the house. We all sat with hats and overcoats on, and the woman cooked in bonnet and shawl. As I sat in the chimney-corner I could put both my hands out, one laid on the other, between the stones of the fire-place and the logs of the wall.

A pallet of quilts and blankets was spread for us in the lean-to, just between the two doors. We slept in all our clothes, including overcoats, hats, and boots, and covered entirely with blankets. At seven in the morning, when we threw them off, the mercury in the thermometer in our saddle-bags, which we had used for a pillow, stood at 25° Fahrenheit.

We contrived to make cloaks and hoods from our blankets, and after going through with the fry, coffee, and pone again, and paying one dollar each for the entertainment of ourselves and horses, we continued our journey.

Caldwell.—Late in the same evening we reached a hamlet, the "seat of justice" of Burleson County. We were obliged to leave our horses in a stable, made up of a roof, in which was a loft for the storage of provender, set upon posts, without side-boarding, so that the norther met with no obstruction. It was filled with horses, and ours alone were blanketed for the night. The mangers were very shallow and narrow, and as the corn was fed on the cob, a considerable proportion of it was thrown out by the horses in their efforts to detach the edible portion. With laudable economy, our landlord had twenty-five or thirty pigs running at large in the stable, to prevent this overflow from being wasted.

The "hotel" was an unusually large and fine one; the principal room had glass windows. Several panes of these were, however, broken, and the outside door could not be closed from without; and when closed, was generally pried open with a pocket-knife by those who wished to go out. A great part of the time it was left open. Supper was served in another room, in which there was no fire, and the outside door was left open for the convenience of the servants in passing to and from the kitchen, which, as usual here at large houses, was in a detached building. Supper was, however, eaten with such rapidity that nothing had time to freeze on the table.

There were six Texans, planters and herdsmen, who had made harbour at the inn for the norther, two German shopkeepers and a young lawyer, who were boarders, besides our party of three, who had to be seated before the fire. We kept coats and hats on, and gained as much warmth, from the friendly manner in which we drew together, as possible. After ascertaining, by a not at all impertinent or inconsiderate method of inquiry, where we were from, which way we were going, what we thought of the country, what we thought of the weather, and what were the capacities and the cost of our fire-arms, we were considered as initiated members of the crowd, and "the conversation became general."

The matter of most interest came up in this wise: "The man made a white boy, fourteen or fifteen years old, get up and go out in the norther for wood, when there was a great, strong nigger fellow lying on the floor doing nothing. God! I had an appetite to give him a hundred, right there."

"Why, you wouldn't go out into the norther yourself, would you, if you were not obliged to?" inquired one, laughingly.

"I wouldn't have a nigger in my house that I was afraid to set to work, at anything I wanted him to do, at any time. They'd hired him out to go to a new place next Thursday, and they were afraid if they didn't treat him well, he'd run away. If I couldn't break a nigger of running away, I wouldn't have him any how."

"I can tell you how you can break a nigger of running away, certain," said another. "There was an old fellow I used to know in Georgia, that always cured his so. If a nigger ran away, when he caught him, he would bind his knee over a log, and fasten him so he couldn't stir; then he'd take a pair of pincers and pull one of his toe-nails out by the roots; and tell him that if he ever run away again, he would pull out two of them, and if he run away again after that, he told them he'd pull out four of them, and so on, doubling each time. He never had to do it more than twice—it always cured them."

One of the company then said that he was at the present time in pursuit of a negro. He had bought him of a relative in Mississippi, and had been told that he was a great runaway. He had, in fact, run away from his relative three times, and always when they caught him he was trying to *get back to Illinois;* [1] that was the reason he sold him. "He offered him to me cheap," he continued, "and I bought him because he was a first-rate nigger, and I thought perhaps I could break him of running away by bringing him down to this new country. I expect he's making for Mexico now. I am a-most sure I saw his tracks on the road about twelve miles back, where he was a-coming on this way. Night before last I engaged with a man who's got some first-rate nigger dogs to meet me here to-night; but I suppose the cold keeps him back." He then asked us to look

[1] Many freemen have been kidnapped in Illinois and sold into slavery.

out for him as we went on west, and gave us a minute description of him that we might recognize him. He was "a real black nigger," and carried off a double-barrelled gun with him. Another man, who was going on by another road westward, offered to look for him that way, and to advertise him. Would he be likely to defend himself with the gun if he should try to secure him? he asked. The owner said he had no doubt he would. He was as humble a nigger when he was at work as ever he had seen; but he was a mighty resolute nigger—there was no man had more resolution. "Couldn't I induce him to let me take the gun by pretending I wanted to look at it, or something? I'd talk to him simple; make as if I was a stranger, and ask him about the road, and so on, and finally ask him what he had got for a gun, and to let me look at it." The owner didn't believe he'd let go of the gun; he was a "nigger of sense—as much sense as a white man; he was not one of your kinkey-headed niggers." The chances of catching him were discussed. Some thought they were good, and some that the owner might almost as well give it up, he'd got such a start. It was three hundred miles to the Mexican frontier, and he'd have to make fires to cook the game he would kill, and could travel only at night; but then every nigger or Mexican he could find would help him, and if he had so much sense, he'd manage to find out his way pretty straight, and yet not have white folks see him.

We slept in a large upper room, in a company of five, with a broken window at the head of our bed, and another at our side, offering a short cut to the norther across our heads.

We were greatly amused to see one of our bed-room companions gravely *spit* in the candle before jumping into bed, explaining to some one who made a remark, that he always did so, it gave him time to see what he was about before it went out.

The next morning the ground was covered with sleet, and the gale still continued (a pretty steady close-reefing breeze) during the day.

We wished to have a horse shod. The blacksmith, who was a white man, we found in his shop, cleaning a fowling-piece. It was too d—d cold to work, he said, and he was going to shoot some geese; he, at length, at our urgent request, consented to earn a dollar; but, after getting on his apron, he found that we had lost a shoe, and took it off again, refusing to make a shoe while this d—d norther lasted, for any man. As he had no shoes ready made, he absolutely turned us out of the shop, and obliged us to go seventy-five miles further, a great part of the way over a pebbly road, by which the beast lost three shoes before he could be shod.

This respect for the north wind is by no means singular here. The publication of the week's newspaper in Bastrop was interrupted by the norther, the editor mentioning, as a sufficient reason for the irregularity, the fact that his printing-office was in the north part of the house.

Austin.—Before leaving Eastern Texas behind us, I must add a random note or two, the dates of which it would have been uncivil to indicate.

We stopped one night at the house of a planter, now twenty years settled in Eastern Texas. He was a man of some education and natural intelligence, and had, he told us, an income, from the labour of his slaves, of some $4,000. His residence was one of the largest houses we had seen in Texas. It had a second story, two wings and a long gallery. Its windows had been once glazed, but now, out of eighty panes that originally filled the lower windows, thirty only remained unbroken. Not a door in the house had been ever furnished with a latch or even a string; when they were closed, it was necessary to *claw* or to ask some one inside to push open. (Yet we happened to hear a neighbour expressing serious admiration of the way these doors fitted.) The furniture was of the rudest description.

One of the family had just had a hæmorrhage of the lungs; while we were at supper, this person sat between the big fire-place and an open outside door, having a window, too, at his side, in which only three panes remained. A norther was blowing, and ice forming upon the gallery outside. Next day at breakfast, the invalid was unable to appear on account of a "bad turn."

On our supper-table was nothing else than the eternal fry, pone and coffee. Butter, of dreadful odour, was here added by exception. Wheat flour they never used. It was "too much trouble."

We were waited upon by two negro girls, dressed in short-waisted, twilled-cotton gowns, once white, now looking as if they had been worn by chimney-sweeps. The water for the family was brought in tubs upon the heads of these two girls, from a creek, a quarter of a mile distant, this occupation filling nearly all their time.

This gentleman had thirty or forty negroes, and two legitimate sons. One was an idle young man. The other was, at eight years old, a swearing, tobacco-chewing bully and ruffian. We heard him whipping a puppy behind the house, and swearing between the blows, his father and mother being at hand. His language and tone was an evident imitation of his father's mode of dealing with his slaves.

"I've got an account to settle with you; I've let you go about long enough; I'll teach you who's your master; there, go now, God damn you, but I haven't got through with you yet."

"You stop that cursing," said his father, at length, "it isn't right for little boys to curse."

"What do *you* do when you get mad?" replied the boy; "reckon you cuss some; so now you'd better shut up."

In the whole journey through Eastern Texas, we did not see one of the inhabitants look into a newspaper or a book, although we spent days in houses where men were lounging about the fire without occupation. One evening I took up a paper which had been lying unopened upon the table of the inn where we were staying, and smiled to see how painfully news items dribbled into the Texas country papers, the loss of the tug-boat "Ajax," which occurred before we left New York, being here just given as the loss of the "splendid steamer Ocax."

A man who sat near said—

"Reckon you've read a good deal, hain't you?"

"Oh, yes; why?"

"Reckon'd you had."

"Why?"

"You look as though you liked to read. Well, it's a good thing. S'pose you take a pleasure in reading, don't you?"

"That depends, of course, on what I have to read. I suppose everybody likes to read when they find anything interesting to them, don't they?"

"No; it's damn tiresome to some folks, I reckon, any how, 'less you've got the habit of it. Well, it's a good thing; you can pass away your time so."

The sort of interest taken in foreign affairs is well enough illustrated by the views of a gentleman of property in Eastern Texas, who was sitting with us one night, "spitting in the fire," and talking about cotton. Bad luck he had had—only four bales to the hand; couldn't account for it—bad luck; and next year he didn't reckon nothing else but that there would be a general war in Europe, and then he'd be in a pretty fix, with cotton down to four cents a pound. Curse those Turks! If he thought there would be a general war, he would take every d—d nigger he'd got, right down to New Orleans, and sell them for what they'd bring. They'd never be so high again as they were now, and if there should come a general war they wouldn't be worth half as much next year. There always were infernal rascals somewhere in the world trying to prevent an honest man from getting a living. Oh, if they got to fighting, he hoped they'd eat each other up. They just ought to be, all of them—Turks, and Russians, and Prussians, and Dutchmen, and Frenchmen—just be put in a bag together, and slung into hell. That's what he'd do with them.

Remarking, one day, at the house of a woman who was brought up at the North, that there was much more comfort at her house than any we had previously stopped at, she told us that the only reason the people didn't have any comfort here was, that they wouldn't *take any trouble* to get anything. Anything that their negroes could make they would eat; but they would take no pains to instruct them, or to get anything that didn't grow on the plantation. A neighbour of hers owned fifty cows, she supposed, but very rarely had any milk and scarcely ever any butter, simply because his people were too lazy to milk or churn, and he wouldn't take the trouble to make them.

This woman entirely sustained the assertion that Northern people, when they come to the South, have less feeling for the negroes than Southerners themselves usually have. We asked her (she lived in a village) whether she hired or owned her servants. They owned them all, she said. When they first came to Texas they hired servants, but it was very troublesome; they would take no interest in anything; and she couldn't get along with them. Then very often their owners, on some pretext (ill-treatment, perhaps), would take them away. Then they bought negroes. It was very expensive: a good negro girl cost seven or eight hundred dollars, and that, we must know, was a great deal of money to be laid out in a thing that might lie right down the next day and die. They were not much better either than the hired servants.

Folks up North talked about how badly the negroes were treated; she wished they could see how much work her girls did. She had four of them, and she knew they didn't do half so much work as one good Dutch girl such as she used to have at the North. Oh! the negroes were the laziest things in creation; there was no knowing how much trouble they gave to look after them. Up to the North, if a girl went out into the garden for anything, when she came back she would clean her feet, but these nigger girls will stump right in and track mud all over the house. What do they care? They'd just as lief clean the mud after themselves as anything else—their time isn't any value to themselves. What do they care for the trouble it gives you? Not a bit. And you may scold 'em and whip 'em—you never can break 'em into better habits.

I asked what were servants' wages when they were hired out to do housework? They were paid seven or eight dollars a month; sometimes ten. She didn't use to pay her girl at the North but four dollars, and she knew she would do more work than any six of the niggers, and not give half so much trouble as one. But you couldn't get any other help here but niggers. Northern folks talk about abolishing slavery, but there wouldn't be any use in that; that would be ridiculous, unless you could some way get rid of the niggers. Why, they'd murder us all in our beds—that's what they'd do. Why, over to Fannin, there was a negro woman that killed her mistress with an axe, and her two little ones. The people just flocked together, and hung her right up on the spot; they ought to have piled some wood round her, and burned her to death; that would have been a good lesson to the rest. We afterwards heard her scolding one of her girls, the girl made some exculpatory reply, and getting the best of the argument, the mistress angrily told her if she said another word she would have two hundred lashes given her. She came in and remarked that if she hadn't felt so nervous she would have given that girl a good whipping herself; these niggers are so saucy, it's very trying to one who has to take care of them.

Servants are, it is true, "a trial," in all lands, ages, and nations.

But note the fatal reason this woman frankly gives for the inevitable delinquencies of slave-servants, "Their time isn't any value to themselves!"

The women of Eastern Texas seemed to us, in general, far superior to their lords. They have, at least, the tender hearts and some of the gentle delicacy that your "true Texan" lacks, whether mistresses of slaves, or only of their own frying-pan. They are overworked, however, as soon as married, and care gives them thin faces, sallow complexions, and expressions either sad or sour.

Another night we spent at the house of a man who came here, when a boy, from the North. His father was a mechanic, and had emigrated to Texas just before the war of Independence. He joined the army, and his son had been brought up—rather had grown up—Southern fashion, with no training to regular industry. He had learned no trade. What need? His father received some thousand acres of land in payment of his services. The son earned some money by driving a team; bought some cattle, took a wife, and a house, and now had been settled six years, with a young family. He had nothing to do but look after his cattle, go to the nearest town and buy meal and coffee occasionally, and sell a few oxen when the bill was sent in. His house was more comfortless than nine-tenths of the stables of the North. There were several windows, some of which were boarded over, some had wooden shutters, and some were entirely open. There was not a pane of glass. The doors were closed with difficulty. We could see the stars, as we lay in bed, through the openings of the roof; and on all sides, in the walls of the room, one's arm might be thrust out. Notwithstanding, that night the mercury fell below 25° of our Fahrenheit thermometer. There was the standard food and beverage, placed before us night and morning. We asked if there was much game near him? There were a great many deer. He saw them every day. Did he shoot many? He never shot any; 'twas too much trouble. When he wanted "fresh," 'twas easier to go out and stick a hog (the very words he used). He had just corn enough to give our horses one feed—there was none left for the morning. His own horses could get along through the winter on the prairie. He made pets of his children, but was cross and unjust to his wife, who might have been pretty, and was affectionate. He was without care—thoughtless, content, with an unoccupied mind. He took no newspaper—he read nothing. There was, indeed, a pile of old books which his father had brought from the North, but they seemed to be all of the Tract Society sort, and the dust had been undisturbed upon them, it might have been, for many years.

Manchac Spring.—We found a plantation that would have done no discredit to Virginia. The house was large and well constructed, standing in a thick grove, separated from the prairie by a strong worm-fence. Adjacent, within, was the spring, which deserved its prominence of mention upon the maps. It had been tastefully grotted with heavy limestone rocks, now water-stained and mossy, and the pure stream came gurgling up, in impetuous gallons, to pour itself in a bright current out upon the prairie. The fountains of Italy were what came to mind, and "Fontana de Manciocco" would have secured a more natural name.

Everything about the house was orderly and neat. The proprietor came out to receive us, and issued orders about the horses, which we felt, from their quiet tone, would be obeyed without our supervision. When we were ushered into a snug supper-room and found a clean table set with wheat-bread, ham, tea, and preserved fruits, waited on by tidy and ready girls, we could scarce think we had not got beyond the bounds of Texas. We were, in fact, quit, for some time to come, of the lazy poverty of Eastern Texas.

Lower Guadalupe.—Not finding a suitable camping place, we stumbled, after dark, into a large plantation upon the river bottom.

The irruption of our train within the plantation fences caused a furious commotion among the dogs and little negroes, and it was with no little difficulty we could explain to the planter, who appeared with a candle, which was instantly blown out upon the porch, our peaceable intentions. Finally, after a general striking out of Fanny's heels and the master's boots, aided by the throwing of our loose lariats into the confused crowd, the growling and chattering circle about us was sufficiently enlarged and subdued for us to obtain a hearing, and we were hospitably received.

"Ho, Sam! You Tom, here! Call your missus. Suke! if you don't stop that infernal noise I'll have you drowned! Here, Bill! Josh! some of you! why don't you help the gentleman? Bring a lantern here! Packed, are you, sir? Hold on, you there; leave the gun alone. Now, clear out with you, you little devils, every one of you! Is there

no one in the house? St! after 'em, Tiger! Can't any of you find a
lantern? Where's Bill, to take these horses? What are you doing
there? I tell you to be off, now, every one of you! Tom! take a rail
and keep 'em off there!"

In the midst of the noise we go through the familiar motions, and
land our saddles and hampers upon the gallery, then follow what
appears to be the headmost negro to the stable, and give him a hint
to look well out for the horses.

This is our first reintroduction to negro servants after our German
experiences, and the contrast is most striking and disagreeable.[2]
Here were thirty or forty slaves, but not an order could be executed
without more reiteration, and threats, and oaths, and greater trouble
to the master and mistress, than would be needed to get a squadron
under way. We heard the master threaten his negroes with flogging,
at least six times, before we went to bed. In the night a heavy rain
came up, and he rose, on hearing it, to arrange the cistern spout,
cursing again his infernal niggers, who had turned it off for some
convenience of their own. In the morning, we heard the mistress
scolding her girls for having left articles outside which had been
spoiled by the wet, after repeated orders to bring them in. On visiting the stables we found the door fastened by a board leaned
against it.

All the animals were loose, except the mule, which I had fastened
myself. The rope attached to my saddle was stolen, and a shorter
one substituted for it, when I mentioned the fact, by which I was
deceived, until we were too far off to return. The master, seeing the
horses had yet had no fodder, called to a boy to get some for them,
then, countermanding his order, told the boy to call some one else,
and go himself to drive the cows out of the garden. Then, to another
boy, he said, "Go and pull two or three bundles of fodder out of
the stack and give these horses." The boy soon came with two small
bundles. "You infernal rascal, couldn't you tote more fodder than
that? Go back and bring four or five bundles, and be quick about it,
or I'll lick you." The boy walked slowly back, and returned with
four bundles more.

But on entering at night we were struck with the air of comfort
that met us. We were seated in rocking-chairs in a well-furnished

---

[2] For Olmsted's favorable impressions of the Germans in the New Braunfels
district of Western Texas, see *Journey through Texas*, chap. iii.—Editor.

room, before a blazing fire, offered water to wash, in a little lean-to bed-room, and, though we had two hours to wait for our supper, it was most excellent, and we passed an agreeable evening in intelligent conversation with our host.

After his curiosity about us was satisfied, we learned from him that, though a young man, he was an old settler, and had made a comfortable fortune by his plantation. His wife gave us a picturesque account of their waggon journey here with their people, and described the hardships, dangers, and privations they had at first to endure. Now they were far more comfortable than they could have ever hoped to have been in the State from which they came. They thought their farm the best cotton land in the world. It extended across a mile of timbered bottom land from the river, then over a mile of bottom prairie, and included a large tract of the big prairie "for range." Their field would produce, in a favourable season, three bales to the acre; ordinarily a bale and a half: the "bale" 400 lbs. They had always far more than their hands could pick. It was much more free from weeds than the States, so much so, that three hands would be needed there to cultivate the same area as two here; that is, with the same hands the crop would be one-third greater.

But so anxious is every one in Texas to give all strangers a favourable impression, that all statements as to the extreme profit and healthfulness of lands must be taken with a grain of allowance. We found it very difficult, without impertinent persistence, to obtain any unfavourable facts. Persons not interested informed us, that from one-third to one-half the cotton crop on some of these rich plantations had been cut off by the worm, on several occasions, and that negroes suffered much with dysentery and pneumonia.

It cost them very little to haul their cotton to the coast or to get supplies. They had not been more sickly than they would have been on the Mississippi. They considered that their steady sea-breeze was almost a sure preventive of such diseases as they had higher up the country.

They always employed German mechanics, and spoke well of them. Mexicans were regarded in a somewhat unchristian tone, not as heretics or heathen, to be converted with flannel and tracts, but rather as vermin, to be exterminated. The lady was particularly strong in her prejudices. White folks and Mexicans were never made to live together, anyhow, and the Mexicans had no business here. They were getting so impertinent, and were so well protected by the laws, that the Americans would just have to get together and drive them all out of the country.

On the Chockolate [February 27, 1854].—"Which way did you come?" asked some one of the old man.

"From ——."

"See anything of a runaway nigger over there, anywhar?"

"No, sir. What kind of a nigger was it?"

"A small, black, screwed-up-faced nigger."

"How long has he been out?"

"Nigh two weeks."

"Whose is he?"

"Judge ——'s, up here. And he cut the judge right bad. Like to have killed the judge. Cut his young master, too."

"Reckon, if they caught him, 'twould go rather hard with him."

"Reckon 'twould. We caught him once, but he got away from us again. We was just tying his feet together, and he give me a kick in the face, and broke. I had my six-shooter handy, and I tried to shoot him, but every barrel missed fire. Been loaded a week. We shot at him three times with rifles, but he'd got too far off, and we didn't hit, but we must have shaved him close. We chased him, and my dog got close to him once. If he'd grip'd him, we should have got him; but he had a dog himself, and just as my dog got within about a yard of him, his dog turned and fit my dog, and he hurt him so bad we couldn't get him to run him again. We run him close, though, I tell you. Run him out of his coat, and his boots, and a pistol he'd got. But 'twas getting towards dark, and he got into them bayous, and kept swimming from one side to another."

"How long ago was that?"

"Ten days."

"If he's got across the river, he'd get to the Mexicans in two days, and there he'd be safe. The Mexicans'd take care of him."

"What made him run?"

"The judge gave him a week at Christmas, and when the week was up, I s'pose he didn't want to go to work again. He got unruly, and they was a goin' to whip him."

"Now, how much happier that fellow'd 'a' been, if he'd just stayed and done his duty. He might have just worked and done his duty, and his master'd 'a' taken care of him, and given him another week when Christmas come again, and he'd 'a' had nothing to do but enjoy himself again. These niggers, none of 'em, knows how much happier off they are than if they was free. Now, very likely, he'll starve to death, or get shot."

"Oh, the judge treats his niggers too kind. If he was stricter with them, they'd have more respect for him, and be more contented, too."

"Never do to be too slack with niggers."

We were riding in company, to-day [February 28], with a California drover, named Rankin. He was in search of cattle to drive across the plains. He had taken a drove before from Illinois, and told us that people in that State, of equal circumstances, lived ten times better than here, in all matters of comfort and refinement. He had suffered more in travelling in Texas, than ever on the plains or the mountains. Not long before, in driving some mules with his partner, they came to a house which was the last on the road for fourteen miles. They had nothing in the world in the house but a few ears of corn, they were going to grind in their steel mill for their own breakfast, and wouldn't sell on any terms. "We hadn't eaten anything since breakfast, but we actually could get nothing. The only other thing in the cabin, that could be eaten, was a pile of deer-skins, with the hair on. We had to stake our mules, and make a fire, and coil around it. About twelve o'clock there came a norther. We heard it coming, and it made us howl. We didn't sleep a wink for cold."

Houston.—We were sitting on the gallery of the hotel. A tall, jet black negro came up, leading by a rope a downcast mulatto, whose hands were lashed by a cord to his waist, and whose face was horribly cut, and dripping with blood. The wounded man crouched and leaned for support against one of the columns of the gallery—faint and sick.

"What's the matter with that boy?" asked a smoking lounger.

"I run a fork into his face," answered the negro.

"What are his hands tied for?"

"He's a runaway, sir."

"Did you catch him?"

"Yes, sir. He was hiding in the hay-loft, and when I went up to throw some hay to the horses, I pushed the fork down into the mow and it struck something hard. I didn't know what it was, and I pushed hard, and gave it a turn, and then he hollered, and I took it out."

"What do you bring him here for?"

"Come for the key of the jail, sir, to lock him up."

"What!" said another, "one darkey catch another darkey? Don't believe that story."

"Oh yes, mass'r, I tell for true. He was down in our hay-loft, and so you see when I stab him, I *have to* catch him."

"Why, he's hurt bad, isn't he?"

"Yes, he says I pushed through the bones."

"Whose nigger is he?"

"He says he belong to Mass'r Frost, sir, on the Brazos."

The key was soon brought, and the negro led the mulatto away to jail. He walked away limping, crouching, and writhing, as if he had received other injuries than those on his face. The bystanders remarked that the negro had not probably told the whole story.

We afterwards happened to see a gentleman on horseback, and smoking, leading by a long rope through the deep mud, out into the country, the poor mulatto, still limping and crouching, his hands manacled, and his arms pinioned.

There is a prominent slave-mart in town, which holds a large lot of likely-looking negroes, waiting purchasers. In the windows of shops, and on the doors and columns of the hotel, are many written advertisements, headed "A likely negro girl for sale." "Two negroes for sale." "Twenty negro boys for sale," etc.

South-eastern Texas.—We were unable to procure at Houston any definite information with regard to our proposed route. The known roads thence are those that branch northward and westward from their levee, and so thoroughly within lines of business does local knowledge lie, that the eastern shore is completely terra incognita. The roads east were said to be bad after heavy rains, but the season had been dry, and we determined to follow the direct and the distinct road, laid down upon our map.

Now that I am in a position to give preliminary information, however, there is no reason why the reader should enter this region as ignorant as we did.

Our route took us by Harrisburg and San Jacinto to Liberty, upon the Trinity; thence by Beaumont to the Sabine at Turner's ferry; thence by the Big Woods and Lake Charles to Opelousas, the old capital of St. Landry Parish, at the western head of the intricate navigation from New Orleans.

This large district, extending from the Trinity River to the bayous of the Mississippi, has, throughout, the same general characteristics, the principal of which are, lowness, flatness, and wetness. The soil is variable, but is in greater part a loose, sandy loam, covered with coarse grasses, forming level prairies, which are everywhere broken by belts of pine forests, usually bordering creeks and bayous, but often standing in islands. The surface is but very slightly elevated above the sea; I suppose, upon an average, less than ten feet. It is, consequently, imperfectly drained, and in a wet season a large proportion is literally covered with water, as in crossing it, even in a dry time, we were obliged to wade through many miles of marshy pools. The river-bottoms, still lower than the general level, are subject to constant overflow by tide-water, and what with the fallen timber, the dense undergrowth, the mire-quags, the abrupt gullies, the patches of rotten or floating corduroy, and three or four feet of dirty salt water, the roads through them are not such as one would choose for a morning ride. The country is sparsely settled, containing less than one inhabitant to the square mile, one in four being a slave.

The many pools, through which the usual track took us, were swarming with venomous water-snakes, four or five black moccasins often lifting at once their devilish heads above the dirty surface, and wriggling about our horses' heels. Beyond the Sabine, alligator holes are an additional excitement, the unsuspicious traveller suddenly sinking through the treacherous surface, and sometimes falling a victim, horse and all, to the hideous jaws of the reptile, while overwhelmed by the engulfing mire in which he lurks.

Upon the whole, this is not the spot in which I should prefer to come to light, burn, and expire; in fact, if the nether regions, as was suggested by the dream-gentleman of Natchitoches, be "a boggy country," the avernal entrance might, I should think, with good probabilities, be looked for in this region.

We passed, on both sides the Sabine, many abandoned farms, and the country is but thinly settled. We found it impossible to obtain any information about roads, and frequently went astray upon cattle paths, once losing twenty miles in a day's journey. The people were chiefly herdsmen, cultivating a little cotton upon river-banks, but ordinarily only corn, with a patch of cane to furnish household sugar. We tried in vain to purchase corn for our horses, and were told that "folks didn't make corn enough to bread them, and if anybody had corn to give his horse, he carried it in his hat and went out behind somewhere." The herds were in poor condition, and must in winter be reduced to the verge of starvation. We saw a few hogs, converted, by hardship, to figures so unnatural, that we at first took them for goats. Most of the people we met were old emigrants, from Southern Louisiana and Mississippi, and more disposed to gaiety and cheer than the Texan planters. The houses showed a tendency to Louisiana forms, and the table to a French style of serving the jerked beef, which is the general dish of the country. The meat is dried in strips, over smoky fires, and, if untainted and well prepared, is a tolerably savoury food. I hardly know whether to chronicle it as a border barbarism, or a Creolism, that we were several times, in this neighbourhood, shown to a bed standing next to that occupied by the host and his wife, sometimes with the screen of a shawl, sometimes without.

We met with one specimen of the Virginia habit of "dipping," or snuff-chewing, in the person of a woman who was otherwise neat and agreeable, and observed that a young lady, well-dressed, and apparently engaged, while we were present, in reading, went afterward to light her pipe at the kitchen fire, and had a smoke behind the house.

The condition of the young men appeared to incline decidedly to barbarism. We stopped a night at a house in which a drover, bringing mules from Mexico, was staying; and, with the neighbours who had come to look at the drove, we were thirteen men at table. When speaking with us, all were polite and respectful, the women especially so; but among one another, their coarseness was incredible. The master of the house, a well-known gentleman of the county, who had been absent when we arrived, and at supper-time, came afterwards upon the gallery and commenced cursing furiously, because some one had taken his pipe. Seeing us, he stopped abruptly, and after lighting the pipe, said, in a rather peremptory and formal, but not uncourteous tone: "Where are you from, gentlemen?"

"From Beaumont, sir, last."

"Been out West?"

"Yes, sir."

"Travelling?"

"Yes, sir."

After pausing a moment to make up his mind—

"Where do you live when you are at home, gentlemen, and what's your business in this country?"

"We live in New York, and are travelling to see the country."

"How do you like it?"

"Just here we find it flat and wet."

"What's your name?"

"Olmsted."

"And what's this gentleman's name?"

"Olmsted."

"Is it a Spanish name?"

"No, sir."

He then abruptly left us, and the young men entertained one another with stories of fights and horse-trades, and with vulgar obscenities.

Shortly he returned, saying—

"Show you to bed now, gentlemen, if you wish."

"We are ready, sir, if you will be good enough to get a light."

"A light?"

"Yes, sir."

"*A light?*"

"Yes, sir."

"Get a light?"

"Yes, sir."

"Well" (after a moment's hesitation), "I'll get one."

On reaching the bed-room, which was in a building adjoining, he stood awaiting our pleasure. Thanking him, I turned to take the light, but his fingers were the candlestick. He continued to hold it, and six young men, who had followed us, stood grouped around while we undressed, placing our clothes upon the floor. Judy advanced to lie down by them. One of the young men started forward, and said—

"I've got a right good knife."

"What?"

"I've got a right good knife, if you want it."

"What do you mean?"

"Nothing, only I've got a right good knife, and if you'd like to kill that dog, I'll lend it to you."

"Please to tell me what you mean?"

"Oh, nothing."

"Keep your dog quiet, or I'll kill her," I suppose was the interpretation. When we had covered ourselves in bed, the host said—

"I suppose you don't want the light no more?"

"No, sir"; and all bade us good night; but leaving the door open, commenced feats of prolonged dancing, or stamping upon the gallery, which were uproariously applauded. Then came more obscenities and profanities, apropos to fandango frolics described by the drovers. As we had barely got to sleep, several came to occupy other beds in our room. They had been drinking freely, and continued smoking in bed.

Upon the floor lay two boys of fourteen, who continued shouting and laughing after the others had at length become quiet. Some one soon said to one of them—

"You had better stop your noise; Frank says he'll be damn'd if he don't come in and give you a hiding."

Frank was trying to sleep upon the gallery.

"By ——," the boy cried, raising himself, and drawing a coat from under the pillow, "if he comes in here, I'll be damn'd if I don't kill him. He dare not come in here. I would like to see him come in here," drawing from his coat pocket a revolver, and cocking it. "By ——, you may come in here now. Come in here, come in here! Do you hear that?" (revolving the pistol rapidly). "—— damn me, if I don't kill you, if you come near the door."

This continued without remonstrance for some time, when he lay down, asking his companion for a light for his pipe, and continuing the noisy conversation until we fell asleep. The previous talk had been much of knife and pistol fights which had taken place in the county. The same boy was obliging and amiable the next morning, assisting us to bring in and saddle the horses at our departure.

One of the men here was a Yankee, who had lived so long in the Slave States that he had added to his original ruralisms a very complete collection of Southernisms, some of which were of the richest we met with. He had been in the Texas Rangers, and, speaking of the West, said he had been up round the head of the Guadalupe "heaps and cords of times," at the same time giving us a very picturesque account of the county. Speaking of wolves, he informed us that on the San Jacinto there were "*any dimensions* of them." Obstinacy, in his vocabulary, was represented by "damnation *cussedness.*" He was unable to conceive of us in any other light than as two peddlers who had mistaken their ground in coming here.

At another house where we stopped (in which, by the way, we ate our supper by the light of pine knots blazing in the chimney, with an apology for the absence of candles), we heard some conversation upon a negro of the neighbourhood, who had been sold to a free negro, and who refused to live with him, saying he wouldn't be a servant to a nigger. All agreed that he was right, although the man was well known to be kind to his negroes, and would always sell any of them who wished it. The slave had been sold because he wouldn't mind. "If I had a negro that wouldn't mind," said the woman of the house, "I'd break his head, or I'd sell him; I wouldn't have one about me." Her own servant was standing behind her. "I do think it would be better if there wasn't any niggers in the world, they do behave so bad, some of 'em. They steal just like hogs."

South-western Louisiana.—Soon after crossing the Sabine, we entered a "hummock," or tract of more fertile, oak-bearing land, known as the Big Woods. The soil is not rich, but produces cotton, in good seasons nearly a bale to the acre, and the limited area is fully occupied. Upon one plantation we found an intelligent emigrant from Mississippi, who had just bought the place, having stopped on his way into Texas, because the time drew near for the confinement of his wife. Many farms are bought by emigrants, he said, from such temporary considerations: a child is sick, or a horse exhausted; they stop for a few weeks; but summer comes, and they conclude to put in a crop, and often never move again.

It was before reaching the Big Woods, that alligator-holes were first pointed out to us, with a caution to avoid them. They extend from an aperture, obliquely, under ground, to a large cavern, the walls of which are puddled by the motions of the animal; and, being partly filled with water, form a comfortable amphibious residence. A horseman is liable, not only to breaking through near the orifice, but to being precipitated into the den itself, where he will find awaiting him, a disagreeable mixture of mire and angry jaws. In the deep water of the bottoms, we met with no snakes; but the pools were everywhere alive with them. We saw a great variety of long-legged birds, apparently on friendly terms with all the reptiles.

A day's journey took us through the Big Woods, and across Calcasieu to Lake Charles. We were not prepared to find the Calcasieu a superb and solemn river, two hundred and thirty yards across and forty-five feet deep. It is navigable for forty miles, but at its mouth has a bar, on which is sometimes only eighteen inches of water, ordinarily thirty inches. Schooners of light draft ascend it, bringing supplies, and taking out the cotton raised within its reach. Lake Charles is an insignificant village, upon the bank of a pleasant, clear lakelet, several miles in extent.

From the Big Woods to Opelousas, there was no change in the monotonous scenery. Everywhere extended the immense moist plain, being alternate tracts of grass and pine. Nearer Opelousas, oak appears in groups with the pine, and the soil is darker and more fertile. Here the land was mostly taken up, partly by speculators, in view of the Opelousas Railway, then commenced. But, in all the western portion of the district, the land is still government property, and many of the people squatters. Sales are seldom made, but the estimated price of the land is fifty cents an acre.

Some of the timbered land, for a few years after clearing, yields good crops of corn and sweet potatoes. Cotton is seldom attempted, and sugar only for family use. Oats are sometimes grown, but the yield is small, and seldom thrashed from the straw. We noted one field of poor rye. So wet a region and so warm a climate suggested rice, and, were the land sufficiently fertile, it would, doubtless, become a staple production. It is now only cultivated for home use, the bayou bottoms being rudely arranged for flowing the crop. But without manure no profitable return can be obtained from breaking the prairie, and the only system of manuring in use is that of ploughing up occasionally the cow-pens of the herdsmen.

The road was now distinctly marked enough, but had frequent and embarrassing forks, which occasioned us almost as much annoyance as the clouds of musquitoes which, east of the Sabine, hovered continually about our horses and our heads. Notions of distance we found incredibly vague. At Lake Charles we were informed that the exact distance to Opelousas was ninety-six miles. After riding eight hours, we were told by a respectable gentleman that the distance from his house was one hundred and twenty miles. The next evening the distance was forty miles; and the following evening a gentleman who met us stated first that it was "a good long way"; next, that it was "thirty or forty miles, and damn'd long ones, too." About four miles beyond him, we reached the twentieth mile-post.

Across the bayous of any size, bridges had been constructed, but so rudely built of logs that the traveller, where possible, left them for a ford.

The people, after passing the frontier, changed in every prominent characteristic. French became the prevailing language, and French the prevailing manners. The gruff Texan bidding, "Sit up, stranger; take some fry!" became a matter of recollection, of which "Monsieur, la soupe est servie," was the smooth substitute. The good-nature of the people was an incessant astonishment. If we inquired the way, a contented old gentleman waddled out and showed us also his wife's house-pet, an immense white crane, his big crop of peaches, his old fig-tree, thirty feet in diameter of shade, and to his wish of "bon voyage" added for each a bouquet of the jessamines we were admiring. The homes were homes, not settlements on speculation; the house, sometimes of logs, it is true, but hereditary logs, and more often of smooth lumber, with deep and spreading galleries on all sides for the coolest comfort. For form, all ran or tended to run to a peaked and many-chimneyed centre, with, here and there, a suggestion of a dormer window. Not all were provided with figs and jessamines, but each had some inclosure betraying good intentions.

The monotonous landscape did not invite to loitering, and we passed but three nights in houses by the road. The first was that of an old Italian-French emigrant, known as "Old Man Corse." He had a name of his own, which he recalled for us, but in forty years it had been lost and superseded by this designation, derived from his birth-place, the island of Corsica. This mixture of nationalities in language must be breeding for future antiquaries a good deal of amusing labour. Next day we were recommended to stop at Jack Bacon's, and, although we would have preferred to avoid an American's, did so rather than go further, and found our Jack Bacon a Creole, named Jacques Béguin. This is equal to Tuckapaw and Nakitosh, the general pronunciation of Attakapas and Natchitoches.

The house of Old Man Corse stood in the shade of oaks, figs, and cypresses, upon the bank of a little bayou, looking out upon the broad prairie. It was large and comfortable, with wide galleries and dormer windows, supported by a negro-hut and a stable. Ornamental axe-work and rude decorative joinery were abundant. The roof was of large split shingles, much warped in the sun. As we entered and took seats by the fire, the room reminded us, with its big fire-place, and old smoke-stained and time-toned cypress beams and ceiling, and its rude but comfortable aspect, of the Acadian fireside:

> In doors, warm by the wide-mouthed fire-place, idly the farmer
> Sat in his elbow-chair, and watched how the flames and the smoke-wreaths
> Struggled together, like foes in a burning city. Behind him,
> Nodding and mocking along the wall, with gestures fantastic,
> Darted his own huge shadow, and vanished away into darkness,
> Faces, clumsily carved in oak, on the back of his arm-chair,
> Laughed in the flickering light, and the pewter plates on the dresser
> Caught and reflected the flame, as shields of armies the sunshine.

The tall, elderly, busy housewife bustled about with preparations for supper, while we learned that they had been settled here forty years, and had never had reason to regret their emigration. The old man had learnt French, but no English. The woman could speak some "American," as she properly termed it. Asking her about musquitoes, we received a reply in French, that they were more abundant some years than others; then, as no quantitative adjective of sufficient force occurred to her, she added, "Three years ago, oh! heaps of musquitoes, sir, *heaps!* worse as now."

She laid the table to the last item, and prepared everything nicely, but called a negro girl to wait upon us. The girl stood quiet behind us, the mistress helping us, and practically anticipating all our wants.

The supper was of venison, in ragoût, with a sauce that savoured of the south of France; there was a side dish of hominy, a jug of sweet milk, and wheat-bread in loaf—the first since Houston.

In an evening smoke, upon the settle, we learned that there were many Creoles about here, most of whom learned English, and had their children taught English at the schools. The Americans would not take the trouble to learn French. They often intermarried. A daughter of their own was the wife of an American neighbour. We asked if they knew of a distinct people here called Acadians. Oh yes, they knew many settled in the vicinity, descended from some nation that came here in the last century. They had now no peculiarities. There were but few free negroes just here, but at Opelousas and Niggerville there were many, some of whom were rich and owned slaves, though a part were unmixed black in colour. They kept pretty much by themselves, not attempting to enter white society.

As we went to look at our horses, two negroes followed us to the stable.

"Dat horse a Tennessee horse, mass'r," said one.

"Yes, he was born in Tennessee."

"Born in Tennessee and raised by a Dutchman," said the other, sotto voce, I suppose, quoting a song.

"Why, were you born in Tennessee?" I asked.

"No, sar, I was born in dis State."

"How comes it you speak English so much better than your master?"

"Ho, ho, my old mass'r, he don' speak it at all; my missus she speak it better'n my mass'r do, but you see I war raised on de parara, to der eastward, whar thar's heaps of 'Mericans; so I larned it good."

He spoke it, with a slight accent, while the other, whom he called Uncle Tom, I observed did not. I asked Uncle Tom if he was born in the State.

"*No, sar!* I was born in *Varginny!* in ole Varginny, mass'r. I was raised in —— county [in the West]. I was twenty-two year ole when I came away from thar, and I've been in this country, forty year come next Christmas."

"Then you are sixty years old."

"Yes, sar, amos' sixty. But I'd like to go back to Varginny. Ho, ho! I 'ould like to go back and live in ole Varginny, again."

"Why so? I thought niggers generally liked this country best— I've been told so—because it is so warm here."

"Ho, ho! it's mos' too warm here, sometime, and I can't work at my trade here. Sometimes for three months I don' go in my shop, on'y Sundays to work for mysef."

"What is your trade?"

"I'm a blacksmith, mass'r. I used to work at blacksmithing all the time in ole Varginny, ironin' waggons, and shoein' horses for the folks that work in the mines. But here, can't get nothun' to do. In this here sile, if you sharpen up a plough in the spring o' the year, it'll last all summer, and horses don' want shoeing once a year, here on the parara. I've got a good mass'r here, tho'; the ole man ain't hard on his niggers."

"Was your master hard in Virginia?"

"Well, I wos hired to different mass'rs, sar, thar, afore I wos sole off. I wos sole off to a sheriff's sale, mass'r: I wos sole for fifteen hunerd an' fifty dollars; I fetched that on the block, cash, I did, and the man as bought me he brung me down here, and sole me for two thousand two hunerd dollars."

"That was a good price; a very high price in those days."

"Yes, sar, it was that—ho, ho, ho! It was a man by the name of ——, from Tennessee, what bought me. He made a business of goin' roun' and buyin' up people, and bringin' 'em down here, speculatin' on 'em. Ho, ho! he did well that time. But I'd 'a' liked it better, for all that, to have stayed in ole Varginny. 'Tain't the heat, tho' it's too hot here sometimes; but you know, sar, I was born and raised in Varginny, and seems like 'twould be pleasanter to live thar. It's kinder natural to people to hanker arter the place they wos raised in. Ho, ho! I'd like it a heap better, tho' this ole man's a good mass'r; never had no better mass'r."

"I suppose you became a Catholic after you got here?"

"Yes, sar" (hesitatingly).

"I suppose all the people are Catholics here?"

"Here? Oh, no, sar; they wos whar I wos first in this here country; they wos all Catholics there."

"Well, they are all Catholics here, too—ain't they?"

"Here, sar? Here, sar? Oh, no, sar!"

"Why, your master is not a Protestant, is he?"

After two deep groans, he replied in a whisper:

"Oh, sar, they don' have no meetin' o' no kind, roun' here!"

"There are a good many free negroes in this country, ain't there?"

"What! here, sar? Oh, no, sar; no such good luck as that in this country."

"At Opelousas, I understood, there were a good many."

"Oh, but them wos born free, sar, under old Spain, sar."

"Yes, those I mean."

"Oh, yes, there's lots o' *them;* some of 'em rich, and some of 'em— a good many of 'em—goes to the penitentiary—you know what that is. White folks goes to the penitenti'ry, too—ho! ho!—sometimes."

"I have understood many of them were quite rich."

"Oh, yes, o' course they is: they started free, and ain't got nobody to work for but theirselves; of course they gets rich. Some of 'em owns slaves—heaps of 'em. That ar ain't right."

"Not right! why not?"

"Why, you don' think it's right for one nigger to own another nigger! One nigger's no business to sarve another. It's bad enough to have to sarve a white man without being paid for it, without having to sarve a black man."

"Don't they treat their slaves well?"

"No, sar, they don't. There ain't no nations so bad masters to niggers as them free niggers, though there's some, I've heard, wos very kind; but—I wouldn't sarve 'em if they wos—no!—Does you live in Tennessee, mass'r?"

"No—in New York."

"There's heaps of Quakers in New York, ain't there, mass'r?"

"No—not many."

"I've always heard there was."

"In Philadelphia there are a good many."

"Oh, yes! in Philadelphia, and in Winchester, and in New Jarsey. I know—ho! ho! I've been in those countries, and I've seen 'em. I wos raised nigh by Winchester, and I've been all about there. Used to iron waggons and shoe horses in that country. Dar's a road from Winchester to Philadelphia—right straight. Quakers all along. Right good people, dem Quakers—ho! ho!—I know." [3]

We slept in well-barred beds, and awoke long after sunrise. As soon as we were stirring, black coffee was sent in to us, and at

---

[3] Evidently an allusion to the "underground railroad," or smuggling of runaway slaves, which is generally supposed to be managed mainly by Quakers. This shows how knowledge of the abolition agitation must be carried among the slaves to the most remote districts.

breakfast we had *café au lait* in immense bowls in the style of the *crémeries* of Paris. The woman remarked that our dog had slept in their bed-room. They had taken our saddle-bags and blankets with them for security, and Judy had insisted on following them. "Dishonest black people might come here and get into the room," explained the old man. "Yes; and some of our own people in the house might come to them. Such things have happened here, and you never can trust any of them," said the woman, her own black girl behind her chair.

At Mr. Béguin's (Bacon's) we stopped on a Saturday night: and I was obliged to feed my own horse in the morning, the negroes having all gone off before daylight. The proprietor was a Creole farmer, owning a number of labourers, and living in comfort. The house was of the ordinary Southern double-cabined style, the people speaking English, intelligent, lively, and polite, giving us good entertainment at the usual price. At a rude corn-mill belonging to Mr. Béguin, we had noticed among the negroes an Indian boy, in negro clothing, and about the house were two other Indians—an old man and a young man; the first poorly clad, the other gaily dressed in a showy printed calico frock, and worked buckskin leggings, with beads and tinsel ornaments, a great turban of Scotch shawl-stuff on his head. It appeared they were Choctaws, of whom a good many lived in the neighbourhood. The two were hired for farm labour at three bits (37½ cents) a day. The old man had a field of his own in which stood handsome corn. Some of them were industrious, but none were steady at work—often refusing to go on, or absenting themselves from freaks. I asked about the boy at the mill. He lived there and did work, getting no wages, but "living there with the niggers." They seldom consort; our host knew but one case in which a negro had an Indian wife.

At Lake Charles we had seen a troop of Alabamas, riding through the town with baskets and dressed deerskins for sale. They were decked with feathers, and dressed more showily than the Choctaws, but in calico: and over their heads, on horseback—curious progress of manners—all carried open, black cotton *umbrellas.*

Our last night in this region was spent in a house which we reached at sundown of a Sunday afternoon. It proved to be a mere cottage, in a style which has grown to be common along our road.

The walls are low, of timber and mud; the roof, high, and sloping from a short ridge in all directions; and the chimney of sticks and mud. The space is divided into one long living-room, having a kitchen at one end and a bed-room at the other. As we rode up, we found only a little boy, who answered us in French. His mother was milking, and his father out in the field.

We rode on to the fence of the field, which enclosed twenty acres, planted in cotton, corn, and sweet potatoes, and waited until the proprietor reached us and the end of his furrow. He stopped before replying, to unhitch his horse, then gave consent to our staying in his house, and we followed his lead to the yard, where we unsaddled our horses. He was a tall, stalwart man in figure, with a large intellectual head, but as uninformed, we afterwards discovered, as any European peasant; though he wore, as it were, an ill-fitting dress of rude independence in manner, such as characterises the Western man.

The field was well cultivated, and showed the best corn we had seen east of the Brazos. Three negro men and two women were at work, and continued hoeing until sunset. They were hired, it appeared, by the proprietor, at four bits (fifty cents) a day. He was in the habit of making use of the Sundays of the slaves of the neighbourhood in this way, paying them sometimes seventy-five cents a day.

On entering the house, we were met by two young boys, gentle and winning in manner, coming up of their own accord to offer us their hands. They were immediately set to work by their father at grinding corn, in the steel-mill, for supper. The task seemed their usual one, yet very much too severe for their strength, as they were slightly built, and not over ten years old. Taking hold at opposite sides of the winch, they ground away, outside the door, for more than an hour, constantly stopping to take breath, and spurred on by the voice of the papa, if the delay were long.

They spoke only French, though understanding questions in English. The man and his wife—an energetic but worn woman—spoke French or English indifferently, even to one another, changing, often, in a single sentence. He could not tell us which was his mother tongue; he had always been as much accustomed to the one as to the other. He said he was not a Frenchman, but a native, American-born; but afterwards called himself a "Dutch-American," a phrase he was unable to explain. He informed us that there were many "Dutch-French" here, that is, people who were Dutch, but who spoke French.

The room into which we were ushered, was actually without an article of furniture. The floor was of boards, while those of the other two rooms were of trodden clay. The mud-walls had no other relief than the mantel, on which stood a Connecticut clock, two small mirrors, three or four cheap cups and saucers, and a paste brooch in the form of a cross, pinned upon paper, as in a jeweller's shop. Chairs were brought in from the kitchen, having deer-hide seats, from which sprang forth an atrocious number of fresh fleas.

We had two or three hours to wait for our late supper, and thus more than ample time to converse with our host, who proceeded to twist and light a shuck cigar. He made, he said, a little cotton, which he hauled ten miles to be ginned and baled. For this service he paid seventy-five cents a hundred weight, in which the cost of bagging was not included. The planter who baled it, also sold it for him, sending it, with his own, to a factor in New Orleans, by steamboat from Niggerville, just beyond Opelousas. Besides cotton, he sold every year some beef cattle. He had a good many cows, but didn't exactly know how many. Corn, too, he sometimes sold, but only to neighbours, who had not raised enough for themselves. It would not pay to haul it to any market. The same applied to sweet potatoes, which were considered worth seventy-five cents a barrel.

The "range" was much poorer than formerly. It was crowded, and people would have to take their stock somewhere else in four or five years more, or they would starve. He didn't know what was going to become of poor folks, rich people were taking up the public land so fast, induced by the proposed railroad to New Orleans.

More or less stock was always starved in winter. The worst time for them was when a black gnat, called the "eye-breaker," comes out. This insect breeds in the low woodlands, and when a freshet occurs in winter is driven out in swarms upon the prairies, attacking cattle terribly. They were worse than all manner of musquitoes, flies, or other insects. Cattle would herd together then, and wander wildly about, not looking for the best feed, and many would get killed. But this did not often happen.

Horses and cattle had degenerated much within his recollection. No pains were taken to improve breeds. People, now-a-days, had got proud, and when they had a fine colt would break him for a carriage or riding-horse, leaving only the common scurvy sort to run with the mares. This was confirmed by our observation, the horses about here being wretched in appearance, and the grass short and coarse.

When we asked to wash before supper, a shallow cake-pan was brought and set upon the window-seat, and a mere rag offered us for towel. Upon the supper-table, we found two wash-bowls, one filled with milk, the other with molasses. We asked water, which was given us in one battered tin cup. The dishes, besides the bacon and bread, were fried eggs and sweet potatoes. The bowl of molasses stood in the centre of the table, and we were pressed to partake of it, as the family did, by dipping in it bits of bread. But how it was expected to be used at breakfast, when we had bacon and potatoes, with spoons, but no bread, I cannot imagine, the family not breakfasting with us.

The night was warm, and musquitoes swarmed, but we carried with us a portable tent-shaped bar, which we hung over the feather bed, upon the floor, and rested soundly amid their mad singing.

The distance to Opelousas, our Frenchman told us, was fifteen miles by the road, though only ten miles in a direct line. We found it lined with farms, whose division-fences the road always followed, frequently changing its course in so doing at a right angle. The country was very wet and unattractive. About five miles from the town, begin plantations on an extensive scale, upon better soil, and here were large gangs of negroes at work upon cotton, with their hoes.

At the outskirts of the town, we waded the last pool, and entered, with a good deal of satisfaction, the peaceful shaded streets. Reaching the hotel, we were not so instantly struck as perhaps we should have been, with the overwhelming advantages of civilization, which sat in the form of a landlord, slapping with an agate-headed, pliable cane, his patent leather boots, poised, at easy height, upon one of the columns of the gallery. We were suffered to take off our saddle-bags, and to wait until waiting was no longer a pleasure, before civilization, wringing his cane against the floor, but not removing his cigar, brought his patent leathers to our vicinity.

After some conversation, intended as animated upon one side and ineffably indifferent on the other, our horses obtained notice from that exquisitely vague eye, but a further introduction was required before our persons became less than transparent, for the boots walked away, and became again a subject of contemplation upon the column, leaving us, with our saddle-bags, upon the steps. After inquiring of a bystander if this glossy individual were the actual landlord, we attacked him in a tone likely to produce either a revolver-shot or a room, but whose effect was to obtain a removal of the cigar and a gentle survey, ending in a call for a boy to show the gentlemen to number thirteen.

After an hour's delay, we procured water, and were about to enjoy very necessary ablutions, when we observed that the door of our room was partly of uncurtained glass. A shirt was pinned to this, and ceremonies were about beginning, when a step came down the passage, and a gentleman put his hand through a broken pane, and lifted the obstruction, wishing "to see what was going on so damn'd secret in number thirteen." When I walked toward him hurriedly, *in puris naturalibus,* he drew back hastily and entered the next room.

On the gallery of the hotel, after dinner, a fine-looking man—who was on the best of terms with every one—familiar with the judge— and who had been particularly polite to me, at the dinner-table, said to another:

"I hear you were very unlucky with that girl you bought of me, last year?"

"Yes, I was; very unlucky. She died with her first child, and the child died, too."

"Well, that was right hard for you. She was a fine girl. I don't reckon you lost less than five thousand dollars, when she died."

"No, sir, not a dollar less."

"Well, it came right hard upon you—just beginning so."

"Yes, I was foolish, I suppose, to risk so much on the life of a single woman; but I've got a good start again now, for all that. I've got two right likely girls; one of them's got a fine boy, four months old, and the other's with child—and old Pine Knot's as hearty as ever."

"Is he? Hasn't been sick at all, eh?"

"Yes; he was sick very soon after I bought him of you; but he got well soon."

"That's right. I'd rather a nigger would be sick early, after he comes into this country; for he's bound to be acclimated, sooner or later, and the longer it's put off, the harder it goes with him."

The man was a regular negro trader. He told me that he had a partner in Kentucky, and that they owned a farm there, and another one here. His partner bought negroes, as opportunity offered to get them advantageously, and kept them on their Kentucky farm; and he went on occasionally, and brought the surplus to their Louisiana plantation—where he held them for sale.

"So-and-so is very hard upon you," said another man, to him as he still sat, smoking his cigar, on the gallery, after dinner.

"Why so? He's no business to complain; I told him just exactly what the nigger was, before I sold him" (laughing, as if there was a concealed joke). "It was all right—all right. I heard that he sold him again for a thousand dollars; and the people that bought him, gave him two hundred dollars to let them off from the bargain. I'm sure he can't complain of me. It was a fair transaction. He knew just what he was buying."

An intelligent man whom I met here, and who had been travelling most of the time during the last two years in Louisiana, having business with the planters, described the condition of the new slave-holders and the poorer planters as being very miserable.

He had sometimes found it difficult to get food, even when he was in urgent need of it, at their houses. The lowest class live much from hand to mouth, and are often in extreme destitution. This was more particularly the case with those who lived on the river; those who resided on the prairies were seldom so much reduced. The former now live only on those parts of the river to which the back-swamp approaches nearest; that is, where there is but little valuable land, that can be appropriated for plantation-purposes. They almost all reside in communities, very closely housed in poor cabins. If there is any considerable number of them, there is to be always found, among the cluster of their cabins, a church, and a billiard and a gambling-room—and the latter is always occupied, and play going on.

They almost all appear excessively apathetic, sleepy, and stupid, if you see them at home; and they are always longing and waiting for some excitement. They live for excitement, and will not labour, unless it is violently, for a short time, to gratify some passion.

This was as much the case with the women as the men. The

women were often handsome, stately, and graceful, and, ordinarily, exceedingly kind; but languid, and incredibly indolent, unless there was a ball, or some other excitement, to engage them. Under excitement, they were splendidly animated, impetuous, and eccentric. One moment they seemed possessed by a devil, and the next by an angel.

The Creoles [4] are inveterate gamblers—rich and poor alike. The majority of wealthy Creoles, he said, do nothing to improve their estate; and are very apt to live beyond their income. They borrow and play, and keep borrowing to play, as long as they can; but they will not part with their land, and especially with their home, as long as they can help it, by any sacrifice.

The men are generally dissolute. They have large families, and a great deal of family affection. He did not know that they had more than Anglo-Saxons; but they certainly manifested a great deal more, and, he thought, had more domestic happiness. If a Creole farmer's child marries, he will build a house for the new couple, adjoining his own; and when another marries, he builds another house—so, often his whole front on the river is at length occupied. Then he begins to build others, back of the first—and so, there gradually forms a little village, wherever there is a large Creole family, owning any considerable piece of land. The children are poorly educated, and are not brought up to industry, at all.

The planters living near them, as their needs increase, lend them money, and get mortgages on their land, or, in some way or other, if it is of any value, force them to part with it. Thus they are every year reduced, more and more, to the poorest lands; and the majority now are able to get but a very poor living, and would not be able to live at all in a Northern climate. They are nevertheless—even the poorest of them—habitually gay and careless, as well as kind-hearted, hospitable, and dissolute—working little, and spending much of their time at church, or at balls, or the gaming-table.

There are very many wealthy Creole planters, who are as cultivated and intelligent as the better class of American planters, and usually more refined. The Creoles, he said, did not work their slaves as hard as the Americans; but, on the other hand, they did not feed

[4] Creole means simply native of the region, but in Louisiana (a vast region purchased, by the United States, of France, for strategic reasons, and now proposed to be filibustered away from us), it generally indicates French blood.

or clothe them nearly as well, and he had noticed universally, on the Creole plantations, a large number of "used-up hands"—slaves, sore and crippled, or invalided for some cause. On all sugar plantations, he said, they work the negroes excessively, in the grinding season; often cruelly. Under the usual system, to keep the fires burning, and the works constantly supplied, eighteen hours' work was required of every negro, in twenty-four—leaving but six for rest. The work of most of them, too, was very hard. They were generally, during the grinding season, liberally supplied with food and coffee, and were induced, as much as possible, to make a kind of frolic of it; yet, on the Creole plantations, he thought they did not, even in the grinding season, often get meat.

I remarked that the law, in Louisiana, required that meat should be regularly served to the negroes.

"O, those laws are very little regarded."

"Indeed?"

"Certainly. Suppose you are my neighbour; if you maltreat your negroes, and tell me of it, or I see it, am I going to prefer charges against you to the magistrates? I might possibly get you punished according to law; but if I did, or did not, I should have you, and your family and friends, far and near, for my mortal enemies. There is a law of the State that negroes shall not be worked on Sundays; but I have seen negroes at work almost every Sunday, when I have been in the country, since I have lived in Louisiana.⁵ I spent a Sunday once with a gentleman, who did not work his hands at all on Sunday, even in the grinding season; and he had got some of his neighbours to help him build a school-house, which was used as a church on Sunday. He said, there was not a plantation on either side of him, as far as he could see, where the slaves were not generally worked on Sunday; but that, after the church was started, several of them quit the practice, and made their negroes go to the meeting. This made others discontented; and after a year or two, the planters voted new trustees to the school, and these forbid the house to be used for any other than school purposes. This was done, he had no doubt, for the purpose of breaking up the meetings, and to lessen the discontent of the slaves which were worked on Sunday.

⁵ I also saw slaves at work every Sunday that I was in Louisiana. The law permits slaves to be worked, I believe, on Sunday; but requires that some compensation shall be made to them when they are—such as a subsequent holiday.

It was said that the custom of working the negroes on Sunday was much less common than formerly; if so, he thought that it must have formerly been universal.

He had lived, when a boy, for several years on a farm in Western New York, and afterwards, for some time, at Rochester, and was well acquainted with the people generally, in the valley of the Genesee.

I asked him if he thought, among the intelligent class of farmers and planters, people of equal property lived more happily in New York or Louisiana. He replied immediately, as if he had carefully considered the topic, that, with some rare exceptions, farmers worth forty thousand dollars lived in far greater comfort, and enjoyed more refined and elegant leisure, than planters worth three hundred thousand, and that farmers of the ordinary class, who laboured with their own hands, and were worth some six thousand dollars, in the Genesee valley, lived in far greater comfort, and in all respects more enviably, than planters worth forty thousand dollars in Louisiana. The contrast was especially favourable to the New York farmer, in respect to books and newspapers. He might travel several days, and call on a hundred planters, and hardly see in their houses more than a single newspaper apiece, in most cases; perhaps none at all: nor any books, except a Bible, and some government publications, that had been franked to them through the post-office, and perhaps a few religious tracts or school-books.

The most striking difference that he observed between the Anglo-Americans of Louisiana and New York, was the impulsive and unreflective habit of the former, in doing business. He mentioned, as illustrative of this, the almost universal passion among the planters for increasing their negro-stock. It appeared evident to him, that the market price of negroes was much higher than the prices of cotton and sugar warranted; but it seemed as if no planter ever made any calculation of that kind. The majority of planters, he thought, would always run in debt to the extent of their credit for negroes, whatever was asked for them, without making any calculation of the reasonable prospects of their being able to pay their debts. When any one made a good crop, he would always expect that his next one would be better, and make purchases in advance upon such expectation. When they were dunned, they would attribute their inability to pay, to accidental short crops, and always were going ahead risking everything, in confidence that another year of luck would favour them, and a big crop make all right.

If they had a full crop, probably there would be good crops everywhere else, and prices would fall, and then they would whine and complain, as if the merchants were to blame for it, and would insinuate that no one could be expected to pay his debts when prices were so low, and that it would be dangerous to press such an unjust claim. And, if the crops met with any misfortune, from floods, or rot, or vermin, they would cry about it like children when rain fell upon a holiday, as if they had never thought of the possibility of such a thing, and were very hard used.[6]

He had talked with many sugar-planters who were strong Cuba war and annexation men, and had rarely found that any of these had given the first thought to the probable effect the annexation of Cuba would have on their home interests. It was mainly a romantic excitement and enthusiasm, inflamed by senseless appeals to their patriotism and their combativeness. They had got the idea, that patriotism was necessarily associated with hatred and contempt of any other country but their own, and the only foreigners to be regarded with favour were those who desired to surrender themselves to us. They did not reflect that the annexation of Cuba would necessarily be attended by the removal of the duty on sugar, and would bring them into competition with the sugar-planters of that island,

---

[6] The following resolutions were proposed (I am not sure that they were adopted) in the Southern Commercial Convention, at New Orleans, in 1855:

"*Resolved,*—That this Convention strongly recommends the Chambers of Commerce and Commission Merchants of our Southern and South-western cities to adopt such a system of laws and regulations as will put a stop to the dangerous practice, heretofore existing, of making advances to planters, in anticipation of their crops—a practice entirely at variance with everything like safety in business transactions, and tending directly to establish the relations of master and slave between the merchant and planter, by bringing the latter into the most abject and servile bondage.

"*Resolved,*—That this Convention recommend, in the most urgent manner, that the planters of the Southern and South-western States patronize exclusively our home merchants, and that our Chambers of Commerce, and merchants generally, exert all their influence to exclude foreign agents from the purchase and sale of produce in any of our Southern and South-western cities.

"*Resolved, further,*—That this Convention recommend to the legislatures of the Southern and South-western States to pass laws, making it a penitentiary offence for the planters to ask of the merchants to make such pecuniary advances."

where the advantages for growing cane were so much greater than in Louisiana.

To some of the very wealthy planters who favoured the movement, and who were understood to have taken some of the Junta [7] stock, he gave credit for greater sagacity. He thought it was the purpose of these men, if Cuba could be annexed, to get possession of large estates there: then, with the advantages of their greater skill in sugar-making, and better machinery than that which yet was in use in Cuba, and with much cheaper land and labour, and a far better climate for cane growing than that of Louisiana, it would be easy for them to accumulate large fortunes in a few years; but he thought the sugar-planters who remained in Louisiana would be ruined by it.

The principal subscribers to the Junta stock at the South, he thought, were land speculators; persons who expected that, by now favouring the movement, they would be able to obtain from the revolutionary government large grants of land in the island as gratuities in reward of their services or at nominal prices, which after annexation would rise rapidly in value; or persons who now owned wild land in the States, and who thought that if Cuba were annexed the African slave-trade would be re-established, either openly or clandestinely, with the States, and their lands be increased in value, by the greater cheapness with which they could then be stocked with labourers.

I find these views confirmed in a published letter from a Louisiana planter, to one of the members of Congress, from that State; and I insert an extract of that letter, as it is evidently from a sensible and far-thinking man, to show on how insecure a basis rests the prosperity of the slave-holding interest in Louisiana. The fact would seem to be, that, if it were not for the tariff on foreign sugars, sugar could not be produced at all by slave-labour; and that a discontinuance of sugar culture would almost desolate the State.

The question now naturally comes up to you and to me, Do we Louisianians desire the possession of Cuba? It is not what the provision dealers of the West, or the shipowners of the North may wish for, but what the State of Louisiana, as a State, may deem consistent with her best interests. My own opinion on the subject is not a new one. It was long ago ex-

[7] The Junta was a filibustering conspiracy against Cuba.

pressed to high officers of our Government, neither of whom ever hesitated to acknowledge that it was, in the main, correct. That opinion was and is, *that the acquisition of Cuba would prove the ruin of our State.* I found this opinion on the following reasons: Cuba has already land enough in cultivation to produce, when directed by American skill, energy, and capital, twenty millions of tons of sugar. In addition to this she has virgin soil, only needing roads to bring it, with a people of the least pretension to enterprise, into active working, sufficient nearly to double this; all of which would be soon brought into productiveness were it our own, with the whole American market free to it. If any man supposes that the culture of sugar in our State can be sustained in the face of this, I have only to say that he can suppose anything. We have very nearly, if not quite, eighty millions invested in the sugar culture. My idea is that *three-fourths of this would, so far as the State is concerned, be annihilated at a blow.* The planter who is in debt, would find his negroes and machinery sold and despatched to Cuba for him, and he who is independent would go there in self-defence. What will become of the other portion of the capital? It consists of land, on which I maintain there can be produced no other crop but sugar, under present auspices, that will bear the contest with cocoa,[8] and the expense and risk of levees, as it regards the larger part of it, and the difficulty of transportation for the remainder. But supposing that it will be taken up by some other cultivation, that in any case must be a work of time, and in this case a very long time for unacclimated men. It is not unreasonable, then, to suppose that the whole capital will, for purposes of taxation, be withdrawn from Louisiana. From whence, then, is to come the revenue for the support of our State government, for the payment of the interest on our debt, and the eventual redemption of the principal? Perhaps repudiation may be recommended; but you and I, my dear sir, are too old-fashioned to rob in that manner, or in any other. The only resort, then, is double taxation on the cotton planter, which will drive him, without much difficulty, to Texas, to Arkansas, and Mississippi.

Washington [Louisiana].—The inn, here, when we arrived, was well filled with guests, and my friend and I were told that we must sleep together. In the room containing our bed there were three other beds; and although the outside of the house was pierced with windows, nowhere more than four feet apart, not one of them

---

[8] Cocoa is a grass much more pernicious, and more difficult of extirpation when it once gets a footing upon a sugar plantation, than the Canada thistle, or any other weed known at the North. Several plantations have been ruined by it, and given up as worthless by their owners.

opened out of our room. A door opened into the hall, another into the dining-room, and at the side of our bed was a window into the dining-room, through which, betimes in the morning, we could, with our heads on our pillows, see the girls setting the breakfast-tables. Both the doors were provided with glass windows, without curtains. Hither, about eleven o'clock, we "retired." Soon afterwards, hearing something moving under the bed, I asked, "Who's there?" and was answered by a girl, who was burrowing for eggs; part of the stores of the establishment being kept in boxes, in this conveni-ent locality. Later, I was awakened by a stranger attempting to enter my bed. I expostulated, and he replied that it was his bed, and no-body else had a right to his place in it. Who was I, he asked, angrily, and where was his partner? "Here I am," answered a voice from an-other bed; and without another word, he left us. I slept but little, and woke feverish, and with a headache, caused by the want of ven-tilation.

While at the dinner-table, a man asked, as one might at the North, if the steamer had arrived, if there had been "any fights to-day?" After dinner, while we were sitting on the gallery, loud cursing, and threatening voices were heard in the direction of the bar-room, which, as at Natchitoches, was detached, and at a little distance from the hotel. The company, except myself and the other New-Yorker, immediately ran towards it. After ten minutes, one re-turned, and said—

"I don't believe there'll be any fight; they are both cowards."

"Are they preparing for a fight?"

"O, yes; they are loading pistols in the coffee-room, and there's a man outside, in the street, who has a revolver and a knife, and who is challenging another to come out. He swears he'll wait there till he does come out; but in my opinion he'll think better of it, when he finds that the other feller's got pistols, too."

"What's the occasion of the quarrel?"

"Why, the man in the street says the other one insulted him this morning, and that he had his hand on his knife, at the very moment he did so, so he couldn't reply. And now he says he's ready to talk with him, and he wants to have him come out, and as many of his friends as are a mind to, may come with him; he's got enough for all of 'em, he says. He's got two revolvers, I believe."

We did not hear how it ended; but, about an hour afterwards,

I saw three men, with pistols in their hands, coming from the bar-room.

The next day, I saw, in the streets of the same town, two boys running from another, who was pursuing them with a large, open dirk-knife in his hand, and every appearance of ungovernable rage in his face.

The boat, for which I was waiting, not arriving, I asked the land-lady—who appeared to be a German Jewess—if I could not have a better sleeping-room. She showed me one, which she said I might use for a single night; but, if I remained another, I must not refuse to give it up. It had been occupied by another gentleman, and she thought he might return the next day, and would want it again; and, if I remained in it, he would be very angry that they had not reserved it for him, although they were under no obligation to him. "He is a dangerous man," she observed, "and my husband, he's a quick-tempered man, and, if they get to quarrelling about it, there'll be knives about, sure. It always frightens me to see knives drawn."

A Texas drover, who stayed over night at the hotel, being asked, as he was about to leave in the morning, if he was not going to have his horse shod, replied:

"No sir! it'll be a damn'd long spell 'fore I pay for having a horse shod. I reckon, if God Almighty had thought it right hosses should have iron on thar feet, he'd a put it thar himself. I don't pretend to be a pious man myself; but I a'nt a-goin' to run agin the will of God Almighty, though thar's some, that calls themselves ministers of Christ, that does it."

CHAPTER XI

A Trip into Northern Mississippi

Vicksburg, March 18th [1854].—I arrived at this place last night, about sunset, and was told that there was no hotel in the town except on the wharf-boat, the only house used for that purpose having been closed a few days ago on account of a difference of opinion between its owner and his tenant.

There are no wharves on the Mississippi, or any of the Southern rivers. The wharf-boat is an old steamboat, with her paddle boxes and machinery removed and otherwise dismantled, on which steamboats discharge passengers and freight. The main deck is used as a warehouse, and, in place of the furnace, has in this case a dram shop, a chandler's shop, a forwarding agency, and a telegraph office. Overhead, the saloon and state-rooms remain, and with the bar-room and clerk's office, kitchen and barber's shop, constitute a stationary though floating hostelry.

Though there were fifty or more rooms, and not a dozen guests, I was obliged, about twelve o'clock, to admit a stranger who had been gambling all the evening in the saloon, to occupy the spare shelf of my closet. If a disposition to enjoy occasional privacy, or to exercise a choice in one's room-mates were a sure symptom of a monomania for incendiarism, it could not be more carefully thwarted than it is at all public-houses in this part of the world.

Memphis, March 20th.—I reached this place to-day in forty-eight hours by steamboat from Vicksburg.

Here, at the "Commercial Hotel," I am favoured with an unusually good-natured room-mate. He is smoking on the bed—our bed—now, and wants to know what my business is here, and whether I carry a pistol about me; also whether I believe that it isn't lucky to play cards on Sundays; which I do most strenuously, especially as this is a rainy Sunday, and his second cigar is nearly smoked out.

This is a first-class hotel, and has, of course, printed bills of fare, which, in a dearth of other literature, are not to be dropped at the first glance. A copy of to-day's is presented on the opposite page.

Being in a distant quarter of the establishment when a crash of

COMMERCIAL HOTEL.

BY D. COCKRELL.

BILL OF FARE.

MARCH 20.

SOUP.

Oyster.

FISH.

Red.

BOILED.

Jole and Green.
Ham.
Corned beef.
Bacon and turnips.
Codfish egg sauce.
Beef heart egg sauce.
Leg of mutton caper sauce.
Barbecued rabits.
Boiled tongue.

ROAST.

Veal.
Roast pig.
Muscovie ducks.
Kentucky beef.
Mutton.
Barbecued shoat.
Roast bear meat.
Roast pork.

ENTREES.

Fricasee pork.
Calf feet mushroom sauce.
Bear sausages.
Harricane tripe.
Stewed mutton.
Browned rice.
Calf feet madeira sauce.
Stewed turkey wine sauce.
Giblets volivon.
Mutton omelett.
Beef's heart fricaseed.
Cheese macaroni.
Chicken chops robert sauce.
Breast chicken madeira sauce.
Beef kidney pickle sauce.
Cod fish baked.
Calf head wine sauce.

FRUIT.

Almonds.
Raisins.
Pecans.

VEGETABLES.

Boiled cabbage.
Turnips.
Cold slaugh.
Hot slaugh.
Pickled beets.
Creole hominy.
Crout cabbage.
Oyster plant fried.
Parsneps gravied.
Stewed parsneps.
Fried cabbage.
Sweet potatoes spiced.
Carrot.
Sweet potatoes baked.
Cabbage stuffed.
Onions, boiled.
Irish potatoes creamed and mashed.
Irish potatoes browned.
Boiled shellots.
Scolloped carrots.
Boiled turnips drawn butter.
White beans.

PASTRY.

Currant pies.
Lemon custard.
Rice pudding.
Cocoanut pie.
Cranberry pies.
Sliced potato pie.
Chess cake.
Irish pudding.
Orange custard.
Cranberry shapes.
Green peach tarts.
Green peach puff paste.
Grape tarts.
Huckle berry pies.
Pound cake.
Rheubarb tarts.
Plum tarts.
Calves feet jelly.
Blamonge.
Orange jelly.

the gong announced dinner, I did not get to the table as early as some others. The meal was served in a large, dreary room exactly like a hospital ward; and it is a striking illustration of the celerity with which everything is accomplished in our young country, that beginning with the soup, and going on by the fish to the roasts, the first five dishes I inquired for—when at last I succeeded in arresting one of the negro boys—were "all gone"; and as the waiter had to go to the head of the dining-room, or to the kitchen, to ascertain this fact upon each demand, the majority of the company had left the table before I was served at all. At length I said I would take anything that was still to be had, and thereupon was provided immediately with some grimy bacon, and greasy cabbage. This I commenced eating, but I no sooner paused for a moment, than it was suddenly and surreptitiously removed, and its place supplied, without the expression of any desire on my part, with some other Memphitic chef d'œuvre, a close investigation of which left me in doubt whether it was that denominated "sliced potato pie," or "Irish pudding."

I congratulate myself that I have lived to see the day in which an agitation for reform in our GREAT HOTEL SYSTEM has been commenced, and I trust that a Society for the Revival of Village Inns will ere long form one of the features of the May anniversaries.

A stage-coach conveyed the railroad passengers from the hotel to the station, which was a mile or two out of town. As we were entering the coach the driver observed with a Mephistophelean smile that we "needn't calk'late we were gwine to ride very fur," and, as soon as we had got into the country he stopped and asked all the men to get out and walk, for, he condescended to explain, "it was as much as his hosses could do to draw the ladies and the baggage." It was quite true; the horses were often obliged to stop, even with the diminished load, and as there was a contract between myself and the proprietors by which, for a stipulated sum of money by me to them in hand duly paid, they had undertaken to convey me over this ground, I thought it would have been no more than honest if they had looked out beforehand to have either a stronger team, or a better road, provided. As is the custom of our country, however, we allowed ourselves to be thus robbed with great good-nature, and waded along ankle-deep in the mud, joking with the driver and ready to put our shoulders to the wheels if it should be

necessary. Two portmanteaus were jerked off in heavy lurches of
the coach; the owners picked them up and carried them on their
shoulders till the horses stopped to breathe again. The train of
course had waited for us, and it continued to wait until another
coach arrived, when it started twenty minutes behind time.

After some forty miles of rail, nine of us were stowed away
in another stage-coach. The road was bad, the weather foul. We
proceeded slowly, were often in imminent danger of being upset, and once were all obliged to get out and help the horses
drag the coach out of a slough; but with smoking, and the occasional circulation of a small black bottle, and a general disposition
to be as comfortable as circumstances would allow, four hours
of coaching proved less fatiguing than one of the ill-ventilated
rail-cars.

Among the passengers was a "Judge," resident in the vicinity,
portly, dignified, and well-informed; and a young man, who was a
personal friend of the member of Congress from the district, and
who, as he informed me, had, through the influence of this friend,
a promise from the President of honourable and lucrative employment under Government. He was known to all the other passengers,
and hailed by every one on the road-side, by the title of Colonel.
The Judge was ready to converse about the country through which
we were passing, and while perfectly aware, as no one else seemed
to be, that it bore anything but an appearance of prosperity or attractiveness to a stranger, he assured me that it was really improving in all respects quite rapidly. There were few large plantations, but many small planters or rather farmers, for cotton, though
the principal source of cash income, was much less exclusively an
object of attention than in the more southern parts of the State.
A larger space was occupied by the maize and grain crops. There
were not a few small fields of wheat. In the afternoon, when only
the Colonel and myself were with him, the Judge talked about
slavery in a candid and liberal spirit. At present prices, he said,
nobody could afford to own slaves, unless he could engage them
almost exclusively in cotton-growing. It was undoubtedly a great
injury to a region like this, which was not altogether well adapted
to cotton, to be in the midst of a slaveholding country, for it prevented efficient free labour. A good deal of cotton was nevertheless
grown hereabouts by white labour—by poor men who planted an

acre or two, and worked it themselves, getting the planters to gin and press it for them. It was not at all uncommon for men to begin in this way and soon purchase negroes on credit, and eventually become rich men. Most of the plantations in this vicinity, indeed, belonged to men who had come into the country with nothing within twenty years. Once a man got a good start with negroes, unless the luck was much against him, nothing but his own folly could prevent his becoming rich. The increase of his negro property by births, if he took good care of it, must, in a few years, make him independent. The worst thing, and the most difficult to remedy, was the deplorable ignorance which prevailed. Latterly, however, people were taking more pride in the education of their children. Some excellent schools had been established, the teachers generally from the North, and a great many children were sent to board in the villages—county-seats—to attend them. This was especially true of girls, who liked to live in the villages rather than on the plantations. There was more difficulty in making boys attend school, until, at least, they were too old to get much good from it.

The "Colonel" was a rough, merry, good-hearted, simple-minded man, and kept all the would-be sober-sides of our coach body in irrepressible laughter with queer observations on passing occurrences, anecdotes and comic songs. It must be confessed that there is no charge which the enemies of the theatre bring against the stage, that was not duly illustrated, and that with a broadness which the taste of a metropolitan audience would scarcely permit. Had Doctor —— and Doctor —— been with me they would thereafter for ever have denied themselves, and discountenanced in others, the use of such a means of travel. The Colonel, notwithstanding, was of a most obliging disposition, and having ascertained in what direction I was going, enumerated at least a dozen families on the road, within some hundred miles, whom he invited me to visit, assuring me that I should find pretty girls in all of them, and a warm welcome, if I mentioned his name.

He told the Judge that his bar-bill on the boat, coming up from New Orleans, was forty dollars—seventeen dollars the first night. But he had made money—had won forty dollars of one gentleman. He confessed, however, that he had lost fifteen by another, "but he saw how he did it. He did not want to accuse him publicly, but he saw it and he meant to write to him and tell him of it. He did not want to insult the gentleman, only he did not want to have him think that he was so green as not to know how he did it."

While stopping for dinner at a village inn, a young man came into the room where we all were, and asked the coachman what was to be paid for a trunk which had been brought for him. The coachman said the charge would be a dollar, which the young man thought excessive. The coachman denied that it was so, said that it was what he had often been paid; he should not take less. The young man finally agreed to wait for the decision of the proprietor of the line. There was a woman in the room; I noticed no loud words or angry tones, and had not supposed that there was the slightest excitement. I observed, however, that there was a profound silence for a minute afterwards, which was interrupted by a jocose remark of the coachman about the delay of our dinner. Soon after we re-entered the coach, the Colonel referred to the trunk owner in a contemptuous manner. The Judge replied in a similar tone. "If I had been in the driver's place, I should have killed him sure," said the Colonel. With great surprise, I ventured to ask for what reason. "Did not you see the fellow put his hand to his breast when the driver denied that he had ever taken less than a dollar for bringing a trunk from Memphis?"

"No, I did not; but what of it?"

"Why, he meant to frighten the driver, of course."

"You think he had a knife in his breast?"

"Of course he had, sir."

"But you wouldn't kill him for that, I suppose?"

"When a man threatens to kill me, you wouldn't have me wait for him to do it, would you, sir?"

The roads continued very heavy; some one remarked, "There's been a heap of rain lately," and rain still kept falling. We passed a number of cotton waggons which had stopped in the road; the cattle had been turned out and had strayed off into the woods, and the drivers lay under the tilts asleep on straw.

The Colonel said this sight reminded him of his old camp-meeting days. "I used to be very fond of going to camp-meetings. I used to go first for fun, and, oh Lord! haint I had some fun at camp-meetings? But after a while I got a conviction—needn't laugh, gentlemen. I tell you it was sober business for me. I'll never make fun of that. The truth just is, I am a melancholy case; I thought I was a pious man once, I did—I'm damn'd if I didn't. Don't laugh at what I say, now; I don't want fun made of that; I give you my word I experienced religion, and I used to go to the meetings with as much sincerity and soberness as anybody could. That was the time I learned to sing—learned to pray too, I did; could pray right smart. I did think I was a converted man, but of course I ain't, and I 'spose 'twarnt the right sort, and I don't reckon I shall have another chance. A gentleman has a right to make the most of this life, when he can't calculate on anything better than roasting in the next. Ain't that so, Judge? I reckon so. You mustn't think hard of me, if I do talk wicked some. Can't help it."

I was forced by the stage arrangements to travel night and day. The Colonel told me that I should be able to get a good supper at a house where the coach was to stop about midnight—"good honest fried bacon, and hot Christian corn-bread—nothing like it, to fill a man up and make him feel righteous. You get a heap better living up in this country than you can at the St. Charles, for all the fuss they make about it. It's lucky you'll have something better to travel on to-night than them French friterzeed Dutch flabbergasted hell-fixins: for you'll have the—" (another most extraordinary series of imprecations on the road over which I was to travel).

Before dark all my companions left me, and in their place I had but one, a young gentleman with whom I soon became very intimately acquainted. He was seventeen years old, so he said; he looked older; and the son of a planter in the "Yazoo bottoms." The last year he had "follered overseein'" on his father's plantation, but he was bound for Tennessee, now, to go to an academy, where he could learn geography. There was a school near home at which he had studied reading and writing and ciphering, but he thought a gentleman ought to have some knowledge of geography. At ten o'clock the next morning, the stage-coach having progressed at the rate of exactly two miles and a half an hour, for the previous sixteen hours, during which time we had been fasting, the supper-house, which we should have reached before midnight, was still ten miles ahead, the driver sulky and refusing to stop until we reached it. We had been pounded till we ached in every muscle. I had had no sleep since I left Memphis. We were passing over a hill country which sometimes appeared to be quite thickly inhabited, yet mainly still covered with a pine forest, through which the wind moaned lugubriously.

I had been induced to turn this way in my journey in no slight degree by reading the following description in a statistical article of De Bow's Review:

The settling of this region is one among the many remarkable events in the history of the rise of the Western States. Fifteen years ago it was an Indian wilderness, and now it has reached and passed in its population, other portions of the State of ten times its age, and this population, too, one of the finest in all the West. Great attention has been given to schools and education, and here, [at Oxford,] has been located the University of Mississippi; so amply endowed by the State, and now just going into operation under the auspices of some of the ablest professors from the eastern colleges. There is no overgrown wealth among them, and yet no squalid poverty; the people being generally comfortable, substantial, and independent farmers. Considering its climate, soil, wealth, and general character of its inhabitants, I should think no more desirable or delightful residence could be found than among the hills and sunny valleys of the Chickasaw Cession.[1]

And here among the hills of this Paradise of the South-west, we were, Yazoo and I—he, savagely hungry, as may be guessed from his observations upon "the finest people of the West," among whose cabins in the pine-wood toiled our stage-coach.

The whole art of driving was directed to the discovery of a passage for the coach among the trees and through the fields, where there were fields, adjoining the road—the road itself being impassable. Occasionally, when the coachman, during the night, found it necessary, owing to the thickness of the forest on each side, to take to the road, he would first leave the coach and make a survey with his lantern, sounding the ruts of the cotton-waggons, and finally making out a channel by guiding-stakes which he cut from the underwood with a hatchet, usually carried in the holster. If, after diligent sounding, he found no passage sufficiently shallow, he would sometimes spend half an hour in preparing one, bringing rails from the nearest fence, or cutting brushwood for the purpose. We were but once or twice during the night called upon to leave the coach, or to assist in road-making, and my companion fre-

[1] See "Resources"; article, "Mississippi," etc. [*The Industrial Resources, etc., of the Western and Southern States*, II, 42].

quently expressed his gratitude for this—gratitude not to the driver but to Providence, who had made a country, as he thought, so unusually well adapted for stage-coaching. The night before, he had been on a much worse road, and was half the time, with numerous other passengers, engaged in bringing rails, and prying the coach out of sloughs. They had been obliged to keep on the track, because the water was up over the adjoining country. Where the wooden causeway had floated off, they had passed through water so deep that it entered the coach body. With our road of to-day, then, he could only express satisfaction; not so with the residents upon it. "Look at 'em!" he would say. "Just look at 'em! What's the use of such people's living? 'Pears to me I'd die if I couldn't live better'n that. When I get to be representative, I'm going to have a law made that all such kind of men shall be took up by the State and sent to the penitentiary, to make 'em work and earn something to support their families. I pity the women; I haint nuthin agin them; they work hard enough, I know; but the men—I know how 'tis. They just hang around groceries and spend all the money they can get—just go round and live on other people, and play keerds, and only go home to nights; and the poor women, they hev to live how they ken."

"Do you think it's so? It is strange we see no men—only women and children."

"Tell you they're off, gettin' a dinner out o' somebody. Tell you I know it's so. It's the way all these people do. Why there's one poor man I know, that lives in a neighbourhood of poor men, down our way, and he's right industrious, but he can't get rich and he never ken, cause all these other poor men live on him."

"What do you mean? Do they all drop in about dinner time?"

"No, not all on 'em, but some on 'em every day. And they keep borrowin' things of him. He haint spunk enough to insult 'em. If he'd just move into a rich neighbourhood and jest be a little sassy, and not keer so much about what folks said of him, he'd get rich; never knew a man that was industrious and sassy in this country that didn't get rich, quick, and get niggers to do his work for him. Anybody ken that's smart. Thar's whar they tried to raise some corn. Warn't no corn grew thar; that's sartin. Wonder what they live on? See the stalks. They never made no corn. Ploughed right down the hill! Did you ever see anything like it? As if this sile

warn't poor enough already. There now. Just the same. Only look
at 'em! 'Pears like they never see a stage afore. This ain't the right
road, the way they look at us. No, sartin, they never see a stage.
Lord God! see the babies. They never see a stage afore. No, the
stage never went by here afore, I know. This damn'd driver's just
taken us round this way to show off what he can do and pass away
the time before breakfast. Couldn't get no breakfast here if he
would stop—less we ate a baby. That's right! step out where you
ken see her good; prehaps you'll never see a stage again; better
look now, right sharp. Yes, oh yes, sartin; fetch out all the babies.
Haint you got no more? Well, I should hope not. Now, what is the
use of so many babies? That's the worst on't. I'd get married to-
morrow if I wasn't sure I'd hev babies. I hate babies, can't bear 'em
round me, and won't have 'em. I would like to be married. I know
several gals I'd marry if 'twarn't for that. Well, it's a fact. Just so.
I hate the squallin' things. I know I was born a baby, but I couldn't
help it, could I? I wish I hadn't been. I hate the squallin' things. If I
had to hev a baby round me I should kill it."

"If you had a baby of your own, you'd feel differently about it."

"That's what they tell me. I s'pose I should, but I don't want to
feel differently. I hate 'em. I hate 'em."

The coach stopped at length. We got out and found ourselves on
the bank of an overflowed brook. A part of the bridge was broken
up, the driver declared it impossible to ford the stream, and said
he should return to the shanty, four miles back, at which we had
last changed horses. We persuaded him to take one of his horses
from the team and let us see if we could not get across. I succeeded
in doing this without difficulty, and turning the horse loose he returned. The driver, however, was still afraid to try to ford the
stream with the coach and mails, and after trying our best to persuade him, I told him if he returned he should do it without me,
hoping he would be shamed out of his pusillanimity. Yazoo joined
me, but the driver having again recovered the horse upon which he
had forded the stream, turned about and drove back. We pushed on,
and after walking a few miles, came to a neat new house, with a
cluster of old cabins about it. It was much the most comfortable
establishment we had seen during the day. Truly a "sunny valley"
home of northern Mississippi. We entered quietly, and were received by two women who were spinning in a room with three out-

side doors all open, though a fine fire was burning, merely to warm the room, in a large fire-place, within. Upon our asking if we could have breakfast prepared for us, one of the women went to the door and gave orders to a negro, and in a moment after, we saw six or seven black boys and girls chasing and clubbing a hen round the yard for our benefit. I regret to add that they did not succeed in making her tender. At twelve o'clock we breakfasted, and were then accommodated with a bed, upon which we slept together for several hours. When I awoke I walked out to look at the premises.

The house was half a dozen rods from the high road, with a square yard all about it, in one corner of which was a small enclosure for stock, and a log stable and corn-crib. There were also three negro cabins; one before the house, and two behind it. The house was a neat building of logs, boarded over and painted on the outside. On the inside, the logs were neatly hewn to a plane face, and exposed. One of the lower rooms contained a bed, and but little other furniture; the other was the common family apartment, but also was furnished with a bed. A door opened into another smaller log house in the rear, in which were two rooms—one of them the family dining-room; the other the kitchen. Behind this was still another log erection, fifteen feet square, which was the smoke-house, and in which a great store of bacon was kept. The negro cabins were small, dilapidated, and dingy; the walls were not chinked, and there were no windows—which, indeed, would have been a superfluous luxury, for there were spaces of several inches between the logs, through which there was unobstructed vision. The furniture in the cabins was of the simplest and rudest imaginable kind, two or three beds with dirty clothing upon them, a chest, a wooden stool or two made with an axe, and some earthenware and cooking apparatus. Everything within the cabins was coloured black by smoke. The chimneys of both the house and the cabins were built of splinters and clay, and on the outer side of the walls. At the door of each cabin were literally "heaps" of babies and puppies, and behind or beside it a pig-sty and poultry coop, a ley-tub, and quantities of home-carded cotton placed upon boards to bleach. Within each of them was a woman or two, spinning with the old-fashioned great wheel, and in the kitchen another woman was weaving coarse cotton shirting with the ancient rude hand-loom. The mistress herself was spinning in the living-room, and asked, when we had grown acquainted, what women at the North could find to do, and how they could ever pass the time, when they gave up spinning and weaving. She made the common every-day clothing for all her family and her servants. They only bought a few "store-goods" for their "dress-up" clothes. She kept the negro girls spinning all through the winter, and at all times when they were not needed in the field. She supposed they would begin to plant corn now in a few days, and then the girls would go to work out of doors. I noticed that all the bed-clothing, the towels, curtains, etc., in the house, were of homespun.

The proprietor, who had been absent on a fishing excursion, during the day, returned at dusk. He was a man of the fat, slow-and-easy style, and proved to be good-natured, talkative, and communicative. He had bought the tract of land he now occupied, and moved upon it about ten years before. He had made a large clearing, and could now sell it for a good deal more than he gave for it. He intended to sell whenever he could get a good offer, and move on West. It was the best land in this part of the country, and he had got it well fenced, and put up a nice house: there were a great many people that like to have these things done for them in advance—and he thought he should not have to wait long for a purchaser. He liked himself to be clearing land, and it was getting too close settled about here to suit him. He did not have much to do but to hunt and fish, and the game was getting so scarce it was too much trouble to go after it. He did not think there were so many cat in the creek as there used to be either, but there were more gar-fish. When he first bought this land he was not worth much—had to run in debt— hadn't but three negroes. Now, he was pretty much out of debt and owned twenty negroes, seven of them prime field-hands, and he reckoned I had not seen a better lot anywhere.

During the evening, all the cabins were illuminated by great fires, and, looking into one of them, I saw a very picturesque family group; a man sat on the ground making a basket, a woman lounged on a chest in the chimney corner smoking a pipe, and a boy and two girls sat in a bed which had been drawn up opposite to her, completing the fireside circle. They were talking and laughing cheerfully.

The next morning when I turned out I found Yazoo looking with the eye of a connoisseur at the seven prime field-hands, who at half-past seven were just starting off with hoes and axes for their day's work. As I approached him, he exclaimed with enthusiasm:—

"Aren't them a right keen lookin' lot of niggers?"

And our host soon after coming out, he immediately walked up to him, saying:—

"Why, friend, them yer niggers o' yourn would be good for seventy bales of cotton, if you'd move down into our country."

Their owner was perfectly aware of their value, and said everything good of them.

"There's something ruther singlar, too, about my niggers; I don't know as I ever see anything like it anywhere else."

"How so, sir?"

"Well, I reckon it's my way o' treatin' 'em, much as anything. I never hev no difficulty with 'em. Hen't licked a nigger in five year, 'cept maybe sprouting some of the young ones sometimes. Fact, my niggers never want no lookin' arter; they jus tek ker o' themselves. Fact, they do tek a greater interest in the crops than I do myself. There's another thing—I 'spose 'twill surprise you—there ent one of my niggers but what can read; read good, too—better 'n I can, at any rate."

"How did they learn?"

"Taught themselves. I b'lieve there was one on 'em that I bought, that could read, and he taught all the rest. But niggers is mighty apt at larnin', a heap more 'n white folks is."

I said that this was contrary to the generally received opinion.

"Well, now, let me tell you," he continued; "I had a boy to work, when I was buildin', and my boys jus teachin' him night times and such, he warn't here more'n three months, and he larned to read as well as any man I ever heerd, and I know he didn't know his letters when he come here. It didn't seem to me any white man could have done that; does it to you, now?"

"How old was he?"

"Warn't more'n seventeen, I reckon."

"How do they get books—do you get them for them?"

"Oh, no; get 'em for themselves."

"How?"

"Buy 'em."

"How do they get the money?"

"Earn it."

"How?"

"By their own work. I tell you my niggers have got more money 'n I hev."

"What kind of books do they get?"

"Religious kind a books ginerally—these stories; and some of them will buy novels, I believe. They won't let on to that, but I expect they do it."

They bought them of peddlers. I inquired about the law to prevent negroes reading, and asked if it allowed books to be sold to negroes. He had never heard of any such law—didn't believe there was any. The Yazoo man said there was such a law in his country. Negroes never had anything to read there. I asked our host if his negroes were religious, as their choice of works would have indicated.

"Yes; all on 'em, I reckon. Don't s'pose you'll believe it, but I tell you it's a fact; I haint heerd a swear on this place for a twelvemonth. They keep the Lord's day, too, right tight, in gineral."

"Our niggers is mighty wicked down in Yallerbush county," said my companion; "they dance."

"Dance on Sunday?" I asked.

"Oh, no, we don't allow that."

"What do they do, then—go to meeting?"

"Why, Sundays they sleep mostly; they've been at work hard all the week, you know, and Sundays they stay in their cabins, and sleep and talk to each other. There's so many of 'em together, they don't want to go visiting off the place."

"Are your negroes Baptists or Methodists?" I inquired of our host.

"All Baptists; niggers allers want to be ducked, you know. They ain't content to be just titch'd with water; they must be ducked in all over. There was two niggers jined the Methodists up here last summer, and they made the minister put 'em into the branch; they wouldn't jine 'less he'd duck 'em."

"The Bible says baptize, too," observed Yazoo.

"Well, they think they must be ducked all under, or 'tain't no good."

"Do they go to meeting?"

"Yes, they hev a meeting among themselves."

"And a preacher?"

"Yes; a nigger preacher."

"Our niggers is mighty wicked; they dance!" repeated Yazoo.

"Do you consider dancing so very wicked, then?" I asked.

"Well, I don't account so myself, as I know on, but they do, you know—the pious people, all kinds, except the 'Piscopers; some o' them, they do dance themselves, I believe. Do you dance in your country?"

"Yes."

"What sort of dances—cotillions and reels?"

"Yes; what do you?"

"Well, we dance cotillions and reels too, and we dance on a plank; that's the kind of dancin' I like best."

"How is it done?"

"Why, don't you know that? You stand face to face with your partner on a plank and keep a dancin'. Put the plank up on two barrel heads, so it'll kind o' spring. At some of our parties—that's among common kind o' people, you know—it's great fun. They dance as fast as they can, and the folks all stand round and holler, '*Keep it up, John!*' '*Go it, Nance!*' '*Don't give it up so!*' '*Old Virginny never tire!*' '*Heel and toe, ketch a fire!*' and such kind of observations, and clap and stamp 'em."

"Do your negroes dance much?"

"Yes, they are mighty fond on't. Saturday night they dance all night, and Sunday nights too. Daytime they sleep and rest themselves, and Sunday nights we let 'em dance and sing if they want. It does 'em good, you know, to enjoy theirselves."

"They dance to the banjo, I suppose?"

"Banjos and violins; some of 'em has got violins."

"I like to hear negroes sing," said I.

"Niggers is allers good singers nat'rally," said our host. "I reckon they got better lungs than white folks, they hev such powerful voices."

We were sitting at this time on the rail fence at the corner of a hog-pen and a large half-cleared field. In that part of this field nearest the house, among the old stumps, twenty or thirty small fruit trees had been planted. I asked what sorts they were.

"I don't know—good kinds tho', I expect; I bought 'em for that at any rate."

"Where did you buy them?"

"I bought 'em of a feller that came a peddlin' round here last fall; he said I'd find 'em good."

"What did you pay for them?"

"A bit apiece."

"That's very cheap, if they're good for anything; you are sure they're grafted, aren't you?"

"Only by what he said—he said they was grafted kinds. I've got a paper in the housen he gin me, tells about 'em; leastways, he said it did. They's the curosest kinds of trees printed into it you ever heerd on. But I did not buy none, only the fruit kinds."

Getting off the fence I began to pick about the roots of one of them with my pocket-knife. After exposing the trunk for five or six inches below the surface, I said, "You've planted these too deep, if they're all like this. You should have the ground dished about it or it won't grow." I tried another, and after picking some minutes without finding any signs of the "collar," I asked if they had all been planted so deeply.

"I don't know—I told the boys to put 'em in about two feet, and I expect they did, for they fancied to have apple-trees growin'."

The catalogue of the tree-peddler, which afterwards came into my possession, quite justified the opinion my host expressed of the kinds of trees described in it. The reader shall judge for himself, and I assure him that the following is a literal transcript of it, omitting the sections headed "Ancebus new," "Camelias," "Rhododendrums," "Bubbs Pæony," "Rosiers," "Wind's flowers of the greatest scarcity," "Bulbous Roots, and of various kinds of graines."

"But come," said the farmer, "go in; take a drink. Breakfast'll be ready right smart."

"I don't want to drink before breakfast, thank you."

"Why not?"

"I'm not accustomed to it, and I don't find it's wholesome."

Not wholesome to drink before breakfast! That was "a new kink" to our jolly host, and troubled him as much as a new "ism" would an old fogy. Not wholesome? He had always reckoned it warn't very wholesome not to drink before breakfast. He did not expect I had seen a great many healthier men than he was, had I? and he always took a drink before breakfast. If a man just kept himself well strung up, without ever stretching himself right tight, he didn't reckon damps or heat would ever do him much harm. He had never had a

SPECIAL CATALOGUE
OF THE PLANTS, FLOWERS, SHRUBS IMPORTED BY
ROUSSET
MEMBER OF SEVERAL SOCIETIES
At Paris (France), boulevard of Hopital, and at Chambery, faubourg de Mache.

MR ROUSSET beg to inform they are arrived in this town, with a large assortment of the most rare vegetable plants, either flowerd on fruit bearer, onion bulbous, seeds, &c., &c. Price very moderate.

Their store is situated

CHOIX D'ARBRES A FRUIT.

CHOICE OF FRUIT TREES.
PEAR TREES.

1 Good Louisa from Avranche.
2 Winter's Perfume.
3 Saint-John-in-Iron.
4 Leon-the-Clerc.
5 Bergamot from England.
6 Duchess of Angoulème.
7 Goulu-Morceau.
8 Tarquin Pear.
9 Summer's Good (large) Christian.
10 Good Turkisk Christian.
11 Grey (large) Beurré.
12 Royal Beurré from England.

1 Bon-Chrétien d'été,
2   —   d'hiver.
3   —   de Pâque.
4 Doyenné blanc.
5 Duchesse d'Angora-New.
6 Belle Angevine, fondante.
7 Crassane d'hiver.
8 Louise d'Orleans, sucré.
9 Double fleur hâtif.
10 Angélique de Tour.

1 Borgamotte de Milan, Gros.
2   —   d'Aiençon, très-gros.
3 Beurrê gris d'hiver.
4   —   Amanlis.
5   —   d'Hardenpont, précoce.
6 Fortunè, fondant.
7 Josephine, chair fine.
8 Martin-sec, sucrè.
9 Messire, gris.

10 Muscat d'etè.
11 Doyenné d'automne.
12   —   d'hiver, sucré.
13 Virgouleuse fondonte.
14 Bezy-Lamotte.
15 Gros-Blanquet.

APPLES.

1 Renetto of Spain.
2   —   Green.
3 Apple Coin.
4   —   Friette.
5 Calville, white, winter's fruit.
6   —   red, autumn's fruit.
7   —   red, winter's fruit.
8 Violet or of the Four-Taste.
9 Renette from England, or Gold-Apple.
10 Golded Renette, a yellow backward plant.
11 White   —   of a great perfume.
12 Renette, red, winter's fruit.

1 Renette, yellow, heavy fruit.
2   —   grey, very delicate.
3   —   Princess noble.
4 Apple d'Api.
5   —   d'Eve.
6 Winter's Postophe.
7 Plein gney fenouillet.
8 Renette franc.
9   —   of St. Laurent.
10 Sammers Numbourg.
11 Belle du Havre.
12 Belle Hollandaise.

1 Violet Apple or of the 4 taste; the fruit may be preserved 2 years.

2 Princess Renette, of a gold yellow, spotted with red of a delicious taste.
3 White Renette from Canada, of which the skin is lite scales strange by its size.
4 The Cythère Apple.
5 The Caynoite Apple.
6 Apple Trees with double flowers. Blooms twice a year, Camélia's flowers like.
106 others kinds of Apples of the newest choice.

Apricots.

1 The Ladie's Apricots.
2 The Peack Apricots.
3 The Royal Apricots.
4 The Gros Muscg Apricots.
5 The Pourret Apricots.
6 Portugal Apricots.
7 Apricats monstruous from America, of a gold yellow, of an enormous size, and of the pine's apple taste.

Peach Trees.

1 Peach Grosse Mignonne.
2 —   Bello Beauty.
3 —   Godess.
4 —   Beauty of Paris.
4 —   From Naples! said without stone,
6 Brugnon, musc taste.
7 Admirable; Belle of Vitry.
8 The Large Royal.
9 Monstruous Pavie.
10 The Cardinal, very forward.
11 Good Workman.
12 Lètitia Bonaparte.
13 The Prince's Peach, melting in the mouth.
14 The Prince's Peach from Africa, with large white fruit, weighing pound and half each; hearly, new kind.
50 others new kinds of Peach Trees.

Plum Trees.

1 Plum Lamorte.
2 Surpasse Monsieur.

3 Damas with musc taste.
4 Royale of Tonrs.
5 Green Gage, of a violet colour.
6 Large Mirabelle.
7 Green gage, golded.
8 Imperial, of a violet colour.
9 Empress, of a white colour.
10 Ste-Catherine, zellow, sugar taste like.

Cherry Trees.

1 Cherry from the North.
2 —   Royal, gives from 18 to 20 cherries weihing one pound, 4 differentes kinds.
3 Cherry Reina Hortense.
4 —   Montmorency.
5 —   with thort stalk (Gros-Gobet),
6 —   Le Mercier.
7 —   Four for a pound.
8 Cherry Beauty of Choicy.
9 —   The English.
10 Cherry-Duck.
11 —   Créole with bunches.
12 —   Bigarrot or monster of new Mézel.

Currant Trees.

1 Currant Three with red bunches (grapes).
2 —   — with white bunches.
3 Gooseberries of 1st choice (Raspherries six kinds of alégery.
4 New kind of currants, of which the grapes are as big as the wine grapes.

Grapes Wines.

1 Chasselas of Fountainebleau, with large gold grains.
2 Chasselas, black very good.
3 —   red, of musc teste.
4 Verdal, the sweetest and finest fruit for desert.
5 White Muscadine grape, or of Frontignan.
6 Muscat of Alexandrie, musc taste.
7 Cornichon, white, sweet sugar like, very good.

8 Tokay, red and white.
9 Verjus from Bordeaux, large yellow fruit.
10 St. Peter large and fine fruit.
11 Red Muscadine Graper.
12 Raisin of Malaga.
13 The Celestial Wine Mree, or the amphibious grain, weighing two ounces, the grain of a red and violet colour.

NEW STRAWBERRY PLANTS.

1 The Strawberry Cremont.
2 — — the Queen.
3 — — monster, new kind.
4 — — from Cllili.
5 Caperon of a raspberry taste.
6 Scarlat from Venose, very forward plant.
7 Prince Albert, fruit of very greatz beauty.
8 Grinston colalant, very large.
9 Rose-Berry, big fruit and of a long form.
10 Bath chery, very good.
11 The Big Chinese Strawberry, weihing 16 to a pound, produce fruit all year round, of the pine apple's taste.
12 Vilmoth full.

NEW FIG TREES OF A MONSTRUOUS SIZE.

1 Diodena white, of a large size.
2 Duchess of Maroc, green fruit.
3 Donne-à-Dieu, blue fruit.
4 La Sanspareille, yellow fruit.

The Perpetual Raspberry Tree, imported from Indies producing a fruit large as an egg, taste delicious 3 kinds, red, violet and white.

The Rapsberry Tree from Fastolff, red fruit, very good of an extraordinary size, very hearly forward plant.

Cherry Currant Tree, with large bunches, it has a great production. Its numerous and long bunches cover entirely the old wood and looks like grapes; the fruit of a cherry pink colour is very large and of the best quality.

Asparagus from Africa, new kinds, good to eat the same year of their planting (seeds of two years). 1000 varieties of annual and perpetual flower's grains also of kitchen garden grains.

PAULNOVIA INPERIALIS. Magnificent hardy plant from 12 to 15 yards of higth: its leave come to the size of 75 to 80 centimeter and its fine and larg flowers of a fine blue, gives when the spring comes, a soft and agréable perfume.

Besides these plants the amateur will fine at M. ROUSSET, _stores, a great number of other Plants and Fruit Trees of which would be to long to describe._

NOTICE.

The admirable and strange plant called _Trompette du Jugement_ (The Judgment Trompette) of that name having not yet found its classification.

This marvellous plant was send to us from China by the cleuer and courageous botanist collector M. Fortune, from l'Himalaya, near summet of the Chamalari Macon.

This splendid plant deserves the first rank among all kinds of plant wich the botanical science has produce till now in spite of all the new discoveries.

This bulbous plant gives several stems on the same subject. It grows to the height of 6 feet. It is furnished with flowers from bottom to top. The bud looks by his from like a big cannon ball of a heavenly blue. The center is of an aurora yellewish colour. The vegetation of that plant is to fouitfull that when it is near to blossom it gives a great heat when tassing it in hand and when the bud opens it produces a naite Similar to a pistole shot. Immediately the vegetation takes fire and burns like alcohol about an hour and a half. The flowers succeeding one to the other gives the satisfaction of having flowers during 7 or 8 months.

The most intense cold can not hurt this plant and can be cultivated in pots, in appartments or gpeen houses.

Wa call the public attention to this plant as a great curiosity.

Havre—Printed by F. HUE, rue de Paris, 89.

sick day since he came to this place, and he reckoned that this was owin' considerable to the good rye whisky he took. It was a healthy trac' of land, though, he believed, a mighty healthy trac'; everything seemed to thrive here. We must see a nigger-gal that he was raisin'; she was just coming five, and would pull up nigh upon a hundred weight.

"Two year ago," he continued, after taking his dram, as we sat by the fire in the north room, "when I had a carpenter here to finish off this house, I told one of my boys he must come in and help him. I reckoned he would larn quick, if he was a mind to. So he come in, and a week arterwards he fitted the plank and laid this floor, and now you just look at it; I don't believe any man could do it better. That was two year ago, and now he's as good a carpenter as you ever see. I bought him some tools after the carpenter left, and he can do anything with 'em—make a table or a chest of drawers or anything. I think niggers is somehow nat'rally ingenious; more so 'n white folks. They is wonderful apt to any kind of slight."

I took out my pocket-map, and while studying it, asked Yazoo some questions about the route East. Not having yet studied geography, as he observed, he could not answer. Our host inquired where I was going, that way. I said I should go on to Carolina.

"Expect you're going to buy a rice-farm, in the Carolinies, aint you? and I reckon you're up here speckylating arter nigger stock, aint you now?"

"Well," said I, "I wouldn't mind getting that fat girl of yours, if we can make a trade. How much a pound will you sell her at?"

"We don't sell niggers by the pound in this country."

"Well, how much by the lump?"

"Well, I don't know; reckon I don't keer about sellin' her just yet."

After breakfast, I inquired about the management of the farm. He said that he purchased negroes, as he was able, from time to time. He grew rich by the improved saleable value of his land, arising in part from their labour, and from their natural increase and improvement, for he bought only such as would be likely to increase in value on his hands. He had been obliged to spend but little money, being able to live and provide most of the food and clothing for his family and his people, by the production of his farm. He made a little cotton, which he had to send some distance to be ginned and baled, and then waggoned it seventy miles to a market; also raised some wheat, which he turned into flour at a neighbouring mill, and sent to the same market. This transfer engaged much of the winter labour of his man-slaves.

I said that I supposed the Memphis and Charleston railroad, as it progressed east, would shorten the distance to which it would be necessary to draw his cotton, and so be of much service to him. He did not know that. He did not know as he should ever use it. He expected they would charge pretty high for carrying cotton, and his niggers hadn't anything else to do. It did not really cost him anything now to send it to Memphis, because he had to board the niggers and the cattle anyhow, and they did not want much more on the road than they did at home.

He made a large crop of corn, which, however, was mainly consumed by his own force, and he killed annually about one hundred and fifty hogs, the bacon of which was all consumed in his own family and by his people, or sold to passing travellers. In the fall, a great many drovers and slave-dealers passed over the road with their stock, and they frequently camped against his house, so as to buy corn and bacon of him. This they cooked themselves.

There were sometimes two hundred negroes brought along together, going South. He didn't always have bacon to spare for them, though he killed one hundred and fifty swine. They were generally bad characters, and had been sold for fault by their owners. Some of the slave-dealers were high-minded, honourable men, he thought; "high-toned gentlemen, as ever he saw, some of 'em, was."

Niggers were great eaters, and wanted more meat than white folks; and he always gave his as much as they wanted, and more too. The negro cook always got dinner for them, and took what she liked for it; his wife didn't know much about it. She got as much as she liked, and he guessed she didn't spare it. When the field-hands were anywhere within a reasonable distance, they always came up to the house to get their dinner. If they were going to work a great way off, they would carry their dinner with them. They did as they liked about it. When they hadn't taken their dinner, the cook called them at twelve o'clock with a conch. They ate in the kitchen, and he had the same dinner that they did, right out of the same frying-pan; it was all the same, only they ate in the kitchen, and he ate in the room we were in, with the door open between them.

I brought up the subject of the cost of labour, North and South. He had no apprehension that there would ever be any want of labourers at the South, and could not understand that the ruling price indicated the state of the demand for them. He thought negroes would increase more rapidly than the need for their labour. "Niggers," said he, "breed faster than white folks, a 'mazin' sight, you know; they begin younger."

"How young do they begin?"

"Sometimes at fourteen, sometimes at sixteen, and sometimes at eighteen."

"Do you let them marry so young as that?" I inquired. He laughed, and said, "They don't very often wait to be married."

"When they marry, do they have a minister to marry them?"

"Yes, generally one of their own preachers."

"Do they with you?" I inquired of Yazoo.

"Yes, sometimes they hev a white minister, and sometimes a black one, and if there aren't neither handy, they get some of the pious ones to marry 'em. But then very often they only just come and ask our consent, and then go ahead, without any more ceremony. They just call themselves married. But most niggers likes a ceremony, you know, and they generally make out to hev one somehow. They don't very often get married for good, though, without trying each other, as they say, for two or three weeks, to see how they are going to like each other."

I afterwards asked how far it was to the post-office. It was six miles. "One of my boys," said our host, "always gets the paper every week. He goes to visit his wife, and passes by the post-office every Sunday. Our paper hain't come, though, now, for three weeks. The mail don't come very regular." All of his negroes, who had wives off the place, left an hour before sunset on Saturday evening. One of them, who had a wife twenty miles away, left at twelve o'clock Saturday, and got back at twelve o'clock Monday.

"We had a nigger once," said Yazoo, "that had a wife fifteen miles away, and he used to do so; but he did some rascality once, and he was afraid to go again. He told us his wife was so far off, 't was too much trouble to go there, and he believed he'd give her up. We was glad of it. He was a darned rascally nigger—allers getting into scrapes. One time we sent him to mill, and he went round into town and sold some of the meal. The storekeeper wouldn't pay him for't, 'cause he hadn't got an order. The next time we were in town, the storekeeper just showed us the bag of meal; said he reckoned 't was stole; so when we got home we just tied him up to the tree and licked him. He's a right smart nigger; rascally niggers allers is smart. I'd rather have a rascally nigger than any other—they's so smart allers. He is about the best nigger we've got."

"I have heard," said I, "that religious negroes were generally the most valuable. I have been told that a third more would be given for a man if he were religious." "Well, I never heerd of it before," said he. Our host thought there was no difference in the market value of sinners and saints.

"Only," observed Yazoo, "the rascalier a nigger is, the better he'll work. Now that yer nigger I was tellin' you on, he's worth more'n any other nigger we've got. He's a yaller nigger."

I asked their opinion as to the comparative value of black and yellow negroes. Our host had two bright mulatto boys among his—didn't think there was much difference, "but allers reckoned yellow fellows was the best a little; they worked smarter. He would rather have them." Yazoo would not; he "didn't think but what they'd work as well; but he didn't fancy yellow negroes 'round him; would rather have real black ones."

I asked our host if he had no foreman or driver for his negroes, or if he gave his directions to one of them in particular for all the rest. He did not. They all did just as they pleased, and arranged the work among themselves. They never needed driving.

"If I ever notice one of 'em getting a little slack, I just talk to him; tell him we must get out of the grass, and I want to hev him stir himself a little more, and then, maybe, I slip a dollar into his hand, and when he gits into the field he'll go ahead, and the rest seeing him, won't let themselves be distanced by him. My niggers never want no lookin' arter. They tek more interest in the crop than I do myself, every one of 'em."

Religious, instructed, and seeking further enlightenment; industrious, energetic, and self directing; well fed, respected, and trusted by their master, and this master an illiterate, indolent, and careless man! A very different state of things, this, from what I saw on a certain great cotton planter's estate, where a profit of $100,000 was made in a single year, but where five hundred negroes were constantly kept under the whip, where religion was only a pow-wow or cloak for immorality, and where the negro was considered to be of an inferior race, especially designed by Providence to be kept in the position he there occupied! A very different thing; and strongly suggesting what a very different thing this negro servitude might be made in general, were the ruling disposition of the South more just and sensible.

About half-past eleven, a stage-coach, which had come earlier in the morning from the East, and had gone on as far as the brook, returned, having had our luggage transferred to it from the one we had left on the other side. In the transfer a portion of mine was omitted and never recovered. Up to this time our host had not paid the smallest attention to any work his men were doing, or even looked to see if they had fed the cattle, but had lounged about, sitting upon a fence, chewing tobacco, and talking with us, evidently very glad to have somebody to converse with. He went in once again, after a drink; showed us the bacon he had in his smokehouse, and told a good many stories of his experience in life, about a white man's "dying hard" in the neighbourhood, and of a tree falling on a team with which one of his negroes was ploughing cotton, "which was lucky"—that is, that it did not kill the negro—and a good deal about "hunting" when he was younger and lighter.

Still absurdly influenced by an old idea which I had brought to the South with me, I waited, after the coach came in sight, for Yazoo to put the question, which he presently did, boldly enough.

"Well; reckon we're goin' now. What's the damage?"

"Well; reckon seventy-five cents 'll be right."

Chapter XII

The Interior Cotton Districts
Central Mississippi, Alabama, etc.

Central Mississippi, May 31st [1854].—Yesterday was a raw, cold day, wind north-east, like a dry north-east storm at home. Fortunately I came to the pleasantest house and household I had seen for some time. The proprietor was a native of Maryland, and had travelled in the North; a devout Methodist, and somewhat educated. He first came South, as I understood, for the benefit of his health, his lungs being weak.

His first dwelling, a rude log cabin, was still standing, and was occupied by some of his slaves. The new house, a cottage, consisting of four rooms and a hall, stood in a small grove of oaks; the family were quiet, kind, and sensible.

When I arrived, the oldest boy was at work, holding a plough in the cotton-field, but he left it and came at once, with confident and affable courtesy, to entertain me.

My host had been in Texas, and after exploring it quite thoroughly, concluded that he much preferred to remain where he was. He found no part of that country where good land, timber, and a healthy climate were combined: in the West he did not like the vicinage of the Germans and Mexicans; moreover, he didn't "fancy" a prairie county. Here, in favourable years, he got a bale of cotton to the acre. Not so much now as formerly. Still, he said, the soil would be good enough for him here, for many years to come.

I went five times to the stable without being able to find a servant there. I was always told that "the boy" would feed my horse, and take good care of him, when he came; and so at length I had to go to bed, trusting to this assurance. I went out just before breakfast next morning, and found the horse with only ten *dry* cobs in the manger. I searched for the boy; could not find him, but was told that my horse had been fed. I said, "I wish to have him fed more—as much as he will eat." Very well, the boy should give him more. When I went out after breakfast the boy was leading out the horse. I asked if he had given him corn this morning.

"Oh yes, sir."

"How many ears did you give him?"

"Ten or fifteen—or sixteen, sir; he eats very hearty."

I went into the stable and saw that he had not been fed; there were the same ten cobs (dry) in the manger. I doubted, indeed, from their appearance, if the boy had fed him at all the night before. I fed him with leaves myself, but could not get into the corn crib. The proprietor was, I do not doubt, perfectly honest, but the negro had probably stolen the corn for his own hogs and fowls.

The next day I rode more than thirty miles, having secured a good feed of corn for the horse at midday. At nightfall I was much fatigued, but had as yet failed to get lodging. It began to rain, and grew dark, and I kept the road with difficulty. About nine o'clock I came to a large, comfortable house.

An old lady sat in the verandah, of whom I asked if I could be accommodated for the night. "Reckon so," she replied: then after a few moments' reflection, without rising from her chair she shouted, "Gal!—gal!" Presently a girl came.

"Missis?"

"Call Tom!"

The girl went off, while I remained, waiting for a more definite answer. At length she returned: "Tom ain't there, missis."

"Who is there?"

"Old Pete."

"Well, tell him to come and take this gentleman's horse."

Pete came, and I went with him to the gate where I had fastened my horse. Here he called for some younger slave to come and take him down to "the pen," while he took off the saddle.

All this time it was raining, but any rapidity of movement was out of the question. Pete continued shouting. "Why not lead the horse to the pen yourself?" I asked. "I must take care of de saddle and tings, massa; tote 'em to de house whar dey'll be safe. Dese niggers is so treacherous, can't leave nothin' roun' but dey'll hook suthing off of it."

Next morning, at dawn of day, I saw honest Pete come into the room where I was in bed and go stealthily to his young master's clothes, probably mistaking them for mine. I moved and he dropped them, and slunk out to the next room, where he went loudly to making a fire. I managed to see the horse well fed night and morning.

There were three pretty young women in this house, of good manners and well dressed, except for the abundance of rings and jewelry which they displayed at breakfast. One of them surprised me not a little at the table. I had been offered, in succession, fried ham and eggs, sweet potatoes, apple-pie, corn-bread, and molasses; this last article I declined, and passed it to the young lady opposite, looking to see how it was to be used. She had, on a breakfast plate, fried ham and eggs and apple-pie, and poured molasses between them.

June 1st.—I stopped last evening at the house of a man who was called "Doctor" by his family, but who was, to judge from his language, very illiterate. His son, by whom I was first received, followed me to the stable. He had ordered a negro child to lead my horse, but as I saw the little fellow couldn't hold him I went myself. He had no fodder (corn-leaves), and proposed to give the horse some shucks (corn-husks) dipped in salt water, and, as it was now too late to go further, I assented. Belshazzar licked them greedily, but would not eat them, and they seemed to destroy his appetite for corn, for late in the evening, having groped my way into the stable, I found seven small ears of corn, almost untasted, in the manger. I got the young man to come out and give him more.

The "Doctor" returned from "a hunt," as he said, with no game but a turtle, which he had taken from a "trot line"—a line, with hooks at intervals, stretched across the river.

The house was large, and in a good-sized parlour or common room stood a handsome centre table, on which were a few books and papers, mostly Baptist publications. I sat here alone in the evening, straining my eyes to read a wretchedly printed newspaper, till I was offered a bed. I was very tired and sleepy, having been ill two nights before. The bed was apparently clean, and I gladly embraced it.

My host, holding a candle for me to undress by (there was no candlestick in the house), called to a boy on the outside to fasten the doors, which he did by setting articles of furniture against them. When I had got into bed he went himself into an inner room, the door of which he closed and fastened in the same manner. No sooner was the light withdrawn than I was attacked by bugs. I was determined, if possible, not to be kept awake by them, but they soon conquered me. I never suffered such incessant and merciless persecution from them before. In half an hour I was nearly frantic, and leaped from bed. But what to do? There was no use in making a disturbance about it; doubtless every other bed and resting place in the house was full of them. I shook out my day clothes carefully and put them on, and then pushing away the barricade, opened the door and went into the parlour. At first I thought that I would arrange the chairs in a row and sleep on them; but this I found impracticable, for the seats of the chairs were too narrow, and moreover of deerskin, which was sure to be full of fleas if not of bugs. Stiff and sore and weak, I groaningly lay down where the light of the moon came through a broken window, for bugs feed but little except in darkness, and with my saddle-bags for a pillow, again essayed to sleep. Fleas! instantly. There was nothing else to be done; I was too tired to sit up, even if that would have effectually removed the annoyance. Finally I dozed—not long, I think, for I was suddenly awakened by a large insect dropping upon my eye. I struck it off, and at the moment it stung me. My eyelid swelled immediately, and grew painful, but at length I slept in spite of it. I was once more awakened by a large beetle which fell on me from the window; once more I got asleep, till finally at four o'clock I awoke with that feverish dryness of the eyes which indicates a determination to sleep no more. It was daylight, and I was stiff and shivering; the inflammation and pain of the sting in my eyelid had in a great degree subsided. I pushed back the bolt of the outside door-lock, and went to the stable. The negroes were already at work in the field. Belshazzar had had a bad night too: that was evident. The floor of the stall, being of earth, had been trodden into two hollows at each end, leaving a small rough hillock in the centre. Bad as it was, however, it was the best in the stable; only one in four of the stalls having a manger that was not broken down. A wee little black girl and boy were cleaning their master's horses—mine they were afraid of. They had managed to put some fresh corn in his manger, however, and as he refused to eat, I took a curry-comb and brush, and in the next two hours gave him the first thorough grooming he had enjoyed since I owned him. I could not detect the reason of his loss of appetite. I had been advised by an old Southern traveller to examine the corn when my horse refused to eat—if corn were high I might find that it had been greased. From the actions of the horse, then and subsequently, I suspect some trick of this kind was here practised upon me. When I returned to the house and asked to wash, water was given me in a vessel which, though I doubted the right of my host to a medical diploma, certainly smelt strongly of the shop—it was such as is used by apothecaries in mixing drugs. The title of Doctor is often popularly given at the South to druggists and venders of popular medicines; very probably he had been one, and had now retired to enjoy the respectability of a planter.

June 2nd.—I met a ragged old negro, of whom I asked the way, and at what house within twelve miles I had better stop. He advised me to go to one more than twelve miles distant.

"I suppose," said I, "I can stop at any house along the road here, can't I? They'll all take in travellers?"

"Yes, sir, if you'll take rough fare, such as travellers has to, sometimes. They're all damn'd rascals along dis road, for ten or twelve miles, and you'll get nothin' but rough fare. But I say, massa, rough fare's good enough for dis world; ain't it, massa? Dis world ain't nothin; dis is hell, dis is, I calls it; hell to what's a comin' arter, ha! ha! Ef you's prepared? you says. I don't look much's if I was prepared, does I? nor talk like it, nuther. De Lord he cum to me in my cabin in de night time, in de year '45."

"What?"

"De Lord! massa, de bressed Lord! He cum to me in de night time, in de year '45, and he says to me, says he, 'I'll spare you yet five year longer, old boy!' So when '50 cum round I thought my time had cum, sure; but as I didn't die, I reckon de Lord has 'cepted of me, and I 'specs I shall be saved, dough I don't look much like it, ha! ha! ho! ho! de Lord am my rock, and he shall not perwail over me. I will lie down in green pastures and take up my bed in hell, yet will not His mercy circumwent me. Got some baccy, master?"

A little after sunset I came to an unusually promising plantation, the dwelling being within a large enclosure, in which there was a well-kept southern sward shaded by fine trees. The house, of the usual form, was painted white, and the large number of neat outbuildings seemed to indicate opulence, and, I thought, unusual good taste in its owner. A lad of sixteen received me, and said I could stay; I might fasten my horse, and when the negroes came up he would have him taken care of. When I had done so, and had brought the saddle to the verandah, he offered me a chair, and at once commenced a conversation in the character of entertainer. Nothing in his tone or manner would have indicated that he was not the father of the family, and proprietor of the establishment. No prince royal could have had more assured and nonchalant dignity. Yet a Northern stable-boy, or apprentice, of his age, would seldom be found as ignorant.

"Where do you live, sir, when you are at home?" he asked.

"At New York."

"New York is a big place, sir, I expect?"

"Yes, very big."

"Big as New Orleans, is it, sir?"

"Yes, much bigger."

"Bigger 'n New Orleans? It must be a bully city."

"Yes; the largest in America."

"Sickly there now, sir?"

"No, not now; it is sometimes."

"Like New Orleans, I suppose?"

"No, never so bad as New Orleans sometimes is."

"Right healthy place, I expect, sir?"

"Yes, I believe so, for a place of its size."

"What diseases do you have there, sir?"

"All sorts of diseases—not so much fever, however, as you have hereabouts."

"Measles and whooping-cough, sometimes, I reckon?"

"Yes, 'most all the time, I dare say."

"All the time! People must die there right smart. Some is dyin' 'most every day, I expect, sir?"

"More than a hundred every day, I suppose."

"Gosh! a hundred every day! Almighty sickly place 't must be?"

"It is such a large place, you see—seven hundred thousand people."

"Seven hundred thousand—expect that's a heap of people, ain't it?"

His father, a portly, well-dressed man, soon came in, and learning that I had been in Mexico, said, "I suppose there's a heap of Americans flocking in and settling up that country along on the line, ain't there, sir?"

"No, sir, very few. I saw none, in fact—only a few Irishmen and Frenchmen, who called themselves Americans. Those were the only foreigners I saw, except negroes."

"Niggers! Where were they from?"

"They were runaways from Texas."

"But their masters go there and get them again, don't they?"

"No, sir, they can't."

"Why not?"

"The Mexicans are friendly to the niggers, and protect them."

"But why not go to the Government?"

"The Government considers them as free, and will not let them be taken back."

"But that's stealing, sir. Why don't our Government make them deliver them up? What good is the Government to us if it don't preserve the rights of property, sir? Niggers are property, ain't they? and if a man steals my property, ain't the Government bound to get it for me? Niggers are property, sir, the same as horses and cattle, and nobody's any more right to help a nigger that's run away than he has to steal a horse."

He spoke very angrily, and was excited. Perhaps he was indirectly addressing me, as a Northern man, on the general subject of fugitive slaves. I said that it was necessary to have special treaty stipulations about such matters. The Mexicans lost their *peóns*—bounden servants; they ran away to our side, but the United States Government never took any measures to restore them, nor did the Mexicans ask it. "But," he answered, in a tone of indignation, "those are not niggers, are they? They are white people, sir, just as white as the Mexicans themselves, and just as much right to be free."

My horse stood in the yard till quite dark, the negroes not coming in from the cotton-field. I twice proposed to take him to the stable, but he said, "No: the niggers would come up soon and attend to him." Just as we were called to supper, the negroes began to make their appearance, getting over a fence with their hoes, and the master called to one to put the horse in the stable, and to "take good care of him." "I want him to have all the corn he'll eat," said I. "Yes, sir; feed him well; do you hear there?"

The house was meagrely furnished within, not nearly as well as the most common New England farm-house. I saw no books and no decorations. The interior wood-work was unpainted.

At supper there were three negro girls in attendance—two children of twelve or fourteen years of age, and an older one, but in a few moments they all disappeared. The mistress called aloud several times, and at length the oldest came, bringing in hot biscuit.

"Where's Suke and Bet?"

"In the kitchen, missus."

"Tell them both to come to me, right off."

A few minutes afterwards, one of the girls slunk in and stood behind me, as far as possible from her mistress. Presently, however, she was discovered.

"You Bet, you there? Come here! come here to me! close to me! (*Slap, slap, slap.*) Now, why don't you stay in here? (*Slap, slap, slap,* on the side of the head.*) I know! you want to be out in the kitchen with them Indians! (*Slap, slap, slap.*) Now see if you can stay here." (*Slap!*) The other girl didn't come at all, and was forgotten.

As soon as supper was over my hostess exclaimed, "Now, you Bet, stop crying there, and do you go right straight home; mind you run every step of the way, and if you stop one minute in the kitchen you'd better look out. Begone!" During the time I was in the house she was incessantly scolding the servants, in a manner very disagreeable for me to hear, though they seemed to regard it very little.

The Indians, I learned, lived some miles away, and were hired to hoe cotton. I inquired their wages. "Well, it costs me about four bits (fifty cents) a day," (including food, probably). They worked well for a few days at a time; were better at picking than at hoeing. "They don't pick so much in a day as niggers, but do it better." The women said they were good for nothing, and her husband had no business to plant so much cotton that he couldn't 'tend it with his own slave hands.

While at table a young man, very dirty and sweaty, with a ragged shirt and no coat on, came in to supper. He was surly and rude in his actions, and did not speak a word; he left the table before I had finished, and lighting a pipe, laid himself at full length on the floor of the room to smoke. This was the overseer.

Immediately after supper the master told me that he was in the habit of going to bed early, and he would show me where I was to sleep. He did so, and left me without a candle. It was dark, and I did not know the way to the stables, so I soon went to bed. On a feather bed I did not enjoy much rest, and when I at last awoke and dressed, breakfast was just ready. I said I would go first to look after my horse, and did so, the planter following me. I found him standing in a miserable stall, in a sorry state; he had not been cleaned, and there were no cobs or other indications of his having been fed at all since he had been there. I said to my host—

"He has not been fed, sir!"

"I wonder! hain't he? Well, I'll have him fed. I s'pose the overseer forgot him."

But, instead of going to the crib and feeding him at once himself, he returned to the house and blew a horn for a negro; when after a long time one came in sight from the cotton-fields, he called to him to go to the overseer for the key of the corn-crib and feed the gentleman's horse, and asked me now to come to breakfast. The overseer joined us as at supper; nothing was said to him about my horse, and he was perfectly silent, and conducted himself like an angry or sulky man in all his actions. As before, when he had finished his meal, without waiting for others to leave the table, he lighted a pipe and lay down to rest on the floor. I went to the stable and found my horse had been supplied with seven poor ears of corn only. I came back to ask for more, but could find neither master nor overseer. While I was packing my saddle-bags preparatory to leaving, I heard my host call a negro to "clean that gentleman's horse and bring him here." As it was late, I did not interpose. While I was putting on the bridle, he took off the musquito tent attached to the saddle and examined it. I explained why I carried it.

"You won't want it any more," said he; "no musquitoes of any account where you are going now; you'd better give it to me, sir; I should like to use it when I go a-fishing; musquitoes are powerful bad in the swamp." After some further solicitation, as I seldom used it, I gave it to him. Almost immediately afterwards he charged me a dollar for my entertainment, which I paid, notwithstanding the value of the tent was several times that amount. Hospitality to travellers is so entirely a matter of business with the common planters.

I passed the hoe-gang at work in the cotton-field, the overseer lounging among them carrying a whip; there were ten or twelve of them; not one looked up at me. Within ten minutes I passed five who were ploughing, with no overseer or driver in sight, and each stopped his plough to gaze at me.

June 3rd.—Yesterday I met a well-dressed man upon the road, and inquired of him if he could recommend me to a comfortable place to pass the night.

"Yes, I can," said he; "you stop at John Watson's. He is a real good fellow, and his wife is a nice, tidy woman; he's got a good house, and you'll be as well taken care of there as in any place I know."

"What I am most concerned about is a clean bed," said I.

"Well, you are safe for that, there."

So distinct a recommendation was unusual, and when I reached the house he had described to me, though it was not yet dark, I stopped to solicit entertainment.

In the gallery sat a fine, stalwart man, and a woman, who in size and figure matched him well. Some ruddy, fat children were playing on the steps. The man wore a full beard, which is very uncommon in these parts. I rode to a horse-block near the gallery, and asked if I could be accommodated for the night. "Oh, yes, you can stay here if you can get along without anything to eat; we don't have anything to eat but once a week." "You look as if it agreed with you, I reckon I'll try it for one night." "Alight, sir, alight. Why, you came from Texas, didn't you? Your rig looks like it," he said, as I dismounted. "Yes, I've just crossed Texas, all the way from the Rio Grande." "Have you though? Well, I'll be right glad to hear something of that country." He threw my saddle and bags across the rail of the gallery, and we walked together to the stable.

"I hear that there are a great many Germans in the western part of Texas," he said presently.

"There are a great many; west of the Guadalupe, more Germans than Americans born."

"Have they got many slaves?"

"No."

"Well, won't they break off and make a Free State down there, by and by?"

"I should think it not impossible that they might."

"I wish to God they would; I would like right well to go and settle there if it was free from slavery. You see Kansas and all the Free States are too far north for me; I was raised in Alabama, and I don't want to move into a colder climate; but I would like to go into a country where they had not got this curse of slavery."

He said this not knowing that I was a Northern man. Greatly surprised, I asked, "What are your objections to slavery, sir?"

"Objections! The first's here" (striking his breast); "I never could bring myself to like it. Well, sir, I know slavery is wrong, and God'll put an end to it. It's bound to come to an end, and when the end does come, there'll be woe in the land. And, instead of preparing for it, and trying to make it as light as possible, we are doing nothing but make it worse and worse. That's the way it appears to me, and I'd rather get out of these parts before it comes. Then I've another objection to it. I don't like to have slaves about me. Now, I tell a nigger to go and feed your horse; I never know if he's done it unless I go and see; and if he didn't know I would go and see, and would whip him if I found he hadn't fed him, would he feed him? He'd let him starve. I've got as good niggers as anybody, but I never can depend on them; they will lie, and they will steal, and take advantage of me in every way they dare. Of course they will, if they are slaves. But lying and stealing are not the worst of it. I've got a family of children, and I don't like to have such degraded beings round my house while they are growing up. I know what the consequences are to children, of growing up among slaves."

I here told him that I was a Northern man, and asked if he could safely utter such sentiments among the people of this district, who bore the reputation of being among the most extreme and fanatical devotees of slavery. "I've been told a hundred times I should be killed if I were not more prudent in expressing my opinions, but, when it comes to killing, I'm as good as the next man, and they know it. I never came the worst out of a fight yet since I was a boy. I never am afraid to speak what I think to anybody. I don't think I ever shall be."

"Are there many persons here who have as bad an opinion of slavery as you have?"

"I reckon you never saw a conscientious man who had been brought up among slaves who did not think of it pretty much as I do—did you?"

"Yes, I think I have, a good many."

"Ah, self-interest warps men's minds wonderfully, but I don't believe there are many who don't think so, sometimes—it's impossible, I know, that they don't."

Were there any others in this neighbourhood, I asked, who

avowedly hated slavery? He replied that there were a good many mechanics, all the mechanics he knew, who felt slavery to be a great curse to them, and who wanted to see it brought to an end in some way. The competition in which they were constantly made to feel themselves engaged with slave-labour was degrading to them, and they felt it to be so. He knew a poor, hard-working man who was lately offered the services of three negroes for six years each if he would let them learn his trade, but he refused the proposal with indignation, saying he would starve before he helped a slave to become a mechanic.[1] There was a good deal of talk now among them about getting laws passed to prevent the owners of slaves from having them taught trades, and to prohibit slave-mechanics from being hired out. He could go out to-morrow, he supposed, and in the course of a day get two hundred signatures to a paper alleging that slavery was a curse to the people of Mississippi, and praying the Legislature to take measures to relieve them of it as soon as practicable. (The county contains three times as many slaves as whites.)

He considered a coercive government of the negroes by the whites, forcing them to labour systematically, and restraining them from a reckless destruction of life and property, at present to be necessary. Of course, he did not think it wrong to hold slaves, and the profits of their labour were not more than enough to pay a man for looking after them—not if he did his duty to them. What was wrong, was making slavery so much worse than was necessary. Negroes would improve very rapidly, if they were allowed, in any con-

---

[1] At Wilmington, North Carolina, on the night of the 27th of July (1857), the frame-work of a new building was destroyed by a number of persons, and a placard attached to the disjointed lumber, stating that a similar course would be pursued in all cases, against edifices that should be erected by negro contractors or carpenters, by one of which class of men the house had been constructed. There was a public meeting called a few days afterwards, to take this outrage into consideration, which was numerously attended. Resolutions were adopted, denouncing the act, and the authorities were instructed to offer a suitable reward for the detection and conviction of the rioters. "The impression was conveyed at the meeting," says the *Wilmington Herald*, "that the act had been committed by members of an organized association, said to exist here, and to number some two hundred and fifty persons, and possibly more, who, as was alleged, to right what they considered a grievance in the matter of negro competition with white labour, had adopted the illegal course of which the act in question was an illustration." Proceedings of a similar significance had occurred at various points, especially in Virginia.

siderable measure, the ordinary incitements to improvement. He knew hosts of negroes who showed extraordinary talents, considering their opportunities: there were a great many in this part of the country who could read and write, and calculate mentally as well as the general run of white men who had been to schools. There were Colonel ——'s negroes, some fifty of them; he did not suppose there were any fifty more contented people in the world; they were not driven hard, and work was stopped three times a day for meals; they had plenty to eat, and good clothes; and through the whole year they had from Friday night to Monday morning to do what they liked with themselves. Saturdays, the men generally worked in their patches (private gardens), and the women washed and mended clothes. Sundays, they nearly all went to a Sabbath School which the mistress taught, and to meeting, but they were not obliged to go; they could come and go as they pleased all Saturday and Sunday; they were not looked after at all. Only on Monday morning, if there should any one be missing, or any one should come to the field with ragged or dirty clothes, he would be whipped. He had often noticed how much more intelligent and sprightly these negroes all were than the common run; a great many of them had books and could read and write; and on Sundays they were smartly dressed, some of them better than he or his wife ever thought of dressing. These things were purchased with the money they made out of their patches, working Saturdays.

There were two other large plantations near him, in both of which the negroes were turned out to work at half-past three every week-day morning—I might hear the bell ring for them—and frequently they were not stopped till nine o'clock at night, Saturday nights the same as any other. One of them belonged to a very religious lady, and on Sunday mornings at half-past nine she had her bell rung for Sunday School, and after Sunday School they had a meeting, and after dinner another religious service. Every negro on the plantation was obliged to attend all these exercises, and if they were not dressed clean they were whipped. They were never allowed to go off the plantation, and if they were caught speaking to a negro from any other place, they were whipped. They could all of them repeat the catechism, he believed, but they were the dullest, and laziest, and most sorrowful looking negroes he ever saw.

As a general rule, the condition of the slaves, as regards their material comfort, had greatly improved within twenty years. He did not know that it had in other respects. It would not be a bit safer to turn them free to shift for themselves, than it would have been twenty years ago. Of this he was quite confident. Perhaps they were a little more intelligent, knew more, but they were not as capable of self-guidance, not as much accustomed to work and contrive for themselves, as they used to be, when they were not fed and clothed nearly as well as now.

Beyond the excessive labour required of them on some plantations, he did not think slaves were often treated with unnecessary cruelty. It was necessary to use the lash occasionally. Slaves never really felt under any moral obligation to obey their masters. Faithful service was preached to them as a Christian duty, and they pretended to acknowledge it, but the fact was that they were obedient just so far as they saw that they must be to avoid punishment; and punishment was necessary, now and then, to maintain their faith in their master's power. He had seventeen slaves, and he did not suppose that there had been a hundred strokes of the whip on his place for a year past.

He asked if there were many Americans in Texas who were opposed to slavery, and if they were free to express themselves. I said that the wealthy Americans there were all slaveholders themselves; that their influence all went to encourage the use of slave-labour, and render labour by whites disreputable. "But are there not a good many Northern men there?" he asked. The Northern men, I replied, were chiefly merchants or speculators, who had but one idea, which was to make money as fast as they could; and nearly all the little money there was in that country was in the hands of the largest slaveholders.

If that was the way of things there, he said, there could not be much chance of its becoming a Free State. I thought the chances were against it, but if the Germans continued to flock into the country, it would rapidly acquire all the characteristic features of a free-labour community, including an abundance and variety of skilled labour, a home market for a variety of crops, denser settlements, and more numerous social, educational, and commercial conveniences. There would soon be a large body of small proprietors, not so wealthy that the stimulus to personal and active industry would have been lost, but yet able to indulge in a good many luxuries, to

found churches, schools, and railroads, and to attract thither tradesmen, mechanics, professional men, and artists. Moreover, the labourers who were not landholders would be intimately blended with
them in all their interests; the two classes not living dissociated from
each other, as was the case generally at the South, but engaged in a
constant fulfilment of reciprocal obligations. I told him that if such
a character of society could once be firmly and extensively established before the country was partitioned out into these little independent negro kingdoms, which had existed from the beginning
in every other part of the South, I did not think any laws would be
necessary to prevent slavery. It might be a slave State, but it would
be a free people.

On coming from my room in the morning, my host met me with a
hearty grasp of the hand. "I have slept very little with thinking of
what you told me about western Texas. I think I shall have to go
there. If we could get rid of slavery in this region, I believe we
would soon be the most prosperous people in the world. What a
disadvantage it must be to have your ground all frozen up, and to
be obliged to fodder your cattle five months in the year, as you do
at the North. I don't see how you live. I think I should like to buy a
small farm near some town where I could send my children to
school—a farm that I could take care of with one or two hired men.
One thing I wanted to ask you, are the Germans learning English
at all?" "Oh, yes; they teach the children English in their schools."
"And have they good schools?" "Wherever they have settled at all
closely they have. At New Braunfels they employ American as well
as German teachers, and instruction can be had in the classics, natural history, and the higher mathematics." "Upon my word, I think I
must go there," he replied. (Since then, as I hear, an educational
institution of a high character, has been established by German
influence in San Antonio, teachers in which are from Harvard.)

When I left he mounted a horse and rode on with me some miles,
saying he did not often find an intelligent man who liked to converse
with him on the question of slavery. It seemed to him there was an
epidemic insanity on the subject. It is unnecessary to state his views
at length. They were precisely those which used to be common
among all respectable men at the South.

As we rode an old negro met and greeted us warmly. My companion hereupon observed that he had never uttered his sentiments

in the presence of a slave, but in some way all the slaves in the country had, he thought, been informed what they were, for they all looked to him as their special friend. When they got into trouble, they would often come to him for advice or assistance. This morning before I was up, a negro came to him from some miles distant, who had been working for a white man on Sundays till he owed him three dollars, which, now that the negro wanted it, he said he could not pay. He had given the negro the three dollars, for he thought he could manage to get it from the white man.

He confirmed an impression I had begun to get of the purely dramatic character of what passed for religion with most of the slaves. One of his slaves was a preacher, and a favourite among them. He sometimes went to plantations twenty miles away—even further—on a Sunday, to preach a funeral sermon, making journeys of fifty miles a day on foot. After the sermon, a hat would be passed round, and he sometimes brought home as much as ten dollars. He was a notable pedestrian; and once when he had committed some abominable crime for which he knew he would have to be punished, and had run away, he (Mr. Watson) rode after him almost immediately, often got in sight of him, but did not overtake him until the second day, when starting early in the morning he overhauled him crossing a broad, smooth field. When the runaway parson saw that he could not escape, he jumped up into a tree and called out to him, with a cheerful voice, "I gin ye a good run dis time, didn't I, massa?" He was the most rascally negro, the worst liar, thief, and adulterer on his place. Indeed, when he was preaching, he always made a strong point of his own sinfulness, and would weep and bellow about it like a bull of Bashan, till he got a whole camp meeting into convulsions.

The night after leaving Mr. Watson's I was kindly received by a tradesman, who took me, after closing his shop, to his mother's house, a log cabin, but more comfortable than many more pretentious residences at which I passed a night on this journey. For the first time in many months tea was offered me. It was coarse Bohea, sweetened with honey, which was stirred into the tea as it boiled in a kettle over the fire, by the old lady herself, whose especial luxury it seemed to be. She asked me if folks ever drank tea at the North, and when I spoke of green tea said she had never heard of that kind of tea before. They owned a number of slaves, but the young man looked after my horse himself. There was a good assortment of books and newspapers at this house, and the people were quite intelligent and very amiable.

The next day, I passed a number of small Indian farms, very badly cultivated—the corn nearly concealed by weeds. The soil became poorer than before, and the cabins of poor people more frequent. I counted about ten plantations, or negro-cultivated farms, in twenty miles. A planter, at whose house I called after sunset, said it was not convenient for him to accommodate me, and I was obliged to ride until it was quite dark. The next house at which I arrived was one of the commonest sort of cabins. I had passed twenty like it during the day, and I thought I would take the opportunity to get an interior knowledge of them. The fact that a horse and waggon were kept, and that a considerable area of land in the rear of the cabin was planted with cotton, showed that the family were by no means of the lowest class, yet, as they were not able even to hire a slave, they may be considered to represent very favourably, I believe, the condition of the poor whites of the plantation districts. The whites of the county, I observe, by the census, are three to one of the slaves; in the nearest adjoining county, the proportion is reversed; and within a few miles the soil was richer, and large plantations occurred.

It was raining, and nearly nine o'clock. The door of the cabin was open, and I rode up and conversed with the occupant as he stood within. He said that he was not in the habit of taking in travellers, and his wife was about sick, but if I was a mind to put up with common fare, he didn't care. Grateful, I dismounted and took the seat he had vacated by the fire, while he led away my horse to an open shed in the rear—his own horse ranging at large, when not in use, during the summer.

The house was all comprised in a single room, twenty-eight by twenty-five feet in area, and open to the roof above. There was a large fireplace at one end and a door on each side—no windows at all. Two bedsteads, a spinning-wheel, a packing-case, which served as a bureau, a cupboard, made of rough hewn slabs, two or three deer-skin seated chairs, a Connecticut clock, and a large poster of Jayne's patent medicines, constituted all the visible furniture, either useful or ornamental in purpose. A little girl, immediately, without having had any directions to do so, got a frying-pan and a chunk of bacon from the cupboard, and cutting slices from the latter, set it frying for my supper. The woman of the house sat sulkily in a chair tilted back and leaning against the logs, spitting occasionally at the fire, but took no notice of me, barely nodding when I saluted her. A baby lay crying on the floor. I quieted it and amused it with my watch till the little girl, having made "coffee" and put a piece of corn-bread on the table with the bacon, took charge of it.

I hoped the woman was not very ill.

"Got the headache right bad," she answered. "Have the headache a heap, I do. Knew I should have it to-night. Been cuttin' brush in the cotton this arternoon. Knew't would bring on my headache. Told him so when I begun."

As soon as I had finished my supper and fed Jude, the little girl put the fragments and the dishes in the cupboard, shoved the table into a corner, and dragged a quantity of quilts from one of the bedsteads, which she spread upon the floor, and presently crawled among them out of sight for the night. The woman picked up the child—which, though still a suckling, she said was twenty-two months old—and nursed it, retaking her old position. The man sat with me by the fire, his back towards her. The baby having fallen asleep was laid away somewhere, and the woman dragged off another lot of quilts from the beds, spreading them upon the floor. Then taking a deep tin pan, she filled it with alternate layers of corn-cobs and hot embers from the fire. This she placed upon a large block, which was evidently used habitually for the purpose, in the centre of the cabin. A furious smoke arose from it, and we soon began to cough. "Most *too* much smoke," observed the man. "Hope 'twill drive out all the gnats, then," replied the woman. (There is a very minute flying insect here, the bite of which is excessively sharp.)

The woman suddenly dropped off her outer garment and stepped from the midst of its folds, in her petticoat; then, taking the baby from the place where she had deposited it, lay down and covered herself with the quilts upon the floor. The man told me that I could take the bed which remained on one of the bedsteads, and kicking off his shoes only, rolled himself into a blanket by the side of his wife. I ventured to take off my cravat and stockings, as well as my boots, but almost immediately put my stockings on again, drawing their tops over my pantaloons. The advantage of this arrangement was that, although my face, eyes, ears, neck, and hands, were immediately attacked, the vermin did not reach my legs for two or three hours. Just after the clock struck two, I distinctly heard the man and the woman, and the girl and the dog scratching, and the horse out in the shed stamping and gnawing himself. Soon afterward the man exclaimed, "Good God Almighty—mighty! mighty! mighty!" and jumping up pulled off one of his stockings, shook it, scratched his foot vehemently, put on the stocking, and lay down again with a groan. The two doors were open, and through the logs and the openings in the roof, I saw the clouds divide and the moon and stars reveal themselves. The woman, after having been nearly smothered by the smoke from the pan which she had originally placed close to her own pillow, rose and placed it on the sill of the windward door, where it burned feebly and smoked lustily, like an altar to the Lares, all night. Fortunately the cabin was so open that it gave us little annoyance, while it seemed to answer the purpose of keeping all flying insects at a distance.

When, on rising in the morning, I said that I would like to wash my face, water was given me for the purpose in an earthen pie-dish. Just as breakfast, which was of exactly the same materials as my supper, was ready, rain began to fall, presently in such a smart shower as to put the fire out and compel us to move the table under the least leaky part of the roof.

At breakfast occured the following conversation:—

"Are there many niggers in New York?"

"Very few."

"How do you get your work done?"

"There are many Irish and German people constantly coming there who are glad to get work to do."

"Oh, and you have them for slaves?"

"They want money and are willing to work for it. A great many American-born work for wages, too."

"What do you have to pay?"

"Ten or twelve dollars a month."

"There was a heap of Irishmen to work on the railroad; they was paid a dollar a day; there was a good many Americans, too, but mostly they had little carts and mules, and hauled dirt and sich like. They was paid twenty-five or thirty dollars a month and found."

"What did they find them?"

"Oh, blanket and shoes, I expect; they put up kind o' tents like for 'em to sleep in altogether."

"What food did they find them?"

"Oh, common food; bacon and meal."

"What do they generally give the niggers on the plantations here?"

"A peck of meal and three pound of bacon is what they call 'lowance, in general, I believe. It takes a heap o' meat on a big plantation. I was on one of William R. King's plantations over in Alabamy, where there was about fifty niggers, one Sunday last summer, and I see 'em weighin' outen the meat. Tell you, it took a powerful heap on it. They had an old nigger to weigh it out, and he warn't no ways partickler about the weight. He just took and chopped it off, middlins, in chunks, and he'd throw them into the scales, and if a piece weighed a pound or two over he wouldn't mind it; he never took none back. Ain't niggers all-fired sassy at the North?"

"No, not particularly."

"Ain't they all free, there? I hearn so."

"Yes."

"Well, how do they get along when they 's free?"

"I never have seen a great many, to know their circumstances very well. Right about where I live they seem to me to live quite comfortably; more so than the niggers on these big plantations do, I should think."

"Oh, they have a mighty hard time on the big plantations. I 'd ruther be dead than to be a nigger on one of these big plantations."

"Why, I thought they were pretty well taken care of on them."

The man and his wife both looked at me as if surprised, and smiled.

"Why, they are well fed, are they not?"

"Oh, but they work 'em so hard. My God, sir, in pickin' time on these plantations they start 'em to work 'fore light, and they don't give 'em time to eat."

"I supposed they generally gave them an hour or two at noon."

"No, sir; they just carry a piece of bread and meat in their pockets and they eat it when they can, standin' up. They have a hard life on 't, that 's a fact. I reckon you can get along about as well withouten slaves as with 'em, can't you, in New York?"

"In New York there is not nearly so large a proportion of very rich men as here. There are very few people who farm over three hundred acres, and the greater number—nineteen out of twenty, I suppose—work themselves with the hands they employ. Yes, I think it's better than it is here, for all concerned, a great deal. Folks that can't afford to buy niggers get along a great deal better in the Free States, I think; and I guess that those who could afford to have niggers get along better without them."

"I no doubt that's so. I wish there warn't no niggers here. They are a great cuss to this country, I expect. But 'twouldn't do to free 'em; that wouldn't do nohow!"

"Are there many people here who think slavery a curse to the country?"

"Oh, yes, a great many. I reckon the majority would be right glad if we could get rid of the niggers. But it wouldn't never do to free 'em and leave 'em here. I don't know anybody, hardly, in favour of that. Make 'em free and leave 'em here and they'd steal everything we made. Nobody couldn't live here then."

These views of slavery seem to be universal among people of this class. They were repeated to me at least a dozen times.

"Where I used to live [Alabama], I remember when I was a boy—must ha' been about twenty years ago—folks was dreadful frightened about the niggers. I remember they built pens in the woods where they could hide, and Christmas time they went and got into the pens, 'fraid the niggers was risin'."

"I remember the same time where we was in South Carolina," said his wife; "we had all our things put up in bags, so we could tote 'em, if we heerd they was comin' our way."

They did not suppose the niggers ever thought of rising now, but could give no better reason for not supposing so than that "everybody said there warn't no danger on't now."

Hereabouts the plantations were generally small, ten to twenty negroes on each; sometimes thirty or forty. Where he used to live they were big ones—forty or fifty, sometimes a hundred on each. He had lived here ten years. I could not make out why he had not accumulated wealth, so small a family and such an inexpensive style of living as he had. He generally planted twenty to thirty acres, he said; this year he had sixteen in cotton and about ten, he thought, in corn. Decently cultivated, this planting should have produced him five hundred dollars' worth of cotton, besides supplying him with bread and bacon—his chief expense, apparently. I suggested that this was a very large planting for his little family; he would need some help in picking time. He ought to have some now, he said; grass and bushes were all overgrowing him; he had to work just like a nigger; this durnation rain would just make the weeds jump, and he didn't expect he should have any cotton at all. There warn't much use in a man's trying to get along by himself; everything seemed to set in agin him. He'd been trying to hire somebody, but he couldn't, and his wife was a sickly kind of a woman.

His wife reckoned he might hire some help if he'd look round sharp.

My horse and dog were as well cared for as possible, and a "snack" of bacon and corn-bread was offered me for noon, which has been unusual in Mississippi. When I asked what I should pay, the man hesitated and said he reckoned what I had had, wasn't worth much of anything; he was sorry he could not have accommodated me better. I offered him a dollar, for which he thanked me warmly. It is the first instance of hesitation in charging for a lodging which I have met with from a stranger at the South.

Northern Alabama, June 15th.—I have to-day reached a more distinctly hilly country—somewhat rocky and rugged, but with inviting dells. The soil is sandy and less frequently fertile; cotton-fields are seen only at long intervals, the crops on the small proportion of cultivated land being chiefly corn and oats. I notice also that white men are more commonly at work in the fields than negroes, and this as well in the cultivation of cotton as of corn.

The larger number of the dwellings are rude log huts, of only one room, and that unwholesomely crowded. I saw in and about one of them, not more than fifteen feet square, five grown persons, and as many children. Occasionally, however, the monotony of these huts is agreeably varied by neat, white, frame houses. At one such, I dined to-day, and was comfortably entertained. The owner held a number of slaves, but made no cotton. He owned a saw mill, was the postmaster of the neighbourhood, and had been in the Legislature.

I asked him why the capital had been changed from Tuscaloosa to Montgomery. He did not know. "Because Montgomery is more central and easy of access, probably," I suggested. "No, I don't think that had anything to do with it." "Is Tuscaloosa an unhealthy place?" "No, sir; healthier than Montgomery, I reckon." "Was it then simply because the people of the southern districts were stronger, and used their power to make the capital more convenient of access to themselves?" "Well, no, I don't think that was it, exactly. The fact is, sir, the people here are not like you Northern people; they don't reason out everything so. They are fond of change, and they got tired of Tuscaloosa; the Montgomery folks wanted it there and offered to pay for moving it, so they let 'em have it; 'twas just for a change." "If there really was no better reason, was it not rather wasteful to give up all the public buildings at Tuscaloosa?" "Oh, the Montgomery people wanted it so bad they promised to pay for building a new State House; so it did not cost anything."

Quite on a par with the economics of Southern commercial conventions.

I passed the night at the second framed house that I saw during the day, stopping early in order to avail myself of its promise of comfort. It was attractively situated on a hill-top, with a peach orchard near it. The proprietor owned a dozen slaves, and "made cotton," he said, "with other crops." He had some of his neighbours at tea and at breakfast; sociable, kindly people, satisfied with themselves and their circumstances, which I judged from their conversation had been recently improving. One coming in, remarked that he had discharged a white labourer whom he had employed for some time past; the others congratulated him on being "shet" of him; all seemed to have noticed him as a bad, lazy man; he had often been seen lounging in the field, rapping the negroes with his hoe if they didn't work to suit him. "He was about the meanest white man I ever see," said a woman; "he was a heap meaner 'n niggers. I reckon niggers would come somewhere between white folks and such as he." "The first thing I tell a man," said another, "when I hire him, is, 'if there's any whippin' to be done on this place I want to do it myself.' If I saw a man rappin' my niggers with a hoe-handle, as I see him, durned if I wouldn't rap him—the lazy whelp."

One of the negroes complimented my horse. "Dar's a heap of genus in dat yar hoss's head!" The proprietor looked after the feeding himself.

These people were extremely kind; inquiring with the simplest good feeling about my domestic relations and the purpose of my journey. When I left, one of them walked a quarter of a mile to make sure that I went upon the right road. The charge for entertainment, though it was unusually good, was a quarter of a dollar less than I have paid before, which I mention, not as Mr. De Bow would suppose,[2] out of gratitude for the moderation, but as an indication of the habits of the people, showing, as it may, either closer calculation, or that the district grows its own supplies, and can furnish food cheaper than those in which attention is more exclusively given to cotton.

June 17th.—The country continues hilly, and is well populated by farmers, living in log huts, while every mile or two, on the more level and fertile land, there is a larger farm, with ten or twenty negroes at work. A few whites are usually working near them, in the same field, generally ploughing while the negroes hoe.

About noon, my attention was attracted towards a person upon a ledge, a little above the road, who was throwing up earth and stone with a shovel. I stopped to see what the purpose of this work might be, and perceived that the shoveller was a woman, who, presently discovering me, stopped and called to others behind her, and immediately a stout girl and two younger children, with a man, came to the edge and looked at me. The woman was bareheaded, and otherwise half-naked, as perhaps needed to be, for her work would have been thought hard by our stoutest labourers, and it was the hottest weather of the summer, in the latitude of Charleston, and on a hill-side in the full face of the noon sun. I pushed my horse up the hill until I reached them, when another man appeared, and in answer to my inquiries told me that they were getting out iron ore. One was picking in a vein, having excavated a short adit; the other man picked looser ore exterior to the vein. The women and children shovelled out the ore and piled it on kilns of timber, where they roasted it to make it crumble. It was then carted to a forge, and they were paid for it by the load. They were all clothed very meanly and

[2] See De Bow's Review, for August, 1857, p. 117.

scantily. The women worked, so far as I could see, as hard as the men. The children, too, even to the youngest—a boy of eight or ten—were carrying large lumps of ore, and heaving them into the kiln, and shovelling the finer into a screen to separate the earth from it.

Immediately after leaving them I found a good spot for nooning. I roped my horse out to graze, and spread my blanket in a deep shade. I noticed that the noise of their work had ceased, and about fifteen minutes afterwards, Jude suddenly barking, I saw one of the men peering at me through the trees, several rods distant. I called to him to come up. He approached rather slowly and timidly, examined the rope with which my horse was fastened, eyed me vigilantly, and at length asked if I was resting myself. I replied that I was; and he said that he did not know but I might be sick, and had come to see me. I thanked him, and offered him a seat upon my blanket, which he declined. Presently he took up a newspaper that I had been reading, looked at it for a moment, then he told me he couldn't read. "Folks don't care much for edication round here; it would be better for 'em, I expect, if they did." He began then to question me closely about my circumstances—where I came from, whither I was going, etc.

When his curiosity was partially appeased he suddenly laughed in a silly manner, and said that the people he had been working with had watched me after I left them; they saw me ride up the hill and stop, ride on again, and finally take off my saddle, turn my horse loose and tote my saddle away, and they were much frightened, thinking I must be crazy at least. When he started to come toward me they told him he wouldn't dare to go to me, but he saw how it was, well enough—I was just resting myself.

"If I should run down hill now," said he, "they'd start right off and wouldn't stop for ten mile, reckoning you was arter me. That would be fun; oh, we have some good fun here sometimes with these green folks. There's an amazin' ignorant set round here."

I asked if they were foreigners.

"Oh, no; they are common, no account people; they used to live over the hill, here; they come right nigh starvin' thar, I expect."

They had not been able to get any work to do, and had been "powerful poor," until he got them to come here. They had taken an old cabin, worked with him, and were doing right well now. He didn't let them work in the vein—he kept that for himself—but they worked all around, and some days they made a dollar and a half—the man, woman, and children together. They had one other girl, but she had to stay at home to take care of the baby and keep cattle and hogs out of their "gardien." He had known the woman when she was a girl; "she was always a good one to work. She'd got a voice like a bull, and she was as smart as a wild cat; but the man warn't no account."

He had himself followed this business (mining) since he was a young man, and could earn three dollars a day by it if he tried; he had a large family and owned a small farm: never laid up anything, always kept himself a little in debt at the store.

He asked if I had not found the people "more friendly like" up in this country to what they were down below, and assured me that I would find them grow more friendly as I went further North, so at least he had heard, and he knew where he first came from (Tennessee) the people were more friendly than they were here. "The richer a man is," he continued, pursuing a natural association of ideas, "and the more niggers he's got, the poorer he seems to live. If you want to fare well in this country you stop to poor folks' housen; they try to enjoy what they've got, while they ken, but these yer big planters they don' care for nothing but to save. Now, I never calculate to save anything; I tell my wife I work hard, and I mean to enjoy what I earn as fast as it comes."

Sometimes he "took up bee-huntin' for a spell," and made money by collecting wild honey. He described his manner of finding the hives and securing the honey, and, with a hushed voice, told me a "secret," which was, that if you carried three leaves, each of a different tree (?) in your hand, there was never a bee would dare to sting you.

I asked about his children. He had one grown-up son, who was doing very well; he was hired by the gentleman who owned the forge, to cart ore. He had nothing to do but to drive a team; he didn't have to load, and he had a nigger to take care of the horses when his day's teaming was done.

His wages were seven dollars a month, and board for himself and wife. They ate at the same table with the gentleman, and had good living, besides having something out of the store, "tobacco and so on—tobacco for both on 'em, and two people uses a good deal of tobacco you know; so that's pretty good wages—seven dollars a month besides their keep and tobacco." Irishmen, he informed me, had been employed occasionally at the forge. "They do well at first, only they is apt to get into fights all the time; but after they've been here a year or two, they get to feel so independent and keerless-like, you can't get along with 'em." He remained about half an hour, and not till he returned did I hear again the noise of picking and shovelling, and cutting timber.

At the forges, I was told, slave labour is mainly employed—the slaves being owned by the proprietors of the forges.

I spent that night at a large inn in a village. In the morning as I sat waiting in my room, a boy opened the door. Without looking up I asked, "Well?"

"I didn't say nuthin', sar," with a great grin.

"What are you waiting there for?" "Please, massa, I b'leve you's owin' me suthin', sar." "Owing you something? What do you mean?" "For drying yer clothes for yer, sar, last night." I had ordered him immediately after tea to go up stairs and get my clothes, which had been drenched in a shower, and hang them by the kitchen fire, that they might be dry if I should wish to leave early in the morning. When I went to my bedroom at nine o'clock I found the clothes where I had left them. I went down and reported it to the landlord, who directly sent the boy for them. In the morning, when I got them again I found they were not dry except where they were burned. I told him to be gone; but with the door half open, he stood putting in his head, bowing and grinning. "Please, sar, massa sent me out of an errand, and I was afeard you would be gone before I got back; dat's the reason why I mention it, sar; dat's all, sar; I hope you'll skuse me, sar."

During the afternoon I rode on through a valley, narrow and apparently fertile, but the crops indifferent. The general social characteristics were the same that I met with yesterday.

At night I stopped at a large house having an unusual number of negro cabins and stables about it. The proprietor, a hearty old farmer, boasted much of his pack of hounds, saying they had pulled down five deer before he had had a shot at them. He was much interested to hear about Texas, the Indians and the game. He reckoned there was "a heap of big varmint out thar."

His crop of cotton did not average two bales to the hand, and corn not twenty bushels to the acre.

He amused me much with a humorous account of an oyster supper to which he had been invited in town, and his attempts to eat the "nasty things" without appearing disconcerted before the ladies.

An old negro took my horse when I arrived, and half an hour afterward, came to me and asked if I wanted to see him fed. As we walked toward the stables, he told me that he always took care not to forget gentlemen's hosses, and to treat them well; "then," he said, bowing and with emphasis, "they looks out and don't forget to treat me well."

The same negro was called to serve me as a candlestick at bedtime. He held the candle till I got into bed. As he retired I closed my eyes, but directly afterward, perceiving the light return, I opened them. Uncle Abram was bending over me, holding the candle, grinning with his toothless gums, winking and shaking his head in a most mysterious manner.

"Hush! massa," he whispered. "You hain't got something to drink, in dem saddle-bags, has you, sar?"

The farmer told me something about "nigger dogs"; they didn't use foxhounds, but bloodhounds—not pure, he thought, but a cross of the Spanish bloodhound with the common hounds, or curs. There were many men, he said, in the country below here, who made a business of nigger-hunting, and they had their horses trained, as well as the dogs, to go over any common fence, or if they couldn't leap it, to break it down. Dogs were trained, when pups, to follow a nigger—not allowed to catch one, however, unless they were quite young, so that they couldn't hurt him much, and they were always taught to hate a negro, never being permitted to see one except to be put in chase of him. He believed that only two of a pack were kept kenneled all the time—these were old, keen ones, who led the rest when they were out; they were always kept coupled together with a chain, except when trailing. He had seen a pack of thirteen who would follow a trail two days and a half old, if rain had not fallen in the mean time. When it rained immediately after a negro got off, they had to scour the country where they supposed he might be, till they scented him.

When hard pushed, a negro always took to a tree; sometimes,

however, they would catch him in an open field. When this was the case the hunter called off the dogs as soon as he could, unless the negro fought—"that generally makes 'em mad (the hunters), and they'll let 'em tear him a spell. The owners don't mind having them kind o' niggers tore a good deal; runaways ain't much account no-how, and it makes the rest more afraid to run away, when they see how they are sarved." If they caught the runaway within two or three days, they got from $10 to $20; if it took a longer time, they were paid more than that; sometimes $200. They asked their own price; if an owner should think it exorbitant, he supposed, he said in reply to an inquiry, they'd turn the nigger loose, order him to make off, and tell his master to catch his own niggers.

Sunday.—I rode on, during the cool of the morning, about eight miles, and stopped for the day, at a house pleasantly situated by a small stream, among wooded hills. During the forenoon, seven men and three women, with their children, gathered at the house. All of them, I concluded, were non-slaveholders, as was our host him-self; though, as one told me, "with his five boys he makes a heap more crop than Mrs. ——, who's got forty niggers." "How is that?" "Well, she's a woman, and she can't make the niggers work; she won't have a overseer, and niggers won't work, you know, unless there's somebody to drive 'em."

Our host, when I arrived, had just been pulling weeds out of his potato patch, which he mentioned as an apology for not being a little clean, like the rest.

Besides the company I have mentioned, and the large family of the house, there was another traveller and myself to dinner, and three bountiful tables were spread, one after another.

The traveller was said to be a Methodist preacher, but gave no indication of it, except that he said grace before meat, and used the Hebrew word for Sunday. He was, however, a man of superior intelligence to the others, who were ignorant and stupid, though friendly and communicative. He asked me "what a good nigger man could be bought for in New York"; he didn't seem surprised, or make any further inquiry, when I told him we had no slaves there. Some asked me much about crops, and when I told them that my crops of wheat for six years had averaged twenty-eight bushels, and that I had once reaped forty from a single acre, they were amazed beyond expression, and anxious to know how I "put it in." I described the process minutely, which astonished them still more; and one man said he had often thought they might get more wheat if they put it in differently; he had thought that perhaps more wheat would grow if more seed were sown, but he never tried it. The general practice, they told me, was to sow wheat on ground from which they had taken maize, without removing the maize stumps, or ploughing it at all; they sowed three pecks of wheat to the acre, and then ploughed it in—that was all. They used the cradle, but had never heard of reaping machines; the crop was from five to ten bushels an acre; ten bushels was extraordinary, six was not thought bad. Of cotton, the ordinary crop was five hundred pounds to the acre, or from one to two bales to a hand. Of maize, usually from ten to twenty bushels to the acre; last year not over ten; this year they thought it would be twenty-five on the best land.

The general admiration of Jude brought up the topic of negro dogs again, and the clergyman told a story of a man who hunted niggers near where he lived. He was out once with another man, when after a long search, they found the dogs barking up a big cottonwood tree. They examined the tree closely without finding any negro, and concluded that the dogs must have been foiled, and they were about to go away, when Mr. ——, from some distance off, thought he saw a negro's leg very high up in the tree, where the leaves and moss were thick enough to hide a man lying on the top of a limb with his feet against the trunk. He called out, as if he really saw a man, telling him to come down, but nothing stirred. He sent for an axe, and called out again, saying he would cut the tree to the ground if he didn't come down. There was no reply. He then cut half through the tree on one side, and was beginning on the other, when the negro halloed out that if he would stop he would come down. He stopped cutting, and the negro descended to the lowest limb, which was still far from the ground, and asked the hunter to take away his dogs, and promise they shouldn't tear him. But the hunter swore he'd make no conditions with him after having been made to cut the tree almost down.

The negro said no more, but retained his position until the tree was nearly cut in two. When it began to totter, he slid down the trunk, the dogs springing upon him as soon as he was within their reach. He fought them hard, and got hold of one by the ear; that made them fiercer, and they tore him till the hunter was afraid they'd kill him, and stopped them.

"Are dogs allowed to tear the negroes when they catch them?"

"When the hunters come up they always call them off, unless the nigger fights. If the nigger fights 'em that makes 'em mad, and they let 'em tear him good," said the clergyman.

There were two or three young women present, and the young men were sparking with them in the house, sitting on the beds for want of sofas, the chairs being all in use outside; the rest of the company sat on the gallery most of the time, but there was little conversation. It was twice remarked to me, "Sunday's a dull day—nothing to do."

As the Methodist and I were reading after dinner, I noticed that two or three were persuading the others to go with them some-where, and I asked where they purposed to go. They said they wanted to go over the mountain to hunt a bull.

"To shoot him?"

"Oh, no, it's a working bull; they got his mate yesterday. There ain't but one pair of cattle in this neighbourhood, and they do all the hauling for nine families." They belonged, together with their waggon, to one man, and the rest borrowed of him. They wanted them this week to cart in their oats. The stray bull was driven in to-ward night, yoked with another to a waggon, and one of the women, with her family, got into the waggon and was carried home. The bulls were fractious and had to be led by one man, while another urged them forward with a cudgel.

Last night by the way a neighbour came into the house of Uncle Abram's master, and in the course of conversation about crops, said that on Sunday he went over to John Brown's to get him to come out and help him at his harvesting. He found four others there for the same purpose, but John said he didn't feel well, and he reckoned he couldn't work. He offered him a dollar and a half a day to cradle for him; but when he tried to persuade him, John spoke out plainly and said, "he'd be d—d if he was going to work anyhow"; so he said to the others, "Come, boys, we may as well go; you can't make a lazy man work when he's determined he won't." He supposed that remark made him mad, for on Thursday John came running across his cotton patch, where he was ploughing. He didn't speak a word to him, but cut along over to his neighbour's house, and told him that he had shot two deer, and wanted his hounds to catch 'em, promising to give him half the venison if he succeeded. He did catch one of them, and kept his promise.

This man Brown, they told me, had a large family, and lived in a little cabin on the mountain. He pretended to plant a corn patch, but he never worked it, and didn't make any corn. They reckoned he lived pretty much on what corn and hogs he could steal, and on game. The children were described as pitiably "scrawny," half-starved little wretches. Last summer his wife had come to one of them, saying they had no corn, and she wanted to pick cotton to earn some. He had let her go in with the niggers and pick. She kept at it for two days, and took her pay in corn. Afterward he saw her little boy "toting" it to the mill to be ground—much too heavy a load for him.

I asked if there were many such vagabonds.

"Yes, a great many on the mountain, and they make a heap of trouble. There is a law by which they might be taken up [if it could be proved that they have no 'visible means of support'] and made to work to support their families; but the law is never used."

Speaking of another man, one said: "He'll be here to breakfast, at your house to dinner, and at Dr. ——'s to supper, leaving his family to live as best they can." They "reckoned" he got most of his living in that way, while his family had to get theirs by stealing. He never did any work except hunting, and they "reckoned" he killed about as many shoats and yearlings as deer and turkeys.

They said that this sort of people were not often intemperate; they had no money to buy liquor with; now and then, when they'd sold some game or done a little work to raise money, they'd have a spree; but they were more apt to gamble it off or spend it for fine clothes and things to trick out their wives.

June ——. To-day, I am passing through a valley of thin, sandy soil, thickly populated by poor farmers. Negroes are rare, but occasionally neat, new houses, with other improvements, show the increasing prosperity of the district. The majority of dwellings are small log cabins of one room, with another separate cabin for a kitchen; each house has a well, and a garden inclosed with palings. Cows, goats, mules and swine, fowls and doves are abundant. The people are more social than those of the lower country, falling read-

ily into friendly conversation with a traveller. They are very ignorant; the agriculture is wretched and the work hard. I have seen
three white women hoeing field crops to-day. A spinning-wheel is
heard in every house, and frequently a loom is clanging in the gallery, always worked by women; every one wears homespun. The
negroes have much more individual freedom than in the rich cotton
country, and are not unfrequently heard singing or whistling at
their work.

Tennessee, June 29th.—At nightfall I entered a broader and more
populous valley than I had seen before during the day, but for some
time there were only small single room log cabins, at which I was
loath to apply for lodging. At length I reached a large and substantial log house with negro cabins. The master sat in the stoop. I asked
if he could accommodate me.

"What do you want?"

"Something to eat for myself and horse, and room to sleep under
your roof."

"The wust on't is," he said, getting up and coming toward me,
"we haven't got much for your horse."

"You've got corn, I suppose."

"No, hain't got no corn but a little that we want for ourselves,
only just enough to bread us till corn comes again."

"Well, you have oats?"

"Hain't got an oat."

"Haven't you hay?"

"No."

"Then I must go further, for my horse can't travel on fodder."

"Hain't got nary fodder nuther."

Fortunately I did not have to go much further before I came to
the best house I had seen during the day, a large, neat, white house,
with negro shanties, and an open log cabin in the front yard. A stout,
elderly, fine-looking woman, in a cool white muslin dress, sat upon
the gallery, fanning herself. Two little negroes had just brought a
pail of fresh water, and she was drinking of it with a gourd, as I
came to the gate. I asked if it would be convenient for her to accommodate me for the night, doubtingly, for I had learned to distrust the accommodations of the wealthy slaveholders.

"Oh yes, get down; fasten your horse there, and the niggers will take care of him when they come from their work. Come up here and take a seat."

I brought in my saddle-bags.

"Bring them in here, into the parlour," she said, "where they'll be safe."

The interior of the house was furnished with unusual comfort. "The parlour," however, had a bed in it. As we came out, she locked the door.

We had not sat long, talking about the weather (she was suffering much from the heat), when her husband came. He was very hot also, though dressed coolly enough in merely a pair of short-legged, unbleached cotton trousers, and a shirt with the bosom spread open —no shoes nor stockings. He took his seat before speaking to me, and after telling his wife it was the hottest day he ever saw, squared his chair toward me, threw it back so as to recline against a post, and said gruffly, "Good evening, sir; you going to stay here to-night?"

I replied, and he looked at me a few moments without speaking. He was, in fact, so hot that he spoke with difficulty. At length he got breath and asked abruptly: "You a mechanic, sir, or a dentist, eh— or what?"

Supper was cooked by two young women, daughters of the master of the house, assisted by the two little negro boys. The cabin in front of the house was the kitchen, and when the bacon was dished up, one of the boys struck an iron triangle at the door. "Come to supper," said the host, and led the way to the kitchen, which was also the supper-room. One of the young ladies took the foot of the table, the other seated herself apart by the fire, and actually waited on the table, though the two negro boys stood at the head and foot, nominally waiters, but always anticipated by the Cinderella, when anything was wanted.

A big lout of a youth who came from the field with the negroes, looked in, but seeing me, retired. His father called, but his mother said, " 'twouldn't do no good—he was so bashful."

Speaking of the climate of the country, I was informed that a majority of the folks went barefoot all winter, though they had snow much of the time four or five inches deep, and the man said he didn't think most of the men about here had more than one coat, and they never wore any in winter except on holidays. "That was the healthiest way," he reckoned, "just to toughen yourself and not wear no coat"; no matter how cold it was, he didn't wear no coat.

The master held a candle for me while I undressed, in a large room above stairs; and gave me my choice of the four beds in it. I found one straw bed (with, as usual, but one sheet), on which I slept comfortably. At midnight I was awakened by some one coming in. I rustled my straw, and a voice said, "Who is there in this room?"

"A stranger passing the night; who are you?"

"All right; I belong here. I've been away and have just come home."

He did not take his clothes off to sleep. He turned out to be an older son who had been fifty miles away, looking after a stray horse. When I went down stairs in the morning, having been wakened early by flies, and the dawn of day through an open window, I saw the master lying on his bed in the "parlour," still asleep in the clothes he wore at supper. His wife was washing her face on the gallery, being already dressed for the day; after using the family towel, she went into the kitchen, but soon returned, smoking a pipe, to her chair in the doorway.

Yet everything betokened an opulent and prosperous man—rich land, extensive field crops, a number of negroes, and considerable herds of cattle and horses. He also had capital invested in mines and railroads, he told me. His elder son spoke of him as "the squire."

A negro woman assisted in preparing breakfast (she had probably been employed in the field labour the night before), and both the young ladies were at the table. The squire observed to me that he supposed we could buy hands very cheap in New York. I said we could hire them there at moderate wages. He asked if we couldn't buy as many as we wanted, by sending to Ireland for them and paying their passage. He had supposed we could buy them and hold them as slaves for a term of years, by paying the freight on them. When I had corrected him, he said, a little hesitatingly, "You don't have no black slaves in New York?" "No, sir." "There's niggers there, ain't there, only they're all free?" "Yes, sir." "Well, how do they get along so?" "So far as I know, the most of them live pretty comfortably." (I have changed my standard of comfort lately, and am inclined to believe that the majority of the negroes at the North live more comfortably than the majority of whites at the South.) "I wouldn't like that," said the old lady. "I wouldn't like to live where niggers was free, they are bad enough when they are slaves: it's hard enough to get along with them here, they're so bad. I reckon that niggers are the meanest critters on earth; they are so mean and nasty" (she expressed disgust and indignation very strongly in her face). "If they was to think themselves equal to we, I don't think white folks could abide it—they're such vile saucy things." A negro woman and two boys were in the room as she said this.

North Carolina, July 13th.—I rode late last night, there being no cabins for several miles in which I was willing to spend the night, until I came to one of larger size than usual, with a gallery on the side toward the road and a good stable opposite it. A man on the gallery was about to answer (as I judged from his countenance), "I reckon you can," to my inquiry if I could stay, when the cracked voice of a worryful woman screeched out from within, "We don't foller takin' in people."

"No, sir," said the man, "we don't foller it."

"How far shall I have to go?"

"There's another house a little better than three quarters of a mile further on."

To this house I proceeded—a cabin of one room and a loft, with a kitchen in a separate cabin. The owner said he never turned anybody away, and I was welcome. He did not say that he had no corn, until after supper, when I asked for it to feed my horse. The family were good-natured, intelligent people, but very ignorant. The man and his wife and the daughters slept below, the boy and I in the cock-loft. Supper and breakfast were eaten in the detached kitchen. Yet they were by no means poor people. The man told me that he had over a thousand acres of rich tillable land, besides a large extent of mountain range, the most of which latter he had bought from time to time as he was able, to prevent the settlement of squatters near his valley-land. "There were people who would be bad neighbours, I knew," he said, "that would settle on most any kind of place, and everybody wants to keep such as far away from them as they can." (When I took my bridle off, I hung it up by the stable-door; he took it down and said he'd hang it in a safer place. He'd never had anything stolen from here, and he didn't mean to have—it was just as well not to put temptation before people, and he took it into the house and put it under his bed.)

Besides this large tract of land here, he owned another tract of two hundred acres with a house upon it, rented for one-third the produce, and another smaller farm, similarly rented; he also owned a grist mill, which he rented to a miller for half the tolls. He told me that he had thought a good deal formerly of moving to new countries, but he had been doing pretty well and had stayed here now so long, he didn't much think he should ever budge. He reckoned he'd got enough to make him a living for the rest of his life, and he didn't know any use a man had for more'n that.

I did not see a single book in the house, nor do I think that any of the family could read. He said that many people here were talking about Iowa and Indiana; "was Iowa (Hiaway) beyond the Texies?" I opened my map to show him where it was, but he said he "wasn't scollar'd enough" to understand it, and I could not induce him to look at it. I asked him if the people here preferred Iowa and Indiana to Missouri at all because they were Free States. "I reckon," he replied, "they don't have no allusion to that. Slavery is a great cuss, though, I think, the greatest there is in these United States. There ain't no account of slaves up here in the west, but down in the east part of this State about Fayetteville there's as many as there is in South Carolina. That's the reason the West and the East don't agree in this State; people out here hates the Eastern people."

"Why is that?"

"Why, you see they vote on the slave basis, and there's some of them nigger counties where there ain't more'n four or five hundred white folks, that has just as much power in the Legislature as any of our mountain counties where there'll be some thousand voters."

He made further remarks against slavery and against slaveholders. When I told him that I entirely agreed with him, and said further, that poor white people were usually far better off in the Free than in the Slave States, he seemed a little surprised and said, "New York ain't a Free State, is it?"

Labourers' wages here, he stated, were from fifty cents to one dollar a day, or eight dollars a month. "How much by the year?" "They's never hired by the year."

"Would it be $75 a year?"

"'Twouldn't be over that, anyhow, but 'tain't general for people to hire here only for harvest time; fact is, a man couldn't earn his board, let alone his wages, for six months in the year."

"But what do these men who hire out during harvest time do during the rest of the year; do they have to earn enough in those two or three months to live on for the other eight or nine?"

"Well, they gets jobs sometimes, and they goes from one place to another."

"But in winter time, when you say there's not work enough to pay their board?"

"Well, they keeps a goin' round from one place to another, and gets their living somehow."

"The fact on't is," he said at length, as I pressed the inquiry, "there ain't anybody that ever means to work any in this country, except just along in harvest—folks don't keep working here as they do in your country, I expect."

"But they must put in their crops?"

"Yes, folks that have farms of their own, they do put in their craps and tend 'em, but these fellows that don't have farms, they won't work except in harvest, when they can get high wages [$8 a month]. I hired a fellow last spring for six months; I wanted him to help me plant and tend my corn. You see I had a short crap last year, and this spring I had to pay fifty cents a bushel for corn for bread, and I didn't want to get caught so again, not this year, so I gin this fellow $6 a month for six months—$36 I gin him in hard silver."

"Paid it to him in advance?"

"Yes, he wouldn't come 'less I'd pay him right then. Well, he worked one month, and maybe eight days—no, I don't think it was more than six days over a month, and then he went away, and I hain't seen a sight on him since. I expect I shall lose my money—reckon he don't ever intend to come back; he knows I'm right in harvest, and want him now, if ever I do."

"What did he go away for?"

"Why, he said he was sick, but if he was, he got well mighty easy after he stopped working."

"Do you know where he is now?"

"Oh, yes, he's going round here."

"What is he doing?"

"Well, he's just goin' round."

"Is he at work for any one else?"

"Reckon not—no, he's just goin' round from one place to another."

At supper and breakfast surprise was expressed that I declined coffee, and more still that I drank water instead of milk. The woman observed, 'twas cheap boarding me. The man said he must get home a couple more cows; they ought to drink milk more, coffee was so high now, and he believed milk would be just as healthy. The woman asked the price of coffee in New York; I could not tell her, but said I believed it was uncommonly high; the crops had been short. She asked how coffee grew. I told her as well as I was able, but concluded by saying I had never seen it growing. "Don't you raise coffee in New York?" she asked; "I thought that was where it came from."

The butter was excellent. I said so, and asked if they never made any for sale. The woman said she could make "as good butter as any ever was made in the yarth," but she couldn't get anything for it; "there warn't many of the merchants would buy it, and those that did, would only take it at eight cents a pound for goods." The man said the only thing he could ever sell for ready money was cattle. Drovers bought them for the New York market, and lately they were very high—four cents a pound. He had driven cattle all the way to Charleston himself, to sell them, and only got four cents a pound there. He had sold corn here for twelve and a half cents a bushel.

Although the man could not read, he had honoured letters by calling one of his children "Washington Irving"; another was known as Matterson (Madison?). He had never tried manuring land for crops, but said, "I do believe it is a good plan, and if I live I mean to try it sometime."

July 16th.—I stopped last night at the pleasantest house I have yet seen in the highlands; a framed house, painted white, with a log kitchen attached. The owner was a man of superior standing. I judged from the public documents and law books on his table, that he had either been in the Legislature of the State, or that he was a justice of the peace. There were also a good many other books and newspapers, chiefly of a religious character. He used, however, some singularly uncouth phrases common here. He had a store, and carried on farming and stock raising. After a conversation about his agriculture, I remarked that there were but few slaves in this part of the country. He wished that there were fewer. They were not profitable property here, I presumed. They were not, he said, except to raise for sale; but there were a good many people here who would not have them if they were profitable, and yet who were abundantly able to buy them. They were horrid things, he thought; he would not take one to keep it if it should be given to him. 'Twould be a great deal better for the country, he believed, if there was not a slave in it. He supposed it would not be right to take them away from those who had acquired property in them, without any remuneration, but he wished they could all be sent out of the country —sent to Liberia. That was what ought to be done with them. I said it was evident that where there were no slaves, other things being equal, there was greater prosperity than where slavery supplied the labour. He didn't care so much for that, he said; there was a greater objection to slavery than that, in his mind. He was afraid that there was many a man who had gone to the bad world, who wouldn't have gone there if he hadn't had any slaves. He had been down in the nigger counties a good deal, and he had seen how it worked on the white people. It made the rich people, who owned the niggers, passionate and proud, and ugly, and it made the poor people mean. "People that own niggers are always mad with them about something; half their time is spent in swearing and yelling at them."

"I see you have 'Uncle Tom's Cabin' here," said I; "have you read it?"

"Oh, yes."

"And what do you think of it?"

"Think of it? I think well of it."

"Do most of the people here in the mountains think as you do about slavery?"

"Well, there's some thinks one way and some another, but there's hardly any one here that don't think slavery's a curse to our country, or who wouldn't be glad to get rid of it."

I asked what the people about here thought of the Nebraska Bill. He couldn't say what the majority thought. Would people moving from here to Nebraska now, be likely to vote for the admission of slavery there? He thought not; "most people would much rather live in a Free State." He told me that he knew personally several persons who had gone to California, and taken slaves with them, who had not been able to bring them back. There were one or two cases where the negroes had been induced to return, and these instances had been made much of in the papers, as evidence that the slaves were contented.

"That's a great lie," he said; "they are not content, and nine-tenths of 'em would do 'most anything to be free. It's only now and then that slaves, who are treated unusual kind, and made a great deal of, will choose to remain in slavery if freedom is put in their way." He knew one man (giving his name) who tried to bring two slaves back from California, and had got started with them, when some white people suspecting it, went on board the ship and told him it was against the law to hold negroes as slaves in California, and his negroes shouldn't go back with him unless they were willing to. Then they went to the slaves and told them they need not return if they preferred to stay, and the slaves said they had wanted very much to go back to North Carolina, yet they would rather remain in California, if they could be free, and so they took them ashore. He had heard the slave owner himself relating this, and cursing the men who interfered. He had told him that they did no more than Christians were obliged to do.

I overtook upon the road, to-day, three young men of the poorest class. Speaking of the price of land and the profit of farming, one of them said, believing me to be a Southerner—

"We are all poor folks here; don't hardly make enough to keep us in liquor. Anybody can raise as much corn and hogs on the mountains as he'll want to live on, but there ain't no rich people here. Nobody's got any black ones—only three or four; no one's got fifty or a hundred, like as they have down in the East." "It would be better," interrupted another, somewhat fiercely, "there warn't any at all; that's my mind about it; they're no business here; they ought to be in their own country and take care of themselves, that's what I believe, and I don't care who hears it." But let the reader not be deceived by these expressions; they indicate simply the weakness and cowardice of the class represented by these men. It is not slavery they detest; it is simply the negro competition, and the monopoly of the opportunities to make money by negro owners, which they feel and but dimly comprehend.

If you meet a man without stopping, the salutation here always is, "How d'ye do, sir?" never "Good morning"; and on parting it is, "I wish you well, sir," more frequently than "Good-bye." You are always commanded to appear at the table, as elsewhere throughout the South, in a rough, peremptory tone, as if your host feared you would try to excuse yourself.

"Come in to supper." "Take a seat." "Some of the fry?" "Help yourself to anything you see that you can eat."

They ask your name, but do not often call you by it, but hail you "Stranger," or "Friend."

Texas is always spoken of in the plural—"the Texies." "Bean't the Texies powerful sickly?"

"Ill" is used for "vicious." "Is your horse ill?" "Not that I am aware of. Does he appear so?" "No; but some horses will bite a stranger if he goes to handling on 'em."

"Is your horse ill?" "No, I believe not." "I see he kind o' drapt his ears when I came up, 'zif he was playful."

Everybody I've met in the last three counties—after ascertaining what parts I came from, and which parts I'm going to, where I got my horse, what he cost, and of what breed he is, what breed the dog is, and whether she's followed me all the way from the Texies, if her feet ain't worn out, and if I don't think I'll have to tote her if I go much further, and if I don't want to give her away, how I like the Texies, etc.—has asked me whether I didn't see a man by the name of Baker in the Texies, who was sheriff of —— county, and didn't behave exactly the gentleman, or another fellow by the name of ——, who ran away from the same county, and cut to the Texies. I've been asked if they had done fighting yet in the Texies, referring to the war with Mexico, which was ended ten years ago. Indeed the ignorance with regard to everything transpiring in the world outside, and the absurd ideas and reports I hear, are quite incredible. It cannot be supposed that having been at home in New York, there should be any one there whom I do not personally know, or that, having passed through Texas, I should be unable to speak from personal knowledge of the welfare of every one in that State.

North-eastern Tennessee, ——. —Night before last I spent at the residence of a man who had six slaves; last night, at the home of a farmer without slaves. Both houses were of the best class common in this region; two-story framed buildings, large, and with many beds, to accommodate drovers and waggoners, who, at some seasons, fill the houses which are known to be prepared with stabling, corn, and beds for them. The slaveholder was much the wealthier of the two, and his house originally was the finer, but he lived in much less comfort than the other. His house was in great need of repair, and was much disordered; it was dirty, and the bed given me to sleep in was disgusting. He and his wife made the signs of pious people, but were very morose or sadly silent, when not scolding and re-ordering their servants. Their son, a boy of twelve, was alternately crying and bullying his mother all the evening till bed-time, because his father had refused to give him something that he wanted. He slept in the same room with me, but did not come to bed until after I had once been asleep, and then he brought another boy to sleep with him. He left the candle burning on the floor, and when, in five minutes after he had got into bed, a girl came after it, he cursed her with a shocking volubility of filthy blackguardism, demanding why she had not come sooner. She replied gently and entreatingly, "I didn't think you'd have more'n got into bed yet, master John." The boys were talking and whispering obscenity till I fell asleep again. The white women of the house were very negligent and sluttish in their attire; the food at the table badly cooked, and badly served by negroes.

The house of the farmer without slaves, though not in good repair, was much neater, and everything within was well-ordered and unusually comfortable. The women and girls were clean and neatly dressed; every one was cheerful and kind. There was no servant. The table was abundantly supplied with the most wholesome food— I might almost say the first wholesome food—I have had set before me since I was at the hotel at Natchez; loaf bread for the first time; chickens, stewed instead of fried; potatoes without fat; two sorts of simple preserved fruit, and whortleberry and blackberry tarts. (The first time I have had any of these articles at a private house since I was in Western Texas.) All the work, both within and without the house, was carried on regularly and easily, and it was well done, because done by parties interested in the result, not by servants interested only to escape reproof or punishment.

Doubtless two extreme cases were thus brought together, but

similar, if less striking, contrasts are found the general rule, according to my experience. It is a common saying with the drovers and waggoners of this country, that if you wish to be well taken care of, you must not stop at houses where they have slaves.

The man of the last described house was intelligent and an ardent Methodist. The room in which I slept was papered with the "Christian Advocate and Journal," the Methodist paper of New York.[3] At the slaveholder's house, my bedroom was partially papered with "Lottery Schemes."

The free labouring farmer remarked, that, although there were few slaves in this part of the country, he had often said to his wife that he would rather be living where there were none. He thought slavery wrong in itself, and deplorable in its effects upon the white people. Of all the Methodists whom he knew in North-eastern Tennessee and South-western Virginia, he believed that fully three fourths would be glad to join the Methodist Church North, if it were "convenient." They generally thought slavery wrong, and believed it the duty of the church to favour measures to bring it to an end. He was not an Abolitionist, he said; he didn't think slaves could be set free at once, but they ought to be sent back to their own country, and while they were here they ought to be educated. He had perceived that great injustice was done by the people both of the North and South, towards each other. At the South, people were very apt to believe that the Northerners were wanting not only to deprive them of their property, but also to incite the slaves to barbarity and murder. At the North, people thought that the negroes were all very inhumanely treated. That was not the case, at least hereabouts, it wasn't. If I would go with him to a camp meeting here, or to one of the common Sunday meetings, I would see that the negroes were generally better dressed than the whites. He believed that they were always well fed, and they were not punished

---

[3] RELIGION IN VIRGINIA.—A mass meeting of citizens of Taylor County, Virginia, was held at Boothesville recently, at which the following, among other resolutions, was passed unanimously:

"That the five *Christian Advocates*, published in the cities of New York, Pittsburg, Cincinnati, St. Louis, and Chicago, having become Abolition sheets of the rankest character, we ask our commonwealth's attorneys and postmasters to examine them, and, if found to be of an unlawful character, to deal with them and their agents as the laws of our State direct."—*Washington Republic.*

severely. They did not work hard, not nearly as hard as many of the white folks; they were fat and cheerful. I said that I had perceived this, and it was so generally, to a great degree, throughout the country; yet I was sure that on the large plantations it was necessary to treat the slaves with great severity. He "expected" it was so, for he had heard people say, who had been on the great rice and cotton plantations in South Carolina, that the negroes were treated very hard, and he knew there was a man down here on the railroad, a contractor, who had some sixty hands which he had hired in Old Virginny ("that's what we call Eastern Virginia here"), and everybody who saw them at work, said he drove them till they could hardly stand, and did not give them half what they ought to have to eat. He was opposed to the Nebraska Bill, he said, and to any further extension of slavery, on any pretext; the North would not do its Christian duty if it allowed slavery to be extended; he wished that it could be abolished in Tennessee. He thought that many of the people who went hence to Kansas would vote to exclude slavery, but he wasn't sure that they would do it generally, because they would consider themselves Southerners, and would not like to go against other Southerners. A large part of the emigration from this part of the country went to Indiana, Illinois, and Iowa; those States being preferred to Missouri, because they were Free States. There were fewer slaves hereabouts now, than there were when he was a boy. The people all thought slavery wrong, except, he supposed, some slaveholders who, because they had property in slaves, would try to make out to themselves that it was right. He knew one rich man who had owned a great many slaves. He thought slavery was wrong, and he had a family of boys growing up, and he knew they wouldn't be good for anything as long as he brought them up with slaves; so he had told his slaves that if they wanted to be free, he would free them, send them to Liberia, and give them a hundred dollars to start with, and they had all accepted the offer. He himself never owned a slave, and never would own one for his own benefit, if it were given to him, "first, because it was wrong; and secondly, because he didn't think they ever did a man much good."

I noticed that the neighbours of this man on each side owned slaves; and that their houses and establishments were much poorer than his.

Chapter XIII

The Exceptional Large Planters

Feliciana [Louisiana, May 1854].[1]—A deep notch of sadness marks in my memory the morning of the May day on which I rode out of the chattering little town of Bayou Sara, and I recollect little of its immediate suburbs but the sympathetic cloud-shadows slowly going before me over the hill of St. Francis. At the top is an old French hamlet.

One from among the gloomy, staring loungers at the door of the tavern, as I pass, throws himself upon a horse, and overtaking me, checks his pace to keep by my side. I turn towards him, and being full of aversion for the companionship of a stranger, nod, in such a manner as to say, "Your equality is acknowledged; go on." Not a nod; not the slightest deflection of a single line in the austere countenance; not a ripple of radiance in the sullen eyes, which wander slowly over, and, at distinct intervals, examine my horse, my saddlebags, my spurs, lariat, gloves, finally my face, with such stern deliberation that, at last, I should not be sorry if he would speak. But he does not; does not make the smallest response to the further turning of my head, which acknowledges the reflex interest in my own mind; his eyes rest as fixedly upon me as if they were a dead man's. I can, at length, no longer endure this in silence, so I ask, in a voice attuned to his apparent humour—

"How far to Woodville?"

The only reply is a slight grunt, with an elevation of the chin.

"You don't know?"

"No."

"Never been there."

"No."

"I can ride there before night, I suppose?"

No reply.

[1] "This latter received its beautiful and expressive name from its beautifully variegated surface of hills and valleys, and its rare combination of all the qualities that are most desired in a planting country. It is a region of almost fairy beauty and wealth. Here are some of the wealthiest and most intelligent planters and the finest plantations in the State, the region of princely taste and more than patriarchal hospitality," etc.—*Norman's New Orleans.*

"Good walker, your horse?"

Not a nod.

"I thought mine pretty good."

Not a sneer, or a gleam of vanity, and Belshazzar and I warmed up together. Scott's man of leather occurred to my mind, and I felt sure that I could guess my man's chord. Cotton! I touched it, and in a moment he became animated, civil; hospitable even. I was immediately informed that this was a famous cotton region: "when it was first settled up by 'Mericans, used to be reckoned the gardying of the world. The almightiest rich sile God Almighty ever shuck down. All on't owned by big-bugs." Finally he confided to me that he was an overseer for one of them, "one of the biggest sort." This greatest of the local hemipteras was not now on his plantation, but had "gone North to Paris or Saratogy, or some of them places."

Wearing no waistcoat, the overseer carried a pistol, without a thought of concealment, in the fob of his trousers. The distance to Woodville, which, after he had exhausted his subject of cotton, I tried again to ascertain, he did not know, and would not attempt to guess. The ignorance of the more brutalized slaves is often described by saying of them that they cannot count above twenty. I find many of the whites but little more intelligent. At all events, it is rarely that you meet, in the plantation districts, a man, whether white or black, who can give you any clear information about the roads, or the distances between places in his own vicinity. While in or near Bayou Sara and St. Francisville, I asked, at different times, ten men, black and white, the distance to Woodville (the next town to the northward on the map). None answered with any appearance of certainty, and those who ventured to give an opinion, differed in their estimates as much as ten miles. I found the actual distance to be, I think, about twenty-four miles. After riding by my side for a mile or two the overseer suddenly turned off at a fork in the road, with hardly more ceremony than he had used in joining me.

For some miles about St. Francisville the landscape has an open, suburban character, with residences indicative of rapidly accumulating wealth, and advancement in luxury, or careless expenditure, among the proprietors. For twenty miles to the north of the town, there is on both sides a succession of large sugar and cotton plantations. Much land still remains uncultivated, however. The roadside fences are generally hedges of roses—Cherokee and sweet brier.

These are planted first by the side of a common rail fence, which, while they are young, supports them in the manner of a trellis; as they grow older they fall each way, and mat together, finally forming a confused, sprawling, slovenly thicket, often ten feet in breadth and four to six feet high. Trumpet creepers, grape-vines, greenbriers, and in very rich soil, cane, grow up through the mat of roses, and add to its strength. It is not as pretty as a more upright hedge, yet very agreeable, and, at one or two points, where the road was narrow, deep, and lane like, delightful memories of England were brought to mind.

There were frequent groves of magnolia grandiflora, large trees, and every one in the glory of full blossom. The magnolia does not, however, mass well, and the road-side woods were much finer, where the beech, elm, and liquid amber formed the body, and the magnolias stood out against them, magnificent chandeliers of fragrance. The large-leaved magnolia, very beautiful at this season, was more rarely seen.

The soil seems generally rich, though much washed off the higher ground. The ploughing is directed with some care not to favour this process. Young pine trees, however, and other indications of rapid impoverishment, are seen on many plantations.

The soil is a sandy loam, so friable that the negroes always working in large gangs, superintended by a driver with a whip, continued their hoeing in the midst of quite smart showers, and when the road had become a poaching mud.

Only once did I see a gang which had been allowed to discontinue its work on account of the rain. This was after a heavy thunder shower, and the appearance of the negroes whom I met crossing the road in returning to the field, from the gin-house to which they had retreated, was remarkable. First came, led by an old driver carrying a whip, forty of the largest and strongest women I ever saw together; they were all in a simple uniform dress of a bluish check stuff, the skirts reaching little below the knee; their legs and feet were bare; they carried themselves loftily, each having a hoe over the shoulder, and walking with a free, powerful swing. Behind them came the cavalry, thirty strong, mostly men, but a few of them women, two of whom rode astride on the plough mules. A lean and vigilant white overseer, on a brisk pony, brought up the rear. The men wore small blue Scotch bonnets; many of the women, handkerchiefs, turban fashion, and a few nothing at all on their heads. They were evidently a picked lot. I thought that every one would pass for a "prime" cotton hand.

The slaves generally of this district appear uncommonly well—doubtless, chiefly, because the large incomes of their owners enable them to select the best from the yearly exportations of Virginia and Kentucky, but also because they are systematically well fed.

The plantation residences were of a cottage class, sometimes, but not usually, with extensive and tasteful grounds about them.

An old gentleman, sensible, polite, and communicative, who rode a short distance with me, said that many of the proprietors were absentees—some of the plantations had dwellings only for the negroes and the overseer. He called my attention to a field of cotton which, he said, had been ruined by his overseer's neglect. The negroes had been allowed at a critical time to be careless in their hoeing, and it would now be impossible to recover the ground then lost. Grass grew so rampantly in this black soil, that if it once got a good start ahead, you could never overtake it. That was the devil of a rainy season. Cotton could stand drouth better than it could grass.[2]

The inclosures are not often of less area than a hundred acres. Fewer than fifty negroes are seldom found on a plantation; many

---

[2] "FINE PROSPECT FOR HAY.—While riding by a field the other day, which looked as rich and green as a New England meadow, we observed to a man sitting on the fence, 'You have a fine prospect for hay, neighbour.' 'Hay! that's *cotton, sir,*' said he, with an emotion that betrayed an excitement which we cared to provoke no further; for we had as soon sport with a rattlesnake in the blind days of August as a farmer at this season of the year, badly in the grass. . . .

"All jesting aside, we have never known so poor a prospect for cotton in this region. In some instances the fields are clean and well worked, but the cotton is diminutive in size and sickly in appearance. We have seen some fields so foul that it was almost impossible to tell what had been planted.

"All this backwardness is attributable to the cold, wet weather that we have had almost constantly since the planting season commenced. When there was a warm spell, it was raining so that ploughs could not run to any advantage; so, between the cold and the rain, the cotton crop is very unpromising. . . .

"The low, flat lands this year have suffered particularly. Thoroughly saturated all the time, and often overflowed, the crops on them are small and sickly, while the weeds and grass are luxurious and rank.

"A week or two of dry hot weather will make a wonderful change in our agricultural prospects, but we have no idea that any sort of seasons could bring the cotton to more than an average crop."—*Hernando* (*Miss.*) *Advance*, June 22, 1854.

muster by the hundred. In general the fields are remarkably free from weeds and well tilled.

I arrived shortly after dusk at Woodville, a well-built and pleasant court-town, with a small but pretentious hotel. Court was in session, I fancy, for the house was filled with guests of somewhat remarkable character. The landlord was inattentive, and, when followed up, inclined to be uncivil. At the ordinary—supper and breakfast alike—there were twelve men besides myself, all of them wearing black cloth coats, black cravats, and satin or embroidered waistcoats; all, too, sleek as if just from a hairdresser's, and redolent of perfumes, which really had the best of it with the exhalations of the kitchen. Perhaps it was because I was not in the regulation dress that I found no one ready to converse with me, and could obtain not the slightest information about my road, even from the landlord.

I might have left Woodville with more respect for this decorum if I had not, when shown by a servant to my room, found two beds in it, each of which proved to be furnished with soiled sheets and greasy pillows, nor was it without reiterated demands and liberal cash in hand to the servant, that I succeeded in getting them changed on the one I selected. A gentleman of embroidered waistcoat took the other bed as it was, with no apparent reluctance, soon after I had effected my own arrangements. One wash-bowl, and a towel which had already been used, was expected to answer for both of us, and would have done so but that I carried a private towel in my saddle-bags. Another requirement of a civilized household was wanting, and its only substitute unavailable with decency.

The bill was excessive, and the black hostler, who had left the mud of yesterday hanging all along the inside of Belshazzar's legs, and who had put the saddle on so awkwardly that I resaddled him myself after he had brought him to the door, grumbled, in presence of the landlord, at the smallness of the gratuity which I saw fit to give him.

The country, for some distance north of Woodville, is the most uneven, for a non-mountainous region, I ever saw. The road seems well engineered, yet you are nearly all the time mounting or descending the sides of protuberances or basins, ribs or dykes. In one place it follows along the top of a crooked ridge, as steep-sided and regular for nearly a quarter of a mile, as a high railroad embankment. A man might jump off anywhère and land thirty feet below. The ground being too rough here for cultivation, the dense native forest remains intact.

This ridge, a man told me, had been a famous place for robberies. It is not far from the Mississippi bottoms.

"Thar couldn't be," said he, "a better location for a feller that wanted to foller that business. There was one chap there a spell ago, who built himself a cabin t'other side the river. He used to come over in a dug-out. He could paddle his dug-out up the swamp, you see, to within two mile of the ridge; then, when he stopped a man, he'd run through the woods to his dug-out, and before the man could get help, he'd be t'other side the Mississippi, a sittin' in his housen as honest as you be."

The same man had another story of the ridge:—

"Mr. Allen up here caught a runaway once, and started to take him down to Woodville to the jail. He put him in irons and carried him along in his waggin. The nigger was peaceable and submissive till they got along onto that yer ridge place. When they got thar, all of a sudden he gin a whop like, and over he went twenty foot plum down the side of the ridge. 'Fore Allen could stop his hoss he'd tumbled and rolled himself 'way out of sight. He started right away arter him, but he never cotched a sight on him again."

Not far north of the ridge, plantations are found again, though the character of the surface changes but little. The hill-sides are carefully ploughed so that each furrow forms a contour line. After the first ploughing the same lines are followed in subsequent cultivation, year in and year out, as long as enough soil remains to grow cotton upon with profit. On the hills recently brought into cultivation, broad, serpentine ditches, having a fall of from two to four inches in a rod, have been frequently constructed: these are intended to prevent the formation of gullies leading more directly down the hill during heavy rains. But all these precautions are not fully successful, the cultivated hills, in spite of them, losing soil every year in a melancholy manner.

I passed during the day four or five large plantations, the hill-sides worn, cleft, and channelled like icebergs; stables and negro quarters all abandoned, and everything given up to nature and decay.

In its natural state the virgin soil appears the richest I have ever seen, the growth upon it from weeds to trees being invariably rank and rich in colour. At first it is expected to bear a bale and a half of cotton to the acre, making eight or ten bales for each able field-hand. But from the cause described its productiveness rapidly decreases.

Originally, much of this country was covered by a natural growth of cane, and by various nutritious grasses. A good Northern farmer would deem it a crying shame and sin to attempt to grow any crops upon such steep slopes, except grasses or shrubs which do not require tillage. The waste of soil which attends the practice is much greater than it would be at the North, and, notwithstanding the un-appeasable demand of the world for cotton, its bad economy, considering the subject nationally, cannot be doubted.

If these slopes were thrown into permanent terraces, with turfed or stone-faced escarpments, the fertility of the soil might be preserved, even with constant tillage. In this way the hills would continue for ages to produce annual crops of greater value than those which are at present obtained from them at such destructive expense—from ten to twenty crops of cotton rendering them absolute deserts. But with negroes at fourteen hundred dollars a head, and fresh land in Texas at half a dollar an acre, nothing of this sort can be thought of. The time will probably come when the soil now washing into the adjoining swamps will be brought back by our descendants, perhaps on their heads, in pots and baskets, in the manner Huc describes in China,—and which may be seen also in the Rhenish vineyards,—to be relaid on these sunny slopes, to grow the luxurious cotton in.

The plantations are all large, but, except in their size and rather unusually good tillage, display few signs of wealthy proprietorship. The greater number have but small and mean residences upon them. No poor white people live upon the road, nor in all this country of rich soils are they seen, except *en voyage*. In a distance of seventy-five miles I saw no houses without negro-cabins attached, and I calculated that there were fifty slaves, on an average, to every white family resident in the country under my view. (There is a small sandy region about Woodville, which I passed through after night-fall, and which, of course, my note does not include.)

I called in the afternoon, at a house, almost the only one I had seen during the day which did not appear to be the residence of a planter or overseer, to obtain lodging. No one was at home but a negro woman and children. The woman said that her master never took in strangers; there was a man a few miles further on who did; it was the only place she knew at which I was likely to "get in."

I found the place: probably the proprietor was the poorest white man whose house I had passed during the day, but he had several slaves; one of them, at least, a very superior man, worth fully $2,000.

Just before me, another traveller, a Mr. S., from beyond Natchez, had arrived. Learning that I was from Texas, he immediately addressed me with volubility.

"Ah! then you can tell us something about it, and I would be obliged to you if you would. Been out west about Antonio? Ranchering's a good business, eh, out west there? Isn't it? Make thirty per cent. by it, eh? I hear so. Should think that would be a good business. How much capital ought a man to have to go into ranchering, good, eh? So as to make it a good business?"

He was a middle-aged, well-dressed man, devouring tobacco prodigiously; nervous and wavering in his manner; asking questions, a dozen at a breath, and paying no heed to the answers. He owned a plantation in the bottoms, and another on the upland; the latter was getting worn out, it was too unhealthy for him to live in the bottoms, and so, as he said, he had had "a good notion to go into ranchering. Just for ease and pleasure."

"Fact is, though, I've got a family, and this is no country for children to be raised in. All the children get such foolish notions. I don't want my children to be brought up here. Ruins everybody. Does, sir, sure. Spoils 'em. Too bad. 'Tis so. Too bad. Can't make anything of children here, sir. Can't, sir. Fact."

He had been nearly persuaded to purchase a large tract of land at a point upon a certain creek where, he had been told, was a large court-house, an excellent school, etc. The waters of the creek he named are brackish, the neighbouring country is a desert, and the only inhabitants, savages. Some knavish speculator had nearly got a customer, but could not quite prevail on him to purchase until he examined the country personally, which it was his intention soon to do. He gave me no time to tell him how false was the account he had had, but went on, after describing its beauties and advantages—

"But negro property isn't very secure there, I'm told. How is't? Know?"

"Not at all secure, sir; if it is disposed to go, it will go: the only way you could keep it would be to make it always contented to remain. The road would always be open to Mexico; it would go when it liked."

"So I hear. Only way is, to have young ones there and keep their mothers here, eh? Negroes have such attachments, you know. Don't you think that would fix 'em, eh? No? No, I suppose not. If they got mad at anything, they'd forget their mothers, eh? Yes, I suppose they would. Can't depend on niggers. But I reckon they'd come back. Only be worse off in Mexico—eh?"

"Nothing but—"

"Being free, eh? Get tired of that, I should think. Nobody to take care of them. No, I suppose not. Learn to take care of themselves."

Then he turned to our host and began to ask him about his neighbours, many of whom he had known when he was a boy, and been at school with. A sorry account he got of most. Generally they had run through their property; their lands had passed into new hands; their negroes had been disposed of; two were now, he thought, "strikers" for gamblers in Natchez.

"What is a striker?" I asked the landlord at the first opportunity.

"Oh! to rope in fat fellows for the gamblers; they don't do that themselves, but get somebody else. I don't know as it is so; all I know is, they don't have no business, not till late at night; they never stir out till late at night, and nobody knows how they live, and that's what I expect they do. Fellows that come into town flush, you know —sold out their cotton and are flush—they always think they must see everything, and try their hands at everything—they get hold of 'em and bring 'em in to the gamblers, and get 'em tight for 'em, you know."

"How's ——— got along since his father died?" asked Mr. S.

"Well, ———'s been unfortunate. Got mad with his overseer; thought he was lazy and packed him off; then he undertook to oversee for himself, and he was unfortunate. Had two bad crops. Finally the sheriff took about half his niggers. He tried to work the plantation with the rest, but they was old, used-up hands, and he got mad that they would not work more, and tired o' seein' 'em, and 'fore the end of the year he sold 'em all."

Another young man, whom he inquired about, had had his property managed for him by a relative till he came of age, and had been sent North to college. When he returned and got it into his own hands, the first year he ran it in debt $16,000. The income from it being greatly reduced under his management, he had put it back in the care of his relative, but continued to live upon it. "I see," continued our host, "every time any of their teams pass from town they fetch a barrel or a demijohn. There is a parcel of fellows, who, when they can't liquor anywhere else, always go to him."

"But how did he manage to spend so much," I inquired, "the first year after his return, as you said,—in gambling?"

"Well, he gambled some, and run horses. He don't know anything about a horse, and, of course, he thinks he knows everything. Those fellows up at Natchez would sell him any kind of a tacky for four or five hundred dollars, and then after he'd had him a month, they'd ride out another and make a bet of five or six hundred dollars they'd beat him. Then he'd run with 'em, and of course he'd lose it."

"But sixteen thousand dollars is a large sum of money to be worked off even in that way in a year," I observed.

"Oh, he had plenty of other ways. He'd go into a bar-room, and get tight and commence to break things. They'd let him go on, and the next morning hand him a bill for a hundred dollars. He thinks that's a smart thing, and just laughs and pays it, and then treats all around again."

By one and the other, many stories were then told of similar follies of young men. Among the rest, this:—

A certain man had, as was said to be the custom when running for office, given an order at a grocery for all to be "treated" who applied in his name. The grocer, after the election, which resulted in the defeat of the treater, presented what was thought an exorbitant bill. He refused to pay it, and a lawsuit ensued. A gentleman in the witness box, being asked if he thought it possible for the whole number of people taking part in the election to have consumed the quantity of liquor alleged, answered—

"Moy Goad! Judge!" (reproachfully): "Yes, sir! Why, I've been charged for a hundred and fifty drinks 'fore breakfast, when I've stood treat, and I never thought o' disputin' it."

At supper, Mr. S., looking at the daughter of our host, said—

"What a pretty girl that is. My dear, do you find any schools to go to out here—eh? I reckon not. This isn't the country for schools. There'll not be a school in Mississippi 'fore long, I reckon. Nothing but Institutes, eh? Ha! ha! ha! Institutes, humph! Don't believe there's a school between this and Natchez, is there?"

"No, sir."

"Of course there isn't." [3]

"What sort of a country is it, then, between here and Natchez?" I asked. "I should suppose it would be well settled."

"Big plantations, sir. Nothing else. Aristocrats, Swell-heads, I call them, sir. Nothing but swell-heads, and you can't get a night's lodging, sir. Beyond the ferry, I'll be bound, a man might die on the road 'fore he'd get a lodging with one of them. Eh, Mr. N.? So, isn't it? 'Take a stranger in, and I'll clear you out!' That's the rule. That's what they tell their overseers, eh? Yes, sir; just so inhospitable as that. Swell-heads! Swell-heads, sir. Every plantation. Can't get a meal of victuals or a night's lodging from one of them, I don't suppose, not if your life depended on it. Can you, Mr. N.?"

"Well, I believe Mr. ——, his place is right on the road, and it's half way to the ferry, and I believe he tells his overseer if a man comes and wants something to eat, he must give it to him, but he must not take any pay for it, because strangers must have something to eat. They start out of Natchez, thinking it's as 'tis in other countries; that there's houses along, where they can get a meal, and so they don't provide for themselves, and when they get along about there, they are sometimes desperate hungry. Had to be something done."

"Do the planters not live themselves on their plantations?"

"Why, a good many of them has two or three plantations, but they don't often live on any of them."

[3] "Sectional excitement" had given a great impetus to educational projects in the South, and the Mississippi newspapers about this time contained numerous advertisements of a similar character to the following:

"CALHOUN INSTITUTE—FOR YOUNG LADIES; MACON, NOXUBEE COUNTY, MISSISSIPPI.—W. R. POINDEXTER, A.M., Principal and Proprietor.—The above School, formerly known as the 'Macon Female Institute,' will be reopened on the first of October, 1855, with an entirely new corps of teachers from Principal down. Having purchased the property at public sale, and thus become *sole proprietor,* the Principal has determined to use all means he can now command, as well as he may realize for several years yet to come, in building, refitting and procuring such appurtenances as shall enable him to contribute his full quota, as a professional man, to the progress of the great cause of 'SOUTHERN EDUCATION.'"

"Must have ice for their wine, you see," said Mr. S., "or they'd die. So they have to live in Natchez or New Orleans. A heap of them live in New Orleans."

"And in summer they go up into Kentucky, do they not? I've seen country houses there which were said to belong to cotton-planters from Mississippi."

"No, sir. They go North. To New York, and Newport, and Saratoga, and Cape May, and Seneca Lake. Somewhere that they can display themselves more than they do here. Kentucky is no place for that. That's the sort of people, sir, all the way from here to Natchez. And all round Natchez, too. And in all this section of country where there's good land. Good God! I wouldn't have my children educated, sir, among them, not to have them as rich as Dr. ——, every one of them. You can know their children as far off as you can see them. Young swell-heads! You'll take note of 'em in Natchez. You can tell them by their walk. I noticed it yesterday at the Mansion House. They sort o' throw out their legs as if they hadn't got strength enough to lift 'em and put them down in any particular place. They do want so bad to look as if they weren't made of the same clay as the rest of God's creation."

Some allowance is of course to be made for the splenetic temperament of this gentleman, but facts evidently afford some justification of his sarcasms. This is easily accounted for. The farce of the vulgar-rich has its foundation in Mississippi, as in New York and in Manchester, in the rapidity with which certain values have advanced, especially that of cotton, and, simultaneously, that of cotton lands and negroes.[4] Of course, there are men of refinement and cultivation among the rich planters of Mississippi, and many highly estimable and intelligent persons outside of the wealthy class, but the number of such is smaller in proportion to that of the immoral, vulgar, and ignorant newly-rich, than in any other part of the United

---

[4] As "A SOUTHERN LAWYER," writing for *Harper's Weekly* (February, 1859), observes: "The sudden acquisition of wealth in the cotton-growing region of the United States, in many instances by planters commencing with very limited means, is almost miraculous. Patient, industrious, frugal, and self-denying, nearly the entire amount of their cotton-crops is devoted to the increase of their capital. The result is, in a few years large estates, as if by magic, are accumulated. The fortunate proprietors then build fine houses, and surround themselves with comforts and luxuries to which they were strangers in their earlier years of care and toil."

States. And herein is a radical difference between the social condition of this region and that of the sea-board Slave States, where there are fewer wealthy families, but where among the few people of wealth, refinement and education are more general.

I asked how rich the sort of men were of whom he spoke.

"Why, sir, from a hundred thousand to ten million."

"Do you mean that between here and Natchez there are none worth less than a hundred thousand dollars?"

"No, sir, not beyond the ferry. Why, any sort of a plantation is worth a hundred thousand dollars. The niggers would sell for that."

"How many negroes are there on these plantations?"

"From fifty to a hundred."

"Never over one hundred?"

"No; when they've increased to a hundred they always divide them; stock another plantation. There are sometimes three or four plantations adjoining one another, with an overseer for each, belonging to the same man. But that isn't general. In general, they have to strike off for new land."

"How many acres will a hand tend here?"

"About fifteen—ten of cotton, and five of corn; some pretend to make them tend twenty."

"And what is the usual crop?"

"A bale and a half to the acre on fresh land and in the bottom. From four to eight bales to a hand they generally get: sometimes ten and better, when they are lucky."

"A bale and a half on fresh land? How much on old?"

"Well, you can't tell. Depends on how much it's worn and what the season is so much. Old land, after a while, isn't worth bothering with."

"Do most of these large planters who live so freely, anticipate their crops as the sugar planters are said to—spend the money, I mean, before the crop is sold?"

"Yes, sir, and three and four crops ahead generally."

"Are most of them the sons of rich men? are they old estates?"

"No, sir; lots of them were overseers once."

"Have you noticed whether it is a fact that these large properties seldom continue long in the same family? Do the grandsons of wealthy planters often become poor men?"

"Generally the sons do. Almost always their sons are fools, and soon go through with it."

"If they don't kill themselves before their fathers die," said the other.

"Yes. They drink hard and gamble, and of course that brings them into fights."

This was while they were smoking on the gallery after supper. I walked to the stable to see how my horse was provided for, and took my notes of the conversation. When I returned they were talking of negroes who had died of yellow fever while confined in the jail at Natchez. Two of them were spoken of as having been thus "happily released," being under sentence of death, and unjustly so, in their opinion.

A man living in this vicinity having taken a runaway while the fever was raging in the jail at Natchez, a physician advised him not to send him there. He did not, and the negro escaped; was some time afterward recaptured, and the owner having learned from him that he had been once before taken and not detained according to law, he made a journey to inquire into the matter, and was very angry. He said, "Whenever you catch a nigger again, you send him to jail, no matter what's to be feared. If he dies in the jail, you are not responsible. You've done your duty, and you can leave the rest to Providence."

"That was right, too," said Mr. P. "Yes, he ought to a' minded the law. Then if he'd died in jail, he'd know 'twasn't his fault."

Next morning, near the ferry house, I noticed a set of stocks, having holes for the head as well as the ankles; they stood unsheltered and unshaded in the open road.

I asked an old negro what it was.

"Dat ting, massa?" grinning; "well, sah, we calls dat a ting to put black people, niggers, in, when dey misbehaves bad, and to put runaways in, sah. Heaps o' runaways, dis country, sah. Yes, sah, heaps on 'em round here." [5]

[5] The following is a characteristic newspaper item of this vicinity:—
From the *West Feliciana Whig.*—"On Saturday last, a runaway negro was killed in the parish of East Baton Rouge, just below the line of this parish, under the following circumstances: Two citizens of Port Hudson, learning that a negro was at work on a flat boat, loading with sand, just below that place, who was suspected of being a runaway, went down in a skiff for the purpose of arresting him.

Mr. S. and I slept in the same room. I went to bed some time before him; he sat up late, to smoke, he said. He woke me when he came in, by his efforts to barricade the door with our rather limited furniture. The room being small, and without a window, I expostulated. He acknowledged it would probably make us rather too warm, but he shouldn't feel safe if the door were left open. "You don't know," said he; "there may be runaways around."

He then drew two small revolvers, hitherto concealed under his clothing, and began to examine the caps. He was certainly a nervous man, perhaps a madman. I suppose he saw some expression of this thought in my face, for he said, placing them so they could be easily taken up as he lay in bed, "Sometimes a man has a use for them when he least expects it. There was a gentleman on this road a few days ago. He was going to Natchez. He overtook a runaway, and he says to him, 'Bad company's better'n none, boy, and I reckon I'll keep you along with me into Natchez.' The nigger appeared to be pleased to have company, and went along, talking with him, very well, till they came to a thicket place, about six miles from Natchez. Then he told him he reckoned he would not go any further with him. 'What! you black rascal,' says he; 'you mean you won't go in with me? You step out and go straight ahead, and if you turn your face till you get into Natchez, I'll shoot you.' 'Aha! massa,' says the nigger, mighty good-natured, 'I reckon you ain't got no shootin' irons'; and he bolted off into the thicket, and got away from him."

At breakfast, Mr. S. came late. He bowed his head as he took his seat, and closed his eyes for a second or two; then, withdrawing his

---

"Having seized him and put him into the skiff they started back, but had not proceeded far when the negro, who had been at the oars, seized a hatchet and assaulted one of them, wounding him very seriously. A scuffle ensued, in which both parties fell overboard. They were both rescued by the citizen pulling to them with the skiff. Finding him so unmanageable, the negro was put ashore, and the parties returned to Port Hudson for arms and a pack of negro dogs, and started again with the intention to capture him. They soon got on his trail, and when found again he was standing at bay upon the outer edge of a large raft of drift wood, armed with a club and pistol.

"In this position he bade defiance to men and dogs—knocking the latter into the water with his club, and resolutely threatening death to any man who approached him. Finding him obstinately determined not to surrender, one of his pursuers shot him. He fell at the third fire, and so determined was he not to be captured, that when an effort was made to rescue him from drowning he made battle with his club, and sunk waving his weapon in angry defiance at his pursuers. He refused to give the name of his owner."

quid of tobacco and throwing it in the fire-place, he looked round with a smile, and said:—

"I always think it a good plan to thank the Lord for His mercies. I'm afraid some people'll think I'm a member of the church. I aint, and never was. Wish I was. I am a Son, though [of Temperance?]. Give me some water, girl. Coffee first. Never too soon for coffee. And never too late, I say. Wait for anything but coffee. These swell-heads drink their coffee after they've eaten all their dinner. I want it with dinner, eh? Don't nothing taste good without coffee, I reckon."

Before he left, he invited me to visit his plantations, giving me careful directions to find them, and saying that if he should not have returned before I reached them, his wife and his overseer would give me every attention if I would tell them he told me to visit them. He said again, and in this connection, that he believed this was the most inhospitable country in the world, and asked, as I had been a good deal of a traveller, didn't I think so myself? I answered that my experience was much too small to permit me to form an opinion so contrary to that generally held.

If they had a reputation for hospitality, he said, it could only be among their own sort. They made great swell-head parties; and when they were on their plantation places, they made it a point to have a great deal of company; they would not have anything to do if they didn't. But they were all swell-heads, I might be sure; they'd never ask anybody but a regular swell-head to see them.

His own family, however, seemed not to be excluded from the swell-head society.

Among numerous anecdotes illustrative of the folly of his neighbours, or his own prejudices and jealousy, I remember none which it would be proper to publish but the following:—

"Do you remember a place you passed?" (describing the locality).

"Yes," said I; "a pretty cottage with a large garden, with some statues or vases in it."

"I think it likely. Got a foreign gardener, I expect. That's all the fashion with them. A nigger isn't good enough for them. Well, that belongs to Mr. A. J. Clayborn[?]. He's got to be a very rich man. I suppose he's got as many as five hundred people on all his places. He went out to Europe a few years ago, and sometime after he came back, he came up to Natchez. I was there with my wife at the same time, and as she and Mrs. Clayborn came from the same section of country, and used to know each other when they were girls, she thought she must go and see her. Mrs. Clayborn could not talk about anything but the great people they had seen in Europe. She was telling of some great nobleman's castle they went to, and the splendid park there was to it, and how grandly they lived. For her part, she admired it so much, and they made so many friends among the people of quality, she said, she didn't care if they always stayed there. In fact, she really wanted Mr. Clayborn to buy one of the castles, and be a nobleman himself. 'But he wouldn't,' says she; 'he's such a strong Democrat, you know.' Ha! ha! ha! I wonder what old Tom Jeff. would have said to these swell-head Democrats."

I asked him if there were no poor people in this country. I could see no houses which seemed to belong to poor people.

"Of course not, sir. Every inch of the land bought up by the swellheads on purpose to keep them away. But you go back on to the pine ridge. Good Lord! I've heard a heap about the poor folks at the North; but if you ever saw any poorer people than them, I should like to know what they live on. Must be a miracle if they live at all. I don't see how these people live, and I've wondered how they do a great many times. Don't raise corn enough, great many of them, to keep a shoat alive through the winter. There's no way they can live, 'less they steal."

At the ferry of the Homochitto I fell in with a German, originally from Düsseldorf, whence he came seventeen years ago, first to New York; afterward he had resided successively in Baltimore, Cincinnati, New Orleans, Pensacola, Mobile, and Natchez. By the time he reached the last place he had lost all his money. Going to work as a labourer in the town, he soon earned enough again to set him up as a trinket peddler; and a few months afterward he was able to buy "a leetle coach-dray." Then, he said, he made money fast; for he would go back into the country, among the poor people, and sell them trinkets, and calico, and handkerchiefs, and patent medicines. They never had any money. "All poor folks," he said; "dam poor; got no money; oh no; but I say, 'dat too bad, I don't like to balk you, my frind; may be so, you got some egg, some fedder, some cheeken, some rag, some sass, or some skin vot you kill.' I takes dem dings vot they's got, and ven I gets my load I cums to Natchez back and sells dem, alvays dwo or dree times so much as dey coss me; and den I buys some more goots. Not bad beesnes—no. Oh, dese poor people dey deenk me is von fool ven I buy some dime deir rag vat dey bin vear; dey calls me de ole Dutch cuss. But dey don't know nottin' vot it is vorth. I deenk dey neever see no money; may be so dey geev all de cheeken vot they been got for a leetle breaspin vot cost me not so much as von beet. Sometime dey be dam crazy fool; dey know not how do make de count at all. Yees, I makes some money, a heap."

From the Homochitto to the suburbs of Natchez, a good half-day's ride, I found the country beautiful; fewer hills than before, the soil very rich, and the land almost all inclosed in plantations, the roadside boundaries of which are old rose-hedges. The road is well constructed, and often, in passing through the hills, with high banks on each side, coped with thick and dark, but free and sportive hedges, out of which grow bending trees, brooding angle-like over the traveller, the sentiment of the most charming Herefordshire lanes is reproduced. There are also frequent oak-woods, the trees often of great height. Sometimes these have been inclosed with neat palings, and slightly and tastefully thinned out, so as to form noble grounds around the residences of the planters, which are always very simple and unostentatious wooden houses. Near two of these are unusually good ranges of negro-houses. On many of the plantations, perhaps most, no residence is visible from the road, and the negro quarters, when seen, are the usual comfortless log-huts.

Within three miles of the town the country is entirely occupied by houses and grounds of a villa character; the grounds usually paltry with miniature terraces, and trees and shrubs planted and trimmed with no regard to architectural or landscape considerations. There is, however, an abundance of good trees, much beautiful shrubbery, and the best hedges and screens of evergreen shrubs that I have seen in America. The houses are cheap and shabby.

I was amused to recognize specimens of the "swell-head" fraternity, described by my nervous friend, as soon as I got into the villa district. First came two boys in a skeleton waggon, pitching along with a racking pony, which ran over Jude; she yelped, I wheeled round, and they pulled up and looked apologetic. She was only slightly hurt, but thereafter gave a quicker and broader sheer to approaching vehicles than her Texas experience had taught her to do.

Then came four youthful riders, and two old, roué-looking men, all upon a match-trot; the young fellows screaming, breaking up, and swearing. After them cantered a mulatto groom, white-gloved and neatly dressed, who, I noticed, bowed politely, lifting his hat and smiling to a very aged and ragged negro with a wheel-barrow and shovel, on the foot path.

Next came—and it was a swelteringly hot afternoon—an open carriage with two ladies taking an airing. Mr. S. had said that the swell-heads had "got to think that their old mammy niggers were not good enough for their young ones"; and here, on the front seat of the carriage, was a white and veritable French bonne, holding a richly-belaced baby. The ladies sat back, good-looking women enough, prettily dressed, and excessively demure. But the dignity of the turn-out chiefly reposed in the coachman, an obese old black man, who had, by some means, been set high up in the sun's face, on the bed-like cushion of the box, to display a great livery top-coat, with the wonted capes and velvet, buttoned brightly and tightly to the chin, and crowned by the proper emblazoned narrow-brimmed hat; his elbows squared, the reins and whip in his hands, the sweat in globules all over his ruefully-decorous face, and his eyes fast closed in sleep.

The houses and shops within the town itself are generally small, and always inelegant. A majority of the names on the signs are German; the hotel is unusually clean, and the servants attentive; and the stable at which I left Belshazzar is excellent, and contains several fine horses. Indeed, I never saw such a large number of fine horses as there is here, in any other town of the size. At the stable and the hotel there is a remarkable number of young men, extraordinarily dressed, like shop-boys on a Sunday excursion, all lounging or sauntering, and often calling at the bar; all smoking, all twisting lithe walking-sticks, all "talking horse."

But the grand feature of Natchez is the bluff, terminating in an abrupt precipitous bank over the river, with the public garden upon it. Of this I never had heard; and when, after seeing my horse dried off and eating his oats with great satisfaction—the first time he has ever tasted oats, I suppose, and I had not seen them before for many months—I strolled off to see the town, I came upon it by surprise.

I entered a gate and walked up a slope, supposing that I was approaching the ridge or summit of a hill, and expecting to see beyond it a corresponding slope and the town again, continuing in terraced streets to the river. I suddenly found myself on the very edge of a great cliff, and before me an indescribably vast expanse of forest, extending on every hand to a hazy horizon, in which, directly in front of me, swung the round, red, setting sun. Through the otherwise unbroken forest, the Father of Waters had opened a passage for himself, forming a perfect arc, the hither shore of the middle of the curve being hidden under the crest of the cliff, and the two ends lost in the vast obscurity of the Great West. Overlooked from such an eminence, the size of the Mississippi can be realized—which is difficult under ordinary circumstances; but though the fret of a swelling torrent is not wanting, it is perceptible only as the most delicate chasing upon the broad, gleaming expanse of polished steel, which at once shamed all my previous conceptions of the appearance of the greatest of rivers.

Coming closer to the edge and looking downward, you see the lower town, of Natchez, its roofs with water flowing all around them, and its pigmy people wading, and labouring to carry upward their goods and furniture, in danger from a rising movement of the great water. Poor people, "emigrants and niggers" only.

I lay down, and would have reposed my mind in the infinite vision westward, but was presently disturbed by a hog which came grunting near me, rooting in the poor turf of this wonderful garden. I rose and walked its length. Little more has been done than to inclose a space along the edge, which it would have been dangerous to build upon, to cut out some curving alleys now recaptured by the grass and weeds, and to plant a few succulent trees. A road to the lower town, cutting through it, is crossed by slight wooden footbridges, and there are some rough plank benches, adorned with stencilled "medical" advertisements. Some shrubs are planted on the crumbling face of the cliff, so near the top that the swine can obtain access to them. A man, bearded and smoking, and a woman with him, sitting at the extreme end, were the only visitors except myself and the swine.

As I am writing there is a bustle in the street. A young man is being lifted up and carried into the bar-room. He is insensible. A beautiful mare, from which he has evidently been thrown, is led back from around the corner, quivering with excitement.

I could find no reading-room; no recent newspapers except the *Natchez Free Trader*, which has nothing but cotton and river news and steamboat puffs; no magazines but aged Harpers; and no recent publications of any sort are for sale or to be seen at the booksellers'; so, after supper, I went to the bluff again, and found it most solemnly beautiful; the young moon shining through rents in the clouds: the great gleaming crescent of water; the dim, ungapped horizon; the earth sensibly a mere swinging globe.

Of all the town, only five Germans, sitting together, but smoking in silence, had gathered for this evening worship.

As I returned up the main street, I stopped opposite a house from which there came the sound of excellent music—a violin and piano. I had heard no music since I was in Western Texas, and I leaned upon a lamp-post for an hour, listening. Many stopped near me for a few minutes, and went on. At length, a man who had remained some time, addressed me, speaking in a foreign tongue. "Can't you speak English?" said I.

"You are not an American?"

"Yes."

"I should tzink it not."

"I am; I am a New Yorker."

"So?—O yes, perhaps, but not zis country."

"What are you?"

"Italian."

"Do you live here?"

"Yes."

"Are there many Italians in Natchez?"

"Yes—some many—seven. All big dam rascaal. Yes. Ha! ha! ha! True. Dam rascaal all of us."

"What do you do for a living here?"

"For me it is a cigar-store; fruit; confectionery."

"And the rest?"

"Oh, everytzing. I don't expect dem be here so much long now."

"Why—what will they do?"

"Dey all go to Cuba. Be vawr zair soon now. All go. All dam

rascaal go, can go, ven ze vawr is. Good ting dat for Natchez, eh?
Yes, I tzink."

He told me the names of the players; the violinist, an Italian, he
asserted to be the best in America. He resided in Natchez, I understood, as a teacher; and, I presume, the town has metropolitan advantages for instruction in all fashionable accomplishments. Yet,
with a population of 18,601, the number of children registered for
the public schools and academies, or "Institutes," of the county seat,
is but 1,015; and among these must be included many sent from
other parts of the State, and from Arkansas and Louisiana; the public libraries contain but 2,000 volumes, and the churches seat but
7,700.[6]

Franklin, the next county in the rear of the county in which
Natchez is situated (Adams), has a population of 6,000, and but
132 children attending school.

Mr. [Robert] Russell (*North America: its Agriculture and Climate*, page 258) states that he had been led to believe that "as refined society was to be found at Natchez as in any other part of the
United States"; but *his personal observation* is, that "the chief fre-
quenters of the best hotel are low, drunken fellows." I find a crowd
of big, silly boys, not drunk, but drinking, smoking, chewing, and
betting, and a few men who look like dissolute fourth-rate come-
dians, who have succeeded in swindling a swell-mob tailor.

The first night after leaving Natchez I found lodging with a German, who, when I inquired if he could accommodate me, at once
said, "Yes, sir, I make it *a business* to lodge travellers."

He had a little farm, and owned four strong negro men and a
woman with several children. All his men, however, he hired out as
porters or servants in Natchez, employing a white man, a native of
the country, to work with him on his farm.

To explain the economy of this arrangement, he said that one of
his men earned in Natchez $30 a month clear of all expenses, and
the others much more than he could ever make their labour worth

[6] This may be compared with the town of Springfield, county of Sangamon,
Illinois, in which, with a population of 19,228 (nearer to that of Natchez than
any other town I observe in the Free States), the number of registered school
children is 3,300, the public libraries contain 20,000 volumes, and the churches
can accommodate 28,000 sitters.

to him. A negro of moderate intelligence would hire, as a house-servant, for $200 a year and his board, which was worth $8 a month; whereas he hired this white fellow, who was strong and able, for $10 a month; and he believed he got as much work out of him as he could out of a negro. If labour were worth so much as he got for that of his negroes, why did the white man not demand more? Well —he kept him in whisky and tobacco besides his wages, and he was content. Most folks here did not like white labourers. They had only been used to have niggers do their work, and they did not know how to manage with white labourers; but he had no difficulty.

I asked if eight dollars would cover the cost of a man's board? He supposed it might cost him rather more than that to keep the white man; eight dollars was what it was generally reckoned in town to cost to keep a negro; niggers living in town or near it were expected to have "extras"; out on the plantations, where they did not get anything but bacon and meal, of course it did not cost so much. Did he know what it cost to keep a negro generally upon the plantations? It was generally reckoned, he said, that a nigger ought to have a peck of meal and three pounds of bacon a week; some didn't give so much meat, but he thought it would be better to give them more.

"You are getting rich," I said. "Are the Germans generally, here-abouts, doing well? I see there are a good many in Natchez."

"Oh yes; anybody who is not too proud to work can get rich here."

The next day, having ridden thirty tedious miles through a sombre country, with a few large plantations, about six o'clock I called at the first house standing upon or near the road which I had seen for some time, and solicited a lodging. It was refused, by a woman. How far was it to the next house? I asked her. Two miles and a half. So I found it to be, but it was a deserted house, falling to decay, on an abandoned plantation. I rode several miles further, and it was growing dark, and threatening rain, before I came in sight of an-other. It was a short distance off the road, and approached by a private lane, from which it was separated by a grass plat. A well dressed man stood between the gate and the house. I stopped and bowed to him, but he turned his back upon me and walked to the house. I opened a gate and rode in. Two men were upon the gallery, but as they paid no attention to my presence when I stopped near them, I doubted if either were the master of the house. I asked, "Could I obtain a lodging here to-night, gentlemen?" One of them answered, surlily, "No." I paused a moment that they might observe me—evidently a stranger benighted, with a fatigued horse, and then asked, "Can you tell me, sir, how far it is to a public-house?" "I don't know," replied the same man. I again remained silent a moment. "No public-houses in this section of the country, I reckon, sir," said the other. "Do you know how far it is to the next house on the road, north of this?" "No," answered one. "You'll find one about two miles, or two miles and a half from here," said the other. "Is it a house in which I shall be likely to get a lodging, do you know?" "I don't know, I'm sure."

"Good night, gentlemen; you'll excuse me for troubling you. I am entirely a stranger in this region."

A grunt, or inarticulate monosyllable, from one of them, was the only reply, and I rode away, glad that I had not been fated to spend an evening in such company.

Soon afterward I came to a house and stables close upon the road. There was a man on the gallery playing the fiddle. I asked, "Could you accommodate me here to-night, sir?" He stopped fiddling, and turned his head toward an open door, asking, "Wants to know if you can accommodate him?" "Accommodate him with what?" demanded a harsh-toned woman's voice. "With a bed of course—what do you s'pose—ho! ho! ho!" and he went on fiddling again. I had, during this conversation, observed ranges of negro huts behind the stables, and perceived that it must be the overseer's house of the plantation at which I had previously called. "Like master, like man," I thought, and rode on, my inquiry not having been even answered.

I met a negro boy on the road, who told me it was about two miles to the next house, but he did not reckon that I would get in there. "How far to the next house beyond that?" "About four miles, sir, and I reckon you can get in there, master; I've heerd they did take in travellers to that place."

Soon after this it began to rain and grow dark; so dark that I could not keep the road, for soon finding Belshazzar in difficulty, I got off and discovered that we were following up the dry bed of a small stream. In trying to get back I probably crossed the road, as I did not find it again, and wandered cautiously among trees for nearly an hour, at length coming to open country and a fence. Keeping this in sight, I rode on until I found a gate, entering at which,

I followed a nearly straight and tolerable good road full an hour, as it seemed to me, at last coming to a large negro "settlement."

I passed through it to the end of the rows, where was a cabin larger than the rest, facing on the space between the two lines of huts. A shout brought out the overseer. I begged for a night's lodging; he was silent; I said that I had travelled far, was much fatigued and hungry; my horse was nearly knocked up, and I was a stranger in the country; I had lost my road, and only by good fortune had found my way here. At length, as I continued urging my need, he said—

"Well, I suppose you must stop. Ho, Byron! Here, Byron, take this man's horse, and put him in *my* stable. 'Light, sir, and come in."

Within I found his wife, a young woman, showily dressed—a caricature of the fashions of the day. Apparently, they had both been making a visit to neighbours, and but just come home. I was not received kindly, but at the request of her husband she brought out and set before me some cold corn-bread and fat bacon.

Before I had finished eating my supper, however, they both quite changed their manner, and the woman apologized for not having made coffee. The cook had gone to bed and the fire was out, she said. She presently ordered Byron, as he brought my saddle in, to get some "light-wood" and make a fire; said she was afraid I had made a poor supper, and set a chair by the fire-place for me as I drew away from the table.

I plied the man with inquiries about his business, got him interested in points of difference between Northern and Southern agriculture, and soon had him in quite a sociable and communicative humour. He gave me much overseer's lore about cotton culture, nigger and cattle maladies, the right way to keep sweet potatoes, etc.; and when I proposed to ride over the plantation with him in the morning, he said he "would be very thankful for my company."

I think they gave up their own bed to me, for it was double, and had been slept in since the sheets were last changed; the room was garnished with pistols and other arms and ammunition, rolls of negro-cloth, shoes and hats, handcuffs, a large medicine chest, and several books on medical and surgical subjects and farriery; while articles of both men's and women's wearing apparel hung against the walls, which were also decorated with some large patent-medicine posters. One of them is characteristic of the place and the times.[7]

We had a good breakfast in the morning, and immediately afterward mounted and rode to a very large cotton-field, where the whole field-force of the plantation was engaged.

It was a first-rate plantation. On the highest ground stood a large and handsome mansion, but it had not been occupied for several years, and it was more than two years since the overseer had seen the owner. He lived several hundred miles away, and the overseer would not believe that I did not know him, for he was a rich man and an honourable, and had several times been where I came from—New York.

The whole plantation, including the swamp land around it, and owned with it, covered several square miles. It was four miles from the settlement to the nearest neighbour's house. There were between thirteen and fourteen hundred acres under cultivation with cotton, corn, and other hoed crops, and two hundred hogs running at large in the swamp. It was the intention that corn and pork enough should be raised to keep the slaves and cattle. This year, however, it has been found necessary to purchase largely, and such was probably usually the case,[8] though the overseer intimated the

[7] "THE WASHINGTON REMEDIES—TO PLANTERS AND OTHERS.—These Remedies, now offered to the public under the title of the Washington Remedies, are composed of ingredients, many of which are not even known to Botany. No apothecary has them for sale; they are supplied to the subscriber by the native redmen of Louisiana. The recipes by which they are compounded have descended to the present possessor, M. A. MICKLEJOHN, from ancestors who obtained them from the friendly Indian tribes, prior to and during the Revolution, and they are now offered to the public with that confidence which has been gained from a knowledge of the fact that during so long a series of years there has never been known an instance in which they have failed to perform a speedy and permanent cure. The subscribers do not profess these remedies will cure *every* disarrangement of the human system, but in such as are enumerated below they feel they cannot fail. The directions for use have only to be strictly followed, and however despairing the patient may have been he will find cause for blissful *hope* and renewed *life*.

"*These preparations are no Northern patent humbug,* but are manufactured in New Orleans by a Creole, who has long used them in private practice, rescuing many unfortunate victims of disease from the grave, after they have been given up by their physicians as incurable, or have been tortured beyond endurance by laceration and painful operations."

[8] "The bacon is almost entirely imported from the Northern States, as well as a considerable quantity of Indian corn. This is reckoned bad management by

owner had been displeased, and he "did not mean to be caught so bad again."

There were 135 slaves, big and little, of which 67 went to field regularly—equal, the overseer thought, to fully 60 prime hands. Besides these, there were 3 mechanics (blacksmith, carpenter, and wheelwright), 2 seamstresses, 1 cook, 1 stable servant, 1 cattle-tender, 1 hog-tender, 1 teamster, 1 house servant (overseer's cook), and one midwife and nurse. These were all first-class hands; most of them would be worth more, if they were for sale, the overseer said, than the best field-hands. There was also a driver of the hoe-gang who did not labour personally, and a foreman of the plough-gang. These two acted as petty officers in the field, and alternately in the quarters.

There was a nursery for sucklings at the quarters, and twenty women at this time who left their work four times each day, for half an hour, to nurse their young ones. These women, the overseer counted as half-hands—that is, expected to do half the day's work of a prime field-hand in ordinary condition.

He had just sold a bad runaway to go to Texas, he happened to remark. He was whipping the fellow, when he turned and tried to stab him—then broke from him and ran away. He had him caught almost immediately with the dogs. After catching him, he kept him in irons till he had a chance to sell him. His niggers did not very often run away, he said, because they had found that he was almost sure to catch them. As soon as he saw that one was gone he put the dogs on, and if rain had not just fallen, they would soon find him. Sometimes they did manage to outwit the dogs, but then they almost always kept in the neighbourhood, because they did not like to go where they could not sometimes get back and see their families, and he would soon get wind of where they had been; they would come round their quarters to see their families and to get food, and as soon as he knew it, he would find their tracks and put the dogs on again. Two months was the longest time any of them

---

intelligent planters. . . . On this plantation as much Indian corn was raised as was needed, but little bacon, which was mostly imported from Ohio. The sum annually paid for this article was upwards of eight hundred pounds. Large plantations are not suited to the rearing of hogs; for it is found almost impossible to prevent the negroes from stealing and roasting the pigs." Mr. Russell, visiting the plantation of a friend near Natchez.—*North America: its Agriculture,* etc., p. 265.

ever kept out. He had dogs trained on purpose to run after niggers, and never let out for anything else.

We found in the field thirty ploughs, moving together, turning the earth from the cotton plants, and from thirty to forty hoers, the latter mainly women, with a black driver walking about among them with a whip, which he often cracked at them, sometimes allowing the lash to fall lightly upon their shoulders. He was constantly urging them also with his voice. All worked very steadily, and though the presence of a stranger on the plantation must have been a most unusual occurrence, I saw none raise or turn their heads to look at me. Each gang was attended by a "water-toter," that of the hoe-gang being a straight, sprightly, plump little black girl, whose picture, as she stood balancing the bucket upon her head, shading her bright eyes with one hand, and holding out a calabash with the other to maintain her poise, would have been a worthy study for Murillo.

I asked at what time they began to work in the morning. "Well," said the overseer, "I do better by my niggers than most. I keep 'em right smart at their work while they do work, but I generally knock 'em off at 8 o'clock in the morning, Saturdays, and give 'em all the rest of the day to themselves, and I always gives 'em Sundays, the whole day. Pickin' time, and when the crap's bad in grass, I sometimes keep 'em to it till about sunset, Saturdays, but I never work 'em Sundays."

"How early do you start them out in the morning, usually?"

"Well, I don't never start my niggers 'fore daylight, 'less 'tis in pickin' time, then maybe I get 'em out a quarter of an hour before. But I keep 'em right smart to work through the day." He showed an evident pride in the vigilance of his driver, and called my attention to the large area of ground already hoed over that morning; well hoed, too, as he said.

"At what time do they eat?" I asked. They ate "their snacks" in their cabins, he said, before they came out in the morning (that is before daylight—the sun rising at this time at a little before five, and the day dawning, probably, an hour earlier); then at 12 o'clock their dinner was brought to them in a cart—one cart for the plough-gang and one for the hoe-gang. The hoe-gang ate its dinner in the field, and only stopped work long enough to eat it. The plough-gang drove its teams to the "weather houses"—open sheds erected for the purpose in different parts of the plantation, under which were cisterns filled with rain water, from which the water-toters carried drink to those at work. The mules were fed with as much oats (in straw), corn and fodder as they would eat in two hours; this forage having been brought to the weather houses by another cart. The ploughmen had nothing to do but eat their dinner in all this time. All worked as late as they could see to work well, and had no more food nor rest until they returned to their cabins.[9] At half-past nine o'clock the drivers, each on an alternate night, blew a horn, and at ten visited every cabin to see that its occupants were at rest, and not lurking about and spending their strength in fooleries, and that the fires were safe—a very unusual precaution; the negroes are generally at liberty after their day's work is done till they are called in the morning. When washing and patching were done, wood hauled and cut for the fires, corn ground, etc., I did not learn: probably all chores not of daily necessity were reserved for Saturday. Custom varies in this respect. In general, with regard to fuel for the cabins, the negroes are left to look out for themselves, and they often have to go to "the swamp" for it, or at least, if it has been hauled, to cut it to a convenient size, after their day's work is done. The allowance of food was a peck of corn and four pounds of pork per week, each. When they could not get "greens" (any vegetables) he generally gave them five pounds of pork. They had gardens, and raised a good deal for themselves; they also had fowls, and usually plenty of eggs. He added, "the man who owns this plantation does more for his niggers than any other man I know. Every Christmas he sends me up a thousand or fifteen hundred dollars' [equal to eight or ten dollars each] worth of molasses and

---

[9] This would give at this season hardly less than sixteen hours of plodding labour, relieved by but one short interval of rest, during the daylight, for the hoe-gang. It is not improbable. I was accustomed to rise early and ride late, resting during the heat of the day, while in the cotton district, but I always found the negroes in the field when I first looked out, and generally had to wait for the negroes to come from the field to have my horse fed when I stopped for the night. I am told, however, and I believe, that it is usual in the hottest weather, to give a rest of an hour or two to all hands at noon. I never happened to see it done. The legal limit of a slave's day's work in South Carolina is fifteen hours.

coffee, and tobacco, and calico, and Sunday tricks for 'em. Every family on this plantation gets a barrel of molasses at Christmas." [1]

Besides which, the overseer added, they are able, if they choose, to buy certain comforts for themselves—tobacco for instance—with money earned by Saturday and Sunday work. Some of them went into the swamps on Sunday, and made boards (which means slabs worked out with no other instrument than an axe). One man sold last year as much as fifty dollars' worth.

Finding myself nearer the outer gate than the "quarters," when at length my curiosity was satisfied, I did not return to the house. After getting a clear direction how to find my way back to the road I had been upon the previous day, I said to the overseer, with some hesitation, "You will allow me to pay you for the trouble I have given you?" He looked a little disconcerted by my putting the question in this way, but answered in a matter-of-course tone, "It will be a dollar and a quarter, sir."

This was the only large plantation I had an opportunity of seeing at all closely, over which I was not chiefly conducted by an educated gentleman and slave owner, by whose habitual impressions and sentiments my own were probably somewhat influenced. From what I saw in passing, and from what I heard by chance of others, I suppose it to have been a very favourable specimen of those plantations on which the owners do not reside. A merchant of the vicinity recently in New York tells me that he supposes it to be a fair enough example of plantations of its class. There is nothing remarkable in its management, so far as he had heard. When I asked about the molasses and Christmas presents, he said he reckoned the overseer must have rather stretched that part of his story, but the owner was a very good man. A magistrate of the district, who had often been on the plantation, said in answer to an inquiry from me, that the negroes were very well treated upon it, though he did not think they were extraordinarily so. His comparison was with plantations in general. [2] He also spoke well of the overseer. He had

---

[1] I was told by a gentleman in North Carolina, that the custom of supplying molasses to negroes in Mississippi, was usually mentioned to those sold away from his part of the country, to reconcile them to going thither.

[2] In De Bow's Resources of the South, vol i., p. 150, a table is furnished by a cotton-planter to show that the expenses of raising cotton are "generally greatly underrated." It is to be inferred that they certainly are not underrated in the table. On "a well improved and properly organized plantation," the ex-

been a long time on this plantation—I think he said ever since it had begun to be cultivated. This is very rare; it was the only case I met with in which an overseer had kept the same place ten years, and it was a strong evidence of his comparative excellence, that his employer had been so long satisfied with him. Perhaps it was a stronger evidence that the owner of the negroes was a man of good temper, systematic and thorough in the management of his property.[3]

The condition of the fences, of the mules and tools, and tillage, which would have been considered admirable in the best farming district of New York—the dress of the negroes and the neatness and spaciousness of their "quarters," which were superior to those of most of the better class of plantations on which the owners reside, all bore testimony to a very unusually prudent and provident policy.

I made no special inquiries about the advantages for education or means of religious instruction provided for the slaves. As there seems to be much public desire for definite information upon that point, I regret that I did not. I did not need to put questions to the overseer to satisfy my own mind, however. It was obvious that all natural incitements to self-advancement had been studiously removed or obstructed, in subordination to the general purpose of making the plantation profitable. Regarding only the balance-sheet of the owner's ledger, it was admirable management. I am sorry to have to confess to an impression that it is rare, where this is the uppermost object of the cotton-planter, that an equally frugal econ-

<hr>

pense of feeding one hundred negroes, "as deduced from fifteen years' experience" of the writer, is asserted in this table to be $750 per annum, or seven dollars and a half each; in this sum is included, however, the expenses of the "hospital and the overseer's table." This is much less than the expense for the same purposes, if the overseer's account was true, of the plantation above described. Clothing, shoes, bedding, *sacks for gathering cotton, and so forth,* are estimated by the same authority to cost an equal sum—$7.50 for each slave. I have just paid on account of a day labourer on a farm in New York, his board bill, he being a bachelor living at the house of another Irish labourer with a family. The charge is twenty-one times as large as that set down for the slave.

[3] "I was informed that some successful planters, who held several estates in this neighbourhood [Natchez] made it a rule to *change their overseers every year,* on the principle that the *two* years' service system is sure to spoil them."—Russell's *North America: its Agriculture,* etc., p. 258.

"Overseers are changed every year; a few remain four or five years, but the average time they remain on the same plantation does not exceed two years."—*Southern Agriculturist,* vol. iv., p. 351.

omy is maintained; and as the general character of the district along the Mississippi, which is especially noticeable for the number of large and very productive plantations which it contains, has now been sufficiently illustrated, I will here present certain observations which I wish to make upon the peculiar aspect of slavery in that and other districts where its profits to the owners of slaves are most apparent.

Chapter XIV

Slavery in Its Property Aspect
Moral and Religious Instruction of the Slaves, etc.

In a hilly part of Alabama, fifty miles north of the principal cotton-growing districts of that State, I happened to have a tradesman of the vicinity for a travelling companion, when, in passing an unusually large cluster of negro cabins, he called my attention to a rugged range of hills behind them which, he said, was a favourite lurking-ground for runaway negroes. It afforded them numerous coverts for concealment during the day, and at night the slaves of the plantation we were passing would help them to find the necessaries of existence. He had seen folks who had come here to look after niggers from plantations two hundred miles to the southward. "I suppose," said he, " 't would seem kind o' barbarous to you to see a pack of hounds after a human being?"

"Yes, it would."

"Some fellows take as much delight in it as in runnin' a fox. Always seemed to me a kind o' barbarous sport." (A pause.) "It's necessary, though."

"I suppose it is. Slavery is a custom of society which has come to us from a barbarous people, and, naturally, barbarous practices have to be employed to maintain it."

"Yes, I s'pose that's so. But niggers is generally pretty well treated, considering. Some people work their niggers too hard, that's a fact. I know a man at ——; he's a merchant there, and I have had dealings with him; he's got three plantations, and he puts the hardest overseers he can get on them. He's all the time a' buying niggers, and they say around there he works 'em to death. On these small plantations, niggers ain't very often whipped bad; but on them big plantations, they've got to use 'em hard to keep any sort of control over 'em. The overseers have to always go about armed; their life wouldn't be safe, if they didn't. As 't is, they very often get cut pretty bad." (Cutting is knifing; it may be stabbing, in Southwestern parlance.)

He went on to describe what he had seen on some large plantations which he had visited for business purposes—indications, as he thought, in the appearance of "the people," that they were being "worked to death." "These rich men," he said, "are always bidding for the overseer who will make the most cotton; and a great many of the overseers don't care for anything but to be able to say they've made so many bales in a year. If they make plenty of cotton, the owners never ask how many niggers they kill."

I suggested that this did not seem quite credible; a negro was a valuable piece of property. It would be foolish to use him in such a way.

"Seems they don't think so," he answered. "They are always bragging—you must have heard them—how many bales their overseer has made, or how many their plantation has made to a hand. They never think of anything else. You see, if a man did like to have his niggers taken care of, he couldn't bear to be always hearing that all the plantations round had beat his. He'd think the fault was in his overseer. The fellow who can make the most cotton always gets paid the best."

Overseers' wages were ordinarily from $200 to $600, but a real driving overseer would very often get $1,000. Sometimes they'd get $1,200 or $1,500. He heard of $2,000 being paid one fellow. A determined and perfectly relentless man—I can't recall his exact words, which were very expressive—a real devil of an overseer, would get almost any wages he'd ask; because, when it was told round that such a man had made so many bales to the hand, everybody would be trying to get him.

The man who talked in this way was a native Alabamian, ignorant, but apparently of more than ordinarily reflective habits, and he had been so situated as to have unusually good opportunities for observation. In character, if not in detail, I must say that his information was entirely in accordance with the opinions I should have been led to form from the conversations I heard by chance, from time to time, in the richest cotton districts. That his statements as to the bad management of large plantations, in respect to the waste of negro property, were not much exaggerated, I find frequent evidence in Southern agricultural journals. The following is an extract from one of a series of essays published in *The Cotton Planter*, the chief object of which is to persuade planters that they are under no necessity to employ slaves exclusively in the production of cotton. The writer, Mr. M. W. Phillips, is a well-known, intelligent, and benevolent planter, who resides constantly on his estate, near Jackson, Mississippi:—

I have known many in the rich planting portion of Mississippi especially, and others elsewhere, who, acting on the policy of the boy in the fable, who "killed the goose for the golden egg," accumulated property, yet among those who have relied solely on their product in land and negroes, I doubt if this be the true policy of plantation economy. With the former everything has to bend, give way to large crops of cotton, land has to be cultivated wet or dry, negroes to work, cold or hot. Large crops planted, and they must be cultivated, or done so after a manner. When disease comes about, as, for instance, cholera, pneumonia, flux, and other violent diseases, these are more subject, it seemeth to me, than others, or even if not, there is less vitality to work on, and, therefore, in like situations and similar in severity, they must sink with more certainty; or even should the animal economy rally under all these trials, the neglect consequent upon this "cut and cover" policy must result in greater mortality. Another objection, not one-fourth of the children born are raised, and perhaps not over two-thirds are born on the place, which, under a different policy, might be expected. And this is not all: hands, and teams, and land must wear out sooner; admitting this to be only one year sooner in twenty years, or that lands and negroes are less productive at forty than at forty-two, we see a heavy loss. Is this not so? I am told of negroes not over thirty-five to forty-five, who look older than others at forty-five to fifty-five. I know a man now, not short of sixty, who might readily be taken for forty-five; another on the same place full fifty (for I have known both for twenty-eight years, and the last one for thirty-two years), who could be sold for thirty-five, and these negroes are very leniently dealt with. Others, many others, I know and have known twenty-five to thirty years, of whom I can speak of as above. As to rearing children, I can point to equally as strong cases; ay, men who are, "as it were," of one family, differing as much as four and eight bales in cropping, and equally as much in raising young negroes. The one scarcely paying expenses by his crop, yet in the past twenty-five years raising over seventy-five to a hundred negroes, the other buying more than raised, and yet not as many as the first.

I regard the "just medium" to be the correct point. Labour is conducive to health; a healthy woman will rear most children. I favour good and fair work, yet not overworked so as to tax the animal economy, that the woman cannot rear healthy children, nor should the father be over-wrought, that his vital powers be at all infringed upon.

If the policy be adopted, to make an improvement in land visible, to raise the greatest number of healthy children, to make an abundance of provision, to rear a portion at least of work horses, rely on it we will soon find by our tax list that our country is improving. . . .

Brethren of the South, we must change our policy. *Overseers are not interested in raising children, or meat, in improving land, or improving productive qualities of seed, or animals. Many of them do not care whether property has depreciated or improved, so they have made a crop [of cotton] to boast of.*

As to myself, I care not who has the credit of making crops at Log Hall; and I would prefer that an overseer, who has been one of my family for a year or two, or more, should be benefited; but this thing is to be known and well understood. I plant such fields in such crops as I see fit; I plant acres in corn, cotton, oats, potatoes, etc., as I select, and the general policy of rest, cultivation, etc., must be preserved which I lay down. A self-willed overseer may fraudulently change somewhat in the latter, by not carrying out orders—that I cannot help. What I have written, I have written, and think I can substantiate.

From the *Southern Agriculturist*, vol. iv., page 317:—

OVERSEERS.

. . . When they seek a place, they rest their claims entirely on the number of bags they have heretofore made to the hand, and generally the employer unfortunately recognizes the justice of such claims.

No wonder, then, that the overseer desires to have entire control of the plantation. No wonder he opposes all experiments, or, if they are persisted in, neglects them; *presses everything at the end of the lash; pays no attention to the sick, except to keep them in the field as long as possible; and drives them out again at the first moment, and forces sucklers and breeders to the utmost. He has no other interest than to make a big cotton crop.* And if this does not please you, and induce you to increase his wages, he knows men it will please, and secure him a situation with.

From the Columbia *South Carolinian*:—

. . . Planters may be divided into two great classes, viz., those who attend to their business, and those who do not. And this creates corresponding classes of overseers. The planter who does not manage his own business must, of course, surrender everything into the hands of his overseer. Such a planter usually rates the merits of the overseer exactly in proportion to the number of bags of cotton he makes, and of course the overseer cares for nothing but to make a large crop. To him it is of no consequence that the old hands are worked down, or the young ones overstrained; that the breeding women miscarry, and the sucklers lose their children; that the mules are broken down, the plantation tools destroyed, the stock neglected, and the lands ruined: *so that he has the requisite number of cotton bags, all is overlooked;* he is re-employed at an advanced salary, and his reputation increased. Everybody knows that by such a course, a crop may be increased by the most inferior overseer, in any given year, unless his predecessors have so entirely exhausted the resources of the plantation, that there is no part of the capital left which can be wrought up into current income. . . . Having once had the sole management of a plantation, and imbibed the idea that the only test of good planting is to make a large crop of cotton, an overseer becomes worthless. He will no longer obey orders; he will not stoop to details; he scorns all improvements, and *will not* adopt any other plan of planting than simply to work lands, negroes, and mules to the top of their bent, which necessarily proves fatal to every employer who will allow it.

It seems scarcely credible, that any man owning a plantation will so abandon it and his people on it entirely to a hireling, no matter what his confidence in him is. Yet there are numbers who do it habitually; and I have even known overseers to stipulate that their employers should not give any order, nor interfere in any way with their management of the plantation. There are also some proprietors of considerable property and pretension to being planters, who give their overseer a proportion of the crop for his wages; thus bribing him by the strongest inducements of self-interest, to overstrain and work down everything committed to his charge.

No planter, who attends to his own business, can dispense with agents and sub-agents. It is impossible, on a plantation of any size, for the proprietor to attend to all the details, many of which are irksome and laborious, and he requires more intelligence to assist him than slaves usually possess. To him, therefore, a good overseer is a blessing. But an overseer who would answer the views of such a planter is most difficult to find. The men engaged in that occupation who combine the most intelligence, industry, and character, are allured into the service of those who place all power in their hands, and are ultimately spoiled.

An English traveller [Edwin L. Godkin] writes to the London *Daily News* from Mississippi (1857):—

On crossing the Big Block river, I left the sandhills and began to find myself in the rich loam of the valley of the Mississippi. The plantations became larger, the clearings more numerous and extensive, and the roads less hilly, but worse. Along the Yazoo river one meets with some of the richest soil in the world, and some of the largest crops of cotton in the

Union. My first night in that region was passed at the house of a planter who worked but few hands, was a fast friend of slavery, and yet drew for my benefit one of the most mournful pictures of a slave's life I have ever met with. He said, and I believe truly, that the negroes of small planters are, on the whole, well treated, or at least as well as the owners can afford to treat them. Their master not unfrequently works side by side with them in the fields. . . . But on the large plantations, where the business is carried on by an overseer, and everything is conducted with military strictness and discipline, he described matters as being widely different. *The future of the overseer depends altogether on the quantity of cotton he is able to make up for the market.* Whether the owner be resident or non-resident, if the plantation be large, and a great number of hands be employed upon it, the overseer gets credit for a large crop, and blame for a small one. His professional reputation depends in a great measure upon the number of bales or hogsheads he is able to produce, and neither his education nor his habits are such as to render it likely that he would allow any consideration for the negroes to stand in the way of his advancing it. His interest is to get as much work out of them as they can possibly perform. His skill consists in knowing exactly how hard they may be driven without incapacitating them for future exertion. The larger the plantation the less chance there is, of course, of the owner's softening the rigour of the overseer, or the sternness of discipline by personal interference. So, as Mr. H— said, a vast mass of the slaves pass their lives, from the moment they are able to go afield in the picking season till they drop worn out into the grave, in incessant labour, in all sorts of weather, at all seasons of the year, without any other change or relaxation than is furnished by sickness, without the smallest hope of any improvement either in their condition, in their food, or in their clothing, which are of the plainest and coarsest kind, and indebted solely to the forbearance or good temper of the overseer for exemption from terrible physical suffering. They are rung to bed at nine o'clock, almost immediately after bolting the food which they often have to cook after coming home from their day's labour, and are rung out of bed at four or five in the morning. The interval is one long round of toil. Life has no sunny spots for them. Their only refuge or consolation in this world is in their own stupidity and grossness. The nearer they are to the beast, the happier they are likely to be. Any mental or moral rise is nearly sure to bring unhappiness with it.

The same gentleman writes from Columbus:—

One gets better glimpses of the real condition of the negroes from conversations one happens to overhear than from what is told to one's-self—

above all, when one is known to be a stranger, and particularly an Englishman. The cool way in which you hear [of] the hanging of niggers, the
shooting of niggers, and the necessity for severe discipline among niggers
talked of in bar-rooms, speaks volumes as to the exact state of the case. A
negro was shot when running away, near Greensboro', a small town on
my road, the day before I passed through, by a man who had received
instructions from the owner to take him alive, and shoot him if he resisted.
I heard the subject discussed by some "loafers" in the bar, while getting
my horse fed, and I found, to my no small—I do not know whether to say
horror or amusement—that the point in dispute was not the degree of
moral guilt incurred by the murderer, but the degree of loss and damage
for which he had rendered himself liable to the owner of the slave in
departing from the letter of his commission. One of the group summed up
the arguments on both sides, by exclaiming, "Well, this shootin' of niggers
should be put a stop to, that's a fact." The obvious inference to be deduced from this observation was, that "nigger shootin' " was a slight con-
travention of police regulations—a little of which might be winked at, but
which, in this locality, had been carried to such an extent as to call for
the interference of the law.

I do not think that I have ever seen the sudden death of a negro
noticed in a Southern newspaper, or heard it referred to in conversation, that the loss of property, rather than the extinction of life, was
not the evident occasion of interest. Turning over several Southern
papers at this moment, I fall at once upon these examples:—

We are informed that a negro man, the property of Mr. William Mays,
of this city, was killed last Thursday by a youth, the son of Mr. William
Payne, of Campbell county. The following are the circumstances, as we
have received them. Two sons of Mr. Payne were shooting pigeons on the
plantation of Mr. Mays, about twenty miles from this place, and went to
the tobacco-house, where the overseer and hands were housing tobacco;
one of the boys had a string of pigeons and the other had none. On
reaching the house, the negro who was killed asked the boy who had no
pigeons, "where his were." He replied that he killed none, but could kill
him (the negro), and raised his gun and fired. The load took effect in
the head, and caused death in a few hours. *The negro was a valuable one.
Mr. Mays had refused $1,200 for him.—Lynchburg Virginian.*

A valuable negro boy, the property of W. A. Phipps, living in the upper
end of this county, was accidentally drowned in the Holston river a few
days ago.—*Rogersville Times.*

Mr. Tilghman Cobb's barn at Bedford, Va., was set fire to by lightning

on Friday, the 11th, and consumed. Two negroes and three horses perished in the flames.—*New Orleans Daily Crescent.*

I have repeated these accounts, not to convey to the reader's
mind the impression that slaves are frequently shot by their masters,
which would be, no doubt, a mistaken inference, but to show in
what manner I was made to feel, as I was very strongly in my
journey, that what we call the sacredness of human life, together
with a great range of kindred instincts, scarcely attaches at all, with
most white men, to the slaves, and also in order to justify the following observation:—that I found the lives and the comfort of negroes, in the rich cotton-planting districts especially, habitually regarded, by all classes, much more from a purely pecuniary point of
view than I had ever before supposed they could be; and yet that,
as property, negro life and negro vigour were generally much less
carefully economized than I had always before imagined them to be.

As I became familiar with the circumstances, I saw reasons for
this, which, in looking from a distance, or through the eyes of travellers, I had not been able adequately to appreciate. I will endeavour to state them:—

It is difficult to handle simply as property, a creature possessing
human passions and human feelings, however debased and torpid
the condition of that creature may be; while, on the other hand, the
absolute necessity of dealing with property as a thing, greatly embarrassed a man in any attempt to treat it as a person. And it is the
natural result of this complicated state of things, that the system of
slave-management is irregular, ambiguous, and contradictory; that
it is never either consistently humane or consistently economical.

As a general rule, the larger the body of negroes on a plantation
or estate, the more completely are they treated as mere property,
and in accordance with a policy calculated to insure the largest
pecuniary returns. Hence, in part, the greater proportionate profit
of such plantations, and the tendency which everywhere prevails
in the planting districts to the absorption of small, and the augmen-
tation of large estates. It may be true, that among the wealthier
slave-owners there is oftener a humane disposition, a better judgment, and a greater ability to deal with their dependents indul-
gently and bountifully, but the effects of this disposition are chiefly
felt, even on those plantations where the proprietor resides perma-

nently, among the slaves employed about the house and stables, and perhaps a few old favourites in the quarters. It is more than balanced by the difficulty of acquiring a personal interest in the units of a large body of slaves, and an acquaintance with the individual characteristics of each. The treatment of the mass must be reduced to a system, the ruling idea of which will be, to enable one man to force into the same channel of labour the muscles of a large number of men of various and often conflicting wills.

The chief difficulty is to overcome their great aversion to labour. They have no objection to eating, drinking, and resting, when necessary, and no general disinclination to receive instruction. If a man own many slaves, therefore, the faculty which he values highest, and pays most for, in an overseer, is that of making them work. Any fool could see that they were properly supplied with food, clothing, rest, and religious instruction.

The labourers we see in towns, at work on railroads and steamboats, about stations and landings; the menials of our houses and hotels, are less respectable, moral, and intelligent than the great majority of the whole labouring class of the North. The traveller at the South has to learn that there the reverse is the case to a degree which can hardly be sufficiently estimated. I have been obliged to think that many amiable travellers who have received impressions with regard to the condition of the slaves very different from mine, have failed to make a sufficient allowance for this. The rank-and-file plantation negroes are not to be readily made acquaintance with by chance or through letters of introduction.

I have described in detail, in former chapters, two large plantations, which were much the best in respect to the happiness of the negroes, of all that I saw in the South. I am now about to describe what I judged to be the most profitable estate that I visited. In saying this I do not compare it with others noticed in this chapter, my observations of which were too superficial to warrant a com·parison. It was situated upon a tributary of the Mississippi, and accessible only by occasional steamboats; even this mode of communication being frequently interrupted at low stages of the rivers. The slaves upon it formed about one twentieth of the whole population of the county, in which the blacks considerably outnumber the whites. At the time of my visit, the owner was sojourning upon it, with his family and several invited guests, but his usual residence was upon a small plantation, of little productive value, situated in a neighbourhood somewhat noted for the luxury and hospitality of its citizens, and having a daily mail, and direct railroad and telegraphic communication with New York. This was, if I am not mistaken, his second visit in five years.

The property consisted of four adjoining plantations, each with its own negro-cabins, stables, and overseer, and each worked to a great extent independently of the others, but all contributing their crop to one gin-house and warehouse, and all under the general superintendence of a bailiff or manager, who constantly resided upon the estate, and in the absence of the owner, had vice-regal power over the overseers, controlling, so far as he thought fit, the economy of all the plantations.

The manager was himself a gentleman of good education, generous and poetic in temperament, and possessing a capacity for the enjoyment of nature and a happiness in the bucolic life, unfortunately rare with Americans. I found him a delightful companion, and I have known no man with whose natural tastes and feelings I have felt, on so short acquaintance, a more hearty sympathy. The gang of toiling negroes to him, however, was as essential an element of the poetry of nature as flocks of peaceful sheep and herds of lowing kine, and he would no more appreciate the aspect in which an Abolitionist would see them, than would Virgil have honoured the feelings of a vegetarian, sighing at the sight of flocks and herds destined to feed the depraved appetite of the carnivorous savage of modern civilization. The overseers were superior to most of their class, and, with one exception, frank, honest, temperate, and industrious, but their feelings toward negroes were such as naturally result from their occupation. They were all married, and lived with their families, each in a cabin or cottage, in the hamlet of the slaves of which he had especial charge. Their wages varied from $500 to $1,000 a year each.

These five men, each living more than a mile distant from either of the others, were the only white men on the estate, and the only others within several miles of them were a few skulking vagabonds. Of course, to secure their own personal safety and to efficiently direct the labour of such a large number of ignorant, indolent, and vicious negroes, rules, or rather habits and customs, of discipline, were necessary, which would in particular cases be liable to operate unjustly and cruelly. It is apparent, also, that, as the testimony of negroes against them would not be received as evidence in court, there was very little probability that any excessive severity would be restrained by fear of the law. A provision of the law intended to secure a certain privilege to slaves, was indeed disregarded under my own observation, and such infraction of the law was confessedly customary with one of the overseers, and was permitted by the manager, for the reason that it seemed to him to be, in a certain degree, justifiable and expedient under the circumstances, and because he did not like to interfere unnecessarily in such matters.

In the main, the negroes appeared to be well taken care of and abundantly supplied with the necessaries of vigorous physical existence. A large part of them lived in commodious and well-built cottages, with broad galleries in front, so that each family of five had two rooms on the lower floor, and a loft. The remainder lived in log huts, small and mean in appearance, but those of their overseers were little better, and preparations were being made to replace all of these by neat boarded cottages. Each family had a fowl-house and hog-sty (constructed by the negroes themselves), and kept fowls and swine, feeding the latter during the summer on weeds and fattening them in the autumn on corn, *stolen* (this was mentioned to me by the overseers as if it were a matter of course) from their master's corn-fields. I several times saw gangs of them eating the dinner which they had brought, each man for himself, to the field, and observed that they generally had plenty, often more than they could eat, of bacon, corn-bread, and molasses. The allowance of food is weighed and measured under the eye of the manager by the drivers, and distributed to the head of each family weekly: consisting of—for each person, 3 pounds of pork, 1 peck of meal; and from January to July, 1 quart of molasses. Monthly, in addition, 1 pound tobacco, and 4 pints salt. No drink is ever served but water, except after unusual exposure, or to ditchers working in water, who get a glass of whisky at night. All hands cook for themselves after work at night, or whenever they please between nightfall and daybreak, each family in its own cabin. Each family has a garden, the products of which, together with eggs, fowls, and bacon, they frequently sell, or use in addition to their regular allowance of food. Most of the families buy a barrel of flour every year. The manager endeavours to encourage this practice;

and that they may spend their money for flour instead of liquor, he furnishes it to them at rather less than what it costs him at wholesale. There are many poor whites within a few miles who will always sell liquor to the negroes, and encourage them to steal, to obtain the means to buy it of them. These poor whites are always spoken of with anger by the overseers, and they each have a standing offer of much more than the intrinsic value of their land, from the manager, to induce them to move away.

The negroes also obtain a good deal of game. They set traps for raccoons, rabbits, and turkeys; and I once heard the stock-tender complaining that he had detected one of the vagabond whites stealing a turkey which had been caught in his pen. I several times partook of game, while on the plantation, that had been purchased of the negroes. The stock-tender, an old negro, whose business it was to ride about in the woods and keep an eye on the stock cattle that were pastured in them, and who was thus likely to know where the deer ran, had an ingenious way of supplying himself with venison. He lashed a scythe blade or butcher's knife to the end of a pole so that it formed a lance; this he set near a fence or fallen tree which obstructed a path in which the deer habitually ran, and the deer in leaping over the obstacle would leap directly on the knife. In this manner he had killed two deer the week before my visit.

The manager sent to him for some of this venison for his own use, and justified himself to me for not paying for it on the ground that the stock-tender had undoubtedly taken time which really belonged to his owner to set his spear. Game taken by the field-hands was not looked upon in the same light, because it must have been got at night when they were excused from labour for their owner.

The first morning I was on the estate, while at breakfast with the manager, an old negro woman came into the room and said to him, "Dat gal's bin bleedin' agin dis mornin'."

"How much did she bleed?"

"About a pint, sir."

"Very well: I'll call and see her after breakfast."

"I come up for some sugar of lead, masser; I gin her some powdered alum 'fore I come away."

"Very well; you can have some."

After breakfast the manager invited me to ride with him on his usual daily round of inspection through the plantations.

On reaching the nearest "quarters," we stopped at a house, a little larger than the ordinary cabins, which was called the loom-house, in which a dozen negroes were at work making shoes, and manufacturing coarse cotton stuff for negro clothing. One of the hands so employed was insane, and most of the others were cripples, invalids with chronic complaints, or unfitted by age, or some infirmity, for field-work.

From this we went to one of the cabins, where we found the sick woman who had been bleeding at the lungs, with the old nurse in attendance upon her. The manager examined and prescribed for her in a kind manner. When we came out he asked the nurse if any one else was sick.

"Oney dat woman Carline."

"What do you think is the matter with her?"

"Well, I don't tink dere's anyting de matter wid her, masser; I mus' answer you for true, I don't tink anyting de matter wid her, oney she's a little sore from dat whippin' she got."

We went to another cabin and entered a room where a woman lay on a bed, groaning. It was a dingy, comfortless room, but a musquito bar, much patched and very dirty, covered the bed. The manager asked the woman several times what was the matter, but could get no distinct reply. She appeared to be suffering great pain. The manager felt her pulse and looked at her tongue, and after making a few more inquiries, to which no intelligible reply was given, told her he did not believe she was ill at all. At this the woman's groans redoubled. "I have heard of your tricks," continued the manager; "you had a chill when I came to see you yesterday morning; you had a chill when the mistress came here, and you had a chill when the master came. I never knew a chill to last the whole day. So you'll just get up now and go to the field, and if you don't work smart, you'll get a dressing; do you hear?"

We then left. The manager said that he rarely—almost never—had occasion to employ a physician for the people. Never for accouchements; the women, from their labour in the field, were not subject to the difficulty, danger, and pain which attended women of the better classes in giving birth to their offspring. (I do not suppose that there was a physician within a day's journey of the plantations.)

Near the first quarters we visited there was a large blacksmith's

and wheelwright's shop, in which a number of mechanics were at
work. Most of them, as we rode up, were eating their breakfast,
which they warmed at their fires. Within and around the shop there
were some fifty ploughs which they were putting in order. The
manager inspected the work, found some of it faulty, sharply reprimanded the workmen for not getting on faster, and threatened one
of them with a whipping for not paying closer attention to the directions which had been given him.

The overseer of this plantation rode up while we were at the
shop, and in a free and easy style, reported to the manager how all
his hands were employed. There were so many at this and so many
at that, and they had done so much since yesterday. "There's that
girl, Caroline," said the manager; "she's not sick, and I told her she
must go to work; put her to the hoeing; there's nothing the matter
with her, except she's sore with the whipping she got. You must go
and get her out." A woman passing at the time, the manager told
her to go and tell Caroline she must get up and go to work, or the
overseer would come and start her. She returned in a few minutes,
and reported that Caroline said she could not get up. The overseer
and manager rode toward the cabin, but before they reached it, the
girl, who had probably been watching us from the window, came
out and went to the field with her hoe. They then returned to me
and continued their conversation. Just before we left the overseer,
he said, "I think that girl who ran away last week was in her cabin
last night." The manager told me, as we rode on, that the people
often ran away after they had been whipped, or something else had
happened to make them angry. They hide in the swamp, and come
in to the cabins at night to get food. They seldom remain away more
than a fortnight, and when they come in they are whipped. The
woman, Caroline, he said, had been delivered of a dead child about
six weeks before, and had been complaining and getting rid of work
ever since. She was the laziest woman on the estate. This shamming
illness gave him the most disagreeable duty he had to perform.
Negroes were famous for it. "If it was not for her bad character,"
he continued, "I should fear to make her go to work to-day; but her
pulse is steady, and her tongue perfectly smooth. We have to be
sharp with them; if we were not, every negro on the estate would
be a-bed."

We rode on to where the different gangs of labourers were at work, and inspected them one after another. I observed, as we were looking at one of the gangs, that they were very dirty. "Negroes are the filthiest people in the world," said the manager; "there are some of them who would not keep clean twenty-four hours at a time if you gave them thirty suits a year." I asked him if there were any rules to maintain cleanliness. There were not, but sometimes the negroes were told at night that any one who came into the field the next morning without being clean would be whipped. This gave no trouble to those who were habitually clean, while it was in itself a punishment to those who were not, as they were obliged to spend the night in washing.

They were furnished with two suits of summer, and one of winter clothing each year. Besides which, most of them got presents of holiday finery (calico dresses, handkerchiefs, etc.), and purchased more for themselves, at Christmas. One of the drivers now in the field had on a uniform coat of an officer of artillery. After the Mexican war, a great deal of military clothing was sold at auction in New Orleans, and much of it was bought by the planters at a low price, and given to their negroes, who were greatly pleased with it.

Each overseer regulated the hours of work on his own plantation. I saw the negroes at work before sunrise and after sunset. At about eight o'clock they were allowed to stop for breakfast, and again about noon, to dine. The length of these rests was at the discretion of the overseer or drivers, usually, I should say, from half an hour to an hour. There was no rule.

The number of hands directed by each overseer was considerably over one hundred. The manager thought it would be better economy to have a white man over every fifty hands, but the difficulty of obtaining trustworthy overseers prevented it. Three of those he then had were the best he had ever known. He described the great majority as being passionate, careless, inefficient men, generally intemperate, and totally unfitted for the duties of the position. The best overseers, ordinarily, are young men, the sons of small planters, who take up the business temporarily, as a means of acquiring a little capital with which to purchase negroes for themselves.

The ploughs at work, both with single and double mule teams, were generally held by women, and very well held, too. I watched with some interest for any indication that their sex unfitted them for the occupation. Twenty of them were ploughing together, with double teams and heavy ploughs. They were superintended by a negro man who carried a whip, which he frequently cracked at them, permitting no dawdling or delay at the turning; and they twitched their ploughs around on the head-land, jerking their reins, and yelling to their mules, with apparent ease, energy, and rapidity. Throughout the South-west the negroes, as a rule, appear to be worked much harder than in the Eastern and Northern Slave States. I do not think they accomplish as much in the same time as agricultural labourers at the North usually do, but they certainly labour much harder, and more unremittingly. They are constantly and steadily driven up to their work, and the stupid, plodding, machine-like manner in which they labour, is painful to witness. This was especially the case with the hoe-gangs. One of them numbered nearly two hundred hands (for the force of two plantations was working together), moving across the field in parallel lines, with a considerable degree of precision. I repeatedly rode through the lines at a canter, with other horsemen, often coming upon them suddenly, without producing the smallest change or interruption in the dogged action of the labourers, or causing one of them, so far as I could see, to lift an eye from the ground. I had noticed the same thing with smaller numbers before, but here, considering that I was a stranger, and that strangers could but very rarely visit the plantation, it amazed me very much. I think it told a more painful story than any I had ever heard, of the cruelty of slavery. It was emphasized by a tall and powerful negro who walked to and fro in the rear of the line, frequently cracking his whip, and calling out in the surliest manner, to one and another, "Shove your hoe, there! shove your hoe!" But I never saw him strike any one with the whip.

The whip was evidently in constant use, however. There were no rules on the subject, that I learned; the overseers and drivers punished the negroes whenever they deemed it necessary, and in such manner, and with such severity, as they thought fit. "If you don't work faster," or "If you don't work better," or "If you don't recollect what I tell you, I will have you flogged," I often heard. I said to one of the overseers, "It must be disagreeable to have to punish them as much as you do?" "Yes, it would be to those who are not used to it—but it's my business, and I think nothing of it. Why, sir, I wouldn't mind killing a nigger more than I would a dog." I asked if he had ever killed a negro? "Not quite that," he said, but overseers were often obliged to. Some negroes are determined never to let a white man whip them, and will resist you, when you attempt it; of course you must kill them in that case.[1] Once a negro, whom he was about to whip in the field, struck at his head with a hoe. He parried the blow with his whip, and, drawing a pistol, tried to shoot him; but the pistol missing fire, he rushed in and knocked him down with the butt of it. At another time, a negro whom he was punishing insulted and threatened him. He went to the house for his gun, and as he was returning, the negro, thinking he would be afraid of spoiling so valuable a piece of property by firing, broke for the woods. He fired at once, and put six buck-shot into his hips. He always carried a bowie-knife, but not a pistol unless he anticipated some unusual act of insubordination. He always kept a pair of pistols ready loaded over the mantel-piece, however, in case they should be needed. It was only when he first came upon a plantation that he ever had much trouble. A great many overseers were unfit for their business, and too easy and slack with the negroes. When he succeeded such a man, he had hard work for a time to break the negroes in; but it did not take long to teach them their place. His conversation on the subject was exactly like what I have heard said, again and again, by Northern shipmasters and officers, with regard to seamen.

I happened to see the severest corporeal punishment of a negro that I witnessed at the South while visiting this estate. I suppose, however, that punishment equally severe is common; in fact, it must be necessary to the maintenance of adequate discipline on every large plantation. It is much more necessary than on shipboard, because the opportunities of hiding away and shirking labour, and of wasting and injuring the owner's property without danger to themselves, are far greater in the case of the slaves than in that of the sailors, but, above all, because there is no real moral obligation on the part of the negro to do what is demanded of him. The sailor performs his duty in obedience to a voluntary contract; the

[1] "On Monday last, as James Allen (overseer on Prothro's plantation at St. Maurice) was punishing a negro boy named Jack, for stealing hogs, the boy ran off before the overseer had chastised him sufficiently for the offence. He was immediately pursued by the overseer, who succeeded in catching him, when the negro drew a knife and inflicted a terrible gash in his abdomen. The wounds of the overseer were dressed by Dr. Stephens, who pronounces it a very critical case, but still entertains hope of his recovery."—*Natchitoches Chronicle*.

slave is in an involuntary servitude. The manner of the overseer who inflicted the punishment, and his subsequent conversation with me about it, indicated that it was by no means unusual in severity. I had accidentally encountered him, and he was showing me his plantation. In going from one side of it to the other, we had twice crossed a deep gully, at the bottom of which was a thick covert of brushwood. We were crossing it a third time, and had nearly passed through the brush, when the overseer suddenly stopped his horse exclaiming, "What's that? Hallo! who are you, there?"

It was a girl lying at full length on the ground at the bottom of the gully, evidently intending to hide herself from us in the bushes.

"Who are you, there?"

"Sam's Sall, sir."

"What are you skulking there for?"

The girl half rose, but gave no answer.

"Have you been here all day?"

"No, sir."

"How did you get here?"

The girl made no reply.

"Where have you been all day?"

The answer was unintelligible.

After some further questioning, she said her father accidentally locked her in, when he went out in the morning.

"How did you manage to get out?"

"Pushed a plank off, sir, and crawled out."

The overseer was silent for a moment, looking at the girl, and then said, "That won't do; come out here." The girl arose at once, and walked towards him. She was about eighteen years of age. A bunch of keys hung at her waist, which the overseer espied, and he said, "Your father locked you in; but you have got the keys." After a little hesitation, she replied that these were the keys of some other locks; her father had the door-key.

Whether her story was true or false, could have been ascertained in two minutes by riding on to the gang with which her father was at work, but the overseer had made up his mind.

"That won't do," said he; "get down." The girl knelt on the ground; he got off his horse, and holding him with his left hand, struck her thirty or forty blows across the shoulders with his tough, flexible, "raw-hide" whip (a terrible instrument for the purpose).

They were well laid on, at arm's length, but with no appearance of angry excitement on the part of the overseer. At every stroke the girl winced and exclaimed, "Yes, sir!" or "Ah, sir!" or "Please, sir!" not groaning or screaming. At length he stopped and said, "Now tell me the truth." The girl repeated the same story. "You have not got enough yet," said he; "pull up your clothes—lie down." The girl without any hesitation, without a word or look of remonstrance or entreaty, drew closely all her garments under her shoulders, and lay down upon the ground with her face toward the overseer, who continued to flog her with the raw-hide, across her naked loins and thighs, with as much strength as before. She now shrunk away from him, not rising, but writhing, grovelling, and screaming, "Oh, don't, sir! oh, please stop, master! please, sir! please, sir! oh, that's enough, master! oh, Lord! oh, master, master! oh, God, master, do stop! oh, God, master! oh, God, master!"

A young gentleman of fifteen was with us; he had ridden in front, and now, turning on his horse, looked back with an expression only of impatience at the delay. It was the first time I had ever seen a woman flogged. I had seen a man cudgelled and beaten, in the heat of passion, before, but never flogged with a hundredth part of the severity used in this case. I glanced again at the perfectly passionless but rather grim business-like face of the overseer, and again at the young gentleman, who had turned away; if not indifferent he had evidently not the faintest sympathy with my emotion. Only my horse chafed. I gave him rein and spur and we plunged into the bushes and scrambled fiercely up the steep acclivity. The screaming yells and the whip strokes had ceased when I reached the top of the bank. Choking, sobbing, spasmodic groans only were heard. I rode on to where the road, coming diagonally up the ravine, ran out upon the cotton-field. My young companion met me there, and immediately afterward the overseer. He laughed as he joined us, and said:

"She meant to cheat me out of a day's work, and she has done it, too."

"Did you succeed in getting another story from her?" I asked, as soon as I could trust myself to speak.

"No; she stuck to it."

"Was it not perhaps true?"

"Oh no, sir; she slipped out of the gang when they were going to work, and she's been dodging about all day, going from one place to another as she saw me coming. She saw us crossing there a little while ago, and thought we had gone to the quarters, but we turned back so quick, we came into the gully before she knew it, and she could do nothing but lie down in the bushes."

"I suppose they often slip off so."

"No, sir; I never had one do so before—not like this; they often run away to the woods, and are gone some time, but I never had a dodge-off like this before."

"Was it necessary to punish her so severely?"

"Oh yes, sir" (laughing again). "If I hadn't, she would have done the same thing again to-morrow, and half the people on the plantation would have followed her example. Oh, you've no idea how lazy these niggers are; you Northern people don't know anything about it. They'd never do any work at all if they were not afraid of being whipped."

We soon afterward met an old man, who, on being closely questioned, said that he had seen the girl leave the gang as they went to work after dinner. It appeared that she had been at work during the forenoon, but at dinner-time the gang was moved, and as it passed through the gully she slipped out. The driver had not missed her. The overseer said that when he first took charge of this plantation, the negroes ran away a great deal—they disliked him so much. They used to say, 'twas hell to be on his place; but after a few months they got used to his ways, and liked him better than any of the rest. He had not had any run away now for some time. When they ran away they would generally return within a fortnight. If many of them went off, or if they stayed out long, he would make the rest of the force work Sundays, or deprive them of some of their usual privileges until the runaways returned. The negroes on the plantation could always bring them in if they chose to do so. They depended on them for their food, and they had only to stop the supplies to oblige them to surrender.

Accepting the position of the overseer, I knew that his method was right, but it was a red-hot experience to me, and has ever since been a fearful thing in my memory. Strangely so, I sometimes think, but I suppose the fact that the delicate and ingenuous lad who was with me, betrayed not even the slightest flush of shame, and that I constrained myself from the least expression of feeling of any kind, made the impression in my brain the more intense and lasting.

Sitting near a gang with an overseer and the manager, the former would occasionally call out to one and another by name, in directing or urging their labour. I asked if he knew them all by name. He did, but I found that the manager did not know one in five of them. The overseer said he generally could call most of the negroes on a plantation by their names in two weeks after he came to it, but it was rather difficult to learn them on account of there being so many of the same name, distinguished from each other by a prefix. "There's a Big Jim here, and a Little Jim, and Eliza's Jim, and there's Jim Bob, and Jim Clarisy."

"What's Jim Clarisy?—how does he get that name?"

"He's Clarisy's child, and Bob is Jim Bob's father. That fellow ahead there, with the blue rag on his head, his name is Swamp; he always goes by that name, but his real name is Abraham, I believe; is it not, Mr. [Manager]?"

"His name is Swamp on the plantation register—that's all I know of him."

"I believe his name is Abraham," said the overseer; "he told me so. He was bought of Judge ——, he says, and he told me his master called him Swamp because he ran away so much. He is the worst runaway on the place."

I inquired about the increase of the negroes on the estate, and the manager having told me the number of deaths and births the previous year, which gave a net increase of four per cent.—on Virginia estates it is often twenty per cent.—I asked if the negroes began to have children at a very early age. "Sometimes at sixteen," said the manager. "Yes, and at fourteen," said the overseer; "that girl's had a child"—pointing to a girl that did not appear older than fourteen. "Is she married?" "No." "You see," said the manager, "negro girls are not remarkable for chastity; their habits indeed rather hinder them from having children. They'd have them younger than they do, if they would marry or live with but one man, sooner than they do.[2] They often do not have children till they are twenty-

[2] Mr. Russell makes an observation to the same effect with regard to the Cuba plantations, p. 230. On these large cotton plantations there are frequently

five years old." "Are those who are married true to each other?" I asked. The overseer laughed heartily at the idea, and described a disgusting state of things. Women were almost common property, though sometimes the men were not all inclined to acknowledge it; for when I asked: "Do you not try to discourage this?" the overseer answered: "No, not unless they quarrel." "They get jealous and quarrel among themselves sometimes about it," the manager explained, "or come to the overseer and complain, and he has them punished." "Give all hands a damned good hiding," said the overseer. "You punish for adultery, then, but not for fornication?" "Yes," answered the manager, but "No," insisted the overseer, "we punish them for quarrelling; if they don't quarrel I don't mind anything about it, but if it makes a muss, I give all four of 'em a warning."

Riding through a large gang of hoers, with two of the overseers, I observed that a large proportion of them appeared to be thoroughbred Africans. Both of them thought that the "real black niggers" were about three-fourths of the whole number, and that this would hold as an average on Mississippi and Louisiana plantations. One of them pointed out a girl—"That one is pure white; you see her hair?" (It was straight and sandy.) "She is the only one we have got." It was not uncommon, he said, to see slaves so white that they could not be easily distinguished from pure-blooded whites. He had never been on a plantation before, that had not more than one on it.[3] "Now," said I, "if that girl should dress herself well, and run

---

more men than women, men being bought in preference to women for cotton picking.

The contrary is usually the case on the small plantations, where the profits of breeding negroes are constantly in view.

[3] "A woman, calling herself Violet Ludlow, was arrested a few days ago, and committed to jail, on the supposition that she was a runaway slave belonging to A. M. Mobley, of Upshur county, Texas, who had offered through our columns a reward of fifty dollars for her apprehension. On being brought before a justice of the peace, she stated that she was a white woman, and claimed her liberty. She states that she is a daughter of Jeremiah Ludlow, of Pike county, Alabama, and was brought from that country in 1853, by George Cope, who emigrated to Texas. After arriving in Texas, she was sold by George Cope to a Doctor Terry, in Upshur county, Texas, and was soon after sold by him to a Mrs. Hagen, or Hagens, of the same county. Violet says that she protested against each sale made of her, declaring herself a free woman. She names George Gilmer, Thomas Rogers, John Garret, and others, residents of Pike county, Alabama, as persons who have known her from infancy as the daughter of one Jeremiah Ludlow and Rene Martin, a widow at the time of her birth,

away, would she be suspected of being a slave?" (I could see nothing myself by which to distinguish her, as she passed, from an ordinary poor white girl.)

"Oh, yes; you might not know her if she got to the North, but any of us would know her."

"How?"

"By her language and manners."

"But if she had been brought up as house-servant?"

"Perhaps not in that case."

The other thought there would be no difficulty; you could always see a slave girl quail when you looked in her eyes.

I asked if they thought the mulattoes or white slaves were weaker or less valuable than the pure negroes.

"Oh, no; I'd rather have them a great deal," said one. "Well, I had not," said the other; "the blacker the better for me." "The white ones," added the first, "are more active, and know more, and I think they do the most work." "Are they more subject to illness, or do they appear to be of weaker constitutions?" One said they were not, the other that they did not seem to bear the heat as well. The first thought that this might be so, but that, nevertheless, they would do more work. I afterwards asked the manager's opinion. He thought they did not stand excessive heat as well as the pure negroes, but that, from their greater activity and willingness, they would do more work. He believed they were equally strong and no more liable to illness; had never had reason to think them of weaker constitution. They often had large families, and he had not noticed that their children were weaker or more subject to disease than others. He thought that perhaps they did not have so many children as the pure negroes, but he had supposed the reason to be that they did

and as being a free white woman, and her father a free white man. Violet is about instituting legal proceedings for her freedom."—*Shreveport Southwestern.*

"Some days since, a woman named Pelasgie was arrested as a fugitive slave, who has lived for more than twelve years in this city as a free woman. She was so nearly white that few could detect any traces of her African descent. She was arrested at the instance of a man named Raby, who claimed her as belonging to an estate of which he is heir-at-law. She was conveyed to the First District guard-house for safe keeping, and while there she stated to Acting Recorder Filleul that she was free, had never belonged to Raby, and had been in the full and unquestioned enjoyment of her freedom in this city for the above-mentioned period. She also stated that she had a house, well furnished, which she was in the habit of letting out in rooms."—*New Orleans Picayune.*

not begin bearing so young as the others, and this was because they were more attractive to the men, and perhaps more amorous themselves. He knew a great many mulattoes living together, and they generally had large and healthy families.

Afterwards, at one of the plantation nurseries, where there were some twenty or thirty infants and young children, a number of whom were evidently the offspring of white fathers, I asked the nurse to point out the healthiest children to me, and of those she indicated more were of the pure than of the mixed breed. I then asked her to show me which were the sickliest, and she did not point to any of the latter. I then asked if she noticed any difference in this respect between the black and the yellow children. "Well, dey do say, master, dat de yellow ones is de sickliest, but I can't tell for true dat I ever see as dey was."

Being with the proprietor and the manager together, I asked about the religious condition of the slaves. There were "preachers" on the plantations, and they had some religious observances on a Sunday; but the preachers were the worst characters among them, and, they thought, only made their religion a cloak for habits of especial depravity. They were, at all events, the most deceitful and dishonest slaves on the plantation, and oftenest required punishment. The negroes of all denominations, and even those who ordinarily made no religious pretensions, would join together in exciting religious observances. They did not like to have white men preach on the estate; and in future they did not intend to permit them to do so. It excited the negroes so much as to greatly interfere with the subordination and order which were necessary to obtain the profitable use of their labour. They would be singing and dancing every night in their cabins, till dawn of day, and utterly unfit themselves for work.

With regard to the religious instruction of slaves, widely different practices of course prevail. There are some slaveholders, like Bishop [Leonidas] Polk of Louisiana,[4] who oblige, and many others who en-

---

[4] "Bishop Polk, of Louisiana, was one of the guests. He assured me that he had been all over the country on Red River, the scene of the fictitious sufferings of 'Uncle Tom,' and that he had found the temporal and spiritual welfare of the negroes well cared for. He had confirmed thirty black persons near the situation assigned to Legree's estate. He is himself the owner of four hundred slaves, whom he endeavours to bring up in a religious manner. He tolerates no religion

courage, their slaves to engage in religious exercises, furnishing them certain conveniences for the purpose. Among the wealthier slaveowners, however, and in all those parts of the country where the enslaved portion of the population outnumbers the whites, there is generally a visible, and often an avowed distrust of the effect of religious exercises upon slaves, and even the preaching of white clergymen to them is permitted by many with reluctance. The prevailing impression among us, with regard to the important influence of slavery in promoting the spread of religion among the blacks, is an erroneous one in my opinion. I have heard Northern clergymen speak as if they supposed a regular daily instruction of slaves in the truths of Christianity to be general. So far is this from being the case that, although family prayers were held in several of the fifty planters' houses in Mississippi and Alabama, in which I passed a night, I never in a single instance saw a field-hand attend or join in the devotion of the family.

In South Carolina, a formal remonstrance, signed by over three hundred and fifty of the leading planters and citizens, was presented to a Methodist clergyman who had been chosen by the Conference of that State, as being a cautious and discreet person, to preach especially to slaves. It was his purpose, expressly declared beforehand, to confine himself to verbal instruction in religious truth. "Verbal instruction," replied the remonstrants, "will increase the desire of the black population to learn. . . . Open the missionary sluice, and the current will swell in its gradual onward advance. We thus expect *a progressive system of improvement* will be introduced, or will follow from the nature and force of circumstances, which, if not checked (though it may be shrouded in sophistry and disguise), *will ultimately revolutionize our civil institutions.*"

on his estate but that of the Church. He baptizes all the children, and teaches them the Catechism. All, without exception, attend the Church service, and the chanting is creditably performed by them, in the opinion of their owner. Ninety of them are communicants, marriages are celebrated according to the Church ritual, and the state of morals is satisfactory. Twenty infants had been baptized by the bishop just before his departure from home, and he had left his whole estate, his keys, &c., in the sole charge of one of his slaves, without the slightest apprehension of loss or damage. In judging of the position of this Christian prelate as a slave-owner, the English reader must bear in mind that, by the laws of Louisiana, emancipation has been rendered all but impracticable, and, that, if practicable, it would not necessarily be, in all cases, an act of mercy or of

The missionary, the Rev. T. Tupper, accordingly retired from the field. The local newspaper, the *Greenville Mountaineer*, in announcing his withdrawal, stated that the great body of the people were manifestly opposed to the religious instruction of their slaves, even if it were only given orally.

Though I do not suppose this view is often avowed, or consciously held by intelligent citizens, such a formal, distinct, and effective manifestation of sentiment made by so important an integral portion of the slaveholding body, cannot be supposed to represent a merely local or occasional state of mind; and I have not been able to resist the impression, that even where the economy, safety, and duty of some sort of religious education of the slaves is conceded, so much caution, reservation, and restriction is felt to be necessary in their instruction, that the result in the majority of cases has been merely to furnish a delusive clothing of Christian forms and phrases to the original vague superstition of the African savage.

In the county of Liberty, in Georgia, a Presbyterian minister has been for many years employed exclusively in labouring for the moral enlightenment of the slaves, being engaged and paid for this especial duty by their owners. From this circumstance, almost unparalleled as it is, it may be inferred that the planters of that county are, as a body, remarkably intelligent, liberal, and thoughtful for the moral welfare of the childlike wards Providence has placed under their care and tutorship. According to my private information, there is no body of slaveowners more, if any as much so, in the United States. I heard them referred to with admiration of their reputation in this particular, even as far away as Virginia and Kentucky. I believe, that in no other district has there been displayed as general and long-continued an interest in the spiritual well-being of the negroes. It must be supposed that nowhere else are their circumstances more happy and favourable to Christian nurture.[5]

justice."—*The Western World Revisited.* By the Rev. Henry Caswall, M.A., author of "America and the American Church," etc. Oxford, John Henry Parker, 1854.

[5] In [George] White's "Statistics of the State of Georgia" (page 377), the citizens of Liberty county are characterized as "unsurpassed for the great attention paid to the duties of religion."—Dr. Stevens, in his "History of Georgia," describes them as "worthy of their sires," who were, "the moral and intellectual nobility of the province," "whose accession was an honour to Georgia, and has ever proved one of its richest blessings."—In the biography of General Scrivens the county of Liberty is designated "proud spot of Georgia's soil!"—Dr. J. M. B.

After labouring thirteen years with a zeal and judgment which had made him famous, this apostle to the slaves of Liberty was called to the professorship of theology in the University of South Carolina. On retiring from his field of labour as a missionary, he addressed a valedictory sermon to his patrons, which has been published. While there is no unbecoming despondency or absence of proper gratitude for such results as have rewarded his protracted labour, visible in this document, the summing up is not such as would draw unusual cheers if given in the report of an African missionary at the Tabernacle or Exeter Hall [in London]. Without a word on which the most vigilant suspicion could rest a doubt of his entire loyalty to the uttermost rights of property which might be claimed by those whom he addressed, he could not avoid indicating, in the following passages, what he had been obliged to see to be the insurmountable difficulty in the way of any vital elevation of character among those to whom he had been especially charged to preach the Gospel wherewith Christ blessed mankind:—

They [his pastoral charge] are, in the language of Scripture, *"your money."* They are the source, the means of your wealth; by their labour do you obtain the necessaries, the conveniences, and comforts of life. The increase of them is the general standard of your worldly prosperity: without them you would be comparatively poor. *They are consequently sought after and desired as property, and when possessed, must be so taken care of and managed as to be made profitable.*

Now, it is exceedingly difficult to use them as money; to treat them as property, and at the same time render to them that which is just and equal as immortal and accountable beings, and as heirs of the grace of life, equally with ourselves. They are associated in our business, and thoughts, and feelings, with labour, and interest, and gain, and wealth. Under the influence of the powerful feeling of self-interest, there is a tendency to view and to treat them as instruments of labour, as a means of wealth, and to forget or pass over lightly, the fact that they are what they are, under the eye and government of God. There is a tendency to rest satisfied with very small and miserable efforts for their moral im-

---

Harden, in a medical report of the county, says: "The use of intoxicating drinks has been almost entirely given up" by its people.—White says ("Statistics," p. 373), "The people of Liberty, from their earliest settlement, have paid much attention to the subject of education. Excellent schools are found in different portions of the county, and it is believed a greater number of young men from Liberty graduate at our colleges than from any [other] section of Georgia. Indeed, it has been proverbial for furnishing able ministers and instructors."

provement, and to give one's self but little trouble to correct immoralities and reform wicked practices and habits, should they do their work quietly and profitably, and enjoy health, and go on to multiply and increase upon the earth.

This is addressed to a body of "professing evangelical Christians," in a district in which more is done for the elevation of the slaves than in any other of the South. What they are called to witness from their own experience, as the tendency of a system which recognizes slaves as absolute property, mere instruments of labour and means of wealth, "exceedingly difficult" for them to resist, is, I am well convinced, the *entirely irresistible effect* upon the mass of slave-holders. Fearing that moral and intellectual culture may injure their value as property, they oftener interfere to prevent than they endeavour to assist their slaves from using the poor opportunities that chance may throw in their way.

Moreover, the missionary adds:—

The current of the conversation and of business in society, in respect to negroes, runs in the channel of interest, and thus increases the blindness and insensibility of owners. . . . And this custom of society acts also on the negroes, who, seeing, and more than seeing, *feeling and knowing, that their owners regard and treat them as their money—as property only*—are inclined to lose sight of their better character and higher interests, and, in their ignorance and depravity, to estimate themselves, and religion, and virtue, no higher than their owners do.

Again, from the paramount interest of owners in the property quality of these beings, they provide them only such accommodations for spending the time in which they are not actively employed, as shall be favourable to their bodily health, and enable them to comply with the commandment, to "increase and multiply upon the earth," without regard to their moral health, without caring much for their obedience to the more pure and spiritual commands of the Scriptures.

The consequent mingling up of husbands and wives, children and youths, banishes the privacy and modesty essential to domestic peace and purity, and opens wide the door to dishonesty, oppression, violence, and profligacy. The owner may see, or hear, or know little of it. His servants may appear cheerful, and go on in the usual way, and enjoy health, and do his will, yet their actual moral state may be miserable. . . . *If family relations are not preserved and protected, we cannot look for any consid-erable degree of moral and religious improvement.*

It must be acknowledged of slavery, as a system, not only in Liberty county, but as that system finds the expression of the theory on which it is based in the laws of every Southern State, that family relations are not preserved and protected under it. As we should therefore expect, the missionary finds that

One of the chief causes of the immorality of negroes arises from the in-difference both of themselves and of their owners to family relations.

Large planters generally do not allow their negroes to marry off the plantation to which they belong, conceiving "that their own convenience and interest, and," says the missionary, "the comfort and *real* happiness of their people" are thereby promoted. Upon this point, however, it is but just to quote the views of the editor of the *Southern Agriculturist,* who, in urging planters to adopt and strictly maintain such a regulation, says: "If a master has a servant, and no suitable one of the other sex for a companion, he had better give an extra price for such an one as his would be willing to marry, than to have one man owning the husband, and the other the wife."

But this mode of arranging the difficulty seems not to have oc-curred to the Liberty county missionary; and while arguing against the course usually pursued, he puts the following, as a pertinent suggestion:—

Admitting that they are people having their preferences as well as others, *and there be a supply,* can that love which is the foundation and essence of the marriage state be forced?

Touching honesty and thrift among the negroes, he says:

While some discipline their people for every act of theft committed against their interests, they have no care whatever what amount of pilfer-ing and stealing the people carry on *among themselves.* Hence, in some places, thieves thrive and honest men suffer, until it becomes a practice "to keep if you can what is your own, and get all you can besides that is your neighbour's." Things come to such a pass, that the saying of the negroes is literally true, "The people live upon one another."

Referring to the evil of intemperance, it is observed:

Whatever toleration masters use towards ardent spirits in others, they are generally inclined to use none in respect to their servants; and in effecting this reformation, masters and mistresses should set the example;

for without example, precepts and persuasions are powerless. Nor can force effect this reformation as surely and perfectly as persuasion—appealing to the character and happiness of the servant himself, the appeal recognizes him in such a manner as to produce self-respect, and it tends to give elevation of conduct and character. I will not dwell upon this point.

He will not dwell on this point; yet, is it not evident that until this point can be dwelt upon, all effort for the genuine Christianization of the negro race in the South must be ineffectual?

The benefit to the African which is supposed to be incidental to American slavery, is confessedly proportionate to the degree in which he is forced into intercourse with a superior race and made subject to its example. Before I visited the South, I had believed that the advantages accruing from slavery, in this way, far outweighed the occasional cruelties, and other evils incidental to the system. I found, however, the mental and moral condition of the negroes, even in Virginia, and in those towns and districts containing the largest proportion of whites, much lower than I had anticipated; and as soon as I had an opportunity to examine one of the extensive plantations of the interior, although one inherited by its owner, and the home of a large and virtuous white family, I was satisfied that the advantages arising to the blacks from association with their white masters were very inconsiderable, scarcely appreciable, for the great majority of the field-hands. Even the overseer had barely acquaintance enough with the slaves, individually, to call them by name; the owner could not determine if he were addressing one of his own chattels, or whether it was another man's property, he said, when by chance he came upon a negro off the work. Much less did the slaves have an opportunity to cultivate their minds by intercourse with other white people. Whatever of civilization, and of the forms, customs, and shibboleths of Christianity, they were acquiring by example, and through police restraints, might, it occurred to me, after all, but poorly compensate the effect of the systematic withdrawal from them of all the usual influences which tend to nourish the moral nature and develop the intellectual faculties, in savages as well as in civilized free men.

This doubt, as my Northern friends well know, for I had habitually assumed the opposite, in all previous discussions of the slavery question, was unexpected and painful to me. I resisted it long, and it was not till I had been more than twelve months in the South, with my attention constantly fixed upon the point, that I ceased to suspect that the circumstances which brought me to it were exceptional and deceptive. It grew constantly stronger with every opportunity I had of observing the condition, habits, and character of slaves whom I could believe to present fair examples of the working of the system with the majority of those subject to it upon the large plantations.

The frequency with which the slaves use religious phrases of all kinds, the readiness with which they engage in what are deemed religious exercises, and fall into religious ecstasies, with the crazy, jocular manner in which they often talk of them, are striking and general characteristics. It is not at all uncommon to hear them refer to conversations which they allege, and apparently believe themselves to have had with Christ, the apostles, or the prophets of old, or to account for some of their actions by attributing them to the direct influence of the Holy Spirit, or of the devil. It seems to me that this state of mind is fraught with more danger to their masters than any to which they could possibly have been brought by general and systematic education, and by the unrestricted study of the Bible, even though this involved what is so much dreaded, but which is, I suspect, an inevitable accompaniment of moral elevation, the birth of an ambition to look out for themselves. Grossly ignorant and degraded in mind, with a crude, undefined, and incomplete system of theology and ethics, credulous and excitable, intensely superstitious and fanatical, what better field could a cunning monomaniac or a sagacious zealot desire in which to set on foot an appalling crusade?

The African races, compared with the white, at least with the Teutonic, have greater vanity or love of approbation, a stronger dramatic and demonstrative character, more excitability, less exact or analytic minds, and a nature more sensuous, though (perhaps from want of cultivation) less refined. They take a real pleasure, for instance, such as it is a rare thing for a white man to be able to feel, in bright and strongly contrasting colours, and in music, in which nearly all are proficient to some extent. They are far less adapted for steady, uninterrupted labour than we are, but excel us in feats demanding agility and tempestuous energy. A Mississippi steamboat manned by negro deck-hands will wood up a third quicker

than one manned by the same number of whites; but white labourers of equal intelligence and under equal stimulus will cut
twice as much wood, split twice as many rails, and hoe a third more
corn in a day than negroes. On many plantations, religious exercises
are almost the only habitual recreation not purely sensual, from
steady dull labour, in which the negroes are permitted to indulge,
and generally all other forms of mental enjoyment are discouraged.
Religious exercises are rarely forbidden, and a greater freedom to
individual impulse and talent is allowed while engaged in them
than is ever tolerated in conducting mere amusements or educational exercises.

Naturally and necessarily all that part of the negro's nature which
is otherwise suppressed, bursts out with an intensity and vehe-
mence almost terrible to witness, in forms of religious worship and
communion; and a "profession" of piety which it is necessary to
make before one can take a very noticeable part in the customary
social exercises, is almost universal, except on plantations where
the ordinary tumultuous religious meetings are discouraged, or in
towns where other recreations are open to the slaves.[6]

Upon the value of the statistics of "coloured church member-
ship," which are often used as evidence that the evils of slavery are
fully compensated by its influence in Christianizing the slaves, some
light is thrown by the following letter from the white pastor of a
town church in that part of the South in which the whites are most
numerous, and in which the negroes enjoy the most privileges.

To the Editor of the Richmond (Virginia) Religious Herald.

. . . The truth is, the teachings of the pulpit (at least among Baptists)
have nothing to do with the matter. Let me furnish a case in proof. Of

[6] The following newspaper paragraph indicates the wholesale way in which
slaves may be nominally Christianized:—

"REVIVAL AMONG THE SLAVES.—Rev. J. M. C. Breaker, of Beaufort, S.C.,
writes to the *Southern Baptist*, that within the last three months he has baptized by immersion three hundred and fifty persons, *all of them, with a few exceptions, negroes*. These conversions were the result of a revival which has
been in progress during the last six months. On the 12th inst., he baptized two
hundred and twenty-three converts—all blacks but three—and the ceremony,
although performed with due deliberation, occupied only one hour and five
minutes. This is nearly four a minute, and Mr. Breaker considers it a demon-
stration that the three thousand converted on the day of Pentecost could easily
have been baptized by the twelve apostles—each taking two hundred and fifty
—in an hour and thirteen minutes."

two churches which the writer serves, his immediate predecessor was pastor for about twenty-five years. It would be only necessary to give his name, to furnish the strongest and most satisfactory assurance that nothing which ever fell from his lips could be construed into the support of ignorance, superstition, or fanaticism. During the five or six years I have served these churches, whatever may have been my errors and failings (and I am ready to admit that they have been numerous and grievous enough, in all conscience), I know I have never uttered a sentiment which could be tortured into the support of the superstitions prevailing among the coloured people. And yet in both these churches, the coloured members are as superstitious and fanatical as they are elsewhere. Indeed, this was to be expected, for I certainly claim no superiority over my brethren in the ministry, and I am satisfied that many of them are far better qualified than I am to expose error and to root out superstition. This state of things, then, is not due to the teachings of the pulpit. Nor is it the result of private instructions by masters. Indeed, these last have been afforded so sparingly, till within a few years since, they could produce but little effect of any sort. And, besides, those who own servants, and are willing to teach them, are far too intelligent to countenance superstition in any way. I repeat the inquiry, then, Why is it that so many of our coloured members are ignorant, superstitious, and fanatical? It is the effect of instructions received from leading men among themselves, and the churches are responsible for this effect, in so far as they receive into fellowship those who have listened to these instructions, ground their hopes upon them, and guide their lives by them. Whatever we may say against superstition, so long as we receive into our churches those who are its slaves, they will believe that we think them Christians; and naturally relying on our judgment as expressed by their reception, they will live deluded, and die but to be lost.

But some one will say, "We never receive coloured persons when they manifest these superstitions—when they talk of visions, dreams, sounds," etc. This is right as far as it goes. In every such case they should be rejected. But superstition of a fatal character often exists where nothing is said about dreams and visions. It is just as fatally superstitious to trust in prayers and feelings, as in dreams and visions. And this is the sort of superstition which now prevails among the coloured people. They have found that sights and sounds will not answer before the whites, and now (reserving these, perhaps, for some chosen auditory of their own colour), they substitute prayers and feelings. In illustration permit me to record, in no spirit of levity, the stereotyped experience which generally passes current, and, in ninety-nine cases out of a hundred, introduces the coloured candidate into the church. The pastor is informed, by one of the "coloured deacons," that a man wishes to offer to the church with a view to baptism. The fact is announced, a meeting of the church called, and the candidate comes forward.

Pastor.—"Well, John, tell me in a few words, in your own way, your religious experience. What have been your feelings, and what are your present hopes and purposes?"

John.—"I see other people trying, and so I thought I would try too, as I had a soul to save. So I went to pray, and the more I pray the wus I felt; so I kept on praying, and the more I pray the wus I felt. I felt heavy —I felt a weight—and I kept on praying till at last I felt light—I felt easy—I felt like I loved all Christian people—I felt like I loved everybody."

Now this is positively the whole of the experience which is generally related by coloured candidates for baptism. There may be a slight variation of expression now and then, but the sense is almost invariably the same. On this experience, hundreds have been received into the churches —I have received many upon it myself. I am somewhat curious to know how many of the seventy, baptized by my good brother Bagby, told this tale. I'll warrant not less than fifty. Have any of us been right in receiving persons on such a relation as this? In the whole of it, there is not one word of gospel, not one word about sorrow for sin, not one word about faith, not one word about Christ. I know that all these things are subsequently brought out by questions; and were this not the case, I have no idea that the candidate would be in any instance received. *But that these questions may be understood, they are made necessarily "leading questions,"* such as suggest their answers; and consequently these answers are of comparatively little value. . . . I am aware that, as brother Bagby suggests, private instructions by masters have been too much neglected. *But these can accomplish but little good, so long as they are counteracted by the teachings of leading coloured members, in whose views, after all our efforts, the coloured people will have most confidence.*

Not the smallest suggestion, I observe, in all the long article from which the above is derived, is ventured, that the negroes are capable of education, or that their religious condition would improve if their general enlightenment of mind were not studiously prevented.

"I have often heard the remark made," says the Rev. C. C. Jones, in a treatise on the "Religious Instruction of Slaves," printed at Savannah, Georgia, 1842, "by men whose standing and office in the churches afforded them abundant opportunity for observation, that the more they have had to do with coloured members, the less confidence they have been compelled to place in their Christian professions."

A portion of a letter written for publication by the wife of the pastor of a church in the capital of Alabama, given below, naïvely reveals the degree of enlightenment prevailing among the Christianized Africans at a point where their means of instruction are a thousand times better than they are on an average throughout the country.

Having talked to him seriously, and in the strongest light held up to him the enormity of the crime of forsaking his lawful wife and taking another, Colly replied, most earnestly, and not taking in at all the idea of guilt, but deeply distressed at having offended his master:

"Lor, Massa Harry, what was I to do, sir? She tuk all I could git, and more too, sir, to put on her back; and tellin' de truf, sir, dress herself as no poor man's wife hav' any right to. I 'monstrated wid her, massa, but to no purpose; and den, sir, w'y I jis did all a decent man could do—lef' her, sir, for some oder nigger better off 'an I is."

'Twas no use. Colly could not be aroused to conscientiousness on the subject.

Not one in a thousand, I suppose, of these poor creatures have any conception whatever of the sanctity of marriage; nor can they be made to have; yet, strange to say, they are perfect models of conjugal fidelity and devotion while the temporary bondage lasts. I have known them to walk miles after a hard day's work, not only occasionally, but every night, to see the old woman, and cut her wood for her, etc. But to see the coolness with which they throw off the yoke is diverting in the extreme.

I was accosted one morning in my husband's study by a respectable-looking negro woman, who meekly inquired if Mr. B. was at home.

"No, he is not. Is it anything particular you want?—perhaps I can help you."

"Yes, ma'am; it's partickler business wid himself."

Having good reason to believe it was the old story of a "mountain in labour and brought forth a mouse," I pressed the question, partly to save my better half some of the petty annoyances to which he was almost daily subjected by his sable flock, and partly, I own, to gratify a becoming and laudable curiosity, after all this show of mystery. Behold the answer in plain English, or rather nigger English.

"I came to ask, please ma'am, if I might have another husband."

Just at this crisis the oracle entered, who, having authority by a few spoken words, to join together those whom no man may put asunder, these poor people simply imagine him gifted with equal power to annul the contract with a breath of his mouth.

I was heartily amused to find that this woman was really no widow, as I had supposed, but merely from caprice, or some reason satisfactory to herself, no doubt, took it into her head to drop her present spouse and look out for another. The matter was referred to the "Quarterly Conference," where an amusing scene occurred, which resulted in the discomfiture of the disconsolate petitioner, who returned to her home rather crest-fallen.

These Quarterly Conference debates, for flights of oratory, and superlativeness of diction, beggar all description. Be it understood, that negroes, as a class, have more "business" to attend to than any other people—that is, provided they can thereby get a chance to "speak 'fore white folks." To make a speech is glory enough for Sambo, if he happen to have the "gift of gab"; and to speak before the preacher is an honour unparalleled. And, by the way, if the preacher have will and wit enough to manage and control the discordant elements of a negro Quarterly Conference, he will be abundantly rewarded with such respect and gratitude as a man seldom may lay claim to. They account him but a very little "lower than the angels"; and their lives, their fortunes, and their sacred honour, are equally his at command. But wo be to the unfortunate pastor who treats them with undue indulgence; they will besiege him daily and hourly with their petty affairs, and their business meetings will be such a monopoly of his time and patience, that but for the farcical character of the same, making them more like dramatic entertainments than sober realities, he would be in despair. Far into the short hours of morning will they speechify and magnify, until nothing but the voice of stern authority, in a tone of command not to be mistaken, can stop the torrent.

An Alabama gentleman whom I questioned with regard to the chastity of the so-called pious slaves, confessed, that four negro women had borne children in his own house, all of them at the time members in good standing of the Baptist church, and none of them calling any man husband. The only negro man in the house was also a church member, and he believed that he was the father of the four children. He said that he did not know of more than one negro woman whom he could suppose to be chaste, yet he knew hosts who were members of churches.[7]

[7] "A small farmer," who "has had control of negroes for thirty years and has been pursuing his present system with them for twenty years," and who "owning but a few slaves is able," as he observes, "to do better by them" than large planters, writing to Mr. De Bow, says: "I have tried faithfully to break up

A Northern clergyman who had been some years in another town in Alabama, where also the means of instruction offered the slaves were unusually good, answered my inquiry, What proportion of the coloured members of the churches in the town had any clear comprehension of the meaning of the articles of faith which they professed? "Certainly not more than one in seven."

The acknowledgment that "the coloured people will, in spite of all our efforts, have more confidence in the views of leading coloured members," made by the writer of the letter taken from the "Religious Herald," has been generally made by all clergymen at the South with whom I have conversed. A clergyman of the Episcopal Church, of very frank and engaging manners, said in my presence that he had been striving for seven years to gain the confidence of the small number of Africans belonging to his congregation, and with extreme humility he had been lately forced to acknowledge that all his apparent success hitherto had been most delusive. When asked how he accounted for it, he at once ascribed it to the negro's habitual distrust of the white race, and in discussing the causes of this distrust he asked how, if he pretended to believe that the Bible was the Word of God, addressed equally to all the human race, he could explain to a negro's satisfaction why he should fear to put it directly into his hands and instruct him to read it and judge for himself of his duty? A planter present, a member of his church, immediately observed that these were dangerous views, and advised him to be cautious in the expression of them. The laws of the country forbade the education of negroes, and the church was, and he trusted always would remain, the bulwark of the laws. The clergyman replied that he had no design to break the laws, but he must say that he considered that the law which withheld the Bible from the negro was unnecessary and papistical in character.[8]

---

immorality. I have not known an oath to be sworn for a long time. I know of no quarrelling, no calling harsh names, and but little stealing. *Habits of amalgamation, I cannot stop.* I can only check it in name. I am willing to be taught, for I have tried everything I know." He has his field-negroes attend his own family prayers on Sunday, prayer meetings at four o'clock Sunday mornings, etc.— De Bow's *Resources,* vol. ii., p. 337.

[8] The "Southern Presbyterian," in reviewing some observations made before a South Carolina Bible Society, in which it had been urged that if slaves were permitted to read the Bible, they would learn from it to be more submissive to

The "Methodist Protestant," a religious newspaper edited by a clergyman, in Maryland, where the slave population is to the free only in the ratio of one to twenty-five, lately printed an account of a slave auction in Java (translated from a Dutch paper), at which the father of a slave family was permitted to purchase his wife and children at a nominal price, owing to the humanity of the spectators. The account concluded as follows:—

It would be difficult to describe the joy experienced by these slaves on hearing the fall of the hammer which thus gave them their liberty; and this joy was further augmented by the presents given them by numbers of the spectators, in order that they might be able to obtain a subsistence till such time as they could procure employment.

These are the acts of a noble generosity that deserves to be remembered, and which, at the same time, testify that the inhabitants of Java begin to abhor the crying injustice of slavery, and are willing to entertain measures for its abolition.

To give currency to such ideas, even in Maryland, would be fatal to what ministers call their "influence," and which they everywhere value at a rather dangerous estimate; accordingly, in the editorial columns prominence is given to the following salve to the outraged sensibilities of the subscribers:

SLAVE AUCTION IN JAVA

A brief article, with this head, appears on the fourth page of our paper this week. It is of a class of articles we *never select*, because they are very often manufactured by paragraphists for a purpose, and are not reliable. It was put in by our printer in place of something we had *marked out*. We did not see this objectionable substitute until the outside form was worked off, and are therefore not responsible for it.[9]

The habitual caution imposed on clergymen and public teachers must, and obviously does have an important secondary effect, similar to that usually attributed by Protestants to papacy, upon the minds of all the people, discountenancing and retarding the free

---

the authority which the State gives the master over them, says that the speaker "seems to be uninformed of the fact that the Scriptures are read in our churches every Sabbath day, and those very passages which inculcate the relative duties of masters and servants in consequence of their textual, *i. e.* legally prescribed connections, are *more frequently read* than any other portions of the Bible."

[9] Organized action for the abolition of slavery in the island of Java has since been authentically reported.

and fearless exercise of the mind upon subjects of a religious or ethical nature, and the necessity of accepting and apologizing for the exceedingly low morality of the nominally religious slaves, together with the familiarity with this immorality which all classes acquire, renders the existence of a very elevated standard of morals among the whites almost an impossibility.[1]

In spite of the constant denunciations by the Southern newspapers, of those who continued to patronize Northern educational institutions, I never conversed with a cultivated Southerner on the effects of slavery, that he did not express a wish or intention to have his own children educated where they should be free from demoralizing association with slaves. That this association is almost inevitably corrupting and dangerous, is very generally (I may say, excepting by the extremest fanatics of South Carolina, universally) admitted. Now, although the children of a few wealthy men may, for a limited period, be preserved from this danger, the children of the million cannot be. Indeed it requires a man of some culture, and knowledge of the rest of the world, to appreciate the danger sufficiently to guard at all diligently against it. If habitual intercourse with a hopelessly low and immoral class is at all bad in its effects on young minds, the people of the South are, as a people, educated subject to this bad influence, and must bear the consequences. In other words, if the slaves must not be elevated, it would seem to be a necessity that the citizens should steadily degenerate.

---

[1] Twice it happened to come to my knowledge that sons of a planter, by whom I was lodged while on this journey—lads of fourteen or sixteen—who were supposed to have slept in the same room with me, really spent the night, till after daybreak, in the negro cabins. A Southern merchant, visiting New York, to whom I expressed the view I had been led to form of the evil of slavery in this way, replied that he thought I over-estimated the evil to boys on the plantations, but that it was impossible to over-estimate it in towns. "I have personal knowledge," he continued, "that there are but two lads, sixteen years old, in our town [a small market town of Alabama], who have not already had occasion to resort to remedies for the penalty of licentiousness." "When on my brother's plantation, just before I came North," said another Southern merchant, on his annual visit to New York, "I was informed that each of his family-servants were suffering from ――――, and I ascertained that each of my brother's children, girls and boys, had been informed of it, and knew how and from whom it had been acquired. The negroes being their familiar companions, I tried to get my brother to send them North with me to school. I told him he might as well have them educated in a brothel at once, as in the way they were growing up."

Change and grow more marked in their peculiarities with every generation, they certainly do, very obviously. "The South" has a traditional reputation for qualities and habits in which I think the Southern people, as a whole, are to-day more deficient than any other nation in the world. The Southern gentleman, as we ordinarily conceive him to be, is as rare a phenomenon in the South at the present day as is the old squire of Geoffrey Crayon in modern England. But it is unnecessary to argue how great must be the influence, upon people of a higher origin, of habitual association with a race systematically kept at the lowest ebb of intellect and morals. It has been elaborately and convincingly described by Mr. Jefferson, from his personal experience and observation of his neighbours. What he testified to be the effect upon the Virginians, in his day, of owning and associating with slaves, is now to be witnessed to a far greater and more deplorable extent throughout the whole South, but most deplorably in districts where the slave population predominates, and where, consequently, the action of slavery has been most unimpeded.[2]

What proportion of the larger cotton plantations are resided upon by their owners, I am unable to estimate with confidence. Of those having cabin accommodations for fifty slaves each, which came under my observation from the road, while I was travelling through

[2] Jefferson fails to enumerate, among the evils of slavery, one of its influences which I am inclined to think as distinct and as baneful to us nationally as any other. How can men retain the most essential quality of true manhood who daily, without remonstrance or interference, see men beaten, whose position renders effective resistance totally impracticable—and not only men, but women, too! Is it not partially the result of this, that self-respect seldom seems to suggest to an angry man at the South that he should use anything like magnanimity? that he should be careful to secure fair play for his opponent in a quarrel? A gentleman of veracity, now living in the South, told me that among his friends he had once numbered two young men, who were themselves intimate friends, till one of them, taking offence at some foolish words uttered by the other, challenged him. A large crowd assembled to see the duel, which took place on a piece of prairie ground. The combatants came armed with rifles, and at the first interchange of shots the challenged man fell disabled by a ball in the thigh. The other, throwing down his rifle, walked toward him, and kneeling by his side, drew a bowie knife, and deliberately butchered him. The crowd of bystanders not only permitted this, but the execrable assassin still lives in the community, has since married, and, as far as my informant could judge, his social position has been rather advanced than otherwise, from thus dealing with his enemy. In what other English—in what other civilized or half-civilized community would such cowardly atrocity have been endured?

the rich cotton district bordering the Mississippi River, I think more than half were unprovided with a habitation which I could suppose to be the ordinary residence of a man of moderate wealth. I should judge that a large majority of all the slaves in this district, were left by their owners to the nearly unlimited government of hireling overseers the greater part of the time. Some of these plantations are owned by capitalists, who reside permanently and constantly in the North or in Europe. Many are owned by wealthy Virginians and Carolinians, who reside on the "show plantations" of those States—country seats, the exhausted soil of which will scarcely produce sufficient to feed and clothe the resident slaves, whose increase is constantly removed to colonize these richer fields of the West.

A still larger number are merely occasional sojourning places of their owners, who naturally enough prefer to live, as soon as they can afford to do so, where the conveniences and luxuries belonging to a highly civilized state of society are more easily obtained than they can ever be in a country of large plantations. It is rare that a plantation of this class can have a dozen intelligent families residing within a day's ride of it. Any society that a planter enjoys on his estate must, therefore, consist in a great degree of permanent guests. Hence the name for hospitality of wealthy planters. A large plantation is necessarily a retreat from general society, and is used by its owner, I am inclined to think, in the majority of cases, in winter, as Berkshire villas and farms are in summer by rich people of New York and Boston. I have never been on a plantation numbering fifty field-hands, the owner of which was accustomed to reside steadily through the year upon it. Still I am aware that there are many such, and possibly it is a minority of them who are regularly absent with their families from their plantations during any considerable part of the year.

The summer visitors to our Northern watering places, and the European tourists, from the South, are, I judge, chiefly of the migratory, wealthy class. Such persons, it is evident, are much less influenced in their character and habits, by association with slaves, than any other at the South.

The number of the very wealthy is, of course, small, yet as the chief part of the wealth of these consists in slaves, no inconsiderable proportion of all the slaves belong to men who deputize their government in a great measure to overseers. It may be computed, from the census of 1850, that about one half the slaves of Louisiana and one third those of Mississippi, belonged to estates of not less than fifty slaves each, and of these, I believe, nine-tenths live on plantations which their owners reside upon, if at all, but transiently.

The number of plantations of this class, and the proportion of those employed upon them to the whole body of negroes in the country, is, as I have said, rapidly increasing. At the present prices of cotton the large grower has such advantages over the small, that the owner of a plantation of fifty slaves, favourably situated, unless he lives very recklessly, will increase in wealth so rapidly and possess such a credit that he may very soon establish or purchase other plantations, so that at his death his children may be provided for without reducing the effective force of negroes on any division of his landed estate. The excessive credit given to such planters by negro dealers and tradesmen renders this the more practicable. The higher the price of cotton the higher is that of negroes, and the higher the price of negroes the less is it in the power of men of small capital to buy them. Large plantations of course pay a much larger per centage on the capital invested in them than smaller ones; indeed the only plausible economical defence of slavery is simply an explanation of the advantages of associated labour, advantages which are possessed equally by large manufacturing establishments in which free labourers are brought together and employed in the most effective manner, and which I can see no sufficient reason for supposing could not be made available for agriculture did not the good results flowing from small holdings, on the whole, counterbalance them. If the present high price of cotton and the present scarcity of labour at the South continue, the cultivation of cotton on small plantations will by-and-by become unusual, for the same reason that hand-loom weaving has become unusual in the farm houses of Massachusetts.

But whatever advantages large plantations have, they accrue only to their owners and to the buyers of cotton; the mass of the white inhabitants are dispersed over a greater surface, discouraged and driven toward barbarism by them, and the blacks upon them, while rapidly degenerating from all that is redeeming in savage-life, are, it is to be feared, gaining little that is valuable of civilization.

In the report of the Grand Jury of Richland District, South Carolina, in 1854, calling for a re-establishment of the African slave trade,[3] it is observed: "As to the morality of this question, it is scarcely necessary for us to allude to it; when the fact is remarked that the plantations of Alabama, Mississippi, Louisiana, and Texas have been and are daily settled by the removal of slaves from the more northern of the Slave States, and that in consequence of their having been raised in a more healthy climate and in most cases trained to pursuits totally different, the mortality even on the best-ordered farms is so great that in many instances the entire income is expended in the purchase of more slaves from the same source in order to replenish and keep up those plantations, while in *every case* the condition of the slave, if his life is spared, is made worse both physically and morally. . . . And if you look at the subject in a religious point of view, the contrast is equally striking, for when you remove a slave from the more northern to the more southern parts of the slaveholding States, you thereby diminish his religious opportunities."

I believe that this statement gives an exaggerated and calumnious report of the general condition of the slaves upon the plantations of the States referred to—containing, as they do, nearly one half of the whole slave population of the South—but I have not been able to resist the conviction that in the districts where cotton is now grown most profitably to the planters, the oppression and deterioration of the negro race is much more lamentable than is generally supposed by those who like myself have been constrained, by other considerations, to accept it as a duty to oppose temperately but determinately the modern policy of the South, of which this is an immediate result. Its effect on the white race, I still consider to be infinitely more deplorable.

[3] Richland District contains seven thousand white, and thirteen thousand slave population. The Report is published in the *Charleston Standard*, October 12th, 1854.

CHAPTER XV

Slavery as a Poor-law System

IN the year 1846 the Secretary of the Treasury of the United States addressed a circular of inquiries to persons engaged in various businesses throughout the country, to obtain information of the national resources. In reply to this circular, forty-eight sugar-planters, of St. Mary's Parish, Louisiana, having compared notes, made the following statement of the usual expenses of a plantation, which might be expected to produce, one year with another, one hundred hogsheads of sugar:—

Household and family expenses	$1,000
Overseer's salary	400
Food and clothing for 15 working hands, at $30	450
Food and clothing for 15 old negroes and children, at $15	225
1½ per cent. on capital invested (which is about $40,000), to keep it in repair	600
	2,675

50 hogsheads sugar, at 4 cents per pound (net proceeds)	$2,000	
25 hogsheads sugar, at 3 cents per pound (net proceeds)	750	
25 hogsheads sugar, at 2 cents per pound (net proceeds)	500	
4,000 gallons of molasses, at 10 cents	400	
		3,650

Leaving a profit of	$975

Another gentleman furnished the following estimate of the expenses of one of the larger class of plantations, working one hundred slaves, and producing, per annum, four to five hundred hogsheads of sugar:—

Overseer	$1,500
Physician's attendance (by contract, $3 a head, of all ages)	300
Yearly repairs to engine, copper work, resetting of sugar kettles, etc., at least	900
Engineer, during grinding season	200

Pork, 50 pounds per day—say, per annum, 90 hogsheads, at $12	$1,080
Hoops	80
Clothing, two full suits per annum, shoes, caps, hats, and 100 blankets, at least $15 per slave	1,500
Mules or horses, and cattle to replace, at least	500
Implements of husbandry, iron, nails, lime, etc., at least	1,000
Factor's commission, 2½ per cent.	500
	$7,560

(It should be noticed that in this estimate the working force is considered as being equal, in first-class hands, to but one-third of the whole number of slaves.)

In the report of an Agricultural Society, the work of one hand, on a well-regulated sugar-estate, is put down as the cultivation of five acres—producing 5,000 pounds of sugar, and 125 gallons of molasses; the former valued on the spot at 5½ cents per pound, and the latter at 18 cents per gallon—together, $297.50. The annual expenses, per hand, including wages paid, horses, mules, and oxen, physician's bills etc., $105. An estate of eighty negroes annually costs $8,330. The items are as follows—Salt meat and spirits, $830; clothing, $1,200; medical attendance and medicines, $400; Indian corn, $1,090 (total for food and drink of negroes, and other live stock, $24 per head of the negroes, per annum. For clothing $15); overseer and sugar-maker's salary, $1,000; taxes $300. The capital invested in 1,200 acres of land, with its stock of slaves, horses, mules, and working oxen, is estimated at $147,200. One-third, or 400 acres, being cultivated annually in cane, it is estimated, will yield 400,000 pounds, at 5½ cents, and 10,000 gallons molasses at 18 cents—together $23,800. Deduct annual expense, as before, $8,330, an apparent profit remains of $15,470 or 10 3-7 per cent. interest on the investment. The crop upon which these estimates were based, has been considered an uncommonly fine one.

These estimates are all made by persons anxious to maintain the necessity of protection to the continued production of sugar in the United States, and who are, therefore, under strong temptation to over-estimate expenditures.

In the first statement, the cost of clothing and boarding a first-rate, hard-working man is stated to be $30 a year. A suit of winter clothing and a pair of trousers for summer, a blanket for bedding, a pair of shoes and a hat, must all at least be included under the head of clothing; and these, however poor, could not certainly cost, altogether, less than $10. For food, then, $20 a year is a large estimate, which is 5½ cents a day. This is for the best hands; light hands are estimated at half this cost. Does the food of a first-rate labourer, anywhere in the free world, cost less? The lowest price paid by agricultural labourers in the Free States of America for board is 21 cents a day, that is, $1.50 a week; the larger part probably pay at least twice as much as this.

On most plantations, I suppose, but by no means on all, the slaves cultivate "patches," and raise poultry for themselves. The produce is nearly always sold to get money to buy tobacco and Sunday finery. But these additions to the usual allowance cannot be said to be provided for them by their masters. The labour expended in this way for themselves does not average half a day a week per slave; and many planters will not allow their slaves to cultivate patches, because it tempts them to reserve for and to expend in the night-work the strength they want employed in their service during the day, and also because the produce thus obtained is made to cover much plundering of their master's crops, and of his live stock.[1] The free labourer also, in addition to his board, nearly always spends something for luxuries—tobacco, fruit, and confections, to say nothing of dress and luxuries and recreations.

The fact is, that ninety-nine in a hundred of our free labourers, from choice and not from necessity—for the same provisions cost more in Louisiana than they do anywhere in the Northern States—live, in respect to food, at least four times as well as the average of the hardest-worked slaves on the Louisiana sugar-plantations. And

---

[1] "Most persons allow their negroes to cultivate a small crop of their own. For a number of reasons the practice is a bad one. It is next to impossible to keep them from working the crop on the Sabbath. They labour at night when they should be at rest. There is no saving more than to give them the same amount; for, like all other animals, the negro is only capable of doing a certain amount of work without injury. To this point he may be worked at his regular task, and any labour beyond this is an injury to both master and slave. They will pilfer to add to what cotton or corn they have made. If they sell the crop and trade for themselves, they are apt to be cheated out of a good portion of their labour. They will have many things in their possession, under colour of purchases, which we know not whether they have obtained honestly."—*Southern Cultivator*.

for two or three months in the year I have elsewhere shown that these are worked with much greater severity than free labourers at the North ever are. For on no farm, and in no factory, or mine, even when double wages are paid for night-work, did I ever hear of men or women working regularly eighteen hours a day. If ever done, it is only when some accident makes it especially desirable for a few days.

I have not compared the comfort of the light hands, in which, besides the aged and children, are evidently included most of the females of the plantation, with that of factory girls and apprentices; but who of those at the North was ever expected to find board at four cents a day, and obliged to save money enough out of such an allowance to provide him or herself with clothing? But that, manifestly and beyond the smallest doubt of error (except in favour of free labour), expresses the condition of the Louisiana slave. Forty-eight of the most worthy planters of the State attest it in an official document, published by order of Congress.

There is no reason for supposing that the slaves are much, if any, better fed elsewhere than in Louisiana. I was expressly told in Virginia that I should find them better fed in Louisiana than anywhere else. In the same Report of Mr. Secretary [Robert J.] Walker, a gentleman in South Carolina testifies that he considers that the "furnishing" (food and clothing) of "full-tasked hands" costs $15 a year.[2]

The United States army is generally recruited from our labouring class, and a well-conditioned and respectable labourer is not very often induced to join it. The following, taken from an advertisement, for recruits, in the *Richmond Enquirer*, shows the food provided.

"*Daily Rations.*—One and a quarter pounds of beef, one and three-sixteenths pounds of bread; and at the rate of eight quarts of beans, eight pounds of sugar, four pounds of coffee, two quarts of salt, four pounds of candles, and four pounds of soap, to every hundred rations."

From an advertisement for slaves to be hired by the year, to work on a canal, in the *Daily Georgian*:

[2] P. W. Fraser, p. 574, Pub. Doc. VI., 1846.

"*Weekly Allowance.*—They will be provided with three and a half pounds of pork or bacon, and ten quarts of gourd seed corn per week, lodged in comfortable shanties, and attended by a skilful physician."

The expense of boarding, clothes, taxes, and so forth, of a male slave, is estimated by Robert C. Hall, a Maryland planter, at $45 per annum; this in a climate but little milder than that of New York, and in a breeding state. By J. D. Messenger, Jerusalem, Virginia: "The usual estimate for an able-bodied labourer—three barrels of corn, and 250 pounds of well-cured bacon, seldom using beef or pork; peas and potatoes substitute about one-third the allowance of bread" (maize). By R. G. Morris, Amherst County, Va.: "Not much beef is used on our estates; bacon, however, is used much more freely, three pounds a week being the usual allowance. The quantity of milk used by slaves is frequently considerable."—*Pat. Office Report*, 1848.

On the most valuable plantation, with one exception, which I visited in the South, no meat was regularly provided for the slaves, but a meal of bacon was given them "occasionally."

Louisiana is the only State in which meat is required, by law, to be furnished the slaves. I believe the required ration is four pounds a week, with a barrel of corn (flour barrel of ears of maize) per month, and salt. (This law is a dead letter, many planters in the State making no regular provision of meat for their force.) In North Carolina the law fixes "a quart of corn per day" as the proper allowance of food for a slave. In no other States does the law define the quantity, but it is required, in general terms, to be sufficient for the health of the slave; and I have no doubt that suffering from want of food is rare. The food is everywhere, however, coarse, crude, and wanting in variety; much more so than that of our prison convicts.

Does argument, that the condition of free-labourers is, on the whole, better than that of slaves, or that simply they are generally better fed, and more comfortably provided, seem to any one to be unnecessary? Many of our newspapers, of the largest circulation, and certainly of great influence among people—probably not very reflective, but certainly not fools—take the contrary for granted, whenever it suits their purpose. The Southern newspapers, so far as I know, do so, without exception. And very few Southern writers, on any subject whatever, can get through a book, or even a business or friendly letter, to be sent North, without, in some form or other, asserting that Northern labourers might well envy the condition of the slaves. A great many Southern gentlemen—gentlemen whom I respect much for their moral character, if not for their faculties of observation—have asserted it so strongly and confidently, as to shut my mouth, and by assuring me that they had personally observed the condition of Northern labourers themselves, and really knew that I was wrong, have for a time half convinced me against my long experience. I have, since my return, received letters to the same effect: I have heard the assertion repeated by several travellers, and even by Northerners, who had resided long in the South: I have heard it publicly repeated in Tammany Hall, and elsewhere, by Northern Democrats: I have seen it in European books and journals: I have, in times past, taken its truth for granted, and repeated it myself. Such is the effect of the continued iteration of falsehood.

Since my return I have made it a subject of careful and extended inquiry. I have received reliable and unprejudiced information in the matter, or have examined personally the food, the wages, and the habits of the labourers in more than one hundred different farmers' families, in every Free State (except California), and in Canada. I have made personal observations and inquiries of the same sort in Great Britain, Germany, France, and Belgium. In Europe, where there are large landed estates, which are rented by lordly proprietors to the peasant farmers, or where land is divided into such small portions that its owners are unable to make use of the best modern labour-saving implements, the condition of the labourer, as respects food, often is as bad as that of the slave often is—never worse than that sometimes is. But in general, even in France, I do not believe it is generally or frequently worse; I believe it is, in the large majority of cases, much better than that of the majority of slaves. And as respects higher things than the necessities of life—in their intellectual, moral, and social condition, with some exceptions on large farms and large estates in England, bad as is that of the mass of European labourers, the man is a brute or a devil who, with my information, would prefer that of the American slave. As to our own labourers, in the Free States, I have already said enough for my present purpose.

But it is time to speak of the extreme cases, of which so much use has been made, in the process of destroying the confidence of the people of the United States in the freedom of trade, as applied to labour.

In the year 1855, the severest winter ever known occurred at New York, in conjunction with unprecedentedly high prices of food and fuel, extraordinary business depression, unparalleled marine disasters, and the failure of establishments employing large numbers of men and women. At the same time, there continued to arrive, daily, from five hundred to one thousand of the poorer class of European peasantry. Many of these came, expecting to find the usual demand and the usual reward for labour, and were quite unprepared to support themselves for any length of time unless they could obtain work and wages. There was consequently great distress.

We all did what we thought we could, or ought, to relieve it; and with such success, that not one single case of actual starvation is known to have occurred in a close compacted population of over a million, of which it was generally reported fifty thousand were out of employment. Those who needed charitable assistance were, in nearly every case, recent foreign immigrants, sickly people, cripples, drunkards, or knaves taking advantage of the public benevolence, to neglect to provide for themselves. Most of those who received assistance would have thrown a slave's ordinary allowance in the face of the giver, as an insult; and this often occurred with more palatable and suitable provisions. Hundreds and hundreds, to my personal knowledge, during the worst of this dreadful season, refused to work for money-wages that would have purchased them ten times the slave's ordinary allowance of the slave's ordinary food. In repeated instances, men who represented themselves to be suffering for food refused to work for a dollar a day. A labourer, employed by a neighbour of mine, on wages and board, refused to work unless he was better fed. "What's the matter," said my neighbour; "don't you have enough?" "Enough; yes, such as it is." "You have good meat, good bread, and a variety of vegetables; what do you want else?" "Why, I want pies and puddings, too, to be sure." Another labourer left another neighbour of mine, because, as he alleged, he never had any meat offered him except beef and pork; he "didn't see why he shouldn't have chickens."

And these men went to New York, and joined themselves to that army on which our Southern friends exercise their pity—of labourers out of work—of men who are supposed to envy the condition of the slave, because the "slave never dies for want of food." [3]

In the depth of winter, a trustworthy man wrote us from Indiana:—

Here, at Rensselaer, a good mechanic, a joiner or shoemaker, for instance—and numbers are needed here—may obtain for his labour in one week:

2 bushels of corn	25 pounds of pork
1 bushel of wheat	1 good turkey
5 pounds of sugar	3 pounds of butter
½ pound of tea	1 pound of coffee
10 pounds of beef	1 bushel of potatoes

and have a couple of dollars left in his pocket, to start with the next Monday morning.

The moment the ice thawed in the spring, the demand for mechanics exceeded the supply, and the workmen had the master-hand of the capitalists. In June, the following rates were willingly paid to the different classes of workmen—some of the trades being on strike for higher:—

	Dollars per Week		Dollars per Week
Boiler-maker	12 to 20	Cigar-maker	9 to 25
Blacksmith	12 to 20	Car-driver (city cars) ..	10
Baker	9 to 14	Car-conductor " ..	10½
Barber	7 to 10	Engineer, common ..	12 to 15
Bricklayer	14 to 15	Engineer, locomotive ..	15
Boat-builder	15	Harness-maker	10
Cooper	8 to 12	Mason	10 to 15
Carpenter (house) ..	15	Omnibus-driver	10
Confectioner	8 to 12	Printer	10 to 25

[3] Among the thousands of applicants for soup, and bread, and fuel, as charity, I never saw, during "the famine" in New York, one negro. Five Points Pease said to me, "The negro seems to be more provident than the Celt. The poor blacks always manage to keep themselves more decent and comfortable than the poor whites. They very rarely complain, or ask for charity; and I have often found them sharing their food with white people, who were too poor to provide for themselves." A great deal of falsehood is circulated and accredited about the sufferings of the free negroes at the North. Their condition is bad enough, but no worse than that of any men educated and treated as they are, must be; and it is, on an average, far better than that of the slave.

	Dollars per Week		Dollars per Week
Plumber	15	Ship-fastener	18
Painter (house)	15	Shoemaker	16
Pianoforte maker ..	10 to 14	Sign painter	25 to 30
Shipwright	18	Sail-maker	15
Ship-caulker	18	Tailor	8 to 17

At this time I engaged a gardener, who had been boarding for a month or two in New York, and paying for his board and lodging $3 a week. I saw him at the dinner-table of his boarding house, and I knew that the table was better supplied with a variety of wholesome food, and was more attractive, than that of the majority of slaveowners with whom I have dined.

Amasa Walker, formerly Secretary of State in Massachusetts, is the authority for the following table, showing the average wages of a common (field-hand) labourer in Boston (where immigrants are constantly arriving, and where, consequently, there is often a necessity, from their ignorance and accidents, of charity, to provide for able-bodied persons), and the prices of ten different articles of sustenance, at three different periods:—

WAGES OF LABOUR AND FOOD AT BOSTON

	1836. Wages. $1.25 per day	1840. Wages. $1 per day	1843. Wages. $1 per day
	Dollars	Dollars	Dollars
1 barrel flour	9.50	5.50	4.75
25 lbs. sugar, at 9c.	2.25	2.00	1.62
10 gals. molasses, 42½c. ..	4.25	2.70	1.80
100 lbs. pork	4.50	8.50	5.00
14 lbs. coffee, 12½c. ..	1.75	1.50	5.00
28 lbs. rice	1.25	1.00	75
1 bushel corn meal ..	96	65	62
1 do rye meal	1.08	83	73
30 lbs. butter, 22c	6.60	4.80	4.20
20 lbs. cheese, 10c	2.00	1.60	1.40
	44.00	28.98	22.00

This shows that in 1836 it required the labour of thirty-four and a half days to pay for the commodities mentioned; while in 1840 it required only the labour of twenty-nine days, and in 1843 that of only twenty-three and a half days to pay for the same. If we compare the ordinary allowance of food given to slaves per month—as, for instance, sixteen pounds pork, one bushel corn meal, and, say one quart of molasses on an average, and a half pint of salt—with that which it is shown by this table the free labourer is usually able to obtain by a month's labour, we can estimate the comparative general comfort of each.

I am not [at] all disposed to neglect the allegation that there is sometimes great suffering among our free labourers. Our system is by no means perfect; no one thinks it so: no one objects to its imperfections being pointed out. There was no subject so much discussed in New York that winter as the causes, political and social, which rendered us liable to have labourers, under the worst possible combination of circumstances, liable to difficulty in procuring satisfactory food.

But this difficulty, as a serious thing, is a very rare and exceptional one (I speak of the whole of the Free States): that it is so, and that our labourers are ordinarily better fed and clothed than the slaves, is evident from their demands and expectations, when they are deemed to be suffering. When any real suffering does occur, it is mainly a consequence and a punishment of their own carelessness and improvidence, and is in the nature of a remedy.

And in every respect, for the labourer, the competitive system, in its present lawless and uncertain state, is far preferable to the slave system; and any labourer, even if he were a mere sensualist and materialist, would be a fool to wish himself a slave.

One New York newspaper, having a very large circulation at the South, but a still larger at the North, in discussing this matter, last winter, fearlessly and distinctly declared—as if its readers were expected to accept the truth of the assertion at once, and without argument—that the only sufficient prevention of destitution among a labouring class was to be found in slavery; that there was always an abundance of food in the Slave States, and hinted that it might yet be necessary, as a security against famine, to extend slavery over the present Free States. This article is still being copied by the Southern papers, as testimony of an unwilling witness to the benevolence and necessity of the eternal slavery of working people.

The extracts following, from Southern papers, will show what has occurred in the slave country in the meanwhile:

For several weeks past, we have noticed accounts of distress among the poor in some sections of the South, for the want of bread, particularly in Western Georgia, East and Middle Alabama. Over in Coosa, corn-cribs are lifted nightly; and one poor fellow (corn thief) lately got caught between the logs, and killed! It is said there are many grain-hoarders in the destitute regions, awaiting higher prices! The L—d pity the poor, for his brother man will not have any mercy upon his brother.—*Pickens Republican, Carrolton, Ala., June 5, 1855.*

We regret that we are unable to publish the letter of Governor Winston, accompanied by a memorial to him from the citizens of a portion of Randolph county, showing a great destitution of breadstuffs in that section, and calling loudly for relief.

The Claiborne *Southerner* says, also, that great destitution in regard to provisions of all kinds, especially corn, prevails in some portions of Perry county.—*Sunny South, Jacksonville, Ala., May 26, 1855.*

As for wheat, the yield in Talladega, Tallapoosa, Chambers, and Macon, is better even than was anticipated. Flour is still high, but a fortnight will lower the price very materially. We think that wheat is bound to go down to $1.25 to $1.50 per bushel, though a fine article commands now $2.25.

Having escaped famine—as we hope we have—we trust the planting community of Alabama will never again suffer themselves to be brought so closely in view of it. Their want of thrift and foresight has come remarkably near placing the whole country in an awful condition. It is only to a kind Providence that we owe a deliverance from a great calamity, which would have been clearly the result of man's short-sightedness.—*Montgomery Mail, copied in Savannah Georgian, June 25, 1855.*

Wheat crops, however, are coming in good, above an average; but oats are entirely cut off. I am issuing commissary, this week for the county, to distribute some corn bought by the Commissioner's Court, for the destitute of our county; and could you have witnessed the applicants, and heard their stories, for the last few days, I am satisfied you could draw a picture that would excite the sympathy of the most selfish heart. I am free to confess that I had no idea of the destitution that prevails in this county. Why, sir, what do you think of a widow and her children living, for three days and nights, on boiled weeds, called pepper grass?—

yet such, I am credibly informed, has been the case in Chambers County.
—*From a letter to the editor of the Montgomery (Ala.) Journal, from Hon.
Samuel Pearson, Judge of Probate, for Chambers County, Alabama.*

FAMINE IN UPPER GEORGIA.—We have sad news from the north part
of Georgia. The *Dalton Times* says that many people are without corn,
or means to procure any. And, besides, there is none for sale. In some
neighbourhoods, a bushel could not be obtained for love or money. Poor
men are offering to work for a peck of corn a day. If they plead, "Our
children will starve," they are answered, "So will mine, if I part with the
little I have." Horses and mules are turned out into the woods, to wait
for grass, or starve. The consequence is, that those who have land can
only plant what they can with the hoe—they cannot plough. It is seriously
argued that, unless assisted soon, many of the poor class of that section
will perish.—*California Paper.*[4]

No approach to anything like such a state of things as those extracts portray (which extended over parts of three agricultural
States) ever occurred, I am sure, in any rural district of the Free
States. Even in our most thickly-peopled manufacturing districts,
to which the staple articles of food are brought from far-distant regions, assistance from abroad, to sustain the poor, has never been
asked; nor do I believe the poor have ever been reduced, for weeks
together, to a diet of corn. But this famine at the South occurred in
a region where most productive land can be purchased for from
three to seven dollars an acre; where maize and wheat grow kindly;
where cattle, sheep, and hogs may be pastured over thousands of
acres, at no rent; where fuel has no value, and at a season of the
year when clothing or shelter is hardly necessary to comfort.

It is a remarkable fact that this frightful famine, unprecedented
in North America, was scarcely noticed, in the smallest way, by
any of those Southern papers which, in the ordinary course of

[4] In the obscure country papers of Northern Alabama and Georgia, and
Western South Carolina, I have seen many more descriptions, similar to these,
of this famine; but I cannot now lay my hand on them. These I have by accident, not having taken pains to collect them for this purpose. In a district of
the Slave States, where it is boasted that more than a hundred bushels of
maize to the acre has been raised, and where not one out of five hundred
of the people is engaged in any other than agricultural industry, I have myself
bought maize, which had been raised by free labour, in Ohio, at two dollars a
bushel.

things, ever reach the North. In the Charleston, Savannah, and Mobile papers, received at our commercial reading-rooms, I have not been able to find any mention of it at all—a single, short, second-hand paragraph in a market report excepted. But these journals had columns of reports from our papers, and from their private correspondents, as well as pages of comment, on the distress of the labourers in New York City the preceding winter.

In 1837, the year of repudiation in Mississippi, a New Orleans editor describes the effect of the money-pressure upon the planters, as follows:—

They are now left without provisions, and the means of living and using their industry for the present year. In this dilemma, planters, whose crops have been from 100 to 700 bales, find themselves forced to sacrifice many of their slaves, in order to get the common necessaries of life, for the support of themselves and the rest of their negroes. In many places, heavy planters compel their slaves to fish for the means of subsistence, rather than sell them at such ruinous rates. There are, at this moment, thousands of slaves in Mississippi, that know not where the next morsel is to come from. The master must be ruined, to save the wretches from being starved.

Absolute starvation is as rare, probably, in slavery, as in freedom; but I do not believe it is more so. An instance is just recorded in the *New Orleans Delta*. Other papers omit to notice it—as they usually do facts which it may be feared will do discredit to slavery—and even the *Delta*, as will be seen, is anxious that the responsibility of the publication should be fixed upon the coroner:

Iɴǫᴜᴇsᴛ.—Dᴇᴀᴛʜ ꜰʀᴏᴍ ɴᴇɢʟᴇᴄᴛ ᴀɴᴅ sᴛᴀʀᴠᴀᴛɪᴏɴ.—The body of an old negro, named Bob, belonging to Mr. S. B. Davis, was found lying dead in the woods, near Marigny Canal, on the Gentilly Road, yesterday. The coroner held an inquest; and, after hearing the evidence, the jury returned a verdict of "Death from starvation and exposure, through neglect of his master." It appeared from the evidence that the negro was too old to work any more, being nearly seventy; and so they drove him forth into the woods to die. He had been without food for forty-eight hours, when found by Mr. Wilbank, who lives near the place, and who brought him into his premises on a wheelbarrow, gave him something to eat, and endeavoured to revive his failing energies, which had been exhausted from exposure and want of food. Every effort to save his life, however, was unavailing, and he died shortly after being brought to Mr. Wilbank's. The

above statement we publish, as it was furnished us by the coroner.—
Sept. 18, 1855.

This is the truth, then—is it not?—The slaves are generally sufficiently well-fed to be in tolerable working condition; but not as
well as our free labourers generally are: slavery, in practice, affords
no safety against occasional suffering for want of food among
labourers, or even against their starvation, any more than the competitive system; while it withholds all encouragement from the labourer to improve his faculties and his skill; destroys his self-
respect; misdirects and debases his ambition, and withholds all the
natural motives which lead men to endeavour to increase their
capacity of usefulness to their country and the world. To all this,
the *occasional suffering* of the free labourer is favourable, on the
whole. The occasional suffering of the slave has no such advantage.
To deceit, indolence, malevolence, and thievery, it may lead, as
may the suffering—though it is much less likely to—of the free labourer; but to industry, cultivation of skill, perseverance, economy,
and virtuous habits, neither the suffering, nor the dread of it as a
possibility, ever can lead the slave, as it generally does the free
labourer, unless it is by inducing him to run away.

Chapter XVI

Cotton Supply and White Labour in the Cotton Climate

Mr. Russell,[1] although he clearly sees the calamity of the South, fully accepts the cotton planter's opinion, that, after all, the system of slavery is a necessary evil attending upon the great good of cheap cotton. He says (p. 252): "If the climate had admitted of the growing of cotton on the banks of the Ohio, we should have seen that slavery possessed as great advantages over free labour in the raising of this crop as it does in that of tobacco." If this is so, it is important that it should be well understood why it is so as precisely as possible.

In his Notes on Maryland, Mr. Russell (p. 141) says: "Though a slave may, under very favourable circumstances, cultivate twenty acres of wheat and twenty acres of Indian corn, he cannot manage more than two acres of tobacco. The cultivation of tobacco, therefore, admits of the concentration of labour, and thus the superintendence and management of a tobacco plantation will be more perfect and less expensive than a corn one." And this is the only explanation he offers of the supposed advantage of slave labour in the cultivation of tobacco (and of consequence in the cultivation of cotton). The chief expense of raising Indian corn is chargeable to planting and tillage, that of tobacco to the seedbed, the transplanting and nursing of the young plants (which is precisely similar to the same operation with cabbages), the hand-weeding, the hoeing after the plant has "become too large to work without injuring the leaves by the swingle-trees of a horse plough"; [2] "the topping," "the suckering," the selection and removal of valueless leaves, and "the worming," all of them, except hoeing, being operations which can be performed by children and child-bearing women, as they usually are in Virginia.[3]

The chief expense of raising cotton, as of Indian corn, is that of planting and tillage. The principal difference between the method of tillage of cotton and that of Indian corn is occasioned by the

---

[1] "North America, its Agriculture and Climate," by Robert Russell, Kilwhiss, Edinburgh: Adam and Charles Black, 1857.

[2] De Bow's "Resources," vol. iii., p. 342.

[3] See De Bow's "Resources," art. Tobacco.

greater luxuriance of weeds in the Southern climate and the slow growth of the cotton plant in its early stages, which obliges the tillage process to be more carefully and more frequently performed. For this reason, the area of cotton cultivated by each labourer is less than of corn. The area of corn land to a hand is much over-estimated by Mr. Russell. On the other hand, the only mention he makes of the area of cotton land to a hand (being the statement of a negro) would lead to the conclusion that it is often not over three acres, and that five acres is extraordinary. Mr. De Bow says,[4] in an argument to prove that the average production per acre is over-estimated, "In the real cotton region, perhaps the average number of acres per hand is ten."

Mr. Russell observes of worming and leafing tobacco: "These operations can be done as well, and consequently as cheaply, by women and children as by full-grown men." (Page 142.) After reading Mr. Russell's views, I placed myself, through the kindness of Governor [Salmon P.] Chase, in communication with the Ohio Board of Agriculture, from which I have obtained elaborate statistics, together with reports on the subject from twelve Presidents or Secretaries of County Agricultural Societies, as well as from others. These gentlemen generally testify that a certain amount of labour given to corn will be much better repaid than if given to tobacco. "Men are worth too much for growing corn to be employed in strolling through tobacco fields, looking for worms, and even women can, as our farmers think, find something better to do about the house." Children, too, are thought to be, and doubtless are, better employed at school in preparing themselves for more profitable duties, and this is probably the chief reason why coarse tobacco [5] cannot be cultivated with as much profit as corn in Ohio, while the want of intelligent, self-interested labour, is the reason

[4] Vol. i., p. 175, "Resources."

[5] In my Notes on Eastern Virginia, it was mentioned that a tobacco planter informed me that he could not raise the finer sorts of tobacco with profit, because he could not make his slaves take pains enough with it; and in certain localities in Ohio, having a favourable soil for the production of fine or high-priced tobacco, it appears that free labour is engaged more profitably in the cultivation of tobacco than in the cultivation of corn. It is the same in parts of Connecticut and of Massachusetts. Except in these limited districts, however, it is found that the labour of Ohio, as of Connecticut and Massachusetts, is more profitably directed to the cultivation of Indian corn and other crops than of tobacco.

why the corn-field, among the tall broad blades of which a man will work during much of its growth in comparative obscurity, cannot be cultivated with as much profit on soils of the same quality in Virginia as in Ohio. In short, a class of labourers, who are good for nothing else, and who, but for this, would be an intolerable burden upon those who are obliged to support them, can be put to some use in raising tobacco, and, therefore, coarse tobacco continues to be cultivated in some of the principal slaveholding counties of Virginia. But this class of labourers is of no more value in cotton culture than in corn culture. Mr. De Bow says: "The Southwest, the great cotton region, is newly settled, and the number of children, out of all proportion, less than in negroes [regions?] peopled by a natural growth of population.[6] Weak women and children are, in fact, not at all wanted for cotton culture, the cotton planter's inquiry being exclusively for 'prime boys,' or 'A 1 field-hands.'"

Thus in every way cotton culture more resembles corn culture than it does tobacco culture. The production of corn is larger in the aggregate, is considerably larger per man engaged in its cultivation, and is far larger per acre in Ohio than in Virginia.[7] I should, therefore, be inclined to reverse Mr. Russell's statement, and to say that if the climate had admitted of the growing of cotton on both banks

[6] "Resources," vol. i, p. 175.

[7] Virginia, with 10,360,135 acres of improved land, produced, according to the last census returns,

> 35,254,319 bushels of corn,
> 56,803,227 pounds of tobacco.

Ohio, with 9,851,493 acres of improved land, produced

> 59,078,695 bushels of corn,
> 10,454,449 pounds of tobacco.

The aggregate value of these two products alone, at present New York prices, would be

> Ohio $5,127,223,565
> Virginia $3,564,639,385

Actual crops per acre, on the average, as returned by the marshals for 1849–50 ("Census Compilation," p. 178):

	Corn	Tobacco
Ohio . . .	36 bushels . . .	730 pounds
Virginia .	18 "	. . . 630 "

of the Ohio, we should have seen that free-labour possessed as great advantages over slavery in the cultivation of cotton as of corn.

Mr. Russell echoes also the opinion, which every cotton planter is in the habit of urging, that the production of cotton would have been comparatively insignificant in the United States if it had not been for slave labour. He likewise restricts the available cotton region within much narrower limits than are usually given to it, and holds that the slave population must soon in a great measure be concentrated within it. As these conclusions of a scientific traveller unintentionally support a view which has been lately systematically pressed upon manufacturers and merchants both in Great Britain and the Free States, namely, that the perpetuation of slavery in its present form is necessary to the perpetuation of a liberal cotton supply, and also that the limit of production in the United States must be rapidly approaching, and consequently that the tendency of prices must be rapidly upward, the grounds on which they rest should be carefully scrutinized.

Mr. Russell says, in a paragraph succeeding the words just now quoted with regard to the supposed advantages of slave labour in raising tobacco:

The rich upland soils of the cotton region afford a profitable investment for capital, even when cultivated by slaves left to the care of overseers. The natural increase of the slaves, from two to six per cent., goes far to pay the interest of the money invested in them. The richest soils of the uplands are invariably occupied by the largest plantations, and the alluvial lands on the banks of the western rivers are so unhealthy for white labourers that the slaveowners occupy them without competition. Thus the banks of the western rivers are now becoming the great cotton-producing districts. Taking these facts into consideration, it appears that the quantity of cotton which would have been raised without slave labour in the United States would have been comparatively insignificant to the present supply.[8]

The advantages of slave-labour for cotton culture seem from this to have been predicated mainly upon the unwholesomeness to free or white labourers of the best cotton lands, especially of the alluvial lands on the banks of rivers. Reference is made particularly to "the county of Washington, Mississippi State, [which] lies between the

[8] "North America, its Climate," etc., p. 286.

Yazoo and Mississippi rivers. . . . The soil is chiefly alluvial, though a considerable portion is swampy and liable to be flooded." [9]

Mr. Russell evidently considers that it is to this swampy condition, and to stagnant water left by floods, that the supposed insalubrity of this region is to be chiefly attributed. How would he explain, then, the undoubted salubrity of the bottom lands in Louisiana, which are lower than those of the Mississippi, exposed to a more southern sun, more swampy, and which were originally much more frequently flooded, but having been dyked and "leveed," are now inhabited by a white population of several hundred thousand. I will refer to the evidence of an expert:—

"Heat, moisture, animal and vegetable matter, are said to be the elements which produce the diseases of the South, and yet the testimony in proof of the health of the banks of the lower portion of the Mississippi river is too strong to be doubted. Here is a perfectly flat alluvial country, covering several hundred miles, interspersed with interminable lakes, lagunes, and jungles, and still we are informed by Dr. Cartwright, one of the most acute observers of the day, that this country is exempt from miasmatic disorders, and is extremely healthy. His assertion has been confirmed to me by hundreds of witnesses; and we know, from our own observation, that the population presents a robust and healthy appearance." (Statistics are given to prove a greater average length of life for the white race in the South than in the North.)—ESSAY ON THE VALUE OF LIFE IN THE SOUTH, by Dr. J. C. Nott, of Alabama.

To the same effect is the testimony of a far more trustworthy scientific observer, [William] Darby, the surveyor and geographer of Louisiana:—

Between the 9th of July, 1805, to the 7th of May, 1815, incredible as it may appear to many persons, I actually travelled [in Southern Alabama, Mississippi, Louisiana, and, what is now, Texas] twenty thousand miles, mostly on foot. During the whole of this period, I was not confined one month, put all my indispositions together, and not one moment by any malady attributable to climate. I have slept in the open air for weeks together, in the hottest summer nights, and endured this mode of life in the most matted woods, perhaps, in the world. During my survey of the Sabine river, myself, and the men that attended me, existed, for several weeks, on flesh and fish, without bread or salt, and without sickness of

[9] De Bow's "Resources." See "Seaboard Slave States," pp. 463 and 586, for further southern evidence.

any kind. That nine-tenths of the distempers of warm climate may be guarded against, I do not harbour a single doubt.

If climate operates extensively upon the actions of human beings, it is principally their amusements that are regulated by proximity to the tropics. Dancing might be called the principal amusement of both sexes, in Louisiana. Beholding the airy sweep of a Creole dance, the length of time that an assembly will preserve in the sport, at any season of the year, cold or warm, indolence would be the last charge that candour could lodge against such a people.[1]

"Copying from Montesquieu," elsewhere says Mr. Darby, himself a slaveholder, "climate has been called upon to account for stains on the human character, imprinted by the hand of political mistake. No country where Negro Slavery is established but must have parts in the wounds committed on nature and justice."

The unacclimated whites on the sea coast and on the river and bayou banks of the low country, between which and the sea coast there is much inter-communication, unquestionably suffer much from certain epidemic, contagious, and infectious pestilences. This, however, only renders the fact that dense settlements of whites have been firmly established upon them, and that they are remarkably exempt from miasmatic disease, one of more value in evidence of the practicability of white occupation of the upper bottom lands. There are grounds for doubting the common opinion that the negroes at the South suffer less from local causes of disease than whites. (See "Seaboard Slave States," p. 647.) They may be less subject to epidemic and infectious diseases, and yet be more liable to other fatal disorders, due to such influences, than whites. The worst climate for unacclimated whites of any town in the United States is that of Charleston. (This, together with the whole of the

[1] A writer in "Household Words," speaking of the "popular fallacy that a man cannot do a hard day's work in the climate of India," says:—

"I have seen as hard work, real bone and muscle work, done by citizens of the United Kingdom in the East, as was ever achieved in the cold West, and all upon rice and curry—not curry and rice—in which the rice has formed the real meal, and the curry has merely helped to give it a relish, as a sort of substantial Kitchener's zest, or Harvey's sauce. I have seen, likewise, Moormen, Malabars, and others of the Indian labouring classes, perform a day's work that would terrify a London porter, or coal-whipper, or a country navvy, or ploughman; and under the direct rays of a sun that has made a wooden platform too hot to stand on in thin shoes, without literally dancing with pain, as I have done many a day, within six degrees of the line."

rice coast, is clearly exceptional in respect of salubrity for whites.) It happens fortunately that the most trustworthy and complete vital statistics of the South are those of Charleston. Dr. Nott, commenting upon these, says that the average mortality, during six years, has been, of blacks alone, one in forty-four; of whites alone, one in fifty-eight. "This mortality," he adds, "is perhaps not an unfair test, as the population during the last six years has been undisturbed by emigration, and acclimated in greater proportion than at any previous period." If the comparison had been made between native negroes and native or acclimated whites alone, it would doubtless show the climate to be still more unfavourable to negroes.[2]

Upon the very district to which Mr. Russell refers, as offering an extreme case, I quote the testimony of a Mississippi statistician:—

The cotton-planters, deserting the rolling land, are fast pouring in upon the "swamp." Indeed, the impression of the sickliness of the South generally has been rapidly losing ground [*i. e.*, among the whites of the South] for some years back, and that blessing [health] is now sought with as much confidence on the swamp lands of the Yazoo and the Mississippi as among the hills and plains of Carolina and Virginia.—(De Bow's "Resources," vol. ii., p. 43.)

Dr. Barton says:—

In another place I have shown that the direct temperature of the sun is not near so great in the South (during the summer) as it is at the North. I shall recur to this hereafter. In fact, the climate is much more endurable, all the year round, with our refreshing breezes, and particularly in some of the more elevated parts of it, or within one hundred miles of the coast, both in and out of doors, at the South than at the North, which shows most conspicuously the folly of the annual summer migrations, to pursue an imaginary mildness of temperature, which is left at home.

Mr. Russell assumes that slave labour tends, as a matter of course, to the formation of large plantations, and that free labour can only

[2] Dr. [Edward H.] Barton, of New Orleans, in a paper read before the Academy of Science of that city, says: "The class of diseases most fatal in the South are mainly of a '*preventible* nature,' and embraces fevers and intestinal diseases, and depends mostly on conditions under the control of man, as drainage, the removal of forest growth—of personal exposure and private hygiene. The climate further north is too rigid the greater part of the year for personal exposure to the open air, so essential to the enjoyment of health, and when the extremes are great and rapid, another class of maladies predominate—the pulmonary, as well as others arising from crowding, defective ventilation and filth —exacting preventive measures from the public authorities with as much urgency as the worst fevers of the South."

be applied to agricultural operations of a limited scope. Of slaves, he says: "Their numbers admit of that organization and divison of labour which renders slavery so serviceable in the culture of cotton." I find no reason given for this assertion, except that he did not himself see any large agricultural enterprises conducted with free labour, while he did see many plantations of fifty to one hundred slave hands. The explanation, in my judgment, is that the cultivation of the crops generally grown in the Free States has hitherto been most profitable when conducted on the "small holding" system; [3] the cultivation of cotton is, as a general rule, more profitable upon the "large holding" system. [4] Undoubtedly there is a point below which it becomes disadvantageous to reduce the farm in the Free States, and this varies with local circumstances. There is equally a limit beyond which it is acknowledged to be unprofitable to enlarge the body of slaves engaged in cotton cultivation under one head. If cotton were to be cultivated by free labour, it is probable that this number would be somewhat reduced. I have no doubt that the number of men on each plantation, in any case, would, on an average, much nearer approach that which would be most economical, in a free-labour cotton-growing country than in a country on which the whole dependence of each proprietor was on slaves. Is not this conclusion irresistible when we consider that the planter, if he needs an additional slave hand to those he possesses, even if temporarily, for harvesting his crop, must, in most cases, employ at least a thousand dollars of capital to obtain it?

Mr. Russell has himself observed (pp. 266-7) that—

The quantity of cotton which can be produced on a [slave-worked] plantation is limited by the number of hands it can turn into the field during the picking or harvesting of the crop. Like some other agricultural operations, this is a simple one, though it does not admit of being done by machinery, as a certain amount of intelligence must direct the hand.

The same is true of a wheat farm, except that much more can be done by machinery, and consequently the extraordinary demand for

[3] Indian corn has been considered an exception, and there are probably larger corn fields in Indiana than cotton fields in Mississippi.

[4] I believe that plantations or agricultural operations devoted to a single crop are, as a general rule, profitable in proportion to their size in the Free States, unless, indeed, the market is a small one and easily overstocked, which is never the case with the cotton market.

labour at the wheat harvest is much less than it is on a cotton plantation. I have several times been on the Mississippi plantations during picking time, and have seen how everything black, with hands, was then pressed into severe service; but, after all, I have often seen negroes breaking down, in preparation for re-ploughing the ground for the next crop, acres of cotton plants, upon which what appeared to me to be a tolerable crop of wool still hung, because it had been impossible to pick it. I have seen what was confessed to be many hundred dollars' worth of cotton thus wasted on a single Red River plantation. I much doubt if the harvest demand of the principal cotton districts of Mississippi adds five per cent. to their field-hand force. In Ohio, there is a far larger population ordinarily engaged in other pursuits which responds to the harvest demand. A temporary increase of the number of agricultural labourers thus occurs of not less than forty per cent. during the most critical period.

An analogous case is that of the vintage in the wine districts of France. In some of these the "small holding" or *parcellement* system is carried to an unfortunate extreme under the influence of what are, perhaps, injudicious laws. The parcels of land are much smaller, on an average, than the smallest class of farms ordinarily cultivated by free labour in the United States. But can any one suppose that if the slave labour system, as it exists in the United States, prevailed in those districts, that is to say, if the proprietors depended solely on themselves, their families, and their regular servants, as those of Mississippi must, at the picking time, there would not be a disastrous falling off in the commerce of those districts? Substitute the French system, unfortunate as in some respects it is, for the Mississippi system in cotton growing, and who will doubt that the cotton supply of the United States would be greatly increased?

Hop picking and cotton picking are very similar operations. The former is the more laborious, and requires the greater skill. What would the planters of Kent do if they had no one but their regular labourers to call upon at their harvest season?

I observed this advantage of the free labour system exemplified in Western Texas, the cotton fields in the vicinity of the German village of New Braunfels having been picked, when I saw them, far closer than any I had before seen, in fact, perfectly clean, having been undoubtedly gleaned, by the poor emigrants. I was told that some mechanics made more in a day, by going into the field of a slaveowner and picking side by side with his slaves, being paid by measure, than they could earn at their regular work in a week. The degree of intelligence and of practice required to pick to advantage was found to be very slight, less, very much, than in any single operation of wheat harvesters. One woman was pointed out to me who had, in the first year she had ever seen a cotton field, picked more cotton in a day than any slave in the county.

I am reminded, as this page is about to be stereotyped, by observing the letter of a cotton planter in the New Orleans Price Current, of another disadvantage for cotton production, of slave labour, or rather of the system which slavery induces. In my volume on Texas (p. 182), I stated that I was informed by a merchant that the cotton picked by the free labour of the Germans was worth from one to two cents a pound more than that picked by slaves in the same township, by reason of its greater cleanliness. From the letter referred to, I make the following extracts:—

DEAR SIR: . . . There are probably no set of men engaged in any business of life who take as little pains and care to inform themselves with regard to the character and quality of their marketable produce as the cotton-planter. Not one in a thousand knows, nor cares to know, whether the cotton he sends to market is ordinary, good ordinary, or middling. Not one in a hundred spends one hour of each day at his gin in ginning season; never sees the cotton after it is gathered, unless he happens to ride near the scaffold and looks from a distance of a hundred yards, and declares the specimen very white and clean, when, perhaps, it, on the contrary, may be very leafy and dirty. . . .

I have often seen the hands on plantations picking cotton with sacks that would hardly hold stalks, they were so torn and full of holes; these sacks dragging on the ground and gathering up pounds of dirt at every few steps. The baskets, too, were with scarcely any bottoms remaining, having been literally worn out, the cotton lying on the ground. Indeed, some overseers do not forbid the hands emptying their cotton on the ground when their sacks are full, and they some distance from their baskets. When this cotton is taken up, some dirt must necessarily come with it. When gathering in wet weather, the hands get into their baskets with muddy feet, and thus toss in some pounds of dirt, in this way making their task easier. These things are never, or rarely, seen by the proprietor; and, consequently, when his merchant writes him that his cotton is a little dusty, he says how can it be? you are surely mistaken.

Now, sir, for all this there is one simple, plain remedy; let the planter spend his time in ginning season at his gin; let him see every load of cotton as it comes from the field and before it goes through the gin. But, says the man of leisure, the gin is a dirty, dusty place. Yes, sir, and always will be so, until you remedy the evil by staying there yourself. You say your overseer is hired to do this dirty work. *Your overseer is after quantity, sir, and the more extra weight he gets in your cotton, the more bales he will have to brag of having made at the end of the year. Don't trust him at the gin. . . .*

Probably he has a conditional contract with his employer: *gets so many dollars for all he makes over a certain number of bales; thus having every inducement to put up as much leaf and dirt, or, if he is one of the dishonest kind, he may add stones, if they should abound in the neighbourhood.*

Why will not the cotton-planter take pride in his own production? The merchant prides himself on his wares; the mechanic on the work of his hands. All seem to pride themselves on the result of their labour except the cotton-planter. . . .

It cannot be admitted that the absence in the Free States of that organization and division of labour in agriculture which is found on a large slave-worked plantation is a necessity attending the use of free labour. Why should it be any more impossible to employ an army of free labourers in moving the ground with an agricultural design than with the intention of constructing a canal or a road, if it were profitable to so employ the necessary capital? A railroad contractor in one of the best cotton districts of the United States told me that, having begun his work with negroes, he was substituting Irish and German labourers for them as rapidly as possible, with great advantage (and this near midsummer). But if I were convinced with Mr. Russell upon this point, I should still be inclined to think that the advantages which are possessed in a free labour state of society equally by the great hop-planters at picking time and the *petits propriétaires* at vintage, which are also found in our own new States by the wheat farmer, and which are not found under the present system anywhere at the South, for cotton picking, would of themselves be sufficient to turn the scale in favour of the free-labour cotton grower.

The error of the assumption by Mr. Russell, that large gangs of unwilling labourers are essential or important to cotton production in the United States, is, I trust, apparent. And as to the more common and popular opinion, that the necessary labour of cotton tillage is too severe for white men in the cotton-growing climate, I repeat that I do not find the slightest weight of fact to sustain it. The necessary labour and causes of fatigue and vital exhaustion attending any part, or all, of the process of cotton culture does not compare with that of our July harvesting; it is not greater than attends the cultivation of Indian corn in the usual New England method. I have seen a weakly white woman the worse for her labour in the cotton field, but never a white man, and I have seen hundreds of them at work in cotton fields under the most unfavourable circumstances, miserable, dispirited wretches, and of weak muscle, subsisting mainly, as they do, on corn bread. Mr. De Bow estimates one hundred thousand white men now engaged in the cultivation of cotton, being one ninth of the whole cotton force (numerically) of the country.[5] I have just seen a commercial letter from San Antonio, which estimates that the handful of Germans in Western Texas will send ten thousand bales of cotton, the production of their own labour, to market this season. If it should prove to be but half this, it must be considered a liberal contribution to the needed supply of the year, by those who, following Mr. Russell, have considered Western Texas out of the true cotton region, and taking the truth of the common planters' assertion for granted, have thought Africans, working under physical compulsion, the only means of meeting the demand which could be looked to in the future of the United States.

It would not surprise me to learn that the cultivation of cotton by the German settlers in Texas had not, after all, been as profitable as its cultivation by the planters employing slaves in the vicinity. I should attribute the superior profits of the planter, if any there be, however, not to the fitness of the climate for negro labour, and its unfitness for white labour, but to the fact that his expenses for fencing, on account of his larger fields and larger estate, are several hundred per cent. less than those of the farmer; to the fact that his expenses for tillage, having mules and ploughs and other instruments to use at the opportune moment, are less than those of the farmer, who, in many cases, cannot afford to own a single team; to the fact that he has, from experience, a better knowledge of the most successful method of cultivation; to the fact that he has a gin and a press of his own in the midst of his cotton fields, to which he can

[5] Vol. i., p. 175, "Resources."

carry his wool at one transfer from the picking; by which he can put it in order for market expeditiously, and at an expense much below that falling upon the farmer, who must first store his wool, then send it to the planter's gin and press and have it prepared at the planter's convenience, paying, perhaps, exorbitantly therefor; and, finally, to the fact that the planter deals directly with the exporter, while the farmer, the whole profit of whose crop would not pay his expenses in a journey to the coast, must transfer his bale or two to the exporter through two or three middle-men, carrying it one bale at a time, to the local purchaser. Merchants will never give as good prices for small lots as for large. There are reasons for this which I need not now explain. I consider, in short, that the disadvantages of the farmer in growing cotton are of the same nature as I have before explained with those which long ago made firewood of hand-looms, and paupers of those who could be nothing else but hand-loom weavers, in Massachusetts. Exactly how much is gained by the application of labour with the advantage of capital and combination of numbers over its isolated application as directed by individuals without capital in a slaveholding region, I cannot estimate, but no one will doubt that it is considerable. Nevertheless, in all the cotton climate of the United States, if a white farmer has made money without slaves, it will be found that it has been, in most cases, obtained exclusively from the sale of cotton. If cotton is a plant the cultivation of which by free or white labour is especially difficult, how is it that, with the additional embarrassments arising from a lack of capital, his gains are almost exclusively derived from his cotton crop?

But I may be asked, if combination is what is needed to make cotton a source of more general prosperity at the South, why is there no such thing as a joint-stock cotton plantation in Mississippi, as there are joint-stock cotton mills in Massachusetts, the stock in which is in large part owned by those employed in them? I ask, in reply, how is it that the common way of obtaining breadstuffs in Northern Alabama is to sow three pecks of seed wheat on hard stubble ground, plough it under with unbroken bullocks, led with a rope, and a bull-tongue plough, and finally to garner rarely so much as six bushels from an acre? How is it that while in Ohio the spinning-wheel and hand-loom are curiosities, and homespun would be a conspicuous and noticeable material of clothing, half the white population of Mississippi still dress in homespun, and at every second house the wheel and loom are found in operation? The same influences which condemn the majority of free labourers in Alabama to hand-looms, homespun, and three hundred pounds of wheat to the acre, as the limit of production, also condemn them to isolated labour, poor soil, poor tools, bad management, "bad luck," small crops, and small profits in cotton culture.

The following passages from a letter published in the *New York Times* present convincing evidence that it is no peculiarity of the Western Texas climate, but only the exceptional social condition with which its people are favoured, that enables free white labour to be employed in increasing the cotton production of the country. I have ascertained that the author of the letter is known to the editor of the *Times*, and is esteemed a gentleman of veracity and trustworthy judgment.

I am well acquainted with Eastern Mississippi, south of Monroe county, and there are few settlements where my name or face is unknown in the following counties, over the greater part of which I have ridden on horseback, to wit: Lowndes, Oktibbeha, Choctaw, Carroll, Attala, Winston, Noxubee, Kemper, Nashoba, Leake, Scott, Newton, Lauderdale, Clarke, Smith, and Jasper. After four years' travel through these counties, transacting business with great numbers of their inhabitants, stopping at their houses, conversing much with them, and viewing their mode of living, I unhesitatingly answer that white men can and do labour in the cotton field, from Christmas to Christmas following; and that there, as elsewhere, prudence, industry, and energy find their universal reward: success and wealth.

In the counties of Choctaw, Winston, Nashoba, Newton, and Smith, there are very few large plantations; most of those having slaves holding but two or three, while those who own none are in the majority; yet these are all cotton-growing counties, and the staple of their cotton, poor as their lands are, is equal to the average sold in the Mobile market. Where the young farmer is enterprising and go-ahead, his cotton is usually superior. . . .

The rich lands where white labour, even in small numbers, might be profitable, are either in the hands of large planters, or too heavily timbered for a single man. The only thing now preventing any poor white man in the South from gaining a fair competence, and even attaining wealth, is his own laziness, shiftlessness, and ignorance; for the small planters in the counties I have mentioned are deplorably ignorant. . . .

There is one case I remember, which is to the point; the man lives in Choctaw county, and was born in Georgia. He does not own a negro, but has two boys, one sixteen, the other twelve. With the assistance of these boys, and the most imperfect agricultural implements, he made twenty-two bales of cotton, year before last, plenty of corn, and sufficient small grain for himself and family, although the season was more than ordinarily bad in his neighbourhood, while many of his neighbours, with five or six slaves, did not exceed him, and some made even less. He went on to his place without ten dollars in his pocket, gave his notes for eight hundred dollars, payable in one, two, and three years' time, with interest at six per cent. per annum, and the ensuing year he purchased another one hundred and sixty acres for seven hundred and fifty dollars, also on time. This man is, however, far more intelligent and progressive in farming than those about him; he does not plant as did his grandfather, because his father did so, but endeavours to improve, and is willing to try an experiment occasionally.

In my own county, in Alabama, there is a woman whose husband died shortly after the crop was planted, leaving her without a single servant, and no assistance except from a little son of twelve years of age; yet she went into the field, ploughed and picked her cotton, prepared her ground for the coming crop, and raised a second crop thereon.

My conclusion, from the various evidences to which I have referred, must be a widely different one from Mr. Russell's, from that which is generally thought to prevail with our leading capitalists, merchants, and manufacturers, and from that which seems to have been accepted by the Cotton Supply Associations of Liverpool and Manchester. It is this: that there is no physical obstacle in the way of our country's supplying ten bales of cotton where it now does one. All that is necessary for this purpose is to direct to the cotton-producing region an adequate number of labourers, either black or white, or both. No amalgamation, no association on equality, no violent disruption of present relations is necessary. It is not even requisite that both black and white should work in the cotton fields. It is necessary that there should be more objects of industry, more varied enterprises, more general intelligence among the people, and especially that they should become, or should desire to become, richer, more comfortable, than they are.

The simple truth is, that even if we view in the brightest light of Fourth of July patriotism, the character of the whites of the cotton-producing region, and the condition of the slaves, we cannot help seeing that, commercially speaking, they are but in a very small part a civilized people. Undoubtedly a large number of merchants have had, at times, a profitable business in supplying civilized luxuries and conveniences to the South. The same is true of Mexico, of Turkey, of Egypt, and of Russia. Silk, cloth, and calico, shoes, gloves, and gold watches, were sold in some quantity in California, before its golden coffers were forcibly opened ten years ago. The Southern supply to commerce and the Southern demand of commerce is no more what it should be, comparing the resources of the South with those of other lands occupied by an active civilized community, than is that of any half-civilized community, than was that of California. Give the South a people moderately close settled, moderately well-informed, moderately ambitious, and moderately industrious, somewhat approaching that of Ohio, for instance, and what a business it would have! Twenty double-track railroads from the Gulf to the lakes, and twenty lines of ocean steamers, would not sufficiently meet its requirements. Who doubts, let him study the present business of Ohio, and ask upon what, in the natural resources of Ohio, or its position, could, forty years ago, a prediction of its present wealth and business have been made, of its present supply and its present demand have been made, which would compare in value with the commercial resources and advantages of position possessed to-day by any one of the Western cotton States? [6]

[6] Some one can render a service to civilization by publishing precisely what feudal rights, so called, were abolished in large parts of Germany and Hungary in 1848, and what results to the commerce of the districts affected the greater freedom and impulse to industry arising therefrom has had. If I am rightly informed, trade, in many cases, both export and import, has already much more than quadrupled in value, thousands of peasants now demanding numerous articles and being able to pay for them, which before only a few score or hundred proprietors were expected to buy.

CHAPTER XVII

The Condition and Character of the Privileged Classes of the South

SINCE the growth of the cotton demand has doubled the value of slave labour, and with it the pecuniary inducement to prevent negroes from taking care of themselves, hypotheses and easy methods for justifying the everlasting perpetuation of slavery have been multiplied. I have not often conversed with a planter about the condition of the slaves, that he did not soon make it evident, that a number of these were on service in his own mind, naïvely falling back from one to another, if a few inquiries about matters of fact were addressed him without obvious argumentative purpose. The beneficence of slavery is commonly urged by an exposition not only of the diet, and the dwellings, and the jollity, and the devotional eloquence of the negroes, but also by demonstrations of the high mental attainments to which individuals are already found to be arriving. Thus, there is always at hand, some negro mathematician, who is not merely held to be far in advance of the native Africans, but who beats most white men in his quickness and accuracy in calculation, and who is at the same time considered to be so thoroughly trustworthy, that he is constantly employed by his master as an accountant and collecting agent; or some negro whose reputation for ingenuity and skill in the management and repair of engines, sugar-mills, cotton-presses, or other machinery, is so well established that his services are more highly valued, throughout a considerable district, than any white man's; or some negro who really manages his owner's plantation, his agricultural judgment being deferred to, as superior to that of any overseer or planter in the county. Scarcely a plantation did I visit on which some such representative black man was not acknowledged and made a matter of boasting by the owner, who, calling attention perhaps to the expression of intelligence and mien of self-confidence which distinguished his premium specimen, would cheerfully give me a history of the known special circumstances, practically constituting a special mental feeding, by which the phenomenon was to be explained. Yet it might happen that the same planter would presently ask, pointing to the brute-like countenance of a moping field-hand, what good would freedom be to such a creature? And this would be one who had been provided from childhood with food, and shelter, and clothing, with as little consideration of his own therefor as for the air he breathed; who had not been allowed to determine for himself with whom he should associate; with what tools and to what purpose he should labour; who had had no care on account of his children; who had no need to provide for old age; who had never had need to count five-and-twenty; the highest demand upon whose faculties had been to discriminate between cotton and crop-grass, and to strike one with a hoe without hitting the other; to whose intelligence, though living in a civilized land, the pen and the press, the mail and the telegraph, had contributed nothing; who had no schooling as a boy; no higher duty as a man than to pick a given quantity of cotton between dawn and dark; and of whom, under this training and these confinements, it might well be wondered that he was found able to understand and to speak the language of human intelligence any more than a horse.

Again, one would assure me that he had witnessed in his own time an obvious advance in the quality of the slaves generally; they were more active, less stupid, employed a larger and more exact vocabulary, and were less superstitious, obstinate, and perverse in their habits of mind than when he was himself a boy; but I had only to presume that, with this rapid improvement, the negroes would soon be safely allowed to take some step toward freedom, to be assured with much more apparent confidence than before, that in the special quality which originally made the negro a slave, there had been no gain; that indeed it was constantly becoming more evident that he was naturally too deficient in forecasting capacity to be able to learn how to take civilized care of himself.

As a rule, when the beneficence of slavery is argued by Southerners, an advancing intellectual as well as moral condition of the mass of negroes is assumed, and the high attainments of individuals are pointed to as evidence of what is to be expected of the mass, if the system is not disturbed. Suggest that any modification of the system would enlarge its beneficence, however, and an exception to the general rule, as regards the single quality of providence, is at once alleged, and in such a manner, that one cannot but get the impression that, in this quality, the negro is believed to be retrograding as

surely as he is advancing in everything else; and this is one method
by which the unconditional perpetuation of the system, as it is, is
justified. Such a justification must of course involve the supposition
that in the tenth generation of an unremitted training, discipline,
education, and custom in abject dependence upon a voluntary provision by others, for every wish of which the gratification is permitted, *white* men would be able, as a rule, to *gain* in the quality of
providence and capacity for independent self-support.

As to the real state of the case, I find, in my own observation, no
reason for doubting, what must be expected of those interested, that
the general improvement of the slave is usually somewhat over-
rated, and his forecasting ability underrated. Measures intended to
prevent a man from following his natural inclinations often have
the effect of stimulating those inclinations; and I believe that the
system which is designed not merely to relieve the negro from having any care for himself, but, as far as practicable, to forcibly prevent him from taking care of himself, in many particulars to which
he has more or less instinctive inclination, instead of gradually sup-
pressing this inclination, to some extent stimulates it, so that the
Southern negro of to-day, however depraved in his desires, and
however badly instructed, is really a man of more cunning, shrewdness, reticence, and persistence, in what he does undertake for himself, than his father was. The healthful use of these qualities (which
would constitute providence) is, however, in general, successfully
opposed by slavery, and, as far as the slave is concerned, nothing
worse than this can be said of the system.

Admitting that, in this view, slavery is not beneficent, or is no
longer beneficent, or can be but for a time beneficent to the slave,
the present attitude of the South still finds a mode of justification
with many minds, in the broad assertion that the negro is not of the
nature of mankind, therefore cannot be a subject of inhumanity.
This, of course, sweeps the field, if it does anything: thus (from the
Day-Book)—

The wide-spread delusion that Southern institutions are an evil, and
their extension dangerous—the notion so prevalent at the North that there
is a real antagonism, or that the system of the South is hostile to Northern
interests; the weakened union sentiment, and the utter debauchment, the
absolute traitorism of a portion of the Northern people, not only to the
Union, but to Democratic institutions, and to the cause of civilization on

this continent; all these, with the minor and most innumerable mischiefs that this mighty world-wide imposture has engendered or drags in its midst, rest upon the dogma, the single assumption, the sole elementary foundation falsehood, that a negro is a black man.

This bold ground is not as often taken at the South as by desperate bidders for Southern confidence among ourselves. I have heard Christian men, however, when pushed for a justification of the sealing up of the printed Bible, of the legal disregard of marriage, of giving power to rascally traders to forcibly separate families, and so on, refer to it as a hypothesis not at all to be scouted under such circumstances. Yet, as they did so, there stood behind their chairs, slaves, in whose veins ran more Anglo-Saxon blood than of any African race's blood, and among their other slaves, it is probable there were many descendants of Nubians, Moors, Egyptians, and Indians, all interbred with white and true negro tribes, so that it would be doubtful if there remained one single absolutely pure negro, to which animal alone their argument would strictly apply. If the right or expediency of denying the means of preparing themselves for freedom to these beings could even be held to be co-existent with the evident preponderance in them of certain qualities of form, colour, etc., the number of those who are held unjustly or inexpediently in the bonds of a perpetual slavery is already quite large in the South, and is gradually but surely increasing—is increasing much more rapidly than are their means of cultivating habits which are necessary to be cultivated, before the manliest child of white men is capable of enjoying freedom.

There are but two methods of vindicating the habit of depending on the labour of slaves for the development of wealth in the land, which appear to me, on the face of them, entitled to be treated gravely. One of these, assuming the beings held in slavery to be as yet generally incompetent to take care of themselves in a civilized manner, and dangerous to the life as well as to the wealth of the civilized people who hold them in slavery, argues that it is necessary for their humane maintenance, and to prevent them from acquiring an increase of the disposition and strength of mind and will which has always been felt a source of danger to the well-being of their masters, that all the present laws for their mental repression should be rigidly maintained. It is not to be denied, I think, that there is some ground for this assumption. Inasmuch as it is also argued that the same necessity requires that these beings, and with them all these laws, should be carried on to territory now free from them, we are called upon to give a sober consideration to the argument which is based upon it. This I shall do in the last chapter. The other method to which I refer assumes that by having a well-defined class set apart for drudging and servile labour, the remainder of a community may be preserved free from the demeaning habits and traits of character which, it is alleged, servile and menial obligations and the necessity of a constant devotion to labour are sure to fix upon those who are subject to them. Hence a peculiar advantage in morals and in manners is believed to belong to the superior class of a community so divided. I am inclined to think that there is no method of justifying slavery, which is more warmly cherished by those interested to maintain it, than this. I am sure that there is none which planters are more ready to suggest to their guests.[1]

[1] From an *"Address on Climatology,"* before the Academy of Science, by Dr. [Edward H.] Barton, of New Orleans:—"The institution of slavery operates by contrast and comparison; it elevates the tone of the superior, adds to its refinement, allows more time to cultivate the mind, exalts the standard in morals, manners, and intellectual endowments; operates as a safety-valve for the evil disposed, leaving the upper race purer, while it really preserves from degradation, in the scale of civilization, the inferior, which we see is their uniform destiny when left to themselves. The slaves constitute essentially the lowest class, and society is immeasurably benefitted by having this class, which constitutes the offensive fungus—the great cancer of civilized life—a vast burthen and expense to every community, under surveillance and control; and not only so, but under direction as an efficient agent to promote the general welfare and increase the wealth of the community. The history of the world furnishes no institution under similar management, where so much good actually results to the governors and the governed as this in the Southern States of North America."

"It is by the existence of slavery, exempting so large a portion of our citizens from labour, that we have leisure for intellectual pursuits."—*Governor* [*James H.*] *Hammond in South. Literary Mess.*

"Would you do a benefit to the horse or the ox, by giving him a cultivated understanding, or fine feelings? So far as the *mere labourer* has the pride, the knowledge, or the aspirations of a free man, he is unfitted for his situation, and must doubly feel its infelicity. If there are sordid, servile, and laborious offices to be performed, is it not better that there should be sordid, servile, and laborious beings to perform them?"—*Chancellor* [*William*] *Harper; Address to South Carolina Institute.*

"The relations between the North and the South are very analogous to those which subsisted between Greece and the Roman Empire, after the subjugation of Achaia by the Consul Mummius. The dignity and energy of the Roman character, conspicuous in war and in politics, were not easily tamed and adjusted to the arts of industry and literature. The degenerate and pliant Greeks,

No sensible man among us shuts his eyes to the ignorance, mean-ness, vice, and misery which accompanies our general prosperity; no class of statesmen, no politicians or demagogues, no writers deny or ignore it. It is canvassed, published, studied, struggled with, by all honest men, and this not in our closets alone, but in our churches, our legislatures, our colleges, our newspapers, our families. We are constantly urging, constantly using means for discovering it and setting it forth plainly. We commission able men to make a business of bringing it to the light, and we publish the statistics which their labours supply as legislative documents to be circulated at the gen-eral expense, in order that our misfortune may be as well known and as exactly comprehended as possible.

From much of all this, which so painfully and anxiously concerns us, we are told that the South is free. We are told that what we be-wail is seen at the South to be the result of a mistaken social system; that the South escapes that result by slavery. We do not deny, we daily acknowledge that there are mistakes in our system; we en-deavour to remedy them; and we not unfrequently have to acknowl-edge that in doing so, we have made some of our bad things worse. Does slavery relieve all? And without compensation? We often find, upon a thorough review, that our expedients, while they have for a time seemed to produce very valuable results, have in fact corrected one evil by creating or enhancing another. We have borrowed from Peter to pay Paul. In this way we find investigation and discussion to be constantly essential to prevent errors and mis-takes from being exaggerated and persevered in unnecessarily. Thus we—our honestly humane part at least—are ever calling for facts, ever publishing, proclaiming, discussing the facts of our evil. It is only those whose selfish interest is thought by themselves to be served by negligence, who resist investigation and publication, who avoid discussion. Thus we come to habitually associate much ac-tivity of discussion, much consideration, much publication with im-provement—often no doubt erroneously—still it is natural and ra-

---

on the contrary, excelled in the handicraft and polite professions. We learn from the vigorous invective of Juvenal, that they were the most useful and capable of servants, whether as pimps or professors of rhetoric. Obsequious, dexterous, and ready, the versatile Greeks monopolized the business of teach-ing, publishing, and manufacturing in the Roman Empire—allowing their mas-ters ample leisure for the service of the State, in the Senate or in the field."— *Richmond Enquirer.*

tional that when we find no discussion of facts, no publication, no consideration, where we find general consideration and general discussion practically prevented by a forcible resistance to publication, we cannot but suspect there is something sadly needing to be made better. And this last we do find to be the case at the South, and with regard to slavery. Why, if their system has such tangible evidence of its advantages within the personal knowledge of any citizen, do they object to its alleged disadvantages being set forth for consideration, and, if it should happen, discussion? True, we may be wrong, we may be mistaken in supposing that this, our constant publication and challenge to discussion is a good thing. Perhaps if we were better, we should talk less, know less of what evil remained to be gradually grown out of. It might be found that the constant consideration of our evil had had a bad effect upon us. But I have not found that the people of the South are inclined to shut their eyes, and close their ears, and bar their imaginations to the same evil. With the misery which prevails among us, Southerners generally appear to be, indeed, more familiar than the most industrious of our home philanthropists. Great as it is, it is really over-estimated at the South—over-estimated in the aggregate at least; for it is perhaps impossible to over-estimate the sufferings of individuals. South of Virginia, an intelligent man or woman is rarely met who does not maintain, with the utmost apparent confidence, that the people who do the work of the North are, on the whole, harder driven, worse fed, and more destitute of comfort than are the slaves at the South, taking an average of both classes; and this I heard assumed by gentlemen, the yearly cost of maintaining whose own slaves, according to their statement to me, would not equal the average monthly expenses of an equal number of the poorest class of labourers I have ever known at the North. I have heard it assumed by planters, who not only did not themselves enjoy, but who never imagined or aspired to a tithe of the comfort to which most journeymen mechanics whom I have known are habituated. I have heard it assumed by gentlemen, nine-tenths of whose neighbours for a hundred miles around them lived in a manner which, if witnessed at the North, would have made them objects of compassion to the majority of our day-labourers.

A gentleman coming up the Mississippi, just after a recent "Southern Commercial Convention" at Memphis, says:

For three days I have been sitting at a table three times a day opposite four of the fire-eaters. . . . It was evident that they were sincere: for they declared to one another the belief that Providence was directing the South to recommence the importation of Africans, that she might lead the world to civilization and Christianity through its dependence upon her soil for cotton. All their conversation was consistent with this. They believed the South the centre of Christianity and the hope of the world, while they had not the slightest doubt that the large majority of the people of the North were much more to be pitied than their own negroes. Exclusive of merchants, manufacturers, lawyers, and politicians, they evidently imagined the whole population of the North to be quite similar to the poor white population of the South. Yet they had travelled in the North, it appeared. I could only conclude that their observation of northern working men had been confined to the Irish operatives of some half-finished western railroad, living in temporary shanties along the route.

I have even found that conservative men, who frankly acknowledged the many bad effects of slavery, and confessed the conviction that the Northern Slave States were ruined by it; men who expressed admiration of Cassius Clay's course, and acknowledged no little sympathy with his views, and who spoke with more contempt of their own fanatics than of the Abolitionists themselves; that such men were inclined to apologize for slavery, and for their own course in acting politically for its extension and perpetuation, by assuming certain social advantages to exist where it prevailed. "There is a higher tone in Southern society than at the North," they would say, "which is, no doubt, due to the greater leisure which slavery secures to us. There is less anxiety for wealth, consequently more honesty. This also leads to the habit of more generous living and of hospitality, which is so characteristic of the South."

I think that there is a type of character resulting in a secondary way from slavery, of which Mr. Clay is himself a noble example, which attracts admiration and affection in a rare manner. I shall explain this secondary action of slavery by-and-by. I have come to the conclusion that whatever may be the good results of slavery in the way I shall then describe, this so constantly asserted, so generally conceded, of inducing a "higher tone" of breeding, and especially of nourishing the virtue of hospitality, is chimerical.

Some reader may at once be inclined to say that the Southerners whom he has met are unquestionably better bred people than are common at the North, and that they state as their experience that they do not find that hospitality, that honesty, that guilelessness of dealing one with another among the people of the North, to which they are accustomed at home. It would remain a question, whether the Southerners whom the reader has met are of a common or an exceptional class; whether it is to slavery, or to some other circumstance, they owe their breeding; whether this other circumstance is dependent on slavery, or whether it may exist (and, if so, whether, when it does exist, it produces the same fruit) quite independently of slavery. It cannot be said that there are no gentlemen and gentlewomen of first water in free countries. A comparison, then, must be a comparison of numbers. I shall, by-and-by, offer the reader some assistance in making a comparison of this kind. And if, as we hear, free-labour society is still an experiment, and one of the results of that experiment is to be found in the low condition of portions of our community, and it is by comparing this result with the condition of the whites of the South that we must judge of the success of the experiment; it may again be a question of numbers. As to experience of hospitality, that is not a question of quantity or of quality merely. I should wish to ask the reader's Southern authorities, "Where and with whom has your experience been, North and South?" And if with a similar class and in similar circumstances, I should wish to ask further, "What do you mean by hospitality?"

I think that the error which prevails in the South, with regard to the general condition of our working people, is much strengthened by the fact, that a different standard of comfort is used by most persons at the South from that known at the North, and that used by Northern writers. People at the South are content and happy with a condition which few accept at the North unless with great complaint, or with expressions of resignation such as are the peculiar property of slaves at the South. If, reader, you had been travelling all day through a country of the highest agricultural capability, settled more than twenty years ago, and toward nightfall should be advised by a considerate stranger to ride five miles further, in order to reach the residence of Mr. Brown, because Mr. Brown, being a well-to-do man, and a right good fellow, had built an uncommonly good house, and got it well furnished, had a score of servants, and being at a distance from neighbours, was always glad to entertain a respectable stranger—after hearing this, as you continued your ride somewhat impatiently in the evening chill, what consolations would your imagination find in the prospect before you? My New England and New York experience would not forbid the hope of a private room, where I could, in the first place, wash off the dust of the road, and make some change of clothing before being admitted to a family apartment. This family room would be curtained and carpeted, and glowing softly with the light of sperm candles or a shaded lamp. When I entered it, I could expect that a couch or an arm-chair, and a fragrant cup of tea, with refined sugar, and wholesome bread of wheaten flour, leavened, would be offered me. I should think it likely that I could then have the snatch of "Tannhäuser" or "Trovatore," which had been running faintly in my head all day, fingered clearly out to my entire satisfaction upon a pianoforte. I should then look with perfect confidence to being able to refer to Shakespeare, or Longfellow, or Dickens, if anything I had seen or thought during the day had haply led me to wish to do so. I should expect, as a matter of course, a clean, sweet bed, where I could sleep alone and undisturbed, until possibly in the morning a jug of hot water should be placed at my door, to aid the removal of a traveller's rigid beard. I should expect to draw a curtain from before a window, to lift the sash without effort, to look into a garden and fill my lungs with fragrant air; and I should be certain when I came down of a royal breakfast. A man of these circumstances in this rich country, he will be asking my opinion of his fruits. A man of his disposition cannot exist in the country without ladies, and ladies cannot exist in the country without flowers; and might I not hope for the refinement which decks even the table with them? and that the breakfast would be a meal as well as a feed—an institution of mental and moral sustenance as well as of palatable nourishment to the body? My horse I need hardly look after, if he be a sound brute;—good stables, litter, oats, hay, and water, grooming, and discretion in their use, will never be wanting in such a man's house in the country.

In what civilized region, after such advice, would such thoughts be preposterous, unless in the Slave States? Not but that such men and such houses, such family and home comforts may be found in the South. I have found them—a dozen of them, delightful homes. But then in a hundred cases where I received such advice, and heard houses and men so described, I did not find one of the things

imagined above, nor anything ranging with them. In my last journey of nearly three months between the Mississippi and the Upper
James River, I saw not only none of those things, received none of
those attentions, but I saw and met nothing of the kind. Nine times
out of ten, at least, after such a promise, I slept in a room with
others, in a bed which stank, supplied with but one sheet, if with
any; I washed with utensils common to the whole household; I
found no garden, no flowers, no fruit, no tea, no cream, no sugar,
no bread (for corn pone—let me assert, in parenthesis, though possibly as tastes differ, a very good thing of its kind for ostriches—is
not bread: neither does even flour, salt, fat, and water, stirred together and warmed, constitute bread); no curtains, no lifting windows (three times out of four absolutely no windows), no couch—
if one reclined in the family room it was on the bare floor—for there
were no carpets or mats. For all that, the house swarmed with vermin. There was no hay, no straw, no oats (but mouldy corn and
leaves of maize), no discretion, no care, no honesty, at the ——
there was no stable, but a log-pen; and besides this, no other out-
house but a smoke-house, a corn-house, and a range of nigger
houses.

In nine-tenths of the houses south of Virginia, in which I was
obliged, making all reasonable endeavour to find the best, to spend
the night, there were none of these things. And most of these had
been recommended to me by disinterested persons on the road as
being better than ordinary—houses where they "sot up for travellers
and had things." From the banks of the Mississippi to the banks of
James, I did not (that I remember) see, except perhaps in one or
two towns, a thermometer, nor a book of Shakespeare, nor a pianoforte or sheet of music; nor the light of a carcel or other good centre-
table or reading-lamp, nor an engraving or copy of any kind, of a
work of art of the slightest merit. I am not speaking of what are
commonly called "poor whites"; a large majority of all these houses
were the residences of shareholders, a considerable proportion cotton-planters.

Those who watch the enormous export of cotton from the South,
and who are accustomed to reckon up its value, as it goes forward,
million on million, hundred million on hundred million, year after
year, say that it is incomprehensible, if it be not incredible, that
the people of the South are not rich and living in luxury unknown

elsewhere. It is asking too much that such statements as I have made should be received without any explanation. I have found this to be so, and so far as the explanation appears in the attendant social phenomena of the country, I shall endeavour to set it forth, sustaining the accuracy of my report by the evidence of competent Southern witnesses.

William H. Gregg, Esq., a distinguished citizen of Charleston, South Carolina, in a report to the directors of the Graniteville Manufacturing Company of that State, describes at length the condition of the operatives of the company, whom he states to have been drawn originally "from the poor of Edgefield, Barnwell and Lexington districts." These are cotton-growing districts of South Carolina, better supplied than usual with the ordinary advantages of civilized communities. For instance, by reference to the census returns, I find that they are provided with public schools at the rate of one to less than thirty square miles, while within the State, inclusive of its several towns, there is but one public school, on an average, to every forty square miles. There are churches within these districts, one to about seventeen square miles; throughout the State, including Charleston and its other cities, one to every twenty-five square miles. In Georgia the average is one to thirty-two square miles. With the condition of the newer cotton States, in these respects, that of Edgefield, Barnwell, and Lexington, would be found to compare still more favourably for the poor. In Lexington there is even a theological seminary. What, nevertheless, there is not generally available to the people at large, Mr. Gregg indicates by his statement of what advantages they possess who have come to Graniteville.

When they were first brought together, the *seventy-nine* out of a hundred grown girls who could neither read nor write were a by-word around the country; that reproach has long since been removed. We have night, Sunday, and week-day schools. Singing-masters, music-teachers, writing-masters, and itinerant lecturers all find patronage in Graniteville where the people can easily earn all the necessaries of life, and are in the enjoyment of the usual luxuries of country life. . . .

To get a steady supply of workmen, a population must be collected *which will regard themselves as a community;* and two essential elements are necessary to the building up, moral growth, and stability of such a collection of people, namely, a church and a school-house. . . .

I can safely say that it is only necessary to make *comfortable homes* in order to procure families, that will afford labourers of the best kind. A large manufacturing establishment located anywhere in the State, away from a town and in a healthy situation, will soon collect around it a population who, however poor, with proper moral restraints thrown around them, will soon develope all the elements of good society. Self-respect and attachment to the place will soon find their way into the minds of such, while intelligence, morality, and well directed industry, *will not fail to acquire position.*

What the poor people of Edgefield, Barnwell, and Lexington districts needed was, in the first place, to be led "to regard themselves as a community"; for this purpose the nuclei of "a church and a school-house" are declared to be essential, to which must be added, such other stimulants to improvement as "singing and writing schools, itinerant lecturers," etc., etc. In short, the power of obtaining, as the result of their labour, "the necessaries of life," "the usual luxuries of country life," or, in two words, which cover and include church, school, music and lecture, as well as bread, cleanliness, luxuries and necessities, "comfortable homes." It was simply by making possible to them what before had not been possible, the essential conditions of a comfortable civilized home, that Mr. Gregg was enabled in a few years to announce, as he did, that, "from extreme poverty and want, they have become a thrifty, happy, and contented people."

The present system of American slavery, notwithstanding the enormous advantages of wealth which the cotton monopoly is supposed to offer, prevents the people at large from having "comfortable homes," in the sense intended by Mr. Gregg. For nine-tenths of the citizens, comfortable homes, as the words would be understood by the mass of citizens of the North and of England, as well as by Mr. Gregg, are, under present arrangements, out of the question.

Examine almost any rural district of the South, study its history, and this will be as evident as it was to Mr. Gregg in the case of those to which his attention was especially called. These, to be sure, contained, probably, a large proportion of very poor soil. But how is it in a district of entirely rich soil? Suppose it to be of twenty square miles, with a population of six hundred, all told, and with an ordinarily convenient access by river navigation to market. The whole of the available cotton land in this case will probably be owned by three or four men, and on these men the demand for cotton will have had, let us suppose, its full effect. Their tillage land will be comparatively well cultivated. Their houses will be comfortable, their furniture and their food luxurious. They will, moreover, not only have secured the best land on which to apply their labour, but the best brute force, the best tools, and the best machinery for ginning and pressing, all superintended by the best class of overseers. The cotton of each will be shipped at the best season, perhaps all at once, on a boat, or by trains expressly engaged at the lowest rates of freight. It will everywhere receive special attention and care, because it forms together a parcel of great value. The merchants will watch the markets closely to get the best prices for it, and when sold the cash returns to each proprietor will be enormously large. As the expenses of raising and marketing cotton are in inverse ratio to the number of hands employed, planters nearly always immediately reinvest their surplus funds in slaves; and as there is a sufficient number of large capitalists engaged in cotton-growing to make a strong competition for the limited number of slaves which the breeding States can supply, it is evident that the price of a slave will always be as high as the product of his labour, under the best management, on the most valuable land, and with every economical advantage which money can procure, will warrant.

But suppose that there are in the district besides these three or four large planters, their families and their slaves, a certain number of whites who do not own slaves. The fact of their being non-slaveholders is evidence that they are as yet without capital. In this case one of two tendencies must soon be developed. Either being stimulated by the high price of cotton they will grow industrious, will accumulate capital and purchase slaves, and owning slaves will require a larger amount of land upon which to work them than they require for their own labour alone, thus being led to buy out one of the other planters, or to move elsewhere themselves before they have acquired an established improvement of character from their prosperity; or, secondly, they will not purchase slaves, but either expend currently for their own comfort, or hoard the results of their labour. If they hoard they will acquire no increase of comfort or improvement of character on account of the demand. If they spend all their earnings, these will not be sufficient, however profitable their cotton culture may be supposed, to purchase luxuries much superior to those furnished to the slaves of the planters, because the local demand, being limited to some fifty white families, in the whole district of twenty square miles, is not enough to draw luxuries to the neighbourhood, unless they are brought by special order, and at great expense from the nearest shipping port. Nor is it possible for such a small number of whites to maintain a church or a newspaper, nor yet a school, unless it is one established by a planter, or two or three planters, and really of a private and very expensive character.

Suppose, again, another district in which either the land is generally less productive or the market less easy of access than in the last, or that both are the case. The stimulus of the cotton demand is, of course, proportionately lessened. In this case, equally with the last, the richest soils, and those most convenient to the river or the railroad, if there happens to be much choice in this respect, will assuredly be possessed by the largest capitalists, that is, the largest slaveholders, who may nevertheless be men of but moderate wealth and limited information. If so, their standard of comfort will yet be low, and their demand will consequently take effect very slowly in increasing the means of comfort, and rendering facilities for obtaining instruction more accessible to their neighbours. But suppose, notwithstanding the disadvantages of the district in its distance from market, that their sales of cotton, the sole export of the district, are very profitable, and that the demand for cotton is constantly increasing. A similar condition with regard to the chief export of a free labour community would inevitably tend to foster the intelligence and industry of a large number of people. It has this effect with only a very limited number of the inhabitants of a plantation district consisting in large part as they must of slaves. These labourers may be driven to work harder, and may be furnished with better tools for the purpose of increasing the value of cotton which is to be exchanged for the luxuries which the planter is learning to demand for himself, but it is for himself and for his family alone that these luxuries will be demanded. The wages—or means of demanding home comfort—of the workmen are not at all influenced by the cotton demand: the effect, therefore, in enlarging and cheapening the local supply of the means of home comfort will be almost inappreciable, while the impulse generated in the planter's mind is almost wholly directed toward increasing the cotton crop through the labour of his slaves alone. His demand upon the whites of the district is not materially enlarged in any way. The slave population of the district will be increased in number, and its labour more energetically directed, and soon the planters will find the soil they possess growing less productive from their increasing drafts upon it. There is plenty of rich unoccupied land to be had for a dollar an acre a few hundred miles to the West, still it is no trifling matter to move all the stock, human, equine, and bovine, and all the implements and machinery of a large plantation. Hence, at the same time, perhaps, with an importation from Virginia of purchased slaves, there will be an active demand among the slaveholders for all the remaining land in the district on which cotton can be profitably grown. Then sooner or later, and with a rapidity proportionate to the effect of the cotton demand, the white population of the district divides, one part, consisting of a few slaveholders, obtains possession of all the valuable cotton land, and monopolizes for a few white families all the advantages of the cotton demand. A second part removes with its slaves, if it possess any, from the district, while a third continues to occupy the sand hills, or sometimes perhaps takes possession of the exhausted land which has been vacated by the large planters, because they, with all their superior skill and advantages of capital, could not cultivate it longer with profit.[2]

The population of the district, then, will consist of the large landowners and slaveowners, who are now so few in number as to be unnoticeable either as producers or consumers; of their slaves, who are producers but not consumers (to any important extent), and of this forlorn hope of poor whites, who are, in the eyes of the commercial world, neither producers nor consumers. The contemplation from a distance of their condition, is a part of the price

[2] The business committee of the South Carolina State Agricultural Society reported, Aug. 9, 1855:—

"Our old fields are enlarging, our homesteads have been decreasing fearfully in number. . . . We are not only losing some of our most energetic and useful citizens to supply the bone and sinew of other States, but we are losing our slave population, which is the true wealth of the State, our stocks of hogs, horses, mules, and cattle are diminishing in size and decreasing in number, and our purses are strained for the last cent to supply their places from the Northwestern States."

which is paid by those who hold slavery to be justifiable on the ground that it maintains a race of gentlemen. Some occasionally flinch for a moment, in observing it, and vainly urge that something should be done to render it less appalling. Touching their ignorance, for instance, said Governor [W. B.] Seabrook of South Carolina, addressing the Legislature of that State, years ago:—

Education has been provided by the Legislature, but for one class of the citizens of the State, which is the wealthy class. For the middle and poorer classes of society it has done nothing, since no organized system has been adopted for that purpose. You have appropriated seventy-five thousand dollars annually to free schools; but, under the present mode of applying it, that liberality is really the profusion of the prodigal, rather than the judicious generosity which confers real benefit. The few who are educated at public expense in those excellent and truly useful institutions, the Arsenal and Citadel Academies [military schools], form almost the only exception to the truth of this remark. Ten years ago, twenty thousand adults, besides children, were unable to read or write, in South Carolina. Has our free-school system dispelled any of this ignorance? Are there not any reasonable fears to be entertained that the number has increased since that period?

Since then, Governor [J. H.] Adams, in another message to the South Carolina Legislature, vainly urging the appointment of a superintendent of popular education, said:—

Make, at least, this effort, and if it results in nothing—if, in consequence of insurmountable difficulties in our condition, no improvement can be made on the present system, and the poor of the land are hopelessly doomed to ignorance, poverty, and crime—you will, at least, feel conscious of having done your duty, and the public anxiety on the subject will be quieted.

It is not unnatural that there should be some anxiety with at least that portion of the public not accustomed to look at public affairs in the large way of South Carolina legislators, when the travelling agent of a religious tract society can read from his diary in a church in Charleston, such a record as this:—

Visited sixty families, numbering two hundred and twenty-one souls over ten years of age; only twenty-three could read, and seventeen write. Forty-one families destitute of the Bible. Average of their going to church, once in seven years. Several, between thirty and forty-five years old, had heard but one or two sermons in their lives. Some grown-up youths had never heard a sermon or prayer, until my visit, and did not know of such a being as the Saviour; and boys and girls, from ten to fifteen years old, did not know who made them. All of one family rushed away when I knelt to pray, to a neighbour's, begging them to tell what I meant by it. Other families fell on their faces, instead of kneeling.

The following is written by a gentleman, "whose name," says the editor of De Bow's "Review," "has long been illustrious for the services he has rendered to the South."

All of you must be aware of the condition of the class of people I allude to. What progress have they made in the last hundred years, and what is to be their future condition, unless some mode of employment be devised to improve it? A noble race of people! reduced to a condition but little above the wild Indian of the forest, or the European gipsy, without education, and, in many instances, unable to procure the food necessary to develop the natural man. They seem to be the only class of people in our State who are not disposed to emigrate to other countries, while our wealthy and intelligent citizens are leaving us by scores, taking with them the treasures which have been accumulated by mercantile thrift, as well as by the growth of cotton and the consequent exhaustion of the soil.[3]

Says Governor Hammond, also of South Carolina, in an address before the South Carolina Institute:—

According to the best calculations which, in the absence of statistic facts, can be made, it is believed that, of the 300,000 *white* inhabitants of South Carolina, there are not less than 50,000, whose industry, such as it is, and compensated as it is, is not, in the present condition of things, and does not promise, hereafter, to be, adequate to procure them, honestly, such a support as every white person in this country is and feels himself entitled to.

Some cannot be said to work at all. They obtain a precarious subsistence by occasional jobs, by hunting, by fishing, sometimes by plundering fields or folds, and, too often, by what is, in its effects, far worse—trading with slaves, and seducing them to plunder for their benefit.

In another part of the same address, Governor Hammond says, that "$18 or, at the most $19, will cover the whole necessary annual cost of a full supply of wholesome and palatable food, pur-

[3] "De Bow's Review," vol. xviii, p. 790.

chased in the market"; meaning, generally, in South Carolina. From a comparison of these two extracts, it will be evident that $19 per annum is high wages for the labour of one-sixth of all the white population of South Carolina—and that one-sixth exclusive of the classes not obliged to labour for their living.

South Carolina affords the fairest example of the tendency of the Southern policy, because it is the oldest cotton State, and because slavery has been longest and most strongly and completely established there. But the same laws are seen in operation leading to the same sure results everywhere. Some carefully compiled statistics of the seaboard district of Georgia will be found in Appendix (D), showing the comparative condition of the people in the rich sea-island counties, and those in their rear, the latter consisting in large proportion of poor or worn-out lands. I recapitulate here the more exact of these statistics:—

Population.—A large majority of the whole white population resides within the barren counties, of which the slave population is less than one-fourteenth that of the aggregate slave population of the whole.

Wealth.—The personal estate of the whites of these upper counties is, on an average, less than one-sixth that of the others.

Education.—As the wealthy are independent of public schools, the means of education are scarcely more available for those who are not rich in one than the other, the school-houses being, on an average, ten and a half miles apart in the less populous, thirteen and three-quarters miles apart in the more populous.

Religion.—It is widely otherwise as to churches. In the planting counties, there is a house of worship for every twenty-nine white families; in the poor white counties, one for every one hundred and sixty-two white families. Notwithstanding the fact, that to accommodate all, the latter should be six times as large, their average value is less than one-tenth that of the others; the one being eight hundred and ninety-eight dollars, the other eighty-nine dollars.

Commerce.—So wholly do the planters, in whose hands is the wealth, depend on their factors for direct supplies from without, the capital invested in trade, in the coast counties, is but thirty-seven and a half cents to each inhabitant, and in the upper counties it is but one dollar and fifty cents. From the remarks on temperance it would seem that the most of this capital must be held in the form of whisky. One "store" in Liberty county, which I myself entered, contained, so far as I could see, nothing but casks, demijohns, decanters, a box of coffee, a case of tobacco, and some powder and lead; and I believe that nine-tenths of the stock in trade referred to in these statistics is of this character. It was mentioned to me by a gentleman who had examined this district with a commercial purpose, that, off the plantations, there was no money in the country— almost literally, no money. The dealings even of the merchants or tradesmen seemed to be entirely by barter. He believed there were many full-grown men who had never seen so much as a dollar in money in their lives.

The following is a graphic sketch by a native Georgian of the present appearance of what was once the most productive cotton land of the State:—

The classic hut occupied a lovely spot, overshadowed by majestic hickories, towering poplars, and strong-armed oaks. The little plain on which it stood was terminated, at the distance of about fifty feet from the door, by the brow of a hill, which descended rather abruptly to a noble spring, that gushed joyously forth from among the roots of a stately beech, at its foot. The stream from this fountain scarcely burst into view, before it hid itself in the dark shade of a field of cane, which overspread the dale through which it flowed, and marked its windings, until it turned from sight, among vine-covered hills, at a distance far beyond that to which the eye could have traced it, without the help of its evergreen belt. A remark of the captain's, as we viewed this lovely country, will give the reader my apology for the minuteness of the foregoing description: "These lands," said he, "will never wear out. Where they lie level, they will be just as good, fifty years hence, as they are now." Forty-two years afterwards, I visited the spot on which he stood when he made the remark. The sun poured his whole strength upon the bald hill which once supported the sequestered school-house; many a deep-washed gully met at a sickly bog, where had gushed the limpid fountain; a dying willow rose from the soil which had nourished the venerable beech; flocks wandered among the dwarf pines, and cropped a scanty meal from the vale where the rich cane had bowed and rustled to every breeze, and all around was barren, dreary, and cheerless.[4]

---

[4] "Georgia Scenes," by the Rev. and Hon. Judge [A. B.] Longstreet, now President of the University of Mississippi. Harper's edition, p. 76.

I will quote from graver authority: [Erasmus D.] Fenner's Southern Medical Reports:—

The native soil of Middle Georgia is a rich argillaceous loam, resting on a firm clay foundation. In some of the richer counties, nearly all the lands have been cut down, and appropriated to tillage; a large maximum of which have been worn out, leaving a desolate picture for the traveller to behold. Decaying tenements, red, old hills, stripped of their native growth and virgin soil, and washed into deep gullies, with here and there patches of Bermuda grass and stunted pine shrubs, struggling for subsistence on what was once one of the richest soils in America.

Let us go on to Alabama, which was admitted as a State of the Union only so long ago as 1818.

In an address before the Chunnenuggee Horticultural Society, by Hon. C. C. Clay, Jr., reported by the author in De Bow's "Review," December, 1855, I find the following passage. I need add not a word to it to show how the political experiment of the Carolinas, and Georgia, is being repeated to the same cursed result in young Alabama. The author, it is fair to say, is devoted to the sustentation of Slavery, and would not, for the world, be suspected of favouring any scheme for arresting this havoc of wealth, further than by chemical science:—

I can show you, with sorrow, in the older portions of Alabama, and in my native county of Madison, the sad memorials of the artless and exhausting culture of cotton. Our small planters, after taking the cream off their lands, unable to restore them by rest, manures, or otherwise, are going further west and south, in search of other virgin lands, which they may and will despoil and impoverish in like manner. *Our wealthier planters, with greater means and no more skill, are buying out their poorer neighbours, extending their plantations, and adding to their slave force. The wealthy few, who are able to live on smaller profits, and to give their blasted fields some rest, are thus pushing off the many, who are merely independent.*

Of the twenty millions of dollars annually realized from the sales of the cotton crop of Alabama, nearly all not expended in supporting the producers is reinvested in land and negroes. Thus the white population has decreased, and the slave increased, almost *pari passu* in several counties of our State. In 1825, Madison county cast about 3,000 votes; now she cannot cast exceeding 2,300. *In traversing that county one will discover numerous farm-houses, once the abode of industrious and intelligent free-*

men, now occupied by slaves, or tenantless, deserted, and dilapidated; he will observe fields, once fertile, now unfenced, abandoned, and covered with those evil harbingers—foxtail and broom-sedge; he will see the moss growing on the mouldering walls of once thrifty villages; and will find "one only master grasps the whole domain" that once furnished happy homes for a dozen white families. Indeed, a country in its infancy, where, fifty years ago, scarce a forest tree had been felled by the axe of the pioneer, is already exhibiting the painful signs of senility and decay, apparent in Virginia and the Carolinas; the freshness of its agricultural glory is gone; the vigour of its youth is extinct, and the spirit of desolation seems brooding over it.

What inducement has capital in railroads or shops or books or tools to move into districts like this, or which are to become like this? Why, rather, I shall be asked, does it not withdraw more completely? Why do not all, who are able, remove from a region so desolate? Why was not its impoverishment more complete, more simultaneous? How is it that any slaveholders yet remain? The "venerable Edmund Ruffin," president of the Virginia State Agricultural Society, shall answer: [5]

The causes are not all in action at once, and in equal progress. The labours of exhausting culture, also, are necessarily suspended as each of the cultivators' fields is successively worn out. And when tillage so ceases, and any space is thus left at rest, nature immediately goes to work to recruit and replace as much as possible of the wasted fertility, until another destroyer, after many years, shall return, again to waste, and in much shorter time than before, the smaller stock of fertility so renewed. Thus the whole territory, so scourged, is not destroyed at one operation. But though these changes and partial recoveries are continually, to some extent counteracting the labours for destruction, still the latter work is in general progress. It may require (as it did in my native region) more than two hundred years, from the first settlement, to reach the lowest degradation. But that final result is not the less certainly to be produced by the continued action of the causes.

As to the extent to which the process is carried, Mr. Gregg says: [6]

I think it would be within bounds to assume that the planting capital withdrawn within that period [the last twenty-five years] would, judiciously applied, have drained every acre of swamp land in South Carolina,

---

[5] Address before the South Carolina Institute.
[6] Fifth Annual Report to Directors of Graniteville Company.

besides resuscitating the old, worn-out land, and doubling the crops—thus more than quadrupling the productive power of the agriculture of the State.

It would be consoling to hope that this planters' capital in the new region to which it is driven were used to better results. Does the average condition of the people of western Louisiana and Texas, as I have exhibited it to the reader in a former chapter, justify such a hope? When we consider the form in which this capital exists, and the change in the mode of its investment which is accomplished when it is transferred from South Carolina, we perceive why it does not.

If we are told that the value of one hundred thousand dollars has been recently transferred from Massachusetts to a certain young township of Illinois, we reasonably infer that the people of this township will be considerably benefited thereby. We think what an excellent saw mill and grist mill, what an assortment of wares, what a good inn, what a good school, what fine breeding stock, what excellent seeds and fruit trees, what superior machinery and implements, they will be able to obtain there now; and we know that some of these or other sources of profit, convenience, and comfort to a neighbourhood, are almost certain to exist in all capital so transferred. In the capital transferred from South Carolina, there is no such virtue—none of consequence. In a hundred thousand dollars of it there will not be found a single mill, nor a waggon load of "store goods"; it will hardly introduce to the neighbourhood whither it goes a single improvement, convenience, or comfort. At least ninety thousand dollars of it will consist in slaves, and if their owners go with them it is hard to see in what respect their real home comfort is greater.

We must admit, it is true, that they are generally better satisfied, else this transfer would not be so unremitting as it is. The motive is the same at the North as at the South, the prospect of a better interest from the capital, and if this did not exist it would not be transferred. Let us suppose that, at starting, the ends of the capitalist are obtained equally in both cases, that a sale of produce is made, bringing in cash twenty thousand dollars; suppose that five thousand dollars of this is used in each case for the home comfort of the owners, and that as much immediate comfort is attainable with it in the one case as in the other. What, then, is done with the fifteen thousand dollars? At the South, it goes to pay for a further transfer of slaves purchased in the East, a trifle also for new tools. At the North, nearly all of it will go to improvement of machinery of some kind, machinery of transfer or trade, if not of manufacture, to the improvement of the productive value of whatever the original capital had been invested in, much of it to the remuneration of talent, which is thus enabled to be employed for the benefit of many people other than these capitalists—for the home comfort of many people. If five thousand dollars purchased no more comfort in the one case than the other, at starting, in a few years it will purchase double as much. For the fifteen thousand dollars which has gone East in the one case to pay for more labour, will, in the other, have procured good roads and cheap transportation of comforts, or shops and machinery, and thus the cheap manufacture of comforts on the spot where they are demanded. But they who sell the reinforcement of slaves, and to whom comes the fifteen thousand dollars, do they have no increase of home comfort? Taking into consideration the gradual destruction of all the elements of home comfort which the rearing and holding of those slaves has occasioned in the district from which they are sold, it may be doubtful if, in the end, they do. Whither, then, does this capital go? The money comes to the country from those who buy cotton, and somebody must have a benefit of it. Who? Every one at the South says, when you ask this, it is the Northern merchant, who, in the end, gets it into his own hands, and it is only him and his whom it benefits. Mr. Gregg apparently believes this. He says, after the sentence last quoted from him, describing the transfer of capital to the West from South Carolina:—

But this is not all. Let us look for a moment at the course of things among our mercantile classes. We shall not have to go much further back than twenty-five years to count up twenty-five millions of capital accumulated in Charleston, and which has left us with its enterprising owners, who have principally located in northern cities. This sum would build factories enough to spin and weave every pound of cotton made in the State, besides making railroads to intersect every portion of the up-country, giving business facilities to the remotest points.

How comes this capital, the return made by the world for the cotton of the South, to be so largely in the hands of Northern men?

The true answer is, that what these get is simply their fair commercial remuneration for the trouble of transporting cotton, transporting money, transporting the total amount of home comfort, little as it is, which the South gets for its cotton, from one part of the country to the other (chiefly cotton to the coast, and goods returned instead of money from the coast to the plantations), and for the enormous risks and advances of capital which are required in dealing with the South. Is this service over paid? If so, why do not the planters transfer capital and energy to it from the plantations? It is not so. Dispersed and costly labour makes the cost of trade or transfer enormous (as it does the cost of cotton producing). It is only when this wealth is transferred to the Free States or to Europe that it gives great results to human comfort and becomes of great value. The South, as a whole, has at present no advantage from cotton, even planters but little. The chief result of the demand for it, as far as they are concerned, is to give a fictitious value to slaves.

Throughout the South-west I found men, who either told me themselves, or of whom it was said by others, that they settled where I found them, ten or fifteen years ago, with scarcely any property beyond half a dozen negroes, who were then indeed heavily in debt, but who were now quite rich men, having from twenty to fifty negroes. Nor is this at all surprising, when it is considered that cotton costs nothing but labour, the value of the land, however rich, being too inconsiderable to be taken into account, and that the price of cotton has doubled in ten years. But in what else besides negroes were these rich men better off than when they called themselves poor? Their real comfort, unless in the sense of security against extreme want, or immunity from the necessity of personal labour to sustain life, could scarcely have been increased in the least. There was, at any rate, the same bacon and corn, the same slough of a waggon channel through the forest, the same bare walls in their dwellings, the same absence of taste and art and literature, the same distance from schools and churches and educated advisers, and—on account of the distance of tolerable mechanics, and the difficulty of moving without destruction, through such a rough country, anything elaborate or finely finished—the same make-shift furniture. There were, to be sure, ploughs and hoes, and gins and presses, and there were scores of very "likely negroes." Whoever sold such

of these negroes as had been bought must have been the richer, it
will be said. But let us see.

The following picture of the condition of Virginia, the great
breeding ground of slaves, is drawn by the last governor of that
State, Henry A. Wise. It was addressed to a Virginia audience, who
testified to its truthfulness.

You have had no commerce, no mining, no manufactures.

You have relied alone on the single power of agriculture—and such
agriculture! Your sedge-patches outshine the sun. Your inattention to
your only source of wealth has scared the very bosom of mother earth.
Instead of having to feed cattle on a thousand hills, you have had to chase
the stump-tailed steer through the sedge-patches to procure a tough beef-
steak.

The present condition of things has existed too long in Virginia. The
landlord has skinned the tenant, and the tenant has skinned the land,
until all have grown poor together. I have heard a story—I will not locate
it here or there—about the condition of the prosperity of our agriculture.
I was told by a gentleman in Washington, not long ago, that he was
travelling in a county not a hundred miles from this place, and overtook
one of our citizens on horseback, with, perhaps, a bag of hay for a saddle,
without stirrups, and the leading line for a bridle, and he said: "Stranger,
whose house is that?" "It is mine," was the reply. They came to another.
"Whose house is that?" "Mine, too, stranger." To a third: "And whose
house is that?" "That's mine, too, stranger; but don't suppose that I'm so
darned poor as to own all the land about here."

But more to the purpose is the following statement of "the venerable Edmund Ruffin," President of the Virginia Agricultural Society.

A gang of slaves on a farm will increase to four times their original
number in thirty or forty years. If a farmer is only able to feed and
maintain his slaves, their increase in value may double the whole of his
capital originally invested in farming before he closes the term of an
ordinary life. But few farms are able to support this increasing expense,
and also furnish the necessary supplies to the family of the owner; whence
very many owners of large estates, in lands and negroes, are throughout
their lives too poor to enjoy the comforts of life, or to incur the expenses
necessary to improve their unprofitable farming. A man so situated may
be said to be a slave to his own slaves. If the owner is industrious and
frugal, he may be able to support the increasing numbers of his slaves,
and to bequeath them undiminished to his children. But the income of

few persons increases as fast as their slaves, and, if not, the consequence must be that some of them will be sold, that the others may be supported, and the sale of more is perhaps afterwards compelled to pay debts incurred in striving to put off that dreaded alternative. The slave at first almost starves his master, and at last is eaten by him—at least, he is exchanged for his value in food.

A large proportion of the negroes sold to these South-western planters, then, had probably been bought by traders at forced sales in the older States, sales forced by merchants who had supplied the previous owners of the negroes, and who had given them credit, not on account of the productive value of their property as then situated, but in view of its cash value for sale, that is, of the value which it would realize when applied to cotton on the new soils of the South-west.

The planters of the South-west are then, in fact, supplying the deficit of Eastern production, taking their pay almost entirely in negroes. The free West fills the deficit of the free Eastern cereal production, but takes its pay in the manufactured goods, the fish, the oil, the butter, and the importations of the free East.

Virginia planters owning twenty to forty slaves, and nominally worth as many thousand dollars, often seem to live generously; but according to Northern standards, I do not think that the comforts and advantages for a rationally happy life, which they possess, compare with those of the average of Northern farmers of half that wealth. When they do, they must be either supplying slaves for the new cotton fields or living on credit—credit based on an anticipation of supplying that market.

Of course it cannot be maintained that no one, while living at the South, is actually richer from the effects of the cotton demand. There are a great many very wealthy men at the South, and of planters, as well as land dealers, negro dealers, and general merchants, but, except in or near those towns which are, practically, colonies of free labour, having constant direct communication and intimate relationship with free countries, the wealth of these more fortunate people secures to them but a small proportion of the advantages which belong to the same nominal wealth anywhere in the Free States, while their number is so small that they must be held of no account at all in estimating the condition of the people, when it is compared with the number of those who are exceedingly destitute, and at whose expense, quite as much as at the expense of their slaves, the wealth of the richer class has been accumulated.

This cannot be rightly deemed extravagant or unjust language. I should not use it if I did not feel satisfied that it was warranted, not only by my own personal observations, but by the testimony of persons whose regard for the pride of the South, whose sympathy with wealthy planters, and whose disposition not to underrate the good results of slavery, if not more sincere than mine, is more certain not to be doubted. I quote, for instance, a single passage from the observations of Mr. [Robert] Russell, an English gentleman, who, travelling with a special view of studying the agricultural condition and prospects of the country, was, nevertheless, so much limited in time that he was obliged to trust in a great degree to the observations of planters for his facts.

In travelling through a fertile district in any of the Southern States, the appearance of things forms a great contrast to that in similar districts in the Free States. During two days' sail on the Alabama river from Mobile to Montgomery, I did not see so many houses standing together in any one spot as could be dignified with the appellation of village: [7] but I may possibly have passed some at night. There were many places where cotton was shipped and provisions were landed, still there were no signs of enterprise to indicate that we were in the heart of a rich cotton region. . . . The planters supply themselves directly through agents in the large towns, and comparatively little of the money drawn for the cotton crop is spent in the Southern States. Many of the planters spend their incomes by travelling with their families in the Northern States or in Europe during the summer, and a large sum is required to pay the hog-raiser in Ohio, the mule-breeder in Kentucky, and, above all, the Northern capitalists who have vast sums of money on mortgage over the estates. *Dr. Cloud, the editor of the Cotton Plant* [Alabama], assured me that, after all these items are paid out of the money received for the whole cotton and sugar crops of the South, there did not remain one-fourth part of it to be spent in the Southern States. Hence, the Slave States soon obtain a comparatively stationary condition, and, further, the progress they make is in proportion to the increase of freemen, whose labour is rend-

[7] Mr. Russell uses the language of England. There are several collections of houses on this river bank, the inhabitants of which would consider it an insult if they should hear such a humble term as "village" applied to their pseudo towns and cities.

ered comparatively unproductive, seeing that the most fertile land is occupied by slaveholders.[8]

I questioned the agent of a large land speculation in Mississippi, a Southerner by birth, with regard to the success of small farmers. In reply he made the following statement, allowing me to take notes of it, understanding they were for publication:—

The majority of our purchasers have been men without capital. To such we usually sell one hundred and sixty acres of land, at from two to three dollars an acre, the agreement being to pay in one, two, and three years, with six per cent. interest. It is very rare that the payments are made when due, and much the largest proportion of this class fail even to pay their interest punctually. Many fail altogether, and quit their farms in about ten years. When crops are generally good, and planters in the same neighbourhood make seven bales to a hand, poor people will not make over two bales, with their whole family. There is ―― ――, in ―― county, for instance. We sold him one hundred and sixty acres of land in 1843. He has a family of good-sized boys—young men now. For ten years he was never able to pay his interest. He sold from two to four bales a year, but he did not get much for it, and after taking out the cost of bagging and rope, and ginning and pressing, he scarcely ever had two hundred dollars a year coming to him, of which he had to pay his store bills, chiefly for coffee and molasses, sometimes a little clothing—some years none at all. They made their own cloth mostly in the house, but bought sheeting sometimes. He has made one payment on the principal, from a sale of hogs. Almost the only poor people who have kept up to their agreement have been some near ――, since the cotton factory was started there. It is wonderful what a difference that has made, though it's but a picayune affair. People who have no negroes in this country generally raise corn enough to bread them through the year, and have hogs enough ranging in the swamps to supply them with bacon. They do not often buy anything except coffee and molasses and tobacco. They are not generally drunkards, but the men will spend all the money they may have and get gloriously drunk once or twice a year, at elections or at court time, when they go to the county town. I think that two bales of cotton a year is as much as is generally made by people who do not own negroes. They are doing well if they net over fifty dollars a year from their labour, besides supplying themselves with corn. A real smart man, who tends his crop well, and who knows how it ought to be managed, can make five bales, almost always. Five bales are worth two hundred and fifty dollars,

[8] "North America; its Agriculture and Climate," pp. 289–90.

but it's very rare that a white man makes that. They have not got the right kind of tools, and they don't know how. Their crops are never half tended. If folks generally tended their crops as some do, there would be more than twice as much cotton raised as there is.

With regard to the enlargement of estates by successful planters, having stated what were my impressions, the same gentleman replied that I was entirely right, and gave an instance, as follows, from his personal knowledge:—

J. B. moved into —— county within my recollection. He has bought out, one after another, and mainly since 1850, more than twenty small landowners, some of them small slaveholders, and they have moved away from the vicinity. I do not know how many negroes he has now, but several hundred, certainly. His surplus must have averaged twenty thousand dollars a year for several years, and, as far as I know, the whole is expended in purchasing negroes or land. He spends no money for anything else in the county, I am sure. It is a common thing to hear a man say, "J. B. has bought up next to me, and I shall have to quit soon." He never gets the land alongside of a man that within two years he does not buy him out. In the last ten years I know of but one exception, and that is a man who has shot two of B.'s niggers who were stealing his corn. This man swears he won't sell at any price, and that he will shoot any of J. B.'s niggers whom he catches coming on his place. B.'s niggers are afraid of him, and let him alone. J. B. will pay more for land than its worth to anybody else, and his negroes are such thieves that nobody can live in comfort on any place adjoining one of his. There are two other men in the county who are constantly buying up the land around there. The white population of the county is diminishing, and the trade of the place [the county town] is not so good as it was ten years ago.

The following is an extract from a letter [in the *New York Times*, June 7, 1861] written by a worthy farmer of Illinois, whose name and address is in my possession [N. C. Meeker, near Cairo], and who is deemed by those who have known him for many years a sound trustworthy man:—

What might be made of this country if the people were free, and the labourer everywhere owned the land, one may speculate upon; and when he sees the homes of Yankees who go thither often with small means, and make old worn-out places blossom and bloom, he begins to suspect that there is something in men as well as in climate.

I now come to speak of the wealth of the people of the South-western

Slave States, and, for fear I may be thought to exaggerate, I here say I will not tell the whole truth. I'll keep some back for another time. Now, men who go through on boats and cars, and stop in cities and large hotels, know nothing to what I do—I who have gone among the people of every class, I who have stayed with them hundreds of nights, Sundays and all, and gone to meetings and frolics, and travelled hours in the woods, where sometimes there was a road, and sometimes not, trying to find a place to stay over night—and, having visited more than a thousand plantations, and slept and eat in I know not how many hovels, and talked with them all, and, if I choose, can talk precisely as they do, and they wouldn't suspect I was born up North—I say, I think I ought to know something about them.

The impression which one gets on going South is the general dilapidation or carelessness which appears, even upon some of the best plantations. The nice white houses so common at the North, even in the remotest agricultural districts, with green blinds, with clean door-yards, and well-kept shrubbery, snug barns, green meadows, and corner schoolhouses, are nowhere seen. The furniture of the houses is of the commonest description; and to make short work with it, I estimate that there are not decent chairs enough in the whole South to give half a set to each family. For there are to-day, and there have been for every day for more than ten years past, more than 30,000 people in Tennessee alone, who have not a foot of land or a bit of work to do. I am speaking of whites, and not of negroes at all. A bushel of corn-meal, a side of bacon, and a little coffee, will be all that a family of this class can ever expect to get beforehand, and it is often they get neither coffee nor bacon. If they have a cow, and she "comes up," they may have milk, but as for butter, some have heard of it, some have seen it, few have eaten it. And the fact is, many, yes, many who own from two to five slaves, are little better off. I stayed with a man who had fifteen slaves and 400 acres of land, where he had lived forty years, and his house was not worth fifty cents; what my fare was you may guess. I have seen hundreds of families living in log cabins, ten or twelve feet square, where the children run around as naked as ever they were born, and a bedstead or chair was not in the house, and never will be. I have seen the children eat wheat and grass, growing in the field. I have seen them eat dirt. I saw children here on my own place, in Southern Illinois, last year, eat dirt, they were so hungry. Southern Illinois has been a city of refuge for the poor people of the Slave States. Folks thought Humboldt told a big story when he gave an account of the clay-eating Indians of South America. Of course where poverty is so general, and where the slaves are few, the slaves cannot fare much worse than their masters. It is generally said by the people of the Slave States that they prefer corn bread, but, place the two kinds before them, and you will see which they like best. No class of people like corn bread, and no people, as a general thing, are worth much who can get nothing else.

For the most part, the people of these regions manufacture all their every-day clothing, and their garments look as though they were made for no other purpose than to keep them warm and to cover their nakedness; beauty of colouring and propriety in fitting are little regarded. Every man who is not rich is a shoemaker. Blacksmith-shops are innumerable, and yet I have sent a boy over eighty miles from shop to shop, and then did not get a horse shod. Men call themselves gunsmiths, but they only stock guns. There are carpenters, and cabinet-makers, and chair-makers, and all this working badly with poor tools. The sum is, there is no real discipline of mind among them, no real ingenuity, no education, no comfortable houses, no good victuals, nor do they know how to cook; and when I go among them, what troubles me most is, they have *no grass, no clover, no hay.*

And yet, as fine and well-disposed men, and as anxious to improve, are to be found in the South-western States as are to be found anywhere. They are as honest as men ever are, and they will treat a stranger the best they know how. The trouble is, the large slaveholders have got all the good land. There can be no schools, and if the son of a poor man rises above his condition there is no earthly chance for him. He can only hope to be a slave-driver, for an office is not his, or he must leave and go to a Free State. *Were there no Free States, the white people of the South would to-day be slaves.*

I will here call upon just one more witness, whose evidence I cite at this point, not merely because, in very few words, having reference to the very heart of the planter's prosperity, it practically endorses all I have said, but for another reason which will presently appear.

First as to the non-slaveholders:—

I am not aware that the relative number of these two classes has ever been ascertained in any of the States, but I am satisfied that the non-slaveholders far outnumber the slaveholders, perhaps by three to one.[9] In the more southern portion of this region ["the South-west," of which Mississippi is the centre], the non-slaveholders possess generally but very small means, and the land which they possess is almost universally poor, and so sterile that a scanty subsistence is all that can be derived from its

---

[9] It was not long since estimated in the Legislature of Kentucky as seven to one in that State.

cultivation, and the more fertile soil, being in the hands of the slave-holders, must ever remain out of the power of those who have none. . . . And I lament to say that I have observed of late years that an evident deterioration is taking place in this part of the population, the younger portion of it being less educated, less industrious, and, in every point of view, less respectable than their ancestors.—J. D. B. DE Bow, *Resources of the South and West*, vol. ii. p. 108.

Again as to the cotton-planters and slaveholders:—

If one unacquainted with the condition of the South-west were told that the cotton-growing district alone had sold the crop for fifty million dollars for the last twenty years he would naturally conclude that this must be the richest community in the world. . . . But what would be his surprise when told that so far from living in palaces, many of these planters dwell in habitations of the most primitive construction, and these so inartificially built as to be incapable of defending the inmates from the winds and rains of heaven. That instead of any artistical improvement, this rude dwelling was surrounded by cotton fields, or probably by fields exhausted, washed into gullies, and abandoned; that instead of canals, the navigable streams remain unimproved, to the great detriment of transportation; that the common roads of the country were scarcely passable; that the edifices erected for the purposes of learning and religion were frequently built of logs and covered [roofed] with boards.—J. D. B. DE Bow, *Resources of the South and West*, vol. ii. pp. 113–14.

Do a majority of Northern working men dwell in habitations having no more elements of comfort, even taking difference of climate into consideration, than Mr. De Bow ascribes to the residences of the slaves' owners? No Northern man can for a moment hold such an opinion. What, then, becomes of the theory by which the planters justify slavery to themselves and recommend it to us? If the ennobling luxuries which the institution of slavery secures to the "superior class," and by which it is supposed to be "qualified for the higher duties of citizenship," are, at the most, sugar, instead of molasses, in its coffee; butter, with its pone; cabbage, with its bacon, and two sheets to its bed—and the traveller who goes where I travelled, month after month, with the same experience, cannot help learning to regard these as luxuries indeed,—if "freedom from sordid and petty cares," and "leisure for intellectual pursuits," means a condition approaching in comfort that of the keeper of a lightship on an outer bar, what is the exact value of such words as "hospitality," "generosity," and "gallantry"? What is to be understood from phrases in such common use as "high toned," "well bred," "generous," "hospitable," and so on, when used in argument to prove the beneficence of slavery and to advocate its extension?

From De Bow's Review, vol. xiii, 113 *et seq.*

Mr. Frederick Law Olmsted, after signalizing himself by two very wordy volumes, abounding in bitterness and prejudice of every sort, and misrepresentations upon the "Seaboard Slave States," finding how profitable such literature is in a pecuniary point of view, and what a run is being made upon it throughout the entire limits of abolitiondom, vouchsafes us now another volume, entitled a "Journey through Texas, or a Saddle-trip on the South-western Frontier." Here, again, the opportunity is too tempting to be resisted to revile and abuse the men and the society whose open hospitality he undoubtedly enjoyed, and whom we have no doubt, like every other of his tribe travelling at the South, he found it convenient at the time to flatter and approve. We have now grown accustomed to this, and it is not at all surprising that here and there it is producing its effect in some violent exhibition of feeling like that displayed by our worthy old friend Dr. Brewer, of Montgomery county, Maryland, who persistently refuses, on all occasions, to allow a Yankee even to cross his fields, or like that of John Randolph, who said in the House, "Mr. Speaker, I would not allow one of my servants to buy as much as a toothorn from one of these people." . . .

Somewhat further on, the parties rest for the night. "For this the charge was $1.25 each person, including breakfast and horse-feed." At the end of every page or two our tourist repeats these growlings over the enormous exactions. It is the refrain from one cover of the book to the other. What a series of martyrdoms. Could such a journey by any possibility be made "to pay"? Perhaps, friend traveller, you have heard of the lavish hospitality of the South, and imagined that people there moved out upon the high road for the sole purpose of sharing the society which gentlemen, like yourself, could furnish, believing every arrival to be an act of special providence! When you offered to pay the woman on Red River, and "feared she was offended by your offering her money for her hospitality," you paid the highest compliment to the South; for heaven knows you would have had no such apprehension on the banks of the Connecticut.

I cannot but be gratified that so much importance should have been attached to my earlier volumes as to induce the Superintendent of the Census to devote to their consideration a leading article in

the first economico-political review of the country; and I can feel
nothing but regret that he should be obliged to attribute to an un-
worthy motive even those of my labours the result of which he
does me the honour to designate as valuable and trustworthy. I
have often had occasion to refer to Mr. De Bow, and, I believe, have
always done so in a manner consistent with the respect which I feel
for the class of men among whom he has had the honourable ambition to rank himself. That a man, while occupying a position which
properly belongs to the most able and just-minded statistician in
the country, should think it proper to write under his own name in
the manner of which the above extracts are a sample, about a work
which assumes to relate calmly and methodically, the result of a
personal study of the condition of the people of a certain State, is a
note-worthy circumstance in illustration of the present political history of our country. I cite them now, however, chiefly to show what
need there is for a discussion upon which I propose to enter, myself,
little further than is necessary to enable me to clearly set forth certain facts in their more important significance, the right of publishing which can hardly be denied me, in view of the insinuations
made by Mr. De Bow, who in this follows what has got to be a
general custom of Southern reviewers and journalists towards travellers with whose expressed judgments upon any matter observed
within the Slave States they differ. There are numerous homes in
the South the memory of which I cherish tenderly. There are numbers of men in the South for whom I have a warm admiration, to
whom I feel grateful, whose respect I wish not to lose. There are
others for whom I have a quite different feeling. Of a single individual of neither class have I spoken in these two volumes, I believe,
by his true name, or in such a manner that he could be recognized,
or his home pointed out by any one who had not been previously
familiar with it and with him, being, as a rule, careful to so far differ from the actual order of the events of my journey in narrating
them, that facts of private life could not be readily localized. From
this rule I do not intend now to depart further than is necessary to
exhibit the whole truth of the facts to which I have referred, but
since the charge of ingratitude and indelicacy is publicly made
against me, as it has frequently been of late against better men on
similar grounds, I propose to examine those grounds in the light of
certain actual experiences of myself and others, and let it be judged

whether there must always exist a peculiar moral obligation upon travellers to be mealy-mouthed as to the habits of the people of the South, either on account of hospitality or in reciprocation of the delicate reserve which, from the tenor of Mr. De Bow's remarks, it might be supposed was habitually exercised in the South with regard to the habits of their own people. These experiences shall be both special and general. What immediately follows is of the former class, but, in the end, it will be found to have a general significance.

On a hot morning in July a Northern traveller left the town of Lynchburg, the chief market-town of Virginia tobacco, and rode eastwardly towards Farmville. Suddenly taken severely ill, and no house being in sight, he turned from the road into the shade of the wood, dismounted, reclined against a sturdy trunk, took an anodyne, which he fortunately had with him, and at length found relief in sleep. Late in the day he awoke, somewhat recovered, but with a sharp headache and much debilitated. He managed, however, to mount, and rode slowly on to find a shelter for the night. In half an hour the welcome sight of an old plantation mansion greeted his eyes. There was a large court, with shade trees and shrubbery between the road and the house, and in the corner of this court, facing the road, a small warehouse or barn, in and around which were a number of negroes moving casks of tobacco. A white man, evidently their owner, was superintending their labour, and to him the traveller applied for lodging for the night.

"We don't take in strangers."

The traveller informed the planter of his illness and inability to ride further.

"You'll have to try to ride as far as the next house, sir; we don't take in travellers here," was the reply.

"Really I don't feel able. I should not like to put you to inconvenience, sir, but I am weak and faint. My horse, too, has eaten nothing since early in the morning."

"Sorry for you, but we have no accommodation for travellers here," was the only reply, and the planter stepped to the other side of a tobacco cask.

The traveller rode on. About half an hour afterwards he came in sight of another house. It was at a distance from the road, and to reach it he was obliged to let down and put up again three different sets of fence-bars. The owner was not at home, and his wife said

that they were not accustomed to take in strangers. It was not far
to the next house, she added, as the traveller hesitated.

He reached, at length, the next house, which proved to be the
residence of another large tobacco planter, who sat smoking in its
verandah, as the traveller rode near and made his petition.

"We don't take in travellers," was again his answer.

The sick man stated his special claims to kindness, and the planter
good-naturedly inquired the particulars, asked how far he had ridden, where he got his horse and his dog, whither he was bound, and
so on (did not ask where he was born or what were his politics).
The traveller again stated that he was ill, unable to ride further, and
begged permission to remain for the night under the planter's roof,
and again the planter carelessly replied that they didn't take in travellers; anon, asked how crops were looking further west, and talked
of guano, the war news, and the prospect for peaches. It became
dusk while the traveller lingered, and the negroes came in with
their hoes over their shoulders from the fields across the road, but
the planter continued chatting and smoking, not even offering the
traveller a cigar, till at length the latter said, "If you really cannot
keep me to-night, I must go on, sir; I cannot keep my horse much
longer, I fear."

"It is not far to the next house."

"But I have already called at three houses to-night, sir."

"Well, you see, since the railroad was done, people here don't
reckon to take in travellers as they once did. So few come along they
don't find their account in being ready for them."

The traveller asked for a drink of water, which a negro brought
in a calabash, bade good night to the planter, and rode on through
the woods. Night presently set in; the road crossed a swamp and
was difficult to follow, and for more than an hour he rode on—seeing
no house—without stopping. Then crossing water, he deliberated
whether he should not bivouac for the night where he was. He had
with him a few biscuits and some dried figs. He had not eaten
hitherto, hoping constantly to come to a habitation where it might
happen he could get a cup of tea, of which he felt more particularly
in need. He stopped, took some nourishment, the first he had tasted
in fifteen hours, and taking also a little brandy, gained strength and
courage to continue his journey. A bright light soon cheered him,
and after a time he made his way to a large white house, in the

rear of which was an old negro woman stirring the contents of a caldron which stood over the fire, by which he had been guided. The old woman had the appearance of a house servant, and he requested her to ask her master if he would favour him with lodging for the night.

Her master did not take in travellers, she said, besides, he was gone to bed; and she stirred on, hardly looking at the traveller till he put his hand in his pocket, and, holding forth silver, said—

"Now, aunty, mind what I tell you. Do you go in to your master, and say to him, 'There is a gentleman outside who says he is sick, and that his horse is tired and has had nothing to eat to-day; that he is a stranger and has been benighted, don't know the roads, is not well enough to ride further, and wants to know if you won't be so kind as to let him stay here to-night.'"

"Yes, massa, I'll tell him; 'twon't do no good, though, and he'll be almighty cross."

She went in, returned after a few minutes, seized her paddle, and began stirring before she uttered the words—

"Says yer ken go on to de store, he reckon."

It was after ten o'clock when the traveller reached the next house. It stood close upon the road, and the voice of a woman answered a knock upon the door, and, in reply to the demand, said it was not far to the store, and she reckoned they accommodated travellers there.

Finally, at the store, the traveller succeeded in getting admittance, was comfortably lodged and well entertained by an amiable family. Their kindness was of such a character that he felt, in the position of an invited guest, unable to demand and unwilling to suggest any unvolunteered service. There was no indication that the house was an inn, yet the traveller's experience left him little room to hesitate to offer money, nor was there the slightest hesitation on the part of the storekeeper in naming the amount due for the entertainment he had, or in taking it.

If the reader will accept the traveller's judgment of himself, he will assume that there was nothing in his countenance, his dress, his language, or his bearing, by which he could readily be distinguished from a gentleman of Southern birth and education, and that he was not imagined to be anything else, certainly not on his first inquiry, at any one of the plantations where he was thus refused shelter.

So far as this inhospitality (for this is, I think, what even the Southern reader will be inclined to call it) needed explanation, it was supposed to be sufficiently given in the fact that the region had, by the recent construction of a railroad through it, approximated the condition of a well-settled and organized community, in which the movements of travellers are so systematized, that the business of providing for their wants, as a matter of pecuniary profit, can no longer be made a mere supplement of another business, but becomes a distinct occupation.

This, then, but a small part of the whole land being thus affected by railroads, was an exception in the South. True; but what is the rule to which this is the exception?

Mr. De Bow says, that the traveller would have had no apprehension that the offer of money for chance entertainment for the night furnished him at a house on the banks of the Connecticut, would give offence; yet in the Connecticut valley, among people having no servants, and not a tithe of the nominal wealth of the Red River planter, or of one of these Virginia planters, such has been a frequent experience of the same traveller. Nor has he ever, when calling benighted at a house, anywhere in the State of Connecticut, far from a public-house, escaped being invited with cordial frankness to enjoy such accommodation as it afforded; and this, he is fully convinced, without any thought in the majority of cases of pecuniary remuneration. In several instances a remuneration in money has been refused in a manner which conveyed a reproof of the offer of it as indelicate; and it thus happens that it was a common experience of that, of the possibility of which Mr. De Bow is unable to conceive, that led in no small degree to the hesitation upon which this very comment was made.

This simple faith in the meanness of the people of the North, and especially of New England, is no eccentricity of Mr. De Bow's. It is in accordance with the general tone of literature and of conversation at the South, that penuriousness, disingenuousness, knavish cunning, cant, cowardice, and hypocrisy are assumed to be the prevailing traits by which they are distinguished from the people of the South—not the poor people of New England from the planters of the South, but the people generally from the people generally. Not the tone of the political literature and of the lower class of the South, but of its wealthy class, very generally, really of its "better class." Mr. De Bow is himself the associate of gentlemen as well informed and as free from narrow prejudices as any at the South. No New England man, who has travelled at the South, would be surprised, indeed, if, at a table at which he were a guest, such an assumption as that of Mr. De Bow should be apparent in all the conversation, and that the gist of it should be supposed to be so well understood and generally conceded, that he could not be annoyed thereat.

I need hardly say that this reference to Mr. De Bow is continued, not for the purpose of vindicating the North any more than myself from a mistaken criticism. I wish only to demonstrate how necessary it must soon be to find other means for saving the Union than these commonplace flatteries of Southern conceit and apologies for Southern folly, to which we have not only become so accustomed ourselves, as to hardly believe our eyes when we are obliged to meet the facts (as was my own case), but by which we have so successfully imposed upon our friends, that a man like Mr. De Bow actually supposes that the common planters of the teeming and sunny South, are, as a rule, a more open-handed, liberal, and hospitable class than the hard-working farmers of the bleak and sterile hills of New England; so much so, that he feels warranted not merely in stating facts within his personal knowledge, illustrating the character of the latter and arguing the causes, but in incidentally referring to their penuriousness as a matter of proverbial contempt. Against this mistake, which, I doubt not, is accomplishing constant mischief to our nation, I merely oppose the facts of actual experience. I wish to do so with true respect for the good sense of the South.

Presenting myself, and known only in the character of a chance traveller, most likely to be in search of health, entertainment, and information; usually taken for and treated as a Southerner, until I stated that I was not one, I journeyed nearly six months at one time (my second journey) through the South. During all this journey, I came not oftener than once a week, on an average, to public-houses, and was thus generally forced to seek lodging and sustenance at private houses. Often it was refused me; not unfrequently rudely refused. But once did I meet with what Northern readers could suppose Mr. De Bow to mean by the term (used in the same article), "free road-side hospitality." Not once with the slightest appearance of what Noah Webster defines hospitality—the "practice of receiving or entertaining strangers without reward."

Only twice, in a journey of four thousand miles, made independently of public conveyances, did I receive a night's lodging or a repast from a native Southerner, without having the exact price in money which I was expected to pay for it stated to me by those at whose hands I received it.

If what I have just narrated had been reported to me before I travelled in the manner I did in my second journey at the South, I should have had serious doubts of either the honesty or the sanity of the reporter. I know, therefore, to what I subject myself in now giving my own name to it. I could not but hesitate to do this, as one would be cautious in acknowledging that he believed himself to have seen the sea-serpent, or had discovered a new motive power. By drawing out the confidence of other travellers, who had chanced to move through the South in a manner at all similar, however, I have had the satisfaction of finding that I am not altogether solitary in my experience. Even this day I met one fresh from the Southwest, to whom, after due approach, I gave the article which is the text of these observations, asking to be told how he had found it in New England and in Mississippi. He replied:

During four winters, I have travelled for a business purpose two months each winter in Mississippi. I have generally spent the night at houses with whose inmates I had some previous acquaintance. Where I had business transactions, especially where debts were due to me, which could not be paid, I sometimes neglected to offer payment for my night's lodging, but in no other case, and never in a single instance, so far as I can now recollect, where I had offered payment, has there been any hesitation in taking it. A planter might refrain from asking payment of a traveller, but it is universally expected. In New England, as far as my limited experience goes, it is not so. I have known New England farmers' wives take a small gratuity after lodging travellers, but always with apparent hesitation. I have known New England farmers refuse to do so. I have had some experience in Iowa; money is there usually (not always) taken for lodging travellers. The principal difference between the custom at private houses there and in Alabama and Mississippi being, that in Iowa the farmer seems to carefully reckon the exact value of the produce you have consumed, and to charge for it at what has often seemed to me an absurdly low rate; while in Mississippi, I have usually paid from four to six times as much as in Iowa, for similar accommodations. I consider the usual charges of planters to travellers extortionate, and the custom the reverse of hospitable. I knew of a Kentucky gentleman travelling from Eutaw to Greensboro' [twenty miles] in his own conveyance. He was taken sick at the crossing of the Warrior River. It was nine o'clock at night. He averred to me that he called at every plantation on the road, and stated that he was a Kentuckian, and sick, but was refused lodging at each of them.

This the richest county of Alabama, and the road is lined with valuable plantations!

The following is an extract from a letter dated Columbus, Mississippi, November 24, 1856, published in the London *Daily News*. It is written by an Englishman [E. L. Godkin] travelling for commercial purposes, and tells what he has learned by experience of the custom of the country:

It is customary in travelling through this country, where towns are few and taverns scarce and vile, to stop at the planters' houses along the road, and pay for your bed and board in the morning just as if you had stayed at an inn. The custom is rather repugnant to our Old World notions of hospitality, but it appears to me an excellent one for both the host and his guest. The one feels less bored by demands upon his kindness, as soon as it ceases to be merely a kindness to comply with them, and the other has no fear about intruding or being troublesome when he knows he will have to pay for his entertainment. It is rarely, however, that the *entrée* can be obtained into the houses of wealthy planters in this way. They will not be bothered by your visits, and, if you apply to them, have no hesitation in politely passing you on to such of their neighbours as have less money or more generosity.

The same writer afterwards relates the following experience:—

About nineteen miles from Canton, I sought lodging at nightfall at a snug house on the roadside, inhabited by an old gentleman and his two daughters, who possessed no slaves and grew no cotton, and whose two sons had been killed in the Mexican war, and who, with the loudest professions of hospitality, cautiously refrained from giving himself any personal trouble in support of them. He informed me that there was corn in the husk in an almost inaccessible loft, there was fodder in an un-get-at-able sort of a cage in the yard, water in a certain pond about half a mile off, and a currycomb in a certain hole in the wall. Having furnished me with this intelligence, he left me to draw my own conclusions as to what my conduct ought to be under the circumstances.

A naturalist, the author of a well-known standard work, who has made several tours of observation in the Slave States, lately confided to me that he believed that the popular report of Southern hospitality must be a popular romance, for never, during all his travels in the South, had he chanced to be entertained for a single night, except by gentlemen to whom he was formally presented by letter, or who had previously been under obligations to him, without paying for it in money, and to an amount quite equal to the value received. By the wealthier, a night's entertainment had been frequently refused him, under circumstances which, as must have been evident to them, rendered his further progress seriously inconvenient. Once, while in company with a foreign naturalist—a titled man—he had been dining at the inn of a small county-town, when a certain locally distinguished judge had seen fit to be eloquent at the dinner-table upon the advantages of slavery in maintaining a class of "high-toned gentlemen," referring especially to the proverbial hospitality of Southern plantations, which he described as quite a bewilderment to strangers, and nothing like which was to be found in any country unblessed with slavery, or institutions equivalent to it. It so happened that the following night the travellers, on approaching a plantation mansion in quest of lodging, were surprised to find that they had fallen upon the residence of this same judge, who recognized them, and welcomed them and bade them be at home. Embarrassed by a recollection of his discourse of hospitality, it was with some difficulty that one of them, when they were taking leave next morning, brought himself to inquire what he might pay for the entertainment they had received. He was at once relieved by the judge's prompt response, "Dollar and a quarter apiece, I reckon."

It is very true that the general custom of the South which leads a traveller to ask for a lodging at any private house he may chance to reach near nightfall, and to receive a favourable answer not merely as a favour but as a matter of business, is a convenient one, is one indeed almost necessary in a country so destitute of villages, and where, off certain thoroughfares of our merchants, there are so few travellers. It is a perfectly respectable and entirely sensible custom, but it is not, as is commonly represented to be, a custom of hospitality, and it is not at all calculated to induce customs of hospitality with the mass of citizens. It is calculated to make inhospitality of habit and inhospitality of character the general rule; hospitality of habit and of character the exception. Yet the common misapplication of the word to this custom is, so far as I can ascertain, the only foundation of the arrogant assumption of superiority of character in this respect of the Southerners over ourselves—the only ground of the claim that slavery breeds a race of more generous and hospitable citizens than freedom.

The difficulty of giving anything like an intelligent and exact estimate of the breeding of any people or of any class of people is almost insurmountable, owing to the vagueness of the terms which must be used, or rather to the quite different ideas which different readers will attach to these terms. The very word which I have employed to designate my present subject has itself such a varied signification that it needs to be defined at the outset. I mean to employ it in that sense wherein, according to Webster, it covers the ground of "nurture, instruction, and the formation of manners." It is something more than "manners and customs," then, and includes, or may include, qualities which, if not congenital, are equally an essential part of character with those qualities which are literally in-bred of a man. Such qualities are mainly the result of a class of circumstances, of the influence of which upon his character and manners a man, or a child growing to a man, is usually unconscious, and of which he cannot be independent if he would.

The general difficulty is increased in dealing with the people of the Slave States, because among themselves all terms defining social rank and social characteristics are applied in a manner which can be understood only after considerable experience; and also because the general terms of classification, always incomplete in their significance, fail entirely with a large class of Southerners, whose manners have some characteristics which would elsewhere be thought "high bred," if they had not others which are elsewhere universally esteemed low and ruffianly.

There are undoubted advantages resulting from the effects of slavery upon the manners of some persons. Somewhat similar advantages I have thought that I perceived to have resulted in the

Free States, where a family has been educated under favourable influences in a frontier community. There is boldness, directness, largeness, confidence, with the effect of the habitual sense of superiority to most of the community; not superiority of wealth, and power from wealth merely, but of a mind well stocked and refined by such advantages of education as only very unusual wealth, or very unusual individual energy, rightly directed, can procure in a scattered and frontier community. When to this is added the effect of visits to the cultivated society of denser communities; when refined and polished manners are grafted on a natural, easy abandon; when there is high culture without effeminacy either of body or mind, as not unfrequently happens, we find a peculiarly respectable and agreeable sort of men and women. They are the result of frontier training under the most favourable circumstances. In the class furthest removed from this on the frontier—people who have grown up without civilized social restraints or encouragements, and always under what in a well-conditioned community would be esteemed great privations—happens, on the other hand, the most disagreeable specimen of mankind that the world breeds; men of a sort almost peculiar to America and Australia; border ruffians, of whom the "rowdies" of our Eastern towns are tame reflections. Cooper has well described the first class in many instances. I know of no picture of the latter which represents them as detestable as I have found them.

The whole South is maintained in a frontier condition by the system which is apologized for on the ground that it favours good breeding. This system, at the same time, tends to concentrate wealth in a few hands. If there is wisdom and great care in the education of a family thus favoured, the result which we see at the North, under the circumstances I have described, is frequently reproduced. There are many more such fruits of frontier life at the South than the North, because there is more frontier life. There is also vastly more of the other sort, and there is everything between, which degrees of wealth and degrees of good fortune in education would be expected to occasion. The bad breed of the frontier, at the South, however, is probably far worse than that of the North, because the frontier condition of the South is everywhere permanent. The child born to-day on the Northern frontier, in most cases, before it is ten years old, will be living in a well organized and tolerably well provided community; schools, churches, libraries, lecture and concert halls, daily mails and printing presses, shops and machines in variety, having arrived within at least a day's journey of it; being always within an influencing distance of it. There are improvements, and communities loosely and gradually cohering in various parts of the South, but so slowly, so feebly, so irregularly, that men's minds and habits are knit firm quite independently of this class of social influences.

There is one other characteristic of the Southerner, which is far more decided than the difference of climate merely would warrant, and which is to be attributed not only to the absence of the ordinary restraints and means of discipline of more compact communities in his education, but unquestionably also to the readiness and safety with which, by reason of slavery, certain passions and impulses may be indulged. Every white Southerner is a person of importance; must be treated with deference. Every wish of the Southerner is imperative; every belief undoubted; every hate, vengeful; every love, fiery. Hence, for instance, the scandalous fiend-like street fights of the South. If a young man feels offended with another, he does not incline to a ring and a fair stand-up set-to, like a young Englishman; he will not attempt to overcome his opponent by logic; he will not be content to vituperate, or to cast ridicule upon him; he is impelled straightway to strike him down with the readiest deadly weapon at hand, with as little ceremony and pretence of fair combat as the loose organization of the people against violence will allow. He seems crazy for blood. Intensity of personal pride—pride in anything a man has, or which connects itself with him, is more commonly evident. Hence, intense local pride and prejudice; hence intense partisanship; hence rashness and over-confidence; hence visionary ambition; hence assurance in debate; hence assurance in society. As self-appreciation is equally with deference a part of what we call good breeding, and as the expression of deference is much more easily reduced to a matter of manners and forms, in the commonplace intercourse of society, than self-appreciation, this characteristic quality of the Southerner needs to be borne in mind in considering the port and manners he commonly has, and judging from them of the effects of slavery.

It must be also considered that the ordinary occupations and amusements of people of moderate wealth at the North are seldom resorted to at the South, that public entertainments of any kind, for instance, are impracticable to a sparse population; consequently that where men of wealth are socially disposed, all intercourse with others is highly valued, prepared for, and made the most of. Hence, with these, the act of social intercourse is more highly esteemed, and is much more frequently carried to a nice perfection of manner than it usually is with men otherwise of corresponding education, and habits at the North.

In a Northern community a man who is not greatly occupied with private business is sure to become interested in social enterprises and to undertake duties in them which will demand a great deal of time and strength. School, road, cemetery, asylum, and church corporations; bridge, ferry, and water companies; literary, scientific, art, mechanical, agricultural, and benevolent societies; all these things are managed chiefly by the unpaid services of gentlemen during hours which they can spare from their private interests. In the successful operations of such enterprises they find much of the satisfaction of their life. So, too, our young men, who are not obliged to devote their thoughts chiefly to business success, are members and managers of reading rooms, public libraries, gymnasiums, game clubs, boat clubs, ball clubs, and all sorts of clubs, Bible classes, debating societies, military companies; they are planting road-side trees, or damming streams for skating ponds, or rigging diving-boards, or getting up firework displays, or private theatricals; they are always doing something, not conversing for the entertainment of the moment. Planters, the details of whose business fall into the hands of overseers, and young men of fortune, at the South, have, when at home on the plantation, none of these occupations. Their talents all turn into two channels, politics and sociality; the very paucity of society making it the more esteemed and the more carefully used. Social intercourse at the North is a relaxation from the ordinary bent of men's talents; at the South, it is that to which mainly their talents are bent. Hence, with men who are otherwise on a par, in respect of natural advantages and education, the Southerner will have a higher standard of manners than the Northerner, because, with him, social intercourse is the grand resource to which all other possible occupations of his mind become subordinate. The Northerner, being troubled by no monotony, unquestionably too much neglects at present this, the highest and final art of every type of civilization. In making this comparison, however, it must not be forgotten that it is made between men who are supposed to be equal in all respects, except in the possession of this advantage, and who are equally at leisure from any necessary habitual occupation for a livelihood.

Having conceded to the South certain elements of advantage in this respect, for a single class, it still remains to inquire where is the greatest weight of advantage for this class, and for all classes of our citizens. In attempting to make such a general comparison, I shall begin at the bottom of the social ladder, and return to the class who can in a great degree choose how they will be occupied.

In the North at the Revolution we scarcely had a distinct class corresponding to the lowest white class of Virginia, as described by Jefferson, our labourers being less ignorant and coarse in their habits, and associating much more familiarly with their betters. We have now a class more nearly corresponding to it furnished by the European peasant immigration. It is, however, a transient class, somewhat seldom including two generations, and, on an average, I trust, not one. It is therefore practically not an additional class, but, overlooking the aged and diseased, a supplement to our lowest normal class. Out of twenty Irish emigrants, landing in New York, perfectly destitute, of whose history I have been intimately cognizant, only two, both of whom were over fifty years of age, have lived out five years here without beginning to acquire wealth and becoming superior in their ambition and habits to the lowest order, which I believe to include a majority of the whites in the plantation districts of the South.[1] Our lowest class, therefore, has a higher standard than the lowest class of the Slave States. This, I understand, is made very evident where the two come together at the West, as in southern Illinois. The very poorest and lowest New England women who go there are frequently offended by the inconsiderate rudeness and coarseness of the women immigrating from the South, and shocked by their "shiftless," comfortless, vagrant habits, so much so that families have often removed, after having been once established, to

[1] I fear that it must be confessed that this general rule has now a multitude of exceptions in our large towns, where, in New York, especially, we seem taking some pains to form a permanent lower class. With the present great and apparently permanent falling off in the European emigration it can hardly last, however.

escape being bored and annoyed by their Southern-born neighbours.

Referring to the lowest class, North and South, as the fourth, I
class as third, the lowest rank in society, North or South, in which
regard is had by its members to the quality of their associates from
other than moral motives, or the prejudices of locality, race, sec-
tarianism, and politics. In other words, that in which there is a distinct social selectiveness and pride. I think that everywhere in the
Free States men of this class would almost universally feel their
position damaged—be a little ashamed—if obliged to confess that
they did not take a newspaper, or were unable to read it with a
clear understanding of the intelligence it was intended to communicate. Allusions to the main facts of American history, to any
clause of the Bible, to the provisions of the Constitution, and the
more important laws, State and National, would be understood in
most cases by those whom I refer to as the third class in Northern
society. In few families of this class would you fail to find some
volumes of the English poets, or some works of great novelists or
renowned travellers. Nothing like this would you find, however, in a
grade of society distinctly superior to the lowest at the South.

The ratio of the number of the citizens who cannot read at all to
the whole, appears, by the census returns, to be only three times
larger at the South than at the North. I believe it to be much greater
at the South than these returns indicate.[2] The comparative education of the third class "North" and of the third class "South," however, cannot be at all judged from these statistics, supposing them
correct. Those who can read and who do not read, or whose reading is confined within extremely narrow limits, are a much larger
number at the South than at the North, owing to the much poorer
supply of books and newspapers which commerce can afford to put
within the reach of the former. The census returns two million newspapers, for instance, printed annually in Virginia, one hundred and

---

[2] The ratio of white illiterate to white population, per cent., as returned,
is, { Free States, 3.36
     { Slave   "   8.27   Of the native population, over twenty years old, it
is, { Free States, 4.12
    { Slave   "   17.23   (Census Compendium, pp. 152, 153). The ability to
merely read and write may itself be of little value, but the fact of a child's having had the painstaking necessary to so far instruct him is in some degree a
means of measuring his other inherited wealth, and thus his breeding.

fifteen million in New York. There is a post-office to every fourteen square miles in New York, one to forty-seven square miles in Virginia; over five hundred publishers and booksellers in New York, but forty in Virginia. Thirty thousand volumes in public libraries in Virginia, eight hundred thousand in New York. The area occupied by the population of Virginia being much the largest, it may be inferred that with the disposition and the ability to read anything in particular, the Virginian of the third class will have to travel more than thirty times as far as the New Yorker to procure it. The same proposition will hold good in regard to most other means of cultivation, and the third class of the South generally has seemed to me to be as much more narrow-minded, rude, coarse, "dangerous," and miserable, than the third class of the Free States, as the most sanguine friend of popular education could anticipate from these facts.

The great difference in character between the third class of the South and that of the North, as indicated by their respective manners, is found in the much less curiosity and ready intelligent interest in matters which have not an immediate personal bearing in that of the South. Apathetic carelessness rather than simple indifference, or reckless incivility as to your comfort, is what makes the low Southerner a disagreeable companion. It is his impertinent shrewdness which makes you wish to keep the Yankee at a distance. The first seems without object, spiritless; the latter keen to better himself, if with nothing else, with information which he can draw from you, and by gaining your good opinion.

The next or second class would include, both North and South, those with whose habits and character I am most familiar, and of whom I can speak with the best right to confidence. It would include in New England and New York the better-educated farmers —these owning, I should say, half the agricultural land—the permanently established manufacturers and merchants of moderate capital; most of the shopkeepers and the better-educated master mechanics and artisan foremen; most of the preachers, physicians, and lawyers (some ranking higher). It would correspond most nearly to what in England would be called the lower-middle class, but any higher grade being very ill-defined, existing distinctly but in few localities, and rarely recognized as existing at all, it is in a great measure free from the peculiar vulgarity of its English parallel.

The number of those at the South who correspond in education and refinement of manners and habits to the average of this class of the North, it will be evident, from a similar mode of reasoning to that before employed, must be very much smaller relatively, either to the territory or the whole white population of their respective regions.

In the comparison commonly made by Southern writers between the condition of the people of a sparsely-settled country and another, it is usually assumed that the advantages of the latter are confined exclusively to towns, and to large and crowded towns. By contrasting the evils which concentrate in such towns with the favourable circumstances of localities where at least wood, water, and air are abundant, and corn enough to support life can usually be got by any one with a little occasional labour, an argument of some force to ignorant people is easily presented. The advantages possessed by a people living in moderately well-occupied rural districts, who are even more free from the evils of great towns than their own people, are entirely overlooked by most Southern writers. Such is the condition, however, of more white people in the Free States than the whole white population of the Slave States. A majority of our farmers' daughters can walk from their dwellings to schools of a quality such as at the South can be maintained not twice in five hundred square miles. These schools are practically a part of their homes. Probably, in more than half the families of the South, the children of which are instructed to the least degree which would be considered "respectable," among this second class of the North, private governesses are obliged to be employed, or the children must be for many years at boarding-schools. We all know that the young women who go to the South, to meet the demand thus occasioned for home education, are not generally, though they may be in cases, our own most esteemed and successful instructresses; and we also know from their report that their skill and labour has necessarily to be long chiefly employed in laying those simple foundation habits of *instructability*, which our Northern children acquire imperceptibly from association with those of the neighbourhood slightly in advance of them. Churches and the various sub-organizations centring in them, in which class distinctions are much lost sight of, to the great advantage of the manners of the lower classes, and little chance of injury to the higher; libraries; literary societies; lecture arrangements; dramatic and musical, art and scientific entertainments, and also highly educated professional men, with whom, for various purposes, many persons are brought often in contact, are correspondingly more frequent at the North, correspondingly more accessible; in other words, the advantages to be derived from them are cheaper, and so more influential on the manners of the people at large.

The common opinion has been that the Southerners or planters of the class now under consideration, are more social, more generous, more heartily kind and genial than Northerners. According to my experience, the reverse of all this is true, as a general rule. Families live so isolatedly at the South, that any social contact, out of the family, is of course much more eventful and stimulating than it is ordinarily at the North, and this accounts for the common opinion. I could not but think, however, that most persons at the South looked to the voluntary good offices and conversation of others, both within and without their families, for their enjoyment of the world, much less than most at the North. It may be that when in towns they attach a greater value to, and are more careful to make use of the opportunities for social gathering afforded by towns, than are Northerners. In towns they attach more consequence to forms, are more scrupulous in matters of etiquette, more lavish in expenditure for dress, and for certain other things which are the signs of luxury rather than luxury itself, such as plate and fancy brands of wines. They make less show of fine art and less pretence of artistic judgment; more of respect and regard for their associates, and of indifference or superiority to all others.

As to manner or deportment simply, with the same impulse and intention, that of the Southerner will habitually, under ordinary circumstances, be best, more true, more composed, more dignified. I have said that the second class at the North is without the pervading vulgarity of the class to which it most nearly corresponds in England, the reason being that those which constitute it seldom wish or attempt to appear to belong to a superior class, not clearly recognizing a superior class. Individuals, however, very generally have a strong desire to be thought better informed, more ingenious, more witty, as well as more successful in their enterprises than they are, and this stamps them with a peculiar quality of manners vulgarly called "smartness," the absence of which makes Southern men and women generally much more agreeable companions than Northerners of the same degree of education and accomplishments in other respects. Not but that snobs abound; of these it will be more convenient to speak under the next division, however.

The traditional "old family," stately but condescending, haughty but jovial, keeping open house for all comers on the plantations of Virginia or South Carolina, is not wholly a myth.

There really was something which, with some sort of propriety, could be termed a gentry in Carolina and Virginia in their colony days; yet of the names which are now thought to have belonged to it, as descended of brave, loyal, and adventurous cavaliers, some. I once saw in London upon an old freight-list of a ship outward bound for Virginia, with the addition of tinker and tailor, poacher and pickpocket, all to be sold for life, or a term of years, to the highest bidder when they should arrive. A large majority of the fathers of Virginia were unquestionably of this class.

What was properly to be termed the gentry in Virginia and South Carolina previous to the Revolution, was very small in number. A large proportion of the families who composed it, and who remained after the Revolution in the country (for many were Tories) have since passed in all their branches through a poverty-stricken period, very dissipating in its influence upon hereditary breeding, novelists and dramatic old servants to the contrary notwithstanding. Many of those who have retained wealth and family pride in succession to the present time, have undeniably, from various causes, degenerated wofully in breeding. Coarse tastes and brutal dispositions cannot be disguised under a cavalier address, and the most assured readiness in the established forms of polite society. Of the real "old families" which remain at all "well bred" in their qualities, habits, and manners, by reason of their lineage, I think it will be difficult for most readers who have not studied the matter at all to form a sufficiently small estimate; call them a dozen or a hundred, what does it matter in a region much larger than the old German empire? Associating with these are a few hundred more new or recuperated families, in which there is also the best breeding, and in certain few parts or districts of the South, to be defined and numbered without difficulty, there is a wealthy, distinct, generous, hospitable, refined, and accomplished first class, clinging with some pertinacity, although with too evident an effort, to the traditional manners and customs of an established gentry.

There was a gentry in the North as well as in Virginia and Carolina in the colony period, though a less important and numerous one. As the North has been much more prosperous, as the value of its property has much more rapidly increased than that of the South, the advantages of wealth have, I believe, been more generally retained in families, and probably the number of those who could trace their breeding in an uninterrupted parental influence from the colonial gentry, is now larger at the North than the South.

Including new families, in whose habits and manners and conversation the best bred people of Europe would find nothing more offensive and inharmonious with themselves than might be ascribed to local fashion or a desire to avoid appearances which, though perfectly proper in an aristocratic society, would be snobbish in a republic, there is unquestionably at this time a very much larger number of thoroughly well-bred people in the Free than in the Slave States. It is equally certain that the proportion of such people to the whole population of whites is larger at the North than the South.

The great majority of wealthy planters who at the present day assume for themselves a special social respectability and superiority to the class I have defined as the second, are, as a general rule, not only distinguished for all those qualities which our satirists and dramatists are accustomed to assume to be the especial property of the newly rich of the Fifth Avenue, but, as far as I have had opportunity to observe both classes, are far more generally and ridiculously so than the would-be fashionable people of New York, or of any other part of the United States. It is a part of the *rôle* they undertake to act, to be hospitable and generous, as it was lately that of our fops to be sleepy and critical. They are not hospitable and generous, however; they know not the meaning of these terms. They are absurdly ostentatious in entertainment, and extravagant in the purchase of notoriety; possibly they have more tact in this than our Potiphars, but such has not been my personal observation.

Chapter XVIII

The Danger of the South

Before the advent of modern science, any idea of systematic laws of human improvement would have been deemed alike impossible and absurd; but the constant observation of facts, the exact statistics recorded, the progress of science in all departments, has made it possible to conceive of, and probable that there actually exist *uniform laws of social movement*, based upon any given condition of society. If the *elementary social* condition be different in regard to religion, government, arts, science, industry, the resulting movements of society will be different. Hence, when we have ascertained by accurate observation upon and record of the social phenomena, that the social movement is uniformly in a certain direction, and that certain results uniformly follow, we shall know in what *elements* the conditions of society must be changed, in order to change the results. Hence, when this law of social movements is ascertained, the philanthropist, legislator, and jurist will know precisely what must be done, and how, in order to remove the evils, or reform the wrongs, or produce the results they desire. They will know that *certain elementary conditions of society* must be changed, and they well know that by removing temptations, or laying restraints, or enlightening the mind, or changing the course of industry, or producing new arts, they will change the social tendency, and thus change the results. . . . Society, or that part of it which thinks and acts, can change the results by changing the elementary conditions which produce them. When you know exactly what the change ought to be, it is not very difficult to produce it; nor does it follow that because a thousand crimes must be committed in Ohio, that a thousand particular individuals *must* commit them. It is true that the individual frequently acts from motives, but is it not just as true that the individual frequently seeks these motives, and presents them to himself?—*From the Report of the Ohio State Commissioner of Statistics,* 1859.

If there is a first principle in intellectual education it is this—that the discipline which does good to the mind is that in which the mind is active, not that in which it is passive. The secret for developing the faculties is to give them much to do, and much inducement to do it.—[John Stuart] Mill's *Political Economy*.

The field-hand negro is, on an average, a very poor and very bad creature, much worse than I had supposed before I had seen him and grown familiar with his stupidity, indolence, duplicity, and sensuality. He seems to be but an imperfect man, incapable of taking care of himself in a civilized manner, and his presence in large numbers must be considered a dangerous circumstance to a civilized people.

A civilized people, within which a large number of such creatures has been placed by any means not within its own control, has claims upon the charity, the aid, if necessary, of all other civilized peoples in its endeavours to relieve itself from the danger which must be apprehended from their brutal propensities, from the incompleteness of their human sympathies—their inhumanity—from their natural love of ease, and the barbaric want of forethought and providence, which would often induce desperate want among them. Evidently the people thus burthened would have need to provide systematically for the physical wants of these poor creatures, else the latter would be liable to prey with great waste upon their substance. Perhaps the very best thing to do would be to collect them into small herds, and attach each herd to a civilized family, the head of which should be responsible for its safe keeping. Such a superintendent should of course contrive, if possible, to make his herd contribute in some way to the procuring of its necessary sustenance; and if, besides this, he even turned their feeble abilities to such good account by his superior judgment, that they actually procured a considerable surplus of food and clothing for the benefit of others, should not Christendom applaud and encourage his exertions, even if a certain amount of severity and physical constraint had been found necessary to accomplish this success?

Let us endeavour to assume a similar difficulty for ourselves. Let us suppose that a large part—the proportion varying with the locality—of our own community should next year suffer from some new malady, the result of which should in no case be fatal, but which should, like the *goitre* of Savoy, leave all who were affected by it permanently injured in their intellects, with diminished bodily activity, and fiercer animal propensities. (I take this method of stating the case, because some of us who only see the negro as he exists at the North might find it difficult to imagine him as he is known to the planters.)

Suppose, further, that this malady should be confined to certain families, as if its seed had been received hundreds of years ago by numerous individuals, and only their descendants (but all of these to the most distant trace of the blood) now suffered from it. Also, that some of our doctors should be of the opinion that the effects of the malady upon the intellect would descend to the children, and to all descendants of those who suffered. Suppose that these unfortunates should be subject to certain hallucinations, that they should be liable to think themselves sane and able to take care of themselves, and that when possessed with these ideas they should be quite cunning and dangerous in attempting to exercise the usual prerogatives of sane men.

What should we do with them?

Finding them in a degree tractable; and sensible enough, after all, to yield readily, if not cheerfully, to superior force, we might herd them together on a sort of farm-hospitals, and let them earn their living, giving especially capable men charge of many, and rewarding them with good salaries, and ordinary small farmers, smaller numbers, with smaller compensations for overseeing them.

Of course, we should place every possible legislative guard and check upon these superintendents and overseers to secure fair and honest dealing, to prevent them from making perquisites for themselves at the expense of a reasonable comfort in their institutions. Careful instructions to secure economical sustenance, and how to turn such labour as could be got from the unfortunates to the best account, in defraying the cost of their keeping, would also be framed by talented men and furnished each keeper.

And having regard to national wealth, to the temporal good of the commonwealth, this is about all that common sense would lead us to do, at least through the agency of government.

Is this all, reader?

You have too much overlooked our small matters of State, if you think so. We have a few crazy people, a few fools, not enough to be a matter of much consideration to our statesmen or legislators, yet we have a State system in our dealing with them, such as it is, and such as it is it puts our dealing with them on a little different footing than would the system I have above imagined. What I have imagined is not quite all we have for some time been in the habit of doing when we did anything with this class. And judging from what we have done, it does not seem as if it would be all that we should do in such an emergency as I have supposed, engaging as it would all the talent of the country to diminish as much as possible the necessary results of the calamity.

We should, it appears, call upon our learned doctors eagerly to study; we should each of us eagerly observe for ourselves whether the fearful infirmity by which so many were incapacitated for their former usefulness, were not only absolutely incurable, but also absolutely not possible to be alleviated. And if our observation should satisfy us, if our doctors could not deny that, with judicious treatment, a considerable alleviation could be effected, so much so indeed, that with a very large part a close approximation to the normal condition of sane and capable mankind could be obtained, there are doubtless those amongst us who would think this a dangerous and an infidel presumption. Just as every year some miserable wretch is found in our dark places to have a crazy father or brother whom he keeps in a cage in his garret, and whose estate he takes care of, and who is of the opinion that it will be of no use, but, on the contrary, a manifest defiance of Divine Providence, and most dangerous to life and property to let this unfortunate out of his cage, to surround him with comforts, and contrive for him cheerful occupation, as our State requires shall be done. But would the average common sense and humanity of the people of the Free States allow them to refuse all reduction from their usual annual incomes; refuse to suffer all necessary addition to their usual taxes; refuse to burden their minds with the difficulties of the all-absorbing problem, in order to initiate a remedial system? Our worst and most cowardly legislature would never dare adjourn leaving this duty incompletely performed. There are thousands on thousands of our citizens who would not only spare from their incomes, but would divide their estates for such a purpose. There is not a county that would not submit to the highest war taxes for it.

Suppose that the doctors and that the universal observation of the community should determine that the defective class were not only capable of being improved, but that so far as their limited intellects permitted, the laws of improvement were the same for them as for healthy men; that they were found to be influenced by a liking for food and drink, for the society of each other and of sane men, for the admiration and respect of each other and of sane men, for their ease, for dancing, for music and other amusements; and that their imperfect natures could be acted upon, drawn out, and enlarged by means of these likings. Suppose that it were found that nearly all of them had still some knowledge of religion, that although they were inclined sometimes to consider sane men as their enemies, they were yet, in most cases, by judicious play upon their inclinations and disinclinations, capable of being trained quite beyond the most sagacious of our domestic animals, even to read intelligently. Should we, because there were so many of them, go back two hundred years in our civilization, denying ourselves the addition which this capacity would give to their powers of usefulness, and consequently of economy of maintenance; denying them the advantages for improvement which we now in every State give to our hopelessly insane, to our blind and mute, to our fools, to our worst and most dangerous criminals?

Why do we not pass laws forbidding criminals and maniacs to read? Our fathers did not allow them to read when negroes were introduced in Virginia. But every man among us whom we call well informed, now knows that it is a profitable business for the State, which has so little profitable business, even to provide teachers and books for a portion of her criminals, to allow books and encourage reading with all. To provide books, to provide physicians, to provide teachers, to provide halls and gardens of recreations, as stimulants to healthful thought for our madmen and our fools; to this the State is impelled equally by considerations of safety and of economy. Even Kentucky has its State institution for the development of manhood in fools born of white women.

Does not every such man know, too, that, given an improvable mind with a sound body, possessed of the natural instincts, the usual desires, appetites, aversions, no matter if at starting the being is even what we call an idiot, a drivelling imbecile, disgusting all who see him, a sheer burden upon society, the process of making him clean in his habits, capable of labouring with a good and intelligent purpose, and of associating inoffensively with others, is just as certain in its principles and in its progress—infinite progress—as the navigation of a ship or the building of a house?

This is even so with a cretin, whose body is deformed beyond remedy, whose brain is contracted, whose face is contorted, whose limbs are half paralyzed, whose every organ is defective, and who has inherited these conditions from goitrous parents and grand-parents.

Dr. [Edouard] Seguin says: "The idiot wishes for nothing, he wishes only to remain in his vacuity."

Even so thinks Dr. [Samuel A.] Cartwright of the negro; and surely nothing worse can be thought of him.[1]

But Dr. Seguin adds: "To treat successfully this ill-will [indisposition to take care of himself], the physician wills that the idiot should act *and think himself, of himself, and, finally, by himself*. The incessant volition of the moral physican urges incessantly the idiot into the sphere of activity of thinking, of labour, of duty, and affectionate feelings."

Is there no such law of progression of capacity for the black imbeciles? All the laws of the South have the contrary aims: to withdraw them as much as possible from the sphere of self-willed activity, thought, labour—to prevent the negro from thinking by himself, of himself, for himself; and the principle on which these laws are based is thus defined by Mr. De Bow:—

The Almighty has thought well to place certain of His creatures in certain *fixed positions* in this world of ours, for what cause He has not seen fit to make quite clear to our limited capacities; and why an ass is not a man, and a man is not an ass, will probably for ever remain a mystery. God made the world; God gave thee thy place, my hirsute brother, and, according to all earthly possibilities and probabilities, it is thy destiny there to remain, bray as thou wilt. From the same great power have our sable friends, Messrs. Sambo, Cuffee, & Co., received their position also. . . . Alas, my poor black brother! thou, like thy hirsute friend, must do thy braying in vain.[2]

Are there laws on our statute-books to prevent asses from being taught to read?

The *Richmond Examiner* says—

These immigrants do not, like our ancestors, fly from religious and political persecution; they come merely as animals in search of a richer and fresher pasture. They come to gratify physical want—for moral, intellectual, or religious wants they have not acquired. They will settle in large masses, and, for ages to come, will practise and inculcate a pure (or

---

[1] De Bow's "Resources," vol. ii, p. 203.
[2] "Resources," vol. ii., pp. 197, 198.

rather impure) materialism. Mormonism is a fit exponent, proof, and illustration of our theory. The mass of them are sensual, grovelling, low-minded agrarians, and nine-tenths of them would join the Mormons, or some such brutal, levelling sect, if an opportunity offered to do so.

European writers describe a large class of population throughout England and the Continent as being distinguished by restless, wandering, nomadic habits, and by a peculiar conformation of the skull and face. Animal and sensual nature largely predominates, with them, over the moral and intellectual. It is they who commit crimes, fill prisons, and adorn the gallows. They will not submit to the restraints of law or religion, nor can they be educated. From their restless and lawless habits, we should infer they composed a large part of the northern immigration.

If all this were true, and were felt by us to be true, should we think it necessary to put the minds of these beings in fetters? Should we hold it to be dangerous if one should undertake to strengthen their intellects, to give them larger ideas?

If all the slaves in the United States were "real Congo niggers," which not one in a thousand is, and if all real Congo niggers were as incapable, and as beastly, and as savage in their propensities as the very worst of them are asserted to be, would the method of dealing with them which the legislation of the Slave States, and which a large part of the labour of the Congress and Executive of our nation is directed to the purpose of perpetuating, be felt to be strictly in accordance with sound and well-established economico-political principles? The purpose of that legislation is avowed to be merely to secure safety with economy. Would a project for establishing an institution planned upon the principles of the ancient Bedlam and the ancient Bridewell be felt to-day to be completely justified among us, by the statement that highwaymen and maniacs will endanger life and the security of our property if they are not somehow taken care of?

If there had been no Mettray with its Demetz, no Norfolk Island with its Machonochie, no Hanwell with its Connolly, no Abendberg with its Guggenbuhl; if the courage, devotion, and labour of Pinel, Sicard, and Seguin had been in vain; if there had been no progress in the science of civilized society since the days of Howard, we might listen with merely silent sadness to such an excuse for debilitating the weak, for holding down the fallen; for permitting brutal keepers to exasperate the mad, and mercenary nurses to stupefy the idiotic; we might, if we saw it to be necessary to preserve a civilized community from destruction, even give its object our aid; but with the knowledge which in our time is everywhere else acted upon, it is impossible for us not to feel that such an argument is a specious and a fallacious one, and that no State can long act upon it with safety, much less with economy.

And surely the system by which intellectual demands and ambition are repressed in the negro is as little calculated to produce the security which is its object, as it is to turn his physical abilities to the most profitable use for his owner. How far it fails in this respect, the extra-legal measures of safety and the semi-instinctive habits of unconscious precaution which pervade Southern society evince. I say unconscious precaution, because Southerners themselves seem to have generally a very inadequate idea of the influence of slavery upon their habits in this way, and this is very natural.

"Every habit breeds unconsciousness of its existence in the mind of the man whom it controls, and this is more true of habits which involve our safety than of any others. The weary sailor aloft, on the look-out, may fall asleep; but, in the lurch of the ship, his hands will clench the swaying cordage only the more firmly, that they act in the method of instinct. A hard-hunted fugitive may nod in his saddle, but his knees will not unloose their hold upon his horse. Men who live in powder-mills are said to lose all conscious feeling of habitual insecurity; but visitors perceive that they have acquired a constant softness of manner and of voice.

"If a labourer on a plantation should insolently contradict his master, it may often appear to be no more than a reasonable precaution for his master to kill him on the spot; for, when a slave has acquired such boldness, it may be evident that not merely is his value as property seriously diminished, but that the attempt to make further use of him at all, as property, involves in danger the whole white community. 'If I let this man live, and permit him the necessary degree of freedom to be further useful to me, he will infect with his audacity all my negro property, which will be correspondingly more difficult to control, and correspondingly reduced in value. If he treats me with so little respect now, what have I to anticipate when he has found other equally independent spirits among the slaves? They will not alone make themselves free, but will avenge upon me, and my wife, and my daughters, and upon all our community, the injustice which they will think has been done them, and their women, and children.' Thus would he reason, and shudder to think what might follow if he yielded to an impulse of mercy.

"To suppose, however, that the master will pause while he thus weighs the danger exactly, and then deliberately act as, upon reflection, he considers the necessities of the case demand, is absurd. The mere circumstance of his doing so would nourish a hopeful spirit in the slave, and stimulate him to consider how he could best avoid all punishment. Hence the instinct-like habit of precaution with individuals, and hence the frenzy which often seizes whole communities.

"But 'planters sleep unguarded, and with their bedroom doors open.' So, as it was boasted, did the Emperor at Biarritz, and with greater bravery, because the assassin of Napoleon would be more sure, in despatching him, that there would be no one left with a vital interest to secure punishment for such a deed: and because, if he failed, Napoleon dare never employ such exemplary punishment for his enemies as would the planters for theirs. The emperors of the South are the whole free society of the South, and it is a society of mutual assurance. Against a slave who has the disposition to become an assassin, his emperor has a bodyguard, which, for general effectiveness, is to the Cent Garde as your right hand is to your right hand's glove.

"It is but a few months since, in Georgia or Alabama, a man treated another precisely as Mr. [Preston S.] Brooks treated Mr. [Charles] Sumner—coming up behind him, with the fury of a madman, and felling him with a bludgeon; killing him by the first blow, however, and then discharging vengeance by repeated strokes upon his senseless body.[3] The man thus pitifully abused had been the

---

[3] The late Mr. Brooks' character should be honestly considered, now that personal enmity toward him is impossible. That he was courteous, accomplished, warm-hearted, and hot-blooded, dear as a friend and fearful as an enemy, may be believed by all; but, in the South, his name is yet never mentioned without the term gallant or courageous, spirited or noble, is also attached to it; and we are obliged to ask, why insist on this? The truth is, we include a habit of mind in these terms which slavery has rendered, in a great degree, obsolete in the South. The man who has been accustomed from childhood to see men beaten when they have no chance to defend themselves; to hear men accused, reproved, vituperated, who dare not open their lips in self-defence or reply; the man who is accustomed to see other men whip women without interference, remonstrance,

master of the other, a remarkably confiding and merciful master, it was said—too much so. 'It never does to be too slack with niggers.' By such indiscretion he brought his death upon him. But did his assassin escape? He was roasted, at a slow fire, on the spot of the murder, in the presence of many thousand slaves, driven to the ground from all the adjoining counties, and when, at length, his life went out, the fire was intensified until his body was in ashes, which were scattered to the winds and trampled under foot. Then 'magistrates and clergymen' addressed appropriate warnings to the assembled subjects. It was not thought indiscreet to leave doors open again that night.

"Will any traveller say that he has seen no signs of discontent, or insecurity, or apprehension, or precaution; that the South has appeared quieter and less excited, even on the subject of slavery, than the North; that the negroes seem happy and contented, and the citizens more tranquilly engaged in the pursuit of their business and pleasure? Has that traveller been in Naples? Precisely the same remarks apply to the appearance of things there at this moment [the moment of this writing—it was in 1857].

"The massacre of Hayti opened in a ball-room. Mr. Cobden judged there was not the smallest reason in the French king's surrounding himself with soldiers the day before the hidden force of insubordination broke forth and cast him forth from his kingdom. It is true, however, that the tranquillity of the South is the tranquillity of Hungary and of Poland, rather than of France or the Two Sicilies; the tranquillity of hopelessness on the part of the subject race. But, in the most favoured regions, this broken spirit of despair is as carefully preserved by the citizens, and with as confident and unhesitating an application of force, when necessary to teach humility, as it is by the army of the Czar, or the omnipresent police of the Kaiser. In Richmond, and Charleston, and New Orleans, the citi-

---

or any expression of indignation, must have a certain quality, which is an essential part of personal honour with us, greatly blunted, if not entirely destroyed. The same quality which we detest in the assassination of an enemy, is essentially constant in all slavery. It is found in effecting one's will with another, when he cannot, if he would, defend himself. Accustomed to this in every hour of their lives, Southerners do not feel magnanimity and the "fair-play" impulse to be a necessary part of the quality of "spirit," courage, and nobleness. By spirit they apparently mean only passionate vindictiveness of character, and by gallantry mere intrepidity.

zens are as careless and gay as in Boston or London, and their servants a thousand times as childlike and cordial, to all appearance, in
their relations with them as our servants are with us. But go to the
bottom of this security and dependence, and you come to police
machinery such as you never find in towns under free government:
citadels, sentries, passports, grape-shotted cannon, and daily public
whippings for accidental infractions of police ceremonies. I happened myself to see more direct expression of tyranny in a single
day and night at Charleston, than at Naples [under Bomba] in a
week; and I found that more than half the inhabitants of this town
were subject to arrest, imprisonment, and barbarous punishment, if
found in the streets without a passport after the evening 'gun-fire.'
Similar precautions and similar customs may be discovered in every
large town in the South.

"Nor is it so much better, as is generally imagined, in the rural districts. Ordinarily there is no show of government any more than at
the North: the slaves go about with as much apparent freedom as
convicts in a dockyard. There is, however, nearly everywhere, always prepared to act, if not always in service, an armed force, with
a military organization, which is invested with more arbitrary and
cruel power than any police in Europe. Yet the security of the
whites is in a much less degree contingent on the action of the 'pa-
trols' than upon the constant, habitual, and instinctive surveillance
and authority of all white people over all black. I have seen a gentleman, with no commission or special authority, oblige negroes to
show their passports, simply because he did not recognize them as
belonging to any of his neighbours. I have seen a girl, twelve years
old, in a district where, in ten miles, the slave population was fifty
to one of the free, stop an old man on the public road, demand to
know where he was going, and by what authority, order him to
face about and return to his plantation, and enforce her command
with turbulent anger, when he hesitated, by threatening that she
would have him well whipped if he did not instantly obey. The man
quailed like a spaniel, and she instantly resumed the manner of a
lovely child with me, no more apprehending that she had acted un-
becomingly, than that her character had been influenced by the
slave's submission to her caprice of supremacy; no more conscious
that she had increased the security of her life by strengthening the
habit of the slave to the master race, than is the sleeping seaman

that he tightens his clutch of the rigging as the ship meets each new billow.

"There is no part of the South in which the people are more free from the direct action of slavery upon the character, or where they have less to apprehend from rebellion, than Eastern Tennessee. Yet, after the burning of a negro near Knoxville, a few years ago, the deed was justified, as necessary for the maintenance of order among the slaves, by the editor of a newspaper (the *Register*), in the following terms:—'It was,' he observed, 'a means of absolute, necessary self-defence, which could not be secured by an ordinary resort to the laws. Two executions on the gallows have occurred in this county within a year or two past, and the example has been unavailing. Four executions by hanging have taken place, heretofore, in Jefferson, of slaves guilty of similar offences, and it has produced no radical terror or example for the others designing the same crimes, and hence any example less horrible and terrifying would have availed nothing here.'

"The other local paper (the *Whig*), upon the same occasion, used the following language:—

" 'We have to say in defence of the act, that it was not perpetrated by an excited multitude, but by one thousand citizens—good citizens at that—who were cool, calm, and deliberate.'

"And the editor, who is a Methodist preacher, presently adds, after explaining the enormity of the offence with which the victim was charged—'We unhesitatingly affirm that the punishment was unequal to the crime. Had we been there we should have taken a part, and even suggested the pinching of pieces out of him with red-hot pincers—the cutting off of a limb at a time, and then burning them all in a heap. The possibility of his escaping from jail forbids the idea of awaiting the tardy movements of the law.' [Although one thousand trusty citizens volunteered to guard him at the stake.]

"How much more horrible than the deed are these apologies for it. They make it manifest that it was not accidental in its character, but a phenomenon of general and fundamental significance. They explain the paralytic effect upon the popular conscience of the great calamity of the South. They indicate a necessary tendency of people living under such circumstances to return in their habits of thought to the dark ages of mankind. For who, from the outside, can fail to see that the real reason why men in the middle of the nineteenth century, and in the centre of the United States, are publicly burned at the stake, is one much less heathenish, less disgraceful to the citizens than that given by the more zealous and extemporaneous of their journalistic exponents—the desire to torture the sinner proportionately to the measure of his sin. Doubtless, this reverend gentleman expresses the utmost feeling of the ruling mind of his community. But would a similar provocation have developed a similar avenging spirit in any other nominally Christian or civilized people? Certainly not. All over Europe, and in every Free State—California, for significant reasons, temporarily excepted—in similar cases, justice deliberately takes its course; the accused is systematically assisted in defending or excusing himself. If the law demands his life, the infliction of unnecessary suffering, and the education of the people in violence and feelings of revenge, are studiously avoided. Go back to the foundation of the custom which thus neutralizes Christianity among the people of the South, which carries them backward blindly against the tide of civilization, and what do we find it to be? The editor who still retains moral health enough to be suspected—as men more enlightened than their neighbours usually are—of heterodoxy, answers. To follow the usual customs of civilization elsewhere would not be felt safe. To indulge in feelings of humanity would not be felt safe. To be faithful to the precepts of Christ would not be felt safe. To act in a spirit of cruel, inconsiderate, illegal, violent, and pitiless vengeance, must be permitted, must be countenanced, must be defended by the most conservative, as a 'means of absolute, necessary self-defence.' To educate the people practically otherwise would be felt to be suicidal. Hence no free press, no free pulpit, no free politics can be permitted in the South. Hence every white stripling in the South may carry a dirk-knife in his pocket, and play with a revolver before he has learned to swim." [4]

I happened to pass through Tennessee shortly after this tragedy, and conversed with a man who was engaged in it—a mild, commonsense native of the country. He told me that there was no evidence against the negro but his own confession. I suggested that he might have been crazy. "What if he was?" he asked with a sudden as-

[4] From the Introduction to T. H. Gladstone's "The Englishman in Kansas" (by the author of this work).

perity. What if he was, to be sure? The slaves who were brought together to witness his torture were not insane. They were at least capable of instruction. That day they were given a lesson; were taught to know their masters better; were taught that when ordinary and legal discipline failed, resort would be had to more potent means of governing them. A better informed man, having regard to the ignorance of a stranger, might have answered me: "It was of no consequence, practically, whether he were sane or mad. We do not wish our slaves to study the right and the wrong of every exciting occurrence. To say that being mad the negro was not responsible, therefore not guilty of a crime, therefore not to be punished, would be proclaiming to them that only that which is wrong is to be dreaded. Whatever offends us, whatever is against our will and pleasure, is what a slave must be made to dread."

Constantly, and everywhere throughout the South, are there occurrences of this significance; I do not say as horrible, though I can answer for it, that no year in the last ten has passed without something as bad; [5] but constantly and everywhere of the same nature, of the same impulse, the same reasoning, the same purposes, the same disregard of principles of society, which no people can ever set aside and not have reason to feel their situation insecure. It is false, it is the most dangerous mistake possible to assume that this feeling of insecurity, this annihilation of the only possible basis of security in human society, is, in the slightest degree, the result of modern agitation. It is the fundamental law of slavery, as distinctly appears in the decision of Justice [Thomas] Ruffin, of North Carolina, in the case of the State v. Mann.[6] The American system of slavery from its earliest years (as shown p. 496, "Seaboard Slave States"), and without cessation to the present time, has had this accompaniment. Less in the last twenty years, if anything, than before. Would it not be more just to say that this element of the present system was the cause of agitation? Must not the determined policy of the South to deal with slavery on the assumption that it is, in its present form, necessary, just, good, and to be extended, strengthened, and perpetuated indefinitely, involve constant agitation as a

[5] That slaves have ever been burned alive has been indignantly denied. The late Judge [William] Jay told me that he had evidence in his possession of negro burnings every year in the last twenty.

[6] 2 Devereaux's North Carolina Reports, 263.

necessary incident of the means used to carry it out? I do not say
with you or with me, reader, but with a goodly number of any civilized community? Do you not, who wish to think otherwise, consider that it will always require what you must deem a superior
mind not to be overcome by incidents necessary to the carrying out
of this determination? And will not such agitation give renewed
sense of danger, and occasion renewed demands for assurance
from us?

I have remarked before that in no single instance did I find an
inquiry of the owner or the overseer of a large plantation about the
poor whites of its vicinity fail to elicit an expression indicating habitual irritation with them. This equally with the polished and
tranquil gentleman of South Carolina and the rude pioneer settler
of Texas, himself born a dirt-eating sand-hiller. It was evident in
most cases, and in one it was distinctly explained to me by a Louisi-
anian planter, that the reason of this was not merely the bad effect
upon the discipline of the plantation, which was had by the intercourse between these people and the slaves, but that it was felt that
the contrast between the habits of the former—most of the time idle,
and when working, working only for their own benefit and without
a master—constantly offered suggestions and temptations to the
slaves to neglect their duty, to run away and live a vagabond life,
as these poor whites were seen to. Hence, one of the acknowledged
advantages of very large and isolated plantations, and hence, in
part, the desire of every planter to get possession of the land of any
poor non-slaveholding neighbour.

As few Southern writers seem to have noticed this, I suppose that
few Southerners are aware how universal with planters is this feeling. My attention being early directed to the causes of the condition of the poor whites, I never failed to make inquiries of planters,
and of intelligent men especially, about those in their neighbourhood; and being soon struck by the constant recurrence of similar
expressions with regard to them, I was the more careful to introduce the subject at every proper opportunity, and, I repeat, always
with the same result. I am afraid that the feeling of the South to the
North is (more or less defined in individual minds) of the same nature, and that the contiguity of a people whose labourers take care
of themselves, and labour industriously without being owned, can
never be felt to be safe by slaveholders. That it must always be

looked upon with apprehension, with a sense of danger, more or less vague, more or less well defined, but always sufficient to lead to efforts intended to counteract its natural influence—its influence not so much with slaves, certainly not alone with the slaves, but also with that important element of population which reaps no profit from the good behaviour of the slaves.

In De Bow's "Review" for January, 1850, will be found the following passage in an article discussing the practicability of employing the non-slaveholding whites in factories, the argument being that there will be less danger of their becoming "Abolitionists" under such circumstances than at present exists:—

The great mass of our poor white population begin to understand that they have rights, and that they, too, are entitled to some of the sympathy which falls upon the suffering. They are fast learning that there is an almost infinite world of industry opening before them by which they can elevate themselves and their families from wretchedness and ignorance to competence and intelligence. It is this great upheaving of our masses that we have to fear, so far as our institutions are concerned.

It is, in the nature of things, while slaveholders refuse the slightest concession to the spirit of the age—while, in their legislation, they refuse to recognize, in the slightest degree, the principles of social science under which we live, and must live, and which every civilized people has fully adopted, that they should endeavour to make it appear the fault of others that they do not feel assured of safety and at ease with themselves; that they should try to make their own ignorant people believe that it is from without all danger is to be apprehended—all assurance of safety to be clamoured for—that they should endeavour to make themselves believe it.[7]

Those who seriously propose to stop all agitation on the subject of slavery, by causing the Abolitionists to refrain from proceedings

[7] The real object of the systematic mail robbery which is maintained throughout the South, and of the censorship of the press which is otherwise attempted, was once betrayed by a somewhat distinguished Southern editor, Duff Green, in the *United States Telegraph*, in the following words:—

"The real danger of this [slave insurrection] is remote. We believe we have most to fear from the organized action upon the consciences and fears of the slaveholders themselves; from the insinuation of their dangerous heresies into our schools, our pulpits, and our domestic circles. It is only by alarming the consciences of the weak and feeble, and diffusing among our people a morbid sensibility on the question of slavery, that the Abolitionists can accomplish their object."

which cause apprehension at the South, by silencing all who entertain sentiments the utterance of which is deemed a source of "danger to Southern institutions," by refraining themselves from all
proceedings which will be looked upon with alarm by their fellow-
citizens of the Slave States, can know very little of what would be
required before the South were satisfied. The destruction of some
million dollars' cost in school and text books would be one of the
first things, and yet but a small item in the undertaking. Books
which directly comment upon slavery are considered comparatively
safe, because their purpose being defined, they can be guarded
against. As is well understood, it is the insidious attacks of a free
press that are most feared. But is it well understood what are felt
to be "insidious attacks"? Some idea may be formed from the following passages which I take, not from the heated columns of a daily
newspaper, but from the cool pages of the deliberate De Bow's "Review." The apprehension they express is not of to-day; in the first
article from which I quote (which was published in the middle of
Mr. Pierce's presidential term), reference is made to warnings of
the same character which have been sounded from time to time before; and this very number of the "Review" contains a testimonial
from fifty-five Southern senators and representatives in Congress to
the "ability and accuracy" of its "exposition of the working of the
system of polity of the Southern States."

Our text books are abolition books. They are so to the extent of their
capacity. . . . We have been too careless and indifferent to the import
of these things.

And so long as we use such works as "Wayland's Moral Science," and
the abolition geographies, readers, and histories, overrunning, as they do,
with all sorts of slanders, caricatures, and blood-thirsty sentiments, let us
never complain of their [northern Church people's] use of that transitory
romance ["Uncle Tom's Cabin"]. They seek to array our children, by false
ideas, against the established ordinance of God; and it sometimes takes
effect. A professor in one of our Southern seminaries, not long since
placed in the hands of a pupil "Wayland's Moral Science," and informed
her that the chapter on slavery was heretical and unscriptural, and that
she would not be examined on that chapter, and need not study it. *Perhaps* she didn't. But on the day of examination she wished her teacher
to tell her "if that chapter was heretical how she was to know but they
were all so?" We might enumerate many other books of similar character
and tendencies. But we will refer to only one more— it is "Gilbert's Atlas"

—though the real author's name does not appear on the title page. On the title page it is called "Appleton's Complete Guide of the World"; published by D. Appleton & Co., New York. This is an elegant and comprehensive volume, endorsed by the Appletons and sent South, containing hidden lessons of the most fiendish and murderous character that enraged fanaticism could conceive or indite.[8] It is a sort of literary and scientific infernal machine. And whatever the design may have been, the tendency is as shocking as the imagination can picture. . . . This is the artillery and these the implements England and our own recreant sister States are employing to overturn the order of society and the established forms of labour that date back beyond the penning of the decalogue. . . . This book, and many other Northern school-books scattered over the country, come within the range of the statutes of this State, which provide for the imprisonment for life or the infliction of the penalty of death upon any person who shall "publish or distribute" such works; and were I a citizen of New Orleans, this work should not escape the attention of the grand jury. But need I add more to convince the sceptical of the necessity there is for the production of our own text-books, and, may I not add, our own literature? Why should the land of domestic servitude be less productive in the great works of the mind now than when Homer evoked the arts, poetry, and eloquence into existence? Moses wrote the Genesis of Creation, the Exodus of Israel, and the laws of mankind? and when Cicero, Virgil, Horace, St. John, and St. Paul became the instructors of the world? [9] . . . They will want no cut-throat literature, no fire-brand moral science . . . nor Appleton's "Complete Atlas," to encourage crimes that would blanch the cheek of a pirate, nor any of the ulcerous and polluting agencies issuing from the hot-beds of abolition fanaticism.

From an article on educational reform at the South, in the same "Review," 1856, I take the following indications of what, among other Northern doings, are considered to imperil the South:—

"Lovell's United States Speaker," the "National Reader," the "Young Ladies' Reader," "Columbian Orator," "Scott's Lessons," the "Village Reader," and numerous others, have been used for years, and are all, in some respects, valuable compilations. We apprehend, however, there are

---

[8] Elsewhere the Messrs. Appleton are spoken of as "the great Abolition publishers of New York."

[9] Note the argument, I pray you, reader. Why, indeed? Why is there not a Feejee Iliad? Are not the Feejees heathen, as Homer was? Why should not the Book of Mormon be as good a thing as the Psalms of David? Was not Joseph Smith also a polygamist?

few parents or teachers who are familiar with the whole of their contents, or they would demand expurgated editions for the use of their children. *The sickly sentimentality of the poet Cowper*, whose ear became so "pained," and his soul "sick with every day's report of wrong and outrage," that it made him cry out in agony for "a lodge in some vast wilderness," where he might commune with howling wolves and panthers on the blessings of *liberty*(?), stamps its infectious poison upon many of the pages of these works. . . .

From the American First Class Book, page 185, we quote another more modern sentiment, which bears no less higher authority than the name of the great Massachusetts statesman, Mr. Webster:

Having burnt or expurgated Webster and Cowper, is it to be imagined that the leaders of opinion in the South would yet be willing to permit familiar intercourse between themselves and a people who allowed a book containing such lines as these to circulate freely?—

> *What is a man*
> *If his chief good and market of his time*
> *Be but to sleep and feed? A beast, no more.*
> *Sure, He that made us with such large discourse,*
> *Looking before and after, gave us not*
> *That capability and Godlike reason,*
> *To rust unused.*

What a dangerous sentiment to come by any chance to a slave! Is it not? Are you, then, prepared to burn your Shakespeare? I will not ask if you will have another book "expurgated," of all passages the tendency of which is to set the bondmen free.

If the security of life and property at the South must for ever be dependent on the thoroughness with which the negro population is prevented from acquiring knowledge; from thinking of themselves and for themselves, it will never be felt to be greater than it is to-day. Efforts made to increase this security will of themselves occasion agitation, and agitation must counteract those efforts. Knowledge, knowledge of what is going on elsewhere, of the condition of men elsewhere, of what is thought elsewhere, must have increased currency with every class of mankind in all parts of this continent, as it increases in population, and the movements of its population increase in activity and importance. No human laws, embargoes, or armies and navies can prevent it. Do our utmost, we cannot go back of the steam-engine, the telegraph, the cotton-gin, and the cylinder press. The South has admitted steamboats and railroads. It was not practicable to stop with these, and bar out all the rest that is peculiar to the nineteenth century. Is it practicable to admit the machinery of modern civilized life, and not stir up its free people? Is it practicable to stir up its intermediate class, and keep its lowest torpid? Assuredly the security which depends upon preventing either of these steps can never be permanently increased; spite of all possible further extension of slave territory, and dispersion and disconnection of plantations, it must gradually lessen. As it lessens, the demand upon the nation to supply new grounds of security must increase—increase continually, until at length, this year, next year, or another, they conclusively and hopelessly fail. It may cost us much or it may cost us little to reach that point, but it is inevitably to be reached. It may be after long and costly civil war, or longer and more costly foreign wars, or it may be peaceably, sensibly, and soon, but it must come. The annexation of Cuba, international fugitive slave laws,[1] the African slave trade, judgments of the Supreme Court, and whatever else may be first asked and given, will not prevent it—nothing the North will do, nothing the North can do, will prevent it. The proximity of a people who cannot hold labour in contempt; who cannot keep labourers in ignorance and permanent dependence each upon another man; who cannot have an effective censorship of the press, or a trustworthy army of *mouchards,* prevents, and must always prevent, the South from standing with the slightest confidence of safety on that policy which it proclaims to be its only ground of safety. Nothing but a reversal of the current of our Northern history for half a century, nothing, in fact, but the

---

[1] From the *Columbia* (S.C.) *Times,* quoted without dissent in the conservative South Carolina paper, the *Charleston Mercury:*—

"The loss that the South annually sustains by the running of slaves into Canada, is of sufficient importance to justify her public men in insisting upon some action of the Government of the United States in the premises. And we confess our surprise that Southern statesmen have submitted with so much patience to the annual robbery of thousands of dollars' worth of property to which she has as good a right as the land they cultivate. The time is propitious for the acquisition of all disputed rights from European powers. They cannot afford to break just now with the United States. Let our public men move in the matter, and we question not but that the President and the American Minister at St. James's will give the movement a cordial support. Besides, this is a golden moment which may never return. Before we get another sound man in the presidential chair, peace may be made in Europe, and the European powers be less inclined to look with favour upon the demands of America."

enslavement of labour at the North, could in the nature of things give that security, even temporarily, to the capitalists of labour at the South which they need.[2] Some demand of the South upon the nation, acquiescence in which it holds essential to its safety, must then at length be distinctly refused. And when, ten or twenty years hence, if so be, this shall come to pass, what then is to happen to us?

Dissolution?

This is what many Southern politicians avow, whenever they contemplate such a contingency.

Why?

Because it is known that the people of the North are unwilling that the Union should be dissolved, whereas they have no indisposition to the only course which it will then be possible for the South to adopt, for the sake of increasing the security of its citizens, against insurrectionary movements of its slaves. This plainly would be to arrange a systematic opportunity and method for the slaves to labour, whenever they chose, and as much as they might choose, in an orderly, peaceable, and wise way, for their own release and improvement, each man for himself and those most dear to him; each man by himself, independently, openly, with no occasion for combination, secrecy, plots, or conspiracy. To prepare, for those disposed to avail themselves of it, a field, either here or elsewhere, in which their capability and Godlike reason, such as it may be, little or great, need not be forced by law to rust unused, or brighten *only* to the material advantage of a master. This I must think to be consciously, even now, the only final course of safety before every reflective Southern mind. This, or—dissolution, and the chances of war.

(The above was written before Mr. Lincoln was spoken of as a candidate for the Presidency.)

[2] "While it is far more obvious that negroes should be slaves than whites, for they are only fit to labour, not to direct; yet the principle of slavery is itself right, and does not depend upon difference of complexion. Difference of race, lineage, of language, of habits, and customs, all tend to render the institution more natural and durable; and although slaves have been generally whites, still the masters and slaves have generally been of different national descent. Moses and Aristotle, the earliest historians, are both authorities in favour of this difference of race, but not of colour."—*Richmond Enquirer.*

APPENDIX

(A)

The Condition of Virginia—Statistics

1

THE *Richmond Enquirer*, a strong and influential pro-slavery news-paper of Virginia, in advocating some railroad projects, thus describes the progress of the State relatively to that of some of the Free States, since the Revolution. (Dec. 29, 1852.)

Virginia, anterior to the Revolution, and up to the adoption of the Federal Constitution, contained more wealth and a larger population than any other State of this Confederacy. . . .

Virginia, from being first in point of wealth and political power, has come down to the fifth in the former, and the fourth in the latter. New York, Pennsylvania, Massachusetts, and Ohio stand above her in wealth, and all, but Massachusetts, in population and political power. Three of these States are literally chequered over with railroads and canals; and the fourth (Massachusetts) with railroads alone. . . .

But when we find that the population of the single city of New York and its environs exceeds the whole free population of Eastern Virginia, and the valley between the Blue Ridge and Alleghany, we have cause to feel deeply for our situation. Philadelphia herself contains a population far greater than the whole free population of Eastern Virginia. The little State of Massachusetts has an aggregate wealth exceeding that of Virginia by more than one hundred and twenty-six millions of dollars—a State, too, which is incapable of subsisting its inhabitants from the production of its soil. And New York, which was as much below Massachusetts, at the adoption of the Federal Constitution, in wealth and power, as the latter was below Virginia, now exceeds the wealth of both. While the aggregate wealth of New York, in 1850, amounted to $1,080,309,216, that of Virginia was $436,701,082—a difference in favour of the former of $643,608,134. The unwrought mineral wealth of Virginia exceeds that of New York. The climate and soil are better; the back country, with equal improvements, would contribute as much.

The same journal adds, on another occasion:—

In no State of the Confederacy do the facilities for manufacturing operations exist in greater profusion than in Virginia. Every condition essential to success in these employments is found here in prodigal abundance, and in a peculiarly convenient combination. First, we have a limitless supply of water power—the cheapest of motors—in localities easy of access. So abundant is this supply of water power that no value is attached to it distinct from the adjacent lands, except in the vicinity of the larger towns. On the Potomac and its tributaries; on the Rappahannock; on the James and its tributaries; on the Roanoke and its tributaries; on the Holston, the Kanawha, and other streams, numberless sites may now be found where the supply of water power is sufficient for the purposes of a Lawrence or a Lowell. Nor is there any want of material for building at these localities; timber and granite are abundant; and, to complete the circle of advantages, the climate is genial and healthful, and the soil eminently productive. . . . Another advantage which Virginia possesses, for the manufacture of cotton, is the proximity of its mills to the raw material. At the present prices of the staple, the value of this advantage is estimated at 10 per cent.

The *Lynchburg Virginian*, another newspaper of respectability, having a similar purpose in hand, namely, to induce capitalists to invest their money in enterprises that shall benefit the State, observes that—

The coal fields of Virginia are the most extensive in the world, and her coal is of the best and purest quality. Her iron deposits are altogether inexhaustible, and in many instances so pure that it is malleable in its primitive state; and many of these deposits in the immediate vicinity of extensive coal-fields. She has, too, very extensive deposits of copper, lead, and gypsum. Her rivers are numerous and bold, generally with fall enough for extensive water power.

A remarkable feature in the mining and manufacturing prospects of Virginia is, the ease and economy with which all her minerals are mined; instead of being, as in England and elsewhere, generally imbedded deep within the bowels of the earth, from which they can be got only with great labour and at great cost, ours are found everywhere on the hills and slopes, with their ledges dipping in the direction of the plains below. Why, then, should not Virginia at once employ at least half of her labour and capital in mining and manufacturing? Richmond could as profitably manufacture all cotton and woollen goods as Lowell, or any other town in New England. Why should not Lynchburg, with all her promised facility of getting coal and pig metal, manufacture all articles of iron and steel just as cheaply, and yet as profitably, as any portion of the Northern States? Why should not every town and village on the line of every railroad in the State, erect their shops, in which they may manufacture a thousand articles of daily consumption, just as good and cheap as they may be made anywhere? . . .

Dependent upon Europe and the North for almost every yard of cloth, and every coat, and boot, and hat we wear; for our axes, scythes, tubs, and buckets—in short, for everything except our bread and meat!—it must occur to the South that if our relations with the North should ever be severed—and how soon they may be, none can know (may God avert it long!)—we would, in all the South, not be able to clothe ourselves. We could not fell our forests, plough our fields, nor mow our meadows. In fact, we would be reduced to a state more abject than we are willing to look at even prospectively. And yet, with all these things staring us in the face, we shut our eyes, and go on blindfold.

At the Convention for the formation of the Virginia State Agricultural Society, in 1852, the draft of an address to the farmers of the State was read, approved, and once adopted by the Convention. The vote by which it was adopted was soon afterwards reconsidered, and it was again approved and adopted. A second time it was reconsidered; and finally it was rejected, on the ground that there were admissions in it that would feed the fanaticism of the Abolitionists. No one argued against it on the ground of the falsity or inaccuracy of these admissions. Twenty of the most respectable proprietors in the State, immediately afterwards, believing it to contain "matter of grave import," which should not be suppressed for such a reason, united in requesting a copy of it for publication. In the note of these gentlemen to the author, they express the belief that Virginia now "possesses the richest soil, most genial climate, and cheapest labour on earth." The author of the address, in his reply, says: "Fanaticism is a fool for whose vagaries I am not responsible. I am a pro-slavery man—I believe it, at this time, impossible to abolish it, and not desirable if it were possible."

The address was accordingly published, and I make the following extracts from it:—

ADDRESS TO THE FARMERS OF VIRGINIA

"The Southern States stand foremost in agricultural labour, though they hold but the third rank in population." At the head of these Southern States, in production, in extent of territory, in climate, in soil, and in population, stands the Commonwealth of Virginia. She is a nation of farmers. Eight-tenths of her industry is expended upon the soil; but less than one-third of her domain is in pasturage, or under the plough.

Out of somewhat more than thirty-nine millions of acres, she tills but little over ten millions of acres, or about twenty-six and a quarter per cent., whilst New York has subdued about forty-one per cent., or twelve and a quarter out of her twenty-nine and a half millions of acres: and Massachusetts, with her sterile soil and inhospitable climate, has reclaimed from the forest, the quarry, and the marsh, about forty-two and a half per cent., or two and one-eighth out of her little territory of five millions of acres. Yet, according to the census of 1840, only six-tenths of the labour of New York, and four-tenths of that of Massachusetts, or, relatively, one-fifth and two-fifths less than our own, is expended upon agriculture. . . .

The live stock of Virginia are worth only three dollars and thirty-one cents for every arable acre; but in New York they are worth six dollars and seven cents, and in Massachusetts four dollars and fifty-two cents.

The proportion of hay for the same quantity of land is, for Virginia, eighty-one pounds; for New York, six hundred and seventy-nine pounds; for Massachusetts, six hundred and eighty-four pounds. . . .

With access to the same markets, and with hundreds of mechanics of our own, who can vie with the best Northern manufacturers, we find that our implements are inferior, that the New York farmer spends upon his nearly three times as much as we do upon ours, and the Massachusetts farmer more than double. . . .

Manure is indispensable to good husbandry. Judging from the history of agriculture in all other countries, we may safely say, that farming can never attain to continued perfection where manure is not put on with an unsparing hand. By far the larger part of this can only be made by stock, which should, at the same time, be made the source of profit, at least sufficient to pay the cost of their keep, so that, *other things being equal,* it is a safe rule to estimate the condition of a farming district by the amount of live stock it may possess, and the provision made for their sustenance. Applied in this instance, we see that the New York farmer has invested in live stock two dollars and seventy-six cents, and the Massachusetts farmer one dollar and twenty-one cents per acre more than the Virginia farmer. In pasturage we cannot tell the difference. It is well, perhaps, for the honour of the State, that we cannot. But in hay, New York has five hundred and ninety-eight pounds, and Massachusetts six hundred and three pounds more per acre than we have. This, however, does not present the true state of the case. Land-locked by mountain barriers, as yet impassable for the ordinary agricultural staples, or debarred from their production by distance and prohibitory rates of transportation, most of the wealth and exports of many considerable portions of our State consists of live stock alone. What proportion these parts bear to the whole, we have been unable definitely to ascertain; but it is, no doubt, so great as to warrant us in assuming a much more considerable disparity than the statistics show in the live stock of the whole Atlantic slope, as compared with New York and Massachusetts. And we shall appreciate, still more highly, the skill of the Northern farmer, if we reflect that a readier market for every, the most trivial, product of his farm, operates as a constant temptation to break up his rotation and diminish his stock.

In the above figures, carefully calculated from the data of authentic documents,[1] we find no cause for self-gratulation, but some food for meditation. They are not without use to those who would improve the future by the past. They show that we have not done our part in the bringing of land into cultivation; that, notwithstanding natural advantages which greatly exceed those of the two States drawn into parallel with Virginia, we are yet behind them both—that with forty and sixty per cent. respectively of their industry devoted to other pursuits, into which it has been lured by prospects of greater gain, they have done more than we have done. . . .

Whilst our population has increased for the last ten years, in a ratio of 11.66, that of New York has increased in a ratio of 27.52, and that of Massachusetts at the still heavier and more startling rate of 34.81. With a territorial area thirty per cent. larger than New York, we have but little more than one-third of her Congressional representation; and Massachusetts, only one-eighth our size, comes within two of our number of representatives, we being cut down to thirteen, while she rises to eleven. And thus we, who once swayed the councils of the Union, find our power gone, and our influence on the wane, at a time when both are of vital importance to our prosperity, if not to our safety. As other States accumulate the means of material greatness, and glide past us on the road to wealth and empire, we slight the warnings of dull statistics, and drive lazily along the field of ancient customs, or stop the *plough*, to speed the *politician*—should we not, in too many cases, say with more propriety, the *demagogue?*

State pride is a good thing; it is one mode in which patriotism is manifested. But it is not always a wise one. Certainly not, when it makes us content on small grounds. And when it smothers up improvement in self-satisfaction, it is a most pernicious thing. We have much to be proud of in Virginia. In intellect and fitness to command, in personal and social qualities, in high tone and noble bearing, in loyalty, in generosity, and magnanimity, and disinterestedness, above all, in moral purity, we once

[1] Abstract of the Seventh Census, and the able work of Professor [George] Tucker, on the "Progress of the United States in Population and Wealth."

stood—let us hope, still stand—pre-eminent among our sister States. But the possession and practice of these virtues do not comprise our whole duty as men or as citizens. The great decree which has gone forth ordaining that we shall "increase, and multiply, and replenish the earth," enjoins upon us quite other duties, which cannot be neglected with impunity; so we have found out by experience—for we *have* neglected these duties. And when we contemplate our field of labour, and the work we have done in it, we cannot but observe the sad contrast between capacity and achievement. With a wide-spread domain, with a kindly soil, with a climate whose sun radiates fertility, and whose very dews distil abundance, we find our inheritance so wasted that the eye aches to behold the prospect.

2

The Census of 1850 gives the following values to agricultural land in the adjoining States of Virginia and Pennsylvania.

	In Virginia	In Pennsylvania
No. of acres improved land in farms,	10,360,135	8,626,619
" unimproved,	15,792,176	6,294,728
Cash value of farms,	$216,401,543—$8 an acre.	$407,876,099—$25 an acre.

Considering that, at the Revolution, Virginia had nearly twice the population of Pennsylvania, was in possession of much more wealth or disposable capital, and had much the best natural facilities for external commerce and internal communication, if her political and social constitution had been and had continued equally good, and her people equally industrious and enterprising with those of Pennsylvania, there is no reason why the value of her farms should not have been, at this time, at least equal to those of Pennsylvania. Were it so, it appears that Virginia, in that particular alone, would now be richer than she is by four hundred and thirty millions of dollars.

If it should be thought that this difference between the value of land in Virginia and Pennsylvania is in some degree due to more fertile soils in the latter, a similar comparison may be made with the other adjoining Free State, and old State of New Jersey, the climate of which, owing to its vicinity to the ocean, differs imperceptibly from that of Virginia, while its soil is decidedly less fertile, taking both States on an average. The average value of farming-land in New Jersey is recorded at $44.

Give this value to the Virginia farms, and the difference between it and their present value would buy, at a large valuation, all the slaves now in the State, send them to Africa, provide each family of them five hundred dollars to start with when they reach there, and leave still a surplus which, divided among the present white population of the State, would give between two and three thousand dollars to each family.

Some Southern writers have lately objected to comparisons of density of population, as indications of the prosperity of communities. Between two adjoining communities, however, where there are no restrictions upon the movements of the populations, and when the people are so ready to move as both those of Pennsylvania, and New Jersey, and of Virginia have shown themselves to be, the price of land must indicate with considerable exactness the comparative value or desirableness of it, all things considered, to live upon. The Virginians do not admit, and have no occasion to do so, that Pennsylvania and New Jersey have any advantage over Virginia, in soil, in climate, or in any natural quality.

3

In intellectual productions, the same general comparative barrenness is noticeable.

From the Richmond Whig

We receive nearly all our books from Northern or foreign authors—gotten up, printed by Northern or foreign publishers—while we have among us numberless men of ripe scholarship, profound acquirements, elegant and forcible writers—men willing to devote themselves to such labour, *only a Southern book is not patronized.* The North usually scowls at it, ridicules it, or damns it with faint praise; and the South takes on a like hue and complexion and neglects it. We have printers and publishers able, willing, and competent to publish, but, such is the *apathy* on the part of Southern people, that it involves hazard to Southern publishers to put them out. Indeed, until recently, almost all the publications, even of Southern books, issued (and that was their only hope of success) from Northern houses. The last chance now of getting a Southern book sold, is to manage to secure the favourable notice of the Northern press, and then the South buys it. Our magazines and periodicals languish for support.

Mr. [Robert R.] Howison, "The Virginia Historian," observes:

The question might be asked, Where is the literature of Virginia? and it would not be easily answered. It is a melancholy fact, that her people have never been a reading people. In the mass they have shown an indifference to polite literature and education in general, depressing to the mind that wishes to see them respectable and happy.

"It is with pain," says the same authority, "that we are compelled to speak of the horrible cloud of ignorance that rests on Virginia," and he computes that (1848) there are in the State 166,000 youth, between seven and sixteen years of age, and of these 126,000 attend no school at all, and receive no education except what can be imparted by poor and ignorant parents. Besides these, he reckons 449,087 slaves and 48,852 free negroes, with few exceptions, wholly uneducated.

The policy which discourages further extension of knowledge among them is necessary: but the fact remains unchanged, that they exist among us, *a huge mass of mind, almost entirely unenlightened.* We fear that the most favourable estimates will leave, in our State, 683,000 rational beings who are destitute of the merest rudiments of knowledge.

Appendix

(B)

The Slave Trade in Virginia

From Chambers' Journal, October, 1853

The exposure of ordinary goods in a store is not more open to the public than are the sales of slaves in Richmond. By consulting the local newspapers, I learned that the sales take place by auction every morning in the offices of certain brokers, who, as I understood by the terms of their advertisements, purchased or received slaves for sale on commission.

Where the street was in which the brokers conducted their business, I did not know; but the discovery was easily made. Rambling down the main street in the city, I found that the subject of my search was a narrow and short thoroughfare, turning off to the left, and terminating in a similar cross thoroughfare. Both streets, lined with brick houses, were dull and silent. There was not a person to whom I could put a question. Looking about, I observed the office of a commission agent, and into it I stepped. Conceive the idea of a large shop with two windows, and a door between; no shelving or counters inside; the interior a spacious, dismal apartment, not well swept; the only furniture a desk at one of the windows, and a bench at one side of the shop, three feet high, with two steps to it from the floor. I say, conceive the idea of this dismal-looking place, with nobody in it but three negro children, who, as I entered, were playing at auctioneering each other. An intensely black little negro, of four or five years of age, was standing on the bench, or block, as it is called, with an equally black girl, about a year younger, by his side, whom he was pretending to sell by bids to another black child, who was rolling about the floor.

My appearance did not interrupt the merriment. The little auctioneer continued his mimic play, and appeared to enjoy the joke of selling the girl, who stood demurely by his side.

"Fifty dolla for de gal—fifty dolla—fifty dolla—I sell dis here fine gal for fifty dolla," was uttered with extraordinary volubility by the woolly-headed urchin, accompanied with appropriate gestures, in imitation, doubtless, of the scenes he had seen enacted daily on the spot. I spoke a few words to the little creatures, but was scarcely understood, and the fun went on as if I had not been present: so I left them, happy in rehearsing what was likely soon to be their own fate.

At another office of a similar character, on the opposite side of the

street, I was more successful. Here, on inquiry, I was respectfully informed, by a person in attendance, that the sale would take place the
following morning at half-past nine o'clock.

Next day I set out accordingly, after breakfast, for the scene of operations, in which there was now a little more life. Two or three persons
were lounging about, smoking cigars; and, looking along the street, I
observed that three red flags were projected from the doors of those
offices in which sales were to occur. On each flag was pinned a piece of
paper, notifying the articles to be sold. The number of lots was not great.
On the first was the following announcement:—"Will be sold this morning, at half-past nine o'clock, a Man and a Boy."

It was already the appointed hour; but as no company had assembled,
I entered and took a seat by the fire. The office, provided with a few deal
forms and chairs, a desk at one of the windows, and a block accessible by
a few steps, was tenantless, save by a gentleman who was arranging papers at the desk, and to whom I had addressed myself on the previous
evening. Minute after minute passed, and still nobody entered. There
was clearly no hurry in going to business. I felt almost like an intruder,
and had formed the resolution of departing, in order to look into the
other offices, when the person referred to left his desk, and came and
seated himself opposite to me at the fire.

"You are an Englishman," said he, looking me steadily in the face; "do
you want to purchase?"

"Yes," I replied, "I am an Englishman; but I do not intend to purchase.
I am travelling about for information, and I shall feel obliged by your
letting me know the prices at which negro servants are sold."

"I will do so with much pleasure," was the answer; "do you mean field-
hands or house-servants?"

"All kinds," I replied; "I wish to get all the information I can."

With much politeness, the gentleman stepped to his desk, and began
to draw up a note of prices. This, however, seemed to require careful
consideration; and while the note was preparing, a lanky person, in a
wide-awake hat, and chewing tobacco, entered, and took the chair just
vacated. He had scarcely seated himself, when, on looking towards the
door, I observed the subjects of sale—the man and boy indicated by the
paper on the red flag—enter together, and quietly walk to a form at the
back of the shop, whence, as the day was chilly, they edged themselves
towards the fire, in the corner where I was seated. I was now between the
two parties—the white man on the right, and the old and young negro on
the left—and I waited to see what would take place.

The sight of the negroes at once attracted the attention of Wide-awake.
Chewing with vigour, he kept keenly eyeing the pair, as if to see what

they were good for. Under this searching gaze, the man and boy were a little abashed, but said nothing. Their appearance had little of the repulsiveness we are apt to associate with the idea of slaves. They were dressed in a gray woollen coat, pants, and waistcoat, coloured cotton neckcloths, clean shirts, coarse woollen stockings, and stout shoes. The man wore a black hat; the boy was bareheaded. Moved by a sudden impulse, Wide-awake left his seat, and rounding the back of my chair, began to grasp at the man's arms, as if to feel their muscular capacity. He then examined his hands and fingers; and, last of all, told him to open his mouth and show his teeth, which he did in a submissive manner. Having finished these examinations, Wide-awake resumed his seat, and chewed on in silence as before.

I thought it was but fair that I should now have my turn of investigation, and accordingly asked the elder negro what was his age. He said he did not know. I next inquired how old the boy was. He said he was seven years of age. On asking the man if the boy was his son, he said he was not—he was his cousin. I was going into other particulars, when the office-keeper approached, and handed me the note he had been preparing; at the same time making the observation that the market was dull at present, and that there never could be a more favourable opportunity of buying. I thanked him for the trouble which he had taken; and now submit a copy of his price-current:

Best Men, 18 to 25 years old . . .	1200 to 1300	dollars
Fair do. do. do. . . .	950 to 1050	"
Boys, 5 feet	850 to 950	"
Do., 4 feet 8 inches	700 to 800	"
Do., 4 feet 5 inches	500 to 600	"
Do., 4 feet	375 to 450	"
Young Women	800 to 1000	"
Girls, 5 feet	750 to 850	"
Do., 4 feet 9 inches	700 to 750	"
Do., 4 feet	350 to 450	"

(Signed) _____

Richmond, Virginia

Leaving this document for future consideration, I pass on to a history of the day's proceedings. It was now ten minutes to ten o'clock, and Wide-awake and I being alike tired of waiting, we went off in quest of sales further up the street. Passing the second office, in which also nobody was to be seen, we were more fortunate at the third. Here according to the announcement on the paper stuck to the flag, there were to be sold, "A woman and three children; a young woman, three men, a middle-aged woman, and a little boy." Already a crowd had met, composed, I should think, of persons mostly from the cotton-plantations of the South. A few were seated near a fire on the right-hand side, and others stood round an iron stove in the middle of the apartment. The whole place had a dilapidated appearance. From a back window, there was a view into a ruinous court-yard; beyond which, in a hollow, accessible by a side lane, stood a shabby brick house, on which the word *Jail* was inscribed in large black letters on a white ground. I imagined it to be a depôt for the reception of negroes.

On my arrival, and while making these preliminary observations, the lots for sale had not made their appearance. In about five minutes afterwards, they were ushered in, one after the other, under the charge of a mulatto, who seemed to act as principal assistant. I saw no whips, chains, or any other engine of force. Nor did such appear to be required. All the lots took their seats on two long forms near the stove; none showed any signs of resistance; nor did any one utter a word. Their manner was that of perfect humility and resignation.

As soon as all were seated, there was a general examination of their respective merits, by feeling their arms, looking into their mouths, and investigating the quality of their hands and fingers—this last being evidently an important particular. Yet there was no abrupt rudeness in making these examinations—no coarse or domineering language was employed. The three negro men were dressed in the usual manner—in gray woollen clothing. The woman, with three children, excited my peculiar attention. She was neatly attired, with a coloured handkerchief bound around her head, and wore a white apron over her gown. Her children were all girls, one of them a baby at the breast three months old, and the others two and three years of age respectively, rigged out with clean white pinafores. There was not a tear or an emotion visible in the whole party. Everything seemed to be considered as a matter of course; and the change of owners was possibly looked forward to with as much indifference as ordinary hired servants anticipate a removal from one employer to another.

While intending purchasers were proceeding with personal examinations of the several lots, I took the liberty of putting a few questions to the mother of the children. The following was our conversation:—

"Are you a married woman?"

"Yes, sir."

"How many children have you had?"

"Seven."

"Where is your husband?"

"In Madison county."

"When did you part from him?"

"On Wednesday—two days ago."

"Were you sorry to part from him?"

"Yes, sir," she replied, with a deep sigh; "my heart was a'most broke."

"Why is your master selling you?"

"I don't know—he wants money to buy some land—suppose he sells me for that."

There might not be a word of truth in these answers, for I had no means of testing their correctness; but the woman seemed to speak unreservedly, and I am inclined to think that she said nothing but what, if necessary, could be substantiated. I spoke, also, to the young woman who was seated near her. She, like the others, was perfectly black, and appeared stout and healthy, of which some of the persons present assured themselves by feeling her arms and ankles, looking into her mouth, and causing her to stand up. She told me she had several brothers and sisters, but did not know where they were. She said she was a house-servant, and would be glad to be bought by a good master—looking at me, as if I should not be unacceptable.

I have said that there was an entire absence of emotion in the looks of men, women, and children, thus seated preparatory to being sold. This does not correspond with the ordinary accounts of slave-sales, which are represented as tearful and harrowing. My belief is, that none of the parties felt deeply on the subject, or at least that any distress they experienced was but momentary—soon passed away, and was forgotten. One of my reasons for this opinion rests on a trifling incident which occurred. While waiting for the commencement of the sale, one of the gentlemen present amused himself with a pointer dog, which, at command, stood on its hind legs, and took pieces of bread from his pocket. These tricks greatly entertained the row of negroes, old and young; and the poor woman, whose heart three minutes before was almost broken, now laughed as heartily as any one.

"Sale is going to commence—this way, gentlemen," cried a man at the door to a number of loungers outside; and all having assembled, the mulatto assistant led the woman and her children to the block, which he helped her to mount. There she stood, with her infant at the breast, and one of her girls at each side. The auctioneer, a handsome, gentlemanly personage, took his place, with one foot on an old deal chair with a broken back, and the other raised on the somewhat more elevated block. It was a striking scene.

"Well, gentlemen," began the salesman, "here is a capital woman and her three children, all in good health—what do you say for them? Give me an offer. (Nobody speaks.) I put up the whole lot at 850 dollars—

850 dollars—850 dollars (speaking very fast)—850 dollars. Will no one advance upon that? A very extraordinary bargain, gentlemen. A fine, healthy baby. Hold it up. (Mulatto goes up the first step of the block; takes the baby from the woman's breast, and holds it aloft with one hand, so as to show that it was a veritable sucking baby.) That will do. A woman, still young, and three children, all for 850 dollars. An advance, if you please, gentlemen. (A voice bids 860.) Thank you, sir, 860; any one bids more? (A second voice says, 870; and so on the bidding goes as far as 890 dollars, when it stops.) That won't do, gentlemen. I cannot take such a low price. (After a pause, addressing the mulatto): She may go down." Down from the block the woman and her children were therefore conducted by the assistant, and, as if nothing had occurred, they calmly resumed their seats by the stove.

The next lot brought forward was one of the men. The assistant beckoning to him with his hand, requested him to come behind a canvas screen, of two leaves, which was standing near the back window. The man placidly rose, and having been placed behind the screen, was ordered to take off his clothes, which he did without a word or look of remonstrance. About a dozen gentlemen crowded to the spot while the poor fellow was stripping himself, and as soon as he stood on the floor, bare from top to toe, a most rigorous scrutiny of his person was instituted. The clear black skin, back and front, was viewed all over for sores from disease; and there was no part of his body left unexamined. The man was told to open and shut his hands, asked if he could pick cotton, and every tooth in his head was scrupulously looked at. The investigation being at an end, he was ordered to dress himself; and having done so, was requested to walk to the block.

The ceremony of offering him for competition was gone through as before, but no one would bid. The other two men, after undergoing similar examinations behind the screen, were also put up, but with the same result. Nobody would bid for them, and they were all sent back to their seats. It seemed as if the company had conspired not to buy anything that day. Probably some imperfections had been detected in the personal qualities of the negroes. Be this as it may, the auctioneer, perhaps a little out of temper from his want of success, walked off to his desk, and the affair was so far at an end.

"This way, gentlemen—this way!" was heard from a voice outside, and the company immediately hived off to the second establishment. At this office there was a young woman, and also a man, for sale. The woman was put up first at 500 dollars; and possessing some recommendable qualities, the bidding for her was run as high as 710 dollars, at which she was knocked down to a purchaser. The man, after the customary examination behind the screen, was put up at 700 dollars; but a small imperfection having been observed in his person, no one would bid for him; and he was ordered down.

"This way, gentlemen, this way—down the street, if you please!" was now shouted by a person in the employment of the first firm, to whose office all very willingly adjourned—one migratory company, it will be perceived, serving all the slave-auctions in the place. In going in the crowd, I went to see what should be the fate of the man and boy, with whom I had already had some communication.

There the pair, the two cousins, sat by the fire, just where I had left them an hour ago. The boy was put up first.

"Come along, my man—jump up; there's a good boy!" said one of the partners, a bulky and respectable looking person, with a gold chain and bunch of seals; at the same time getting on the block. With alacrity the little fellow came forward, and, mounting the steps, stood by his side. The forms in front were filled by the company; and as I seated myself, I found that my old companion, Wide-awake, was close at hand, still chewing and spitting at a great rate.

"Now, gentlemen," said the auctioneer, putting his hand on the shoulder of the boy, "here is a very fine boy, seven years of age, warranted sound—what do you say for him? I put him up at 500 dollars—500 dollars (speaking quick, his right hand raised up, and coming down on the open palm of his left)—500 dollars. Any one say more than 500 dollars? (560 is bid.) 560 dollars. Nonsense! Just look at him. See how high he is. (He draws the lot in front of him, and shows that the little fellow's head comes up to his breast.) You see he is a fine, tall, healthy boy. Look at his hands."

Several step forward, and cause the boy to open and shut his hands—the flexibility of the small fingers, black on the one side, and whitish on the other, being well looked to. The hands, and also the mouth, having given satisfaction, an advance is made to 570, then to 580 dollars.

"Gentlemen, that is a very poor price for a boy of this size. (Addressing the lot)—Go down, my boy, and show them how you can run."

The boy, seemingly happy to do as he was bid, went down from the block, and ran smartly across the floor several times; the eyes of every one in the room following him.

"Now that will do. Get up again. (Boy mounts the block, the steps being rather deep for his short legs; but the auctioneer kindly lends him a hand.) Come, gentlemen, you see this is a first-rate lot. (590—600—610—620—630 dollars are bid.) I will sell him for 630 dollars. (Right hand coming down on left.) Last call. 630 dollars, once—630 dollars, twice. (A pause; hand sinks.) Gone!"

The boy having descended, the man was desired to come forward; and after the usual scrutiny behind a screen, he took his place on the block.

"Well, now, gentlemen," said the auctioneer, "here is a right prime lot. Look at this man; strong, healthy, able-bodied; could not be a better hand for field-work. He can drive a waggon or anything. What do you say for him? I offer the man at the low price of 800 dollars—he is well worth 1200 dollars. Come, make an advance, if you please. 800 dollars said for the man (a bid); thank you; 810 dollars—810 dollars—810 dollars (several bids)—820—830—850—860—going at 860—going. Gentlemen, this is far below his value. A strong-boned man, fit for any kind of heavy work. Just take a look at him. (Addressing the lot): Walk down. (Lot dismounts, and walks from one side of the shop to the other. When about to reascend the block, a gentleman, who is smoking a cigar, examines his mouth with his fingers. Lot resumes his place.) Pray, gentlemen, be quick (continues the auctioneer); I must sell him, and 860 dollars are only bid for the man—860 dollars. (A fresh run of bids to 945 dollars.) 945 dollars, once—945 dollars, twice (looking slowly round, to see if all were done), 945 dollars. Going—going—(hand drops)—gone!"

Such were a forenoon's experiences in the slave-market of Richmond. Everything is described precisely as it occurred, without passion or prejudice. It would not have been difficult to be sentimental on a subject which appeals so strongly to the feelings, but I have preferred telling the simple truth. In a subsequent chapter I shall endeavour to offer some general views of slavery in its social and political relations.

Appendix

(C)

Cost of Labour in the Border States

From a native Virginian, who has resided in New York: [1]

To the Editor of the N. Y. Daily Times

Sir—You will not object, I think, to receive an endorsement from a Southern man, of the statements contained in number seven of "Letters on the Productions, Industry, and Resources of the Southern States" [by Mr. Olmsted], published in your issue on Thursday last. . . .

Where you would see one white labourer on a Northern farm, scores of blacks should appear on the Virginian plantation, *the best of them only performing each day one-fourth a white man's daily task, and all requiring an incessant watch to get even this small modicum of labour.* Yet they eat as much again as a white man, must have their two suits of clothes and shoes yearly, and although the heartiest, healthiest looking men and women anywhere on earth, actually lose for their owners or employers one-sixth their time on account of real or pretended sickness. Be assured, our model Virginia farmer has his hands full, and is not to be envied as a jolly fox-hunting idler, lording it over "ranks of slaves in chains." No, sir; he must be up by "the dawn's early light," and head the column, direct in person the commencing operations, urging, and coaxing; must praise and punish—but too glad to reward the meritorious, granting liberty (*i. e.* leave of absence) often to his own servant, that he dare not take himself, because he must not leave home for fear something will go wrong ere his return. Hence but too many give up, to overseers or other irresponsible persons, the care and management of their estates, rather than undergo such constant annoyance and confinement. Poor culture, scanty crops, and worn-out land, is the inevitable result; and yet, harassed and trammeled as they are, no one but a Southerner regards them with the slightest degree of compassion or even forbearance; and our good friends, the Abolitionists, would have "all the rest of mankind" rank them with pirates and cutthroats. But my object in this communication is not to sympathize with nor ask sympathy on behalf of slaveholders. For, however sinning or sinned against, they seem quite able to take their own part, if molested; and are remarkably indifferent, withal, as to the opinions expressed by ignorant ranters concerning them.

[1] *New York Times*, March 22, 1853.

If I have the ability, my desire is to draw a parallel between the state and condition of Northern and Southern farmers and farming. The Northern farmer does undoubtedly experience a full share of those troubles and cares attendant even upon the most easy and favourable system of farming; but, sir, can he have any such responsibility as that resting upon the owner of from 50 to 300 ignorant, lazy negroes? . . .

You must plough deep, follow up quickly, and sow with powerful fertilizers, attend closely to the growing crop, gather in rapidly before blight or mildew can come and destroy, says our Northern farmer. On a farm of three hundred acres, thus managed with five hands, two extra during harvest, I can raise thirty bushels of wheat to the acre. Now picture the condition of him South, and hear his answer. With from three to fifteen hundred acres of land, and a host of negroes great and small, his cares and troubles are without end. "The hands," able men and women, to say nothing of children, and old ones laid by from age or other infirmity, have wants innumerable. Some are sick, others pretend to be so, many obstinate, indolent, or fractious—each class requires different treatment; so that without mentioning the actual daily wants, as provisions, clothing, etc., etc., the poor man's time, and thoughts—indeed, every faculty of mind—must be exercised on behalf of those who have no minds of their own.

His answer, then, to the Northern farmer is: "I have not one hand on my place capable and willing to do the work you name." They tell me that "five of them could not perform the task required of one." They have never been used to do it, and no amount of force or persuasion will induce them to try. Their task is so much per day; all over that I agree to pay them for, at the same rate I allow free labourers—but 'tis seldom they make extra time, except to get money enough to buy tobacco, rum, or sometimes fine clothes. Can it be wondered at that systematic farming, such as we see North and East, is unknown or not practised to any great degree South? The two systems will not harmonize.

R. J. W.

From a native New Yorker, who has resided in Virginia: [2]

To the Editor of the New York Daily Times

I have read with deep interest the series of letters from the South, published in your columns. Circumstances have made me quite familiar with the field of your correspondent's investigation, much more familiar than he is at present, and yet I am happy to say, that his letters are more satisfactory than any I have ever seen relating to the South. It is now about

[2] *New York Times*, April 7, 1853.

ten years since, going from this State, I first became familiar with those facts in regard to the results of slave labour, etc., that your correspondent and his readers are so much surprised at. I have talked those subjects over as he is doing, with the planters along the shores of the Chesapeake, and on both sides of the James River, through the Tidewater, the middle and the mountainous districts east of the Blue Ridge, and in many of those rich counties in the Valley of Virginia. I may add that, subsequently, spending my winters at the South for my health, I have become well nigh as familiar with the States of North and South Carolina, and Georgia, as I am with Virginia. I have, therefore, almost of necessity, given not a little thought to the questions your correspondent is discussing.

His statement, in regard to the comparative value of slave and free-labour, will surprise those who have given little or no attention to the subject. I wish to confirm his statements on this subject. In Eastern Virginia I have repeatedly been told that the task of one cord of wood a day, or five cords a week, rain or shine, is the general task, and one of the most profitable day's work that the slave does for his master. And this, it should be remembered, is generally pine wood, cut from trees as straight and beautiful as ever grew. The reason of this "profitableness" is the fact that the labour requires so little mental effort. The grand secret of the difference between free and slave labour is, that the latter is without intelligence, and without motive. If the former, in Western New York, has a piece of work to perform, the first thought is, how it can be done with the least labour, and the most expeditiously. He thinks, he plans, before he commences, and while about his labour. His mind labours as much as his body, and this mental labour saves a vast deal of physical labour. Besides this, he is urged on by the strongest motives. He enjoys the products of his labour. The more intelligent and earnest his labours, the richer are his rewards. Slave labour is exactly the opposite of this. It is unintelligent labour—labour without thought—without plan—without motive. It is little more than brute force. To one who has not witnessed it, it is utterly inconceivable how little labour a slave, or a company of slaves, will accomplish in a given time. Their awkwardness, their slowness, the utter absence of all skill and ingenuity in accomplishing the work before them, are absolutely painful to one who has been accustomed to seeing work done with any sort of spirit and life. Often they spend hours in doing what, with a little thought, might be despatched in a few moments, or perhaps avoided altogether. This is a necessary result of employing labour which is without intelligence and without motive. I have often thought of a remark made to me by a planter, in New Kent County, Virginia. We were riding past a field where some of his hands were making a sort of wicker-work fence, peculiar to Eastern Virginia. "There," said he, in a decidedly fretted tone, "those 'boys' have been —— days in making that piece of fence." I expressed my astonishment that they could have spent so much time, and yet have accomplished so very little. He assured me it was so—and after a slight pause, the tones of his voice entirely changed, said: "Well, I believe they have done as well as I would in their circumstances!" And so it is. The slave is without motive, without inducement to exertion. His food, his clothing, and all his wants are supplied as they are, without care on his part, and when these are supplied he has nothing more to hope for. He can make no provision for old age, he can lay up nothing for his children, he has no voice at all in the disposal of the results of his earnings. What cares he whether his labour is productive or unproductive. His principal care seems to be to accomplish just as little as possible. I have said that the slaves were without ingenuity—I must qualify that remark. I have been amused and astonished at their exceeding ingenuity in avoiding and slighting the work that was required of them. It has often seemed to me that their principal mental efforts were in this direction, and I think your correspondent will find universal testimony that they have decided talent in this line.

H. W. P.

In a volume entitled "Notes on Uncle Tom's Cabin; being a Logical Answer to its Allegations and Inferences against Slavery as an Institution," by the Rev. E. J. Stearns, of Maryland (much the most thorough review of that work made from the Southern stand-point), the author, who is a New-Englander by birth, shows, by an elaborate calculation, that in Maryland, the cost of a negro, at twenty-one years of age, has been, to the man who raised him, eight hundred dollars. Six *per cent.* interest on this cost, with one and three-quarters per cent. for life insurance, per annum, makes the lowest wages of a negro, under the most favourable circumstances, sixty-two dollars a year (or five dollars a month), *paid in advance,* in the shape of food and clothing. The author, whose object is to prove that the slaveholder is not guilty, as Mrs. Stowe intimates, of *stealing* the negroes' labour, proceeds, as follows, to show that he pays a great deal more for it than Mrs. Stowe's neighbours in New England do, for the labour they hire:—

If now we add to this (what every New-Englander who has lived at the South *knows*), that Quashy does not do more than one-third, or, at the very utmost, one-half as much work as an able-bodied labourer on a farm at the North; and that, for this he receives, besides the five dollars above mentioned, his food, clothing, and shelter, with medical attendance and nursing when sick, and no deduction for lost time, even though he should be sick for years, while the "farm-hand" at the North gets only ten or twelve dollars, and has to clothe himself out of it, and pay his own doctor's and nurse's bill in sickness, to say nothing of lost time, I think we shall come to the conclusion if there has been stealing anywhere, it has not been from Quashy.—P. 25.

I recollect, the first time I saw Quashy at work in the field, I was struck by the lazy, listless manner in which he raised his hoe. It reminded me of the working-beam of the engine on the steam-boat that I had just landed from—fifteen strokes a minute; but there was this difference: that, whereas the working-beam kept steadily at it, Quashy, on the contrary, would stop about every five strokes and lean upon his hoe, and look around, apparently congratulating himself upon the amount of work he had accomplished.

Mrs. Stowe may well call Quashy "shiftless." One of my father's hired men—who was with him seven years—did more work in that time than an average negro would do in his whole life. Nay, I myself have done more work in a day,—and followed it up, too—than I ever saw a negro do, and I was considered remarkably lazy with the plough or hoe.—P. 142.

APPENDIX

(D)

Statistics of the Georgia Seaboard

THE notes here following are derived from a volume entitled [George] White's "Statistics of Georgia," a large octavo of seven hundred pages, compiled and published in the State. A special section of the book is devoted to the condition of the trade of each county, while a comparison is also attempted to be given, from the personal observation of the compiler, of the comparative social, moral, and religious properties of the people. Thus, so far as the plan has been thoroughly executed, an estimate is presented, not only of the ordinary commercial demand of the citizens, but, so to speak, of the state of their intellectual and moral market.

The counties referred to by Mr. Gregg are in the second tier from the sea in South Carolina. I shall give statistics from Mr. White, and other authorities named in the note,[1] with regard to all the second tier counties of Georgia. What of good soil to be brought into cultivation, without a heavy expenditure at starting, there was originally in these counties begun to be first occupied by whites about 1740. It was not till nearly twenty years after this that slavery obtained the slightest footing in them, and it was not till about thirty years ago that they had begun to seriously deteriorate in production. There is yet some rich land upon the alluvial bottoms of the numerous rivers, which, rising above, pass through these counties toward the ocean; and here many wealthy planters still remain, owning a large number of slaves, and there has been recently a considerable increase of production of some parts owing to the employment of capital in draining marshes, the riches of which have previ-

---

[1] The population, following Mr. White, is given in round numbers, from the State Census of 1845; average personal estate, per family of citizens, reckoned from an official return, published in the "Soil of the South" (Columbus, Georgia, 1852, p. 210), the amount given for each county being divided by one-fifth the number of its population (for families). Observations on education and the character of the people, from White's "Statistics of Georgia" (generally in quotations). School, library, and church statistics, in figures from official United States Census, 1850.

ously been considered impregnable.[2] In general, however, this whole range of country is now quite barren, and most of the land at present cultivated will not probably yield one third as large a crop for the same expenditure of labour as would fair Mississippi cotton land. The slaves formerly owned here have therefore been very largely transferred westward, and the land they have worn out is left for the non-slaveholding whites to make the best of.

As an instructive contrast, I place in an adjoining column with the statistics of these counties those of the counties which bound each of them on the east. In these there is a much larger proportion of rich alluvial soil, and they contain the famous "sea island" cotton plantations, as well as the Georgian rice plantations. The valuable soil is still entirely possessed, as will be evident, by large planters and slave owners, the usual monopolizing effect of slavery being in this instance increased by the peculiar local insalubrity of the coast.

SECOND TIER COUNTIES

Bullock County.—(The Central Railroad, the best conducted road in all the South, passes either through this county or close beside its northern boundary, for a distance of fifty miles. It is watered by the Ogeechee and Connauchee and a number of smaller rivers. On the larger rivers there is yet a considerable amount of productive land.)

Population.—Whites, 2,000; slaves, 1,000. Average amount of property to each white family,

COAST COUNTIES

Bryan County, adjoining Bullock County, on the coast.

Population.—Whites, 1,000; slaves, 2,400. Average amount of property to each white family,

---

[2] The presence of these few planters, with their valuable human property, makes the average nominal wealth of each white family, at first sight, appear large. If, however, the slaves had been appraised at only $500 each, which would be low, they would alone amount in value in some counties to the sum assigned for the whole personal property of the citizens. This item is not, therefore, trustworthy, but, in comparing the coast and second tier counties, it serves to show the great difference in the average wealth of the citizens of each. A similar division of personal estate, as officially returned for the city of New York, would give $4,660 to each family.

SECOND TIER COUNTIES

$1,570. State tax for each white family, $2.95.

Mr. White omits his usual statistics of trade. Both in this and the adjoining coast county of Bryan, the poor people, as well as the planters, are in the habit of dealing directly with Savannah, as described in "Seaboard Slave States," p. 414, and there are probably no established tradesmen in either.

The *soil* is described by Mr. White as generally poor, with some productive "hummock" and river tracts.

Education.—"No newspapers are taken, and few books read. The school fund was once sufficient to educate many poor children, but owing to bad management it has become exhausted." Thus says Mr. White. The census returns show, however, a public school expenditure of $150 per annum, and a private expenditure of $3,000, divided among fifteen schools, which is one for eighty square miles. This is so much better than usual that, with Mr. White's remarks, I am inclined to think it an error.

COAST COUNTIES

$5,302 (fourfold what it is in Bullock County). State tax to each white family, $7.

No statistics of trade, again.

Soil.—"The soil, under the present system of culture, cannot, without rest and manure, be made to produce more than one half as much as when new." This appears to refer particularly to the rice plantations.

Education.—There is no academy, and there are no schools, except those supported by the "Poor School Fund" (a State provision for the children of indigent parents). "The children of the wealthy are either educated by private teachers or sent to school in the more favoured portions of the country; [the vicinity of Savannah, where there is a celebrated and well endowed academy, and of Liberty, where there are others, accounts for this;] the population is too sparse to furnish pupils enough to sustain a regular school" (large tracts of land being held by the planters, though wholly unproductive, to prevent the settlement of poor whites near their negroes, as one in this county informed me). According to the census returns,

SECOND TIER COUNTIES

Character of the people.—"By industry and economy, they manage to supply their wants, which, however, are few. Many rely a great deal on game. . . . As far as temperance is concerned, they are behind the times. Whiskey has its votaries. Those who have attempted to show the citizens the folly and ill consequences of intemperance have been insulted and threatened. Even ministers of our holy religion have publicly denounced the motives and efforts of those who have attempted to form temperance societies."

Religion.—"The most numerous [sects] are the Anti-Missionary [hard shell?] Baptists." Ten church edifices; average value, $145. No Sunday school or other public libraries.

Tatnall County.
Population.—Whites, 2,000; slaves, 600. Average amount of property to each white family, $901.

Capital invested in trade, $4,200.
Soil.—"Light and sandy, except on the streams, which is stiff."

Education.—"Education is neg-

COAST COUNTIES

there were eight schools (one to twenty-five square miles) of all kinds, with an average of twelve pupils each. Total expenditure for each school, $38 per annum.
Character of the people.—No remarks.

Religion.—The county contains eleven church edifices; average value, $500. No Sunday school or other public libraries.

Liberty County.
Population.—Whites, 2,000; slaves, 6,000. Average amount of property each white family, $6,330.

State tax to each white family, $10.
Capital invested in trade, $3,850.
Soil.—"The practice has been to wear out the virgin soils, and clear new lands. . . . Much waste land."

Education.—"Excellent schools

SECOND TIER COUNTIES

lected." Eight public schools (1 to 148 square miles), with sixteen pupils each. Annual cost of maintenance of each school, $150. No other schools; no Sunday school or other libraries.

COAST COUNTIES

are found. . . . And it is believed that a greater number of young men from Liberty county graduate from our *colleges* than from any other section of Georgia." There are five "academies," with an average of nineteen pupils each. Five public schools (1 to 160 square miles), maintained at an average expenditure of $15.40 per annum each. No libraries found in the census canvass of 1849. Mr. White states that the Medway and Newport Library Society had, in 1845, "about seven hundred volumes, in a very bad state of preservation." This library was established by some New England immigrants before the prohibition of slavery was annulled in the province. The early settlers of the county were chiefly from Massachusetts.

Character of the people.—"Sober, industrious and hospitable" (phrases applied to every county not specially noted as conspicuous for some vice or virtue of its inhabitants).

Religion.—Sixteen church edifices, valued at $938 each. According to Mr. White, however, there are "about thirty churches" in the county.

Character of the people.—"Generally upright and virtuous, and they are unsurpassed for the great attention paid to the duties of religion."

Religion.—Ten church edifices; average value, $1,200.

Wayne County.

Population.—Whites, 930; slaves, 350. Average amount of property for each white family, $898.

McIntosh County, broadest on the sea.

Population.—Whites, 1,300; slaves, 4,400. Average amount of property for each white family, $7,287, or eight times as much as in Wayne.

SECOND TIER COUNTIES

State tax, $1.23.

Capital invested in trade, $4,200.

Soil.—"Generally poor, barren pine land; when manured, will produce about twenty bushels of corn per acre."

Education.—"Few schools"; two academies (one Baptist, and the other Methodist, probably), with thirteen pupils between them. Four public schools (1 to 148 square miles), averaging ten pupils each; expense of maintenance not habitants).

Character of the people.—"High for morality and hospitability"; "poor, but honest." At the seat of justice "are many beautiful pine hills, affording delightful summer residences to the wealthy planters of Glynn" (hence the academical advantages).

Religion.—Eight church edifices; average value, $240.

Ware County.—(About one fifth of this county is occupied by the Okefenokee Swamp.)

Population.—Whites, 2,000; slaves, 300. Average amount of personal property for each white family, $480.

State tax, $4.05.

Stock in trade, $2,200.

COAST COUNTIES

State tax, $2.77.

Capital invested in trade, $1,200.

Soil.—Poor turpentine pine land in the rear; on the Altamaha, "of inexhaustible fertility."

Education.—One academy, with thirty-eight scholars; four public schools, twelve and a half miles apart, averaging twenty pupils each. Expense of maintaining each school, $78 per annum. "The wealthier classes are highly educated; but, generally, little interest is felt in the subject of education."

Character of the people.—"Like all parts of Lower Georgia, the citizens of McIntosh are generally intelligent and hospitable."

Religion.—Twelve church edifices; average value, $1,041.

Camden County.—Much the largest part of this county, which is L shaped, with but one arm on the sea, is inland, and unfertile.

Population.—Whites, 3,000; slaves, 4,000. Average amount of personal property for each white family, $4,428.

State tax, $13.

"Amount of business done at St. Mary's is about $30,000 per annum," nearly all in lumber, and done by New Englanders. No other trade statistics.

SECOND TIER COUNTIES

Soil.—"Light and tolerably productive."

Education.—"Very little interest is taken in the subject of education." No academies; six public schools (1 to 485 square miles), sixteen pupils each. Wages of teachers, etc., yearly, $41 each school. No Sunday school or other libraries.

Character of the people.—"The citizens are said to be hardy, industrious, and honest." "Much good might be done by the organization of temperance societies."

Religion.—Fifteen church edifices, fourteen miles apart, each accommodating one hundred sitters, and valued at $56 each.

COAST COUNTIES

Soil.—"Of celebrated fertility."

Education.—No remarks on education or character by Mr. White. Four public schools (1 to 280 square miles), with seventeen pupils each, maintained at an average expenditure of $290 per annum. Two academies, with forty-five pupils. Five Sunday school libraries, with one hundred and ten volumes each.

Character of the people.—No remarks.

Religion.—Ten churches (five of which are in the town of St. Mary's, a beautiful and healthy village, resorted to by consumptives); average value, $850.

I have purposely omitted Effingham County in the above arrangement, because the adjoining coast county of Chatham contains the city of Savannah, an aggregate agency of Northern and foreign merchants, through which is effected the commercial exchanges of a great extent of back country, the population of which can therefore afford no indication as to the point under consideration. Effingham, the county above Chatham, and one of the second tier, is worthy of notice, from some other important exceptional features of its constitution. Owing to the amount of rich soil in the county, along the Savannah River, there is a larger proportion of slaves to the whole population than is usual in the second tier, their number being sixteen hundred against only eighteen hundred whites; the non-slaveholders, however, appear to possess unusual privileges. There is an academy, with fifty pupils, which Mr. White describes as "a fine school." The public schools, eight in number, are less than eight miles apart, with an average attendance of sixteen pupils. Each school costs one hundred and twelve dollars a year. There are twenty-one churches, less than five miles apart, and valued at over twelve hundred dollars apiece. Mr. White says that honesty and industry are leading characteristics of the people, who, notwithstanding the poverty of the soil, are generally in comfortable circumstances.

The reason of this is partially the close vicinity of Savannah, affording a cash market for a variety of productions and household manufactures, among which, as distinguishing the county from any other in the State, are mentioned fruits, silk, fishing lines, and cowbells, "the latter," Mr. White is told, "superior to any manufactured in the North or in Europe." But an equally important reason for the better character and condition of the people is to be found in the fact that a majority of them [3] are descendants and heirs of the land of those very early settlers who most strenuously and to the last resisted the introduction of slaves into the colony, being convinced that, if permitted, it would, as they said in their memorials, "prove a scourge" to the poor people who were persuaded to petition for it.[4] It is most gratifying to perceive that all traces of the habits of industry, honesty, and manly self-reliance, in which they thus educated their children, are not wholly lost in the lapse of a century.

[3] White's "Statistics," p. 224.

[4] Alexander Hewatt's "Historical Account of the Rise and Progress of the Colonies of South Carolina and Georgia"; "Seaboard Slave States," p. 528.

Editor's Appendix

(E)

Olmsted on the Northern and Southern Characters [1]

THE WEALTHY and educated, and especially the fashionable people of all civilized countries, are now so nearly alike in their ordinary manners and customs, that the observations of a passing traveler upon them, must commonly be of much too superficial a character to warrant him in deducing from them, with confidence, any important conclusions. I have spent an evening at the plantation residence of a gentleman in Louisiana, in which there was very little in the conversation or customs and manners of the family to distinguish them from others whom I have visited in Massachusetts, England and Germany. I shall, therefore, undertake with diffidence to describe certain apparently general and fundamental peculiarities of character in the people, which it is a part of my duty to notice, from their importance with reference to the condition and prospects of the Slave States and their institution.

Slavery exerts an immense quiet influence upon the character of the master, and the condition of the slave is greatly affected by the modifications of character thus effected. I do not believe there are any other people in the world with whom the negro would be as contented, and, if contentment is happiness, so happy, as with those who are now his masters. The hopeless perpetuation of such an intolerable nuisance as this labor-system, it is, however, also apparent, depends mainly upon the careless, temporizing, *shiftless* disposition, to which the negro is indebted for this mitigation of the natural wretchedness of Slavery.

The calculating, indefatigable New-Englander, the go-ahead Western man, the exact and stern Englishman, the active Frenchman, the studious, observing, economical German would all and each lose patience with the frequent disobedience and the con-

[1] This penetrating essay was one of Olmsted's concluding articles in the series on his first Southern trip. It appeared in the *New York Times*, January 12, 1854, under the title: "Slavery in Its Effects on Character, and the Social Relations of the Master Class." It was not later reprinted.

stant indolence, forgetfulness and carelessness, and the blundering, awkward, brute-like manner of work of the plantation-slave. The Southerner, if he sees anything of it, generally disregards it and neglects to punish it. Although he is naturally excitable and passionate, he is less subject to impatience and passionate anger with the slave, than is, I believe, generally supposed, because he is habituated to regard him so completely as his inferior, dependent and subject. For the same reason, his anger, when aroused, is usually easily and quickly appeased, and he forgives him readily and entirely, as we do a child or a dog who has annoyed us. And, in general, the relation of master and slave on small farms, and the relations of the family and its household servants everywhere, may be considered a happy one, developing, at the expense of decision, energy, self-reliance and self-control, some of the most beautiful traits of human nature. But it is a great error,—although one nearly universal with Southerners themselves,—to judge of Slavery by the light alone of the master's fireside.

The direct influence of Slavery is, I think, to make the Southerner indifferent to small things; in some relations, we should say rightly, *superior* to small things; prodigal, improvident, and ostentatiously generous. His ordinarily uncontrolled authority, (and from infancy the Southerner is more free from control, in all respects, I should judge, than any other person in the world,) leads him to be habitually impulsive, impetuous, and enthusiastic: gives him self-respect and dignity of character, and makes him bold, confident, and true. Yet it has not appeared to me that the Southerner was frank as he is, I believe, commonly thought to be. He seems to me to be very secretive, or at least reserved, on topics which most nearly concern himself. He minds his own business, and lets alone that of others; not in the English way, but in a way peculiarly his own; resulting partly, perhaps, from want of curiosity, in part from habits formed by such constant intercourse as he has with his inferiors, (negroes,) and partly from the caution in conversation which the "rules of honor" are calculated to give. Not, I said, in the English way, because he meets a stranger easily, and without timidity, or thought of how he is himself appearing, and is ready and usually accomplished in conversation. He is much given to vague and careless generalization, and greatly disinclined to exact and careful reasoning. He follows his natural impulses nobly, has nothing to be ashamed of, and is, therefore, habitually truthful; but his careless-ness, impulsiveness, vagueness, and want of exactness in every-thing, make him speak from his mouth that which is in point of fact untrue, rather oftener than any one else.

From early intimacy with the negro, (an association fruitful in other respects of evil,) he has acquired much of his ready, artless and superficial benevolence, good nature and geniality. The com-paratively solitary nature and somewhat monotonous duties of plantation life, make guests usually exceedingly welcome, while the abundance of servants at command, and other circumstances, make the ordinary duties of hospitality very light. The Southerner, how-ever, is greatly wanting in hospitality of mind, closing his doors to all opinions and schemes to which he has been bred a stranger, with a contempt and bigotry which sometimes seems incompatible with his character as a gentleman. He has a large but unexpansive mind.

The Southerner has no pleasure in labor except with reference to a result. He enjoys life itself. He is content with being. Here is the grand distinction between him and the Northerner; for the North-erner enjoys progress in itself. He finds his happiness in doing. Rest, in itself, is irksome and offensive to him, and however graceful or beatific that rest may be, he values it only with reference to the power of future progress it will bring him. Heaven itself will be dull and stupid to him, if there is no work to be done in it—nothing to struggle for—if he reaches perfection at a jump, and has no chance to make an improvement.

The Southerner cares for the end only; he is impatient of the means. He is passionate, and labors passionately, fitfully, with the energy and strength of anger, rather than of resolute will. He fights rather than works to carry his purpose. He has the intensity of character which belongs to Americans in general, and therefore enjoys excitement and is fond of novelty. But he has much less curiosity than the Northerner; less originating genius, less inventive talent, less patient and persevering energy. And I think this all comes from his want of aptitude for close observation and his dis-like for application to small details. And this, I think, may be rea-sonably supposed to be mainly the result of habitually leaving all matters not either of grand and exciting importance, or of imme-diate consequence to his comfort, to his slaves, and of being accustomed to see them slighted or neglected as much as he will, in his indolence, allow them to be by them.

Of course, I have been speaking of the general tendencies only of character in the North and the South. There are individuals in both communities in whom these extreme characteristics are reversed, as there are graceful Englishmen and awkward Frenchmen. There are, also, in each, those in whom they are more or less harmoniously blended. Those in whom they are the most enviably so— the happiest and the most useful in the social sphere—are equally common, so far as I know, in both; and the grand distinction remains in the mass—manifesting itself, by strikingly contrasting symptoms, in our religion, politics and social life.

In no way more than this: The South endeavors to close its eyes to every evil the removal of which will require self-denial, labor and skill. If, however, an evil is too glaring to be passed by unnoticed, it is immediately declared to be constitutional, or providential, and its removal is declared to be either treasonable or impious—usually both; and, what is worse, it is improper, impolite, ungentlemanly, unmanlike. And so it is ended at the South. But, at the North this sort of opposition only serves to develop the reform, by ridding it of useless weight and drapery.

Northern social life usually leaves a rather melancholy and disagreeable feeling upon the minds of our Southern friends, as many have confessed to me. I think the different tendency of life at the North from that of existence at the South, which I have asserted, will give a key to this unfavorable impression which the Southerner obtains of our social character.

The people of the North are generally well aware of their social deficiencies, and of the unfitness of many of the customs and mannerisms, required by conventional politeness, to their character and duties. A man comes to our house, and custom requires that our countenance should brighten, and that we should say we are glad to see him. This custom makes it unkind in us towards him not to do so. We have no unkindness in our hearts, to the man, but entirely the contrary; yet it happens that we are *not* glad to see him, and such is our constitution that we have no impulsive and natural brightening up under hardly any circumstances. Now we have to choose between a forced, artificial, formal and false expression of a true kindness, and truth and simplicity. Amiable people take sides with kindness—the silent and reliable sort—with truth. Each are constantly aware, to a greater or less degree, of the difficulty they are engaged with. Some attach an absurd importance to the value of expression, and become "affected"; others rebel against the falseness of the conventional forms of expression, and become supercilious or sour and forbidding. Both classes are constantly led to make awkward attempts to compromise their quarrel with themselves.

The Southerner can understand nothing of all this. He naturally accepts the institutions, manners and customs in which he is educated, as necessities imposed upon him by Providence. He is loyal to "Society," and it is opposed to his fundamental idea of a gentleman to essentially deduct from them or add to them. This "clothes philosophy" of the North, he does not in the least comprehend, or if he does he sees nothing in it but impudent and vulgar quackery. And yet I think there is, perhaps, good to come out of it. We believe not, in our day, in good WILLIAM of Wickham's maxim. This new Democratic man is not "made of manners"; it may be best he should make manners to suit himself. Between this slavish conformity and anarchical non-conformity—it is to be hoped that the good sense of our society is drifting towards both a nobler and a happier social life.

But, at the present, the social intercourse of the wealthy people of the South is certainly more agreeable, rational, and to be respected, than that of the nearest corresponding class at the North. I should be sorry to think this the highest compliment it deserved.

The wealthy class is the commanding class in most districts of the South, and gives character to all the slaveholding class. Wealth is less distributed, and is more retained in families at the South than the North. With the slaveholding class there is a pride of birth and social position, much more than in any class at the North. This affects the character and conduct of individuals, and reacts on their associates, and on the whole community—in some respects perniciously, but in many respects favorably.

The "high-toned gentleman" (a Southern expression) of the South is rare at the North. He is not an article of city manufacture, as the most cultivated people of the North are. He has a peculiar character, and peculiar habits—more like those of the "old English gentleman" than any class to be found now, perhaps, even in England itself. He rides much, and hunts, and is given to field sports, and never knows the want of oxygen; for, even in Winter, his windows and doors are always forgotten to be closed. Accordingly, though his diet is detestable, he is generally well physically developed—lighter and more delicate of frame than the English squires, but tall and sinewy. His face would commonly be handsome but that his mouth is made gross, lifeless, and inexpressive, by his habit of using tobacco excessively. He has a peculiar pride and romance, and, though he often appears laughably Quixotic, he is, in the best sense of the word, also chivalrous. He is brave and magnanimous, courteous and polite, to all white people. If he often values his comfort, or the success of his designs, or the gratification of his passions, more than he does a strict adherence to the received rules of Christian morality, he never values life or aught else more than he does his honor. This "honor"—though if you analyze it, it comes to be little else than a conventional standard of feelings and actions, which must be habitual to entitle a man to consider himself a gentleman—is often really far nobler, and makes a nobler man than what *often* passes for religion at the North—at least in this world.

There is, however, a quality, or perhaps it is a faculty of the soul, which is distinct, though seldom separate, from love to the person of God and love to man, or in our time from the Christian faith, which is most nearly defined by the term, an enlightened conscience,—a spontaneous requisite perception and loyal love of the fundamental laws of Right—the laws that God himself is subject to. This quality or faculty is the noblest endowment of man, and is essential to the noblest character. I think it is strongly developed in more individuals at the North than at the South, and I think there are obvious causes for its absence at the South. The habitual reference of the Southerner in his judgment of conduct, whether of himself or another, whether past or contemplated, to the conventional standard of honor, prevents the ascendancy of a higher standard. This habitual contemplation of a relation so essentially wrong as that of slavery, as a permanent and necessary one not reformable, not in progress of removal and abolition, destroys or prevents the development of his sense of any standard of right and wrong above a mere code of laws, or conventional rules.

But to the Southern gentleman, (by distinction,) as I have often met him, I wish to pay great respect. The honest and unstudied dignity of character, the generosity and the real nobleness of habitual impulses, and the well-bred, manly courtesy which distinguish him in all the relations and occupations of life, equally in his business, in his family, and in general society, are sadly rare at the North—much more rare at the North than at the South. I acknowledge it freely but with deep regret and melancholy. There are qualities of character, (not of deportment, merely,) which are common among the planters of many parts of the South, as they are among the aristocratic classes of Europe, which are incompatible with the possession of nothing else that a man should glory in, which the mass of the people of the North have nearly lost, or have failed to gain.

This has been often observed by intelligent travelers visiting us, and is sometimes thought sufficient to condemn our democratic form of government, and our approximately democratic state of society. This is the judgment of many Southerners, (for the government and society of the South is the most essentially aristocratic in the world,) and I have reason to believe that there are many whose confidence in the democracy of the North is so small that they anticipate, and are acting politically with reference to, a division of the present Union and the formation of another great Southern republic—that is, a republic of white capitalists, in which the slavery of the working classes shall be provided for, and every means taken to make it complete and permanent.

But acknowledging the rarity of the thoroughbred gentleman at the North; is an inference to be drawn from it unfavorable to Democratic Institutions? I think not. Without regard to the future, and to what we may yet become under Democracy, the condition and character of our people *as a whole,* to the best of my judgment, is better, more gentlemanly even, far more entitled to respect than that of the people, *including all classes,* of any other nation. Very much more so than of those of the South. I do not say more happy. The people of the Northern States, as a whole, probably enjoy life less than any other civilized people. Perhaps it would be equally true to add —or than any uncivilized people. Those who consider that, if so, the uncivilized people (perchance slaves) are to be envied, will do right to condemn Democracy.

But the only conclusion which the fact seems to me to suggest, with regard to our Democratic Government, is perhaps this: that simple protection to capital and letting-alone to native genius and talent is not the whole duty of Government; possibly that patent laws, and the common schools, with their common teachers, and common instruction, (not education) such as our institutions as yet give to the people, are not enough. That the æsthetic faculties need to be educated—drawn out; that taste and refinement need to be encouraged as well as the useful arts. That there need to be places and time for *re-unions,* which shall be so attractive to the nature of all but the most depraved men, that the rich and the poor, the cultivated and *well-bred,* and the sturdy and self-made people shall be attracted together and encouraged to assimilate.

I think there is no sufficient reason why the aid of the State should not be given to assist corporations and voluntary associations for such purposes, on the same principle, and with the same restrictions, that it is in New-York to schools, to colleges, and to agricultural societies. Thus, I think, with a necessity for scarcely any additional governmental offices, or increase of the friction of governmental machinery, might be encouraged and sustained, at points so frequent and convenient that they would exert an elevating influence upon all the people, public parks and gardens, galleries of art and instruction in art, music, athletic sports and healthful recreations, and other means of cultivating taste and lessening the excessive materialism of purpose in which we are, as a people, so cursedly absorbed, that even the natural capacity for domestic happiness, and, more obviously, for the enjoyment of simple and sensible social life in our community, seems likely to be entirely destroyed. The enemies of Democracy could bring no charge more severe against it, than that such is its tendency, and that it has no means of counteracting it.

Slavery is claimed at the South to be the remedy for this evil. In some respects it is a remedy. But (disregarding the slaves and the poor whites) where there is one true gentleman, and to be respected, at the South, there are two whose whole life seems to be absorbed in sensualism and sickly excitements. Everywhere you meet them, well dressed and spending money freely, constantly drinking, smoking and chewing; card-playing and betting; and unable to converse upon anything that is not either grossly sensual or exciting, such as street rencounters, filibustering schemes, or projects of disunion or war. These persons are, however, gentlemen, in the sense that they are familiar with the forms and usages of the best society, that they are deferential to women, and that (except in money matters) their word is to be implicitly relied upon. They far exceed in numbers any class of at all similar habits that we yet have at the North.

They are invariably politicians, and they generally rule in all political conventions and caucuses. They are brave, in the sense that they are reckless of life, and they are exceedingly fond of the excitement of the hazard of life. They are as careless of the life of others as of themselves. They are especially ambitious of military renown, and in the Mexican war they volunteered almost to a man, many of those who went as privates taking with them several negro servants. If they were not dependent on the price of cotton for the means of their idleness, they would keep the country incessantly at war. Being so, however, they are as conservative in the policy they favor towards any powerful nation as the cotton lords of England or the land lords of Austria. They hate and despise the Democrats of Europe as much as FRANCIS JOSEPH himself. They glorify NAPOLEON, and they boast of the contempt with which they were able to treat the humbug KOSSUTH.

They call themselves Democrats, and sometimes Democratic Whigs. Call them what you will, they are a mischievous class,—the dangerous class at present of the United States. They are not the legitimate offspring of Democracy, thanks to God, but of slavery under a Democracy.

YEOMAN

Editor's Appendix

(F)

General Bibliography

1. Olmsted's Works on the South

The Cotton Kingdom: a Traveller's Observations on Cotton and Slavery in the American Slave States. 2 v. New York, 1861.

"Introduction" to T. H. Gladstone's *The Englishman in Kansas; or Squatter Life and Border Warfare.* London, 1857.

A Journey in the Back Country (*Our Slave States,* III). New York, 1860. New ed. 2 v. New York, 1907.

A Journey in the Seaboard Slave States, with Remarks on Their Economy (*Our Slave States,* I). New York, 1856. New ed., with "Introduction" by W. P. Trent and "Biographical Sketch" by F. L. Olmsted, Jr. 2 v. New York, 1904.

A Journey through Texas; or, a Saddle-Trip on the South-western Frontier: with a Statistical Appendix (*Our Slave States,* II). New York, 1857.

2. Principal Books Cited by Olmsted in *The Cotton Kingdom*

Caswall, Henry: *The Western World Revisited.* Oxford, 1854.

De Bow, J. D. B.: *The Industrial Resources, etc., of the Southern and Western States.* 3 v. New Orleans, 1852.

Gladstone, T. H.: *The Englishman in Kansas; or Squatter Life and Border Warfare.* With "Introduction" by F. L. Olmsted. London, 1857.

Hewatt, Alexander: *Historical Account of the Rise and Progress of the Colonies of South Carolina and Georgia.* 2 v. London, 1779.

Howison, R. R.: *History of Virginia.* 2 v. Philadelphia, 1846; Richmond, 1848.

Huc, E. R.: *Travels in Tartary, Thibet, and China.* Tr. from the French by W. Hazlitt. London, 1852.

JONES, C. C.: *Religious Instruction of the Negroes in the United States.* Savannah, 1842.

LONGSTREET, A. B. (" A Native Georgian"): *Georgia Scenes, Characters, Incidents, &c., in the First Half Century of the Republic.* 2nd ed. New York, 1851.

MILL, J. S.: *Principles of Political Economy.* 2 v. London, 1848.

NORMAN, B. M.: *Norman's New Orleans and Environs.* New York, 1845.

RUSSELL, ROBERT: *North America, Its Agriculture and Climate.* Edinburgh, 1857.

SÉGUIN, EDOUARD: *Traitement Moral, Hygiéne et Éducation des Idiots.* Paris, 1846.

STEARNS, E. J.: *Notes on Uncle Tom's Cabin; Being a Logical Answer to Its Allegations and Inferences against Slavery as an Institution.* 2nd ed. Philadelphia, 1853.

STEVENS, W. B.: *History of Georgia.* 2 v. New York, 1847; Philadelphia, 1859.

WHITE, GEORGE: *Statistics of the State of Georgia.* Savannah, 1849.

3. BOOKS AND ARTICLES CITED IN EDITOR'S INTRODUCTION

ABBOTT, J. B.: "The Abbott Howitzer—Its History," Kansas State Historical Society, *Transactions*, I–II (1881), 221–6.

ADAMS, E. D.: *Great Britain and the American Civil War.* 2 v. New York, 1925.

BERGER, MAX: "American Slavery as Seen by British Visitors," *Journal of Negro History*, XXX (1945), 181–202.

BEVERIDGE, A. J.: *Abraham Lincoln.* 2 v. Boston, 1928.

BIDWELL, P. W. *See* F. L. OLMSTED: "The New England Emigrant Aid Company and English Cotton Supply Associations."

BONNER, J. C.: "Profile of a Late Ante-Bellum Community," *American Historical Review*, XLIX (1944–5), 663–80.

BRACE, EMMA: *The Life of Charles Loring Brace Chiefly Told in His Own Letters.* London, 1894.

BROOKS, VAN WYCK: *New England: Indian Summer.* New York, 1940.

CAIRNES, J. E.: *The Revolution in America.* 5th ed. Dublin, n.d.

——: *The Slave Power.* London, 1862.

CARY, EDWARD: *George William Curtis.* Boston, 1894.

CLARK, T. H.: See F. L. OLMSTED: "Frederick Law Olmsted on the South, 1889."

DARWIN, FRANCIS: *The Life and Letters of Charles Darwin.* 2 v. New York, 1888.

DODD, W. E.: *The Cotton Kingdom.* New Haven, 1919.

EATON, CLEMENT: *A History of the Old South.* New York, 1949.

GLADSTONE, T. H.: *The Englishman in Kansas: or Squatter Life and Border Warfare.* With "Introduction" by F. L. Olmsted. London, 1857.

GRAY, L. C.: *History of Agriculture in the Southern United States to 1860.* 2 v. Washington, 1933.

HART, A. B.: *Slavery and Abolition.* New York, 1906.

HENRY, H. M.: *The Police Control of the Slave in South Carolina.* Emory, Va., 1914.

HOFSTADTER, RICHARD: "U. B. Phillips and the Plantation Legend," *Journal of Negro History,* XXIX (1944), 109–24.

JAMESON, J. F.: "Senator Beveridge, J. Franklin Jameson, and Abraham Lincoln," Elizabeth Donnan and L. F. Stock, eds., *Mississippi Valley Historical Review,* XXXV (1948–9), 639–73.

JORDAN, DONALDSON, and E. J. PRATT: *Europe and the American Civil War.* Boston, 1931.

KIGER, J. H.: "Federal Government Propaganda in Great Britain during the American Civil War," *Historical Outlook,* XIX (1928), 204–9.

LARNED, J. N., ed.: *The Literature of American History.* Boston, 1902.

MITCHELL, BROADUS: *Frederick Law Olmsted, a Critic of the Old South.* Baltimore, 1924.

MONAGHAN, JAY: *Diplomat in Carpet Slippers.* Indianapolis, 1945.

MORLEY, JOHN: *The Life of William Ewart Gladstone.* 3 v. London, 1903.

NEVINS, ALLAN: *The Emergence of Lincoln.* 2 v. New York, 1950.

NORTON, C. E.: *Letters.* Sara Norton and M. A. De W. Howe, eds. 2 v. Boston, 1913.

OGDEN, ROLLO: *Life and Letters of Edwin Lawrence Godkin.* 2 v. New York, 1907.

OLMSTED, F. L.: *Frederick Law Olmsted, Landscape Architect,*

1822–1903. F. L. Olmsted, Jr., and Theodora Kimball, eds. 2 v. New York, 1922–8.

OLMSTED, F. L.: "Frederick Law Olmsted on the South, 1889," T. H. Clark, ed., *South Atlantic Quarterly*, III (1904), 11–15.

——: "The New England Emigrant Aid Company and English Cotton Supply Associations: Letters of Frederick L. Olmsted, 1857," P. W. Bidwell, ed., *American Historical Review*, XXIII (1917–18), 114–19.

——: *Walks and Talks of an American Farmer in England.* New York, 1852. Rev. ed., Columbus, Ohio, 1859.

OLMSTED, F. L., Jr., and THEODORA KIMBALL. *See* F. L. OLMSTED: *Frederick Law Olmsted, Landscape Architect.*

OWSLEY, F. L.: *King Cotton Diplomacy.* Chicago, 1931.

——: *Plain Folk of the Old South.* Baton Rouge, 1949.

PERRY, BLISS: *Life and Letters of Henry Lee Higginson.* 2 v. Boston, 1921.

PHILLIPS, U. B.: *American Negro Slavery.* New York, 1918.

RHODES, J. F.: *History of the United States from the Compromise of 1850.* 7 v. New York, 1893–1906.

ROPER, LAURA WOOD: "Frederick Law Olmsted and the Western Texas Free-Soil Movement," *American Historical Review*, LVI (1950–1), 58–64.

——: "Frederick Law Olmsted in the 'Literary Republic,'" *Mississippi Valley Historical Review*, XXXIX (1952–3), no. 3.

SIMKINS, F. B.: *The South Old and New.* New York, 1947.

SMITH, G. W.: "The Banks Expedition of 1862," *Louisiana Historical Quarterly*, XXVI (1943), 341–60.

TOCQUEVILLE, ALEXIS DE: *Democracy in America.* Phillips Bradley, ed. 2 v. New York, 1945.

TUCKERMAN, H. T.: *America and Her Commentators.* New York, 1864.

VAN RENSSELAER, M. G. (MRS. SCHUYLER): "Frederick Law Olmsted," *Century*, XLVI (1893), 860–7.

WHITE, LAURA A.: "The South in the 1850's as Seen by British Consuls," *Journal of Southern History*, I (1935), 29–45.

WILLIAMSON, H. F.: *Edward Atkinson.* Boston, 1934.

WORMELEY, KATHARINE P.: *The Other Side of War with the Army of the Potomac.* Boston, 1889.

INDEX